Schriftenreihe
Informatik

52

Doucek Petr ■ Sonntag Michael ■
Nedomova Lea (Editors)

IDIMT-2023
New Challenges for ICT and Management

31st Interdisciplinary Information
Management Talks
Sept. 6–8, 2023
Hradec Králové, Czech Republic

Impressum

Schriftenreihe Informatik

Doucek Petr ■ Sonntag Michael ■
Nedomova Lea (Editors)
IDIMT-2023
New Challenges for ICT and Management
31st Interdisciplinary Information Management Talks

This publication was partially supported by the Prague University of Economics and Business – project IGA 409033 and institutional support for the long-term conceptual development of science and research at Faculty of Informatics and Statistics (IP400040), and the Johannes Kepler University Linz.

The Conference IDIMT-2023
took place September 6–8, 2023
in Hradec Králové, Czech Republic

Programme Committee
Aumayr Georg, AT
Delina Radoslav, SK
Doucek Petr, CZ
Fischer Jakub, CZ
Höller Tobias, AT
Jantos Anne, DE
Lisnik Anton, SK
Maryška Miloš, CZ
Neubauer Georg, AT
Pavlíček Antonín, CZ
Pucihar Andreja, SI
Rainer Karin, AT
Schoitsch Erwin, AT
Sonntag Michael, AT
Tkáč Michal, SK

© 2023
The Author(s) 2023

Herausgeber:
Prague University of Economics and Business
nám. W. Churchilla 1938/4
130 67 Praha 3
Czech Republic

Kommissionsverlag:
TRAUNER Verlag + Buchservice GmbH
Köglstraße 14, 4020 Linz
Österreich/Austria

Herstellung:
paco Medienwerkstatt,
1160 Wien, Österreich/Austria

DOI:10.35011/IDIMT-2023

ISBN 978-3-99151-176-2
www.trauner.at

TABLE OF CONTENS

CRISIS MANAGEMENT AND ICT

DECISION SUPPORT FOR APPLICATION OF LABORATORY PLATFORMS IN PANDEMICS 13
Georg Neubauer, Gerald Schimak, Johannes R. Peham, Florian Gehre, Muna Affara, Karin Rainer, Georg Duscher, Alois Leidwein, Angeliki Vlachostergiou, Eva Jaho

ADVANCEMENTS IN GENOMICS WORKFLOWS FOR PANDEMIC MANAGEMENT IMPROVING OUTBREAK INVESTIGATION AND SURVEILLANCE CAPACITY IN AUSTRIA AND BEYOND 21
Karin Rainer, Werner Ruppitsch, Adriana Cabal-Rosel, Julia Steger, Nicole Kramreither, Daniel Polzer, Patrick Hyden, Nadine Peischl, Krista Rathammer, Ivana Ferenčak, Irena Tabain, Kyriaki Tryfinopoulou, Gregory Spanakos, Judit Henczkó, Bernadett Pályi

FROM STRATEGIC PLANNING TO TACKLING PANDEMICS 29
Karin Rainer, Cosmas Grosser, Melissa Hagendorn, Antonia Hafner, Alois Leidwein, Nadine Sturm, Constanze Geyer, Gabriele Salomon, Rainer Prüller, Florian Schöggl

THE ETHICAL EVALUATION STANDARD FOR SECURITY RESEARCH (EESSR) MODEL 39
Constanze Geyer, Gudrun Ringler, Georg Aumayr, Nadine Sturm

CYBER SECURITY

AN EVIDENCE COLLECTION SYSTEM FOR ROBOT-SUPPORTED INSPECTION OF CRITICAL INFRASTRUCTURE 51
Michael Sonntag, Stefan Schraml

A LARGE-SCALE DATA COLLECTION AND EVALUATION FRAMEWORK FOR ANDROID DEVICE SECURITY ATTRIBUTES 63
Ernst Leierzopf, Michael Roland, René Mayrhofer, Florentin Putz

INTRUSION DETECTION AND PREVENTION WITH NEURAL NETWORKS 73
Marie Kovářová, Milos Maryska

DORA AND NIS2 AND THEIR IMPACT ON DATABASE SECURITY 81
Felix Espinoza, Milos Maryska, Petr Doucek, Marie Kovářova

CYBERSECURITY CONTRACTS: A CRITICAL REVIEW 89
Regina Hučková, Laura Bachňáková Rózenfeldová, Pavol Sokol, Soňa Briškárová

EXPLORING THE LINK BETWEEN ACCESSIBLE WEBSITE DESIGN AND USER EXPERIENCE FOR HUMANS WITH BLINDNESS AND VISUAL IMPAIRMENT: A QUALITATIVE STUDY 101
David Henkelmann, Tobias Fertig

VIRTUAL COLLABORATION, TEACHING & LEARNING

SELF-TEST AS A BLENDED ASSESSMENT STRATEGY TO FOSTER STUDENT ENGAGEMENT AND SATISFACTION IN HIGHER EDUCATION 111
Anne Jantos

"YOU CANNOT BE BOTH A GOOD EDUCATOR AND A GOOD RESEARCHER": DATA-SUPPORTED CONTRIBUTIONS AND COMMENTS ON THE BIG QUESTION 121
Lubomír Štěpánek, Filip Habarta, Ivana Malá, Luboš Marek

AUTONOMOUS VEHICLES AND SMART ENVIRONMENTS

AUTONOMOUS SYSTEMS AND SMART ENVIRONMENTS FOR A SUSTAINABLE LIFE 133
Erwin Schoitsch

OVERVIEW OF AI STANDARDIZATION 143
Christoph Schmittner, Abdelkader Magdy Shaaban

A COMPARISON OF CLOUD COMPUTING VS FOG VS EDGE FOR IIOT SENSORS 151
Nikola Kuchtíková, Milos Maryska

FIBER OPTIC ACOUSTIC SENSING (FOAS) FOR AUTOMATIC TRAFFIC JAM QUEUE END DETECTION 161
Carmina Coronel, Martin Litzenberger, Kilian Wohlleben

ERASMUS+ PROJECT 'BENEFIT' – BOOSTING INNOVATION IN DIGITAL FARMING 169
Roman Danel, Marta Harničárová, Walid Khalilia, Zuzana Palková, Khalid Hardan, Talat Tamimi, Yahya Istaitih, Jan Valíček, Michal Řepka

MANAGEMENT OF ICT SYSTEMS

DIGITAL SERVICES AND PUBLIC ADMINISTRATION 179
Petr Doucek, Lea Nedomova

DIGITAL TRANSFORMATION AT THE NATIONAL, REGIONAL, AND LOCAL LEVELS OF PUBLIC ADMINISTRATION: A CASE OF THE CZECH REPUBLIC 187
Martin Lukáš, Tereza Burešová, Miloš Ulman, Martin Havránek, Jan Jarolímek

ASSESSMENT OF AN OPEN GOVERNMENT DATA READINESS – A CASE OF SLOVENIA 195
Mirjana Kljajić Borštnar, Andreja Pucihar

UNRAVELING THE PROCESSES AND CHALLENGES OF ARTIFICIAL INTELLIGENCE IMPLEMENTATION IN THE SWISS PUBLIC SECTOR: A TOE FRAMEWORK ANALYSIS 203
Václav Pechtor, Josef Basl

SECURITY SOFTWARE AS A HYGIENE FACTOR 217
Tomáš Sigmund

THE SIGNIFICANCE OF SOC2 TYPE 2 AND ISO 27001 REGULATIONS FOR CC SERVICE PROVIDERS IN THE CZECH REPUBLIC 227
Vlasta Svatá

THE TOPIC OF AI CHATBOTS IN HIGHER EDUCATION 235
Martin Potančok, Věra Radváková

SOCIAL MEDIA

SOCIAL MEDIA AND INNOVATIONS: CASE STUDIES IN AUTOMOTIVE INDUSTRY 243
Antonín Pavlíček

MARKETING COMMUNICATION TARGETING CHILDREN ON ONLINE MEDIA 255
Jitka Burešová

COMPARATION OF EU POLITICS ACTIVITY ON TWITTER (YEARS 2020 AND 2022) 265
Jana Syrovátková, Jiří Korčák

ARTS NEWS AGENDA SETTING ON SOCIAL MEDIA 273
Tereza Willoughby

DIGITAL TRANSFORMATION OF SUPPLY CHAIN MANAGEMENT

EXAMINING THE EFFECTS OF SUPPLIER LOCALIZATION ON PUBLIC PROCUREMENT PERFORMANCE 283
Radoslav Delina, Gabriel Demeter

ANALYSIS OF PUBLIC PROCUREMENT IN STRATEGY RESOURCE SOURCING: DOES RELATION OF MATTER IN LONG RUN CONTRACTS? 293
Michal Tkáč, Jakub Sieber

THE ANALYSIS OF THE PUBLIC PROCUREMENT ENVIRONMENT BEFORE AND AFTER COVID-19 BREAKTHROUGH: CASE OF SLOVAKIA 303
Michal Tkáč, Michal Tkáč, Juraj Till

ANALYSIS OF UNIVERSITY STUDENTS' ATTITUDES TOWARD WORK IN PROCUREMENT 313
Markéta Zajarošová, Jaroslav Urminský, Anežka Šenkýřová, Marek Macík

BENEFITS OF E-AUCTION: REAL USERS EVALUATION 321
Jaroslav Urminský, Markéta Zajarošová, Adam Vávra, Ondřej Karady

ONLINE REPUTATION OF SELECTED E-COMMERCE ENTITIES THROUGH THE LENS OF PANDEMIC AND POST-PANDEMIC COMPARISON 329
František Pollák, Peter Markovič, Kristián Kalamen

ONLINE REPUTATION OF PUBLIC CHARGING STATIONS OPERATORS: AN EMPIRICAL STUDY ON THE CZECH MARKET 337
Michal Konečný, Michal Ruschak, Yaroslava Kostiuk

BUILDING A SUSTAINABLE BATTERY SUPPLY CHAIN WITH DIGITAL BATTERY PASSPORTS 347
Veronika Siska, Astrid Al-Akrawi, Mats Zackrisson

ETHICAL ASPECTS OF WORKING WITH DATA

ETHICAL ASPECTS OF WORKING WITH DATA 357
Anton Lisnik, Martina Kuperova

ETHICAL IMPLICATIONS OF ARTIFICIAL INTELLIGENCE DATA USAGE: A CASE STUDY OF SLOVAKIA AND GLOBAL PERSPECTIVES 365
Ivan Katrenčík, Boris Mucha, Monika Zatrochová

SPECIFICS OF ETHICAL PRINCIPLES OF SYSTEM DATA PROTECTION IN THE SERVICE SEGMENT 373
Anton Lisnik, Patrik Bretz, Miroslav Warhol, Milan Majerník

SPECIAL SESSION: EARLY CAREER & STUDENT SHOWCASE

E-PORTFOLIOS TO FOSTER REFLECTIVE LEARNING – A SYSTEMATIC LITERATURE ANALYSIS TO EXAMINE CURRENT RESEARCH 383
Julia Schwope, Anne Jantos

DEEP LEARNING FOR CYBER SECURITY IN THE INTERNET OF THINGS (IOT) NETWORK 391
Dawit Dejene Bikila

COBIT 2019 CONTRIBUTION TO DIGITAL LITERACY 399
Karel Maršálek

ANNEX

STATEMENT OF THE PUBLICATION ETHICS AND PUBLICATION MALPRACTICE 409
LIST OF AUTHORS 411

SPONSORS OF IDIMT 2023

CRISIS MANAGEMENT AND ICT

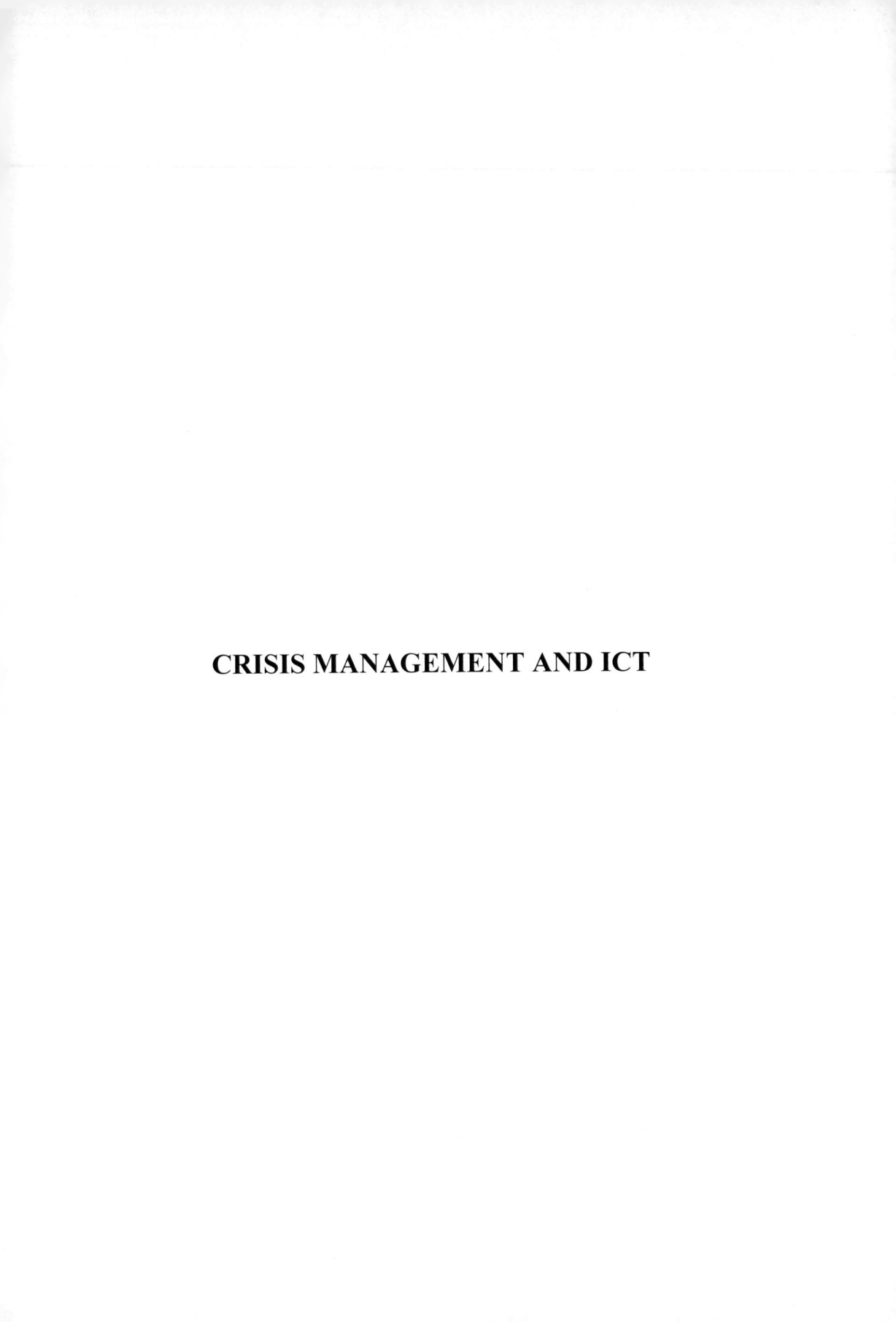

DECISION SUPPORT FOR APPLICATION OF LABORATORY PLATFORMS IN PANDEMICS

Georg Neubauer, Gerald Schimak, Johannes R. Peham

AIT Austrian Institute of Technology GmbH
georg.neubauer@ait.ac.at

Florian Gehre, Muna Affara

Bernhard Nocht Institute
gehre@bnitm.de

Karin Rainer, Georg Duscher, Alois Leidwein

AGES Austrian Agency for Health and Food Safety
karin.rainer@ages.at

Angeliki Vlachostergiou, Eva Jaho

EXUS
a.vlachostergiou@exus.ai

DOI: 10.35011/IDIMT-2023-13

Keywords

pandemic, arbovirus, decision support, BSL4, MOBILISE, STAMINA

Abstract

Climate change and other factors like population increase, inhabitance of new areas, deforestation and agricultural expansion and roll back of living environment of species make transmission of viruses in particular from animal to humans and outbreak of pandemics more likely. To respond adequately to such threats arising from pathogens like emerging arboviruses such as the Crimean-Congo haemorrhagic fever virus or the West Nile virus, mobile one health laboratories with the highest bio-safety level 4 (BSL4) are becoming increasingly important. For the coordination of several mobile laboratories a decision support system is needed. To identify the optimized locations for the operation of these resources, the results on the local incidence of specific pathogens provided by the mobile laboratories needs to be combined with data from different provenience such as modelling of the trend of incidence of pathogens, information provided by international stakeholders such as European Center for Disease Prevention and Control (ECDC) as well as analysis of data coming from sources such as social media. Based on a set of indicators decision makers can be supported in taking time-critical decisions. Within the project MOBILISE a BSL4 mobile laboratory and decision support system (DSS) is developed, using a set of indicators for assistance in taking time-critical decisions. The DSS extends the relevant system built in the STAMINA project for pandemic management, adopting the One Health approach to balance and optimize the health of people, animals and the environment.

1. Introduction

1.1. Gaps in decision support

The relevance of decision support for crisis management and, in particular for pandemic management has been demonstrated in different ways. For instance, an online survey performed in 2020 showed that information distribution and a common operational picture, both key elements to realize decision support were considered to be a central requirement in pandemic management (Neubauer et al, 2020). Among several other gaps, the International Forum to Advance First Responder Innovation (IFAFRI) specified in 2019 a capability gap focusing on the generation of actionable intelligence based on data and information from multiple sources. In detail, IFAFRI specifies that responders need solutions that provide information that can be used to make more effective decisions across many responder tasks. Such body of information should be visible on different technological platforms, evaluation of data should be done in real time and updated in case of incoming new information. Another capability gap is related to the ability to incorporate information from multiple and nontraditional sources into incident command operations. This is reflecting the broad range of data and information such as field observations, sensor data, model outputs or media reports that can provide valuable input for decision support (IFAFRI, 2023). In the frame of the European lighthouse project DRIVER+ one of the identified strategic gaps points to the necessity that information from multiple and non – traditional sources needs to be in cooperated to support decision making, the motivation for this gap is triggered by the insufficiency to report on dangerous areas and situations. This can be based on the overview from multiple and nontraditional sources such as crowdsourcing into response operations (Gaps Explorer, 2019).

From the point of view of pandemic management in the H2020 project STAMINA end user requirements were assessed based on desk research as well as a questionnaire. Key identified gaps encompassed the development of a clear operational picture, strategic information management and decision making as well as communication. Aligned with these outcomes, a strategic gap specifying the need for cross-agency decision support tools was specified by the pandemic experts from STAMINA (Gaps Explorer, 2019). To address these gaps an intelligent, and flexible decision support toolset was built in STAMINA, with central elements such as a Common Operational Picture (COP) tool as well as modelling or diagnostic tools (STAMINA, 2023). In view of the One Health approach, which recognizes that human health is intimately connected to the health of animals and the environment (WHO, 2017), it becomes necessary to improve detection capabilities of zoonotic diseases in humans and improve response times to epidemics. The use of mobile laboratories and associated DSS is a crucial step in this direction.

1.2. Mobile laboratories for pathogen detection

Mobile laboratories are becoming increasingly important for quick response to epidemic outbreaks in remote areas or at any locations where diagnostic capacity is missing. Triggered by climate change as well as other factors such as reduction of wildlife habitats, arboviruses (e.g. Crimean-Congo haemorrhagic fever virus, West Nile virus or Rift Valley fever virus or any other virus that is transmitted via arthropods) are propagating more frequently towards Europe through arthropod vectors (e.g. mosquitoes, ticks), and are increasingly becoming a major public health concern in Europe. Improved monitoring of zoonotic outbreaks needs a one health approach, in which not only human, but also animal and environmental samples are analysed (according to the WHO, one health is an integrated, unifying approach to balance and optimize the health of people, animals and the environment (WHO, 2017)). Travelers might also carry arboviruses. Currently, out of 193 identified European mobile laboratories, only 3% have the highest biosafety level BSL4 needed for haemorrhagic arbovirus handling and 88% are exclusively designed for human diagnostics, only. The Horizon Europe project MOBILISE aims to close this diagnostic gap, by developing a novel, quality-assured, mobile one health laboratory (MOHL) solution, to provide BSL4 capacity to many European countries (MOBILISE, 2023). This laboratory from MOBILISE will include a novel emergency operating centre and decision support system assisting decision makers such as health authorities in coordinating capacities including mobile labs across Europe and manage future outbreaks in real-time.

2. A common understanding on how to share testing capacities in pandemics

2.1. A concept for a decision support system to manage BSL4 testing capacities

At the beginning of the design of a decision support system, a helpful approach is to answer the key questions depicted in Figure 1. Several of these are related to the different users of such a system and their intended roles. First of all, one needs to know which actors have the necessary data and information available to provide the basis for decision support. Data sources are usually available at health organisations and authorities, but in the last years they have been extended by non-traditional sources, such as news articles, social media, blogs, and other internet sources, where users can report incidents of zoonotic diseases. This extension of data sources brings additional challenges about how to process and validate these data, and combine them with data from authorities to provide actionable information. Apart from the question on the availability of information another key question is related to actors that needs to be informed. It is a quality criterion of any information sharing system that the users of such a system do not receive all information, but only what is aligned with their role. For example, decision makers do not need all data available in the system, but exactly the information that is necessary to support them in their decisions. This is reflected by the questions "who is going to decide?", "what do they need to decide?" and "on what do they decide?".

Another important aspect is the identification of relevant sources for the decision support process. Typically, several data or information types need to be considered and integrated, e.g. data from modelling tools on the expected incidence rates in specific regions, environmental data having potential influence on the propagation of a disease (e.g. weather), data on the available resources to manage a threat such as capacities available in hospitals (e.g. free beds), information from international organizations as well as non-conventional information such as information extracted from social media such as Twitter or Facebook or RSS feeds. All these parameters may have an influence on the decision and can be represented by indicators. It is up to the decision makers to give different weights to the multitude of indicators, e.g. on a data dashboard. This process is reflected by the question "how do they decide?".

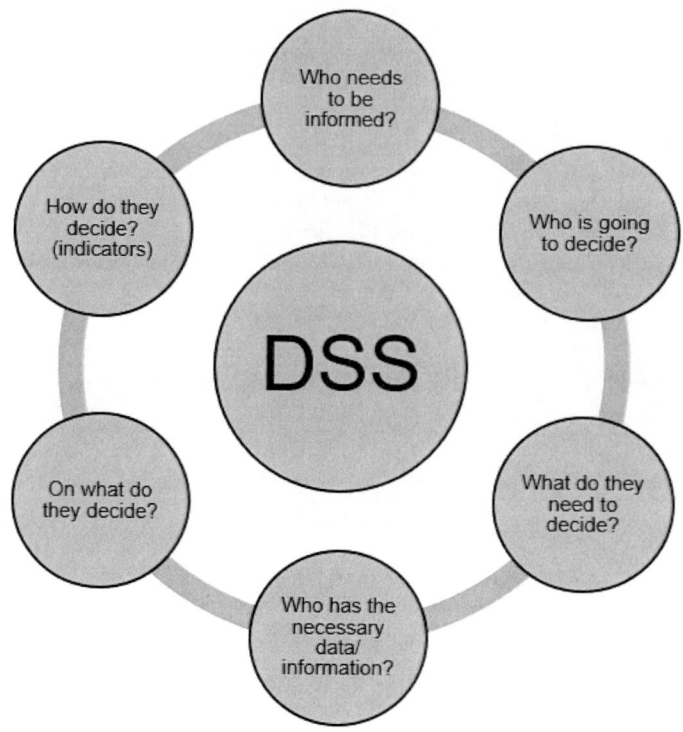

Figure 1. Key questions for the development of a concept of a decision support system

From the moment the decision-making process is known in principle, including actors and their roles as well as the requested input data and information, it is possible to set up a concept of a decision support system, such as the one for mobile laboratories shown in Figure 2.

The functionality of the information distribution system is provided by the Public Safety Hub (PSH). PSH provides standardised information exchange while connecting with arbitrary systems (PSH, 2023). As a result, involved stakeholders can use their legacy system. Moreover, it enables easy integration of their IT systems. The PSH is intended to allow resilient and secure information exchange making it possible to compensate even the failure of one information management unit by another neighbored one. Via PSH, acting also as information distribution system (see Figure 2), systems can send messages to specific recipients or topics, so that each user receives all the information they need for their role, while avoiding unauthorized access.

A central element of the DSS is a predictive modelling tool designed to generate predictions of the progression of an outbreak of a pathogen such as West Nile virus or Crimean-Congo haemorrhagic fever virus. Such predictions may concern the near, short or even long-term future. In addition to data on disease prevalence, the tool can incorporate demographic data such as number of residents of an affected area, their age or their employment. It is intended to combine such data with animal outbreak parameters to respond according to the one health approach. In MOBILISE, a data analytic engine and an "early warning system" module will be integrated. The latter consists of a recommendation engine, which returns relevant information regarding information of the state of the outbreak of a disease to end users, based on the collected and integrated data. Artificial intelligence algorithms based on machine learning techniques and particular deep neural networks will be applied. A central element of the mobile laboratory is the laboratory information system (LIMS). The LIMS will allow tracking barcode samples from reception to result verification by operators, the management and calibration of the equipment as well as storage/biobanking of human, veterinary and environmental samples. A document management system is aligned to the LIMS catalogues version controlled standard operating procedures. The LIMS system provides automated information output at regular levels, that needs to be interfaced with the analytics engine. Other sources like information provided by international agencies such as the World Health Organisation (WHO) or Health Emergency Preparedness and Response (HERA) are also taken as input for decision support. Two other central elements are interfaces for information export to external stakeholders as well a repository. Finally, the decision support will be completed with a module providing the common operational picture (COP) and an information distribution system. For the provision of a COP serving also as user interface (see Figure 2), the Emergency Mapping Tool (EMT) is going to be used. It is a module that is widely tested for providing very different type of information relevant for pandemic management such as results from modelling tools or location of operational units in the field.

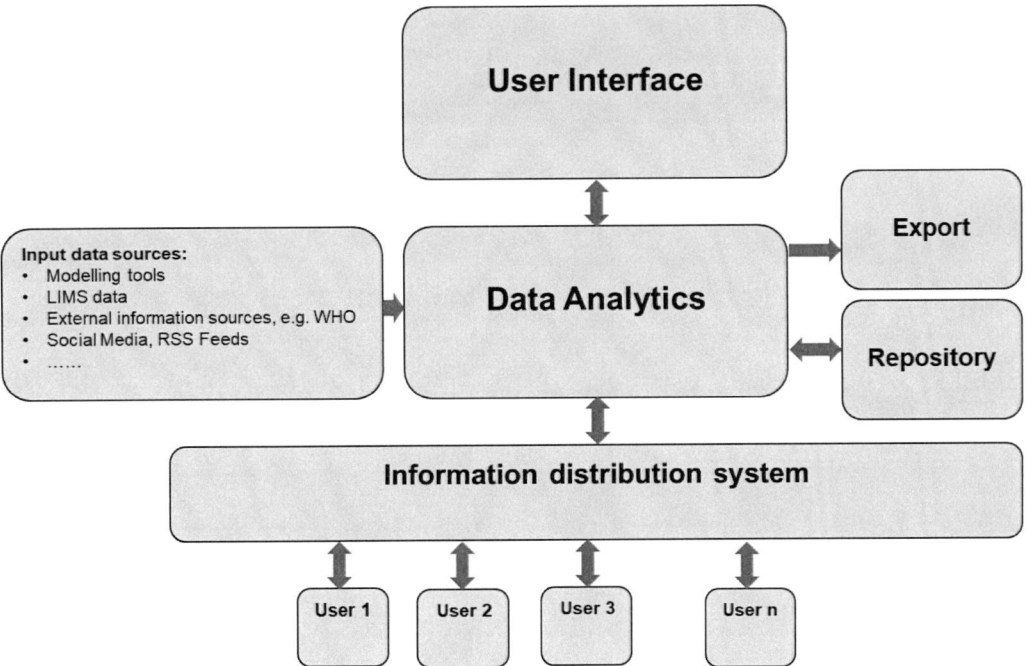

Figure 2. Concept of a decision support system for a mobile laboratory

2.2. Data management requirements of decision support for a one health laboratory

Within the MOBILISE project, a mobile one health laboratory (MOHL) for emerging infectious disease outbreaks is developed, including an emergency operating centre and a decision support system (see chapter 1). Aligned with the quality management system of the MOHL a data management plan needs to be developed. The data management plan defines the general policy and approach to data management and handles related issues on the administrative and technical level.

This includes topics like data and metadata collection, processing, publication and deposition of open data, the data repository infrastructure and compliance to the open access infrastructure for research in Europe (OpenAIRE). As a general guideline, the data management policy shall follow three main principles:

- *KISS: "Keep it Short and Simple"* – the data management within the project including identification, access, retrieval, storage, and reuse of data during and after the project will be made as simple as possible.
- *FAIR:* all data used in the project must be easily Findable, Accessible, Interoperable and Reusable.
- *Societally Responsible:* data produced by the project will be made publicly available unless there is a compelling ethical, legal, or commercial reason against such publication. All project outputs (e.g., data, algorithms) will be explicitly checked for ethical issues.

Key rules of data management encompass:

1. All public data sets will be referenced in an open repository such as Zenodo, to assure that the information can be easily identified and can be referenced by unique DOI – during and after the project.
2. All open data produced in the project or published by the project for the first time will be also published in Zenodo, to assure its long-term storage through OpenAIRE.
3. Some of the data sets used by the project may not be suitable for publication as Open Data, e.g. due to ethical / legal / security / general data protection or commercial confidentiality concerns. For data that cannot be made public, the reasons for non-disclosure and conditions and procedures for accessing the data will be clearly stated both in Zenodo and in the data management plan. Such data will be managed by the owner and kept for at last five years after the project end. IPR restrictions may limit publication of specific data.

On a more general level, for the specific dataset description central elements of requested information encompass

- Dataset name
- Main source of dataset
- Ownership
- Country
- Restrictions
- Access URL
- Responsible partner
- Dataset description
- Purpose
- Additional comments

Updates of the description of the datasets and the data management process needs to be made throughout any project's lifecycle as these datasets become available, collected, updated, or newly identified for covering the ongoing future needs.

3. Validation of the Mobile One Health Laboratory

Within MOBILISE, the end user needs will be systematically collected and followed by gap analysis. The laboratory platform will be customized to the needs of the different end users, such as national health agencies like the Austrian Agency for Health and Food Safety (AGES), health authorities or the operating staff of the mobile laboratory. A standardized methodology is applied for this purpose. We will also apply the so-called STAMINA demonstration methodology (STADEM) for trialing, developed in STAMINA (Fonio, Widera, 2020, Neubauer et al, 2021) and based on the Trial Guidance Methodology (TGM). The main difference between STADEM and TGM is, that the solution selection process can be omitted following STADEM. This fits MOBILISE, because only the solutions provided by the project will be trialed. The trialing methodology is separated in three phases: preparation, execution and validation. It is described in detail in the CEN Workshop Agreement 17514, (CWA, 2020) or in the Trial Guidance Methodology Handbook (Fonio, Widera, 2020). At the time this paper is written, the project is in the early stages of the trial, i.e. step zero and the beginning of the six step approach encompassing elements such as scenario specification or definition of trial objectives. At the stage this paper is written, context and the central gaps of a trial need to be specified. In MOBILISE four trials with the MOHL are going to be executed, taking place in Austria, Greece, Romania and East Africa.

4. Conclusion and Outlook

In this paper a concept for a decision support system for a biological safety level BSL4 mobile one health laboratory is specified. In addition, data management requirements for such a system are given. The development of the system and the integration of already available modules such as COP tool is going to take place aligned with the standardized planning and execution of four trials to ensure that the platform fulfils both technical and socio technical requirements from the involved stakeholders from Austria, Greece, Romania and East Africa. One example of a socio-technical aspect is the user friendliness of a system, this work will be performed according to the STADEM methodology in the frame of the Horizon Europe project MOBILISE. On one hand MOBILISE builds on the outcome of previous projects such as STAMINA, on the other hand it paves the way towards improved solutions for interoperability and situational awareness for future pandemic management. Major challenges to be considered are related to data access from both an organizational (willingness to cooperate, legal, etc.) and technical point of view (interfaces). Quality and completeness of data are imperative for validation of the whole system. In the light of digital transformation, the vision beyond the project is to establish cooperation in common data spaces to enhance future pandemic management. Central objectives are to establish a one health data management with common rules, uniform standards and data sovereignty for public safety stakeholders. This encompasses the establishment of collaboration instead of competence silos, open data ecosystems instead of closed platforms and distribution and sharing of information instead of centralisation.

Acknowledgment

The research leading to these results has received funding from the European Union`s Horizon 2020 research and innovation programme under Grant Agreement n°883441 (STAMINA) and the European Union`s Horizon Europe research and innovation programme under Grant Agreement n°101073982 (MOBILISE).

The authors acknowledge Mrs. Veronika Siska for proof-reading this paper and for their multiple valuable comments.

References

CWA (2020) CEN Workshop Agreement 17514, Systematic assessment of innovative solutions for crisis management - Trial guidance methodology [pdf]. Retrieved from https://ftp.cencenelec.eu/EN/ResearchInnovation/CWA/CWA17514_2020.pdf.

Fonio, C., Widera, A. (Ed.), (2020) Trial Guidance Methodology Handbook. DRIVER+ (Driving Innovation in Crisis Management for European Resilience), Brussels, 2020.

Gaps Explorer (2019), [online], https://pos.driver-project.eu/en/gaps, [Accessed 12 April 2023]

IFAFRI (2023), Capability Gaps, [online], https://www.internationalresponderforum.org/capability-gaps-overview, [Accessed 12 April 2023]

MOBILISE (2023), A novel and green mobile one health laboratory for (re-)emerging infectious disease outbreaks, Cordis Website, [online], https://cordis.europa.eu/project/id/101073982, [Accessed 12 April 2023]

Neubauer, G., Preinerstorfer, A., Martin, A., Rainer, K., van Berlo, M. (2020). Analysis of gaps arising while managing the COVID-19 crisis, IDIMT 2020 – Digitalized Economy, Society and Information Management, Vol. 49, pp165

Neubauer, G., Ignjatovic, D., Schimak, G., Widera, A., Middelhoff, M., Scheuer, S., Aumayr, G., Jaho, E., Rainer, K. (2021). The benefits of trials for pandemic management, IDIMT 2021 – Pandemics: Impacts, Strategies and Responses, Vol. 50, pp 197

PSH (2023), Public Safety Hub, https://www.ait.ac.at/themen/cooperative-digital-technologies/loesungen-projekte/public-safety-defence/public-safety-hub [Accessed 19. April 2023]

STAMINA (2023), Smart support platform for pandemic prediction and management. [online], Available at: https://stamina-project.eu/about/, [Accessed 12 April 2023].

WHO (2017). [online], Available at: https://www.who.int/news-room/questions-and-answers/item/one-health, [Accessed 14 April 2023].

ADVANCEMENTS IN GENOMICS WORKFLOWS FOR PANDEMIC MANAGEMENT IMPROVING OUTBREAK INVESTIGATION AND SURVEILLANCE CAPACITY IN AUSTRIA AND BEYOND

Karin Rainer, Werner Ruppitsch, Adriana Cabal-Rosel, Julia Steger, Nicole Kramreither, Daniel Polzer, Patrick Hyden, Nadine Peischl, Krista Rathammer

Austrian Agency for Health and Food Safety (AGES), Vienna, Austria,
karin.rainer@ages.at

Ivana Ferenčak, Irena Tabain

Microbiology Department, Croatian Institute of Public Health, Zagreb, Croatia,
ivana.ferencak@hzjz.hr

Kyriaki Tryfinopoulou, Gregory Spanakos

Central Public Health Laboratory department and Regional Public Health Laboratories department, National Public Health Organisation, Athens, Greece,
k.tryfinopoulou@eody.gov.gr

Judit Henczkó, Bernadett Pályi

National Biosafety Laboratory, Department for Microbiological Reference Laboratory, National Public Health Center, Budapest, Hungary
henczko.judit@nnk.gov.hu

DOI: 10.35011/IDIMT-2023-21

Keywords

Public health, Crisis preparedness, Pandemic management, Cross border health threats, COVID-19, SARS-CoV-2, whole genome sequencing (WGS), RT-PCR, testing capacity, AGES Austrian Agency for Health and Food Safety

Abstract

The progression through the COVID-19 pandemic in the recent years posed multiple challenges to societies, health systems, economies and policy makers. The lack of epidemiological data hindered decision-making and the implementation of evidence-based measures. In response to this, the SARS-CoV-2 testing- and associated IT-infrastructure had to be enhanced quickly to adapt to the new scale of sample numbers. Therefore, we moved to expand and optimize our WGS and RT-PCR workflows required for high-throughput disease surveillance and outbreak investigation. Since the large amount of sequencing data generated by our pipeline required enhanced data processing and analysis abilities, we implemented a robust data management system. AGES as a key facility received funding by the Health Emergency Preparedness and Response Authority (HERA) of the European Union. We now apply the knowledge gained from this singular action in an international consortium of public health authorities in order to expand our molecular surveillance pipelines to a wider spectrum of candidate pathogens to improve cross-border preparedness for health emergencies.

1. Introduction

1.1. COVID-19 pandemic management

In the past three years, the wide range of actions taken by governments included travel restrictions, social distancing rules, emergency financial aids, the rapid development of medical countermeasures like vaccinations and many more. The constant collection of epidemiological data now allows a systematic exploration of the effects of these policies (Hale et al. 2021). However, at the onset of the pandemic in spring and summer 2020, the general unpreparedness and the lack of evidence-based, trustworthy medical and epidemiological information complicated the decision-making process. The implementation of public health strategies and their communication were marked by uncertainty, strong media interest and public disagreement (Abrams et al. 2020).

Austria was an early hotspot of COVID-19 transmission because of winter tourism (Popa et al. 2020, Kreidl et al. 2020). At that time, the structure of the national pandemic and information management system was not prepared and had to be adapted to a new level. The availability of critical resources such as hospital or intensive care beds and additional resources as the necessary staffing was unsure, and policy measures differed between federal states. This painfully slowed down the response at the national level and obstructed the implementation of efficient pandemic management (Rainer et al. 2022-2020). For this reason, we proposed and successfully received funding in order to start a project focusing on a concept of evidence-based intervention matching for a comprehensive optimization of crisis management, (Rainer et al. 2022). One of the core components of this holistic approach is the generation of a community-driven web database for crisis and disaster management, called Portfolio of Solutions (PoS, Ignjatović et al. 2019). Some of the implemented functions include descriptions of solutions as well as a gaps explorer, which allows the linking of existing gaps with possible solutions. This knowledge management system supports stakeholders such as crisis management professionals in the replacement of gaps in crisis management. This innovative tool is openly accessible (https://pos.driver-project.eu/en/PoS) and facilitates evidence-based measure matching, therefore enhancing our preparedness for future disasters such as pandemics. This generation of a comprehensive crisis management framework is tightly connected to the implementation of specific actions in the public health sector, such as the expansion of viral pathogen sequencing infrastructure. In this regard, we focus on the project titled „Enhancing Whole Genome Sequencing (WGS) and Real-Time Reverse Transcription Polymerase Chain Reaction (RT-PCR) national infrastructures and capacities to respond to the COVID-19 pandemic in the European Union and European Economic Area", in the scope of this paper.

1.2. Whole-genome-sequencing (WGS) capacities at AGES

In Austria, the Austrian Agency of Health and Food Safety (AGES) has been commissioned with securing national public health since 2002 (Austrian Health and Food Security Act, §9a of GesG

2021). It is instructed to prepare emergency plans and to ensure sufficient laboratory capacity to deal with exceptional situations. Among other tasks under a One Health approach (https://onehealthejp.eu), AGES is tasked with the preparation, technical implementation, follow-up maintenance and evaluation of general and special emergency plans required by the relevant European legal acts. For this purpose, AGES provides the technical advice, processing and administrative support for higher-level crisis management.

Before the COVID 19 pandemic outbreak, the public health division at AGES had already established leading Whole Genome Sequencing capacity for disease outbreak characterizations. At this time, the main application was the implementation of a sentinel system for outbreak detection, mostly related to foodborne diseases such as listeriosis and salmonella (Ruppitsch et al. 2015, Schill et al. 2016, Pietzka et al. 2019). Another important field of interest for public health is antimicrobial resistance; in this regard the presence of multi-resistant strains in the environment was monitored (Lepuschitz et al. 2019). Since then, the number of sequenced samples has been increasing constantly, with slight adaptation of equipment and IT infrastructure only added as needed.

This represents the general framework that existed before the arrival of COVID-19. With AGES as the responsible public health agency in Austria, the fast implementation of a nation-wide strategy for WGS and RT-PCR-based testing received high-priority status. Since gaps and upcoming requirements in the entire process were managed by workarounds, a comprehensive optimization of the workflow in terms of speed, efficiency, costs and sample throughput was necessary to increase the capacity to the level needed for intensive SARS-CoV-2 testing. Starting from September 2021, for a span of 13 months, a HERA Incubator Grant supported the enhancement of RT-PCR-based testing and whole genome sequencing infrastructure to facilitate SARS-CoV-2 surveillance in Austria.

An initial analysis of the widest gaps in our workflow identified two key areas: The automatisation of the sample and sequencing library preparation and an upgrade of the IT infrastructure. In addition to the upscaling of the technical capacity for handling large sample numbers, the second key aspect was the integration of sequencing data as a solid resource for national decision-making. Furthermore, the publication of this epidemiological data on a national dashboard (https://covid19-dashboard.ages.at) in a format accessible to the general public was a widely used information tool, providing epidemiological details about the current situation. One of our key aims was the sustainability of the newly implemented infrastructure. Due to the characteristics of our current lives in times of climate change and global interconnectedness, the risk of infectious disease outbreaks keeps on increasing (Baker et al. 2022). Therefore, high-performance pathogen sequencing and ICT technologies that ensure epidemic and pandemic surveillance are required for an efficient response to future health threats.

2. Results

2.1. Identification of the main aims of the enhancement of the WGS and RT-PCR pipeline

The main target of the HERA-funded action at AGES was the rapid implementation of improved laboratory-, IT- and database infrastructure to create efficient and powerful RT-PCR and WGS workflows. The increased sample processing numbers were set up to facilitate enhanced monitoring of known variants and safeguarded the early detection of newly emerging SARS-CoV-2 variants. In addition, we were able to use the data generated in the project to improve our understanding of infectious disease outbreaks. In the long term, this project will strengthen pandemic preparedness by building the capacity needed to respond to cross-border infectious disease outbreaks in a timely and efficient manner. In order to address the most obvious shortcomings in our pre-existing infrastructure, we defined five specific targets:

SO1: Improvement of sample logistics parameters for external sample providers who require analysis at AGES WGS facilities.

SO2: Implementation of automation facilities for sample preparation and processing.

SO3: Establishment of a stable, high-demand data analysis IT workflow.

SO4: Optimization of sample data logistics, data analysis and reporting workflows.

SO5: Preparedness of the IT infrastructure for data transmission to supra-national institutions and the establishment of an accessible computational tool for data sharing.

2.2. Implementation of identified objectives

The upgrade of our technical equipment was centered around the automation of our WGS and RT-PCR workflows, which required the installation of liquid-handling robots and specialized PCR sample pooling machines. Since multiple external stakeholders submitted different types of samples to our centralized sequencing facility, a comprehensive sample labelling system had to be implemented.

To deal with the increased need for computational resources, two servers (32 cores/1TB RAM/Nvidia Tesla A100 GPU) were newly purchased and added to the virtualized server-pool AGES already maintained. The virtual machines allocated to this hardware are composed to a SLURM-managed compute-cluster, which allows full scalability and the possibility to easily increase the dedicated resources (or reduce if the demand is not as high anymore). As for a national public health agency, such as AGES, independence of third-party service providers is important, a potentially more affordable cloud-based solution was not considered the optimal solution.

Bioinformatic workflows for analysis of WGS data were written in NextFlow, which facilitates parallelization and distributed computing, whether via the queue management system SLURM (Simple Linux Utility for Resource Management) or via cloud provider. Typing results are linked to sequencing data (paths) in a MariaDB-database and are accessible in a user-friendly way via newly implemented Django/Python programmed web UI. Access to this resource is however limited to internal personnel. Our workflow contains a module to automatically upload all SARS-CoV-2 genomes to GISAID. Plugins were implemented into our web UI for manually sharing data via ENA, NextCloud or to upload to the EFSA-One Health WGS platform.

2.3. Results of the stakeholder analysis

AGES performs the function of a national reference laboratory for different pathogens. During the COVID-19 pandemic, external medical institutions, from now on referred to as our stakeholders (SH), submitted their samples to AGES for further analysis. Therefore, the involvement of our stakeholders and their satisfaction with our collaboration was an essential part of this project. To ensure the efficiency of our sample data logistics and data analysis workflows, we performed interviews with all external stakeholders. Our analysis included 12 independent testing facilities, located in 5 federal states. The broad range of sample numbers, which they submitted to the AGES testing pipeline, was classified into 4 categories, spanning <99 to >1000 samples per month (Figure 1).

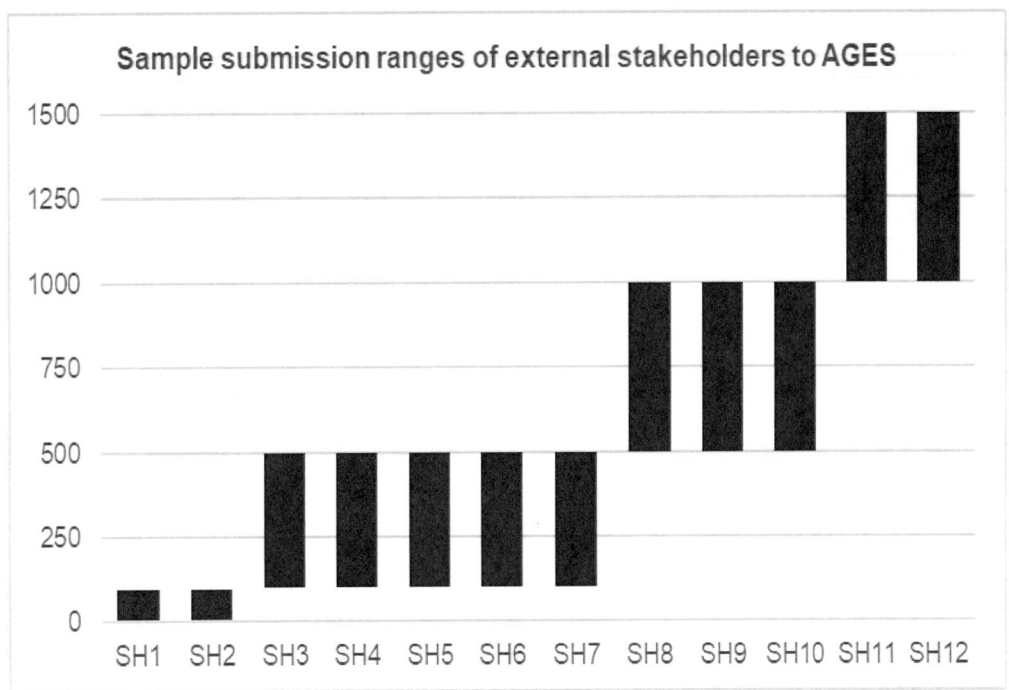

Figure 1. Average monthly sample procession number across 12 external stakeholders (SH1-12). The 4 categories include 0-99, 100-499, 500-999, >1000 samples/month submitted to AGES.

The cooperation with these regional stakeholders spanned from more than 15 years to recently implemented partnerships and included both our SARS-CoV-2 and microbial testing pipelines, which increased the diversity of feedback. The questionnaire consisted of 16 open questions and was conducted in the form of a standardised, quality-controlled telephone interview. The aim was to identify the components of our testing pipeline that needed to be updated and optimised (Table 1). The central areas determined by the stakeholder analysis were sample data logistics and the exchange of data and information. Our stakeholders demanded an increase in bi-directional information flow, especially the accessibility of the sequencing data acquired from their submitted samples. During the submission process, especially the sample labelling system needs to be improved and streamlined. The aim is an automated and digitalized labelling procedure that is consistent across all submitting institutions. In addition, the implementation of a central platform as an interface for the exchange of data and feedback was proposed. In conclusion, the experience of our stakeholders was overall positive, however, optimization of data accessibility and transparency on all steps of the pipeline would highly improve their experience and benefits. In the future, this information exchange will extend beyond the national level and link to international databases such as the EpiPulse platform, the ECDC's European infectious disease surveillance portal.

3. Discussion and Outlook

The molecular surveillance of the spread of SARS-CoV-2 challenged the diagnostic capacities at public health institutes. Therefore, we implemented a centralized and up-scaled testing pipeline at the Austrian Agency for Health and Food Safety. It combines RT-PCR workflows, which are necessary for the rapid detection of known and circulating mutations, and whole genome sequencing for the identification of newly emerging variants. In combination with the optimisation of these technical workflows, we also enhanced our sequencing technology and bioinformatics capacities to ensure thorough epidemiological surveillance.

Table 1. Stakeholders experience of their collaboration with AGES. Results of SWOT-analysis.

STRENGTHS	WEAKNESSES
Expertise in diagnostics and pathogens	Absence of an automated and digital sample labelling system
State-of-the-art technical equipment	Complicated administrative processes
Specific methodologies	Lack of and/or late transmission of results, absence of a data platform
Straightforward dispatch system (medlog)	Uncertainty about personal responsibilities in special cases
OPPORTUNITIES	**THREATS**
Improved background information about sample requirements and their submitting organisation	Inadequate analysis capacity
	Susceptibility to errors due to manual administrative tasks
Simpler and semi-automated sample handling system (technical and digital)	Lack of scientific expertise and guidance

However, our long-term goal is to create a powerful and sustainable infrastructure that can easily adapt to other emerging public health challenges after COVID-19. In addition to the wide range of bacterial pathogens (WHO 2017), the WHO recently released a prioritized list of fungal pathogens (WHO 2022), thus expanding possible future health threats. Currently, the availability of WGS and RT-PCR-based characterisation pipelines is restricted to a small number of viral and bacterial strains. Hence, it is essential to adapt and establish sequencing protocols for a wide range of pathogens and to create resilient workflows that can be applied quickly and efficiently in the event of an outbreak.

In addition, the diversity of bacterial, viral and fungal pathogens requires a technology that is capable of detecting a broad spectrum of microorganisms simultaneously in a single sample (Ko et al. 2022). The implementation of metagenomics-based surveillance methods is therefore crucial to improve our preparedness for epi- and pandemics. As disease outbreaks are cross-border issues, the integration of this expertise at the international level is necessary for thorough surveillance systems and an efficient response to emerging outbreaks and informed public health decisions.

References

Abrams, E. M., Shaker, M., Oppenheimer, J., Davis, R. S., Bukstein, D. A., & Greenhawt, M. (2020). The challenges and opportunities for shared decision making highlighted by COVID-19. The Journal of Allergy and Clinical Immunology: In Practice, 8(8), 2474-2480.

Baker, R. E., Mahmud, A. S., Miller, I. F., Rajeev, M., Rasambainarivo, F., Rice, B. L., ... & Metcalf, C. J. E. (2022). Infectious disease in an era of global change. Nature Reviews Microbiology, 20(4), 193-205.

Hale T, et al. (2021) A global panel database of pandemic policies (Oxford COVID-19 Government Response Tracker). Nat Hum Behav 5, 529–538. https://doi.org/10.1038/s41562-021-01079-8

Ignjatović, D., Havlik, D., Neubauer, G., Turptil, S., Gonzales, F., & Regeczi, D. (2019). The portfolio of solutions. Proceedings of the 27th Interdisciplinary Information Management Talks, Kutná Hora, Czech Republic, 4-6.

Lepuschitz, S., Schill, S., Stoeger, A., Pekard-Amenitsch, S., Huhulescu, S., Inreiter, N., ... & Ruppitsch, W. (2019). Whole genome sequencing reveals resemblance between ESBL-producing and carbapenem resistant Klebsiella pneumoniae isolates from Austrian rivers and clinical isolates from hospitals. Science of the Total Environment, 662, 227-235.

Ko, K. K., Chng, K. R., & Nagarajan, N. (2022). Metagenomics-enabled microbial surveillance. Nature Microbiology, 7(4), 486-496.

Kreidl, P., Schmid, D., Maritschnik, S., Richter, L., Borena, W., Genger, J. W., ... & Allerberger, F. (2020). Emergence of coronavirus disease 2019 (COVID-19) in Austria. Wiener Klinische Wochenschrift, 132, 645-652.

Pietzka, A., Allerberger, F., Murer, A., Lennkh, A., Stöger, A., Cabal Rosel, A., ... & Schmid, D. (2019). Whole genome sequencing based surveillance of L. monocytogenes for early detection and investigations of listeriosis outbreaks. Frontiers in public health, 7, 139.

Popa, A. et al. (2020). Genomic epidemiology of superspreading events in Austria reveals mutational dynamics and transmission properties of SARS-CoV-2.Sci. Transl. Med.12,eabe2555. DOI:10.1126/scitranslmed.abe2555

Rainer, K., Leidwein, A., Hoffmann, M., Kramreither, N., Neubauer, G., Bürger, B., Ignjatovic, Aumayr, G., Kutalek, R., Saretzky, J.. (2022) Requirement focused Intervention-matching for Pandemic Management. National perspectives for involvement of evidence based lessons learned. In: Petr Doucek et al. (Eds.). IDIMT 2022. Information Technology, Society and Economy Strategic Cross-Influences. 30th interdisciplinary Information Management Talks. Trauner Linz. 163-174.

Rainer, K., Fastl, C., Leidwein, A., Nemenz, P., Hoffmann, M., Rathammer, K., Kundratitz, V., Neubauer, G., Preinerstorfer, A., Aumayr, G., Scheuer, S., Eisenberger, I., Hofer, A., Scholz, S. (2021) Digital Transformation in Crisis Management. Risk, Vulnerability and Resilience Analyses for Pandemic Management: Challenges and Perspectives of Approaches for the Future. In: Petr Doucek et al. (Eds.). IDIMT 2021. Information Technology, Society and Economy Strategic Cross-Influences. 29th interdisciplinary Information Management Talks. Trauner Linz. 163-174.

Rainer, K., Leidwein, A., Nemenz, P., Hoffmann, M., Neubauer, G., & Aumayr, G. (2020). Interoperability and crisis management in pandemic outbreak scenarios an overview on different case studies of the Austrian approach to tackle the SARS-CoV-2 spread and adherent management challenges. IDIMT 2020: Digitalized Economy, Society and Information Management-28th Interdisciplinary Information Management Talks.

Ruppitsch, W., et al. (2015) Defining & Evaluating a Core Genome Multilocus Sequence Typing Scheme for WGS-Based Typing of Listeria monocytogenes. J Clin Microbiol 53:2869-76.

Ruppitsch, W., et al. (2015) Ongoing outbreak of invasive listeriosis, Germany, 2012-2015. Euro Surveill 20:doi:10.2807/1560-7917.

Schill, S., Lepuschitz, S., Blaschitz, M., Maritschnik, S., Schmid, D., Allerberger, F., ... & Ruppitsch, W. (2016). Use of genome wide gene-by-gene comparison for *Salmonella enterica* outbreak investigation in Austria. International Journal of Infectious Diseases, 53, 118.

WHO. Prioritization of pathogens to guide discovery, research and development of new antibiotics for drug-resistant bacterial infections, including tuberculosis. Geneva: World Health Organization; 2017(WHO/EMP/IAU/2017.12).

WHO. WHO fungal priority pathogens list to guide research, development and public health action. Geneva: World Health Organization; 2022.

FROM STRATEGIC PLANNING TO TACKLING PANDEMICS

Karin Rainer, Cosmas Grosser, Melissa Hagendorn, Antonia Hafner, Alois Leidwein

AGES Austrian Agency for Health and Food Safety GmbH
karin.rainer@ages.at

Georg Neubauer

AIT Austrian Institute of Technology GmbH
georg.neubauer@ait.ac.at

Nadine Sturm, Constanze Geyer, Gabriele Salomon

JOAFG Johanniter Österreich Ausbildung und Forschung GmbH
nadine.sturm@johanniter.at

Rainer Prüller, Florian Schöggl

pentamap GmbH
rainer.prueller@pentamap.com

DOI: 10.35011/IDIMT-2023-29

Keywords

Pandemic management, strategic planning, lessons learned, intervention-matching, coordination of data, SARS-CoV-2, COVID, decision support approach, analysis integration, validation, taxonomy, AGES Austrian Agency for Health and Food Safety

Abstract

COVID-19 has led to the world's largest virus-induced crisis in recent decades. Like many other countries, Austria was inadequately prepared for a pandemic in some areas. The pandemic management was therefore in most respects reactive instead of pro-active. This led to measures that were sometimes difficult for the population to understand. The need for a clear-cut pandemic management plan that includes feasible recommendations for decision makers was already evident in early stages of the pandemic. "ROADS to Health" aims to work out a holistic, technologically supported system that draws onto lessons learned from the COVID-19 outbreak to tackle future epidemics and pandemics that provides adequate decisions at all times.

The objectives of "ROADS to Health" concentrate on generating the basis for situation-based measure matching in an infection scenario, or more precisely, in an epidemic or pandemic *outbreak. Different aspects of the project include project management, requirements and scenarios, measures, tool conceptioning, testing and validation.*

In the initial project phase, the focus of ROADS lies upon working out certain impacts of bundles of measures that were set over the last years and how they align with strategic aims in pandemic management. The requirements and scenarios that are of utmost importance for the project and are based on background analysis of pandemic parameters, baseline studies, cataloguing and assessment of current practices.

It posed to be difficult to match broad strategic aims with specific means and measures, since the former are not communicated publicly by decision makers. Another challenge hereby was that various organisations, communities, etc. may have different (underlying) strategic plans behind their reasoning for actions.

Hence, our multi-disciplinary team is currently working out categorisations of measures and parameters within pandemic management that can ultimately be traced back to strategic objectives, which dictate the overarching direction decision makers want to head towards in tackling a pandemic outbreak.

1. Background and motivation for enhancements for pandemic management

Early in the COVID-19 pandemic the need for enhancements, amendments and a stable structure behind the management and tackling of the health crisis became clear (Rainer et al. 2021 and 2022). During the focus on operational countering the pandemic, the call for projects including evidence based solutions arose, but could not be transferred into practice due to a lack of possibilities to implement evolving lessons learned. Core activities were based on ongoing operational handling and uncertainties regarding further development of the outbreak in its initial phases. Now, there is the possibility for a fruitful analysis to use lessons learned from the COVID-19 pandemic and work out, how decision makers can set the right measures at the right time during an epidemic or pandemic.

Thus, the ROADS project was selected by the KIRAS Security Research Program to facilitate identifying and analysing short- and long-term effects of strategic aims and operational measures implemented within pandemic management. Due to the high importance of a holistic approach of this issue, psychological, socio-economic, ethical, and legal effects are taken into account as well throughout the project.

ROADS got accepted in the second round for submissions within the FFG call for proposals and was launched on January the 23rd 2023 with a joint workshop at the Austrian Agency for Health and Food Safety (AGES). Project partner organisations are the Austrian Institute of Technology GmbH (AIT), Federal Ministry of Social Affairs, Health, Care and Consumer Protection (BMSGPK), Gesundheit Österreich GmbH (GÖG), Johanniter Österreich Ausbildung und Forschung GmbH (JOAFG), Medical University of Vienna (MUW) and Pentamap GmbH (ROADS website).

ROADS also involves stakeholders and a high level advisory board from different fields of work, such as public health, health management, technology development, public administration, and social as well as preventive medicine. The collaboration draws on the experience and knowledge of these high-level organisations and ensures a cross-cutting, interdisciplinary approach to optimise future pandemic management.

The objectives of ROADS are arranged in several work packages that focus on different aspects of the project. In detail, it is comprised of the identification of national and international strategic, tactical and operative aims by literature research, conducting guided interviews and surveys targeting health and security agencies and infrastructures like hospitals. The information obtained are leading to a functional analysis of aims in different phases of a pandemic and thus build the basis for requirements of a technological decision support tool. Further literature research and document analysis for cataloguing, assessment (efficacy and direct/indirect medical, infrastructural, economic, gender-specific effects) and ex-post analysis of selected objectives in recent national and international pandemic management are being sorted into a self-developed matrix as a basis for the following work packages that determine measures, tool modelling and validation.

Pandemic, epidemic and infection parameters are being described and defined by typing and sorting by relevance, using meta-studies from renowned organisations, e. g. ECDC (European Centre for Disease prevention and Control) and WHO (World Health Organization). Besides, measures and parameters that are related to the experiences, behaviour and actions displayed by the civilian population in the course of the pandemic are compared on national and international levels. Indicators of vulnerability and resilience will be defined with the help of the CAVE (Community Engagement and Vulnerabilities in Coping with Epidemics) project, an interdisciplinary applied pandemic research project in Austria.

By means of stakeholders and renowned experts, the obtained results will be catalogued, assessed and system requirements elaborated. Furthermore, the impact of the obtained pandemic measures and parameters and the associated implications for society as a whole can further be classified according to costs and benefits.

Finally, the previous findings on management strengths and weaknesses in pandemic management with a focus on Austria are included in a matrix in the course of a classic SWOT (Strengths, Weaknesses, Opportunities and Threats, Schawel & Billing 2009) analysis. The underlying procedure of the SWOT analysis is based on the comparison of four basic overall properties of the project: opportunities and threats against strengths and weaknesses. In particular, it serves as an objective assessment of the obtained results of the ROADS-approach and therefore consolidates the starting point for the decision support tool, especially with regard to the measures that need improvement and lessons learned.

Concerning pandemic management, Austria was as inadequately prepared as many other countries. Decision-making regarding public health strategy and measures was intricate and varied highly from state to state and time to time and were highly disputed (Abrams et al. 2020), especially at the beginning, facing an uncertain medical and epidemiological information landscape.

Hence, the measures set in the course of pandemic management led to massive side effects with regards to social, economic (Corona relief measures: info, relief and simplification, 2023), political and psychological matters.

Measures taken during the COVID-19 pandemic varied from country to country, also within the European Union and even on a regional level.

Specifically in Austria, pandemic planning of Sars-CoV-19 was a big issue as the planning was based on the 1913 Act on the Prevention and Control of Communicable Diseases and focused on specific pathogens like *Influenza* and *Ebola* on a reactive instead of a pro-reactive or even preventive basis (BMGF 2006) and thus resulted in the evidence, that developing a more occasion-based legislation was essential.

However, a steep learning curve was evident in the course of finding measures for COVID-19 management, as they led to a flattening of the epidemic curve during the first three COVID waves, prevention of health care systems overload and curtailed excess mortality (e.g. AGES COVID dashboard, 2023; GÖG data platform, 2023).

It is critical in pandemic management to take the right action at the right time and to have knowledge and availability of resources: Supporting this is the overall approach of the ROADS concept. To successfully master prospective challenges of this kind, ROADS aims at developing a foundation for optimised risk and crisis management for future pandemics and epidemics.

2. Challenges to analyse strategic aims in pandemic management

The matching of broad strategic aims with specific tactical and operative interventions and measures posed to be difficult, especially since the former are not communicated publicly by decision makers. Another challenge hereby was that various organisations, communities, etc. may have different (underlying) strategic plans behind their reasoning for actions. Due to those difficulties in getting a hold of general constructs, it was decided by the multi-disciplinary ROADS research team to conduct a document analysis of government announcements from the management level. The initial analysis therefore includes putting together a matrix to trace implemented measures to overarching strategies in pandemic management.

It is also key to be aware of the structure of pandemic management in contrast to traditional crisis or disaster management. The transition from pandemic response to recovery in a spiral fashion, as visualised in Figure 1, is depicting the dynamics of the current system: Each new wave pushes the disaster risk reduction cycle from the recovery back to response phase with a high probability of a second and even third wave of a pandemic if there is no vaccine or immunization at hand.

Pandemics are multifactorial, leading to highly-specific and demanding challenges at times, especially in the development and implementation of a technology-enabled system that strives to improve measures of pandemic management. The following factors therefore have to be considered:

(a) Pandemics are dynamic and it is often difficult to predict how they evolve. In this context, it is crucial to aim at enabling dynamically adaptable scenarios of pandemics.

(b) Pandemics are not spatially limited, in a globalised setting, they have the potential to spread rapidly and at the beginning mostly unnoticed by public health authorities. Thus, the ROADS concept has to aim at enabling dynamically adaptable management solutions and finding to-the-point measures more quickly.

(c) Public acceptance and cooperation are crucial, which results in the utmost importance of maintaining credibility of the authorities that propagate and implement countermeasures, and decision makers that proclaim adequate risk communication strategies. The ROADS-approach is now set up to facilitate the promotion of transparent communication of measures based on the context of scientific findings.

(d) To determine and estimate vulnerable groups in advance poses the greatest risk. Accordingly, ROADS includes the aspect of vulnerable and marginalized groups on purpose (Rainer et al. 2016). Key is the inclusion of the findings of the FFG project CAVE, which focuses on these aspects as well as how to reach those groups by community engagement activities.

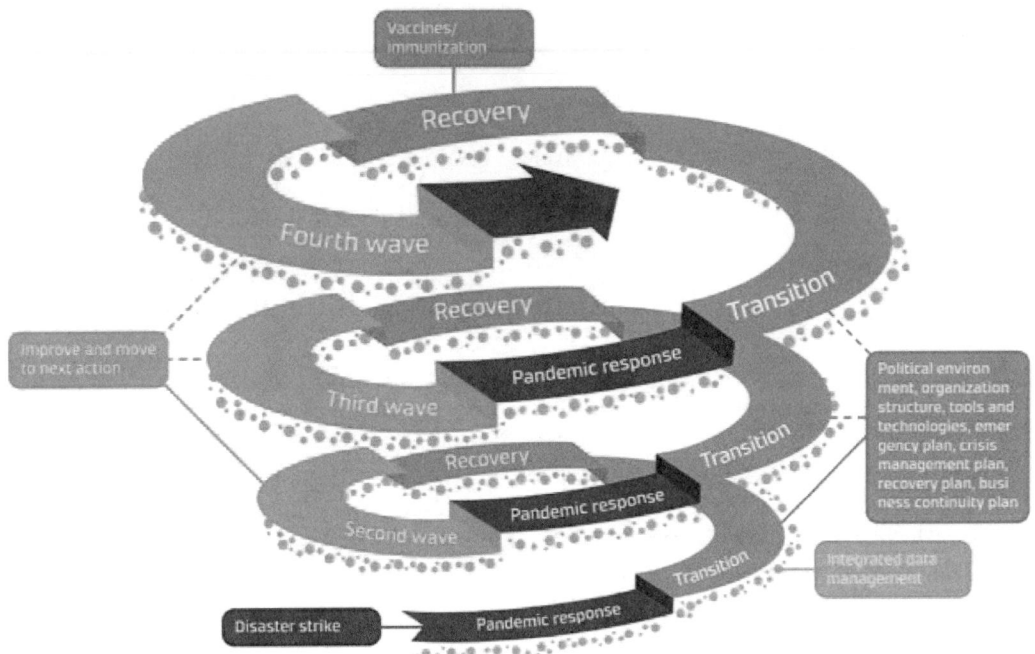
Figure 1. Pandemic management cycle (Fakhruddin et al. 2020)

(e) The integration of legal parameters into the development and implementation of technological solutions was only parenthetically considered. ROADS incorporates aspects of legal, ethical, and gender/diversity matters into its research from the outset.

(f) It is challenging to support the decision-making of pandemic managers. The processes that need to be considered in decision-making are manifold and go far beyond medical aspects, including e. g. socio-economic dimensions. This leads to a great variability in possible scenarios that can be used for comparison with the current situation. The innovative ROADS concept provides a comprehensive set of indicators for this multi-factorial and essential support.

As different crisis situations have to be clearly separated in their measures, there is exigency for further research on pandemic-specific problems in order to uncover vulnerabilities and develop resilience strategies that can be used to identify measures within an evidence-based management strategy system.

3. Research gaps, methodology and basis for the requirements analysis

As mentioned above, we created a matrix to analyse underlying strategic aims in accordance with measures set by decision makers to understand different approaches during specific times in a pandemic. The matrix supports a document analysis (Love, 2003) to investigate regulations, reports, statements, etc. that were implemented by decision makers at times. Various factors and components turned out to be important in this analysis, hence we include the following aspects in working with the framework:

(a) What kind of measure was selected/recommended by whom or what institution? In which context and timeframe was the measure facilitated? How was the measure made available e.g. via which type of document, on a website or by media?

(b) What was the strategic aim, including explicit goals, underlying side objectives, unexpected outcomes, and short- as well as long-term visions? In which specific sectors did the strategic aims take effect and are they measureable and verifiable within the SMART goals approach (Specific, Measureable, Achievable, Relevant, Time-Bound –University of California, 2016)?

(c) Which measures were taken to fulfil strategic aims? In what kind of frame were they implemented, and which sectors were affected by them?

(d) How effective were measures in their fields of implementation?

(e) Were those measures socially accepted and epidemiologically justifiable, concerning parameters for pandemics in general and COVID-19 specifically?

Strategic aims were constructing a frame surrounding measures with certain activities to be achieved in order to successfully reach those targets. Ultimately, our analysis aims to work out those strategic objectives and understand which measures were useful in pursing their achievement, but also which ones ended up having no effects or were even taken back due to social pressure or too little epidemiologic justification to uphold.

The initial analysis of the ROADS approach is mainly conducted by AGES and JOAFG, all other project partners are actively involved in a feedback loop to complement the findings. In addition, internal as well as external stakeholders are involved in giving input to work-task outputs and deliverables throughout the project. This contributes to a highly complex and interwoven, constantly growing matrix of determinants and factors that will be further elaborated on in the next section.

Although several meta-analyses were conducted (OECD, 2022), it turned out that a thorough and user friendly approach that supports stakeholders with relevant decision support is still lacking. One of the core focus aims of ROADS therefore is to build up a concept that includes and addresses (a) strategic parameters and objectives, (b) measures and bundles of measures, and (c) critical resources. The inclusion of pandemic strategic management is key, as those parameters are decided politically, e.g. zero COVID (Silver 2021) and plans to pivot from it (Normil 2022). Actions are based on those strategic aims but also on the availability of resources like protective equipment, pharmaceuticals, availabilities in critical infrastructures, etc. (Rainer et. al 2017, 2020, and 2021).

4. Challenges and approaches regarding pandemic management analysis

An early key question in the initial analysis was, if the effectiveness of strategic aims can be traced back to facilitated measures or bundles of interactions. Moreover, the challenge of the ROADS project and any analysis of the management of the COVID-19 pandemic raised the questions if it is possible to determine a measurement of these factors and how work out scientifically sound cause-effect-dependencies.

Due to the vagueness of many of the initially defined categories of pandemic parameters and additional influential factors, it is difficult to pin their holistic essence down in a clear cut way, since the understanding of terms like effectiveness, acceptance and implementation of bundles of measures varies broadly. This is not only the case within different groups in science and society but also in regards of their specific targeting. Thus, the setting of a stable and reliable foundation of the terminology and connotation is key for specifying the categories for the evolving analysis in order to effectively work out content retrieved in relevant documents.

Government policy statements, which were publicly communicated by the Austrian authorities, were found to be the most promising documents to identify strategic aims in pandemic management. These statements hold information on the general direction policies were set, based on expert opinions and model calculations as well as political and societal influences. (Bundles of) Measures were thereby reasoned for, but also questioned by journalists and experts. Government policy statements also offer insight into the development of strategies over time.

A framework to analyse these statements therefore is a key component for a fruitful breakdown of government action at respective times. Once the framework is finalised it will be possible to transparently trace strategic aims to (bundles of) measures and hence deliver a concise overview of ways to define steps that are necessary to take when tackling a pandemic. The following work-step contains working out prioritisations of pandemic parameters to suggest which ones are the most effective and therefore most important to implement.

The software MAXQDA will be used for a qualitative content analysis to categorise findings, identify connections, and understand logics of pandemic management in different situations. By doing so, a coherent overview will be worked out to comprehend means and measures that were set.

Another software that will be used to conduct a keyword search is "Proterm". Certain clusters of wordings not only provide insight into content-related reasoning for setting measures, but also into societal reactions and effects that play a role during a pandemic.

Once the initial setting of the frame is done, the next step of ROADS is to finalise the framework to transparently trace strategic aims to (bundles of) measures. Thus, starting from the experience of COVID-19, it will be the focus to deliver a concise overview of ways, and thereby define modular and adaptable steps that are necessary for tackling future pandemics in all their phases. The next step in the analysis will be to prioritise key parameters of a pandemic event to deduce, which connected measures are the most effective and therefore most important to timely implement by governance and organisation leads. This analysis of the prerequisites, determinants, and necessary knowledge base for a solid, evidence based intervention matching, will show the requirements but also the limitations and dynamic needs of pandemic management decisions, as Figure 2 outlines.

The highly complex interaction of pandemic classification parameters, determinants and other influencing aspects and areas, as the illustration below exemplarily depicts, shows what key factors in pandemic management have to be taken into account. This evolving example of some categories of the matrix, that catalogues the multitude of interacting factors in a pandemic event shows, how closely these key aspects intertwine and influence each other.

This is also one of the reasons, why simplistic cause-effect deductions can and should not easily be drawn and cannot easily be transferred to model recommendations for future health crisis management. However, it is the aim of the ROADS-approach to take up identified gaps and needs and to connect them with responding solutions and resources for a mitigation of the onset, according to the selected strategic aims.

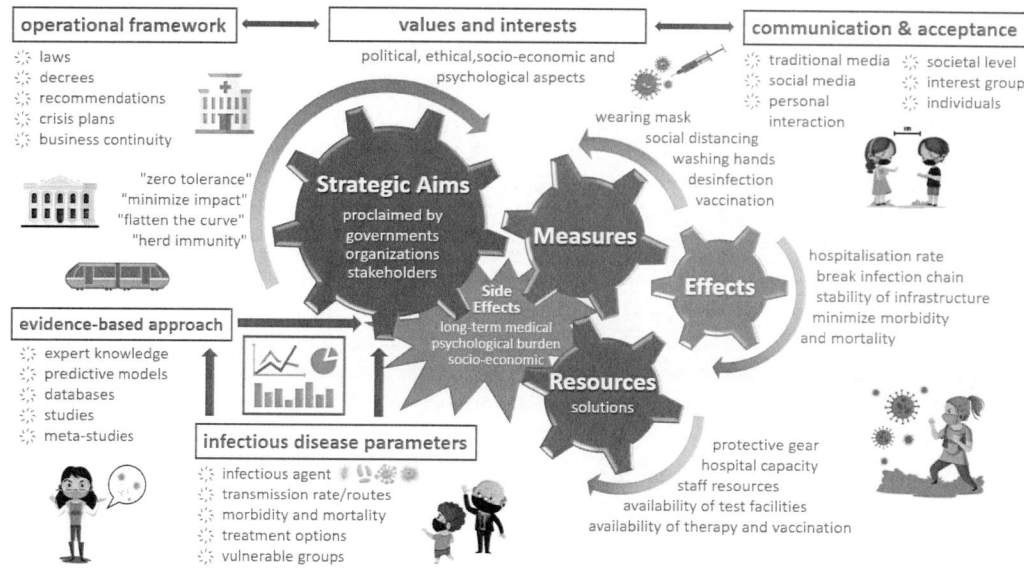

Figure 2. Interaction of pandemic management properties and parameters

Insulated knowledge and singular experience as well as the initial, pressing need for information about an upcoming health threat from infectious diseases – as the experience early in 2020 showed (Pollak, Kowarz, & Partheymüller, 2020) – can lead to measures that have to be modified quickly and very often lack explanation and thorough communication with the public. It also became evident, that the validity and weight of single aspects is highly determined by the dynamic status of the pandemic and its ongoing development and changes by e.g. new virus variants. Up to now, although there are several meta-studies (OECD, 2022) and an evolving necessity for applying the lessons learned from past pandemic management, there is no bundling of current knowledge and also no technologically supported and augmented merging of gained knowledge.

Difficulties are detected in the area of defining strategic aims, since they are not eye-catchingly published by the government or other decision makers but implicitly fostered by outlined measures that have to be implemented (e.g. laws, regulations, etc.). Those measures can ultimately be traced back to underlying strategic aims, they do however leave room for interpretation.

5. Summary and discussion

Pandemic outbreaks are an ongoing challenge that are still not systematically investigated regarding the multiplicity of aspects and holistic approaches that have to be considered. They are however of increasing importance for setting up a strategic, evidence based and still flexible tool set of solutions to foster preparedness and user friendly decision support in the future.

Since measures for fighting the pandemic were set in bundles, there is limited transparency in how efficient and expedient single measures were. Therefore, no simplified cause-effect attributions are possible. Measures do however specifically point out structures in pandemic management that worked well and will most likely work well in future outbreak situations.

Instead, a holistic approach has to strive for validating the impact of bundles of measures or in other words: how a bundle of selected measures was fulfilling strategic aims. Did the bundle of measures close gaps or did they correspond to needs?

Several approaches but also an ample field for further research and development, as well as for political and societal preparation and coordinated effort to prepare for a future pandemic event are shown in the course of the project ROADS up to now. Drawing conclusions between cause and effect poses to be difficult in regards to set feasible, acceptable and targeted measures and underlying strategic aims in pandemic management. The importance of an evidence based approach also became even clearer in the course of the initial research work and the interactive discussion in a multi-disciplinary team. The following period of the ongoing research and the development of a ROADS model for decision support will strive at answering these challenges in a holistic way to support decision makers for future outbreaks.

Acknowledgement

The research leading to these results has received funding from KIRAS Cooperative R&D Projects 2021 with project number FO999899442.

References

Abrams, Elissa M., Marcus Shaker, John Oppenheimer, Ray S. Davis, Don A. Bukstein, Matthew Greenhawt (2020). The Challenges and Opportunities for Shared Decision Making Highlighted by COVID-19, The Journal of Allergy and Clinical Immunology: In Practice, Volume 8, Issue 8, Pages 2474-2480

AGES COVID-Dashboard. (no date). https://covid19-dashboard.ages.at/ retrieved 18.04.2023

BMGF (2006) Influenza Pandemieplan Strategie für Österreich: http://www.bmg.gv.at/cms/site/standard.html?channel=CH0742&doc=CMS112

California, U. o. (2016). University of California: https://www.ucop.edu/local-human-resources/_files/performance-appraisal/How%20to%20write%20SMART%20Goals%20v2.pdf retrieved 13.02.2022

CAVE (2021). https://projekte.ffg.at/projekt/4101160 retrieved 18.04.2023

Corona relief measures: info, relief and simplification. https://www.imf.org/en/Topics/imf-and-covid19/Policy-Responses-to-COVID-19 retrieved 18.04.2023

ECDC. (no date). https://www.ecdc.europa.eu/en/covid-19 retrieved 13.02.2022

Fakhruddin, B.Blanchard, K., Ragupathy, D. (2020). Are we there yet? The transition from response to recovery for the COVID-19 pandemic. https://doi.org/10.1016/j.pdisas.2020.100102 retrieved 14.04.2023

GÖG Datenplattform. (no date). https://datenplattform-covid.goeg.at/ retrieved 18.04.2023

Ignjatović, D., Havlik, D., Neubauer, G., Turptil, S., Gonzales, F., Regeczi, D.: The Portfolio of Solutions. In: Proceedings of the 27th Interdisciplinary Information Management Talks, Kutná Hora, Czech Republic, 4 – 6September 2019, pp199-206

Love, P. (2003). Document Analysis. In P. Love, Research in College Context (S. Chapter 6, 14 pages). New York: Routledge.

Normil, D. (2022). China quietly plans a pivot from "zero COVID". Scientists are studying how to live with the virus while avoiding a crisis like in Hong Kong. Science • 3 Mar 2022 • Vol 375, Issue 6584 • p. 949 • DOI: 10.1126/science.adb1762

OECD Organisaton for Economic Co-operation and Development. https://www.occd.org/coronavirus/policy-responses/first-lessons-from-government-evaluations-of-covid-19-responses-a-synthesis-483507d6/#component-d1e6394 retrieved 18.04.2023

OECD. (21.01.2022). First lessons from government evaluations of COVID-19 responses: A synthesis. OECD Publishing, S. 48.

Pollak, M., Kowarz, N., & Partheymüller, J. (3. June 2020). Universität Wien - Vienna Center for Electoral Research. https://viecer.univie.ac.at/en/projects-and-cooperations/austrian-corona-panel-project/corona-blog/corona-blog-beitraege/blog51/ retrieved 19.04.2023

Rainer, K., Fastl, C., Leidwein, A., Nemenz, P., Hoffmann, M., Rathammer, K., Kundratitz, V., Neubauer, G., Preinerstorfer, A., Aumayr, G., Scheuer, S., Eisenberger, I., Hofer, A., Scholz, S. (2021) Digital Transformation in Crisis Management. Risk, Vulnerability and Resilience Analyses for Pandemic Management: Challenges and Perspectives of Approaches for the Future. In: Petr Doucek et al. (Eds.). Information Technology, Society and Economy Strategic Cross-Influences. 29th interdisciplinary Information Management Talks. Trauner Linz. 163-174

Rainer, K., Leidwein, A., Nemenz, P., Hoffmann, M., Neubauer, G., & Aumayr, G. (2020). Interoperability and crisis management in pandemic outbreak scenarios an overview on different case studies of the austrian approach to tackle the SARS-CoV-2 spread and adherent management challenges. IDIMT 2020: Digitalized Economy, Society and Information Management-28th Interdisciplinary Information Management Talks

Rainer, K., Neubauer, G., Ruzsanyi, V., Silvestru, D., Almer, A. & Lampoltshammer, T. (2017). The Potential of Multiple Types of Sensor Data and Information Exchange. Challenges and Perspectives for an Operational Picture for the Response to Crises with Mass Involvement. In: Petr Doucek et al. (Eds.). IDIMT 2017. Information Technology, Society and Economy Strategic Cross-Influences. 25th interdisciplinary Information Management Talks. Trauner Linz. 111-126

Rainer, K., Neubauer, G., Pointner, K., & Kastel, W. (2016). Inclusion of Marginalized Groups into Crisis Management Processes. Models, Case Studies, and holistic Perspectives. In: Petr Doucek et al. (Eds.). IDIMT 2016. Information Technology, Society and Economy Strategic CrossInfluences. 24th interdisciplinary Information Management Talks. Trauner Linz. 87-100.see e.g. CSH 2020.

ROADS to Health project website (no date). https://www.ages.at/forschung/projekte/roads-to-health retrieved 18.04.2023

Schawel, C., Billing, F. (2009). SWOT-Analyse. In: Top 100 Management Tools. Gabler. https://doi.org/10.1007/978-3-8349-8185-1_79

Silver, A. (2021). Covid-19: Why China is sticking to "zero tolerance" public health measures. BMJ 2021; 375:n2756

Vienna, M. U. (19. April 2023). Austrian Research Promotion Agency (FFG). https://projekte.ffg.at/projekt/4101160 retrieved 19.04.2023

WHO Coronavirus Dashboard (no date). https://covid19.who.int/ retrieved 13.02.2022

THE ETHICAL EVALUATION STANDARD FOR SECURITY RESEARCH (EESSR) MODEL

Constanze Geyer, Gudrun Ringler, Georg Aumayr, Nadine Sturm

Johanniter Österreich Ausbildung und Forschung gGmbH (JOAFG),
Constanze.Geyer@johanniter.at, Gudrun.Ringler@johanniter.at,
Georg.Aumayr@johanniter.at, Nadine.Sturm@johanniter.at

DOI: 10.35011/IDIMT-2023-39

Keywords

Ethical risk assessment, security research, human-technology interaction, data protection, privacy

Abstract

The interaction between humans and technologies in the field of safety and security nowadays makes it crucial to identify ethical and data protection issues in time and - if necessary - to observe them and take measures. In order to be able to analyze technological systems from the beginning as well as during several development phases in a structured way, adequate tools are needed that also make it possible to give application-oriented recommendations. The EESSR model – derived 2019 from Manzeschke et al.'s MEESTAR (2013) – is able to meet these requirements, to create awareness and space for the topic of ethics. Furthermore, the use of the EESSR model in workshops can foster a common understanding of the overall project aim and provide an outlook for the application of the technology.

1. Introduction

The safety and security research sector is at the forefront of many important technological innovations that help first responders do their job more efficiently and safely. Since the use of these inventions often results in unintended and unexpected consequences, the development should be accompanied by a technological assessment to avoid burden in life-saving operations. This directs the focus on analysing the interaction of technological innovation and humans; on individual up to a societal level. Guided by principles such as fairness, accountability, dignity or well-being of those involved, the ethical perspective asks whether the processes of developing, testing and using the technology are justifiable. It is crucial to consider what specific challenges arise with existing moral, norms, values and laws. This means that it is particularly a matter of creating transparency, reflecting on and becoming aware of motives for action, and re-examining and weighing up, what is the right thing to do (Cotton, 2014 and EU, 2021).

The Ethical Evaluation Standard for Security Research (EESSR) model is an adoption for the field of safety and security research based on the evaluation framework Model for the Ethical Evaluation of Socio-Technical Arrangements (MEESTAR). This established instrument is used in the field of technological developments for the health care sector. It is applied for preventing undesired consequences by enabling awareness e.g. about potential malfunctions, or causes for unfair treatment of users (Manzeschke et al., 2013). The EESSR model fosters the identification of ethical issues in each development phase and thus supports an accompanying discussion on ethical matters. Moreover, it enables the users to assess in a structured way and to allocate identified ethical issues to relevant tasks. It facilitates a reflection and the visualizing of ethical aspects. Additional wide-ranging effects are that technical developers get sensitized for the topic and a common understanding about the vision. Further, as it is inherent in its nature, the importance of ethical considerations is created (Ringler, 2019).

2. Derivation of the EESSR model

When the MEESTAR methodology became present in projects funded by the Active and Assisted Living Programme (https://www.aal-europe.eu/) the concept showed its impact in raising awareness of ethical issues and the project aim in a well-structured way, especially at a time when the development can still be adapted. It comprises seven ethical dimensions (*Care, Autonomy, Safety, Justice, Privacy, Participation and Self-Image*), three layers (*individual, organizational and societal*) and four stages of ethical severity (*harmless, sensitive, extremely sensitive, to be opposed*; see *Figure 1*). MEESTAR was considered as a starting point for deriving a similar approach for security research, to cover the gap in ethical discussions and provide a focused methodology for assessing and comparing developments. It was conclusive that adjustments towards related aspects in security research were needed. The derivation is based on the extensive experience from several security research projects and first responder actions (e.g. UEFA EURO 2008, train accidents, search and rescue actions, ambulance service, emergency medical services).

First, the ethical dimensions were transposed from the health focus to the safety and security research area and the conditions of disaster operations: *Care* as a dimension of MEESTAR referred to care services, in the sense of solicitude and welfare. To include first aid and also psycho social support as main services of first responders active in safety as well as in criminal prevention measures, this was adapted to *Care and Support*. *Autonomy* is not an appropriate perspective for emergency situations, as first responders have defined equipment, tasks and hierarchies to follow (INSARAG, 2012). It is important to be aware of the own role and tasks during an operation, the responsibilities and hierarchical structures the first responder needs to comply to. This enables a structured and rapid processing of crisis management (*On-Site Operations Coordination Centre (OSOCC)*, 2017). *Autonomy* was therefore derived to *Self-image of the User*. The dimension *Safety* needs to be understood in the context of operations in difficult and dangerous areas and accident prevention needs to be strongly considered. Therefore, the perspective wars narrowed on *Personal Safety* as a precision towards the conditions in operations. *Justice* was adapted to *Ability of Judgement*. In disaster response, other laws are in place than during daily routines (Aronsson-Storrier & Costa, 2017). Thus, supportive assessment of the situation in a secure manner should be focused, derived decisions must be safe and transparent. The security aspect plays a big role in here, as decisions and processes could be manipulated by, e.g., malfunctions caused by sabotage and vandalism. *Ability of Judgement* (e.g. forced by trainings) enables fair treatment of injured persons, but also promotes justice according from a legal perspective. *Privacy* was excluded due to the same reason of context of application and legal aspects of disaster response (Aronsson-Storrier & Costa, 2017). *Participation* stayed, as it covers an identical concept. According to MEESTAR it involves communication, social acceptance and respectful interaction, which also applies to the field of safety but also security research. As actions in the field of first responders are command driven and mission-oriented (Glass, 2006), the dimension *Self-Image* of MEESTAR, involving e.g. formability of own life or setting limits, was not adopted for EESSR model. The focus of EESSR is to consider roles and persons as well as technology use in the context of disaster response. A holistic analysis of their identities or surrounding factors is not part of the analysis. *Availability* was added as another category to support ethical discussions for safety and security research. The dimension is inspired by restraints of missions in critical areas where sometimes the needed infrastructure is not or hardly available. For example, water purification is an important ethical concern. Nevertheless, in some areas, the requirements cannot be met or are just too expansive to be available for all people in need. This is where an assessment team needs to triage needs onsite (Freeman & Tobin, 2011). Moreover, also security incidents like theft, acts of sabotage and/or vandalism have an effect on availability.

This process logic was implemented with the modification of the three layers in relation to the disaster management cycle (*Tracking the Evolution of the Disaster Management Cycle*, o. J.), adding a time component to the model. The *Societal* layer was adopted to *Strategical Layer*, which refers to long term decisions, comprising the recovery, preparedness and mitigation phase. The *Organizational* layer was modified as *Tactical Layer*, dedicated to the response and recovery phase onsite. The *Individual* layer was changed to *Operational Layer* and relates to the response phase of an incident; accidental and/or criminal. In the MEESTAR, the perspectives involved are covered by the layers. Following on from this, the *affected groups* of people in the safety and security sectors, was initiated (see 3. Methodological approach). The four stages of ethical severity are applied in the same way for EESSR as they have been for MEESTAR. The clearness and understandability are considered accurate also for safety and security research. By applying the EESSR model, it could be further developed with modifications that made it even more practice-oriented. How it is currently used is described in the following chapter.

3. Methodological approach

The EESSR model is applied in workshops with interdisciplinary participants discussing and assessing identified ethical aspects in the context of technology use in a specific scenario. Central to analysis is the creation of a clear vision of the application of the technology in the selected scenario and the corresponding conditions. *Figure 1* below shows the main pillars of analysis with the EESSR model.

In the center of the model, the stages of ethical relevance are set. They allow to concretize needs for action in upcoming steps of the development process. Based on the technology and scenario description in a first step, the roles involved are separated into *Target group*, *Responders* and *Responsible* persons and institutions, as described in Table 1. Previously, one of the roles was titled as *Victim*, which suggests that this role labels a person who is suffering because of some incident. This was changed to *Target group* to make it clear that this role focuses on all people that are at least partly affected by an incident, but not only the ones who need help or rescue (e.g. bystanders). It turned out during the evaluation process that the severity of an issue could strongly differ depending on the (group of) person(s) affected.

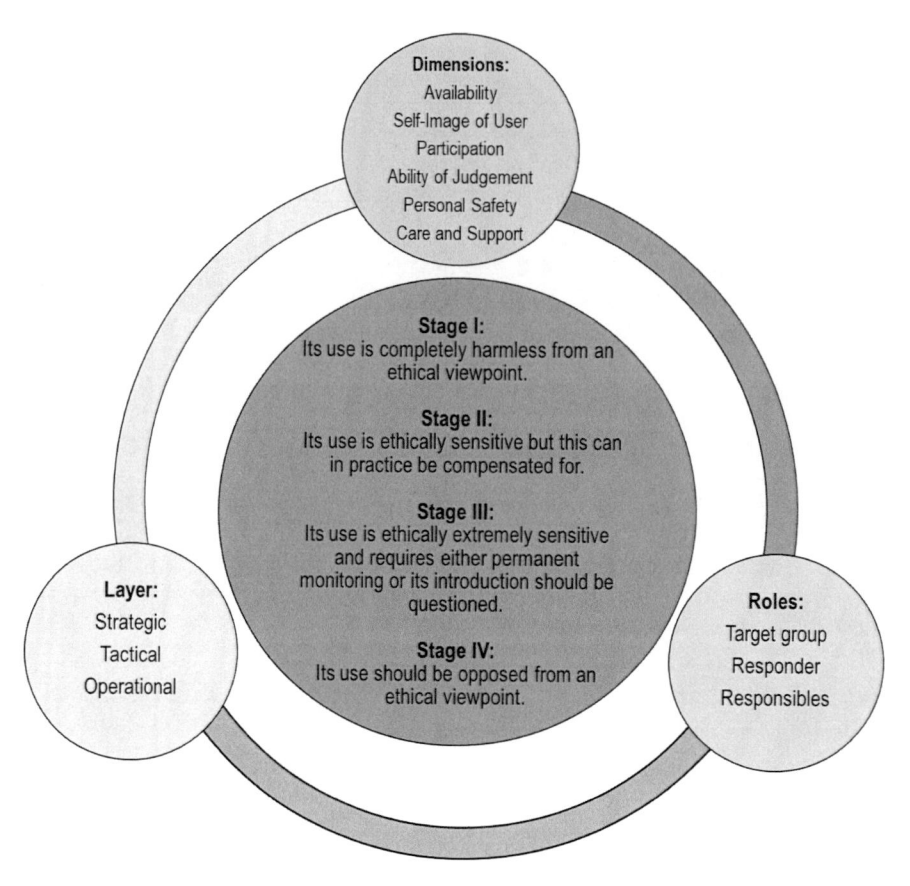

Figure 1. EESSR model   Source: (own illustration)

Table 1. Definition of roles for ethical assessment

Role	Description
Target group	Who is affected due to the consequences of the event?
Responders	Who is reacting to the event to help; also in terms of technology use?
Responsible	Who is responsible for the event on a policy and/or command level in terms of the framework of the operation and possibilities of action?

The dimensions of the ethical assessment at the top of the outer circle of the model serve to operationalise and identify relevant ethical aspects. Thus, ethical questions and problems that arise in the discussion must be categorized accordingly. If an aspect relates to several dimensions, it needs to be formulated from the respective perspective and level. The descriptions in Table 2 are based on general definitions by *Cambridge Free English Dictionary and Thesaurus, n.d. (2022)*, set into the EESSR-context.

Table 2. Dimensions of EESSR model

Dimension	Examples	Description
Availability	Readiness, Capability, Standby, Attendance	Operational readiness of personnel, but also of hardware and software for use. Since in most cases planning and management precede adequate deployment, availability is based on both and can hardly exist without them. Examples for weak availability are a low battery of an applied technology or an unstable internet connection, but also, budgetary needs for procurement.
Self-image of the User	Self-assessment, Weaknesses, Strengths, Skills	Self-perception of the persons defined in "Roles". The more the self-image of the members of the target group, responders and/or responsibles matches their actual values, competencies and responsibilities, the more valuable the person is for other actors and the process. If the self-perception is overestimated, commitment needs limitation as self-regulation cannot be safely achieved. This carries the risk of wrong decisions and requires the engagement of other actors for regulation.
Participation	Teamwork, Cooperation	Commitment and competence to actively cooperate and support the operation and the persons involved. However, it primarily describes the willing of one person being part of a team or also the commitment of a team to cooperate with or be integrated into a larger team (e.g. the operating team of firefighters is incorporated into the disaster-relief team).
Ability of Judgement	Mental Stability, Knowledge, Training	Is built on the pillars of personal characteristics, education and the individual world of experience and strongly influenced by stress and stress resistance. Under pressure the cognitive performance that is needed for assessment tends to be decreased with the risk to lead to wrong decisions.
Personal Safety	Self-Responsibility, Control	The term is aimed at the physical and psychological integrity of all actors, which needs to be preserved at all times of an operation. All actors must contribute to their own safety; they need to act self-responsibly and keep their personal situation under control in the disaster. Additionally, all actors, but especially responders and responsibles, must contribute to the safety of all actors with whom they work with in the disaster.
Care and Support	Helpfulness, Solidarity, Altruism	The ability to care for and support others and use technology can be seen as soft skill. It depends on characteristics and is offered by some individuals to a greater extent than others. In addition, human survival instincts will weigh personal commitment in terms of the personal risks (personal safety) to which help provided might be exposed. Nevertheless, awareness of the need for care and support, as well as knowledge of the methods, can be built through targeted measures, e.g. in the form of training.

To this end, the following research questions are formulated for discussion:
- *Availability:* Which ethical aspects play a role in the area of the performance of the system?
- *Self-image of the User:* How could the system affect the self-assessment of the actors?
- *Participation:* Is there cooperation required for ethical use of the system?
- *Ability of Judgement:* How might the use of the system affect the mental stability and judgement of users?
- *Personal Safety:* Which ethical factors play a role in relation to the external and/or personal responsibility in the use of the system?
- *Care and Support:* Which potential impact could the technology and its use have to support/damage the single roles involved?

Furthermore, a time frame for planning and a concretization of the technology application is given by the strategic, tactical and operative layer, which build the levels of impact shown and described in Table 3. The ethical questions are discussed for each level, and an ethical aspect may be valid at more than one level.

Table 3. Overview levels of impact

Layer	Description
Strategic	Long-term planning for preventing negative consequences
Tactical	Controlling and planning of actions
Operational	Working at the place of action

Linking the model's dimensions and levels of impact with the defined roles and responsibilities involved provides a comprehensive picture of the technology use in the scenario. This enables deeper insight into structural and potential compensations for the assessed risk. Depending on the context, another step could be relevant, which is the assignment of the different identified ethical aspects to the responsible tasks within a development process. The assignment leads to a very concrete distribution of responsibilities and respective time frames.

3.1. Conduction and limitations

It is recommended to apply the EESSR model in a very early stage of development for the first time and afterwards iteratively during the following development process. This aims to manifest participatory design and solidarity ideology in the evaluation and to encourage the development of an invention taking ethical aspects into account. The COVID 19-pandemic made it necessary to change the format of the workshop into an online event. The use of an online whiteboard (e.g. Conceptboard, Miro) is very productive on the levels of visualisation, participation and involvement in collecting ethical issues. The guidance of the workshop by moderators with ethical know how is decisive. However, it is strongly recommended to work with a handful of experts with different professional backgrounds to display several perspectives resulting from various living environments. The EESSR evaluation-process benefits from the participation of a technological project partner who can provide insights into the technological logic of the vision and answers to related questions.

After an introduction of the model with its ethical intent and steps in general, the vision of development and its setting/use case needs to be shared (1), e.g. if a whole system or single innovation is used after an earthquake with people under rubble. Then, roles (see *Table*) involved are discussed (2). This ensures that all participants are on the same level of information about the project and its development, but also about the steps of the model and the aim of the workshop. In the next step, the evaluation of potential ethical issues and their allocation to the dimensions starts (3): All participants are instructed to think about the invention and possible problems that might occur, who could be affected and to what extent and how each problem could be solved or at least curbed. After the categorization according to the layers (4), the ethical gravity has to be assessed with the scale of the four stages (5) and the phases of affected steps of development in the project identified (6). By this, the project team acquires knowledge on issues that must be looked at in detail in upcoming development phases. Awareness for single ethical issues serves as basis to make decisions on development adaptions. In most cases, discussed ethical issues lead to observation and a renewed confrontation in the next EESSR workshop.

Since the development of the EESSR model based on MEESTAR in 2019 not only a proof of concept was implemented. Beyond that several workshops in the context of projects in the field of safety and security research were conducted and limitations and modifications also became apparent. First, the conduction of EESSR workshops takes time (approx. two to three hours each) and almost always some participants have no or low experiences with analyzing ethics and ethical issues yet. Therefore, a clarification - and best practice examples – is needed to impart knowledge of what ethics entails. However, the results of the workshop do not show all ethical issues that might occur in the future. The outcome is based on the experiences and opinions of individuals and therefore do not claim to be representative. In addition, a language barrier cannot be ruled out if a workshop is conducted in English with an international group of participants. Interpretations of dimensions also vary and depend, e.g. on the culture and lifeworld of participants; definitions and examples can support a common understanding and lead out of confusion. Further, the conclusions of the workshops refer to the reference contexts, i.e. a scenario or use case and the conditions described as well as the technology. Some aspects may well be raised to a more abstract level. However, the evaluations are timely punctual collections of possible ethical issues on the timeline of developments and require follow-up in most cases. For this reason, it is emphasized here, that the intention of EESSR workshops is to provide insights and raise awareness, not to achieve completeness. The benefits of such assessment could be shown in several workshops in course of various projects, where an interdisciplinary exchange was enabled, e.g. participants with technical background could exchange with end users and social scientists. Furthermore the ethical evaluation as a stand-alone crucial approach was proven as a possibility to change perspective and open up to new aspects that can be included in future work. This enriching effect was also confirmed several times by positive feedback of participants. The EESSR model provides a well-structured way to evaluate ethical aspects during technological developments enabling a sharpened project vision created by the discussion. In sum the advantages of the model overrule mentioned limitations; especially if awareness could be enabled within the participants.

4. EESSR and Data Protection

Within the framework of various projects with different objectives, the EESSR model could be applied in a targeted manner and its flexibility validated. Most of those projects in the area of security research focus on technology development predominantly in the context of risk assessment and emergency procedures and contain a human-technology interaction. The General Data Protection Regulation (GDPR 2016/679) of the European Parliament and Council initiated awareness and boosted the topic. Developers must by law be more careful with personal data and therefore include data protection issues in their development processes. The close link between ethics and law also brings up data protection as a central topic for analysis using the EESSR model. This allows to identify potential problems and possible measures in this regard. In EESSR workshops, data protection issues almost always raise ethical relevant aspects and need space for discussion. In terms of data protection there are two perspectives which can be covered within EESSR model: Project related activities, i.e. pilots and the outlook of the actual use of the technology in real life operations. Those two situations differ upon others in preparations, briefings, safety measures and supplies (e.g. consent form for participants in research process vs. real life scenario) as well as its aims (testing of technology vs. saving physical integrity). In both environments, considerations of compliance with data protection in human-technology interaction must be made and dealt with – of course best before operation. Data protection issues that were discussed in EESSR workshops until now are about data, which needs to be collected, processed and stored; mostly in an automatic way, e.g. from social media for sentiment analysis. Technologies like imaging systems (e.g. camera drones and satellites) and geo-referencing systems - in combination or as single technology – are able to deliver a more detailed picture not only of major damages but also of persons' looks and motions or mobility behavior. In addition, wearables that record biodata are also often part of systems in the area, e.g. to track first responders. The data required for support conflicts with the question of enabling the privacy of the individual observed, e.g. people who are unknowingly being watched by a drone. These aspects gain weight when technologies are used not only in disasters but also in the daily life for monitoring issues. Thus, when it affects (parts of) the civil society or professional responders or formations that are aware of the technology's application. A simplified example for a potential ethical issue when using the technology on site in Table 4 shall serve as illustration.

Table 4. Example for an ethical relevant aspect, compensation, assigned roles and layers

Technology/ scenario	Description ethical aspect	Dimension	Compensation	Role/layer
Drone/ people trapped under rubble	Personal data of target group is collected and shared without information and consent	Personal Safety	Establishment of a data management plan, access restrictions and communication strategy for transparency	Responsibles/ strategic for compensation Responder/ operational for impact

From this, questions arise for discussion and reflection:

- Is the data generated within projects and subsequently through the use of developed technologies a must in order to fulfill its purpose or can developers do without linking to individuals? Can the impact on privacy be avoided without a loss of needed information? Are anonymizations or pseudonymizations sufficient or should other measures be taken?
- Also, social media posts seem to be useful in the sense of receiving an additional and bigger picture of an event by the civil society on-site: Which additional but not needed data will also be harvested by tapping posts?

By this the process of EESSR allows to raise awareness for data protection and supports the identification and thus avoidance of tasks and/or functions that do not correlate with data protection. Due to the results of EESSR sessions, concrete actions could be set, e.g. the consultation of a data security authority for enabling privacy by design with broad information about the legal situation to be taken into account.

5. Conclusion

In understanding the ethical analysis, it is important to emphasize that the main objective is to identify potential ethical relevant aspects in order to be able to take them into account. However, this does not only mean potential risks, but includes the added value that could be achieved with the technology. Since the research object is in development this kind of evaluation has to be seen in relation to the status and therefore as dynamic and adaptable for changing conditions and processes. A distinction must also be made here between practical implementation, allowing a broader approach and testing within the project framework. With EESSR a structure for a classified uptake of ethical and data protection issues is provided. Moreover, the application of the model fuels regular discussions in interdisciplinary teams and deliver more room for these topics. The compliant outcomes demonstrate that it is useful to analyze ethical aspects and implement control measures. Moreover, it provides a structure to mitigate risks, e.g. thinking along content for necessary training of end users or the GDPR conform communication for the implementation. This makes it easier to address potential issues and e.g. include the right behavior with the technology in the emergency situation. The ethical inquiry and the factors uncovered may also have an impact on the acceptance of the technology (Cotton, 2014). Thus, it also serves as an instrument for the justifiable design of the technology and its handling. In any case, the recommendation is stated to monitor the development properly and validate with end users.

References

Aronsson-Storrier, M., & Costa, K. da. (2017). Regulating disasters? The role of international law in disaster prevention and management. Disaster Prevention and Management, 26(5), 502–513. https://doi.org/10.1108/DPM-09-2017-0218Cambridge Free English Dictionary and Thesaurus. (n.d.) Retrieved 23. February 2022, from: https://dictionary.cambridge.org/dictionary/.

Cambridge Free English Dictionary and Thesaurus. (o. J.). Abgerufen 23. Februar 2022, von https://dictionary.cambridge.org/dictionary/

Cotton, M. (2014). Opening Up Ethical Dialogue. In: Ethics and Technology Assessment: A Participatory Approach. Studies in Applied Philosophy, Epistemology and Rational Ethics, vol 13. Springer, Berlin, Heidelberg. https://doi.org/10.1007/978-3-642-45088-4_6.

European Commission. (2021). Ethics by Design and Ethics of Use Approaches for Artificial Intelligence. https://ec.europa.eu/info/funding-tenders/opportunities/docs/2021-2027/horizon/guidance/ethics-by-design-and-ethics-of-use-approaches-for-artificial-intelligence_he_en.pdf.

Freeman, J. A., & Tobin, G. A. (2011). Assessment of an Emergency Disaster Response to Floods in Agadez, Niger. Risk, Hazards & Crisis in Public Policy, 2(2), 1–19. https://doi.org/10.2202/1944-4079.1072

Glass, T. (2006). INSARAG GUIDELINES AND METHODOLOGY.

INSARAG. (2012). INSARAG Guidelines-2012. 217.

Manzeschke, A., Weber, K., Rother, E., & Fangerau, H. (2013). Ergebnisse der Studie "Ethische Fragen im Bereich Altersgerechter Assistenzsysteme". Berlin: VDI/VDE Innovation + Technik GmbH.

On-Site Operations Coordination Centre (OSOCC). (2017, Februar 24). OCHA. https://www.unocha.org/our-work/coordination/site-operations-coordination-centre-osocc

Ringler, G. (2019). D1.8 Ethics Manual and Guidelines for data protection and safety in passenger ships. PALAEMON. A holistic passenger ship evacuation and rescue ecosystem. EU Horizon 2020 No 814962.

Tracking the evolution of the disaster management cycle: A general system theory approach : original research. (o. J.). Jamba : Journal of Disaster Risk Studies. Abgerufen 5. Juni 2023, von https://journals.co.za/doi/10.4102/jamba.v4i1.54

CYBER SECURITY

AN EVIDENCE COLLECTION SYSTEM FOR ROBOT-SUPPORTED INSPECTION OF CRITICAL INFRASTRUCTURE

Michael Sonntag

Johannes Kepler University Linz
Institute of Networks and Security,
michael.sonntag@jku.at

Stefan Schraml

AIT Austrian Institute of Technology GmbH,
stephan.schraml@ait.ac.at

DOI: 10.35011/IDIMT-2023-51

Keywords

Evidence collection, critical infrastructure, threat model

Abstract

In many sectors, it is necessary to collect evidence in advance, as it may be needed later. While evidence in law enforcement is collected after a crime has occurred to solve it, it needs to be collected in commercial systems in advance to avoid potential future disputes. But can existing data (in the rare case it is needed as such) serve as credible and useful evidence? In this paper we describe the design of a system to collect data for potential use as proof that inspections of critical infrastructure (in this case cable ducts) took place and that certain alarms about potential problems did (or did not) occur. The system consists of two parts, a mobile robot, and a base station. Data needs to be collected independently in both parts and combined later to be able to serve as evidence.

1. Introduction

Inspecting large, physically uniform infrastructures is a complex, tedious and repetitive task – which is nevertheless essential. The owner might have to be able to prove that the inspections have in fact been performed, e.g., to demonstrate compliance to a regulatory authority. Likewise, any findings on the (non-)existence of defects (and consequently the need for repairs) should also be provable to third parties (authorities, courts, etc). A practical example is underground collector ducts for power supply: high-voltage electricity cables, gas pipes, heating/cooling pipes, etc. can run there. In large cities or industrial areas, up to hundreds of kilometers of such ducts may exist, requiring them to be checked regularly by the operating company. Currently, this is typically done manually by sending people in to walk through them and visually inspect for any defects or potential problems. However, this does not take into account, for e.g., small but continuous changes from the previous inspection (nobody can remember after a year the height of the duct in millimeters, or how large the wet spot on the floor was, or whether that was because of recent rain).

Automating these inspections by robots that document the activity (e.g., laser scanning to obtain exact measurements, videos for visual comparison, and various other sensors to detect potential hazards such as gases or fluids) is therefore an alternative being developed in the research project INFRASPEC. This poses several technical challenges (moving the robot – autonomously or manually guided – without collisions, pot. hazardous environments such as gas leaks, high EM radiation…; detecting deviations from previous scans as well as recognizing problems like sintered deposits etc.). This paper, however, focuses on the aspect of evidence collection of these activities: if necessary being able to prove that an inspection took place at a specific location and at a specific time with particular results, and that this data, given its potential sensitivity, is secure.

Specific difficulties of designing and implementing such a system include:

- The mobile robot might not have a very large bandwidth to its base stations for archiving data. Note that anything sent over this connection to/from the robot is also potential evidence, excluding the evidence collected on the robot itself, obviously. Also, for safe and secure operation command&control might have to take priority over evidence in case of reduced connection speed/bandwidth.
- Large amounts of data need to be archived: robots might have multiple high-resolution cameras. And while an operator might only be using 1-2 at any time, all of them continuously produce potential evidence.
- Inspections often take place in locations where external connectivity, such as internet or GPS, is unavailable (e.g., in tunnels far underground). Any such external communication might have to take place before/afterwards and somewhat removed (both in space and time) from the actual inspection. From this follows a lack of synchronous connection to third parties respectively the near impossibility of exporting data in real-time.
- The evidence is held under control of an interested party: the company owning the infrastructure and performing its inspection might be very much interested in claiming that no problems were found ("We could not foresee that damage!"), that numerous problems exist ("We need more funding/price increases!"), or that inspections took place that were never actually performed (to reduce costs while still "fulfilling" requirements of supervisory bodies).
- The resulting data may be sensitive: the exact location and construction of critical infrastructure, together with where to enter/exit, how they are connected to other buildings etc. should not become public. Humans performing an inspection necessarily know this information but making it explicit and storing it opens up new attack vectors.

This paper describes the design of a system for collecting evidence in such circumstances. It also investigates the threat model as a prerequisite to be able to determine details requirements.

2. Related work

Typical evidence collection in computer forensics takes place after the fact: access to some storage medium/mobile device/PC/car/… is obtained and a copy is made (acquisition and identification; Newman 2007), which must be kept secure (chain of custody) and which should provably identical to the original. Here, however, the evidence is to be collected directly as it is created: no (or very little) time delay should exist. This is therefore similar to live forensic investigations, e.g. when an attacker is still active within a system by the time this is discovered and monitoring begins. However, even there the aim is to obtain evidence from "normal" sources, e.g. the RAM. I.e. we collect data that is not originally/mainly intended as evidence, but can later serve as such (see e.g. Al-Sharif et al 2020). Also, in this project we do not need to collect all data, so we might find evidence somewhere therein, but we can specifically gather what might be needed later for various pre-defined scenarios. Another common difficulty of forensics is that data from multiple sources needs to be correlated – not all of them might have a synchronous time (Kotsiuba et al 2019). When we deliberately collect evidence from multiple sources, we can ensure that either no time difference exists or that it is known exactly (and can then be compensated for).

And while many current systems suggest the use of a blockchain for evidence management (e.g. Sathyprakasan et al 2021), the actual utility of a blockchain seems dubious: using a proof-of-stake system requires an enormous amount of work and time and requires disclosing the actual evidence. Therefore, it is necessary to only provide e.g. hash values for the actual inclusion. If, on the other hand, the blockchain is a private/permissioned one (see e.g. Kim/Ihm/Son 2021), then a simple hash chain with (potentially multiple) signatures is functionally mostly equivalent – which is proposed here.

Our system is designed only for the collection of evidence – in reality only rarely it will be needed as such (integrity protection is a much more common and useful side-effect, but could also be reached simpler). This distinguishes us from systems covering the whole lifecycle, including presentation at court (Li/Lal/Conti/Hu 2021).

We draw loosely on the Evidence Management Plan (EMP; Grobler/Lowrens 2010): proactively identifying potential evidence, evaluating risks, and developing a procedure to ensure we have the best evidence possible.

3. Threat model

Before a system can be designed and implemented, the aims of protection need to be defined, which might be attacked by someone. The typical ones are confidentiality, integrity and availability. Privacy is not seen as relevant here, as the only connection to a person will be the person performing the inspection. This will typically be an employee of the infrastructure (operator) and is seen as less critical and not the focus of this project. Other potential aims are non-repudiation, which is important here, and traceability, the possibility to link results to actions/decisions of a person or a system (e.g. in connection with damages caused by the inspection itself), which is also covered in this project. Given the critical nature of the infrastructure being inspected, ensuring safety is crucial. This includes protecting not only the operators themselves but also potentially other individuals who may be affected, as ducts can be lengthy and hazards could extend over long distances. Additionally, it is essential to consider the safety of the recipients of the services provided through the infrastructure. However, this is out of the scope of this paper. It is important to note that these aims need to be handled two-fold: on one hand for the data to be obtained (e.g. integrity of recorded data/events), on the other for the physical environment (e.g. radio transmissions must not lead to incorrect behavior causing physical destruction – environmental integrity). Similar as before, only the first aspect is described here and the second taken care of during implementation – as it is a prototype only in a controlled, albeit real, environment, this is acceptable.

Which persons are considered potential attackers (note that not all the described "attacks" might be illegal; merely considered "undesirable" by someone) and what goals might these actors pursue?

1. Robot owner: the owner of the robot, which might be separate from the operator or the infrastructure owner (leased/rented equipment). He can be interested in hiding any malfunctions or defects of the device or evidence for what caused those. Other aims include evidence for the amount of actual use (e.g. for billing), or the environment it was used in (e.g. more humid than specified; rough handling like falls).
2. Robot operator: who controls the robot during the inspection. Interests range from faking a not-performed inspection (copying/modifying old data, inventing new data), hiding accidents like damages because of incorrect control of the robot, to wrong results (both finding problems as evidence of their diligence as well as hiding anything found to reduce further work or them overlooking it previously).
3. Infrastructure owner: the entity owning/operating the environment which is investigated. They might be interested in providing confirmation that the investigation was performed (when it was not), that no problems were discovered (to avoid having to fix them) or to show numerous defects (e.g. to argue for more funding). Also, even having incorrectly not performed an investigation might be of interest to deny any knowledge of a problem causing a defect that would have been found (and was simply ignored or overlooked when the inspection was done).
4. Terrorists: someone who wants to cause damage to the infrastructure. Identifying weak/vulnerable points, entrance locations, security precautions or the kind/model of equipment used so they can prepare or perform an attack. A secondary goal might be to pretend an attack happens/happened and cause disruption through false alarms.
5. Activists/media: persons intending to cause (bad) press/publicity for the infrastructure operator. They will be especially interested in all problems discovered as well as a history of those and e.g. the duration for which they occurred (i.e. time it took to fix in the past). "Blockading" the infrastructure might also be an aim, e.g. by enforcing a shutdown as a safety measure because of a person entering the area.
6. Criminals: while most cable ducts will not be very interesting, some parts (security elements like sensors, or copper cables) might be of interest for theft. Which things are where and how to get there (and when they are turned off and can be removed without personal danger) is of interest to those actors.
7. Enthusiasts: people that are merely interested in privately collecting (and perhaps visiting) the locations. They want whatever information they can gather. These persons will probably be less dangerous than others, but there is no guarantee the information stays with them and is not passed on to other more serious attackers.
8. Competitors: they will typically be interested in the actual current state of the infrastructure (usually on a larger scale/overall and not for an individual duct), potential failures and the duration/intensity/precision of the investigations. In some cases, the capacity (actual current "transport amount" of energy/water/..., i.e. the utilization at the moment as well as reserve space for potential enlargements resp. already existing spare/reserve conduits) might be of interest, e.g. for future plans of local competition.
9. Product providers: manufacturers of robots, sensors, and other elements of the system. They are perhaps not interested in the specific data, but they might want to acquire as much of it as possible for e.g. training AI systems. Also, in case of defects the data might be used as evidence for (incorrect usage)/against (defective product) them.

10. Communication system: who operates the system for communication between the robot and a base station and/or the company office. They might not really be interested in much of the data, but they do have access to quite a lot: content, location, duration etc. This is therefore rather a secondary attack target like enthusiast (stealing information or DoS) than a potentially malicious actor.

The following kinds of resources may be available to various of the actors identified above:

1. Access to the robot or other equipment before the inspection takes place. This means, manipulations in both hard- and software are possible. Also, additional devices might be hidden.
2. Access to the robot or other equipment after the inspection took place. Any residual data might be copied, but the device(s) could also be used for producing additional scans/measurements/… as replacements or in a fake environment with any original markers, like serial numbers or manufacturing individualities (e.g. dead pixels).
3. Access to similar/identical equipment. Creating fake data is extremely difficult without the hardware, e.g. the same model of sensor. This also allows investigating the modules for any security weaknesses they might possess, too.
4. Access to the recorded data. That data might be copied, modified, or deleted. Such access to the data encompasses access to its storage location, i.e. the possibility to add new data.
5. Access to the location before the inspection takes place: defects might be simulated or traps (dangerous gases, strong EM fields, water, RF jamming...) be built. Also, previous access might allow prediction of what the operator/robot is going to do where, or e.g. when the communication link will be lost.
6. Access to the location after the inspection took place: this allows re-creating the inspection realistically with slight modifications, e.g. after concealing (but not fixing) any discovered defects – in effect creating an alternate history.
7. Access to the communication: this might be during the investigation (i.e. listening in on the communication between robot and operator), as well as outside (before – e.g. any preparations, initializations, downloading base data or previous scans etc – as well as afterwards – uploading the collected data, logs, reports etc).

4. System design

Within the scope of the research project, the system is implemented as a prototype: fully functional, but not production-ready. Therefore, a detailed requirements analysis and a system design is necessary. The system is currently being implemented to be tested later this year. For easier management, the individual elements are programmed as Docker containers, so that they can run on different systems: separately, if necessary because of resource demands, or together with other elements to obviate the need for separate computing hardware if resources are sufficient.

The basic design of the system is a mobile industrial robot, on which various sensors are mounted. Apart from this at one "end" of the duct a base station is located where the operator sits. This contains also the computing equipment: as this is a research project, multiple computers and a small network will be installed; in production use it might simply be a Laptop. The communication with the robot will be implemented via WLAN for simplicity.

4.1. Requirements

To protect against the actors described above with their resources, several functional requirements must be fulfilled, which are broken down into separate elements:

1. Communication between robot and operator needs to be protected. This requires encryption (for secrecy as well as integrity) and reliability (availability). While a physical cable (glass fiber, ethernet etc.) is very secure in this sense, it is often impractical. Radio communication might be suitable in such ducts, but leads to the possibility of comparatively easy jamming and potential breakdowns on (multiple) corners – many, especially modern, cable ducts are long and straight, but there are also often many decades old ones with numerous doors, changes of direction, different floor levels etc. In this project WLAN was selected, which itself is typically secured. However, in a real product, different kinds of communication could be employed, so that a custom protection layer separate from the actual communication system can be demonstrated.

2. Robot and base station need to be authenticated to each other to prevent MitM attacks. This is best integrated into the communication encryption, by both sides knowing exactly which key/certificate to expect. Note that we only identify the endpoints of the communication: what happens inside the network on board of the robot or between potentially multiple systems of the base station is not secured.

3. When an inspection takes place, some metadata must be assigned: the exact location (some static identifier of the duct or its section, so multiple investigations over time can be correlated), start/end time of this inspection, the person performing it (operator) as well as the identity of the equipment (which robot, sensors etc. plus their configuration…). This ties all the different elements together: the hardware, the person(s), the location, and the time.

4. Inspections must be tied to their metadata: the infrastructure owner could trivially perform a second inspection at a later point in time and manipulate the recorded times (or simply copy a previous report and give it a new date). This must be defended against by timestamps created by trustworthy time sources which must be unforgeable integrated with the metadata from above.

5. When errors occur, these should be documented: e.g. (temporary) communication loss must be documented and should not invalidate other security precautions. Similarly, hardware defects may occur and require a premature termination of an inspection, which needs to be documented as such.

6. Data needs to be secured: when an inspection starts, this fact should be available for later verification. This also means, that the documentation of this activity must be present (and cannot simply "disappear"). Data needs to be protected by backups and other measures to render its destruction as difficult as possible.

7. Data must be complete: removing parts of the data later ("the robot was simply standing then"; "there was a communication failure/data loss") should be detectable. Note that actual loss of sensor data (nothing there/sensor did not provide any data) should be logged (ideally as a negative: explicit absence of data). But this is separate from the potential attack of removing data later that was once present.

8. Activity/alarm documentation: when a problem is discovered (e.g. a pipe leaking) and the operator is notified, this notification as well as the response to it must be logged. This similarly applies to the requirement to provably log (implicitly, by providing an unbroken

chain without such an entry) that no such notification took place, i.e. the operator was not notified.

9. If feasible, the whole command & control stream of the robot should be logged. This includes every single (steering, activity, measurement...) command as well as all feedback (position indicators, pictures/videos of cameras, sensor raw data etc). This however, could be too much data for storage and/or handling, so a reduction may be needed. Usually this applies e.g. to video data. Videos might be reduced e.g. to single images every few seconds, or adaptively to e.g. 10 seconds before an "interesting" event – but which would have to be exhaustively defined in advance.

10. Confirmations by a trusted third party: all timestamps as well as the completion of an inspection should be confirmed by a trusted third party, indicating that no further data can be appended at this point, as it marks the end of the technical process. Here we stipulate that this party should not acquire any data: this is not an "external archive" but merely the confirmation of some (to that entity meaningless) data existing at some point in time.

11. Wiping the equipment: Before an inspection takes place, the equipment needs to be set to a defined state which does not contain any data except approved initialization data (i.e. no traces of previous activities) and is appropriate for the inspection planned. Data removal should take place immediately after an investigation has been completed, and initialization only directly before its start.

12. Data must be stored securely, so that hacking does not easily provide access to the data. This means a separate factor should be required for access; access to the file(s) and something else (cryptographic key stored in a different location, password etc). This includes cross-references to the same location/operator/... as for e.g. a quick re-scan of a location might give a hint to a problem discovered and solved. Consequently, the metadata must be encrypted too, and be unavailable without additional authorization (which allows auditing access too).

13. The location of entrances/exits respectively the exact location and trajectory of ducts need to be specially protected at least in some cases. This may conflict with other elements, e.g. when the video of the robot entering/exiting is included in the evidence.

14. Exports of the data collected need to be possible, but they must be able to be redacted, e.g. entrance locations (see previous point), exact locations of specific devices, robot used, operator who performed it, or markings (e.g. which key is to be used for a specific door, serial numbers of devices which may disclose relevant information) may need to be obfuscated. These aspects are not part of this publication as they are separate from the evidence collection and rather its use/disclosure at a later point in time.

15. Sensors need to be checked whether they disclose other data as side-channels: vibrations of elements could reveal the flow speed inside pipes, sensor data variations could enable calculating the amount of current being transported (EM interference) etc. These "slightly incorrect" results might be much too small to be of relevance for what the sensor is intended to sense (so no correction/shielding/... is added), but could give information on potentially useful data the sensor is not built for. This is excluded here as not part of the evidence collection system.

16. Communication should take place via private networks. If public networks are needed, it must be ensured that as little information as possible is disclosed or can be observed. A practical solution for this is again encryption and sending the data as a single aggregated package. Hiding the location is probably extremely difficult (if not impossible) against the

communication provider, unless actual upload to the infrastructure provider takes place at the home/office location (feasible e.g. for performing only a few inspections before returning).

Non-IT requirements include reliable sensors, which are not easily manipulated. E.g. gas sensors should reliably detect the gas they are intended for and be resilient against interpreting other things as that gas. The same applies to cameras (no "insertion" of fake video sources – usually trivial) as well as distance-to-object sensors for robot collision avoidance. Usability of the software for the operator is also important for products, but less for research projects.

4.2. Implementation of the requirements

As part of the prototype, the communication between the robot and the base station is secured. To reduce the impact on the other elements, this is implemented as a transparent tunnel, i.e. on each side a small device is added into the communication path (in this case WLAN), which takes care of encryption by creating a tunnel between them. This tunnel uses smartcard-based key storage. As a consequence, all communication is securely encrypted (fulfilling requirement 1). The two smartcards (one for each side; YubiKeys) are prepared for each inspection separately on the base station: a new key is created on them and the public key exported and imported to the other one. In this way a unique key is used every time. The exchange between them ensures that both the robot and the base station device can securely recognize the other side (→ requirement 2). As the private key cannot be exported from them (secure hardware), MitM attacks are impossible. These smartcards are prepared on the base station and when the one for the robot is moved there, the inspection can be started: the encrypted tunnel is created, and a new empty log is begun (requirement 11) on the "start" command.

When the robot creates log entries (steering commands, sensor data etc; requirement 9), these are stored on the robot during the inspection phase. This reduces the communication needs, as the bandwidth might be required e.g. for videos for steering or transmitting inspection data. These log entries are linked to each other via a hash chain (→ requirement 7). As changing, removing or inserting an element changes the whole rest of the chain, ensuring that the final value is unchanged is important, but sufficient for the integrity of the whole log. For this purpose, the final hash value is signed with the private key from the robot smartcard. As the key cannot be exported, faking this signature would require breaking the cryptosystem. This would not prevent the operator from reusing the key later. After signing the end of the chain and transmitting the resulting data to a "final storage" (in this case the base station; bandwidth is no longer an issue after the inspection is complete), the key on the smartcard is destroyed, preventing these attacks. Additionally, all local data is removed too (requirement 11). Note that the public key is preserved, as it is part of the metadata: verifying the signature is possible indefinitely. After all data has been collected on the base station (the data received from the robot is combined with the data logged in the base station), it is packed into an archive, signed with the base station key, and a timestamp is obtained for the whole set (requirement 10). Finally, the base station private key is destroyed too to prevent reuse. The complete archive is finally encrypted with a separate key/password and can be transmitted to an archive storage.

This would still allow the infrastructure owner/operator to simply create a new key and use this to sign any modified versions by recalculating the hash chain. To prevent this, both public keys and the metadata (see below) are timestamped by a trusted third party *before* the inspection begins (the inclusion of the metadata prevents obtaining "spare" timestamps in advance). This guarantees that both keys existed at a certain point in time and were not created later (requirement 4). The metadata needs to be entered by the operator to create a new inspection log. This may not guarantee its correctness, but it documents the content beforehand and renders it unchangeable (as part of the start of the data chain), fulfilling requirement 3 (currently not implemented is the automatic gathering of hardware serial numbers: this is desirable to potentially discover additional hidden devices; currently needs to be entered manually).

Requirement 6 can only be fulfilled partially at the moment: the trusted third party provides a timestamp when an inspection starts, but it does not get access to the metadata. Consequently, while it can later provide the information that some timestamp was created, it does not know for what purpose. If this is required, then the metadata could be disclosed to this third party, which could archive it. This would require cooperation by the third party and that it is trusted with knowing details about the inspections taking place. The advantage of the current implementation is, that any entity providing timestamps can be used securely and no contractual relationship is necessary.

While some data might be evaluated directly on the robot and cause an alarm (e.g. hardware defects → requirement 5; or gas levels from a sensors → requirement 8), more complex evaluations will take place on the computationally much more powerful base station. Consequently, events from this source must be taken into account too. The log captured as evidence therefore contains not only input from the robot but also from other sources. As it cannot be readily predicted which and how many sources of events will exist (e.g. which alarms are generated by which parts, or what constitutes a "reaction" to them and therefore needs to be logged too), all events from the various sources are inserted by a web service (requirement 8) (push-model as opposed to the silently observing and locally storing data model as used on the robot).

Requirements 13 and 16 involve organizational methods rather than technical solutions, while 14 and 15 are outside the scope of this paper. Requirement 12 refers to the final storage of data at an organization and is therefore not relevant here too; regarding the intermediate storage an encrypted disk is recommended, which can e.g. be implemented by full-disk-encryption combined with MFA.

Performing an inspection, therefore, consists of the following sequence of activities regarding evidence collection: first, the whole system is set up physically. Then on the base station a new investigation is started by entering the metadata and creating the keys on the two smart cards. This initial data is externally timestamped. One key is moved to the robot, the other to the base station encryption device, creating a secure communication channel to the robot. The investigation is then started by a command sent from the base station to the robot (which automatically provides a synchronization point so clocks are synchronized/their difference known) – both sides start collecting evidence (log entries, communication etc). Now the investigation takes place – no further interaction with the evidence collection system is necessary during this period. After the inspection has finished, a "stop" command is transmitted to the robot and both sides stop collecting evidence. The robot prepares its data package (signature etc – see above), which is then transmitted to the base station (via network or a storage medium). The private key on the robot is automatically destroyed. The evidence collection system then integrates the data collected on the base station and finalizes the complete package, which is timestamped and encrypted. The base station private key is automatically destroyed. The evidence is now available for export as a single secure package for download to a mobile device, a USB key, or upload to an online storage etc. Human intervention is therefore limited to some preparatory data input and issuing a start command, signaling the end of the collection, and archiving the final outcome.

4.3. Generalization possibilities

While some elements of the system are peculiar to the concrete scenario, e.g. the specific metadata, other elements can be used in similar systems too. This applies specifically to the approach of combining timestamps, hash chains and metadata – securing the evidence even against manipulation by the holder/owner of it. As discussed, improvements are possible through more tightly integrating the third party: disclosing the metadata to it (and having it stored there as well), does obviously disclose that data (but not the actual investigation log), but renders manipulations absent collusion between those parties even more difficult.

While in this project two entities provide evidence, the robot and the base station, this model is extensible to any number of participants. Note that communication security is again specific to the project, so providing each data source with its own private key and collecting all public keys as the shared starting value is the general requirement. This may prove challenging if the approach taken here – generating all keys on secure devices in a single location and only then distributing these devices – is not possible or suitable. In that case secure exchange of all public keys between all parties needs to be achieved.

To further improve security, intermediate "checkpoints" could be created: the robot could obtain external timestamps at regular intervals (time-/log count-/event-/data amount-/… -based) and insert them in its hash chain. Then any window for manipulation further shrinks. The drawback of that approach is, that an online connection to the Internet is required during the operation too, which can be problematic to guarantee in this scenario, but which might not be problematic at all in others.

5. Summary

We analyzed the requirements for an evidence collection system in a specific setting: distributed collection of data from multiple sources in real-time, which needs to be protected – as far as possible – against manipulations by the operator of the system too. This security can be achieved against later modifications, but not against those made in real-time during the inspection. The system is therefore limited to scenarios, where "problems" that might have to be "removed" occur unpredictably: as soon as they appear, modification is difficult or impossible. Only when known in advance, they can be suppressed. This seems a plausible scenario for many applications, rendering this a useful approach.

Acknowledgements

This publication and the system described in it was developed within the scope of the project INFRASPEC (FFG project number FO999895182), which is funded by the Austrian security research program KIRAS of the Federal Ministry of Finance (BMF).

References

Al-Sharif, Ziad A., Al-Saleh, Mohammed I., Alawneh, Luay M., Jararweh, Yaser I., Gupta, Brij. Live forensics of software attacks on cyber–physical systems. Future Generation Computer Systems, Volume 108, 2020, 1217-1229. https://doi.org/10.1016/j.future.2018.07.028

Grobler, C. P., Louwrens, C. P.. Digital Evidence Management Plan. 2010 Information Security for South Africa, Johannesburg, South Africa, 2010, 1-6. doi: 10.1109/ISSA.2010.5588661

Kim, D., Ihm, S.-Y., Son, Y. Two-Level Blockchain System for Digital Crime Evidence Management. Sensors 2021, 21, 3051. https://doi.org/10.3390/s21093051

Kotsiuba, I., Skarga, I. Bandurova, Giannakoulias, A., Bulda, O. Basic Forensic Procedures for Cyber Crime Investigation in Smart Grid Networks. 2019 IEEE International Conference on Big Data (Big Data), Los Angeles, 2019, 4255-4264

Li, M., Lal, C., Conti, M., Hu, D. LEChain: A blockchain-based lawful evidence management scheme for digital forensics, Future Generation Computer Systems, Volume 115, 2021, 406-420. https://doi.org/10.1016/j.future.2020.09.038

Newman, Robert C., Computer Forensics. Evidence Collection and Management. Taylor & Francis Group 2007

Sathyaprakasan, R., Govindan, P., Alvi, S., Sadath, L., Philip, S., Singh, N. An Implementation of Blockchain Technology in Forensic Evidence Management. 2021 International Conference on Computational Intelligence and Knowledge Economy (ICCIKE), Dubai, United Arab Emirates, 2021, 208-212. doi: 10.1109/ICCIKE51210.2021.9410791

A LARGE-SCALE DATA COLLECTION AND EVALUATION FRAMEWORK FOR ANDROID DEVICE SECURITY ATTRIBUTES

Ernst Leierzopf, Michael Roland, René Mayrhofer

Johannes Kepler University Linz, Austria / Institute of Networks and Security

{leierzopf, roland, rm}@ins.jku.at

Florentin Putz

Technical University of Darmstadt, Germany / Secure Mobile Networking Lab

fputz@seemoo.tu-darmstadt.de

DOI: 10.35011/IDIMT-2023-63

Keywords

Android, Data Mining, Security and Privacy, Webscraping, Crowdsourcing

Abstract

Android's fast-lived development cycles and increasing amounts of manufacturers and device models make a comparison of relevant security attributes, in addition to the already difficult comparison of features, more challenging. Most smartphone reviews only consider offered features in their analysis. Smartphone manufacturers include their own software on top of the Android Open Source Project (AOSP) to improve user experience, to add their own pre-installed apps or apps from third-party sponsors, and to distinguish themselves from their competitors. These changes affect the security of smartphones. It is insufficient to validate device security state only based on measured data from real devices for a complete assessment. Promised major version releases, security updates, security update schedules of devices, and correct claims on security and privacy of pre-installed software are some aspects, which need statistically significant amounts of data to evaluate. Lack of software and security updates is a common reason for shorter lifespans of electronics, especially for smartphones. Validating the claims of manufacturers and publishing the results creates incentives towards more sustainable maintenance and longevity of smartphones. We present a novel scalable data collection and evaluation framework, which includes multiple sources of data like dedicated device farms, crowdsourcing, and webscraping. Our solution improves the comparability of devices based on their security attributes by providing measurements from real devices.

1. Introduction

Android is a rapidly developing open-source mobile operating system. Due to Android's fast-paced development cycles, the heterogeneity of device manufacturers, and the large number of devices with vendor-specific software modifications, it is challenging to evaluate and compare devices with regard to security and functionality. AOSP follows strict release cycles with one major version update per year and monthly security updates including updates for the Android platform, the upstream Linux kernel and fixes from system-on-chip (SOC) manufacturers. These security updates are defined in security patch levels and can be found in the Android Security Bulletins. Smartphone manufacturers include their own software on top of AOSP to improve user experience, to add their own pre-installed apps or apps from third-party sponsors, and to distinguish themselves from their competitors. Consequently, smartphone manufacturers need to adapt these additions and customizations of the AOSP codebase before releasing (security) updates to end user devices. Therefore, a fully automated rollout process from AOSP to the end user is not yet possible. However, Google has started to address this issue. Starting with Android 8, *Project Treble* (Malchev, 2017) aims to separate device-specific vendor implementations from the Android OS framework, which allows for faster Android releases without modification of hardware-specific parts of Android. *Project Mainline* (Siddiqui, 2020) adds modular system components and introduces the Android Pony EXpress (APEX) file format for system component packaging in Android 10. Since then, more and more system components are modularized in later Android versions. Modular system components are a major improvement on the update process, as Google is able to remove dependencies on manufacturers by providing updates of system modules over existing infrastructure like Google Play Store. These developments and increasing commitment to continuous maintenance by smartphone manufacturers for up to 5 years of security updates (Atanassov, 2021; Google, 2023; Samsung Mobile Security, 2022) improve the lifespan of Android devices, as lack of security updates often leads to restricted use in applications with high security requirements. Given such commitments, it is vital to verify if manufacturers keep their promises and if there are discrepancies in the quality of the maintained software across different manufacturers.

In addition to the functional aspects of a device, more-recent Android versions offer improved security and privacy features, which users may want to consider for their purchase decisions. The ever-growing number of Android devices and device manufacturers increase the number of options for consumers ranging from low-budget to high-end flagship devices. Psychology suggests that choice overload decreases the ability of consumers to properly compare and evaluate their options due to decreasing commitment and oversight (Schwartz, 2003). Web services like GSMArena provide the possibility to search for and compare multiple devices from different manufacturers. Most of these websites scrape manufacturer websites for devices and update their internal database. Users are often not able to validate the information from such third-party websites.

This paper presents a scalable data collection and evaluation framework, which includes multiple sources of data like dedicated device farms, crowdsourcing and webscraping, and stores the collected data for analysis and presentation to end users. In addition, data is recorded in a raw file archive to maintain transparency and permit iterative re-processing upon improvements of analysis algorithms. The aggregated database should serve experts as well as average smartphone users, by providing detailed data measured from real devices (to verify manufacturer claims) and a simple total security score for fast comparison (to assist future buying decisions). An initial prototypical frontend for advanced users is available at https://www.android-device-security.org/.

2. Related Work

The Android ecosystem contains a complex, evolving architecture including different security mechanisms. Mayrhofer et al. (2021) describe mechanisms and concepts in AOSP and their development history up to Android version 11. Based on their research, there are many privacy and security related threats like the risk of pre-installed applications with pre-granted permissions.

Lau et al. (2020) propose the Uraniborg risk computation framework as an approach to calculate the security risk of an Android device. Their formula is based on the number of apps with signature permissions, pre-granted permissions, cleartext communication of apps, and a custom risk score for specific permissions defined by the authors.

Ozbay and Bicakci (2023) propose a total device security score based on metrics of pre-installed applications. Each metric has its own security score calculated by multiplying the number of affected pre-installed applications, the difficulty to exploit, and the impact of exploitation. The result is a score based on the normalized sum of all individual metric scores.

Other work focuses on static code analysis of firmware images from different vendors to evaluate the security of Android devices based on pre-installed software, security patch rollout time, verification of security update promises, and the number of vulnerable apps with open CVEs (Elsabagh et al., 2020; Gamba et al., 2020; Hou et al., 2022).

Pöll and Roland (2022) investigated on the reproducibility of AOSP and proposed a framework to analyze the state of reproducibility of AOSP and AOSP-code used in device firmware images. The authors introduced accountable builds as a form of reproducibility permitting explainable differences. They found that pure AOSP is already close to full reproducibility and that Project Treble (Malchev, 2017) helped to get the core operating system (*system.img*) closer to AOSP in actual device firmware by eliminating hardware and manufacturer-specific components.

Wagner et al. (2014) conducted a large-scale crowdsourced data collection of low-level data in 33 different event categories from 12,500 Android users worldwide within a timespan of nearly two years. As a result, Thomas et al. (2015) proposed the Free-Update-Mean (FUM) security metric to rank the performance of device manufacturers and network operators, based on their provision of updates and exposure to critical vulnerabilities. Their conclusion was that the main bottleneck in the latency of the security update processes lies within the manufacturers.

Khokhlov and Reznik (2017) proposed the Overall Security Evaluation Score (OSES) to evaluate device security and to check the validity of sensor data. The metric assumes that the more permissions a user has, the higher the risk of sensor data manipulation.

Many manufacturers publish relevant security update promises, security bulletins, and other information about devices on their websites; often lacking a machine-readable format. Due to the vast quantity of existing device models, it is challenging to collect significant amounts of first-hand information about Android devices. Aside of crowdsourcing, manual or automated webscraping is usually the only way to obtain such information. Third-party websites also offer collections of information about Android devices, but this information is usually not obtained from actual devices, but through other, potentially wrong or outdated sources. Therefore, the information must be validated before usage in security evaluations. Jones et al. (2020) put effort into the investigation of rollout processes of Android security updates and OS upgrades. They used a pseudonymized dataset based on HTTP access logs from a social network app containing request date, hashed user account identifier, user-agent string (including OS and build version, phone model, etc.), country code (derived from IP address), combined with data scraped from Android security bulletins, carrier and manufacturer security update announcements, and device release dates from GSMArena and PhoneArena. Particularly the analysis of metadata from Android security bulletins and CVEs is interesting for this work, because it shows what security updates need to be implemented by manufacturers to fulfill their security update promises (Farhang et al., 2020; Wu et al., 2019).

Previous work provides a solid basis for the evaluation of Android devices from different manufacturers. However, most approaches do not offer an actionable way to evaluate the security of specific devices. Consequently, the results are short-lived and often incomplete. Our approach creates and provides access to a database of security-relevant attributes for specific devices.

3. Collecting Security State of Android Devices

In order to collect and aggregate data about update distribution, supported security and privacy features, device state in general, and promised device features, we create a data collection and processing framework that collects data from controlled lab devices (in the form of device farms), in-field devices (through future crowdsourcing) and from webscraping. A scalable data ingestion pipeline accepts data from all the different sources, stores it for long-term archival and for subsequent post-processing. A modular post-processing pipeline analyzes the data and derives attributes about device security and privacy features to be stored in a database for presentation through a web-based user interface.

3.1. Data Ingestion and Processing

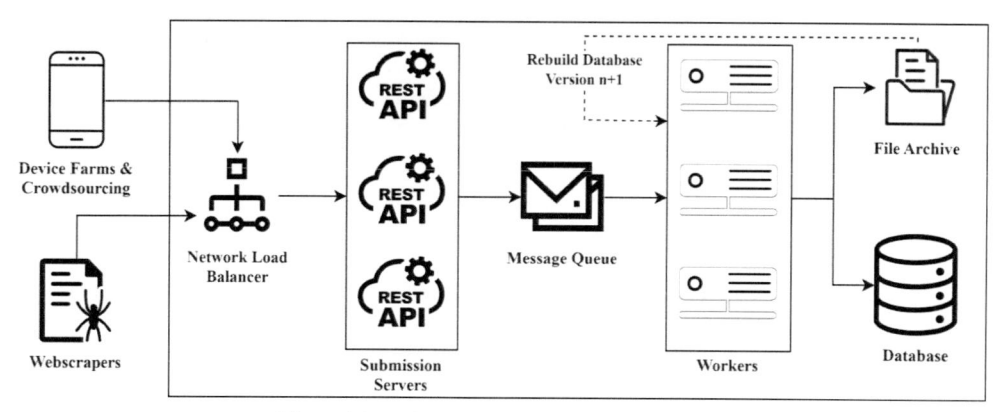

Figure 1. Data Ingestion and Processing Pipeline

The data ingestion and processing pipeline consists of modular server components that receive data from controlled lab devices in device farms, from crowdsourcing, and webscrapers. All components are designed in a modular and scalable manner with the aim of high-throughput processing. To achieve this goal, a load balancer receives distributes incoming requests to one or more submission servers. The submission servers implement a simple REST API, which receives the submissions as JSON objects and writes them into a message queue (MQ). The MQ reduces the risk of dropping incoming requests due to servers being overloaded with processing data.

Depending on its source, the data is labeled with different trust levels distinguishing between trusted data from controlled lab devices, controlled webscrapers and (potentially manipulated) crowdsourced data. An HMAC (hash-based message authentication code) based authentication with shared secrets is used to identify data submitted by trusted sources.

Workers are responsible for the offline processing of data from the MQ. From experience, we have learned that errors may occur in data or the processing implementation that result in inaccurate post-processed data. Manual fixes are time-intensive and the change history is often incomplete and opaque. To tackle this problem, we implemented a file-based archive, which stores all raw data and permits later rebuilding of the post-processed data by feeding the collected raw data into the MQ again. When a new iteration of the database needs to be built, the down time of the frontend can be minimized by reprocessing the raw data into a fresh database, which replaces the old one once the build process is finished. Unique file names based on content hashes allow for an efficient synchronization to backups and between multiple instances of the archive. Figure 1 shows the full pipeline.

3.2. Data Storage

All collected raw JSON data is stored in a file archive. A special folder structure derived from the hexadecimal representation of a SHA-256 hash function allows for efficient searching through the archive. Half of the hexadecimal characters are grouped in pairs, each representing one level in the folder hierarchy. This strategy permits faster searches of specific messages. The filename consists of the archival timestamp, a message-specific index token for file-lookup, and the hexadecimal representation of the authentication HMAC (if one exists).

Each attribute derived from raw data through post-processing is stored as a separate measurement in the database without linking back to the ingested raw dataset. This reduces the risk of device fingerprinting and privacy-relevant data leaks from the processed data through unique attribute combinations. Measurements only include a reference to the device model and its specific firmware version, a validity score, the origin (if from a trusted source), and the measured value. They are grouped into multiple categories. The definition of these categories and the determination of the validity score, which represents the trustworthiness of the measured value based on the source of the data, are subject to future evaluation. By using measurements from actual devices and by comparing those with update expectations (from scraped data), we are able to check how trustworthy manufacturers are with their update promises.

3.3. Android Device Farm

Using controlled lab devices in organized in device farms for measuring state of untainted devices is an effective way to ensure integrity of collected data. It also allows running tests that cannot easily be run on in-field devices via crowdsourcing, e.g. due to relying on access through Android Debug Bridge (ADB) or due to being intensive in terms of screen time, storage, etc.

We have built a device farm consisting of about 30 Android devices with Android versions ranging from 7 to 13. All devices are connected via a set of USB hubs to a Mini PC (Zotac ZBOX CI547 Nano) running Debian/Linux, which gives access to all devices through ADB. Due to their heterogeneity, Android devices have subtle differences in interaction methods and commands required to fulfill a task. Additionally, ADB on its own not efficient for the management of a whole device farm. To overcome these challenges, we implemented a Device Farm Manager with a web interface to monitor the state of devices and to create scheduled tasks for running our attribute collection.

The farm manager allows connecting to and managing multiple distributed device farms simultaneously. In future, the infrastructure will consist of multiple device farms operated by trusted institutions and organizations that contribute measurements to the submission pipeline.

As a first take-away from operating a device farm for several years is that battery management is troublesome. Keeping devices continuously attached to an external USB power supply, resulted in damaged (bloated) batteries for several devices. As a solution, we decided to keep the devices attached to USB (and thus charging) for only one hour per day. We achieve this by switching the power supply of the USB hubs. However, this creates a range of new problems including loss of ADB connectivity (due to unusual default USB configuration after restarting the USB hubs). Also, the battery management of some devices could not handle this alternative charging mode resulting in yet more damaged batteries. Eventually, we replaced batteries on affected phones with supercapacitors by removing the battery, extracting the protection circuit from the battery pack and replacing the Lithium cells with 5-farad capacitors with a dielectric strength of more than 5 volts.

3.4. Attribute Scanner App

We created an app to collect measurements from Android devices. The app can be run on lab devices as well as on devices of volunteers (crowdsourcing). It consists of a lightweight frontend and a modular scanner library. In future, the library may be included in third-party apps to boost crowdsourcing. A plug-in system simplifies the addition of new scanner modules and allows scans with pre-defined subsets of scanner modules using the App settings or ADB arguments. When run via ADB, the app also accepts the HMAC secret for authenticated submission of results.

In the device farm, the farm manager schedules different types of scans at different intervals (e.g. daily, weekly, or monthly), based on the likelihood that scanned data may change (e.g. due to system updates), expected collection effort (processing time to get results) and addition of new scanner modules. The scheduled process interacts with devices over ADB and consists of unlocking the device, installing the latest version of the scanner app, and starting it with scan-specific parameters. After scan completion, the app directly submits the collected data into the ingestion pipeline.

3.5. Crowdsourcing

Despite the advantages of device farms, it is infeasible to achieve full device coverage due to cost and management effort. In addition, staged update rollout processes, regional differences, mobile network operator customizations, etc. may influence measurements. Crowdsourced measurements can cover a broader spectrum of smartphone models across different regions, including less popular or older models that are not part of the device farms. Thus, crowdsourcing helps to fill that gap and to increase the scope of the evaluations.

In an initial attempt towards future crowdsourcing, we designed the scanner app with a GUI that permits volunteers to participate in crowdsourcing by collecting and submitting measurements from their devices. The scanners permitted in the crowdsourcing case are designed to minimize required permissions and to avoid collection of potentially personally identifying or otherwise privacy-sensitive data. Nevertheless, unlike with ADB-based automation, the app informs the user about the contents of collected data and explicitly requests user-consent before submitting any data.

To evaluate our prototype implementation of the crowdsourcing process, we have conducted a pilot measurement campaign with 67 volunteers, covering 52 distinct smartphone models from 12 vendors. These devices were manufactured between 2013 and 2020, and ran Android versions 6 to 11. Most devices were manufactured by Samsung, Huawei, and Google, but we also tested our implementation on smartphones from Sony, OnePlus, and Xiaomi, and even on less common Android smartphones such as the Blackview BV5500 Pro, the Fairphone 3, or the Realme X50 5G.

The downside of crowdsourcing is that measurements are not possible on-demand and instead depend on volunteers' ad-hoc participation and consent. Crowdsourcing is best suited for lightweight measurements rather than long-running scans, in order to encourage volunteers to participate in the collection process. Moreover, in order to attract volunteers, the app will need to offer some incentive. E.g., the app might present a total security score for comparison with other devices or recommendations for device-specific security and privacy improvements.

3.6. Webscraping

Not all data that we aim to collect about Android devices is measurable directly on-device. For instance, some manufacturers distribute data on update promises through their websites; some data about version-specific Android features is available in the AOSP documentation; device certifications (if available) are published by independent labs; additional data about devices is available through third-party device information websites. Webscraping is an obvious choice to acquire such information and to enhance the database with information not (yet) collected and verified through measurements from actual devices. The trustworthiness of data is determined based on its origin. Generally, we consider first-party websites more trustworthy.

We developed a Python-based webscraping framework to collect data about the Android platform (Android versions, builds of Google devices, manifest permissions, permission groups), smartphone certifications (Common Criteria, Samsung Knox), security update promises and update schedules from first-hand source (Google, Samsung, Oppo, Huawei, Nokia, Xiaomi, Motorola, Vivo), and basic device information from third-party websites (GSMArena, PhoneDB, AndroidEnterpriseSolutionsDirectory). We use BeautifulSoup to render websites and and Selenium to automate crawling. Scraped data is normalized into a JSON structure and fed into the ingestion pipeline. To assess the requirements for maintenance of the webscraper components due to structural page-changes, we tested our solution against the history of a website based on data from the Wayback Machine.

3.7. Frontend

One of the main outcomes of the project is a browsable frontend to our database. It can be accessed at https://www.android-device-security.org/ and allows users to query information inferred about device models. Data can be filtered based on a set of basic and advanced filters. Basic filters include manufacturers, device names, device model names, and searched attributes. Advanced filters allow for filtering based on selected attributes and ranges of release dates, Android API levels, and security patch levels. The current design allows users to research attributes of one or multiple smartphones. Future work will include additional selection fields and a configurable scoring algorithm, where users can define their own score by defining feature/attribute sets and their impact to compare devices. Future work may also add different presentations of the data to target different experience levels of users or specific comparison use-cases, eventually aiming for a broad target audience ranging from researchers and experienced users evaluating the capabilities of devices to end users making buying decisions.

4. Conclusion

This research focuses on the very important aspect of security on Android devices. We present a scalable architecture for data mining, evaluation, and presentation purposes. The main aim of this architecture is to create a basis for future research, by collecting large amounts of data on the security and privacy capabilities and features of Android devices. The results of this research may impact future purchase decisions of end users and businesses, and tech-reviewers might use the raw data to include a security comparison, in addition to the feature reviews.

In future work we aim to extend the frontend by including more attributes of devices and grouping them into intuitive clusters. Also, there may be different presentation forms based on the knowledge of the users. Further, we aim for a customizable security evaluation score, where the user is able to select and weight specific attributes or clusters in the calculation of the security score. New types of scanners will check if manufacturers provide correct implementations of security-relevant code like for example EncryptedSharedPreferences.

Acknowledgements

This work has been carried out within the scope of ONCE (FFG grant FO999887054) in the program "IKT der Zukunft" funded by the Austrian Federal Ministry for Climate Action, Environment, Energy, Mobility, Innovation and Technology (BMK). This work has been co-funded by the LOEWE initiative (Hesse, Germany) within the emergenCITY center. We thank Patrick Schmidt (TU Darmstadt) for his contributions to the scanner app and the submission pipeline.

References

Atanassov, M. (2021). OnePlus extends software support for its smartphones. https://www.gsmarena.com/oneplus_extends_software_support_for_its_smartphones-news-49868.php (Retrieved 2023-04-16)

Elsabagh, M., Johnson, R., Stavrou, A., Zuo, C., Zhao, Q., & Lin, Z. (2020). FIRMSCOPE: Automatic Uncovering of Privilege-Escalation Vulnerabilities in Pre-Installed Apps in Android Firmware. 29th USENIX Security Symposium (USENIX Security 20), 2379–2396.

Farhang, S., Kirdan, M.B., Laszka, A., and Grossklags, J. (2020). An Empirical Study of Android Security Bulletins in Different Vendors. Proceedings of The Web Conference 2020. https://doi.org/10.1145/3366423.3380078

Gamba, J., Rashed, M., Razaghpanah, A., Tapiador, J.E., & Vallina-Rodriguez, N. (2020). An Analysis of Pre-installed Android Software. 2020 IEEE Symposium on Security and Privacy. https://doi.org/10.1109/SP40000.2020.00013

Google (2023). Learn when you'll get software updates on Google Pixel phones. https://support.google.com/pixelphone/answer/4457705 (Retrieved 2023-04-16)

Hou, Q., Diao, W., Wang, Y., Liu, X., Liu, S., Ying, L., Guo, S., Li, Y., Nie, M., & Duan, H. (2022). Large-scale Security Measurements on the Android Firmware Ecosystem. 2022 IEEE/ACM 44th International Conference on Software Engineering (ICSE), 1257–1268. https://doi.org/10.1145/3510003.3510072

Jones, K.R., Yen, T.-F., Sundaramurthy, S.C., & Bardas, A.G. (2020). Deploying Android Security Updates: An Extensive Study Involving Manufacturers, Carriers, and End Users. Proceedings of the 2020 ACM SIGSAC Conference on Computer and Communications Security (CCS '20). https://doi.org/10.1145/3372297.3423346

Khokhlov, I., & Reznik, L. (2017). Data Security Evaluation for Mobile Android Devices. 2017 20th Conference of Open Innovations Association (FRUCT), 154–160. https://doi.org/10.23919/FRUCT.2017.8071306

Kumar, R., Virkud, A., Raman, R.S., Prakash, A., & Ensafi, R. (2022). A Large-scale Investigation into Geodifferences in Mobile Apps. 31st USENIX Security Symposium (USENIX Security 22), 1203–1220.

Lau, B., Zhang, J., Beresford, A.R., Thomas, D.R., & Mayrhofer, R. (2020). Uraniborg's Device Preloaded App Risks Scoring Metrics. https://www.android-device-security.org/publications/2020-lau-uraniborg/Lau_2020_Uraniborg_Scoring_Whitepaper_20200827.pdf

Malchev, I. (2017). Here comes Treble: A modular base for Android. https://android-developers.googleblog.com/2017/05/here-comes-treble-modular-base-for.html (Retrieved 2023-04-16)

Mayrhofer, R., Vander Stoep, J., Brubaker, C., & Kralevich, N. (2021). The Android Platform Security Model. ACM Trans. Priv. Secur., 24(3). https://doi.org/10.1145/3448609

Ozbay, A., & Bicakci, K. (2023). Should Users Trust Their Android Devices? A Scoring System for Assessing Security and Privacy Risks of Pre-Installed Applications. https://doi.org/10.48550/arXiv.2203.10583

Pöll, M., & Roland, M. (2022). Automating the Quantitative Analysis of Reproducibility for Build Artifacts Derived from the Android Open Source Project. Proceedings of the 15th ACM Conference on Security and Privacy in Wireless and Mobile Networks (WiSec '22), 6–19. https://doi.org/10.1145/3507657.3528537

Samsung Mobile Security (2022). Announcing up to five (5) years support for Samsung Security Updates on select Galaxy devices. https://security.samsungmobile.com/securityPost.smsb (Retrieved 2023-04-16)

Schwartz, B. (2003). The Paradox of Choice: Why More Is Less. HarperCollins.

Siddiqui, A. (2020). Everything you need to know about Android's Project Mainline. https://www.xda-developers.com/android-project-mainline-modules-explanation (Retrieved 2023-04-16)

Thomas, D.R., Beresford, A.R., & Rice, A. (2015). Security Metrics for the Android Ecosystem. Proceedings of the 5th Annual ACM CCS Workshop on Security and Privacy in Smartphones and Mobile Devices (SPSM '15), 87–98. https://doi.org/10.1145/2808117.2808118

Wagner, D.T., Rice, A., & Beresford, A.R. (2014). Device Analyzer: Large-Scale Mobile Data Collection. ACM SIGMETRICS Performance Evaluation Review, 41(4), 53–56. https://doi.org/10.1145/2627534.2627553

Wu, D., Gao, D., Cheng, E.K.T., Cao, Y., Jiang, J., & Deng, R.H. (2019). Towards Understanding Android System Vulnerabilities: Techniques and Insights. Proceedings of the 2019 ACM Asia Conference on Computer and Communications Security (Asia CCS '19), 295–306. https://doi.org/10.1145/3321705.3329831

INTRUSION DETECTION AND PREVENTION WITH NEURAL NETWORKS

Marie Kovářová, Milos Maryska

Prague University of Economics and Business
Department of Information Technology
marie.kovarova@vse.cz, milos.maryska@vse.cz

DOI: 10.35011/IDIMT-2023-73

Keywords

Cyber security, Intrusion Detection and Prevention Systems (IDPS), Neural Networks, Artificial Intelligence (AI).

Abstract

This paper focuses on cyber security, particularly on Intrusion Detection and Prevention Systems (IDPS) using Neural Networks. The paper discusses the limitations of traditional techniques in IDPS and the growing interest in the use of Machine-Learning (ML) and Deep-Learning (DL) algorithms to detect unknown attacks. The aim of the paper is to analyze the possible usage of neural networks in IDPS from a cyber security data structure perspective. The paper describes the structure of cyber security and its data, methods and techniques used in IDPS with an emphasis on the usage of Artificial Intelligence (AI) related algorithms. The suitability of neural networks for usage in IDPS is analyzed based on cyber security data description. The paper concludes that neural networks implemented within IDPS bring many benefits but also many challenges that need to be addressed. In the context of high-frequency data in IDPS environment a Recurrent Neural Network combined with Attention mechanism was selected for development of future IDPS.

1. Introduction

This paper focuses on cyber security, particularly on Intrusion Detection and Prevention Systems (IDPS) using Neural Networks. With the increasing sophistication and frequency of cyber-attacks, breach detection and prevention have become a critical part of any cybersecurity strategy. IDPS are designed to monitor and analyze network for signs of malicious activity. (Scarfone et al. 2007) Traditional techniques in IDPS include signature-based detection, anomaly-based detection, and behavior-based detection (Scarfone et al. 2007). However, these techniques have limitations and are not able to detect all types of threats. The attack types such as DoS (Denail of Service), U2R (User to Root) and R2L (Remote to Local) already need knowledge from the training phase. Due to these limitations, there is a growing interest in the use of Machine-Learning (Kotenko et al. 2020) and Deep-Learning (Lansky et al. 2021) algorithms. Machine-Learning (ML) algorithms represent supervised and unsupervised learning models and Deep Learning (DL) algorithms represent neural networks. ML and DL algorithms are gradually becoming another part of cyber security. Another future threat is the increase in zero-day attacks, which highlights the need for security mechanisms capable of accurately detecting previously unknown attacks. ML and DL algorithms are suitable to detect just yet unknown attacks.

The aim of this paper is to analyze possible usage of neural networks in IDPS from cyber security data structure perspective. Existing available knowledge of neural networks usage is analyzed in the field of IDPS as preparation for future research and application. As neural networks require data and knowledge of structure which should be learned by them, first is described cyber security structure and data. Next methods and techniques used in IDPS where the emphasis is on usage of Artificial Intelligence (AI) related algorithms. To evaluate usability of neural networks, they are analyzed in relation to intrusion prevention and detection. Based on cyber security data description is selected appropriate type of neural network and analyzed its suitability for usage in IDPS.

2. Methodology

To complete the aim of our paper, we set the following objectives: 1) Conduct literature review on IDPS, known applications of AI related algorithms in the field of IDPS, cyber security, its structure and data. 2) Identify suitable neural network and analyze its applicability for intrusion prevention and detection, especially from cyber security data processing view. For the identification and analysis of neural networks, a combination of previous research (Kovářová 2022) conducted on high-frequency data, which has the same characteristics as cybersecurity data, and a literature review is used.

3. Results

This chapter fulfils the first objective of the methodology. The following subchapters describe the knowledge building blocks that provide the information framework for Chapter 4, which fulfils the second objective.

3.1. Structure of cyber security and its data

This subchapter first describes the structure of cyber security itself focusing on its elements and later the structure and properties of data within cyber security. The basic structure of the cyber security process and their data is a symbiosis that can be unique in each organization. The two domains interact and actively work together to detect and prevent sensitive data. The right symbiosis between a properly set up cyber security process and their data, is the fundamental key to good protection of any online information. Mastering their interconnection is very important for any private or government entity.

3.1.1. Cyber security structure

The structure of Cyber security generally consists of several basic elements. The exact structure may vary depending on the specific organization, system or application that is the subject of protection. The basic elements within cyber security can be as follows (Paloalto, 2023):

a) **Identification** - Processes and technologies used to identify users, devices, systems or applications that have access to protected data (passwords, certificates, biometric).

b) **Protection** - Includes various technical and organizational measures to protect data from unauthorized access, such as firewalls, anti-virus programs, encryption and backups.

c) **Detection** - Is the process of identifying suspicious or unusual activity that could indicate a cyber-attack or threat. Detection tools may include Security Information and Event Management (SIEM) systems, Intrusion Detection Systems (IDS), and other tools to monitor and analyze network or system traffic.

d) **Response** - Actions that are taken upon detection of a potential cyber-attack or threat. This may include rapid incident response, isolation of compromised systems, restoration of data from backups, and other measures to minimize the damage caused by the attack.

e) **Monitoring** - This is a process to monitor cybersecurity in real time, identify new threats, track and evaluate the effectiveness of security measures and collect data for analysis and cybersecurity improvements.

f) **Training and awareness** - Training users who work with data to be familiar with security practices, and education on cyber threats and good practices for data protection.

3.1.2. Data structure in the cyber security area

The data structure within cyber security can be organized into several categories or layers that together form a secure cyber ecosystem. These categories or layers may include:

a) **Data at rest** - This refers to data that is stored or transmitted in an inactive state, such as data stored on a hard drive, data in a database or backups. Protecting data at rest involves using encryption to secure the data from unauthorized access or disclosure. (Atchison 2022)

b) **Data in motion** - It is data that is actively transmitted or received between different systems or networks. Protecting data in motion involves the use of communication encryption, secure channels or protocols that protect data from eavesdropping or attacks during transmission. (Atchison 2022)

c) **Metadata** - This is information about the data that may include metadata, such as information about authors, times, places, and other meta-information that is associated with the data. The protection of metadata involves restricting and securing access to this information to protect it from misuse or unauthorized access. (Villadiego 2020)

d) **Logs and audit trails** - These are records of events and activities that take place on systems or networks, such as security logs, audit trails and event tracking. The protection of logs and audit trails includes the retention, monitoring and analysis of these records to detect cyber threats and identify unusual activity. (Villadiego 2020)

e) **Identification and authentication data** - These are usernames, passwords, certificates or other data used to verify the identity of users or systems. The protection of those data includes encryption, two-factor or multi-factor authentication, and the management of access rights to those data to minimize the risk of unauthorized access or misuse.

3.2. Overview of Intrusion Detection and Prevention Techniques

This subchapter presents existing approaches to detection and prevention in the context of cyber threats, the structure of IDS and IPS (Intrusion Prevention Systems) systems and their methods for detection and prevention.

IDS and IPS or together as IDPS primarily focus on identifying and preventing potential incidents. Incidents can include, for example, a DoS incident, which in the modern digital economy can lead to potential losses of millions in revenue. IPS are security systems that are designed to prevent unauthorized access to a network by monitoring network traffic and identifying potential threats. (Paloalto 2023) IPS can identify and stop attacks in real time, preventing them from reaching their intended targets. IPS can be addressed using both hardware and software. Following solutions are examples of such IPS: Cisco Intrusion Prevention System, McAfee Network Security Platform, Snort and Palo Alto Networks IPS.

On the other hand, IDS are security systems that monitor network traffic or system events for signs of potential security breaches or unauthorized access. (Pankaj 2019) There are four main types of IDS. **NIDS** - Network Intrusion Detection System (network traffic); **HIDS** - Host-based Intrusion Detection System (system logs and events on individual hosts); **PIDS** - Perimeter Intrusion Detection System (perimeter of the critical infrastructure); **VMIDS** - Virtual Machine based Intrusion Detection System. (Uppal et al. 2014)

Examples of IDS systems are following existing solutions: Snort, OSSEC, Suricata, McAfee Network Security Platform. IDPS technologies use basic methodologies to detect incidents. These include signature-based, anomaly detection and behavior-based methodologies. These basic methodologies may no longer be sufficient to detect and prevent cyber-attacks today, and therefore AI approaches namely ML and DL algorithms are coming to the fore.

3.2.1. Basic detection system methods

Signature-Based Detection involves using known attack signatures to identify threats. (Scarfone et al. 2007) However, this approach is limited to detecting only known threats and is not effective against new or previously unknown attacks. Signature-based detection is the simplest detection method because signatures have little knowledge of many network or application technologies.

Anomaly-Based Detection involves creating a profile of normal network behavior and looking for deviations from that profile. It is the process of comparing definitions of activities that are considered normal for deviations detection in behavior profiles. These profiles are created by observing the characteristics of a typical activity over a selected time period. (Scarfone et al. 2007) However, this approach can generate false-positive and false-negative results.

Behavior-based detection involves analyzing network traffic to identify patterns of behavior that may indicate an attack. (Scarfone et al. 2007) This approach is time consuming and may not be effective against sophisticated attacks.

3.2.2. Extension of detection system methodology

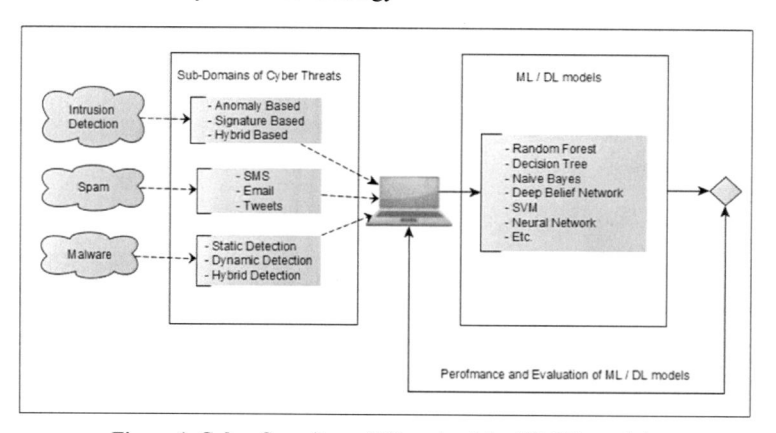

Figure 1. Cyber Security and lifecycle of the ML/DL models

Extensions to the core methodology within the IDPS are an important direction in cyber security. According to a paper (XIN et al. 2018), they conducted a review of which ML algorithms and DL algorithms can be used within Cyber security and for which type of threat. Figure 1 shows the lifecycle of the ML/DL models related to cyber security.

3.3. Artificial Intelligence in Detection and Intrusion Prevention

This subchapter focusses on possible approaches to detecting and preventing cyber threats using AI tools. The aim of this chapter is to provide the basic characteristics of AI algorithms (ML/DL). The use of DL or ML algorithms for intrusion detection and prevention in cyber security has become very popular recently. Several successful implementations of neural network based IDPS or their combination with ML algorithms have been reported in the context of DL/ML algorithms. Example is the Adaptive Multi-Agent System for Intrusion Detection (AMASID), which is a neural network-based system (Kisielewicz et al. 2022) that was developed for the US Navy. The AMASID system was able to detect attacks with high accuracy and low false positive rates. Today we can see a robust solution from OpenAI, which is also used in cyber security in Microsoft Azure and is based on a combination of DL and ML algorithms (Prewitt 2023).

3.3.1. Machine-learning algorithms

ML algorithms are one branch of AI. Algorithms within ML are very closely tied to the statistical approach of data analysis. To give a more concrete idea, ML is divided into supervised and unsupervised learning. Sometimes ML is mistakenly confused with data mining (Louridas et al. 2016), but the subfield of data mining is more focused on exploratory data analysis. ML algorithms primarily focus on classification and regression based on known features in the data, and its learning consists of training model on the historical data. Using ML models, we can detect anomalies in data (Nassif et al. 2021), incident prediction (Sun et al. 2019) and much more.

3.3.2. Deep-learning algorithms

DL algorithms are the second branch of AI, where are included models that can simulate the human brain for analytical learning. They can mimic the mechanism of the human brain in interpreting data such as images, sounds and texts (LeCun et al. 2015). These models include Neural Network in all its forms for example Perceptron, Feed Forward Neural Network, Multilayer Perception, Long Short-Term Memory and Modular Neural Network. (Great Learning 2022)

Neural networks are machine learning algorithms that are modeled after the human brain. They consist of layers of interconnected nodes that are capable of learning and recognizing patterns in data. Neural networks can be trained to recognize patterns in network traffic that indicate an attack. They can also be trained to distinguish between legitimate and malicious traffic, which can be used for detection and prevention of not yet known attacks including zero-day attacks as those create unknown network traffic, which can be blocked as potentially malicious. In IPS, the neural network is integrated into the network architecture and used to make real-time decisions about whether to allow or block traffic. The neural network can be trained to create rules that govern the behavior of the network. These rules can be updated in real time to respond to new incoming threats.

Neural networks can also play an important role in IDS to detect incidents more accurately. The data structure within cyber security can show signs of high frequency data i.e. events recorded in seconds or minutes. High-frequency data takes the form of a time series of consecutive events. It is advisable to use a properly selected type of neural network in the analysis of high-frequency data, which can identify system breaches with a higher degree of accuracy. In analysis on high-frequency data (Kovářová 2022) was found that classical time series approaches (SARIMA, ARIMA etc.) to analyze high-frequency data are not suitable. Similarly, methods designed for data mining are not suitable. In the context of high frequency data analysis, more robust solutions in the form of DL models must be used, which include neural networks in all their forms.

4. Discussion

Data within cyber security, for example logs, has time series features as they represent certain time sequence. Therefore, it is very important to select the right type of ML or DL algorithm to analyze the data to detect and prevent cyber-attacks. ML algorithms themselves focus on classification or regression tasks. DL algorithms are advanced machine learning techniques that use neural networks with multiple layers to extract complex features from data. DL algorithms can process large and complex datasets, extract features and learn independently, therefore DL algorithms are in some cases more advantageous than traditional ML algorithms. In the case of cyber threat detection and prevention, where the input data is in the form of a time series, DL algorithms are more robust with high accuracy. Within DL algorithms, there are several types of neural networks (Great Learning 2022), where each has its own form to handle specific tasks. Recurrent neural networks (RNNs) appear to be a suitable type of neural network for handling high frequency time series data (Hewamalage et al. 2021). RNNs take the previous hidden state of the network as part of their input, allowing the network to have memory. This property of it makes them useful for modeling sequential and time series data such as logs. However, training RNNs on sequences longer than a few hundred-time steps can be difficult, so it is necessary to choose the right type of recurrent neural network based on their properties.

4.1. Analysis of recurrent neural networks for high-frequency data: Benefits and limitations

The data structure within cyber security is very heterogeneous, as noted above. Most of the data within cyber security is high frequency data (log data). According to (Goodfellow et al. 2016) "Recurrent Neural Networks are a class of neural networks that are designed to process sequences of data, such as time series or sequences of words. Unlike feedforward neural networks, which process inputs in a single forward pass, RNNs have connections that loop back on themselves, allowing them to maintain hidden states that capture information from previous time steps. This recurrent architecture endows RNNs with the ability to capture temporal dependencies and learn complex patterns in sequential data, making them particularly suited for tasks such as language modeling, speech recognition, and sequence prediction."

When applying basic RNNs to high-frequency data, however, it can lead to the problem of vanishing gradient or exploding gradient. This problem arises when training long time series, which means that parameters in the hidden layers either do not change as much or lead to numerical instability and chaotic behavior. This can happen when the gradient of the cost function involves the performance, which affects its memory capacity and makes the classical RNNs very computationally expensive. The consequence of this error can then lead to incorrect prediction of future values and bias the result. The classical RNNs suffers from poor memory, which is unable to consider several elements of the past when answering the future. Several other variants of RNNs such as Long Short-Term Memory (LSTM), Gated Recurrent Unit (GRU), Encoder-Decoder Model, and Attention Mechanism can help avoid this problem of vanishing and exploding gradient. It is memory extension that is very crucial in certain domain areas such as finance where a great deal of knowledge of historical events is required.

Within the RNN, LSTM, GRU models, each input corresponds to an output for the same time step. Although in real cases, we rather want to predict the output sequence of a given input sequence of different length, without correspondence between each input and each output. This situation is called a sequential mapping model, and can be found, for example, in language translators, voice devices, or online chatbots. And it is the sequential mapping model that is the focus of the Encoder-Decoder model, which takes a sequence as input and generates the most likely next sequence as output. This model consists of two models, the Encoder model, which is responsible for traversing the input timesteps and encoding the entire sequence into a fixed-length vector called the context vector. And the Decoder model, which is responsible for stepping through the output timesteps when reading from the context vector.

The advantage of the Encoder-Decoder model is that it can map sequences of different lengths to each other, since the inputs and outputs are uncorrelated, and their lengths may be different. But again, this approach can also create another set of problems as it only works well for small sequences. It is very difficult to summarize a long sequence into a single vector, and then the model very often forgets the earlier parts of the input sequence when processing the last parts. This is why many experiments show that the performance of this model decreases as the sequence size increases.

Another way to avoid this problem is to use an extension of the Encoder-Decoder model by adding an attention mechanism model. This extension improves performance for long input sequences. The main idea here is to allow the decoder to selectively access the encoder information during decoding. This is achieved by constructing a different context vector for each time step of the decoder, which is computed depending on the previous hidden state and on all hidden states of the encoder and assigning trainable weights to them. In this way, the Attention mechanism assigns different weights to different elements of the input sequence and gives more relevant inputs more attention. This model achieves very good results because it allows to remember all the information in the input and to recognize the most relevant information when formulating the result. The Attention mechanism comes out as very advantageous in intrusion detection in all the above types of recurrent neural networks. The data structure in cyber security framework mentioned above, i.e., logs, contains sequence of different events in time, hence Attention mechanism appears to be a suitable approach for intrusion detection based on neural networks.

4.2. Conclusion

Neural networks that are implemented within IDPS bring many benefits, but also many challenges that need to be addressed. Each type of neural network has its own unique characteristic. Choosing the appropriate type of neural network always depends on the type of data and what is the subject to be solved. In the context of high-frequency data in IDPS environment, after a thorough analysis, the recurrent neural network in combination with method that uses Attention mechanism was selected.

This work is input for future model creation based on RNNs which will be used on real case scenarios in cyber security field. This future research will verify suitability and limitations of RNNs with Attention mechanism.

In case the model won't be successful, another possible future direction for neural network based IDPS is the use of DL and ML algorithms that can process large amounts of data and learn complex patterns. Another direction within DL algorithms is the integration of multiple data sources e.g., log files and network traffic etc. These enhancements can provide a more comprehensive view of network activity and increase the accuracy of IDPS.

Finally, the development of more robust and adaptable neural network-based systems is the main future interest. But for such an aim is much more research needed than is the limit of this paper.

References

Atchison, L. (2022, July 18). Securing data at rest and data in motion. Retrieved April 17, 2023, from https://www.infoworld.com/article/3666500/securing-data-at-rest-and-data-in-motion.html

Goodfellow, I., Bengio, Y., & Courville, A. (2016). Deep Learning (Illustrated edition). Cambridge, Massachusetts: The MIT Press.

Hewamalage, H., Bergmeir, C., & Bandara, K. (2021). Recurrent Neural Networks for Time Series Forecasting: Current status and future directions. International Journal of Forecasting, 37(1), 388–427. https://doi.org/10.1016/j.ijforecast.2020.06.008

Kisielewicz, T., Stanek, S., & Żytniewski, M. (2022). A Multi-Agent Adaptive Architecture for Smart-Grid-Intrusion Detection and Prevention. Energies, 15, 4726. https://doi.org/10.3390/en15134726

Kotenko, I., Saenko, I., & Branitskiy, A. (2020). Machine Learning and Big Data Processing for Cybersecurity Data Analysis. In L. F. Sikos & K.-K. R. Choo (Eds.), Data Science in Cybersecurity and Cyberthreat Intelligence (pp. 61–85). Cham: Springer International Publishing. https://doi.org/10.1007/978-3-030-38788-4_4

Kovářová, M. (2022). TV CONTENT AUDIENCE PROFILE PREDICTION OPTIONS. 479, č. 201, s. 201–208. https://doi.org/10.35011/IDIMT-2022

Lansky, J., Ali, S., Mohammadi, M., Majeed, M. K., Karim, S. H. T., Rashidi, S., Hosseinzadeh, M., & Rahmani, A. M. (2021). Deep Learning-Based Intrusion Detection Systems: A Systematic Review. IEEE Access, 9, 101574–101599. https://doi.org/10.1109/ACCESS.2021.3097247

LeCun, Y., Bengio, Y., & Hinton, G. (2015). Deep learning. Nature, 521(7553), Article 7553. https://doi.org/10.1038/nature14539

Louridas, P., & Ebert, C. (2016). Machine Learning. IEEE Software, 33, 110–115. https://doi.org/10.1109/MS.2016.114

Nassif, A. B., Talib, M. A., Nasir, Q., & Dakalbab, F. M. (2021). Machine Learning for Anomaly Detection: A Systematic Review. IEEE Access, 9, 78658–78700. https://doi.org/10.1109/ACCESS.2021.3083060

Paloalto. (2023). What is an Intrusion Prevention System? [Cyber security specialist]. Palo Alto Networks. https://www.paloaltonetworks.com/cyberpedia/what-is-an-intrusion-prevention-system-ips

Pankaj. (2019, April 8). Intrusion Detection System (IDS) [Computer Networks]. GeeksforGeeks. https://www.geeksforgeeks.org/intrusion-detection-system-ids/

Prewitt, C. (n.d.). Council Post: Four Ways ChatGPT Is Changing Cybersecurity. Forbes. Retrieved April 14, 2023, from https://www.forbes.com/sites/forbestechcouncil/2023/03/09/four-ways-chatgpt-is-changing-cybersecurity/

Scarfone, K. A., & Mell, P. M. (2007). Guide to Intrusion Detection and Prevention Systems (NIST SP 800-94; 0 ed., p. NIST SP 800-94). National Institute of Standards and Technology. https://doi.org/10.6028/NIST.SP.800-94

Sun, N., Zhang, J., Rimba, P., Gao, S., Zhang, L. Y., & Xiang, Y. (2019). Data-Driven Cybersecurity Incident Prediction: A Survey. IEEE Communications Surveys & Tutorials, 21(2), 1744–1772. https://doi.org/10.1109/COMST.2018.2885561

Great Learning (2022, August 4). Types of Neural Networks and Definition of Neural Network. Great Learning Blog https://www.mygreatlearning.com/blog/types-of-neural-networks/

Uppal, H. A. M., Javed, M., & Arshad, M. J. (2014). An Overview of Intrusion Detection System (IDS) along with its Commonly Used Techniques and Classifications. International Journal of Computer Science and Telecommunications [Volume 5, Issue 2, February 2014], 5(2).

Villadiego, R. (2020). The four insights network metadata can reveal about your compromise level | 2020-10-26 | Security Magazine. https://www.securitymagazine.com/articles/93741-the-four-insights-network-metadata-can-reveal-about-your-compromise-level

Xin, Y., Kong, L., Liu, Z., Chen, Y., Li, Y., Zhu, H., Gao, M., Hou, H., & Wang, C. (2018). Machine Learning and Deep Learning Methods for Cybersecurity. IEEE Access, 6, 35365–35381. https://doi.org/10.1109/ACCESS.2018.2836950

DORA AND NIS2
AND THEIR IMPACT ON DATABASE SECURITY

Felix Espinoza, Milos Maryska, Petr Doucek, Marie Kovářova

Faculty of Informatics and Statistics, Prague University of Economics and Business
Felix.espinoza@vse.cz, milos.maryska@vse.cz, doucek@vse.cz, xbalm21@vse.cz

DOI: 10.35011/IDIMT-2023-81

Keywords

DORA, Digital Operational Resilience Act, NIS2, Network Information Security, Database Security

Abstract

In today's era, digital transformation has become an essential part of every business. With the increasing use of digital technologies, businesses are becoming more dependent on data. This dependency includes areas like from payment systems and online banking to algorithmic trading and risk management. Higher usage of IT technologies increases the risk of cyber-attacks, data breaches, and other security threats. In this article, we will compare the Digital Operational Resilience Act (DORA) and NIS2 and their impact on Database Security. The DORA will seek to harmonies digital resilience in the European Union through the introduction of requirements on ICT risk management and ICT-related incident reporting.

Significant penalties can be imposed for non-compliance companies. Penalties can be presented as a periodic penalty payment of 1% of the average daily global turnover of the company in the previous business year. DORA applies to all financial entities in the EU and to the ICT providers servicing the industry

1. Introduction

In today's era, digital transformation has become an essential part of every business. Companies collect, store, and manage large amounts of data to gain insights, make informed decisions, and improve their operations. With the increasing use of digital technologies, businesses are becoming more dependent on data. This dependency includes areas like from payment systems and online banking to algorithmic trading and risk management. This increased dependence on databases for data management requires a robust security framework to prevent unauthorized access, data breaches, and data loss.

Higher usage of IT technologies increases the risk of cyber-attacks, data breaches, and other security threats. Therefore, it is essential to have a robust digital resilience strategy to protect data and maintain business continuity.

To address these challenges, governments around the world are enacting new regulations to protect critical infrastructure from cyber threats and improve the operational resilience of the financial sector by ensuring that it is better prepared to withstand and recover from major disruptive events, such as cyber-attacks, IT failures, or natural disasters. In the event of a major cyberattack or other disruption, the consequences could be catastrophic, potentially affecting everything from the stability of financial markets to the safety and security of individual account holders.

In this article, we will compare the Digital Resilience Operational Act (DORA) and NIS2 and their impact on Database Security.

The need for both DORA/NIS2 legislation has become increasingly urgent in recent years, as the financial sector has become increasingly reliant on digital technology to conduct its operations as mentioned above.

2. Methodology

The article is based on a detailed analysis of current information from many information sources describing and defining various aspects of Digital Operational Resilience Act, Network Information Security 2 and Database security. The main information sources are directives published by the European Union and other resources describing requirements of database security.

This article analyzes in detail requirements of DORA, NIS2 and standard requirements on database security, compares then and validates them and identifies differences and potentially identical conclusions.

For the purposes of this article, we analyzed more than 16 information sources and 7 of them was used and cited in this paper.

3. DORA, NIS2 and Database Security

3.1. Digital Operational Resilience Act

The Digital Operational Resilience Act (DORA) is a legislative proposal introduced by the European Commission in late 2020. The full name of the DORA is "Regulation (EU) 2022/2554 of the European Parliament and of the Council of 14 December 2022 on digital operational resilience for the financial sector and amending Regulations (EC) No 1060/2009, (EU) No 648/2012, (EU) No 600/2014, (EU) No 909/2014 and (EU) 2016/1011 (Text with EEA relevance). (Europe, 2022; Reynolds, 2023)

Its primary goal is to improve the operational resilience of the financial sector by ensuring that it is better prepared to withstand and recover from major disruptive events, such as cyber-attacks, IT failures, or natural disasters. The DORA proposes a range of measures to enhance the security and reliability of digital networks, systems, and services, particularly in times of crisis or emergency. (*What can we expect from the Digital Operational Resilience Act*, n.d.)

One of the key components of the DORA is the establishment of a framework for operational resilience. (Finextra, 2022)The framework is based on five core areas that organizations need to focus on to build a robust digital resilience strategy:

- identify and manage their operational risks, including those related to their digital infrastructure and operations. This would involve conducting regular risk assessments and developing resilience plans that ensure the continuity of critical services in the event of an attack or other disruption.
- maintain robust incident response and recovery capabilities. This would involve establishing clear procedures for responding to incidents, including cybersecurity breaches, and

recovering from them. The act also proposes that institutions regularly test their incident response and recovery plans to ensure their effectiveness. Pillar Incident Reporting

- enhance the cybersecurity and data protection measures of financial institutions. This includes requirements for robust authentication and authorization mechanisms, secure data storage and transmission, and regular vulnerability assessments and penetration testing. The act also calls for the establishment of a cyber incident reporting framework, which would require institutions to report all significant cyber incidents to the relevant authorities. Pillar Digital Operational Resiliency Testing.

- to enhance analysis, dependency and resiliency of firms that use third party providers to support critical or important functions. DORA newly requires that such Third-part providers must be governed by the law of European Union Member State. Important note is, that in this case DORA is not talking about main provider only but about all sub-providers used by the main provider (including self-employed persons). Pillar ICT Third-party Risk

- enhance cooperation and information sharing between financial institutions and regulators. This includes the establishment of a joint cyber unit, which would serve as a centralized hub for sharing threat intelligence and coordinating response efforts. The act also calls for the creation of a digital operational resilience committee, which would bring together representatives from industry and government to share best practices and coordinate efforts to improve operational resilience. Pillar Information & Intelligence Sharing.

Risk Management	Incident Reporting	Digital Operational Resiliency Testing	ICT Third-party risk	Information & Intelligence Sharing
Business continuity and disaster recovery plans a must	Cybersecurity and reporting processes a requirement	Annually including remediation plans	ICT third parties subject to EU oversight	Encouraged to share threat information and intelligence

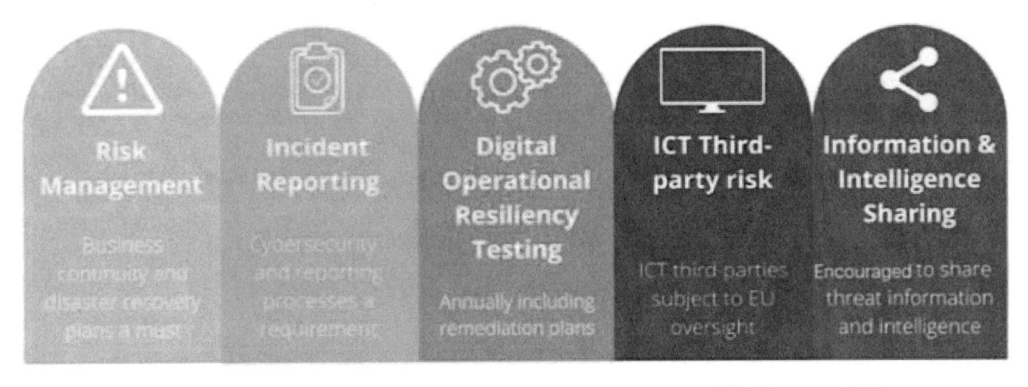

Figure 1. DORA - 5 Pillars   Source: (EU, 2023; Europe, 2022)

3.2. Network Information Security 2

The Network Information Security 2 (NIS2) directive is the European Union (EU) directive that aims to improve the cybersecurity of critical infrastructure in the EU. The directive requires member states to establish a national framework for managing cybersecurity risks and to designate competent authorities responsible for implementing and enforcing the directive. The directive applies to operators of essential services in sectors such as energy, transport, finance, and healthcare. (DataGuidance, 2022)

The (Network Information Security 2 Directive is an update to the existing NIS directive, aimed at improving the level of cybersecurity in the European Union. Key goal of the NIS2 directive is the expansion of the directive's scope to include additional sectors. The current directive only applies to essential service providers, but NIS2 extends its reach to cover digital infrastructure providers and online marketplaces. This expansion reflects the growing importance of the digital economy and the need for more robust cybersecurity measures in these sectors

The proposed directive includes several pillars, which are the focus areas for improving cybersecurity and resilience in the EU's critical infrastructure. Key pillars of NIS2 directive (as a comparison to DORA directive) are (Reynolds, 2023):

- Incident Reporting and Response: NIS2 proposes new rules for incident reporting and response. Essential service providers will be required to report significant cyber incidents to national authorities within 24 hours. This will enable authorities to respond quickly to cyber threats and take appropriate action to mitigate their impact. The proposed directive also includes the establishment of a European Cybersecurity Competence Center to provide technical support and expertise to Member States and essential service providers in the event of a cyber incident.

- Risk Management: The directive requires essential service providers to conduct regular risk assessments and implement appropriate measures to mitigate identified risks. This includes measures to protect against cyber threats, such as implementing multi-factor authentication and encryption.

- Supply Chain Security: NIS2 includes new rules on supply chain security, which is essential as cyber-attacks can often occur through vulnerabilities in the supply chain. Essential service providers will be required to ensure that their suppliers and contractors meet appropriate cybersecurity standards.

- Cooperation and Information Sharing: NIS2 increased cooperation and information sharing between EU Member States. The directive includes measures to facilitate the sharing of threat intelligence and best practices between national authorities and essential service providers. This will enable all parties to learn from each other and improve their cybersecurity posture.

The described pillars of NIS2 are focused on expanding the scope of the NIS2 directive, improving incident reporting and response, focusing on risk management, ensuring supply chain security, and increasing cooperation and information sharing between Member States. These pillars are critical to improving the resilience of the EU's critical infrastructure against cyber threats and protecting essential services.

3.3. Database Security

Database security is the practice of protecting data stored within a database system from unauthorized access, use, disclosure, modification, or destruction. As databases often contain sensitive and confidential information, such as personal identification data, financial records, and trade secrets, securing them is critical to safeguarding the integrity of the data and maintaining the trust of stakeholders. (Technopedia, 2022)

Database security is a critical component of any digital resilience strategy. Databases are used to store sensitive and confidential information, including financial records, customer data, and intellectual property. Therefore, protecting the database from cyber-attacks and data breaches is essential.

Database security involves various technical and organizational measures to ensure the confidentiality, integrity, and availability of data. The key aspects of database security are: Authentication and Authorization, Encryption, Access Controls, Auditing and Monitoring, Backup and Recovery, Physical Security, etc.(Epinoza & Maryska, 2022)

In conclusion, database security is a critical aspect of information security that requires ongoing attention and investment. Organizations should adopt a multi-layered approach to database security that includes technical and organizational measures to protect against a range of threats, including cyberattacks, data breaches, and insider threats. By implementing robust security controls and best practices, organizations can reduce the risk of security incidents, protect sensitive data, and maintain the trust of stakeholders.

4. Results

4.1. Comparison of DORA and NIS2

The DORA and NIS2 directive share several similarities, as both aim to improve the resilience of critical infrastructure and promote cybersecurity best practices. However, there are also key differences between the two pieces of legislation.

The comparison can be in 4 key areas:

- Scope
- Requirements
- Reporting
- Enforcement

One of the most significant *differences* between DORA and the NIS2 directive *is their scope*. DORA focuses exclusively on the financial sector, while the NIS2directive applies to operators of essential services in several sectors. This means that DORA is more narrowly focused than the NIS2 directive and may be less relevant to organizations operating outside the financial sector.

DORA and the NIS2 directive also have *different requirements*. DORA places a greater emphasis on business continuity planning and incident response, while the NIS2 directive requires operators of essential services to implement appropriate security measures to protect their network and information systems.

Both DORA and the NIS2 directive *require organizations to report significant incidents* to their national competent authorities. However, the reporting requirements under DORA are more prescriptive than under the NIS2directive. DORA requires financial institutions to report incidents that meet specific criteria, such as incidents that result in the unavailability of critical services for a specified period.

The *enforcement mechanisms* under DORA and the NIS2 directive also *differ*. DORA is a regulation, which means that it will be directly applicable in all member states without the need for national transposition. The NIS2 directive is a directive, which means that member states must transpose it into national law, which could result in differences in the way it is implemented and enforced across member states.

Table 1. Comparison of DORA and NIS2

	DORA	**NIS2**
Scope	• Financial sector	• Operators of essential services
Requirements	• Business continuity planning • Incident response	• Security measures to protect network Security measures to protect information systems
Reporting	• Report significant incidents • Prescriptive • Report incidents that meet specific criteria	• Report significant incidents
Enforcement	• Regulation • Directly applicable without the need for national transposition	• Directive • Must be transposed it into national law • Transposition could cause differences across states
Validity	• Effective 17.1.2025	• Effective 18.10.2024

4.2. DORA, NIS2 and Database Security

Both DORA and NIS2 have a significant impact on database security. DORA mandates the adoption of measures to improve the resilience of digital assets against cyber threats. When it comes to database security, the DORA proposal includes several provisions that are likely to have a significant impact on how financial institutions manage their databases. Specifically, the proposal includes the following measures (like the rules mentioned above):

- Mandatory reporting of significant IT and cyber incidents: The DORA proposal would require financial institutions to report any significant IT or cyber incidents that have a material impact on their business operations or services. This requirement is likely to increase the visibility of database security incidents, as financial institutions will be required to report them to their regulators.

- Increased regulatory oversight: The DORA proposal would also increase the powers of financial regulators to oversee the operational resilience of financial institutions. Regulators would be empowered to conduct regular assessments of financial institutions' IT and cyber resilience, including their database security measures.

- NIS2 also has a significant impact on database security. To address related challenge, NIS2 provides advanced security features such as role-based access control, data encryption, and secure communication channels.

5. Conclusions

The DORA will seek to harmonise digital resilience in the European Union through the introduction of requirements on ICT risk management and ICT-related incident reporting. (*What can we expect from the Digital Operational Resilience Act*, n.d.)Overall, the Digital Operational Resilience Act represents an important step forward. By promoting collaboration and information sharing between financial institutions and regulators, and promoting best practices in cybersecurity and operational resilience, the act seeks to ensure that the financial sector can withstand even the most serious threats and disruptions.

Significant penalties can be imposed for non-compliance companies. Penalties can be presented as a periodic penalty payment of 1% of the average daily global turnover of the company in the previous business year. This can be applied until compliance is achieved but no more than six months.

DORA applies to all financial entities in the EU and to the ICT providers servicing the industry. The financial entities definition under the DORA proposal is very wide and encompasses all kinds of players in the financial industry, from banks and credit institutions to payment institutions, pension funds, insurance companies, investment firms and all players in capital markets.

References

DataGuidance. (2022, May 27). *International: Legislative cybersecurity updates - NIS2, DORA, and the Second Additional Protocol to the Budapest Convention*. DataGuidance. https://www.dataguidance.com/opinion/international-legislative-cybersecurity-updates-nis2

Epinoza, F., & Maryska, M. (2022). LITERATURE REVIEW OF AUDIT OF DATABASE SECURITY. *Digitalization of Society, Business and Management in a Pandemic: 30th Interdisciplinary Information Management Talks*. IDIMT 2022, Linz. https://doi.org/10.35011/IDIMT-2022-285

EU. (2023). *The EU DORA Digital Operational Resilience Act for digital finance*. I-SCOOP. https://www.i-scoop.eu/eu-dora-digital-operational-resilience/

Europe, I. D. C. (2022, April 21). DORA Making Digital Resilience Real: EU Regulation on Financial Industry Operational Resilience. *IDC Europe Blog*. https://blog-idceurope.com/dora-making-digital-resilience-real/

Finextra. (2022, December 21). *Five key considerations on the Digital Operational Resilience Act (DORA)*. Finextra Research. https://www.finextra.com/blogposting/23444/five-key-considerations-on-the-digital-operational-resilience-act-dora

Reynolds, D. (2023, January 25). Understanding DORA, NIS2 and CER. *Sensible Cyber Security Solutions*. https://commsec.ie/understanding-dora-nis2-cer/

Technopedia. (2022, March 31). *What is Database Security? - Definition from Techopedia*. Techopedia.Com. http://www.techopedia.com/definition/29841/database-security

What can we expect from the Digital Operational Resilience Act. (n.d.). Deloitte Netherlands. Retrieved February 26, 2023,from https://www2.deloitte.com/nl/nl/pages/risk/articles/digital-operational-resilience-act.html

CYBERSECURITY CONTRACTS: A CRITICAL REVIEW

Regina Hučková, Laura Bachňáková Rózenfeldová

Pavol Jozef Šafárik University in Košice, Faculty of Law
regina.huckova@upjs.sk, laura.rozenfeldova@upjs.sk

Pavol Sokol, Soňa Briškárová

Pavol Jozef Šafárik University in Košice, Faculty of Science
pavol.sokol@upjs.sk, sona.briskarova@student.upjs.sk

DOI: 10.35011/IDIMT-2023-89

Keywords

Cybersecurity, contract, service, remuneration, liability, confidential information, personal data

Abstract

The essence of cybersecurity is to ensure the confidentiality, integrity, and availability of an organization's assets. This paper critically reviews contractual relationships concluded in cybersecurity, explicitly focusing on contracts between state-related actors and private providers. The authors aim to consider the nature of the contracts concluded and the application of selected legal institutes, from which certain conclusions regarding the practice of subjects operating in this area can be inferred. The conclusions presented in this paper are based on the analysis of 158 contracts concluded between Slovak public authorities and private providers in the period 2020-2023. The authors identify several areas for improvement in regulating these contractual relationships, including issues related to the pricing, content of services, liability limitation, and sharing of sensitive data.

1. Introduction

The continuing process of digitalization, accelerated in recent years by the pandemic, demonstrated the need to strengthen information and cyber security of the systems and tools we use daily. As the number of cyberattacks and other related threats rises, so does the urgency of this issue. One of the necessary components of ensuring the desired (or possible) level of security is sufficient and qualified personnel that includes experts (technical and legal), in information security, cybersecurity and the protection of information. Numerous studies have highlighted the scarcity of such personnel in practice. To illustrate, the European Union Agency for Cybersecurity points out "*a lack of skilled and qualified personnel in the labour market to work in cybersecurity roles*" (Nurse, 2021). Similarly in Slovakia, the National Security Authority considers the absence of professional staff in its National Cybersecurity Strategy for the years 2021-2025 (NSA, 2021) as a security threat. A recent solution to this problem presents an emerging practice of entrusting the fulfilment of obligations legally imposed on certain subjects to third parties – private providers that have at their disposal qualified personnel – on the basis of a contract. In this paper, we focus on contractual relations established between these entities and identify (dis)advantages of this approach.

Specifically, we look at the relations concluded between state-related actors – different public authorities and their private providers.

Related research can be found primarily in studies that focus on contracts between cyber security service providers and their customers, examining various types of contracts and responsibilities related to the provision of cyber security services and evaluating their effectiveness in protecting information systems. For instance, some papers analyse legal relationships between external service providers and the government in the context of cyber security and suggest important implications for incorporating data confidentiality requirements into security service level agreements (Nugraha, 2022). These papers also address the issue of liability in service provision and propose different types of contracts (Wu, 2021), such as threshold-based liability contracts and variable liability contracts, to achieve optimal outcomes considering post-breach effort verification feasibility (Hui, 2019). The authors of these papers also investigate factors influencing organizational decisions to outsource information security, including organizational factors such as cost-benefit analysis and inability to cope with the threat environment, as well as legal factors such as regulatory and legal compliance (Arshad, 2022). Another group of related studies focuses on contracts related to the security of processed personal data, which are used to ensure compliance with applicable legal regulations. These studies analyse the content, responsibilities, and contractual provisions related to information security and cybersecurity in such contracts. For example, some papers analyse privacy service level agreements, describing the risk assessment process and selection of cloud services (Rios, 2019). Additionally, some articles propose metamodels for privacy-level agreements to support privacy management based on analysing privacy threats, vulnerabilities, and trust relationships in information systems (Diamantopoulou, 2017).

The main objective of this paper is to explore the risks and challenges associated with the outsourcing of information and cyber security to third parties through contractual relationships. The article provides insights into some aspects of information and cyber security outsourcing, which can help readers better understand the potential risks, challenges, and benefits of such practices. We state the following research sub-goals:

1. *what is the extent and nature of cyber security services that are outsourced by public authorities to service providers?*
2. *identification of the degree of limitation of responsibility in the contractual relationships in the field of cyber security.*

This paper is organized into four sections. Section II discusses research methodology. Section III outlines selected legal aspects related to contractual relations in cyber security. Section IV contains discussion and conclusion including our suggestions for future research.

2. Methodology

The scope of this study is limited to the analysis of selected legal aspects of contracts concluded between public authorities and private providers, the object of which is the provision of services in the field of cybersecurity. The analysis is based on a dataset of contracts obtained from the Slovak Central Register of Contracts – a database of contracts that are obligatorily published in accordance with the Act No. 211/2000 Coll. on free access to information ('Freedom of Information Act'). This database currently includes more than 3 million published contracts. The selection of contracts that formed the basis for our analysis was determined by the contract title, specifically the authors focused on contract titles that included the term 'cyber' or 'cybersecurity' or its Slovak abbreviation 'KB' or, alternatively, mentioned the provision of cybersecurity services such as audit.

The authors have analysed 158 contracts concluded in the time period of 2020-2023. These included 5 contracts concluded in 2020, 9 contracts concluded in 2021, 108 contracts concluded in 2022 and 36 contracts concluded in 2023. Data collection ended as of 12.4.2023. Six contracts have been excluded from the final analysis as they did not relate to any cybersecurity issues analysed in this paper (despite the fact that a referral to cybersecurity was included in their title) but focused solely on personal data processing. Another 13 contracts have been excluded from the analysis, as these included contracts that the essential service operator is obligated to conclude according to Article 19 and consequential provisions of the Slovak Act No. 69/2018 Coll. on cybersecurity as amended (hereinafter referred to as 'Cyber Security Act') with the objective to ensure fulfilment of security measures and notification obligations. Due to their subject matter these contracts have a different structure and do not contain several attributes based on which we examine contractual relationships.

The data collected from the individual contracts included information regarding 1) the contractual parties, specifically identification of the supplier (private party) and customer (public authority), 2) the contract identification, namely contract ID, title, date of application and database link and 3) attributes focusing on selected legal aspects analysed in this paper, namely the contractual types utilized in practice (focusing on the common subject of the contracts concluded and the corresponding legal act on the basis of which they were concluded), specification of remuneration, liability aspects and protection of information.

For exploring relationships between individual binary attributes, we used *Pearson's correlation* (Cohen, 2009). We computed the Pearson's correlation coefficient between the respective attributes (as indicated below in the article). The range of this coefficient is from -1 to 1, where:

- 0.2 to -0.2 indicates no or negligible relationship;
- 0.2 to 0.4 or -0.2 to -0.4 indicates a weak to moderate relationship;
- 0.4 to 0.7 or -0.4 to -0.7 indicates a strong relationship; and
- 0.7 to 1 or -0.7 to -1 indicates a very strong relationship.

Subsequently, we tested for statistically significant correlations between the variables using a chi-squared test of the independence of variables in a contingency table. To conduct this analysis, we utilized the SciPy implementation of the chi-squared test in scipy.stats.chi2_contingency (The SciPy community, 2023). The null hypothesis assumed independence between the variables. We then examined whether the calculated p-value was below the threshold of 0.05. If the p-value was lower, we rejected the null hypothesis, indicating a statistically significant correlation between the attributes. Conversely, if the p-value was higher, we accepted the null hypothesis, concluding that there is no statistically significant correlation between the attributes.

3. Selected legal aspects

3.1. Contractual parties

The contractual parties to the analysed contracts include public authorities with specific obligations stemming from the applicable cybersecurity legislation and private providers claiming to be able to ensure the fulfilment of these obligations in practice. As regards public authorities, these include primarily subjects of local self-government (municipalities and regional self-government units) (in 101 contracts), different state institutions such as ministries and other national government bodies (in 22 cases), national health care providers (11) or state companies (5). Whereas 120 different public authorities have been identified as a contractual party in the analyzed dataset of contracts, only 50 different service providers can be distinguished in this regard. Moreover, in 33 cases, the service provider opted for the possibility to use services of subcontractors to ensure contract performance.

3.2. Applicable legal framework

The most referred to legislation establishing the legal framework for the contractual relations between the parties of the contracts analysed in this paper included a referral to the Slovak Act No. 513/1991 Coll. Commercial Code as amended (hereinafter referred to as 'Commercial Code') (in 110 contracts) or the Cyber Security Act (in 75 contracts). In many cases, a referral to the implementing legislation was also included. Such as a referral to the Regulation No. 362/2018 Coll. defining the scope of cybersecurity measures, the content and structure of security documentation and the scope of general security measures (in 56 contracts) and the Regulation No. 78/2020 Coll. on standards for information technologies of public administration (in 30 contracts). It must, however, be noted that in most cases the individual contracts refer to more than one legal act as their legal basis. Moreover, the contracts concluded in this regard present, in most cases, the so-called innominate contracts that lack detailed regulation in legislation. In only 12 cases, a regulated contractual type was used, namely a contract to work done (contracts to work done as defined in the Act No. 513/1991 Coll. Commercial Code as amended (§ 539)) in 9 cases, a license contract (license contracts defined in the Act No. 185/2015 Coll. Copyright Act (§ 65)) in two cases or a contract of control (contracts of control defined in the Act No. 513/1991 Coll. Commercial Code as amended (§ 591)) in one case. This presents a challenge in practice, as such contracts must be formulated without a general basis provided in the legislation focusing on the specificities of the individual case.

3.3. Contract subject-matter

The common subject-matter of the analysed contracts could be divided into four different categories:

1. *provision of a qualified expert personnel,* specifically in the form of:
   a. a cybersecurity manager, e.g. CISO (hereinafter referred to as 'manager') – 78 contracts;
   b. an expert providing consultations regarding information and cyber security in the organization concerned, cybersecurity governance (hereinafter referred to as 'consulting') – 104 contracts;
2. *provision of services related to security events and incidents handling (proactive and reactive measures),* specifically in the form of:
   a. monitoring of infrastructure, servers, service or security operation system capabilities (hereinafter referred to as 'monitoring') – 5 contracts;
   b. cyber security incident handling and response including reporting these incidents (hereinafter referred to as 'IR_IH') – 84 contracts;
3. *provision of services related to implementation of security measures,* specifically:
   a. delivery of infrastructure, including software and hardware (hereinafter referred to as 'infrastructure') – 5 contracts;
   b. security documentation, e. g. risk analysis, business continuity management, security policy (hereinafter referred to as 'documentation') – 16 contracts;
4. *provision of services concerning cybersecurity audit and control,* specifically:

a. preliminary audit or a preparation of the public authority for audit (analysis of cybersecurity in organization – 54 contracts;

b. audit according to Article 29 of the Cyber Security Act - 13 contracts;

In addition to these services, the subject-matter of one of the contracts was also the provision of an expert opinion in the field of information and cyber security, and one contract involved the provision of training in incident response and proactive security measures. Due to the small number of these contracts, we have decided not to consider them in the subsequent analyses.

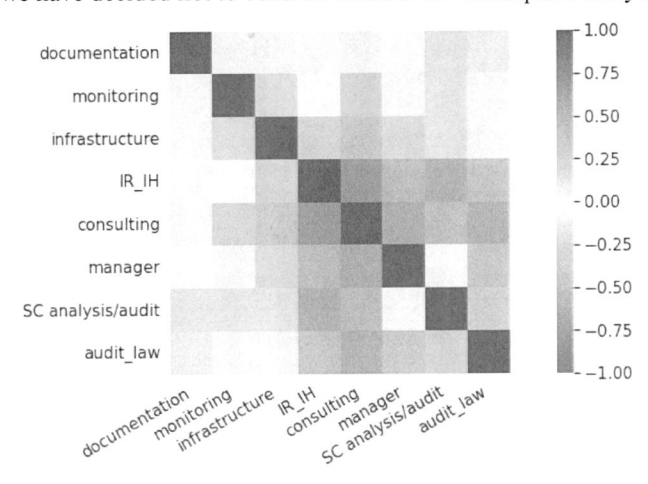

Figure 1. Statistical correlation among contract subject-matter - Pearson's correlation coefficient

On Figure 1, correlations between the different subject matters can be observed. Pearson's correlation method was used for the analysis, following the procedure outlined in the Methodology section. Based on the chi-squared test, we identified 13 significant correlations, which were sorted according to the relationships:

- *strong relationship:* (I) IR_IH - manager (0.441); (II) IR_IH - SC analysis/audit (0.494); (III) consulting - manager (0.522); (IV) audit_law - consulting (-0.554); and (V) IR_IH - consulting (0.649).

- *moderate relationship:* (I) infrastructure - manager (-0.218); (II) infrastructure - IR_IH (-0.239); (III) monitoring - consulting (-0.244); (IV) audit_law - SC analysis/audit (-0.256); (V) infrastructure - consulting (-0.333); (VI) audit_law - manager (-0.363); (VII) consulting - SC analysis/audit (0.394); and (VIII) audit_law - IR_IH (-0.397).

An interesting finding is a higher correlation between the provision of consulting services and the resolution of cyber security incidents (IR_IH) compared to the correlation between the cyber security manager and the resolution of cyber security incidents (IR_IH). According to the Slovak Cyber Security Act, the cyber security manager is the person responsible for managing the incident resolution within the organization and communicating with other relevant stakeholders. The implicit understanding of this responsibility and its omission in the contractual provisions may explain this observation. This is further supported by the repeated obligation of the service provider to inform the cyber security manager about any cyber security incidents that occur. On the other hand, such an approach may pose challenges in identifying the extent of responsibility of an external cyber security manager. A particular group of contracts consists of contracts aimed at conducting audits in accordance with the Cyber Security Act. In almost all correlations, a moderate or strong indirect correlation is evident. This can be explained primarily by the fact that an external audit should be independent. Interestingly, in this context there are situations where an organization offers other services in addition to external audits.

3.4. Remuneration and validity period

Table 1 presents an analysis of the total amount of remuneration defined for specific contract performance per a certain duration. In the analysis we considered the overall sum provided for contract performance in the case of one-time payments or framework agreements. The second group of contracts consisted of services with recurring payments, where we considered the monthly payment and the number of months for which the contract was concluded, or the median of the total number of months for indefinite contracts. Table 1 includes the total number of analysed sums in the dataset categorized by contract item (column count), the maximum amount (column max), the minimum amount (column min), the average amount (column mean), and the median of prices (column median).

Table 1. Comparison of remuneration according to the subject type per a certain duration.

Subject	Count	Max	Min	Mean	Median
Documentation	16	€136 920	€720	€27 395	€2 400
Monitoring	5	€44 928	€5 58	€15 525	€9 600
Infrastructure	5	€155 400	€11 750	€79 874	€58 800
IR_IH	84	€80 352	€144	€3 826	€1 224
consulting	104	€139 300	€144	€8 266	€1 296
manager	78	€101 088	€144	€4 205	€1 296
SC analysis/audit	54	€11 976	€240	€1 851	€864
audit_law	13	€49 000	€2 479	€14 801	€7 800

As regards the contract item 'infrastructure delivery', the table demonstrates a relatively high average price for this item. This may be given by the fact that it includes the adoption of cost-intensive security measures. The second highest average price is specified for the 'delivery of necessary documentation' in accordance with the Cyber Security Act and the corresponding implementing regulations. However, the amounts specified for such performance range from €720 to €136.920. This could be related to the fact that in Slovakia there are three different categories of subjects that must implement security measures, the scope of which is determined by the category the specific subject belongs to. However, another negative explanation of this differing range could be determined from the analysis, specifically the fact that in most cases the provision of documentation is described in only very general terms (e. g., by copying of legal text) without providing detailed content of such documentation to be provided.

Another interesting aspect to note regards the provision of consultation services and services of a cybersecurity manager. Reasons for varying prices could include the size of the organization, the number of information systems, users. etc. Nevertheless, the quality of the service provided at a value of €12 per month is worth considering. 37 contracts specified a remuneration for the provision of these services in the amount of €137 or lower to be paid monthly. Some providers also provided the service of a cybersecurity manager or cybersecurity incident handling in addition to consultations.

3.5. Liability

The design of liability and its individual aspects differentiates the analysed contracts into two categories corresponding to the chosen regime of legal regulation.

One category of contractual relations is regulated by the Commercial Code, which establishes liability for damages based on the principle of objective liability, meaning liability without fault with the possibility of liberation. This means, in general, that the party that infringes its contractual obligation is liable for damages caused to the other party, unless it is demonstrated that the infringement falls under any of the exemptions from liability specified in Art. 374 of the Commercial Code. Establishment of liability in this category is based on the requirement of special qualification. The nature of these relations is determined by the fact that suppliers act as professionals with specific knowledge desired by other parties trusting their expertise. Of particular importance in these relations is the problem of information asymmetry and demonstration of its careful balancing in favour of the weaker party in the contracting process.

Another category of the analysed contracts is regulated not only by the Commercial Code, but also by another legislative act, specifically the Cyber Security Act. As regards the limitation of liability for damages, this is determined by the contractual nature of this institute. The contractual provision that limits liability should be precisely defined by the contractual parties so that their will is unquestionable. The provision follows other contract provisions and there are no contradictions (Šilhán, 2011). The liability for damages is regulated in the analysed contracts in the following ways:

a) 39 contracts (concluded under Art. 269 (2) of the Commercial Code) - *liability is not limited* (hereinafter referred to as 'liability_not_limited');

b) 100 contracts (concluded under Art. 269 (2) of the Commercial Code and Act No. 69/2018 Coll.) (hereinafter referred to as 'liability_limited') – *liability is limited* on the basis of:

   1. *restricting the impact on the organisation*, specifically in these forms:
      - limitation of liability for damages by a specific amount (hereinafter referred to as 'limitation_amount') – 45 contracts, and
      - limitation of liability for damages by the damage caused (hereinafter referred to as 'limitation_damage') – 34 contracts.

   2. *restricting the conditions for the establishment of liability* in case of:
      - failure to cooperate (hereinafter referred to as 'no_cooperate') – 21 contracts;
      - failure to adopt recommendations and/or measures proposed by the supplier (hereinafter referred to as 'non_acceptance') – 11 contracts;
      - provision of incorrect information (hereinafter referred to as 'incorrect_inputs') – 16 contracts;
      - other – For example, not contesting the fine awarded by the competent authority, non-submission of documentation prepared by the service provider to the competent authority etc. – 47 contracts; and
      - explicit referral to the circumstances excluding liability (hereinafter referred to as 'circumstance_excl_liability') – 20 contracts.

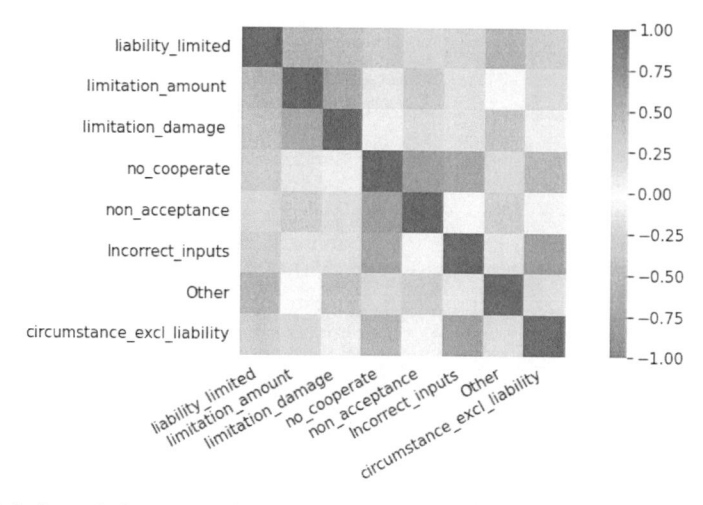

Figure 2. Statistical correlation among circumstances excluding liability – Pearson's correlation coefficient

On Figure 2, correlations between the different circumstances excluding liability can be observed. Pearson's correlation method was used for the analysis, following the procedure outlined in the Methodology section. Based on the chi-squared test, we identified 6 significant correlations, which were sorted according to the relationships:

- *strong positive relationship:* (I) limitation_amount - liability_limited (0.432); (II) liability_limited - Other (0.446); (III) no_cooperate - circumstance_excl_liability (0.457); (IV) limitation_amount - limitation_damage (0.536); (V) no_cooperate - incorrect_inputs (0.540); (VI) no_cooperate - non_acceptance (0.620);

An interesting fact can be observed from the analysis of the correlation table among circumstances excluding liability (Figure 2). High Pearson's correlation coefficient values are seen between limitations of incurred impact for the organization (2 cases mentioned above) and limitations based on facts/assumptions (5 cases mentioned above). It is clear from this that suppliers do not approach the combination of liability limitations but rather utilize one of the mentioned approaches. The most significant correlation in the case of combining both approaches is seen with limitations based on incurred damage and other circumstances. In this case, Pearson's correlation coefficient was -0.371, indicating a moderate negative correlation.

As regards liability regulation and limitation of damages, we conclude that in the analysed contracts an inclination to conclusion of contracts in the special legislative regime with a precise limitation of damages could be distinguished. However, a restriction of damages by the amount of sanction imposed does not reflect other damage components that may emerge in practice. e. g. as a result of a cybersecurity incident (loss of clients, costs for infrastructure renewal etc.).

3.6. Confidential information and personal data

Another aspect to be considered with regard to the analysed contracts is the question whether they regulate, in any way, the management of information exchanged in the scope of the established contractual relations. In this regard, different types of data could be distinguished:

a) *confidential information* including any information defined as confidential that is mutually provided by contractual parties within the scope of the contractual relationship (§ 271 of the Act No. 513/1991 Coll. Commercial code).

b) *personal data* within their definition provided in Art. 4 (1) of GDPR.

c) *classified information* pursuant to § 2 (a) of the Act No. 215/2004 Coll. on the protection of classified information as amended.

As regards confidential information the majority of the analysed contracts (114) included a set of provisions, the objective of which was the protection of such information. Personal data was similarly regulated in the majority of cases (91). This illustrates the public authority's obligation as a controller to ensure the compliance with GDPR regulation, if personal data processed by it is handled by third parties (private providers), e.g. in the course of security incident handling. In this regard, the following forms of contractual regulation could be distinguished:

1. provision of a more complex, but in most cases very general regulation (in 37 contracts),
2. absence of a specific regulation, but inclusion of personal data into the category of confidential information (23 contracts),
3. general referral to the applicable legislation (15 contracts),
4. a mention of personal data regarding one of the supplier's obligations, namely the commitment to build security awareness in the area of personal data protection (7 contracts),
5. referral to the regulation of personal data protection in the future contracts (4 contracts),
6. authorization of the supplier's access to employees' personal data. e. g. for the purposes of cybersecurity audit (2 contracts).

On the other hand, classified information was only mentioned in 6 contracts, firstly as a general obligation to safeguard information protected by legislation (in 4 cases), secondly as an exemption to information to be protected as confidential (1) and lastly, in the contract, the object of which was the provision of an expert opinion with regard to providing of such information to the expert.

As part of our study, we have also examined the relationship between the attributes of confidential information and personal data. The Pearson's correlation coefficient was found to be -0.301, indicating a moderate negative correlation between these attributes. We further conducted a chi-squared test and the resulting p-value was significantly below 0.05, leading to the rejection of the null hypothesis and indicating a statistically significant correlation between these attributes.

The relationship between the contract subject-matter associated with cyber security analysis or internal audit (SC analysis/audit) and personal data protection provisions is worth mentioning. Pearson's correlation coefficient was -0.418, indicating a moderate negative correlation between these attributes. We further conducted a chi-squared test and it showed a statistically significant correlation between these attributes. This is an interesting fact, as internal audits involve exposure to personal data. A slightly weaker indirect dependence was found between the provision of services by a cyber security manager and provisions governing the provision of confidential information (Pearson's correlation coefficient was found to be -0.262). Similar statistically significant correlations (e.g. documentation and personal information, consulting and personal information) also showed Pearson's correlation coefficient values around -0.25, indicating a weak correlation but revealing an exciting fact: none of the contractual subject-matter types showed a moderate or high positive correlation. The paradox is that sensitive assets, including personal data, are not regulated in the contractual relationship when services for securing an organization's cyber security are provided.

4. Discussion and conclusion

The essence of cybersecurity is to ensure confidentiality, integrity, and availability of an organization's assets. The authors conducted a critical review of contractual relationships concluded in cyber security. A limitation of this study was that we only had access to contracts that are obligatorily published. It must be noted that specific rights and obligations of parties should be explicitly stated in the contract. Only then the contractual obligations can be effectively enforced. Our analysis identified several shortcomings in the way these contractual relationships are regulated.

The first issue is the amount charged for the contracted services, which moved in a wide price range. The price naturally depends on the organization's size, the number of users, and the number and importance of information systems. On the other hand, the content of the delivered service is not clearly defined in a significant number of contracts. There needs to be a more detailed specification of obligations arising from legal provisions. One solution is to include attachments to contracts that provide a more detailed description of the contract subject-matter. Another issue was identified with regard to the limitation of service provider's liability. In most cases, some form of liability limitation was included in the analysed contracts, strengthening the position of the service provider, disadvantaging the public authority.

Finally, we have also identified issues with provisions regulating the sharing of sensitive data (such as confidential information and personal data) between contractual parties. In some cases, the regulation of such information was overlooked. These issues showcase the disadvantages of contractual solutions for organization's inability to ensure cybersecurity in its own capacity.

Acknowledgment

This paper was funded by the Slovak Research and Development Agency under contracts No. APVV-21-0336 "Analysis of Judicial Decisions using Artificial Intelligence", and APVV-17-0561 "Human rights related aspects and ethical aspects of the information security".

References

Arshad. A.. Ahmad. A.. & Maynard. S. (2022). Factors Influencing the Organizational Decision to Outsource IT Security: A Review and Research Agenda. arXiv:2208.12875.

Cohen. I. et al. (2009). Pearson correlation coefficient. Noise reduction in speech processing. Vol. 2. Springer Science & Business Media. 1-4.

Diamantopoulou. V.. Angelopoulos. K.. Pavlidis. M.. & Mouratidis. H. (2017. January). A Metamodel for GDPR-based Privacy Level Agreements. In ER Forum/Demos. pp. 285-291

European Parliament (2016). Regulation (EU) 2016/679 of the European Parliament and of the Council of 27 April 2016 on the protection of natural persons with regard to the processing of personal data and on the free movement of such data. and repealing Directive 95/46/EC (General Data Protection Regulation). *OJ L 119. 4.5.2016. p. 1–88.*

European Parliament (2018). Regulation 362/2018 Coll. of the National Security Authority defining the scope of cybersecurity measures. the content and structure of security documentation and the scope of general security measures.

European Parliament (2020). Regulation 78/2020 Coll. on standards for information technologies of public administration.

Hui. K. L. et al. (2019). Bilateral liability-based contracts in information security outsourcing. Information Systems Research. 30(2). 411-429.

National Security Authority (2021). The National Cybersecurity Strategy 2021-2025. Available: https://www.nbu.gov.sk/wp-content/uploads/cyber-security/National_cybersecurity_strategy_2021.pdf [22.4.2023].

Nugraha. Y. & Martin. A. (2022). Cybersecurity service level agreements: understanding government data confidentiality requirements. Journal of Cybersecurity. 8(1).

Nurse. J. R.. Adamos. K.. Grammatopoulos. A. & Di Franco. F. (2021). Addressing the EU cybersecurity skills shortage and gap through higher education. (ENISA) Report.

Rios. E. et al. (2019). Service level agreement-based GDPR compliance and security assurance in (multi) Cloud-based systems. IET Software. 13(3). 213-222.

Slovak Act No. 513/1991 Coll. Commercial Code as amended

Slovak Act No. 18/2018 Coll. on the protection of personal data

Slovak Act No. 69/2018 Coll. on cybersecurity as amended

Slovak Act No. 211/2000 Coll. on free access to information ('Freedom of Information Act')

Slovak Act No. 215/2004 Coll. on the protection of classified information as amended

Šilhán. J. (2011). Náhrada škody v obchodních vztazích a možnosti její smluvní limitace. C.H.Beck.

The SciPy community (2023). SciPy Manual v1.10.1 - stats.chisquare. Available: from https://docs.scipy.org/doc/scipy/reference/generated/scipy.stats.chisquare.html [22.4.2023].

Wu. Y.. Tayi. G. K.. Feng. G.. & Fung. R. Y. (2021). Managing information security outsourcing in a dynamic cooperation environment. Journal of the Association for Information Systems. 22(3).

EXPLORING THE LINK BETWEEN ACCESSIBLE WEBSITE DESIGN AND USER EXPERIENCE FOR HUMANS WITH BLINDNESS AND VISUAL IMPAIRMENT: A QUALITATIVE STUDY

David Henkelmann, Tobias Fertig

Faculty of Computer Science and Business Information Systems
Technical University of Applied Sciences Würzburg-Schweinfurt
{david.henkelmann, tobias.fertig}@thws.de

DOI: 10.35011/IDIMT-2023-101

Keywords

Visually impaired, accessibility, perception, user experience, WCAG guidelines, WAIX-Model

Abstract

In today's digital age, web accessibility and barrier-free design are crucial for individuals with disabilities to fully participate in and benefit from the Internet. Despite existing guidelines, there is room for improvement in their implementation. This qualitative study explores the relationship between accessible website design and user experience for individuals with blindness and visual impairments. Through interviews, it aims to understand their current emotions and perceptions towards the Internet. Additionally, the study discusses the importance of involving individuals with visual impairments in the creation and implementation of accessibility policies and laws. The findings of this study will serve as the foundation for further empirical research to test the hypotheses formed.

1. General

During the early days of the Internet, little attention was given to the diverse health needs of users in website design and development (Universiti Putra Malaysia and Yazid, 2019). Today, individuals with blindness and visual impairment continue to face significant barriers on the World Wide Web, mainly due to the visual-centric design of web applications (Murphy et al., 2008).

The foundation for an accessible internet was established by the World Wide Web Consortium (W3C) with the publication of Web Content Accessibility Guidelines 1.0 (WCAG 1.0) in 1999 (Chisholm et al., 1999). To address the limitations of WCAG 1.0 and WCAG 2.0, the current WCAG 2.1 guidelines were introduced as a more comprehensive standard for web content accessibility (Kirkpatrick et al., 2018; Caldwell et al., 2008). However, research, such as the work of Power et al. (2012), has shown that guidelines alone are insufficient. Only about half of the issues faced by individuals with blindness and visual impairments on the internet are covered by the WCAG 2.0 standard. This indicates that meeting the guidelines does not guarantee sufficient accessibility for users (Aizpurua et al., 2016).

Therefore, it is important to transform concepts that find application in improving the user experience of people without impairments to the needs of people with blindness and visual impairments. A comprehensive approach to this is provided by Yazid et al. with their Web Accessibility Interaction Experience (WAIX) Model (Jantan et al., 2022; Universiti Putra Malaysia, and Yazid, 2019; Yazid and Jantan, 2022). The WAIX model is an integrated model. It fuses Hassenzahl's UX Model (Hassenzahl, 2018a), the CUE model for user experience (Thüring and Mahlke, 2007), the TAM model (Venkatesh and Davis, 2000) for technology acceptance, and approaches to accessibility. The goal of the model is to generate a holistic view of the needs and expectations for web offerings of people with blindness and visual impairments to drive accessible website development (Jantan et al., 2022).

The primary objective of this research paper is to address the following research question: What are the emotional experiences and challenges encountered by visually impaired users when engaging with contemporary web designs, and how can these insights inform the development of accessible web design practices to enhance user experience and promote digital inclusivity? Through qualitative interviews, insights into users' subjective perspectives will be gathered to formulate relevant hypotheses regarding the emotional aspects of web accessibility. The study will focus on investigating both transported emotions and experienced barriers from people with blindness and visual impairments due to accessibility barriers. By exploring visually impaired users' emotional landscape, expectations, and impressions, a comprehensive understanding of their user experience will be gained. The findings and hypotheses derived from this study can inform the development of accessible web design practices that better address the needs and expectations of visually impaired users. Ultimately, this research strives to enhance overall user experience, promote digital inclusivity, and identify common objective hurdles based on the explored emotions.

2. Related Works

2.1. Identified web barriers for individuals with blindness and visual impairments

Despite the significant advancements achieved through guidelines such as the current WCAG 2.1 regulation or the freely accessible Barrier-Free-Information-Technology-Regulation (BITV), people with blindness and visual impairments continue to face barriers in accessing web content. The greatest barrier faced by people with blindness and visual impairments is their own limitation, which conflicts with the basic concept of the Internet (Dobransky and Hargittai, 2006). Websites primarily rely on visual presentation, which is intended to provide an easier access and a more appealing and goal-oriented user experience. However, what provides additional value to the unrestricted user proves to be the opposite for visually impaired users. The implementation of graphics, animated images, tables, frames, or audio and video streams makes it difficult for them to use websites. This is because assistive technologies such as text-to-speech synthesizers and Braille output devices can only inadequately represent these contents (Murphy et al., 2008; The web, 2004).

In addition to the predominantly visual design character of websites, the abundance of information and how this is presented to users with blindness and visual impairment is also a hurdle that should not be neglected. Each website has its own individual structure and character of how the information is presented within the website. Just being able to get an overview of a website is a challenge for visually impaired users (Petrie et al., 2001). The type of presented information is also very different. For example, in addition to the actual content, web pages also present embedded advertisements or cross-references. Evaluating and analyzing the actual information from this flood of non-content information can lead users astray (Murphy et al., 2008). The composition of highly visually dependent information and embedded filler information create another barrier, information loss

(Petrie et al., 2001). The design choices such as different font, text size, or formatting is indistinguishable to screen readers. Thus, valuable context can be lost, impacting the personal user experience of people with blindness and visual impairment (Murphy et al., 2008; Petrie et al., 2001).

2.2. Web Accessibility

"The power of the Web is in its universality. Access by everyone regardless of disability is an essential aspect." - Tim Berners-Lee, W3C Director and inventor of the World Wide Web. Web accessibility should enable everyone, but especially those with disabilities, to make full use of the Internet and all its offerings. This includes navigation, understanding the content presented, and interacting with the website itself (Herny et al., 2016). As described in the introduction, the foundation for web accessibility was laid by the first version of the W3C Web Content Accessibility Guidelines (WCAG). This collection of standards was published in 1999 and has since been the blueprint for laws and regulations in various countries (Abou-Zahra and Brewer, 2019). For example, the WCAG guidelines are the inspiration of the U.S. Section 508 Technical Standard as well as the European EN 301 549 standard (Abou-Zahra and Brewer, 2019).

All WCAG guidelines are formulated in a technology-neutral way and include aspects and manual instructions for code, design, processes, multimedia and text. Likewise, the guidelines apply not only to the Internet, but also to non-web documents and software. The congruence of the guidelines is indicated by a three-level categorization: Level A (lowest), Level AA, and Level AAA (highest). These ratings explain how well a website is adapted to the needs of users with handicaps (visual impairment, motor limitations, etc.). A low accessibility level corresponds to level A, while a medium or high accessibility level corresponds to levels AA and AAA (Kirkpatrick et al., 2018). The current WCAG 2.1 guidelines include 13 guidelines that are structured according to the four basic principles of perceptible, understandable, operable, and robust (Kirkpatrick et al., 2018). The 13 guidelines are underpinned by 78 so-called success criteria, which offer concrete action instructions for accessible implementation (Kirkpatrick et al., 2018). Looking at the four basic principles, it becomes clear what the WCAG guidelines are aiming for at their core. The effort to adhere to these four principles benefits everyone, not just users with limitations. People talk about a "design for all" or an "Internet for all". But to create a design for all, several concepts must be brought together. In addition to accessibility, the general user experience must also be considered when creating web offerings (Aizpurua et al., 2016). Because if accessibility, usability, or a good user experience are not properly integrated, websites can either be accessible but hardly usable, or usable but hardly accessible (Aizpurua et al., 2016).

2.3. User Experience

The concept of user experience remains a complex and debated topic among researchers (Hassenzahl, 2018b). It originated from the need to expand beyond the narrow scope of human interface and usability. Donald Norman, a cognitive scientist, introduced the term "user experience" in 1993 to encompass various aspects, including graphical design and physical interaction with a system. The ISO 9241-210 standard further defines user experience as the perceptions and reactions resulting from the actual or expected use of a product, system, or service (DIN EN ISO 9241-210, 2020). These perceptions and reactions encompass emotions, beliefs, preferences, and behaviors that occur throughout the interaction process (Yazid and Jantan, 2022). In the context of websites, they should be viewed as more than functional features, but as generators of meaningful and holistic experiences. Interaction with websites should aim to create memorable and purposeful experiences, ultimately shaping a positive overall perception (Hassenzahl, 2018a).

Unfortunately, the concept of user experience is not universally lived for all user groups (Dobransky and Hargittai, 2006; Power et al., 2012; The web, 2004). This is because, despite the extensive WCAG guidelines, there is evidence that compliance with these standards does not guarantee a satisfactory user experience. In 2004, Petrie et al. (2004) conducted a user study with 51 participants with disabilities. The result was that 45% of the observed barriers faced by the subjects were not related to a violation of the WCAG 1.0 guidelines. A similar result was found for the extended WCAG 2.0 guidelines (Caldwell et al., 2008). The empirical study by Power et al. (2012) also showed that only 50.4% of the obstacles encountered by the subjects were covered by the WCAG 2.0 guidelines. This indicates that a deeper understanding of how accessibility and UX are related and experienced by blind and visually impaired users is needed (Aizpurua et al., 2016). Aizpurua et al. (2015) have confirmed in previous work that experiential aspects such as memories, expectations, and biases influence the perceptions of blind and visually impaired users. These experiential aspects guide perceptions of website accessibility and other features, and thus directly affect user experience. The work of Jantan et al. (2022), Universiti Putra Malaysia, and Yazid (2019), and Yazid and Jantan (2022) also reached the same conclusion by defining accessibility as an input variable in their conceptual model (WAIX model), which has a significant impact on direct user experience.

3. Methodology and Implementation

A qualitative research method, specifically focused interviews, was chosen as the methodology, since the experienced accessibility of a website and the associated user experience is subjective. The stimuli for the interviews were two websites: https://www.tagesschau.de and https://www.zalando.de. These websites underwent accessibility testing using Google Lighthouse and WAVE, receiving AA to AAA ratings on the WCAG spectrum.

The study included a test group with a sample size of n=4 participants. The participants had different visual impairments. One subject suffered from glaucoma caused by removal of the crystalline lenses due to cataract, two other subjects suffered from progressive cone rod dystrophy with nystagmus, and one subject suffered from brainstem cavernoma resulting in visual impairment due to optic nerve compression. All participants were students of the "bbs nürnberg - Educational Center for the Blind and Visually Impaired".

The interviews were conducted at the institution on site in Nuremberg. At the beginning, the privacy statement was filled out and discussed with the subjects. Afterwards the stimuli were introduced. Each website was presented in two different scenarios, representing Hassenzahl's goal mode and action mode, respectively (Hassenzahl, 2018a). The interviews consisted of 21 questions, categorized into internet usage, accessibility, information presentation, perceived effort and emotions, and navigation. The interviews were recorded, and the participants' data were anonymized. All interviews were transcribed and coded to ensure data reliability.

4. Results

Five categories were identified from the available material. The most concise results are presented below.

Barriers to Websites: The analysis revealed key barriers to website accessibility as identified by the respondents. Participants emphasized that an unclear website structure significantly hampers task completion, leading to increased processing time and a negative user experience. Excessive advertisements were also highlighted as a hindrance, particularly when they disrupt the flow of reading for users relying on screen readers or Braille displays. Additionally, participants expressed frustration when content was not read aloud by screen readers or properly displayed on Braille devices, effectively excluding them from accessing the website's content. For users dependent on these assistive tools, failure to recognize and present the content renders the website inaccessible to them.

Accessibility expectations: A prominent finding from the data analysis was the category of expectations for accessibility. Interviewees expressed a fundamental expectation that assistive devices and peripherals should enable them to perceive website content. They emphasized that all websites should make information interpretable for assistive devices without any exceptions. Furthermore, interviewees advocated for strict adherence to accessibility guidelines such as the WCAG guidelines or the Accessibility Protection Act on all websites. They argued that such compliance is crucial to ensure web accessibility and provide an inclusive and positive user experience, especially for individuals with visual impairments or other physical limitations. However, respondents perceived the current implementation of guidelines and laws to be insufficient in terms of speed and comprehensiveness. They attributed this inadequacy to the vague wording of the guidelines and laws, which they believed only addressed a fraction of all impairments.

Perceived emotions: The emotional experiences of individuals with blindness and visual impairments when using websites have both individual and legal relevance. Participants reported frustration, a sense of exclusion, stress and anger in relation to website barriers and usability issues. They expressed the need for better representation and faster changes in addressing their concerns. The slow pace of progress in web accessibility was a source of frustration and the emotion of being excluded. Usability issues, such as complex menus, broken links, and inconsistent layouts, caused stress, anger, and annoyance.

User behavior: The user behavior category in this research provides valuable insights into the needs and behavior patterns of individuals with accessibility needs when using websites. Participants reported conducting targeted searches on search engines, such as Google, to find specific information instead of navigating through the actual website. They also expressed a preference for familiar websites with well-known structures and functions, as this facilitates easier navigation and task completion. Additionally, participants emphasized the importance of retaining a certain level of control over their website usage.

Suggestions for improving accessibility: The study participants showed a strong sensitivity to accessibility on the Internet. They stressed the importance of homogenizing websites to ensure a consistent user experience. They advocated a tree-like structure to improve navigation and suggested an international standard for keyboard shortcuts to improve usability across websites. Respondents also stressed the importance of aligning the website creation process with the needs of the most vulnerable user group to ensure optimal accessibility for all. They recommended involving more people with disabilities in decision-making bodies to monitor and promote the implementation of accessibility, and creating new legislation. Participants called for the creation of a mandatory international guideline, such as the WCAG guidelines, that would serve as a universal standard to accelerate and standardize accessibility implementation.

5. Discussion

The results highlight the importance of a clear structure on web pages for individuals with blindness, as it facilitates accessible navigation. A well-structured website allows for easy comprehension and understanding with the assistance of screen readers. On the other hand, an unclear structure leads to confusion and navigation difficulties. Interviewees expressed their preference for using familiar websites rather than exploring unknown ones, which aligns with the findings of previous studies (Jantan et al., 2022; Universiti Putra Malaysia and Yazid, 2019). The concept of expectation, as defined in the WAIX model, suggests that familiarity with a website contributes positively to user experience evaluation. Interviewees also utilized workarounds such as using Google search to bypass a website's structure and directly access the desired information, highlighting their interest in clear and user-friendly page structures. They further recommended the implementation of shortcut lists to facilitate uniform and targeted navigation across all pages. However, it is essential to consider that while a homogeneous internet landscape with clear and identical structures benefits users with limitations, it may also result in a loss of individuality for web pages. Regardless of the chosen structure, developers should ensure that it is logical, presenting content in a well-organized and clear manner. A good structure is crucial for website accessibility and a positive user experience. Web designers should prioritize addressing this issue consciously, aiming to enable inclusive and accessible use for all individuals (Horton and Quesenbery, 2013; Kirkpatrick et al., 2018).

A crucial finding is the necessity of programming websites to ensure compatibility with assistive devices such as Braille displays and screen readers. A clear structure and the use of semantic HTML elements facilitate the accurate interpretation of website content by these devices. This enables people with visual impairments to access website content seamlessly, avoiding any barriers or difficulties. Experiencing content that cannot be perceived due to blindness or visual impairment can evoke negative emotions of exclusion. Consequently, establishing trust in a website becomes paramount for individuals with visual impairments. The interviewees emphasized that trust enhances the perception of accessibility, fosters inclusivity, and contributes to an improved user experience. This notion aligns with the findings of Jantan et al. (2022), who identified trust in a website as a significant factor influencing perceived accessibility. In their WAIX model, Jantan et al. (2022) also highlight trust as one of the two non-instrumental qualities that significantly impact user experience.

The implementation of WCAG guidelines and accessibility laws, such as the German Accessibility Protection Act, presents several challenges that impact their effectiveness. Unclear definitions and limited coverage of specific pathologies have been criticized by the interviewees (Kirkpatrick et al., 2018; Power et al., 2012). These ambiguities result in varying interpretations and hinder consistent implementation (Power et al., 2012). Furthermore, organizations often face difficulties in adapting existing technologies and processes to meet WCAG requirements. Additionally, despite the existence of laws and guidelines, there is a gap between theory and practice, with many websites and digital media remaining inaccessible due to inconsistent enforcement (Aizpurua et al., 2016). To address these issues, stakeholders emphasize the importance of greater involvement of individuals with disabilities and advocacy groups in the design and implementation of guidelines and laws. Establishing internationally recognized standards and comprehensive laws with joint commitments from countries is crucial for achieving uniform and barrier-free website usage. Encouraging the active participation of people with blindness and visual impairments in political and governmental organizations is vital, as their insights and experiences can contribute to better representation and the expedited implementation of accessible policies. Their firsthand knowledge of daily challenges enables informed perspectives on the needs and demands of the affected population. By including individuals with blindness and visual impairments in decision-making processes, relevant issues can be actively discussed and adequately addressed. Hence, their participation in policy-making can significantly contribute to the implementation of accessible policies and the proper representation of the interests of this population.

After all results have been discussed, the following hypotheses are formulated based on the findings. These serve as a starting point for further analysis and verification of the assumptions.

Hypothesis 1 (H1): The clearer, more logical, and more uniform the structures of all web pages are, the higher the accessibility and thus also the user experience.

Hypothesis 2 (H2): If people with blindness and visual impairments have a strong sense of trust in a website and its usability, then this increased sense of trust will have a positive effect on the perception of accessibility as well as the user experience.

Hypothesis 3 (H3): If a stronger involvement of affected groups of people in the creation and decision-making processes is realized, this will lead to a more targeted and faster implementation of WCAG guidelines and laws in web accessibility.

6. Conclusion

In summary, the study and available literature demonstrate the direct correlation between accessibility and user experience. However, there is still a need for further research to better understand this correlation, as the concept of user experience is an extremely complex and subjective field of research. To validate or refute H1, future research can conduct usability tests and user studies involving individuals with blindness and visual impairments. Participants would interact with web pages of varying structural complexity, and their feedback and experiences would be collected. Analyzing the data and comparing accessibility and user experience ratings across different structures would determine if there is a significant relationship between web page clarity, logic, uniformity, and accessibility.

Similarly, H2 can be investigated by conducting surveys and interviews with individuals with visual impairments. Participants would be asked about their levels of trust in different websites and how they perceive accessibility and user experience. Analyzing the responses and examining correlations between trust, accessibility, and user experience ratings would provide empirical evidence supporting or refuting the hypothesis.

To explore H3, future studies can employ case studies or implement collaborative design processes involving affected groups in web accessibility initiatives. By comparing outcomes and timelines of projects with and without strong involvement from affected groups, researchers can assess the impact on targeted and timely implementation of WCAG guidelines and laws. Collecting feedback and input from the participants would further strengthen or challenge the hypothesis.

By employing these research methodologies, future work can provide insights into the relationships between web page structures, trust, involvement of affected groups, and their impacts on accessibility and user experience.

References

Abou-Zahra, S., Brewer, J., 2019. Standards, Guidelines, and Trends, in: Yesilada, Y., Harper, S. (Eds.), Web Accessibility, Human–Computer Interaction Series. Springer London, London, pp. 225–246. https://doi.org/10.1007/978-1-4471-7440-0_13

Aizpurua, A., Arrue, M., Vigo, M., 2015. Prejudices, memories, expectations and confidence influence experienced accessibility on the Web. Comput. Hum. Behav. 51, 152–160. https://doi.org/10.1016/j.chb.2015.04.035

Aizpurua, A., Harper, S., Vigo, M., 2016. Exploring the relationship between web accessibility and user experience. Int. J. Hum.-Comput. Stud. 91, 13–23. https://doi.org/10.1016/j.ijhcs.2016.03.008

Caldwell, B., Cooper, M., Guarino Reid, L., Vanderheiden, G., 2008. Web Content Accessibility Guidelines (WCAG 2.0). W3C Recomm. URL https://www.w3.org/TR/WCAG20/ (accessed 11.14.22).

Chisholm, W., Vanderheiden, G., Jacobs, I., 1999. Web Content Accessibility Guidelines 1.0. W3C Recomm. URL https://www.w3.org/TR/WAI-WEBCONTENT/ (accessed 11.14.22).

DIN EN ISO 9241-210:2020-03, Ergonomie der Mensch-System-Interaktion_-_Teil_210: Menschzentrierte Gestaltung interaktiver Systeme (ISO_9241-210:2019); Deutsche Fassung EN_ISO_9241-210:2019, 2020. . Beuth Verlag GmbH. https://doi.org/10.31030/3104744

Dobransky, K., Hargittai, E., 2006. The disability divide in internet access and use. Inf. Commun. Soc. 9, 313–334. https://doi.org/10.1080/13691180600751298

Hassenzahl, M., 2018a. The Thing and I: Understanding the Relationship Between User and Product, in: Blythe, M., Monk, A. (Eds.), Funology 2, Human–Computer Interaction Series. Springer International Publishing, Cham, pp. 301–313. https://doi.org/10.1007/978-3-319-68213-6_19

Hassenzahl, M., 2018b. The Thing and I (Summer of '17 Remix), in: Blythe, M., Monk, A. (Eds.), Funology 2, Human–Computer Interaction Series. Springer International Publishing, Cham, pp. 17–31. https://doi.org/10.1007/978-3-319-68213-6_2

Herny, S.L., Abou-Zahra, S., White, K., 2016. Accessibility, Usability, and Inclusion. Web Accesibility Initiat. URL https://www.w3.org/WAI/fundamentals/accessibility-usability-inclusion/ (accessed 1.23.23).

Horton, S., Quesenbery, W., 2013. A web for everyone: designing accessible user experiences. Rosenfeld Media, Brooklyn, New York.

Jantan, A.H., Yazid, M.A., Husain, W.N.L.W., 2022. Evaluation Criteria and Assessments for Effective User Experiences, Web Accessibility, and Interaction for Visually Impaired Users, in: Alfred, R., Lim, Y. (Eds.), Proceedings of the 8th International Conference on Computational Science and Technology, Lecture Notes in Electrical Engineering. Springer Singapore, Singapore, pp. 881–890. https://doi.org/10.1007/978-981-16-8515-6_67

Kirkpatrick, A., O Connor, J., Cambell, A., Cooper, M., 2018. Web Content Accessibility Guidelines (WCAG) 2.1. W3C Recomm. URL https://www.w3.org/TR/WCAG21/ (accessed 11.14.22).

Murphy, E., Kuber, R., McAllister, G., Strain, P., Yu, W., 2008. An empirical investigation into the difficulties experienced by visually impaired Internet users. Univers. Access Inf. Soc. 7, 79–91. https://doi.org/10.1007/s10209-007-0098-4

Petrie, H., Fisher, W., O'Neill, A., Fisher, W., Di Segni, Y., 2001. Deliverable 2.1: Report on user requirements of mainstream readers and print disabled readers. Available:

Petrie, H., Hamilton, F., King, N., 2004. Tension, what tension? Website accessibility and visual design, in: Proceedings of the International Cross-Disciplinary Workshop on Web Accessibility - W4A. Presented at the the international cross-disciplinary workshop, ACM Press, New York City, New York, p. 13. https://doi.org/10.1145/990657.990660

Power, C., Freire, A., Petrie, H., Swallow, D., 2012. Guidelines are only half of the story: accessibility problems encountered by blind users on the web, in: Proceedings of the SIGCHI Conference on Human Factors in Computing Systems. Presented at the CHI '12: CHI Conference on Human Factors in Computing Systems, ACM, Austin Texas USA, pp. 433–442. https://doi.org/10.1145/2207676.2207736

Thüring, M., Mahlke, S., 2007. Usability, aesthetics and emotions in human–technology interaction. Int. J. Psychol. 42, 253–264. https://doi.org/10.1080/00207590701396674

Universiti Putra Malaysia, Yazid, M.A., 2019. An Integrated Conceptual Model of Visually Impaired Users' Experience and Technology Acceptance of a Website. Int. J. Adv. Trends Comput. Sci. Eng. 8, 313–322. https://doi.org/10.30534/ijatcse/2019/4981.42019

Venkatesh, V., Davis, F.D., 2000. A Theoretical Extension of the Technology Acceptance Model: Four Longitudinal Field Studies. Manag. Sci. 46, 186–204. https://doi.org/10.1287/mnsc.46.2.186.11926

Yazid, M.A., Jantan, A.H., 2022. Systematic Evaluation Approach to Support Effective Web Interaction Among Visually Impaired Users, in: 2022 Applied Informatics International Conference (AiIC). Presented at the 2022 Applied Informatics International Conference (AiIC), IEEE, Serdang, Malaysia, pp. 99–104. https://doi.org/10.1109/AiIC54368.2022.9914579

VIRTUAL COLLABORATION, TEACHING & LEARNING

SELF-TEST AS A BLENDED ASSESSMENT STRATEGY TO FOSTER STUDENT ENGAGEMENT AND SATISFACTION IN HIGHER EDUCATION

Anne Jantos, Iris Vogt, Elena Fleckenstein

TUD Dresden University of Technology
{anne.jantos, iris.vogt, elena.fleckenstein}@tu-dresden.de

DOI: 10.35011/IDIMT-2023-111

Keywords

Higher education, assessment, e-assessment, blended assessment

Abstract

Standard assessment methods in higher education are mostly one-dimensional and leave students and teachers dissatisfied. We propose a blended assessment approach to foster student engagement, self-efficacy, and overall satisfaction by using a digital self-test as preparation for an exam. We designed, implemented, and evaluated a course where students both created and used a self-test. We found that this diverse assessment strategy engages students, increases their learning outcome, and leaves them generally more satisfied. Based on our findings, we derive a guideline to implement self-tests in a course in higher education that enables teachers to use this blended assessment approach in the future. We show that student engagement, satisfaction and learning outcome is perceived to be much increased and that various steps need to be taken to ensure a successful course implementation such as transparent communication and rigorous mentoring by faculty staff.

1. Introduction

The traditional method of assessing students in higher education, via summative assessment, has long been criticized for being outdated and not aligned with current best practices in pedagogy (Schütze et al. 2018). The system's rigid structure, with grades and degrees awarded solely based on the final assessment, puts significant pressure on students and can lead to a negative impact on their well-being. Numerous studies have shown that this method of assessment often creates stress and dissatisfaction among students, leading to a loss of motivation and even dropout rates (Graf et al. 2023; Selkomaa 2022). To address these issues, the concept of formative assessment has been proposed, which emphasizes feedback throughout the learning process rather than just at the end. Formative assessment, as opposed to summative assessment, allows students to receive feedback on their progress throughout the learning journey (Andrade 2010, Black & Wiliam 2010, 2018). This approach provides opportunities for students to identify and address areas of weakness, leading to better retention of information and improved outcomes. Studies have shown that the use of formative assessment can lead to significant gains in student achievement and engagement (Andrade & Cizek 2010). However, implementing formative assessment comprehensively requires a significant effort from educators, and it can be challenging due to the lack of time and resources

(Asamoah 2022; Looney 2019). As a result, a blended approach that combines formative and summative assessment can be an effective solution (Jantos & Langesee 2023). This approach could use digital media to provide students with feedback on their learning progress before the actual exam. Digital tools, such as learning management systems or online quizzes, can provide instant feedback to students and help educators identify areas for improvement (Looney 2019). By adopting a blended approach, educators can promote a more supportive learning environment that provides ongoing feedback and support as well as fair assessment for students (Jantos & Langesee 2023; Jantos & Huettemann 2023). This approach can help to reduce the stress and anxiety often associated with summative assessment, while still maintaining the structure and rigor necessary for higher education. Overall, the use of a Blended Assessment strategy can help to create a more dynamic and engaging learning experience for students in higher education.

2. Theoretical Background

Higher education institutions have the responsibility of providing students with the necessary skills and knowledge to support their lifelong learning, both in the workplace and in other social contexts. However, research by Boud and Falchikov (2006) suggests that current assessment practices in higher education are not adequately preparing students for future learning and assessment challenges. As such, it is crucial to examine assessment methods to ensure that they appropriately equip students to evaluate their learning throughout their lives. To achieve this, Shepard (2006) argues that summative assessments should not only document what students know and can do but also provide learning support if designed appropriately. One way to do this is by ensuring that the content, format, and design of the test provide a rich representation of the subject matter, which can lead to a worthwhile learning experience. Furthermore, taking a test can reinforce the retention of information and slow down the forgetting process (Rohrer & Pashler 2010). In contrast, formative assessment is a process used by teachers and students to provide ongoing feedback on teaching and learning during class to enhance students' achievement of desired outcomes (McManus 2008). It is not a test, but a way to adjust instruction to meet students' needs. Bloom (1969) suggests that formative evaluation provides feedback at different stages of the teaching and learning process, while summative evaluation determines what a student has accomplished after completing a course. However, summative assessment's role and its negative impact on student learning have been criticized heavily in the literature (Knight & Yorke 2003; Ecclestone 1999; Knight 2002). Therefore, it is essential to strike a balance between formative and summative assessments to prepare students adequately for a lifetime of learning and assessment in the workplace. To address this, we designed, implemented, and evaluated the use of a self-test for self-evaluation and feedback for students to prepare for an exam. The self-test served as a formative assessment tool that allowed students to test their knowledge and understanding of the subject matter while providing them with feedback to help adjust their learning strategies. This approach can not only reduce the failure rate but also promote more sustainable learning, especially for lower semester students who may be overwhelmed with what they are expected to learn. Furthermore, the use of self-testing provides a sense of security to students, and by allowing them to conduct the test independently, it reduces the workload for supervisors (Looney 2019). Additionally, it allows for the development of new question ideas, thus diversifying the assessment opportunities available to students (Jantos & Langesee 2023).

3. Self-Test

The course "Existing Buildings" is part of the undergraduate curriculum at the Faculty of Civil Engineering at the Dresden University of Technology. It is offered in the basic studies and attracts around 150 students annually who can earn 5 ECTS credits. The final evaluation is based on a written summative exam at the end of the semester, preceded by a group presentation as a preliminary performance. Additionally, students now have the opportunity to work on creating exam questions as a group, which are derived from the lecture content and serve as a resource for exam preparation. This multi-level and semester-long examination approach was developed based on the Blended Assessment Cube (Jantos and Langesee, 2023). One of our primary goals is to better prepare our students for exams and reduce the failure rate. We also aim to promote more sustainable learning by encouraging students to take an active role in their education. This is particularly important for lower-semester students who often struggle with identifying what they need to learn and feel overwhelmed by the material. By providing opportunities for self-testing, we can give students a sense of security and confidence in their knowledge. Furthermore, self-testing allows students to take more ownership of their learning, which ultimately results in less effort required from us as educators. Additionally, implementing self-testing may spark new ideas about what types of questions to ask, leading to a more diverse and engaging assessment approach. Overall, we believe that a broader assessment strategy centered around self-testing has the potential to enhance student learning outcomes and create a more positive and effective learning environment.

3.1. Student Creation Process of the Self-Test

In the first step, all students were asked if they wanted to be part of a group that would create complex exam questions and associated sample solutions for each lecture unit based on the content covered. 11 people responded. Over the course of the semester, they each created two realistic exam questions per lecture and thus compiled an extensive catalogue of questions. All questions should be as complex as possible and correctly implemented in the learning management system. Members of faculty and teaching support monitored the progress and gave extensive feedback on content and method. Our assessment approach included a variety of question types, such as single and multiple-choice, matching tasks (picture-text), and free text tasks.

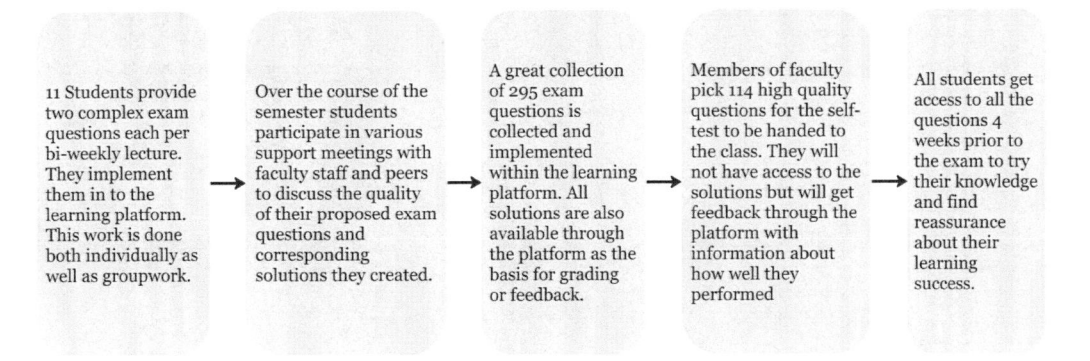

| 11 Students provide two complex exam questions each per bi-weekly lecture. They implement them in to the learning platform. This work is done both individually as well as groupwork. | Over the course of the semester students participate in various support meetings with faculty staff and peers to discuss the quality of their proposed exam questions and corresponding solutions they created. | A great collection of 295 exam questions is collected and implemented within the learning platform. All solutions are also available through the platform as the basis for grading or feedback. | Members of faculty pick 114 high quality questions for the self-test to be handed to the class. They will not have access to the solutions but will get feedback through the platform with information about how well they performed | All students get access to all the questions 4 weeks prior to the exam to try their knowledge and find reassurance about their learning success. |

Figure 1. Process of the Development of the Self-Test

Although we were uncertain of the full range of question types that could be created using our assessment platform, Onyx, we believe that the available types provided a range of assessment opportunities that accommodated the diverse learning styles and abilities of our students. This variety of question types is especially important as research has shown that using a range of question types improves learning outcomes and provides a more comprehensive assessment of student knowledge. The following figure shows the evaluation of the group that created the self-test. Five out of the eleven students who worked on this assignment answered the survey.

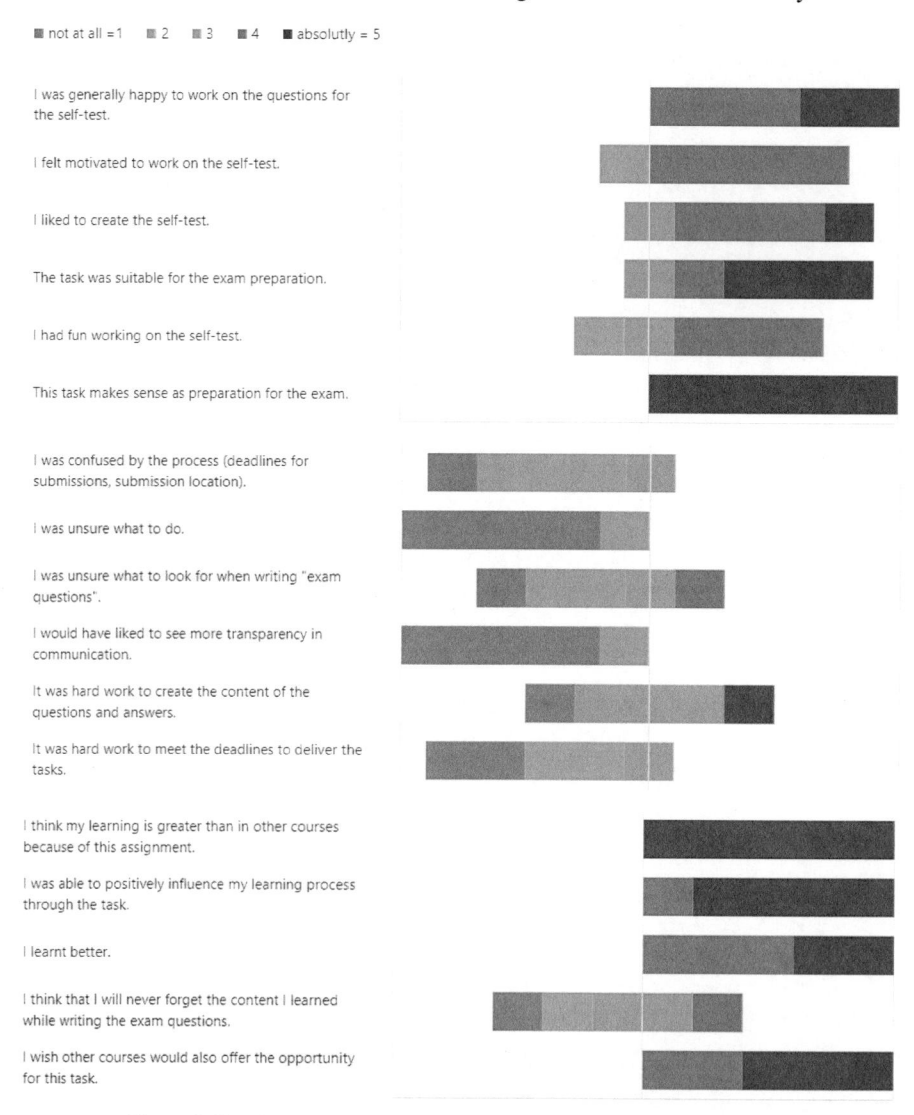

Figure 2. Results of the Evaluation of the group that created the self-test

The respondents generally enjoyed the task, felt motivated, and found it suitable for exam preparation. None were confused by the submission process and neither were they unsure what to do at any time. They are not asking for more transparency in communication. Some found creating the questions and answers hard work and none perceived meeting the deadlines as challenging. The respondents felt that their learning was greater than in other courses and that the task positively influenced their learning process. They learned better and believe they will never forget the content they learned while writing the exam questions. Finally, all of the respondents wished other courses offered a similar opportunity to create self-test exam questions as part of their course work.

3.2. Self-Test as Exam Preparation

For the second step, the sum of the questions was published for the rest of the course to use as a basis for exam preparation. After careful consideration, we have identified the most appropriate questions for each topic, with approximately 5-15 questions per topic. Some questions were deemed irrelevant or redundant, and including them would have resulted in an excessive number of questions. Some questions were chosen quite deliberately. We used the same choice of words in the exam task as in the self-test. We arrived at a final tally of 114 questions for the self-test, out of a total of 295 questions. The test could be taken an unlimited number of times, and results were displayed after each task. Users also had the option to select individual tasks to complete. We cannot view which students took the test or how well they performed, but we can provide anonymous analysis of how well each task was answered. 48 out of the 127 students who were enrolled in the exam answered the survey. The following figures show the results of the evaluation.

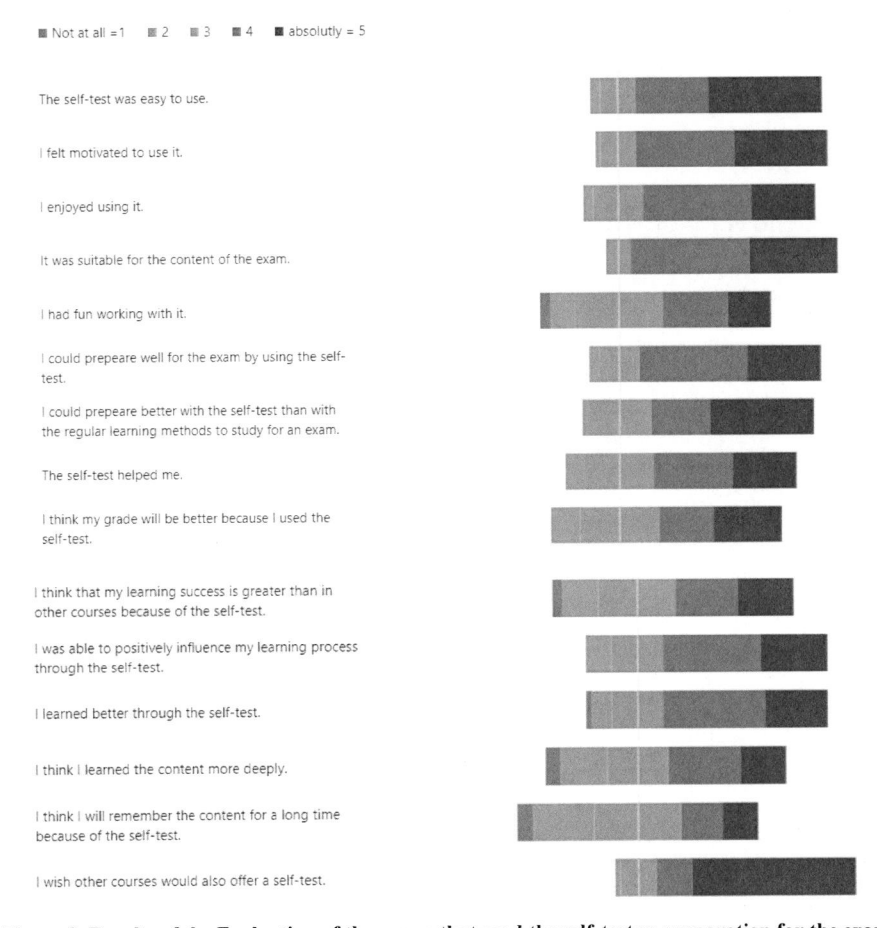

Figure 3. Results of the Evaluation of the group that used the self-test as preparation for the exam

The majority of students felt that the self-test was easy to use, felt motivated to use it, and generally enjoyed using it. Most agree, that this method it suitable for the contents of the exam and that they were able to prepare well and better than with other methods for the exam. In general, they felt helped by the self-test and that their grade would be better because they used it. Both their learning process and success were increased. Most students wished, that other courses would offer a self-test such as the one they used here.

The Self-Test was opened 818 times in preparation for the exam. It was successfully finished 177 times and took a medium of two hours to complete. The majority of the tests were taken within 2-3 days prior to the exam. The exam took place on March 2nd in the afternoon. The following figure shows the distribution of usage of the self-test sorted by days.

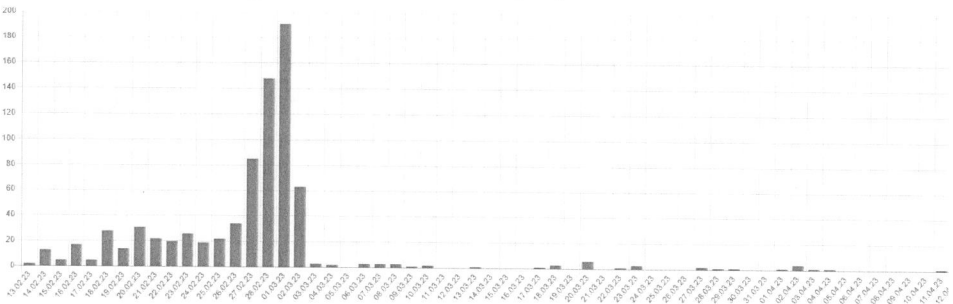

Figure 4. Distribution of Self-Test Usage per day

4. Recommendation for Implementation of Self-Tests Higher Education

We formulated recommendations to be considered when designing and implementing the creation and implementation of a self-test as a form of formative assessment.

Recognize the learner: Numerous studies have shown that students possess diverse learning styles, which require varied instructional strategies for effective learning (Hattie 2009). It is crucial for educators to address the various aspects of different learning types in higher education when offering assessment formats. Assessment is an integral part of the learning process, and it should cater to students' different learning preferences. This ensures that students have equal opportunities to demonstrate their knowledge and skills and can receive meaningful feedback to enhance their learning. Thus, by incorporating diverse assessment formats that consider various learning styles, educators can improve the learning experience of students and enhance their academic performance (Hattie 2009).

Transparency: Overall, transparency in communication is an essential component of effective teaching and learning. By communicating clearly with students about their tasks and expected outcomes, instructors can promote clarity, motivation, and accountability. Transparent communication can facilitate learning by providing students with a framework for understanding the material. When students know what they are expected to learn and how they will be assessed, they are better able to organize their thoughts and make connections between different concepts. For the creation of the self-test, specifically, it is important that students understand their tasks and the expected outcomes, to be better able to focus on what is important content wise and avoid distractions. This clarity helps students to manage their time effectively and prioritize their efforts towards achieving the desired results. We offered bi-weekly support sessions and spontaneous support via text and video chat.

Support by staff: In the process of completing a complex task, like creating questions for the self-test, it is crucial for students to be able to approach their faculty and lecturers. It provides clarification of instructions, expectations, and requirements, which can prevent misunderstandings, confusion, and wasted effort on the part of the students. Faculty and lecturers can provide feedback and support throughout the task, helping students to identify areas of strength and areas for improvement. This can help students stay on track, make progress, and overcome any obstacles they encounter along the way. Furthermore, building a relationship with the lecturer helps students engage with the material and breaking down barriers for open communication at eye level. Additionally, supervisors may need to allocate more time to the process of creating high-quality questions. We encountered a few instances where students submitted questions later than requested or failed to incorporate the desired changes, highlighting the importance of consistent supervision.

Motivation: Students are more motivated to complete their tasks when they know what is expected of them. This motivation can lead to better engagement with the material and a greater sense of accomplishment when the task is completed. That is why we suggest to offer examples of good exam questions to show how a potential result can look like. Also, a bad practice examples can clarify the tasks outcome.

Peer Review: During the process of question selection, we observed that some questions were formulated unclearly, which may have led to confusion among students. To address this issue, it may be beneficial to introduce peer feedback round in the initial weeks to gain insight into how other students interpret the questions and identify any ambiguities.

Know your audience: Before this complex assessment strategy can be successfully implemented, it is necessary to know the students and their level of understanding of various summative and formative task types. Learners who may be just beginning their studies might be overwhelmed by the complexity of the assessment strategy that is required to pass the course. Depending on how the group of students is perceived, the introduction of this blended assessment may be faster or take up more time. We recommend explaining at the beginning of the course exactly where the assessment performance lies and what the requirements are for each task and to give plenty of opportunity to address concerns and questions.

Visualization: Adding visual aids to clarify tasks and deadline can be beneficial because they are processed more quickly. Visual aids such as diagrams and timelines help students to better understand complex concepts such as the combination of lectures, presentation dates, deadline for uploading new exam questions and optional meeting for support. We offered additional visual material using a Miro Board and copied the images into the learning platform to underline the tasks.

Transfer to the next semester and beyond: The curated collection of optimized and selected exam questions can again be used as templates and good practices in subsequent semesters. Teachers and students can draw inspiration and motivation from this collection. It can also be used beyond one's own university as an Open Educational Resource (OER) for students, teachers and practitioners. But we advise to always consider that learning conditions and the impact of a self-test can vary drastically and our results must not be expected in every situation (Bennett 2011)

Don't underestimate the extra effort: The effort that goes into planning, implementation and student support should not be underestimated. Teachers who decide to take this approach must consider that they will have to compensate for the additional communication and coordination efforts required to ensure that the event runs smoothly.

5. Conclusion

We were able to show that the introduction of a student-developed self-test to prepare for a summative examination can significantly improve student engagement and satisfaction. Both students who created the test and those who used it to prepare for the exam reported that their learning process had improved, their learning success had enhanced, their motivation had increased and their overall satisfaction had improved. Furthermore, we were able to illustrate how the multi-level method of the self-test can be introduced and successfully implemented.

This new approach offers several benefits that could fundamentally change how students view exams and assessments. By providing ongoing feedback throughout the learning process, students will have a better understanding of their strengths and weaknesses (Black & Wiliam 2010, 2018). This knowledge can help students identify areas where they need to focus their attention and can ultimately lead to better academic outcomes. As a result, students may be less likely to see exams as a high-stakes event and more as an opportunity to demonstrate their learning. Furthermore, the use of digital tools for formative assessment can provide students with a more interactive and engaging learning experience, especially for remote students.

Digital media, such as online quizzes like this self-test can help to create a more dynamic and collaborative learning environment (Looney 2019). These tools can also provide instant feedback, which can help students stay motivated and engaged. Finally, the blended approach can reduce the stress and anxiety often associated with summative assessment (Graf et al. 2023). This approach can help students feel more in control of their learning and reduce the pressure of having to perform well on a single exam. Overall, the implementation of a blended approach to assessment in higher education can fundamentally change the exam culture by promoting a more supportive and interactive learning environment. By focusing on ongoing feedback and student-centered learning, the new approach can help students feel more engaged, motivated, and confident in their ability to succeed (Jantos & Langesee 2023).

References

Andrade, H. L. (2010): Students as the Definitive Source of Formative Assessment: Academic Self-Assessment and the Self-Regulation of Learning. In: NERA Conference Proceedings. https://www.researchgate.net/publication/50236003.

Andrade, H. L.; Cizek, G. J. (2010): Handbook of formative assessment. Routledge.

Asamoah, D.; Shahrill, M.; Latif, S.N.A. (2022): A Review of Formative Assessment Techniques in Higher Education During COVID-19. In: Qualitative Report. Vol. 27 Issue 2, p475-487. 13p. doi: 10.46743/2160-3715/2022.5145

Bennett, R.E. (2011). Formative Assessment: A critical review. Assessment in Education: Principles, Policy and Practice, Vol. 18, No. 1, 5 — 25.

Black, P. and Wiliam, D. (2010). Inside the Black Box: Raising Standards Through Classroom Assessment, Kappan Magazine, Vol. 92, No. 1, pp. 81 – 90.

Black and Wiliam (2018). Classroom assessment and pedagogy Assessment in Education: Principles, Policy & Practice, Vol. 25, No. 6, 551-575, DOI: 10.1080/0969594X.2018.1441807

Bloom, B. S. (1969): Some theoretical issues relating to educational evaluation. In: Educational evaluation: New roles, new means 69 - The 63rd yearbook of the National Society for the Study of Education, pp. 26–50.

Boud, D.; Falchikov, N. (2006): Aligning assessment with long-term learning. In: Assessment & Evaluation in Higher Education 31 (4), pp. 399–413.

Ecclestone, K. (1999): Empowering or ensnaring? The implications of outcome-based assessment in higher education. In: Higher Education Quarterly 53 (1), pp. 29–48.

Graf, A., Adama, E., Afrifa-Yamoah, E. et al. Perceived Nexus Between Non-Invigilated Summative Assessment and Mental Health Difficulties: A Cross Sectional Studies. J Acad Ethics (2023). https://doi.org/10.1007/s10805-023-09472-w

Hattie, J. (2009). Visible Learning. A Synthesis of over 800 Meta-Analyses Relating to Achievement. London. Routledge.

Jantos, A; Huettemann, S. (2023): Fairness in Blended Assessment in Higher Education – A Quantitative Analysis of Students' Perception. In: Proceedings of Communities in New Media. Digitality and Diversity Overcoming Barriers with digital Transformation: Proceedings of 25th Conference GeNeMe https://doi.org/10.25368/2023.15

Jantos, A.; Langesee, L.-M. (2023): Blended Assessment in Higher Education Collaborative Case Study Work – A Qualitative Study. In Learning in the Age of Digital and Green Transition (pp.44-56) DOI:10.1007/978-3-031-26876-2_5

Knight, P. T. (2002): Summative assessment in higher education: practices in disarray, Studies in Higher Education. In: Studies in Higher Education 27 (3), pp. 275–286.

Knight, P. T.; Yorke, M. (2003): Assessment, learning and employability.

Looney, J. (2019): Digital Formative Assessment: A Review of the Literature. http://www.eun.org/documents/411753/817341/Assess%40Learning+Literature+Review/be02d527-8c2f-45e3-9f75-2c5cd596261d

McManus, S. (2008): Attributes of effective formative assessment. In: Council for Chief State School Officers.

Rohrer, D.; Pashler, H. (2010): Recent research on human learning challenges conventional instructional strategies. In: Educational Researcher 39 (5).

Selkomaa, S.M. (2022): The Relationship Between Students' Experience with Summative Assessment, Emotional Regulation, and Trait Self-Esteem. https://www.duo.uio.no/handle/10852/96261

Schütze, B.; Souvignier, E.; Hasselhorn, M. (2018): Stichwort – Formatives Assessment. In: Z Erziehungswissenschaften 21 (4), pp. 697–715. DOI: 10.1007/s11618-018-0838-7.

Shepard, L. A. (2006): Classroom assessment. In: Educational measurement 4, pp. 623–646.

"YOU CANNOT BE BOTH A GOOD EDUCATOR AND A GOOD RESEARCHER": DATA-SUPPORTED CONTRIBUTIONS AND COMMENTS ON THE BIG QUESTION

Lubomír Štěpánek, Filip Habarta, Ivana Malá, Luboš Marek

Faculty of Informatics and Statistics
Prague University of Economics and Business
lubomir.stepanek@vse.cz, filip.habarta@vse.cz, malai@vse.cz, marek@vse.cz

DOI: 10.35011/IDIMT-2023-121

Keywords

Educator's evaluation, researcher's evaluation, students' inquiry data, publication record, all publications number, total published pages number, impacted publications number, book-like publications number, first authorships number, teaching-research trade-off, teaching-research synergy, COVID-19 possible effect

Abstract

The big question on whether a good researcher could hardly be also a good educator since they dispose with only limited time and have to decide which of the two fields, i.e., teaching or research, focus on, or, on the other hand, a good researcher can also be a good teacher just because of the doing research, advanced concepts' understanding and improving their explanation skills, is not clear for the first impression. References clarifying the question are usually missing or conclude various or ambiguous answers. In this study, we collected large data from student inquiry by which college students from the First Faculty of Medicine, Charles University, evaluate educators at the faculty on an annual basis. The inquiry data comes from the years 2019-2022, i.e., both pre-covid, covid, and post-covid eras, respectively. During the same years, we collected numerous data about educators' research outcomes from the internal database "VĚDA" (i.e., SCIENCE) of Charles University, connected to Web of Science, Scopus, and other scientific databases. We model relationships between educators' ratings of classes they teach, number of publications, number of impacted publications, number of book-like publications, and number of first-authorship, respectively, for each year. While the publication of a paper is usually positively correlated with better evaluation by students, real-time-takers such as a book or textbook authorship or multiple first authorship of an article are correlated rather with negative students' evaluation. Some of the results are consistent over pre-, covid, and post-covid times; some changed significantly, likely, besides others, due to COVID-19's effects on professional activities. Since we received multiple and various results, we do not demolish the myth from the title; we rather comment on them from a managerial point of view, too.

1. Introduction

A university professor is often considered either a good educator or a good researcher, and researchers with extraordinary educational abilities, or vice versa, are rare. Since both college teaching and research is highly time-consuming activity, it tends to enable a professor exceling at most in one of the areas. On the other hand, doing top science could enhance a researcher's skills in teaching since they may deeply understand highly complex concepts, enabling the concepts' easy-to-follow explanations to students. The question from the title, i.e., whether a professor at a university could be a good educator and researcher, has substantial consequences on leading management of the scholar institutions. If it were common for great teachers to be great scientists, they could (or better should) be rewarded for their hard work in both areas. This implies that a scholarly institution should consider adequate foundation sources and create appropriate reserves in advance. Also, universities, as such professors' employers, should consider their time dispositions of them, manage their teaching schedules responsibly, and could not burden them with overtime teaching.

On the other hand, if it is usual that a university could have only great educators or only excellent researchers, but not both of them, it also implies several consequences for the leadership of such an institution. Any evaluations considering each professor's teaching performance and publications record would likely end up with acceptable to great results in one of the dimensions but poor endpoints in the other. Thus, although it is relatively usual at universities in Common Wealth that there are distinct lecturer and research positions with equal prestige, wages similar amount of workload, at German- or Slavonic-speaking universities are typical positions requiring weekly teaching also claiming research results and publications. Indeed, there are also pure research positions, but with depreciated options for high wages or academic progress since teaching is counted as a necessary condition for associate and full professorship tenure and designation.

In worldwide scientific literature, possible answers to the question stated in the manuscript's title differ. Jauch (1976) kicked off the topic and conducted solid research on it; however, it still did not bring a unified answer. Using a large questionnaire study, he agreed with classical academic roles, i.e., educational and research, and supposed that these are complementary and might inspire each other. Also, he confirmed that a time trade-off is there. Thus, good teachers could suffer from detrimental and poor research output, which might even be penalized throughout their academic progress. Analogously, good researchers are strongly motivated to perform highly in that activity since they are attached to a virtual community rewarding for their publications. Consequently, they perform poorly or even ignore their teaching duties. Jauch called for explicitly restoring teaching status and equating the rewards system with research one. Hattie and Marsh (1996) systematically reviewed various approaches to compare college professors' teaching and research performance. They also found that most studies did not provide an explicit answer since they estimated correlations between teaching and research records around zero. DeCorse (1997) refined the question as if a teacher is good, then they should also be a good researcher, particularly due to positive feedback from students, which might be motivating particularly for young teachers that become their research. Feldon et al. (2011) investigated two groups of young researchers so that individuals from the first group also had teaching duties. After the follow-up period, the individuals who both taught and conducted research demonstrated noticeably greater improvement in both abilities. Palali et al. (2018), using data from Maastricht University, revealed that teachers with good research qualities usually tend to improve master students' grades, but their research qualities are not positively evaluated by master students, though. Even more surprisingly, bachelor students tend to evaluate teachers with great research results with lower scores (!).

As we can see, studies bring different or even contradictory results. In this study, we do not have the ambition to bring a final answer to the question; however, using gathered large data from the First Faculty of Medicine, Charles University, we investigate several defined aspects of publication records as a measure of research performance and their effect on the evaluation of the researchers in their teaching academic roles. The manuscript proceeds as follows. The *Data and research methodology* section introduces applied datasets describing education and research performance, their origin, and variables. Also, we shortly depict linear models, which we use to search for relationships between teaching and publication records. In the *Results* and *Discussion and conclusions*, we comment on models we get and discuss possible consequences, also as a point for managerial decision-making of a leadership board of a university. We also plot the investigated relationships and conclude key findings.

2. Data and research methodology

In the following sections, we introduce the dataset we applied and describe the dataset's variables in detail. Also, we shortly revisit multivariate weighted linear models for the relationships between research and teaching performance estimation.

2.1. Datasets used for the teaching versus research performance modeling

Datasets used for the research performance of educators are freely-available for an employee of Charles University at https://is.cuni.cz/veda/portal/. Moreover, teaching evaluation within the First Faculty of Medicine is available for academic employees of the faculty at https://is.cuni.cz/studium/. We collect data from the years 2019—2022; these are completed and contain homogenous scales for teachers' evaluation. Also, while the year 2019 could be considered as the last from the "pre-covid" era, the years 2020—2021 are "covid" years, and the year 2022 is likely a "post-covid" year. That might affect the results we expect, of course. Regarding the datasets:

- in 2019, there were 3805 academic employees on the faculty; of those 1095 received at least one evaluation score for their teaching activities, and of those 625 published at least one publication indexed in Web of Science or Scopus;
- in 2020, there were 3791 academic employees on the faculty; of those 949 received at least one evaluation score for their teaching activities, and of those 542 published at least one publication indexed in Web of Science or Scopus;
- in 2021, there were 3777 academic employees on the faculty; of those 882 received at least one evaluation score for their teaching activities, and of those 520 published at least one publication indexed in Web of Science or Scopus;
- and, finally, in 2022, there were 3775 academic employees on the faculty; of those 1014 received at least one evaluation score for their teaching activities, and of those 568 published at least one publication indexed in Web of Science or Scopus.

For each year, educators are evaluated using a 4-point Likert scale, similar to grammar school marking, i.e., 1 stands for the best teaching performance, 4 stands for the poorest teaching performance. The score for an educator is averaged over all individual student evaluations. Numbers of students evaluating a given educator are used as weights for linear models in the next sections.

Within the datasets depicting publication performance, we created a few of new variables:

- number of all author's publications in a given year;

- number of total pages the author published in a given year;
- number of all author's impacted publications in a given year, i.e., with nonzero impact factor;
- number of all author's book-like publications in a given year, i.e., books and textbooks in a given research domain are considered;
- number of all first authorships in a given year.

The teaching evaluation scores within an academic year "$(r-1)/r$", starting in the fall of previous year $r-1$ and ending in the spring of year r, are matched with publication records of the chronological year r, where $r \in \{2019, 2020, 2021, 2022\}$. This time shift of about one-half of a year well reflects the fact that the publication process is usually delayed within the review routine.

2.2. Multivariate weighted linear model used for the teaching versus research performance modeling

The relationships between teaching and research performance are modeled using a multivariate weighted linear model. In addition, we assume linearity between the teaching performance and all other explanatory variables, i.e., the derived features of the publication record.

Let us mark as X a matrix of all variables' values for each individual, and β a vector of linear coefficients for the variables, i.e., there is

$$\beta = (\beta_1, \beta_2, \beta_3, \beta_4, \beta_5)^T, \tag{1}$$

where β_1 is a linear coefficient for the number of all author's publications in a given year, β_2 for number of total pages the author published in a given year, β_3 for number of all author's impacted publications in a given year, β_4 for number of all author's book-like publications in a given year, and β_5 for number of all first authorships in a given year. Then, let us mark w a vector of weights for each evaluated individual, respectively. Assuming y is a response variable, i.e. all individuals' teaching evaluation, and ε is a vector of residual errors, and β_0 is a vector of an intercept, then, a linear model follows as

$$y = \beta_0 + X\beta + \varepsilon, \tag{2}$$

and, using weighted residual least squares (Charnes, Frome & Yu, 1976), we estimate the linear coefficients as

$$\hat{\beta} = \underset{\beta \in \mathbb{R}^{k+1}}{\mathrm{argmin}} \left\{ \sum_{i=1}^{n} (w_i \varepsilon_i)^2 \right\} = \\ = \underset{\beta \in \mathbb{R}^{k+1}}{\mathrm{argmin}} \left\{ \sum_{i=1}^{n} (w_i (y_i - \beta_0 - x_i \beta))^2 \right\}, \tag{3}$$

where k is number of explanatory variables, i.e., $k = 5$, w_i is i-th value of w, ε_i is i-th value of ε, and x_i is i-th row of X matrix. The quality and performance of the fitted linear models are evaluated both graphically and using p-values that depict a conditional probability of false rejection of a hypothesis that a given linear coefficients is zero. That being said, p-value below 0.05 is sufficiently low for rejecting the hypothesis that such a coefficient is not important for the model. Linear model is estimated for each year r, where $r \in \{2019, 2020, 2021, 2022\}$.

3. Results

For each year r, where $r \in \{2019, 2020, 2021, 2022\}$, we used the weighted least square approach from (3) to enumerate the multivariate weighted linear model that fits a relationship between authors' teaching evaluation as a metric of teaching performance, and explanatory variables measuring research performance, i.e., the number of all author's publications, number of total pages the author published, number of all author's impacted publications, number of all author's book-like publications, and number of all first authorships. Numerical results of the fitted models are in Table 1, while plots for graphical illustration (with their 95% confidence bands in light red) of the relationships are in Figures 1 and 2.

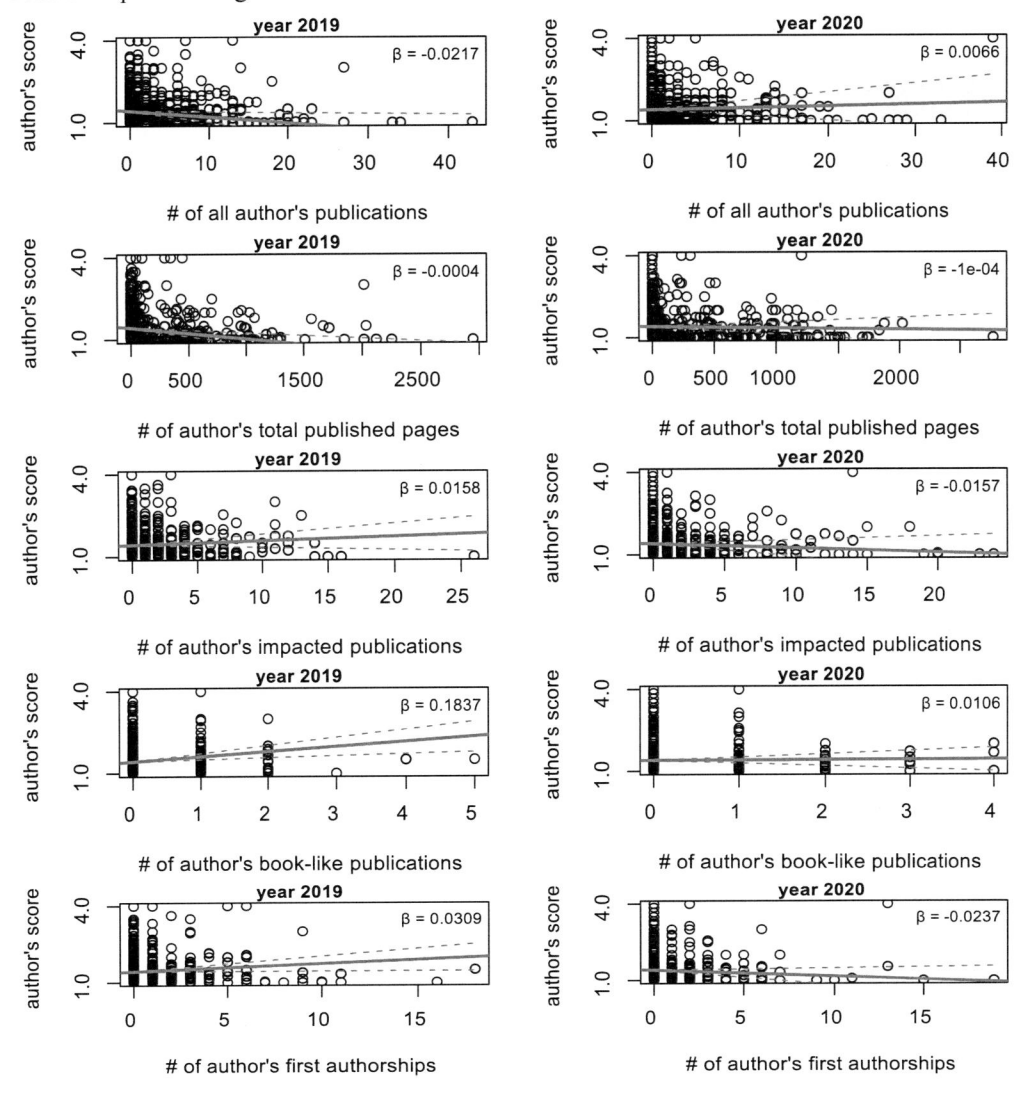

Figure 1. Modeling and plotting of the teaching versus research performance for years 2019 and 2020

Whenever is the linear coefficient β for an explanatory variable depicting research performance greater than zero and significant, i.e. $\hat{\beta} > 0$ and p-value ≤ 0.5, increasing of such an explanatory variable, i.e. higher publication report and research performance, is associated with increased averaged author's teaching evaluation, i.e. poorer teaching scores. That is because of lower values of the teaching performance stand for better teaching performance, according to students' evaluation. Such a linear coefficient has a positive, i.e., increasing slope in Figure 1 or 2. On the other hand, the linear coefficient's estimate lower than zero and significant, i.e., $\hat{\beta} < 0$ and p-value ≤ 0.5, seems – when increases – to decrease the average teaching score, i.e. is as-sociated with improving the teaching performance. The linear coefficient has a negative, i.e., decreasing slope in Figures 1 or 2. Investigating Table 1, we realize that in the year 2019, i.e. in pre-covid era, per each published publication, author's average teaching score seems to decrease (is improved) by 0.022, $p \approx 0.023$. Also, per each published page, author's average teaching performance is associated with a slight decrease of 0.0004, $p \approx 0.001$. Surprisingly, time-consuming research activities such as book or textbook preparation and publication or first authorship claiming increase the averaged teaching score by 0.184 (!) and 0.031, respectively, with $p \approx 0.002$ and $p \approx 0.040$, respectively. The year 2020 was the first year of COVID-19-related changes in many aspects of human being, including education and research. Very likely, since teaching has been "globally" moved online as for the very first time ever, teaching performance evaluation could be biased. In the year 2021, we may assume that online teaching became a new standard and students hopefully evaluated their teachers with an acceptable level of reproducibility. Still, that being said, authors of book-like publications seem to suffer from such of activity – per each book their published in 2021, their teaching performance gets worse by 0.141, $p \approx 0.025$. Finally, in the year 2022, although not significant, $p \approx 0.348$, time-taking research activities such as book or textbook writing and publication still makes author's teaching performance poorer, i.e. increases is by 0.062 per each book. For some reason or another, managing first authorship changed its effect's direction; in 2022, more first authorships an author claimed, the better teaching score they could averagely, in general expect. The association is not significant, $p \approx 0.073$, though. The linear coefficient $\hat{\beta} = -0.0310$ is thus rather zero. All the estimated linear coefficients correspond to slopes of curves in Figures 1 and 2.

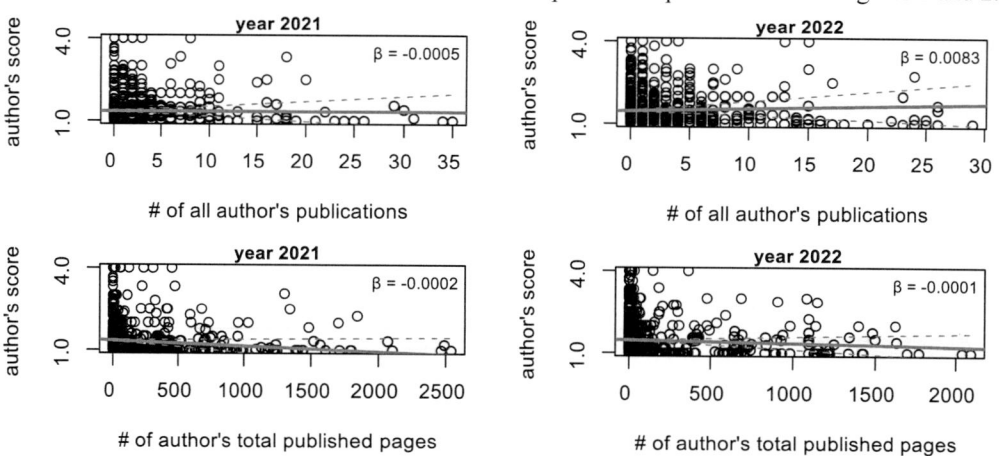

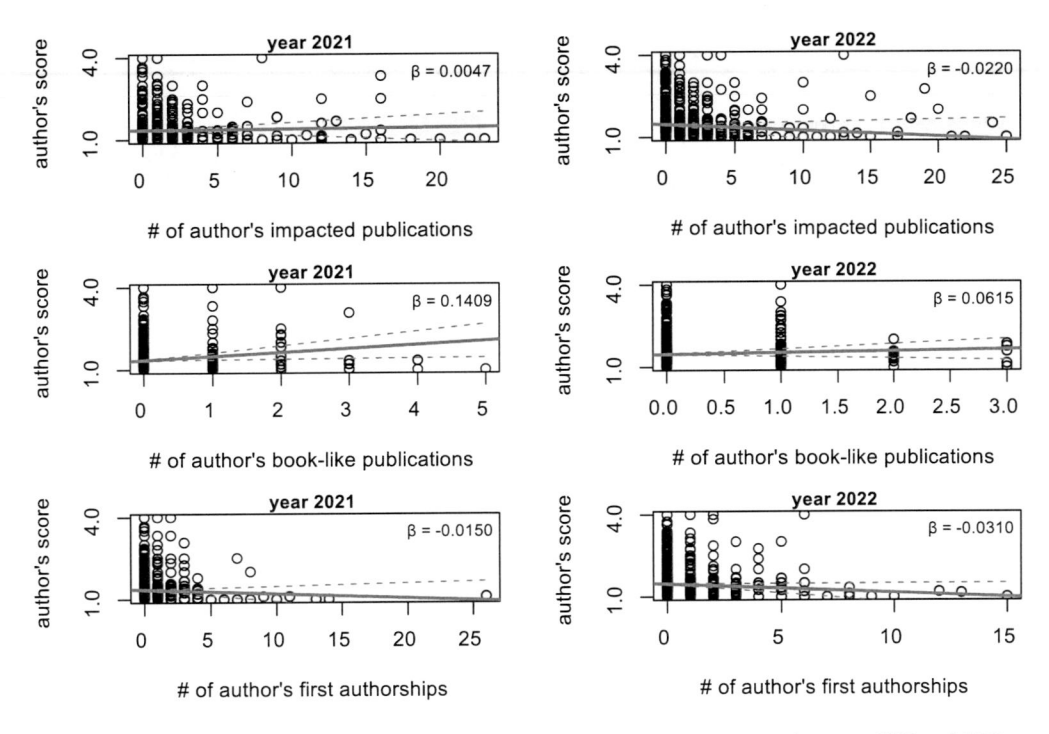

Figure 2. Modeling and plotting of the teaching versus research performance for years 2021 and 2022

Table. 1. Linear coefficients estimated for the multivariate weighted linear models of the teaching versus research performance for years 2019—2022

variable	year							
	2019		2020		2021		2022	
	$\hat{\beta}$	p	$\hat{\beta}$	p	$\hat{\beta}$	p	$\hat{\beta}$	p
intercept	1.4261	0.001	1.4010	0.001	1.3470	0.001	1.4650	0.001
# of all author's publications	-0.0217	0.023	0.0066	0.616	-0.0005	0.959	0.0083	0.532
# of author's total published pages	-0.0004	0.001	-0.0001	0.628	-0.0002	0.106	-0.0001	0.330
# of author's impacted publications	0.0158	0.202	-0.0157	0.303	0.0047	0.701	-0.0220	0.166
# of author's book-like publications	0.1837	0.002	0.0106	0.849	0.1409	0.025	0.0615	0.348
# of author's first authorships	0.0309	0.040	-0.0237	0.149	-0.0150	0.275	-0.0310	0.073

4. Discussion and conclusions

There are reasons why good educators could be good researchers, too; however, there are also notable reasons why it is rather unlikely that a good teacher could perform well also in research and vice versa. While we cannot answer the question properly, it is not the purpose of the manuscript either; surely, there is a relationship between teaching and research performance. Whereas many believe that the quality of teaching is complementary to publication record since both activities are closely related and could potentiate each other, others assume that there is a teaching-research trade-off; simply, one individual could not be really good in both areas since each of them takes much time. Consequently, according to the trade-off, an individual will tend to focus on only one of the areas sooner or later.

We confirmed some of the relationships between teaching and research performance using datasets we obtained and the proposed multivariate weighted linear modeling. Data from the pre-covid era brings intuitive and significant results. The total number of published publications and published pages improved the average teaching scores. If a researcher publishes in their narrow field, which is an expert on, and also teaches in the field, both activities mutually stimulate one to each other. On the other hand, time-expensive research duties such as a book or textbook in a given field preparation and publication, as well as handling first authorship, could be game-changers and may tend to push the teaching to the sideline. Another explanation could be that experienced experts in the field usually publish textbooks and books – typically senior experts. Students could evaluate senior experts with likely high demands and a tough way of teaching rather negatively.

The years 2020 and 2021 changed a lot in teaching and science. Students were forced to join online education for the first time in their life and could evaluate teachers who had never seen and heard in person as a matter of personal feelings. Also, during COVID-19, many conferences as publication platforms for proceedings were canceled. Thus, both teaching evaluation and research performance were affected by COVID-19. Our results do not bring anything significant except for the book published as a feature associated with worsened teaching evaluation. Undoubtedly, the results could vary for data from fields other than medicine or different periods, which is the *study limitation*.

More practically, universities should consider both possible answers to the question from the manuscript title. If great teachers are often also great scientists, i.e., there is teaching-research synergy; they should be supported over usual ways of rewarding. If not, which is in accordance with part of our results, the situation is even more tricky. Regardless of whether teachers or researchers, individuals in academia should be provided with a sufficient time schedule for their focus of interest. While research is often preferred by department and faculty leadership, teaching is still required for everyone intending to career progression in academia. A kind of reorganization would be needed to address the issue. Teaching-research trade-off, usually due to the limited time of an individual, could be addressed by sequential teaching and research, i.e., rotating semester-by-semester between both areas. That approach is experimentally applied within doctoral studies, aiming at promising young researchers with positive attitudes to teaching.

Acknowledgement

This paper is supported by the grant IG410042 with no. 53/2022, which has been provided by the Internal Grant Agency of the Prague University of Economics and Business.

References

Charnes, A., Frome, E. L., & Yu, P. L. (1976). The Equivalence of Generalized Least Squares and Maximum Likelihood Estimates in the Exponential Family. In Journal of the American Statistical Association (Vol. 71, Issue 353, pp. 169–171). Informa UK Limited. https://doi.org/10.1080/01621459.1976.10481508

DeCorse, C. J. B. (1997). "I'm a Good Teacher, Therefore I'm a Good Researcher": Changing Perceptions of Expert and Novice Teachers about Doing Research. Annual Meeting of the American Educational Research Association (pp. 1-19). https://files.eric.ed.gov/fulltext/ED411267.pdf

Feldon, D. F., Peugh, J., Timmerman, B. E., Maher, M. A., Hurst, M., Strickland, D., Gilmore, J. A., & Stiegelmeyer, C. (2011). Graduate Students' Teaching Experiences Improve Their Methodological Research Skills. In Science (Vol. 333, Issue 6045, pp. 1037–1039). American Association for the Advancement of Science (AAAS). https://doi.org/10.1126/science.1204109

Hattie, J., & Marsh, H. W. (1996). The Relationship Between Research and Teaching: A Meta-Analysis. In Review of Educational Research (Vol. 66, Issue 4, pp. 507–542). American Educational Research Association (AERA). https://doi.org/10.3102/00346543066004507

Jauch, L. R. (1976). Relationships of Research and Teaching: Implications for Faculty Evaluation. Research in Higher Education, 5(1), 1–13. http://www.jstor.org/stable/40194981

Palali, A., van Elk, R., Bolhaar, J., & Rud, I. (2018). Are good researchers also good teachers? The relationship between research quality and teaching quality. In Economics of Education Review (Vol. 64, pp. 40–49). Elsevier BV. https://doi.org/10.1016/j.econedurev.2018.03.011

AUTONOMOUS VEHICLES
AND SMART ENVIRONMENTS

AUTONOMOUS SYSTEMS AND SMART ENVIRONMENTS FOR A SUSTAINABLE LIFE

Erwin Schoitsch

Center for Digital Safety & Security
Austrian Institute of Technology
erwin.schoitsch@ait.ac.at

DOI: 10.35011/IDIMT-2023-133

Keywords

Smart Environments, Autonomous Vehicles, Circular Economy, Machine Ethics, Society 5.0, Artificial Intelligence, Trustworthiness, Standardization, Green Deal, UN Sustainable Development Goals, Resilient Society

Abstract

Sustainability and Resilience of Economy and Society are one of the possible benefits which can result from the smart technologies on which the paradigm of "Society 5.0" is based. Smart technologies are the drivers of economic and societal disruptive changes and a chance to shape our future in a beneficial way as enablers of a sustainable, "green" world.

The European "Green Deal" and the European Values of human rights, ethical considerations and societal inclusion are foundation for an update of the Japanese-proposed "Society 5.0" and a "European-type" of implementation of the 17 UN SDGs (Sustainable Development Goals) as a way (contribution) to resolve the current crisis (climate change, aging society, shortage of critical resources resulting in critical dependencies, unbalanced world economy and powers). The paper will show an example which demonstrates mitigation of these risks by smart technologies and high automation including autonomous systems and building of smart environments.

1. Introduction

We are facing a set of long-term challenges just now: Climate change (in an undesirable direction), economic stagnation and high inflation rates, an ageing society, human rights, peace and freedom endangered in many areas of our world, even in developed, democratic countries. Technology change causes disruptive changes for labor forces, customers and economy. Ageing society causes challenges for the health, care and social welfare system in general. Technology promises to help to resolve some of the problems, while creating new threats, e.g., for privacy and security as well as safety. "Cyber-resilience" is one of the new terms pointing at one of the severe threats endangering a society to much dependent on these technologies.

One of the first large initiatives started by science and government in a joint effort was in Japan – the idea of "Society 5.0". The main targets were to fight economic stagnation in a society which for to long a time was governed by the same party and people, and at the same time fighting the consequences of an ageing society. Certain aspects of high automation, e.g., acting robots in healthcare, tagging schoolchildren by RFID devices to monitor their movements, and the like, which are accepted in the Japanese society to an extent unacceptable in Europe under our ideas of privacy ("GDPR") and self-determination. Europe is since the begin of the last period of President Ursula van der Leyen ("No one to leave behind", "AI for the benefit and empowerment of people", strong impact of ethical and societal concerns particularly if looking at the use of AI-technologies) not only targeting the technology challenges from the economic and ethical side part also under the "Green Deal" aspect as a major concern for the future, which was at the beginning not a goal of the Japanese "Society 5.0" movement. For Europe, adaptations to the concept have been undertaken, including also the 17 UN Sustainable Development Goals. "Sustainability" is a rather holistic concept, it requires to take into account all possible long-term effects of any move to meet the challenges – even well-meant ideas (like "bio-fuel" produced from garbage from the fields) could have negative impact – at the moment when mass production required more garbage than available from agricultural waste it lead to misuse of food (maize) to produce fuel!), in a world where still many areas are not able to fight hunger!

2. Society 5.0 (Japan, UNESCO Follow-Up)

It was initiated, on a request by the at this time new government of prime minister Shinzo Abe, by the 5th Science and Technology Basic Plan of the Council for Science, Technology and Innovation 2016. It became an Official Japanese governmental strategy:

- A "Controlled Approach" for the „benefit of all", in an ageing country with depopulation:, to create a sustainable, inclusive socio-economic system by controlled utilization of Cyberspace and integration of cyberspace-physical space
- The strategy was "to balance economic advancement with the resolution of social problems" (includes environmental problems, climate change, as secondary target?).

(Citation from [Japanese Government, 2017]):

- "We aim at creating a society where we can resolve various social challenges by incorporating the innovations of the fourth industrial revolution (e.g. IoT, big data, artificial intelligence (AI), robot, and the sharing economy) into every industry and social life. By doing so the society of the future will be one in which new values and services are created continuously, making peoples' lives more conformable and sustainable.
- This is Society 5.0, a super-smart society. Japan will take the lead to realize this ahead of the rest of the world."

The UNESCO report 2019 praises the approach as „Japan looks into a future without (manual, mechanical) work". Such statements reduce the effort too much to automation, the other aspects for human life and benefits even for people with special needs and independent living are not covered by such statements. AI as particular technology is not expressed explicitly in the reports, but has o be taken up by the currently evolving adaptations, particularly in Europe.

3. Sustainable Development Goals of the UN

The United Nations General Assembly set the "2030 Agenda for Sustainable Development", which came into force on 1 January 2016. These were adopted by the world leaders. This is a commitment for the next fifteen years, to fight hunger, disease, poverty, inequality, and climate change which are real problems that affect millions of people every day, ensuring (hopefully) that no one is left behind.

These 17 GSDs (also called "Global Goals") are a collection of interconnected goals designed to give all of us on our planet a better future, with hundreds of targets and measurement indicators geared toward a date of 2030. The goals were created with businesses in mind, providing a path – what some people refer to as a "Pathway for Humanity" — for any business to harness their power by directing their efforts toward specific global objectives. The reference is downloadable for everybody – it is a booklet describing in a concise manner these 17 goals. More details with further links can be found on https://sdgs.un.org/goals .

The goals themselves are simple but powerful, ranging from ending poverty to building sustainable cities. Technologies are key to realize the most important goals for a still growing world population under pressures like resource exploitation and climate change. An overview is provided in Figure., setting them in context of "Society 5.0" technologies and subgoals.

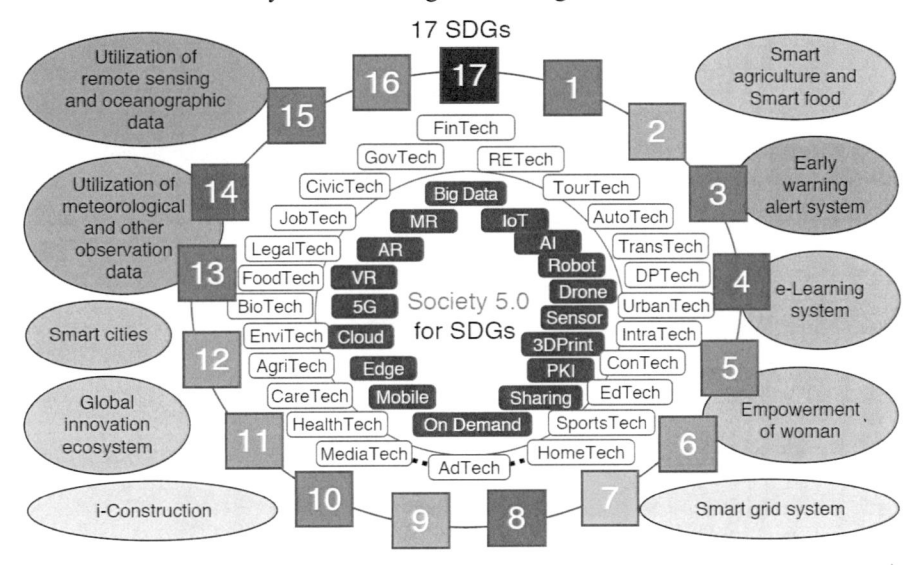

Figure 1. The 17 SDGs and the Society 5.0 Technologies and Sub-Goals Source: (from Japan Business Federation (Keidandren), "Society 5.0 for SDGs")

To monitor and track progress in achieving results towards the SDGS (Sustainable Development Goals), the UN has created a global initiative "Sustainable Development Solutions Network" (https://www.unsdsn.org/sdg-index-and-monitoring). The SDSN methodology (sound metrics, statistical methods, identification of gaps etc.) was audited by the European JRC (Joint Research Center) in July 2019, the results of which are available as a report (see References).

Several regions of the world have developed related reports, e.g., the *Europe Sustainable Development Report* (ESDR) which builds on the methodology of the annual *Sustainable Development Report*, including SDG Index and Dashboards, issued by the SDSN and Bertelsmann Foundation.

International standardization has also taken up the idea: Each new standardization work item proposal shall indicate which "SDGs" are supported by this standard. The ISO/IEC TR5469,

Artificial Intelligence – Functional safety and AI systems, which is explained later, e.g., filled in the table in the following manner:

Please select any UN Sustainable Development Goals (SDGs) that this document will support. For more information on SDGs, please visit our website at www.iso.org/SDGs."
☐ **GOAL 1:** No Poverty
☐ **GOAL 2:** Zero Hunger
☐ **GOAL 3:** Good Health and Well-being
☐ **GOAL 4:** Quality Education
☐ **GOAL 5:** Gender Equality
☐ **GOAL 6:** Clean Water and Sanitation
☐ **GOAL 7:** Affordable and Clean Energy
☒ **GOAL 8: Decent Work and Economic Growth**
☒ **GOAL 9: Industry, Innovation and Infrastructure**
☐ **GOAL 10:** Reduced Inequality
☐ **GOAL 11:** Sustainable Cities and Communities
☐ **GOAL 12:** Responsible Consumption and Production
☐ **GOAL 13:** Climate Action
☐ **GOAL 14:** Life Below Water
☐ **GOAL 15:** Life on Land
☐ **GOAL 16:** Peace and Justice Strong Institutions
N/A GOAL 17: Partnerships to achieve the Goal

Figure 2. Selection of SDGs addressed by TR 5469 (as example)

4. "GREEN DEAL" and "Green Cities" Europe

The declared goal is a "Europe to be the first climate-neutral continent". It is an ambitious commitment to future generations, already under pressure because of strong Lobby-groups (e.g., currently the combustion-engine question).

To overcome these challenges, the **European Green Deal** will transform the EU into a modern, resource efficient and competitive economy, ensuring:

- no net emissions of greenhouse gases by 2050
- economic growth decoupled from resource use
- no person and no place left behind

The European Green Deal action plan (https://eur-lex.europa.eu/legal-content/EN/TXT) wants to

- boost the efficient use of resources by moving to a clean, circular economy
- restore biodiversity and cut pollution

The plan outlines investments needed and financing tools available. It explains how to ensure a just and inclusive transition. The EU aims to be climate neutral in 2050. Reaching this target will require action by all sectors of our economy, including

- investing in environmentally friendly technologies,
- supporting industry to innovate,
- rolling out cleaner, cheaper and healthier forms of private and public transport,
- decarbonising the energy sector,
- ensuring buildings are more energy efficient,
- working with international partners to improve global environmental standards,

The EU will also provide financial support and technical assistance to help those that are most affected by the move towards the green economy. This is called the Just Transition Mechanism. It will help mobilize at least €100 billion over the period 2021-2027 in the most affected regions. A most important part of this huge effort is dedicated to research towards "clean green technologies" to be developed and implemented throughout Europe, converting economy and society.

With respect to "Smart Cities" and "Smart environments", the **European Green Cities movement** strives to support European Cities with projects and advice towards a resilient, sustainable, circular economy and society within much more independence of cities from external resources as today. Research is including (of the EC and the project)

- Mobility and inclusive environments
    - Mobility plans
    - Cycling analysis and strategic solutions
    - Gender sensitive urban planning
    - Solar powered E-mobility and charging infrastructure
- Smart buildings and energy efficiency
- Communication and stakeholder engagement
    - Workshops and Community engagement
    - Stakeholder processes
    - Develop interdisciplinary understanding
    - Webpage and newsletter design and management
- EU Funding and project management

To ensure knowledge sharing across Europe, the organization also manages the non-profit **European Green Cities Network**. The network consists of municipalities, social housing organizations, institutions, companies and universities from more than 19 countries. Concrete examples and current projects can be found at http://greencities.eu/projects.

5. Example Project "AI4CSM" ("Automotive Intelligence for Shared Connected Mobility")

One example for a European research project towards energy-efficient, electric and automated mobility is AI4CSM, funded under the ECSEL JU scheme within Horizon 2020the national authorities of participating partners (41 partners from 10 countries, grant agreement n° 101007326).

The objectives are:

- Develop robust and reliable mobile platforms
- Develop scalable and embedded intelligence for edge and edge/cloud operation
- Design silicon for deterministic low latency and build AI-accelerators for decision and learning
- Solve complexity by trustable AI in functional integrated systems
- Design functional integrated ECS systems
- Build ECAS vehicles for the Green Deal and future connected, shared mobility

Some important demonstrators with AI systems in critical roles are (selected examples):

- Robo-Taxi
- Virtual City Routing
- Lessons from critical scenarios for ADS controllers

Of course, there are about 20 demonstrators, also dealing with Green-Deal objectives and Ethical aspects (see Schoitsch 2022).

One research question for the work in the standardization part of the project was how to support the partners with respect to standards to apply. Almost all demonstrators have AI system developed or integrated in different roles of different criticality with respect to safety. For research purposes, partners active in AI and functional safety standardization, ISO/IEC TR 5469, developed together by ISO/IEC JTC1 SC42, AI, WG 3 (Trustworthiness) and IEC SC65a MT 61508-3 (Functional safety of E/E/PE systems, the basic functional safety standard for SW for safety-related systems in general) informed the partners on the status of the work on this standard. Therefore, the draft standard (it is not published still at the time this paper was written, but almost finished) served as support document to analyze the AI systems in context of their implementation in the demonstrators.

Information on the principles of ISO/IEC DTR 5469:

The approach taken, in short, was to classify AI technology classes and usage classes. The following figure tries to map these and provide recommendations:

AI Technology Class => AI application and usage level	AI technology Class I	AI technology Class II	AI technology Class III
Usage Level A1 (1)	Application of risk reduction concepts of existing functional safety International Standards possible	Appropriate set of requirements (5)	Not recommended
Usage Level A2 (1)		Appropriate set of requirements (5)	
Usage Level B1 (1)		Appropriate set of requirements (5)	
Usage Level B2 (1)		Appropriate set of requirements (5)	
Usage Level C (1,3)		Appropriate set of requirements (5)	
Usage Level D (2)	No specific functional safety requirements for AI technology, but application of risk reduction concepts of existing functional safety International Standards (4)		

1 Static (offline) (during development) teaching or learning only
2 Dynamic (online) teaching or learning possible
3 AI techniques clearly providing additional risk reduction and whose failure is not critical to the level of acceptable risk.
4 Additionally, other safety aspects (not being addressed with functional safety methods) can possibly be adversely affected by AI usage.
5 The appropriate set of requirements for each usage level can be established in consideration of Clauses 8, 9, 10 and 11. Examples are provided in Annex B.

Figure 3. Recommendations for usage of AI Technology Classes at certain Usage Levels Source: (DTR 5469)

AI Technology Classes:

Class I developed and reviewed using existing functional safety methods and standards,

Class II cannot be fully developed and reviewed using existing functional safety methods and standards, but it is still possible to identify a set of available methods and techniques satisfying the properties (e.g., additional V&V).

Class III cannot be developed and reviewed using existing functional safety methods and standards and it is also not possible to identify a set of available methods and techniques satisfying the functional safety properties.

AI Application and Usage Classes:

A1: Used in safety relevant E/E/PE system and automated decision making possible.

A2: Used in safety relevant E/E/PE system and no automated decision making (e.g., for uncritical diagnostics).

B1: Used to develop safety relevant E/E/PE systems (offline support tool). Automated decision making of developed function is possible.

B2: Used to develop safety relevant E/E/PE systems (offline support tool). No automated decision making of the developed function is possible.

C: AI technology is not part of a safety function in the E/E/PE system. Has potential indirect impact on safety (e.g., increase demand placed on a safety system)

D: AI technology is not part of a safety function in the E/E/PE system. No impact on safety due to sufficient segregation and behavior control.

Particularly the "Robo-Taxi" is an ideal example showing all attributes for use of AI standards in safety-relevant implementations, from AI-based control elements and safety analysis, impact on "Green Deal" conformance (reduction of number of vehicles in cities, better usage of infrastructure, reduction of sealed surfaces, optimal support of multi-modal transport, optimization of minimal energy consumption and timing through city-routing, etc.), "inclusion" of people not fit for driving, and reduction of fatalities, as well as ethical and societal concerns because of autonomous decision making impacting people (humans) based on uncertain or unpredictable behavior. The analysis allowed a classification of the various AI-systems and components and will facilitate later testing and final design for an upcoming product-stage. It was also used as part of the tool chain (an AI Training Center, to automatically generate concrete test cases out of an abstract test case to test and validated an ADAS function in an intelligent and structured way).

6. Conclusions

The EC and other international organizations (UN, UNESCO, many governments, standardization organization, research organizations, industry) have a very positive approach and high expectations concerning the benefits of digitisation of economy, industry and society. The "Green Deal" programme and the human implications of these technologies, empowering people through education and skills, and on protecting against the risks of these technologies, are targeting resilience and sustainability of society and economy. They are aware of the risks and of the measures to be taken timely to avoid upcoming problems and even catastrophes (e.g., climate change impact). However, effective action is often prohibited by short-term interests. We should be aware that many of the achievements could be effective too late or used against us as well (and some research projects consider this fact already) or lead to wrong decisions because of badly trained or biased AI systems. We have shown in one example how evolving standards can support development of AI-based systems and integration of such systems in system-of-systems.

Acknowledgements

Part of the work received funding from the EC from the EU Horizon 2020 Programme, the ECSEL Joint Undertaking and the partners' national funding authorities (in Austria FFG (Austrian Research Promotion Agency) on behalf of BMK, The Federal Ministry of Climate Action, Environment, Mobility, Innovation and Technology (BMK)) - (Grant agreements n° 737459-2 (Productive4.0) and n° 737469-2 (AutoDrive), and SECREDAS (783119), iDev40 (783163), AfarCloud (783221) and AI4CSM (101007326-2)). The ADEX (Automated Driving EXaminer) project was funded by the Austrian Research Promotion Agency. TEACHING was funded by Horizon 2020 only (871385).

References[1]

CEN-CENELEC Webinar "Journey towards the UN Sustainable Development Goals – social, economy, environment", https://experts.cen.eu/trainings-materials/events/2022/2022-06-02-webinar-sdgs/

ERCIM News number 127, October 2021, Special Theme "Smart and Circular Cities", Guest editors Schoitsch, E. (AIT, Vienna) and Georgios Mylonas (ISI, Athens), p. 4 – 35, published by ERCIM EEIG, Sophia Antipolis, France, ISSN 0926-4981, https://ercim-news.ercim.eu/en127

European SDSN Network, (2020), "The 2020 Europe Sustainable Development Report (ESDR 2020)", issued by the SDSN (Sustainable Development Solutions Network) and Bertelsmann Foundation, https://www.unsdsn.org/sdg-index-and-monitoring (with further links of other regions)

European Commission, JRC Technical Reports, (2019), JRC Statistical Audit of the Sustainable Development Goals Index and Dashboards, ISBN 978-92-76-08995-7ISSN 1831-9424, https://s3.amazonaws.com/sustainabledevelopment.report/2019/2019_JRC_Audit_SDG_Index.pdf

European Commission, Communication to the European Parliament, the European Council, the Council, the European Economic and Social Committee and the Committee of the Regions, "The European Green Deal", 2019-12-11.

European Commission, High-Level Expert Group, "Ethics Guidelines for Trustworthy AI" (Final report April 2019, HLEG AI), Brussels; https://ec.europa.eu/digital-single-market/en/news/ethics-guidelines-trustworthy-ai

European Green Cities, http://greencities.eu/about; Action Plan https://eur-lex.europa.eu/legal-content/EN/TXT/?qid=1596443911913&uri=CELEX:52019DC0640#document2

Federal Ministry of Transport and Digital Infrastructure, Ethics Commission on "Automated and Connected Driving – Report June 2017", Germany; https://www.bmvi.de/SharedDocs/EN/publications/report-ethics-commission-automated-and-connected-driving.pdf?__blob=publicationFile (Summary available in English)

Hinkelmann, Knut and Gerber, Aurona (Eds), 2022, Proceedings of the Society 5.0 Conference 2022 - Integrating Digital World and Real World to Resolve Challenges in Business and Society, EPiC Series in Computing, Volume 84, https://easychair.org/publications/volume/Society_5.0-2022

Japanese Government, Cabinet Office (2018), Achieving Society 5.0, https://www8.cao.go.jp/cstp/english/society5_0/index.html

Japanese Government, (2017). Realizing Society 5.0. https://www.japan.go.jp/abenomics/_userdata/abenomics/pdf/society_5.0.pdf

Schoitsch, E. (2020). "Towards a Resilient Society – Technology 5.0, Risks and Ethics", IDIMT 2020, Digitalized Economy, Society and Information Management, Proceedings, Trauner Verlag, Linz, Austria, Schriftenreihe Informatik 49, (ISBN 978-3-99062-958-1), p. 403-412,

Schoitsch, E. (2022). "Smart Technology and Circular Economy for a Greener World and Resilient Society", IDIMT 2022, Digitalization of Society, Business and Management in a Pandemic, Trauner Verlag, Linz, Austria, Schriftenreihe Informatik 51, (ISBN 978-3-99113-758-0), p. 357-366.

Schoitsch, E. (2021). "Trustworthy Smart Autonomous Systems-of-Systems – Resilient Technology, Economy and Society", IDIMT 2021, Pandemics: Impacts, Strategies and Responses, Trauner Verlag, Linz, Austria, Schriftenreihe Informatik 50, (ISBN 978-3-99062-958-1), p. 377-388,

United Nations, Transforming our World - The 2030 Agenda for Sustainable Development (2015), https://sustainabledevelopment.un.org/post2015/transformingourworld

Von der Leyen, U. (2019). "A Union that strives for more – My agenda for Europe". https://www.europarl.europa.eu/resources/library/media/20190716RES57231/20190716RES57231.pdf

---

[1] (URL-Links were valid June 19, 2023)

OVERVIEW OF AI STANDARDIZATION

Christoph Schmittner, Abdelkader Magdy Shaaban

Center for Digital Safety & Security
AIT Austrian Institute of Technology
christoph.schmittner@ait.ac.at, abdelkader.shaaban@ait.ac.at

DOI: 10.35011/IDIMT-2023-143

Keywords

Safety, Security, AI, Standardization

Abstract

Artificial Intelligence (AI) is one of the driving forces of Industry 5.0. AI is not restricted to machinery on the shop floor but permeates all areas and is used for diverse topics, ranging from predicting Quality and Yield to Predictive Maintenance, Human-robot collaboration, Generative design, and even Market adaption/supply-chain. With such wide potential usage, trustworthiness is of utmost importance. Safety, security, and privacy need to be considered depending on the usage, processed data, and outputs. With the high pace of technological progress, standardization and regulation try to keep up by developing guidance for AI's ethical, safe, and secure usage. The EU H2020 project TEACHING [1] aims to utilize AI for autonomous, adaptive, and dependable CPSoS applications. AI-related safety and security standards were identified and evaluated during the TEACHING project. This paper summarizes TEACHING results, documented in D6.7, and gives an overview of AI standardization.

1. Introduction

The following chapter lists activities, standardization groups, and new work item proposals to give an overview of the status aim and summarize the results. While we try to cover all aspects, there is currently a very high level of activity in standardization and AI, and we need to rely on the expertise and awareness existing in the project consortium. Many organizations and committees currently treat AI topics. While we will focus on standardization activities, there are also AI-related activities from other groups with differing scopes. Therefore, we only claim completeness or coverage of some AI-related standardization activities, especially when we leave the international (e.g., ISO, IEC, IEEE) or European focus (e.g., ETSI as an example of an ESO).

1.1. AI and Ethics

Especially for topics like ethics, guidance is also developed on national or European levels. This includes the German Ethics Commission for Automated and Connected Driving (Federal Ministry for Digital and Transport, 2017), guidelines on ethics addressed by the EC High-Level Experts Group on "Trustworthy AI" (European Commission, 2019), and other related recommendations as

---

[1] https://teaching-h2020.eu

issued by Informatics and Computer Societies such as IEEE Ethically Aligned Design (IEEE, 2017) and Informatics Europe with ACM Europe (Informatics Europe, 2022).

Moreover, the standards of ISO/IEC JTC1 TR 24368 ("AI - Overview of ethical and societal concerns") (ISO/IEC JTC 1/SC 42, 2022) and on IT Governance.

This is partially caused by differences regarding privacy and human-machine interaction, which challenge the development of international standards. ISO/IEC TR 27563 and ISO/IEC 6089-2 are examples of standards that aim at developing a coherent concept of how privacy in AI can be addressed and managed.

1.2. AI and Security

The ECSO Technical Paper on Artificial Intelligence and Cybersecurity list the following cybersecurity-related usages of AI. AI can be used to improve cybersecurity, e.g., to detect or monitor security incidents or vulnerabilities. An attacker can also use AI to support or conduct attacks. AI is also becoming a potential attack target, e.g., topics like data poisoning for learning or stealing algorithms and contained data. Regarding the threat landscape, the ENISA Ad-Hoc Working Group on Artificial Intelligence Cybersecurity published a report detailing a mapping of the AI cybersecurity ecosystem and its Threat Landscape, including the scope of AI in the context of cybersecurity following a lifecycle approach and detailing assets of the AI ecosystem in the lifecycle (ENISA, 2020). This is complemented by a report containing a detailed analysis of threats targeting machine learning systems, identifying threats like inter alia, data poisoning, adversarial attacks, and data exfiltration (ENISA, 2021). The ETSI Industry Specification Group (ISG) Security Artificial Intelligence (SAI) also has activities in this direction. It published multiple reports identifying paths to protect systems from AI and AI from attack (ETSI, 2021). ISO/IEC 27090 Cybersecurity — Artificial Intelligence — Guidance for addressing security threats and failures in artificial intelligence systems is an example of a standard that focuses on recommendations and guidance on securing AI systems regarding cyber threats, e.g., how to detect and mitigate such threats.

1.3. AI and Sustainability

Besides ethical aspects, there is one additional AI-related aspect that was not covered in detail in previous standardization, "Green and Sustainable AI" has become an issue on an international level too, e.g., CEN/CENELEC JTC21 Ad-Hoc Group Report "Green & Sustainable AI," which will be the basis for a new Work Item on Reducing AI Carbon Footprint, energy, and water consumption or ISO/IEC AWI TR 20226 (under development) Information technology — Artificial intelligence — Environmental sustainability aspects of AI systems.

1.4. AI and Safety

AI challenges existing safety approaches since these rely on an in-depth understanding of the system behavior in all cases, which may impact system safety. Since particularly DNN- and ML-based AI components cannot be evaluated and assured like existing software, the functional safety community relies on specific guidance under which circumstances which type of AI-driven functions can be used in safety-critical systems. For example, Figure provides a summary and a structure of the typical standardized committees and organizations for AI safety in the automotive sector.

The figure illustrates the common AI and safety standards in the automotive industry. The Standard is IEC 61508-3 (IEC, 2010) for the Functional Safety of E/E/PE Systems; it is intended to be applied to any software-defined as a component of any safety-related systems. A functional safety and artificial intelligence system standard, TR 5469 (ISO/IEC CD TR 5469, Standard in development), describes the relationship between safety and AI. Additionally, ISO 22989 (ISO/IEC, 2022) for Artificial intelligence concepts and terminology seeks to standardize terminology for AI and define concepts in the field.

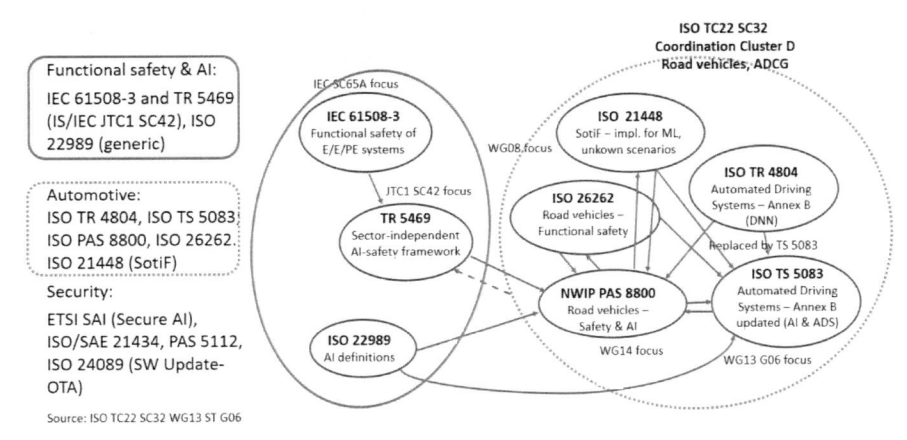

Figure 1. Interrelationships between conventional ISO Safety Standards, automated driving, and AI-Safety Standards

The figure also lists the primary automotive industry safety standards, including the following:

- **ISO 21448**: Road vehicles — Safety of the intended functionality (ISO 21448:2022, 2022).
- **ISO 26262**: Road vehicles — Functional safety (ISO 26262-1, 2018).
- **ISO TR 4804**: Road vehicles — Safety and cybersecurity for automated driving systems — Design, verification, and validation (ISO/TR 4804:2020, 2020).
- **NWIP PAS 8800**: Road Vehicles — Safety and artificial intelligence (ISO/AWI PAS 8800, Standard in development).
- **ISO TS 5083**: Road vehicles — Safety for automated driving systems — Design, verification, and validation (ISO/AWI TS 5083, Standard in development).

The currently predominantly used approach is to classify usage scenarios and AI and recommend restricted usage, e.g., for example, only explainable approaches are recommended for the highest criticality classes. This means many standards like the ISO PAS 8800, which extended ISO 26262 guidance towards AI (ISO/TC 22/SC 32, Standard in development), contain a classification scheme for the applicability of AI in safety-related E/E/PE systems, with a framework of an AI system and related compliance criteria. Such an approach is also chosen in ISO/IEC TR 5469, intended to extend the guidance given in IEC 61508 towards AI safety. The goal is to develop a classification of AI technology classes and usage classes with a mapping, e.g., which AI class is recommended for which usage scenario. AI Technology classes are classified based on the applicability of existing safety risk management technics, e.g., if they can be covered by established and trusted development and V&V activities. AI Application and Usage Classes are classified based on the potential safety impact of the AI component.

2. Ongoing AI-Related Standardization and Guidance Activities

A brief overview of some selected standards is presented, including information on the type of activity, its status, the target domain, a summary, and whether TEACHING partners are involved. ISO/IEC 27090 (ISO/IEC 27090, Standard in development) Cybersecurity — Artificial Intelligence is defined in this section, where a summary of that Standard is defined in Table .

Table 1. ISO/IEC 27090

Name	ISO/IEC 27090 Cybersecurity — Artificial Intelligence — Guidance for addressing security threats and failures in artificial intelligence systems		
Type	International Standard	Domain	Cross Domain
Status	Working draft under development	TEACHING Involvement	No
Summary	Recommendations and guidance on securing AI systems regarding cyber threats, e.g., how to detect and mitigate such threats.		

In addition, the ISO/IEC TR 27563 Cybersecurity — Artificial Intelligence — Impact of security and privacy in artificial intelligence use cases (ISO/IEC 27563, 2023) is investigated in this work. A summary of this Standard is defined in Table 2.

Table 2. ISO/IEC CD TR 27563

Name	ISO/IEC TR 27563 Cybersecurity — Artificial Intelligence — Impact of security and privacy in artificial intelligence use cases.		
Type	Technical Report	Domain:	Cross Domain
Status	Committee draft under development	TEACHING Involvement	No
Summary	Recommendations and guidance on privacy regarding AI usage.		

Our investigation also includes the ISO TS 5083 "Safety for automated driving systems – design, verification, and validation" (ISO/AWI TS 5083, Standard in development), as outlined in Table3.

Table 3. ISO TS 5083

Name	ISO/AWI TS 5083 / Road vehicles — Safety for automated driving systems — Design, verification, and validation		
Type	Technical Specification	Domain	Automated Driving
Status	Working Draft	TEACHING Involvement	Yes

Name	ISO/AWI TS 5083 / Road vehicles — Safety for automated driving systems — Design, verification, and validation
Summary	Based on two documents, the Whitepaper "Safety first for Automated Driving", 2019 and the resulting ISO TR 4804 "Safety and Cybersecurity for automated driving systems — Design, verification and Validation", the development of TS 5083 "Safety for Automated driving systems – design, verification, and validation. TEACHING partners are involved as experts in the development.

ENISA Artificial Intelligence Cybersecurity Challenges (ENISA, 2020) is also defined as part of our investigation, as discussed in Table 4.

Table 4. ENISA Artificial Intelligence Cybersecurity Challenges

Name	ENISA Artificial Intelligence Cybersecurity Challenges		
Type	Technical Paper	Domain	Cross Domain
Status	Published	TEACHING Involvement	No
Summary	ENISA published a report detailing a mapping of the AI cybersecurity ecosystem and its Threat Landscape, including the scope of AI in the context of cybersecurity following a lifecycle approach and detailing assets of the AI ecosystem in the lifecycle, mapped to the AI threat landscape by means of a detailed taxonomy. Threats are classified based on targeted assets, the diverse AI lifecycle stages, relevant threat actors, and impact.		

In addition, ENISA Standardization in Support of AI and Cybersecurity is investigated as part of our work, as discussed in Table .

Table 5. ENISA Standardization in Support of AI and Cybersecurity

Name	ENISA Standardization in Support of AI and Cybersecurity		
Type	Technical Paper	Domain	Cross Domain
Status	Draft	TEACHING Involvement	Yes
Summary	The report considers AI under the classical **CIA** (Confidentiality, Integrity, Availability) paradigm and with a comprehensive view of the trustworthiness of AI. While existing standards mostly cover the CIA paradigm, trustworthiness, defined by ISO/IEC JTC1 SC7 (Software and systems engineering), covers a much broader view and requires new approaches. **TEACHING partners provided comments and inputs to an early draft, especially on the area of trustworthiness of AI and additional methods developed in TEACHING, which can be used to extend from CIA to trustworthiness.**		

In addition, ENISA Securing Machine learning (ENISA, 2021) algorithms are investigated as part of our work, as discussed in Table 6.

Table 6. ISO/IEC 6089-2

Name	ISO/IEC 6089-2 Cybersecurity — Artificial Intelligence — Guidance on addressing privacy protection for artificial intelligence systems		
Type	International Standard	Domain	Cross Domain
Status	NWIP in preparation	TEACHING Involvement	No
Summary	Content not yet known.		

3. Conclusion

We currently see a trend towards harmonization and coordination of developments. Examples are the joint technical committee between ISO and IEC (ISO/IEC JTC1 SC42) to coordinate standardization around Artificial Intelligence (AI). It serves as the focus for ISO/IEC JTC 1's standardization program on AI (General AI standardization). It guides JTC 1, IEC, and ISO committees in developing Artificial Intelligence applications. Under JTC1 SC42 are several Ad-hoc and Working groups, which focus on topics like data (WG2), use cases and applications (WG4) or trustworthiness (WG3), and Computational approaches and computational characteristics of AI systems (WG5), or AI standardization road mapping (AG3).

In addition, the regulation regarding AI is in preparation; examples include the EU Regulation Laying Down Harmonised Rules on Artificial Intelligence (COM/2021/206 final) ("Draft AI Act"). In October 2020, three legislative resolutions on AI covering ethics, civil liability, and intellectual property (IP) were adopted by the European Parliament, and the Commission was asked to establish a comprehensive and future-proof European legal framework of ethical principles for the development, deployment, and use of AI, robotics and related technologies. Like approaches developed by the safety standards, a risk-based classification of AI systems and usages is undertaken, and requirements are defined based on the classification. Besides the restrictions on commercial usage, there is also an impact of AI research expected (Helberger, Natali; Diakopoulos, Nicholas, 2022), since the usage of AI in the highest-risk category is currently intended to be forbidden.

We see this agreement on classification and assessment in most safety-related standards. However, ensuring standardization and regulation keep up with technical developments and potential benefits is challenging in all industrial domains, especially AI. This work will continue to be part of the EdeN project to keep following up on the progress of the development of AI standardizations.

Acknowledgment

This research has received funding from the program "Circular Economy" of the Austrian Research Promotion Agency (FFG) and the Austrian Ministry for Transport, Innovation, and Technology under grant agreement No. 897774 (project EdeN).

References

ENISA. (2020). *Artificial Intelligence Cybersecurity Challenges, Threat Landscape for Artificial Intelligence.* Retrieved from ENISA: https://www.enisa.europa.eu/publications/artificial-intelligence-cybersecurity-challenges

ENISA. (2021). *ENISA Securing Machine learning algorithms.* Retrieved from ENISA: https://www.enisa.europa.eu/publications/securing-machine-learning-algorithms/@@download/fullReport

ETSI. (2021). *Securing Artificial Intelligence (SAI).* Retrieved 01 22, 2023, from ETSI: https://www.etsi.org/technologies/securing-artificial-intelligence

European Commission. (2019). *High-level expert group on artificial intelligence.* Retrieved 02 10, 2023, from https://digital-strategy.ec.europa.eu/en/policies/expert-group-ai

Federal Ministry for Digital and Transport. (2017). *Ethics Commission Automated and Connected Driving.* Retrieved 02 10, 2023, from https://bmdv.bund.de/SharedDocs/EN/publications/report-ethics-commission-automated-and-connected-driving.pdf?__blob=publicationFile

Helberger, Natali; Diakopoulos, Nicholas. (2022). *The European AI Act and How It Matters for Research into AI in Media and Journalism.* Taylor & Francis.

IEC. (2010). *IEC 61508-3:2010 : Functional safety of electrical/electronic/programmable electronic safety-related systems - Part 3: Software requirements.* Retrieved 2 10, 2023, from https://webstore.iec.ch/publication/5517

IEEE. (2017). *Ethically Aligned Design V2.* Retrieved from The IEEE Global Initiative on Ethics of Autonomous and Intelligent Systems: https://standards.ieee.org/wp-content/uploads/import/documents/other/ead_v2.pdf

Informatics Europe. (2022). *Ethics.* Retrieved 2023, from https://www.informatics-europe.org/society/ethics.html

ISO 21448:2022. (2022). *ISO 21448:2022 - Road vehicles — Safety of the intended functionality.* Retrieved 2 10, 2023, from https://www.iso.org/standard/77490.html

ISO 26262-1. (2018). *ISO 26262-1:2011 - Road vehicles — Functional safety — Part 1: Vocabulary.* Retrieved 2 10, 2023, from https://www.iso.org/standard/43464.html

ISO/AWI PAS 8800. (Standard in development). *ISO/AWI PAS 8800 - Road Vehicles — Safety and artificial intelligence.* Retrieved 2 10, 2023, from https://www.iso.org/standard/83303.html

ISO/AWI TS 5083. (Standard in development). *ISO/AWI TS 5083 - Road vehicles — Safety for automated driving systems — Design, verification and validation.* Retrieved 2 10, 2023, from https://www.iso.org/standard/81920.html

ISO/IEC 27090. (Standard in development). *ISO/IEC AWI 27090: Cybersecurity — Artificial Intelligence — Guidance for addressing security threats and failures in artificial intelligence systems.* Retrieved 2 10, 2023, from https://www.iso.org/standard/56581.html

ISO/IEC. (2022). *ISO/IEC 22989:2022 - Information technology — Artificial intelligence — Artificial intelligence concepts and terminology.* Retrieved 2 10, 2023, from https://www.iso.org/standard/74296.html

ISO/IEC 27563. (2023). *ISO/IEC DTR 27563: Security and privacy in artificial intelligence use cases — Best practices.* Retrieved 2 10, 2023, from https://www.iso.org/standard/80396.html

ISO/IEC CD TR 5469. (Standard in development). *ISO/IEC CD TR 5469: Artificial intelligence — Functional safety and AI systems.* (ISO) Retrieved 2 10, 2023, from https://www.iso.org/standard/81283.html

ISO/IEC JTC 1/SC 42. (2022). *ISO/IEC TR 24368 Information technology — Artificial intelligence — Overview of ethical and societal concerns.*

ISO/TC 22/SC 32. (Standard in development). *ISO/AWI PAS 8800 Road Vehicles — Safety and artificial intelligence.* Retrieved 01 08, 2023, from https://www.iso.org/standard/83303.html

ISO/TR 4804:2020. (2020). *ISO/TR 4804:2020: Road vehicles — Safety and cybersecurity for automated driving systems — Design, verification and validation.* Retrieved 2 10, 2023, from https://www.iso.org/standard/80363.html

A COMPARISON OF CLOUD COMPUTING VS FOG VS EDGE FOR IIOT SENSORS

Nikola Kuchtíková, Milos Maryska

Faculty of Informatics and Statistics
Prague University of Economics and Business
nikola.kuchtikova@vse.cz, milos.maryska@vse.cz

DOI: 10.35011/IDIMT-2023-151

Keywords

Industrial IoT, sensors, Cloud computing, Fog computing, Edge computing

Abstract

Cloud computing describes the use of hardware and software delivered via the Internet. The field of cloud computing has been overgrowing rapidly for years, as more organizations seek to work remotely and is closely related to terms Industry 4.0 and smart factory technologies. The idea of Industry 4.0 includes the concept of the Industrial Internet of Things (IIoT) that is the possibility for industrial devices to have an Internet connection and share data obtained from endpoints like sensors. When organizations employ a lot of sensors, they want to avoid a significant increase in data transfer costs and a delay in response times. This is the reason why Fog and edge computing should be considered. This literature review paper provides comparison of selected computing models for use in specific IIoT sensors areas that is currently missing. This paper aims to map the differences between cloud, fog, and edge for IIoT sensor's specific requirements and support strategic decisions when deciding how to implement IIoT sensors in selected industrial areas.

1. Introduction

Cloud computing, fog computing and edge computing may appear similar, but they are just different layers of the IIoT (Winsystems, 2017). The layers are illustrated in Figure 1. Fog and edge layers can be seen as extensions of the cloud layer.

Industrial organizations that rely heavily on data and critical IIoT applications in the cloud do not meet packet latency and reliability requirements (Maldonado et al., 2021) because IIoT sensors generate a massive amount of data (Williams, 2021) that needs to be processed. Cloud computing has limitations like longer outage time, potential loss of data, and a higher risk of attacks (Jagreet, 2021). Fog computing and edge computing can help to provide real-time processing, near-by storage, ultra-low latency, reliability, and high data rate (Basir et al., 2019).

Cloud computing is delivering centralized computing resources over the Internet, "the cloud". Most cloud computing services are divided into three categories: Infrastructure as a service (IaaS), Platform as a service (PaaS) and Software as a service (SaaS) are described for example in Dawis and Watts (2021). They are sometimes called the cloud computing "stack".

Data generated from IoT devices are yet massively processed in a cloud infrastructure. Nevertheless, completely processing IoT and IIoT application requests on the cloud is not an efficient solution for some applications, especially time-sensitive ones (Naha et. al, 2018).

Fog computing delivers a decentralized computing structure in which data, compute, storage, and applications location is between the data source and the cloud. It can optimize data analytics by storing information closer to the data source for real-time analysis (Mahmud et al., 2018). Fog computing means processing data in a fog node or IIoT gateway. Easily said, it involves moving devices closer to the sensors they are talking to.

Fog computing has the potential to support time-sensitive services which request low traffic congestion, low energy consumption and minimum bandwidth, intending to reduce the drain on cloud data centres. Fog computing is not a replacement for cloud computing. It extends the computation, communication, and storage facilities from the cloud to the edge of the networks [Dlamini, 2019].

Edge computing is a distributed information technology architecture in which client data is processed at the edge of the network, as close to the originating source as possible (Shi et. al, 2016). With Edge Computing, we can solve a series of challenges, such as latency or bandwidth. Many claims that the future of the cloud is at the Edge (Gold and Keith, 2021).

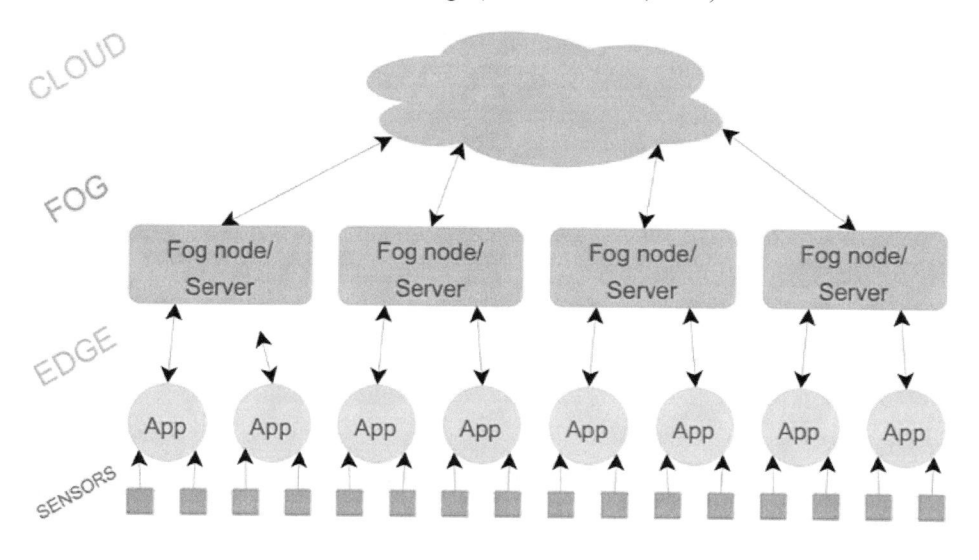

Figure 1. IIoT data processing layers   Source: authors based on Biswas (2019)

Figure 1. shows the discussed computing models: cloud, fog, and edge as a different processing layers of the IIoT.

2. Materials and methods

The basic approach used for this research is the deductive method that is, starting from available theoretical knowledge. The sources are related books and articles filtered based on the presence of keywords "cloud computing", "fog computing" and "edge computing" in combination with the keyword "Industrial IoT" ideally at the title of the document.

At the beginning, two research questions are formulated, the truth of which will be verified at the end.

- **RQ1:** For IIoT sensors, the most secure variant is the use of cloud computing with both extensions, i.e., fog computing and edge computing.
- **RQ2:** The security of cloud computing will be increased by using the expansion of fog computing and/or edge computing.

Based on the literary source analysis of full text information obtained from sources related to defined keywords, the relevant IIoT challenging requirements related to sensors are presented together with a brief explanation of why is chosen challenging requirement relevant. Next step is presenting a matrix table. A matrix table shows relationships between two or more variables in a data set in grid format. Essentially, the matrix chart is a table made up of rows and columns that present data visually (Behrisch et.al, 2016). Here the goal of mentioned table will be to show if the individual models are able to deal with identified requirements.

Further, architecture and interconnection of individual computing models will be presented in detail. The models will then be compared to identify differences in the form of matrix table and subsequently also in the form of individual frameworks.

3. Results and Discussion

At first, we needed to find out what are the most challenging requirements for IIoT sensors.

3.1. Set of challenging IIoT sensor's requirements

As a basis for matrix comparative analysis, we need to define the basic IIoT requirements in a form of simple list completed by detailed related source analysis based on a full text review.

Industrial organizations worldwide are investing to improve production efficiency, **operational reliability**, and supply chain performance (Blanchette, 2016). Reliability and high availability have always been a major concern in distributed systems for information exchange (Willner, 2018). As many processes in industrial environments already depend on real-time cyber-physical systems and embedded sensors, IIoT integration with cognitive computing and **real- time** data exchanges are important for real-time analytics and realization of digital twins in smart environments and services (Koulamas and Laarescu, 2020). IIoT is a challenge for any infrastructure because it generates a large amount of data (Caiza et al., 2020) and its necessarily to reduce **latency and bandwith** of data transmissions and improve response times in the bidirectional link between the end IIoT devices and the data processing servers (Atutxa et. al, 2021), (Trossell, 2017).

Sensors are being deployed in large numbers, in many industries, to harness the power of data and their **power consumption** is a significant concern and limitation. There is increasing consensus among experts that IoT devices need to be self-powered, to be viable at scale, so power consumption in sensors is really challenging topic (Runar, 2020). Utilization of Edge computing in the IoT can have impact on energy consumption of IoT (Mocnej et al, 2018). **Securing** an IIoT as much as possible is the first step an organization should take when it comes to data protection (Rodriguez, 2019). One way to do that could be defence-in-depth strategy which tackle the complexity by providing multiple defense layers (Mosteiro-Sanchez et al, 2022). Many industrial businesses encounter **cost challenges** when they set out to incorporate IIoT technologies, practices, and devices.

Availability is a driver for IIoT. Many factors are related to the availability of standards, platforms, skills, processing power, low-cost sensors, and much more.

3.2. Individual differences Framework/matrix of comparative analysis towards IIoT requirements.

Based on the challenging requirements for IIoT sensors, a matrix of comparative analysis towards Cloud, Fog and Edge computing is performed. The IIoT requirements obtained in a previous step are refined to answer them yes, or no. The values are "YES" in case selected computing can ensure compliance with the chosen IIoT requirement and "NO" if the chosen computing cannot comply with the determined IIoT requirement shown in Table I. For this paper is table shortened mostly to a blunt Yes/No answer for a quick clarity, but this table result could change with time and new technologies.

Table 1. matrix Table of how Cloud, Fog and Edge computing can fulfil the specific IIoT requirements

IIoT Requirement	ID	Cloud	Fog	Edge
High operating reliability	01	Yes	No	Yes
Real-time performance	02	No (difficult)	Yes (achievable)	Yes
Low latency	03	No (high)	Yes	Yes
Low power consumption	04	No	Yes	Yes (offloading)
Bandwith optimisation	05	No	Yes	Yes
Security	06	No (undefined)	Yes (can be defined)	Yes
Availability	07	Yes	Yes	Yes (limited)
Low deployment cost	08	No (planning)	Yes (ad-hoc)	No

Source: authors based on (Elbamby et al., 2019; Naha et. al, 2018; Mijuskovic et al., 2021; Mukherjee et al., 2018; Tariq et al., 2019)

As we can see from the matrix table, cloud computing itself is not a sufficient model to meet the IIoT challenging requirements. Fog and Edge computing can fulfil the requirements in some form, but Fog computing can't function without edge (Overheid, 2020). So, the result coming from this matrix table is that for the use of IIoT sensors, we need to implement at least edge computing or even better fog computing on top of the existing cloud. The way Fog and Edge make it more secure is that fog computing reduces the amount of data being transferred back and forth to the cloud and Edge depersonalizes data which moves out of the local network. Even though the possibility of ensuring security is mentioned in both Fog and Edge, it is of course one of the most complex issues, especially in connection with sensors.

3.3. Framework of how edge computing extends cloud computing.

This framework describes the detailed benefits of edge computing compared to cloud computing for sensors in Industrial IoT. The assumption is that the cloud is the basic approach.

Cloud cannot guarantee the quality of service of real-time IoT analysis services, which can cause a delay between a request from the client and a cloud service provider's response. The edge can process real-time data without connecting to external services because of the closeness to sensors. Additionally, it is not restricted by connection failures with an external network. For this reason, the edge platform can guarantee a better quality of service (Moon et al., 2019). Edge computing places data intelligence closer to where it's needed. That means responses are improved, data, networking, storage, and computing are distributed right through layers of edge computing nodes from IoT and IIoT devices to the data center. The flexibility to choose where to store data improves performance and reduces costs (Bigelow, 2020).

Smart sensors are an essential component of edge systems, providing an area of abilities that improve productivity in the factory and cooperate in driving Industry 4.0 and IIoT.

As already mentioned, Edge computing improves time and reduces latency down to milliseconds while minimizing network bandwidth. Jointly with cloud computing and powered by IIoT sensor technology, these edge systems can profoundly impact industrial system performance and increase productivity and profit for manufacturers (Longbottom, 2020).

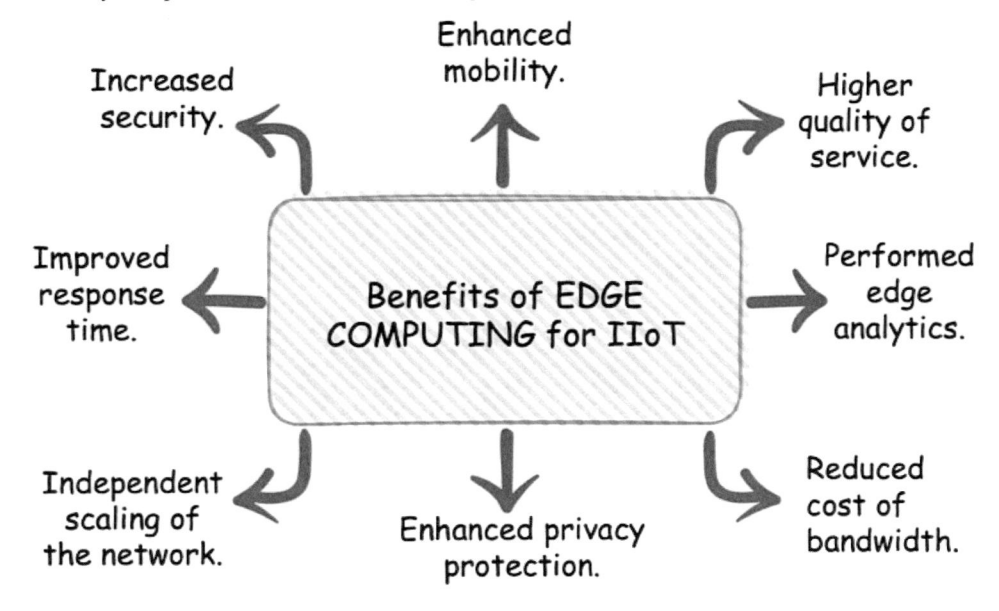

Figure 2. A framework of the benefits of Edge computing in comparison to Cloud computing for the IIoT use case

Source: authors based on (Belyi, 2020; Moon et al., 2019; Kaplunou, 2019; Radford 2021; Zao et al., 2020).

In addition to the positives, it is good to outline even some of the negatives of edge computing. The potential downside to edge computing is that important data could end up being overlooked and discarded in the quest to save bandwidth and reduce latency, never making it to the cloud data center for storage (Marr, 2020).

3.4. Framework of how fog extends the edge computing.

Framework shown in Figure 3 describes the benefits of Fog computing in comparison with edge computing for the use of sensors in Industrial IoT. The assumption is that the Fog is the superstructure of Edge.

Fog and edge computing systems both shift data processing towards the source of data generation, and they attempt to reduce the amount of data sent to the cloud (Pod Group, 2019). Edge computing regards a superset embracing all paradigms where the computation moves to the edge network, including Fog computing (Mahmud et al., 2018).

For example, Cisco, which coined the term "fog computing" in 2012, assumes that "edge computing" indicates the idea of moving computational resources closer to the devices, while "fog computing" refers to the literal implementation and management of this architecture known as "fogging". In a paper by Ren et al. (Ren et al., 2020) fog computing is described as similar to the edge computing, but it has a novel architecture. Fog is originally proposed for the context of IoT with location awareness, timely response, wireless access, and mobility support in mind.

One of the main advantages of fog computing over other approaches to IoT and IIoT integration is represented by security and privacy enforcements, especially concerning the protection of sensitive data. With data storage and processing in LAN in a fog computing architecture, it enables organizations to aggregate data from multi-devices into regional stores (Ismail, 2018).

Fog computing enables real-time data analysis, which can make IoT and IIoT applications work quicker. Fog computing can be used to develop low latency networks between analytics endpoints and devices and using such networks can lead to reduced bandwidth requirements compared to cloud computing. Fog computing can process larger volumes of data compared to edge computing as it can process real-time requests (Joshi, 2019). The best moment to implement fog computing is when we have millions of connected devices sharing data back and forth (Ismail, 2018).

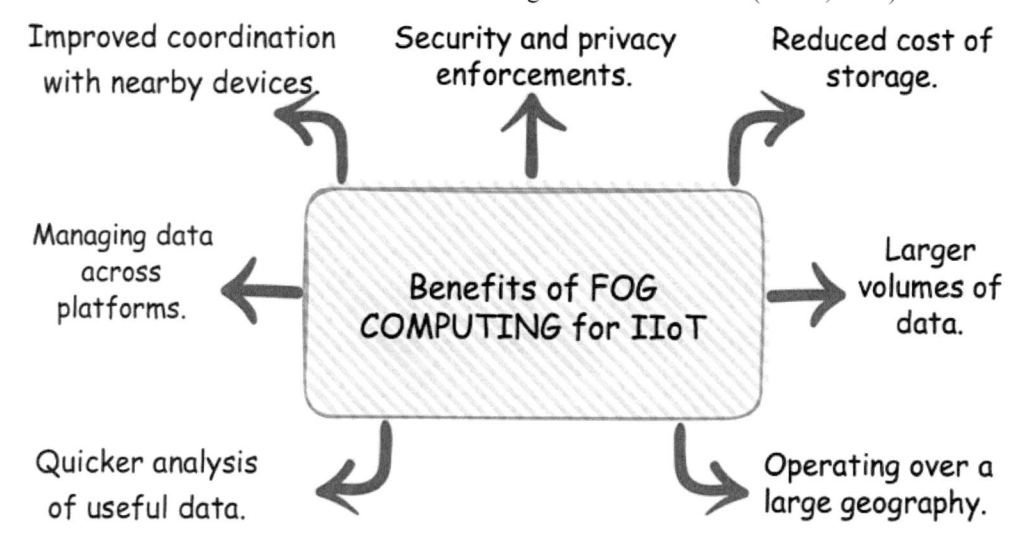

Figure 3. A framework of the benefits of Fog computing in comparison to Edge computing for the IIoT use case

Source: authors based on (Brett, 2021; Curtis, 2021; Ismail, 2018; Joshi, 2019; Mahmud, 2020; Ren et al., 2019).

While fog computing's advantage of connecting with more devices and processing more data than edge computing, this dimension of fog computing is also a potential drawback. More infrastructure and investment are needed, and we are relying on data consistency across an extensive network (Ismail, 2018). Fog computing is dependent on multiple links for transferring data from the physical asset chain to the digital layer, which can be potential points of network failure (Joshi, 2019).

4. Conclusion

Industry 4.0, a revolutionized era, will have many smart devices that will support IIoT applications in every field. This deployment of smart devices will change all domains of human life's perspective. IIoT applications will provide solutions to all areas, such as transportation, healthcare, food supply chain, education, and industry. These IIoT applications will provide efficient, practical solutions for future networks, but there are also challenges in latency, bandwidth, etc. All these advanced IIoT applications will create a massive amount of data, causing a burden on the cloud.

Companies have choices about how to implement Cloud, edge, and fog technologies to best support their needs. It is essential to find out which computing model is best for the organization. In my view, we can't answer the question if fog or edge computing is more useful or efficient. Well-designed IT solutions are optimum solutions that balance requirements, cost, and system/infrastructure capabilities or limitations. Hence either fog or edge computing will qualify as part of an optimum IT solution.

This paper aimed to map the differences between Cloud, Fog, and Edge for IIoT sensor's specific requirements to help organizations decide how to implement IIoT sensors in selected industrial areas and answer to the research question. We can conclude that IIoT is becoming an increasingly popular topic among researchers and both RQ1 and RQ2 are verified.

Nowadays, the Industrial Internet of Things, Cloud computing, Edge computing, and Fog computing represent the most advanced computing paradigms. However, with a first look at the literature, it might be difficult to fully understand their main differences and similarities and how they relate to each other.

This work overviews IIoT applications and their use cases using the Cloud, Fog, and Edge computing. First, I started from this global picture. I focused on each of the paradigms, explaining the main characteristics and features, along with considerations on how they interact and influence each other. I have previewed the works carried out by numerous researchers incorporating any of the mentioned computing models to provide services to IIoT sensors towards Industry 4.0. A critical review of some current work is summarized in Figure 2. This figure can be used to find challenging IIoT requirements for sensors. This is an exciting era to discover what fog and edge computing may contribute to the world of automation in the coming future.

References

Atutxa, A., Franco, D., Sasiain, J., Astorga, J., & Jacob, E. (2021). Achieving Low Latency Communications in Smart Industrial Networks with Programmable Data Planes. Sensors, 21(15), 5199. https://doi.org/10.3390/s21155199

Basir, R., Qaisar, S., Ali, M., Aldwairi, M., Ashraf, M. I., Mahmood, A., & Gidlund, M. (2019). Fog Computing Enabling Industrial Internet of Things: State-of-the-Art and Research Challenges. Sensors, 19(21), 4807. https://doi.org/10.3390/s19214807

Behrisch, M., Bach, B., Henry Riche, N., Schreck, T., & Fekete, J.-D. (2016). Matrix Reordering Methods for Table and Network Visualization. Computer Graphics Forum, 35(3), 693–716. https://doi.org/10.1111/cgf.12935

Belyi, V. (2020, February 4). How Efficient is Edge Computing Compared to Cloud Computing? Dataversity. https://www.dataversity.net/how-efficient-is-edge-computing-compared-to-cloud-computing/#

Bigelow, S. J. (2020, October). What is edge computing? Everything you need to know. Techtarget. https://searchdatacenter.techtarget.com/definition/edge-computing

Biswas, I. (2019, January 24). A Beginner's Guide to Edge Computing. PathPartner. https://www.pathpartnertech.com/a-beginners-guide-to-edge-computing/

Blanchette, B. (2016, October 5). How to implement the Industrial Internet of Things. BControl Engineering. https://www.controleng.com/articles/how-to-implement-the-industrial-internet-of-things/

Brett, D. (2021, February 5). Edge Computing vs. Fog Computing: Is There a Real Difference? Trenton Systems Blog. https://www.trentonsystems.com/blog/edge-computing-fog-computing-benefits-differences

Caiza, G., Saeteros, M., Oñate, W., & Garcia, M. V. (2020). Fog computing at industrial level, architecture, latency, energy, and security: A review. Heliyon, 6(4), e03706. https://doi.org/10.1016/j.heliyon.2020.e03706

Curtis, B. (2021). FOG COMPUTING ADVANTAGES ACROSS DIFFERENT SECTORS. Your Tech Diet. https://www.yourtechdiet.com/blogs/fog-computing-advantages/

Davis, L., & Watts, R. (2021, September 2). What Is Cloud Computing? Everything You Need To Know. Forbes. https://www.forbes.com/advisor/business/what-is-cloud-computing/

Dlamini, S. (2019, August). Optimisation of Fog Computing for Industrial IoT applications. Fog Computing. Southern Africa Telecommunication Networks and Applications Conference (SATNAC).

Elbamby, M. S., Perfecto, C., Liu, C.-F., Park, J., Samarakoon, S., Chen, X., & Bennis, M. (2019). Wireless Edge Computing With Latency and Reliability Guarantees. Proceedings of the IEEE, 107(8), 1717–1737. https://doi.org/10.1109/JPROC.2019.2917084

Gold, J., & Shaw, K. (2021, June 29). What is edge computing and why does it matter? Networkworld. https://www.networkworld.com/article/3224893/what-is-edge-computing-and-how-it-s-changing-the-network.html

Ismail, K. (2018, August 14). Edge Computing vs. Fog Computing: What's the Difference? CMS Wire. https://www.cmswire.com/information-management/edge-computing-vs-fog-computing-whats-the-difference/

Jagreet, K. G. (2021, March 10). Difference between Edge Computing vs Cloud Computing? Akira.AI. https://www.akira.ai/blog/edge-computing-vs-cloud-computing/

Joshi, N. (2019, July 18). Fog vs Edge vs Mist computing. Which one is the most suitable for your business? Allerin. https://www.allerin.com/blog/fog-vs-edge-vs-mist-computing-which-one-is-the-most-suitable-for-your-business

Kaplunou, P. (2019, December 27). Cloud Computing and Edge Computing Compared. Smart IT. https://smart-it.io/blog/cloud-computing-vs-edge-computing-infographic/

Koulamas, C., & Lazarescu, M. T. (2020). Real-Time Sensor Networks and Systems for the Industrial IoT: What Next? Sensors, 20(18), 5023. https://doi.org/10.3390/s20185023

Longbottom, C. (2020, October 2). Comparing edge computing vs. Cloud computing. Techtarget. https://internetofthingsagenda.techtarget.com/tip/Comparing-edge-computing-vs-cloud-computing

Mahmud, R., Kotagiri, R., & Buyya, R. (2018). Fog Computing: A Taxonomy, Survey and Future Directions. In B. Di Martino, K.-C. Li, L. T. Yang, & A. Esposito (Eds.), Internet of Everything (pp. 103–130). Springer Singapore. https://doi.org/10.1007/978-981-10-5861-5_5

Mahmud, R., Ramamohanarao, K., & Buyya, R. (2020). Application Management in Fog Computing Environments: A Taxonomy, Review and Future Directions. ACM Computing Surveys, 53(4), 1–43. https://doi.org/10.1145/3403955

Maldonado, R., Karstensen, A., Pocovi, G., Esswie, A. A., Rosa, C., Alanen, O., Kasslin, M., & Kolding, T. (2021). Comparing Wi-Fi 6 and 5G Downlink Performance for Industrial IoT. IEEE Access, 9, 86928–86937. https://doi.org/10.1109/ACCESS.2021.3085896

Marr, B. (2020, September 16). 3 Advantages (And 1 Disadvantage) Of Edge Computing. Forbes. https://www.forbes.com/sites/bernardmarr/2020/09/16/3-advantages-and-1-disadvantage-of-edge-computing/?sh=3ffec881fc71

Mijuskovic, A., Chiumento, A., Bemthuis, R., Aldea, A., & Havinga, P. (2021). Resource Management Techniques for Cloud/Fog and Edge Computing: An Evaluation Framework and Classification. Sensors, 21(5), 1832. https://doi.org/10.3390/s21051832

Mocnej, J., Miškuf, M., Papcun, P., & Zolotová, I. (2018). Impact of Edge Computing Paradigm on Energy Consumption in IoT. IFAC-PapersOnLine, 51(6), 162–167. https://doi.org/10.1016/j.ifacol.2018.07.147

Moon, J., Kum, S., & Lee, S. (2019). A Heterogeneous IoT Data Analysis Framework with Collaboration of Edge-Cloud Computing: Focusing on Indoor PM10 and PM2.5 Status Prediction. Sensors, 19(14), 3038. https://doi.org/10.3390/s19143038

Mosteiro-Sanchez, A., Barcelo, M., Astorga, J., & Urbieta, A. (2022). Securing IIoT using Defence-in-Depth: Towards an End-to-End Secure Industry 4.0. https://doi.org/10.48550/ARXIV.2201.05415

Mukherjee, M., Shu, L., & Wang, D. (2018). Survey of Fog Computing: Fundamental, Network Applications, and Research Challenges. IEEE Communications Surveys & Tutorials, 20(3), 1826–1857. https://doi.org/10.1109/COMST.2018.2814571

Naha, R. K., Garg, S., Georgakopoulos, D., Jayaraman, P. P., Gao, L., Xiang, Y., & Ranjan, R. (2018). Fog Computing: Survey of Trends, Architectures, Requirements, and Research Directions. IEEE Access, 6, 47980–48009. https://doi.org/10.1109/ACCESS.2018.2866491

Overheid, A. (2020, November 10). Understanding Edge Computing vs. Fog Computing. Onlogic Blog. https://www.onlogic.com/company/io-hub/edge-computing-vs-fog-computing/

Pod Group. (2019, March 4). Fog Vs. Edge Computing: What Are the Differences that Matter? IoT for All. https://www.iotforall.com/fog-vs-edge-computing-do-differences-matter

Radford, A. (2021). 10 Key Benefits of Edge and Fog Computing That You Should Know. Amber Networks. https://amber-networks.com/10-key-benefits-of-edge-and-fog-computing-that-you-should-know/

Ren, J., Zhang, D., He, S., Zhang, Y., & Li, T. (2020). A Survey on End-Edge-Cloud Orchestrated Network Computing Paradigms: Transparent Computing, Mobile Edge Computing, Fog Computing, and Cloudlet. ACM Computing Surveys, 52(6), 1–36. https://doi.org/10.1145/3362031

Rodriguez, L. (2019, September 4). Data Protection Best Practices for IIoT. AutomationWorld. https://www.automationworld.com/factory/iiot/news/13742922/data-protection-best-practices-for-iiot

RUNAR, F. (2020, January 23). Here's why energy-harvesting trumps batteries. Onio. https://www.onio.com/article/energy-harvesting-trumps-batteries.html

Shi, W., Cao, J., Zhang, Q., Li, Y., & Xu, L. (2016). Edge Computing: Vision and Challenges. IEEE Internet of Things Journal, 3(5), 637–646. https://doi.org/10.1109/JIOT.2016.2579198

Tariq, N., Asim, M., Al-Obeidat, F., Zubair Farooqi, M., Baker, T., Hammoudeh, M., & Ghafir, I. (2019). The Security of Big Data in Fog-Enabled IoT Applications Including Blockchain: A Survey. Sensors, 19(8), 1788. https://doi.org/10.3390/s19081788

Trossell, D. (2017, January 18). IoT: How to alleviate bandwidth challenges. ITProPortal. https://www.itproportal.com/features/iot-how-to-alleviate-bandwidth-challenges/

Williams, R. (2021, July 15). IIoT and Sensing on the Edge. Automation.Com. https://www.automation.com/en-us/articles/july-2021/iiot-and-sensing-edge

Willner, A. (2018). The Industrial Internet of Things. In Q. Hassan (Ed.), Internet of Things A to Z (pp. 293–318). John Wiley & Sons, Inc. https://doi.org/10.1002/9781119456735.ch11

Winsystems. (2017, December 4). Cloud, Fog and Edge Computing – What's the Difference? Winsystems. https://www.winsystems.com/cloud-fog-and-edge-computing-whats-the-difference/

Zao, J., Byers, C., Murphy, B., & AbiEzzi, S. (2020). The Industrial Internet of Things Distributed Computing in the Edge. Industrial Internet Consortium. https://www.iiconsortium.org/pdf/IIoT-Distributed-Computing-in-the-Edge.pdf

FIBER OPTIC ACOUSTIC SENSING (FOAS) FOR AUTOMATIC TRAFFIC JAM QUEUE END DETECTION

Carmina Coronel, Martin Litzenberger, Kilian Wohlleben

AIT Austrian Institute of Technology GmbH

martin.litzenberger@ait.ac.at

DOI: 10.35011/IDIMT-2023-161

Keywords

Fiber optic acoustic sensing FOAS, intelligent transportation systems ITS, traffic jam detection

Abstract

Queue end detection in traffic jams is especially important on highways that are prone to traffic jams, and at the same time to fog or other severe weather that can significantly reduce visibility. An automatic warning system for traffic jam build-up needs to work seamlessly over the whole affected road sections. In line with this, we introduce fiber optic acoustic sensing (FOAS) for automated queue end detection in traffic jams. In FOAS systems, series of light pulses are transmitted along a fiber-optic cable and the back-scattered light, which is affected by the mechanical strain of the fiber-optic cables due to ground vibrations, is measured and analyzed. With fiber-optic cables installed parallel to a highway where ground vibrations are induced by passing vehicles, traffic information such strong deceleration can be detected in the FOAS signals. In this paper, we present an algorithm based on image processing methods that estimates strong braking action from image representations of the FOAS signal. We tested the results of the algorithm on FOAS sample data collected on a real highway.

1. Introduction

Traffic jams in combination with severe weather limiting the visibility of the drivers approaching the end of the traffic jam, can result in catastrophic road accidents, when drivers, unaware of the queue ahead of them, crash into the line of stopped vehicles. An accurate, automatic detection and localization of the queue end, independent of visibility conditions and indication to the following traffic, can potentially save lives of road users. To be effective, such a technology needs to monitor the road seamlessly, i.e. without any gaps or "blind spots" along the length of the road. However, on one hand, current road traffic sensors and traffic counters have only a limited field of view, or even measure traffic flow only at one point along the road. A "seamless" installation would require a prohibitive high number of sensors. Video detection on the other hand can cover a few hundred meters of road, but typically fail in the situation of severe weather and limited visibility.

Different technologies are currently used for traffic monitoring systems where sensors are either installed overhead, under, or next to the road to detect traffic flow (Guerrero-Ibáñez et al., 2018). Such sensors could be lasers scanners (Gallego et al., 2009), infrared (Hussain, 1993), radar (Roy, 2022), (Lim, 2021), ultrasonic (Appiah et al., 2020), (Jo et al., 2014), magnetic (Pelegri et al., 2002), (Fimbombaya et al., 2002), acoustic (Lewandowski et al., 2018) or video cameras (Guerrero-Ibáñez et al., 2018), (Roy, 2022). Passing vehicles can cause changes in the magnetic field that are then processed to measure the flow of vehicles (Pelegri et al., 2002), (Fimbombaya et al., 2002). Acoustic-based monitoring measured by a microphone array were also proposed (Na et al., 2015). Another method for traffic monitoring is through crowdsourcing of smartphone connection data (Lewandowski et al., 2018) or from fleets of vehicles equipped with GNSS systems ("floating car") (Astarita et al., 2020). While this technology has in principle the potential for a seamless coverage of the road, it is affected by a certain latency in the detection of the events in question, due to the mathematical models that need to be applied to extrapolate the traffic situation, from the subset of road users that is typically equipped with such a system.

In this study, we demonstrate the application of fiber optic acoustic sensing (FOAS), often also termed distributed acoustic sensing (DAS), for road traffic safety monitoring. FOAS systems work by sending short laser pulses through a fiber optic cable where the light is scattered via Rayleigh scattering and the light returning to the source is analyzed to infer information. In FOAS systems, optical fibers with a length up to 50 kilometers can be used. The fibers used are typically already installed in the ground, parallel to a highway, for telecommunication purposes where it can be kilometers long and any disturbances along the fiber can be measured. An interrogator device connected to one end of the fiber transmits a series of laser light pulses into the fiber cable, where portions of the light pulses are backscattered and are measured by the same interrogator, as shown in Figure 1. The vibrations generated by the passing cars and trucks stretch and compress the optical fiber affecting its optical path length. This induces a measurable phase shift in the back scattered light which is sensed by interferometric methods. In this study, we demonstrate that with these changes in the signal induced by passing vehicles, relevant information on strong braking, as an indicator to traffic jams, can be derived.

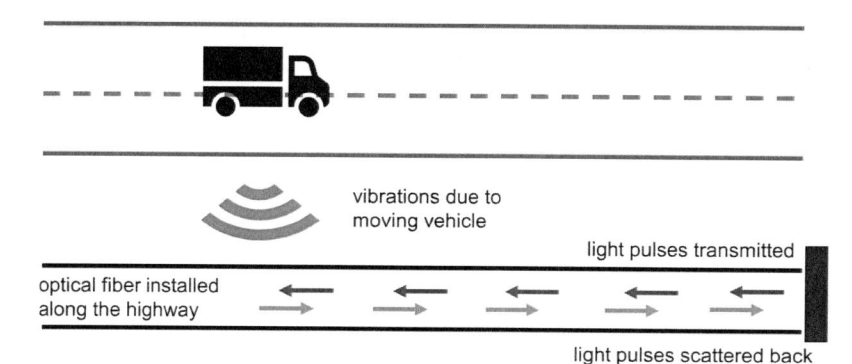

Figure 1. FOAS sensor principle

The use of FOAS systems has been shown to be effective in different monitoring systems such as trains (Kovarik et al., 2020), seismic activity (Dou et al., 2017, Walter et al., 2020), and intrusion sensors (Juarez et al., 2020, Peng et al., 2014, Wang, 2018). FOAS systems only need the passive fiber cable and a single opto-electronic device, the "interrogator". The technology has the potential to become a more economic option than conventional traffic monitoring systems where multiple road-side sensors are needed, where costs of installation, maintenance, and energy supply increase per unit. Another advantage of FOAS is that the fiber cables are not installed over or under the road, but parallel to it. Therefore, the system is not affected by road construction works. The passive nature of the fiber optic cable also makes it insusceptible to electromagnetic interference and lightning strike and therefore does not need as much maintenance and repairs as copper-based cables.

A previous work using FOAS for traffic monitoring has been published using wavelet threshold algorithms tested on moving trucks in a controlled setting (Liu et al., 2018) while another publication presented the application of FOAS-based traffic monitoring given the rise of optic fiber infrastructures in smart cities (Hall & Minto, 2019). In this paper, we employ image and signal processing algorithms to detect strong braking of vehicles as an indicator of traffic jam onset and the exact localization of the actual queue end detection of the traffic jam.

2. FOAS Data Acquisition

For FOAS data acquisition an interrogator from FEBUS OPTICS (Pau, France) has been used. The specific model used is FEBUS A1-R and it provides quantitative phase sensitive FOAS measurements. The device allows configuration of several parameters for the recording. Some of the most important parameters used in this work are collected in Table 1.

Table 1. FOAS signal recording parameters

FOAS Parameter	Value
Pulse Repetition Frequency	2 kHz
Segment Spacing (Spatial Resolution)	4.8 m
Gauge Length	10 m
Laser Pulse Width	6 m
Total Number of segments	5,211
Number of segments used by the algorithm	130

For the recordings, fiber optic cables installed next to the road for telecommunication purposes were used. The cables were buried in the ground, parallel to a 4-lane highway with 2 carriageways, in a few meters up to 10 m distance from the road side. They are capable of picking up vibrations from the environment, such as vibrations caused by vehicles moving along the infrastructure. The optical cables were not installed with the intention of good acoustical coupling with the ground and the installation was heterogeneous along the infrastructure.

The DAS raw signal for the whole highway was sampled at 2 kHz with 5,211 segments, approximately over a range of 25 km. To estimate speed and vehicle flow, we needed to extract the relevant information from the FOAS raw signal. We performed this by analyzing the frequency response of the signal.

To derive the preprocessed FOAS signal, we calculated the frequency response at each segment by discrete fast Fourier transform (FFT) in one-second segments, where we reduced the data by computing the squared energies within the chosen frequency band of 5 – 50 Hz. The preprocessed FOAS signal is then equal to the total energy of the FOAS raw signal within the said frequency band.

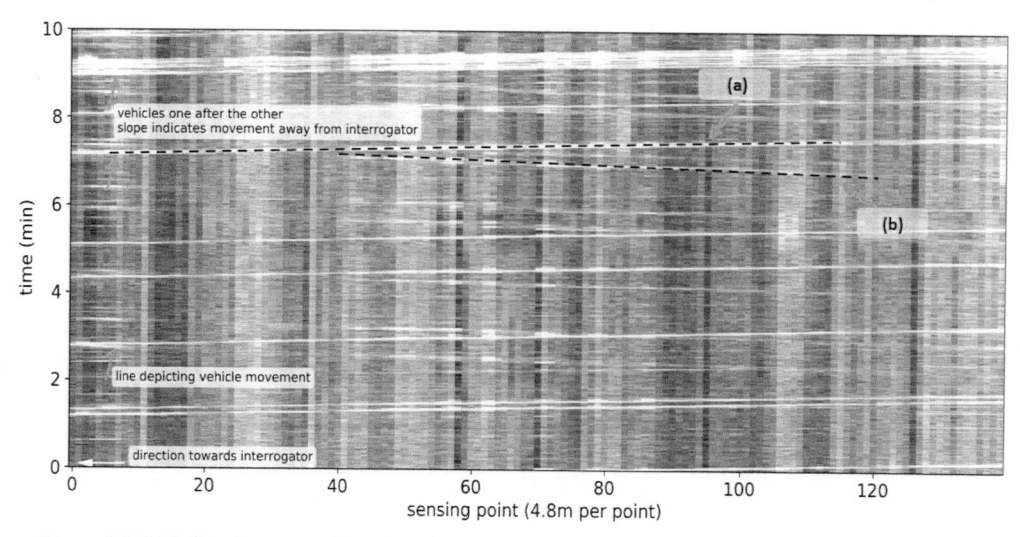

Figure 2. FOAS Signal converted into image matrix representation. Dashed black lines (a) and (b) indicate vehicle trajectories with positive and negative slope, moving away from, and to the interrogator, respectively

Figure 2 shows a typical image matrix calculated by this formula. In this, the energy in 1-second time slots and segments (sensing points) of 4.8m in length are represented as pixels values in an image matrix, where stronger energies are depicted as white. Individual vehicle trajectories appear as lines in the image while the slope of these lines correspond to the speed of a vehicle. The sign of the slope, i.e. either going up or down corresponds to the direction of the vehicle movement. A positive slope corresponds to a vehicle moving away from the interrogator (located at location 0) and a negatively sloped trace corresponds to a vehicle moving towards the interrogator.

3. Detection Algorithm

The algorithm for automatic detection of traffic jam queue end is based on classification of the specific pattern in the image representation that results from braking, i.e. a deceleration of the vehicle. For this the FOAS signal is divided into "image patches" of small size and short duration.

Figure 3 shows four typical examples of image patches containing curved trajectories resulting from multiple braking vehicles (see "positives" in Figure 3) and two examples containing straight, unaccelerated trajectories ("negatives"). The curved lines represent the deceleration from an initial faster speed (indicated by line (a) in Figure 3), visible as a negative slope, to a slower speed with consequently increasing slope (indicated by (b) in Figure 3). Note that in the extreme case stopped vehicles would be represented by vertical lines, but they are not visible in the FOAS signal due to the lack of sufficient vibration energy. The location of the braking event is given by the location of the image patch along the fiber optic cable.

We have intentionally not focused on an average speed estimation, presented elsewhere (Wiesmeyr et al., 2021), as low average speeds will be present over the whole length of the traffic jam, whereas an accumulation of braking "events" will be significant only for the vehicles approaching the end of the queue.

We have also intentionally not relied on tracking algorithms for the individual vehicle trajectories, as this approach frequently fails, to our experience, when multiple vehicle trajectories are overlapping in dense traffic situations.

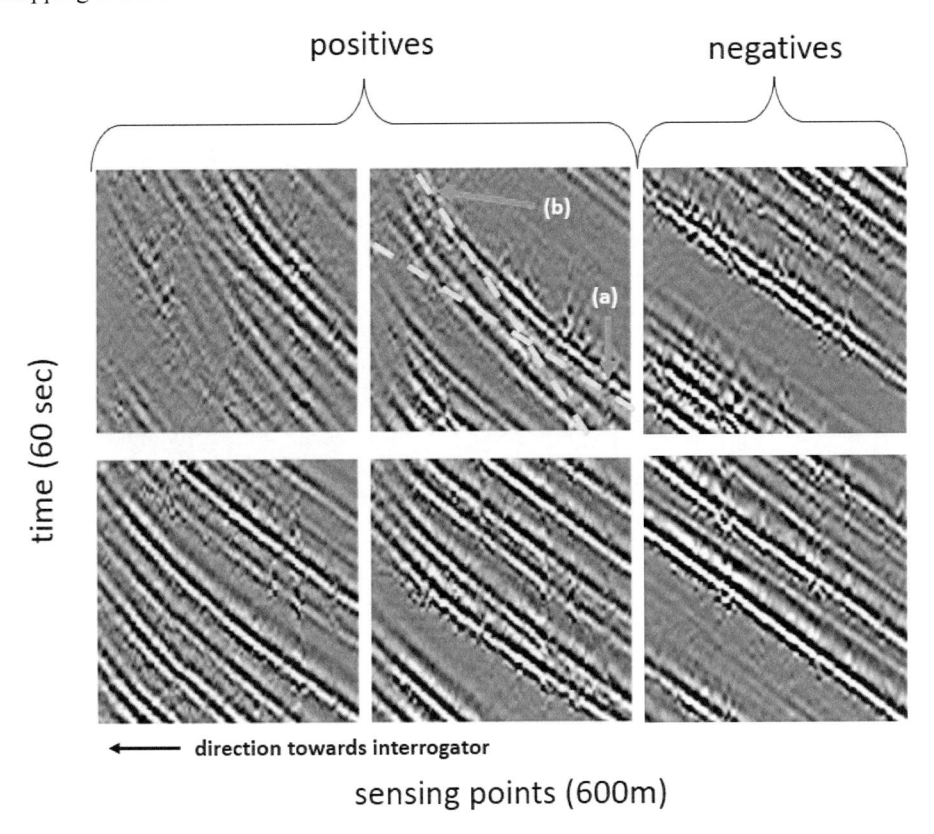

Figure 3. Four samples of FOAS signals in image representation ("patches") having an accumulation of vehicle trajectories with strong deceleration/braking (positives) and two samples without acceleration (negatives)

For this work a 3-layer convolutional neural network (CNN) with 3 fully connected layers has been developed and trained for detecting the patterns of interest, that indicate the braking action in the FOAS image representation. A binary model where an output of 1 indicated deceleration/slowing events and an output value of 0 indicated no braking in the presented FOAS data, has been used. Development and implementation was done using the "TensorFlow" (Abadi et al., 2015) and "Keras" libraries (Chollet et al., 2015) available for the Python programming language. Figure 4 illustrates the data processing flow.

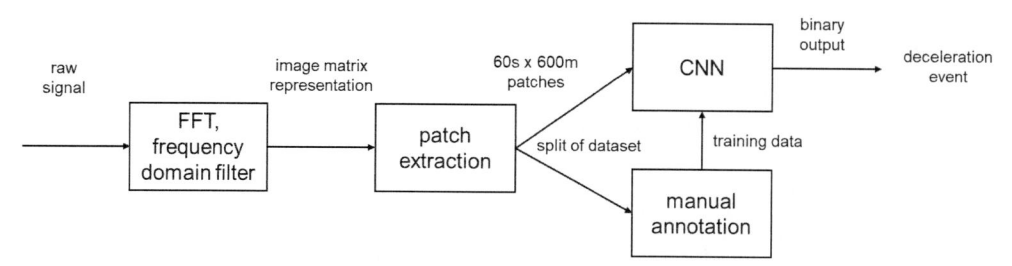

Figure 4. Flow diagram illustrating the algorithm

4. Results

The algorithm was tested with 1803 manually annotated patches of vehicle trajectories of 60 sec duration and 600 m size, where 1675 samples represented free flowing traffic and 128 samples contained trajectories exhibiting strong deceleration. Table 2 shows the confusion matrix of the classifier performance. It shows a true positive rate of 78% and a true negative rate of 95%. The spatial and temporal resolution of the presented results is given by the size of the patches of 600 m and 60 seconds, respectively. It needs to be noted, that this resolution can be further refined by extracting temporally and spatially overlapping patches from the FOAS signal. Choosing a smaller patch size in space or time however, would reduce the probability to resolve the significant curvature of the decelerating trajectory, and is therefore not feasible.

Table 2. Confusion matrix of automatic detection results using a 3-layer CNN

		Model Predicted		Sum
		0	1	
Ground Truth	0	1599	76	1675
	1	28	100	128
Sum		1627	176	

5. Conclusion

We have presented an algorithm for automated queue end detection in traffic jams from FOAS signals by detecting strong braking as a precursor to traffic jam onset and for localization of queue end, that can work seamlessly over the whole length of a road. Our algorithm converts raw FOAS signals into an image representation wherein lines in the image represent the trajectories of the moving vehicles. The algorithm then applies a CNN to classify the patterns of decelerating vehicles from those with constant speed. With 1803 manually annotated samples we have reached detection a rate of 78% and a true negative rate of 95%.

While the true positive rate seems acceptable for the application of issuing traffic jam warnings, the true negative rate of 95% and consequently 5% false positives appear to be too high for a practical application, as this corresponds to one "traffic jam false alarm" at approximately every 20 minutes. For future work we therefore plan to mitigate this by adding plausibility checks, such as combining the result of the CNN detection step with other traffic parameters derived from the FOAS signal, such as traffic density or average speeds (Wiesmeyr et al., 2021).

References

Abadi, M. et al. (2015), "TensorFlow: Large-scale machine learning on heterogeneous systems", 2015. Software available from tensorflow.org.

Appiah, O. et al. (2020), "Ultrasonic sensor based traffic information acquisition system; a cheaper alternative for ITS application in developing countries," Scientific African, vol. 9, p. e00487, Sep. 2020, doi: 10.1016/j.sciaf.2020.e00487.

Astarita, V. et al (2020), "Floating Car Data Adaptive Traffic Signals: A Description of the First Real-Time Experiment with 'Connected' Vehicles," Electronics, vol. 9, no. 1, Art. no. 1, Jan. 2020, doi: 10.3390/electronics9010114.

Chollet, F. et al. (2015), "Keras", GitHub. Retrieved from https://github.com/fchollet/keras

Dou, S. et al. (2017), "Distributed Acoustic Sensing for Seismic Monitoring of The Near Surface: A Traffic-Noise Interferometry Case Study," Sci Rep, vol. 7, no. 1, p. 11620, Dec. 2017, doi: 10.1038/s41598-017-11986-4.

Fimbombaya, H.S., et al. (2018), "Performance Evaluation of Magnetic Wireless Sensor Networks Algorithm for Traffic Flow Monitoring in Chaotic Cities," Modelling and Simulation in Engineering, vol. 2018, pp. 1–11, Oct. 2018, doi: 10.1155/2018/2591304.

Gallego, N. et al. (2009), "Traffic Monitoring: Improving Road Safety Using a Laser Scanner Sensor," in 2009 Electronics, Robotics and Automotive Mechanics Conference (CERMA), Cuernavaca, Morelos, Mexico, Sep. 2009, pp. 281–286, doi: 10.1109/CERMA.2009.11.

Guerrero-Ibáñez, J. et al. (2018), "Sensor Technologies for Intelligent Transportation Systems," Sensors (Basel), vol. 18, no. 4, Apr. 2018, doi: 10.3390/s18041212.

Hall, J. & Minto, C. (2019), "Using Fiber Optic Cables To Deliver Intelligent Traffic Management In Smart Cities," in International Conference on Smart Infrastructure and Construction 2019 (ICSIC), 0 vols., ICE Publishing, 2019, pp. 125–131.

Hussain, T.M. (1993), "Overhead infrared sensor for monitoring vehicular traffic," IEEE Trans. Veh. Technol., vol. 42, no. 4, pp. 477–483, Nov. 1993, doi: 10.1109/25.260764.

Jo, Y. et al. (2014), "Traffic Information Acquisition System with Ultrasonic Sensors in Wireless Sensor Networks," International Journal of Distributed Sensor Networks, vol. 10, no. 5, p. 961073, May 2014, doi: 10.1155/2014/961073.

Juarez J.C., et al. (2005), "Distributed fiber-optic intrusion sensor system," J. Lightwave Technol., vol. 23, no. 6, pp. 2081–2087, Jun. 2005, doi: 10.1109/JLT.2005.849924.

Kowarik,S. et al. (2020), "Fiber Optic Train Monitoring with Distributed Acoustic Sensing: Conventional and Neural Network Data Analysis," Sensors, vol. 20, no. 2, p. 450, Jan. 2020, doi: 10.3390/s20020450.

Lewandowski, M. et al. (2018), "Road Traffic Monitoring System Based on Mobile Devices and Bluetooth Low Energy Beacons," Wireless Communications and Mobile Computing, vol. 2018, pp. 1–12, Jul. 2018, doi: 10.1155/2018/3251598.

Lim, H.-S. (2021), "Lane-by-Lane Traffic Monitoring Using 24.1 GHz FMCW Radar System," IEEE Access, vol. 9, pp. 14677–14687, 2021, doi: 10.1109/ACCESS.2021.3052876.

Liu, H. et al. (2018), "Traffic Flow Detection Using Distributed Fiber Optic Acoustic Sensing," IEEE Access, vol. 6, pp. 68968–68980, 2018, doi: 10.1109/ACCESS.2018.2868418.

Na, Y. et al. (2015), "An Acoustic Traffic Monitoring System: Design and Implementation," in 2015 IEEE 12th Intl Conf on Ubiquitous Intelligence and Computing and 2015 IEEE 12th Intl Conf on Autonomic and Trusted Computing and 2015 IEEE 15th Intl Conf on Scalable Computing and Communications and Its Associated Workshops (UIC-ATC-ScalCom), Aug. 2015, pp. 119–126, doi: 10.1109/UIC-ATC-ScalCom-CBDCom-IoP.2015.41.

Pelegri J. et al. (2002), "Vehicle detection and car speed monitoring system using GMR magnetic sensors," in IEEE 2002 28th Annual Conference of the Industrial Electronics Society. IECON 02, Sevilla, Spain, 2002, vol. 2, pp. 1693–1695, doi: 10.1109/IECON.2002.1185535.

Peng, F. et al. (2014), "Ultra-long high-sensitivity Φ-OTDR for high spatial resolution intrusion detection of pipelines," Opt. Express, vol. 22, no. 11, p. 13804, Jun. 2014, doi: 10.1364/OE.22.013804.

Roy (2022), "Automated traffic surveillance using fusion of Doppler radar and video information," Mathematical and Computer Modelling, vol. 54, no. 1–2, pp. 531–543, Jul. 2011, doi: 10.1016/j.mcm.2011.02.043.

Walter, F. et al. (2020), "Distributed acoustic sensing of microseismic sources and wave propagation in glaciated terrain," Nat Commun, vol. 11, no. 1, p. 2436, Dec. 2020, doi: 10.1038/s41467-020-15824-6.

Wang, C. (2018), "Reliable Leak Detection in Pipelines Using Integrated DdTS Temperature and DAS Acoustic Fiber-Optic Sensor," in 2018 International Carnahan Conference on Security Technology (ICCST), Montreal, QC, Oct. 2018, pp. 1–5, doi: 10.1109/CCST.2018.8585687.

Wiesmeyr, C. et al. (2021), "Distributed Acoustic Sensing for Vehicle Speed and Traffic Flow Estimation", 2021 IEEE 5th International Conference on Intelligent Traffic and Transportation Proceedings (ITSC), p. 2596-2601, doi: 10.1109/ITSC48978.2021.9564517

ERASMUS+ PROJECT 'BENEFIT' – BOOSTING INNOVATION IN DIGITAL FARMING

Roman Danel, Marta Harničárová
VŠTE in České Budějovice
rdanel@mail.vstecb.cz, harnicarova@mail.vstecb.cz

Walid Khalilia
Al Istiqlal University, Palestine
walidkhalilia@pass.ps

Zuzana Palková
Slovak University of Agriculture in Nitra
zuzana.palkova@uniag.sk

Khalid Hardan
Al-Quds Open University, Palestine
khardan@qou.edu

Talat Tamimi
University of Hebron, Palestine
talatt@hebron.edu

Yahya Istaitih
Palestine Technical University - Kadoorie, Palestine
asteteyahya@yahoo.com

Jan Valíček, Michal Řepka
VŠTE in České Budějovice
valicek.jan@mail.vstecb.cz, repka@mail.vstecb.cz

DOI: 10.35011/IDIMT-2023-169

Keywords

BENEFIT, Erasmus+, digital farming, precious agriculture, EU–Palestine cooperation, Agriculture 4.0, aquaponics farm

Abstract

The article presents the Erasmus+ project BENEFIT implemented from 2020 to 2023 as an example of cooperation between universities in the European Union and Palestine. The key objective of the project was to support digital farms and the application of smart technologies in precision agriculture. The project was primarily focused on the university sphere, so one of the main outputs was the preparation of study courses related to precision agriculture at Palestinian universities, where European partners oversaw evaluation to ensure the courses met modern education quality requirements. The project also included developing new technologies and transferring ideas and solutions to the commercial sphere. This paper is focused on the part of the project solved at VŠTE in České Budějovice. Among other things, VŠTE analysed successful digital farm solutions in the Czech Republic and supervised some of the prepared training courses. As part of the project solution, a scientific meeting was also held in Prague in September 2022, where the method of aquaponics fish farming combined with the cultivation of useful plants (Aquaponia Hostomice) was presented to the Palestinian participants.

1. Introduction

In 2020, the project BENEFIT (609544-EPP-1-2019-1-PS-EPPKA-CBHE-JP, http://benefit.edu.ps) was launched. The project was run under the Erasmus+ Capacity Building for Higher Education programme by a consortium of Higher Educational Institutions (HEIs) from European Union (EU) countries – Czechia (VŠTE in České Budějovice), Slovakia (Slovak University of Agriculture in Nitra), Greece (University of Patras) and Bulgaria (University of Ruse) connected with five universities in Palestine (Al-Quds Open University, An-Najah National University, University Hebron, Al-Istiqlal University, Palestine Technical University 'Khadoorie') to address the challenges faced by Palestine regarding applying information and communication technologies (ICT) and technological innovations in agriculture. Digital farming, also called precision agriculture (PA), is an innovative concept in the Middle East, especially in Palestine. Precision agriculture is a whole-farm management approach using innovative technologies such as ICT, global navigation satellite system (GNSS) positioning data, remote sensing and proximal data gathering. This is not specifically only about the technologies but about the overall concept putting an accent on understanding how the technologies can make farming more accurate and controlled (Palková et al., 2022). In 'National Agricultural Sector Strategy 2017-2022 – Resilience and Sustainable Development' (2016), several key factors were identified that negatively impacted the development of (sustainable) agriculture: a weak capacity to keep up with technological progress, low competitiveness of local products and abandoning production processes. Automated robotic systems can bring agriculture flexibility in farmer decision making to select the optimal technological arrangements during the field crop production process, which entails economic, environmental and social aspects.

The main goals of the BENEFIT project are:

- Involve Palestinian HEIs in the PA research movement in Europe.

- Encourage Palestinian researchers and academics to have an interest in topics related to the concept, domains, tools and digital technology of PA (e.g. a wide array of items such as GNSS guidance, control systems, sensors, robotics, drones, autonomous vehicles, variable-rate technology, GNSS-based soil sampling, automated hardware, telematics and software).
- Define a qualification profile and the PA curriculum and elaborate assessment standards.
- Involve Palestinian farmers in PA processes, enhancing them with critical-reflective and creative skills.

Parallel with the abovementioned activities, the installation process was realised for equipment related to digital farming laboratories, including equipment deployment and testing. Al-Quds Open University established an innovative management structure to ensure the successful implementation of all activities and the collaboration of all partners to achieve the intended results and impact.

2. Methodology

The project's innovative character serves to the capacity building of Palestinian HEIs and addresses the challenges EU countries face regarding ICT, technological developments and creating a global research framework that will promote innovation and integration of the newest digital technologies into agriculture and rural development. The following actions have been proposed as possible solutions to these problems:

- Work with the private sector to keep abreast of new technologies and encourage their entry into the local market.
- Continuously train human resources in the agricultural sector to keep current with technical agricultural progress.
- Establish a hub for digital agriculture (BENEFIT Incubator).
- Develop a PA e-Repository.
- Design, pilot and evaluate the initial courses focusing on PA.
- Create an international PA research network.

Palestinian university teachers and researchers represent BENEFIT's primary target group. The second (indirect) group includes students, school teachers, innovators, media-related education and business (i.e. chambers of commerce) and policymakers. These groups will create a dynamic shift to launch the concept of digital farming into different sectors, particularly the commercial sector and practical implementation.

Moreover, having partners from EU countries will help Palestinian HEIs develop their quality of services on many levels, including the capacity building of academic and technical staff, setting up the project to European benchmarking standards and allowing for transparency and efficient monitoring and follow-up. Furthermore, as the project involves a consortium of diverse actors with varied methodologies, knowledge and skills, it would be crucial to have EU partners conduct the change and avoid potential obstacles as they have relatively extensive related experience.

In addition, the EU partnership will ensure that the project will be durable through a dissemination strategy. The EU partners will share the project's outcomes and outputs and create/facilitate new networking possibilities with other EU partners.

3. Case studies of digital farming in Czechia

To involve Palestinian HEIs in the PA research movement in Europe, VŠTE analysed existing PA projects in the Czech Republic. In this chapter, several case studies of successful projects are presented. The ideas of these projects can be a source of best practices for universities that participated in the BENEFIT project.

3.1. CleverFarm

An example of a successful PA startup is the Czech company CleverFarm, founded in 2016 (https://www.cleverfarm.ag/). The company offers a whole range of products and services to Czech farmers, with the company's main product being 'smart maps' in the form of a software application (the basic version is free, but additional modules can be purchased). Data from available maps of agricultural land are linked with data from the cadastre, satellite images and meteorological data. The application then supplements this data with information on compliance with agricultural and ecological regulations (fertilisation records, nitrate directive monitoring, Land Parcel Identification System, etc.). Furthermore, the application provides a three-day weather forecast for the monitored location.

Paid add-on modules allow the application to be connected to smart machines (e.g. tractors communicating via ISOBUS ISO 11783 interface) and thus manage, for example, fertilisation. Another module works with online soil sensors and includes an Internet of Things (IoT) Salinity sensor (measures soil moisture, temperature and conductivity), an Absorb soil sensor (measures water potential in the soil) and a Volumetric sensor (measures the volume of water in the soil). Sensors can be connected using SigFox, LoRa, or NB-IoT networks. They offer protection with an IP68 rating and are powered by batteries that have a lifespan of 1.5 to 2 years. The application can also predict selected plant diseases based on measurements (damage caused by corn borers, septoria and phaeosphaeria wheat spots, fusarium head blight or potato gangrene).

Soil sensor Salinity **Soil sensor Volumetric** **Soil sensor Absorb**

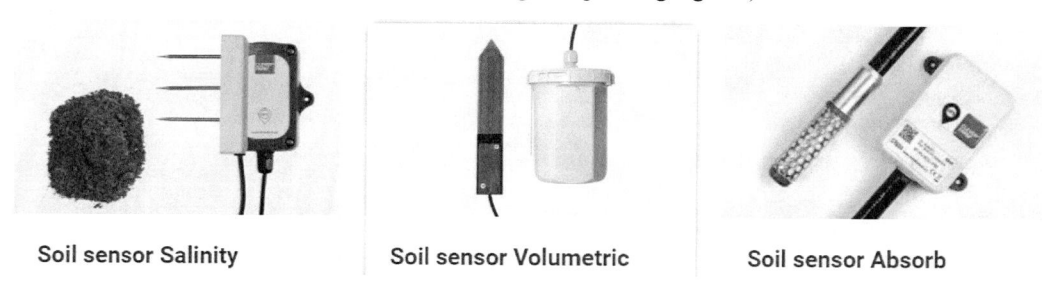

Figure 1. Soil sensors from CleverFarm   Source: (https://www.cleverfarm.ag/products/sensors/)

Another paid module of the application obtains current information from the cadastre (checking the validity of rental contracts, keeping an overview of paid rent, etc.) and creates documents for tax returns.

The CleverFarm system has been deployed in several agricultural enterprises and has references abroad. For example, it has been employed in Chile to cultivate sour cherries in water-scarce areas, where the optimisation of irrigation management has a significant impact on the economics of cultivation.

3.2. FishRAS

The FishRAS is a recirculation aquaculture system (RAS) project of students from the Czech University of Life Sciences, which consists of breeding fish in a system with a closed water cycle. The fish are kept in tanks with a filter system that cleans and oxygenates the water and returns it to the tanks. The main goal of this project is a significant reduction of water consumption, so this solution is especially attractive for countries facing limited water resources. Other advantages of RAS technologies are eliminating the threat of fish predators and preventing the spread of transmissible diseases.

Figure 2. FishRAS   Source: (Ryby-Vlček Facebook, 07-Mar-2019)

3.3. Vertical hydroponics – Feel Greens

A commercial application of vertical hydroponics can be observed in Fosfa a.s.'s Feel Greens farm in Břeclav, South Moravia (https://web.fosfa.cz/en/products/feel-greens/). It took three years to develop this multi-floor farming solution, which is particularly suitable for areas lacking space, such as densely populated regions or urban agglomerations. Compared to classic cultivation, this system only uses a tenth of the water. Hydroponics enables selling plants with a root ball, significantly prolonging their freshness during transport. Due to the closed water circulation and air filtration, no pesticides are needed, and cultivation has no waste. The company has plans to expand production in the near future.

3.4. Varistar

Varistar (https://www.variabilni-aplikace.cz/en/our-services/varistar-portal) offers added value by not selling specific products but a comprehensive service emphasising long-term operation. The company offers an application that integrates data collection from various sources, such as PlanetScope satellite images, soil analysis maps and drainage line maps, which make it possible to create maps of revenue potential and production zones. The system further enhances data utility by enabling Smart Scouting analysis, which helps identify potentially risky areas or zones where plants may fail. Preparing documents for variable soil processing or maps for variable stock fertilisation is also possible. The Varistar system enables connection with spreaders, sprayers and sowing machines of most major manufacturers, including AMAZONE, Bogballe, Fieldstar, Horsch, Kuhn, Kverneland, RDS, Vicon, Väderstad and others. Furthermore, the system supports remote (online) and unattended uploading of created application maps to the terminal of the application device.

3.5. Aquaponics Farm Aquaponia

During the BENEFIT scientific workshop in Prague in September 2022, Palestinian participants visited the aquaponics farm, Aquaponia s.r.o, in Hostomice (near Beroun, 50 km from Prague). The farm focuses on the production of tilapia, trout, sturgeon and African catfish and cultivating herbs such as basil, chives, and baby lettuce. Fish produce natural waste that provides essential nutrients plants require to develop. While the plants absorb nutrients and purify the water, the clean, oxygen-rich water is reintroduced to the fish ponds, reducing water consumption by about 90%. Both the fish and plant production are completely ecological, without any chemical additives. This model could be transferred to Palestine due to considerable water savings and the popularity of tilapia fish in the Jordan Valley.

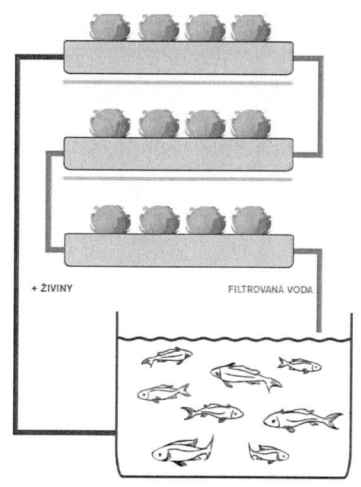

Figure 3. Scheme of aquaponics production Source: (https://aquaponia.cz/jak-to-delame/)

Figure 4. Aquaponics production – fish and plants. Aquaponia Hostomice Source: own

Although the conditions for agriculture in Palestine are different from the Czech Republic (different climate, legislation, etc.), the mentioned case studies of digital farming are focused on transferable technological aspects.

4. New digital farming courses and technologies developed at Palestinian HEIs within the BENEFIT project

Under the supervision of EU project partners, Palestinian universities prepared new courses focused on PA, bought new equipment for PA laboratories and developed new technologies. Some examples of the project BENEFIT outputs are described below.

4.1. AgriLive Monitoring System

A real-time monitoring system based on IoT technology, AgriLive, was developed at Al-Istiqlal University in Jericho to collect data and transmit it to cloud servers.

Figure 5. AgriLive sensor   Source: (Al-Istiqlal University, Dr Walid Khalilia)

AgriLive allows multiuser authentication and wireless connection. It is powered by either solar energy or battery and provides a wide range of hydrological sensors, including temperature, pressure, soil moisture, electrical conductivity (salinity), pH and flow meter, with the ability to control actuators like valves or pumps. Current data is presented as a real-time dashboard, while historical data is in the form of graph reports. This data can be exported to Mircosoft Excel for further processing. The system is currently utilised at student-managed date palm and banana farms.

4.2. Precision Agriculture Course at Palestinian Technical University Kadoorie

The course consists of six modules:

- Measuring Soil Moisture and Temperature in Precision Farming
- Precision Technology in Irrigation Scheduling – water flow in pipelines and open channels, programming and management of irrigation water and irrigation scheduling
- Precision Technology in Fertilizers Management – soil nutrients reaction and transformation, soil nutrients evaluation, methods of fertilisers application and fertiliser programming,
- Big Data Management
- Control of Smart Greenhouses – based on analyses by Gaikwad et al. (2016) and Dwinugroho (2021)

- Precision Technology in Poultry Farms and Hydroponic Units – principles of PA in crop and livestock production, data acquisition and management, the application of the sensor in poultry farms and in the cultivation of hydroponic barley
- Precision Technology in Plant Physiology

4.3. Digital Farming and Environmental Safety Course

This course, prepared by Al-Istiqlal University, reviews the principles of photogrammetry and remote sensing related to agriculture, land surveying, geographic information systems and environmental safety. It includes understanding the necessary mathematics and information technology concepts required for image processing and analysis. Photography and digital photography are covered, emphasising designing and creating the data required to obtain survey information following established standards. In May 2022, a BENEFIT project meeting at SZU Nitra (Slovakia) discussed the usage of unmanned aerial vehicles (UAVs) for detecting plant diseases. Čermáková and Danel (2022) published a detailed analysis of UAVs in PA, and project INVARO, which focuses on detecting invasive plants by UAV, was referenced. These findings can also be applied to the teaching of 'digital farming' courses prepared during the BENEFIT project.

5. Conclusion

Digital farming still represents a new field of science. Even if there are five agricultural faculties in Palestine, there are no specialists at the national level. Therefore, providing researchers at national universities with new experience and knowledge in PA is a national priority for Palestine. To accelerate the adoption of digital farming, researchers and technicians must intensively participate in scientific visits, workshops and training courses. The BENEFIT project and its activities can significantly improve the implementation of innovative technologies in agriculture in Palestine and increase the cooperation between the EU and Palestine.

Acknowledgement

This paper was supported from Erasmus+ project 609544-EPP-1-2019-1-PS-EPPKA-CBHE-JP.

References

Čermáková, I. and Danel, R. (2022). Usage of Unmanned Aerial Vehicles for detection of plant anomalies. 30th Interdisciplinary Information Management Talks: Digitalization of Society, Business and Management in a Pandemic, Prague, pp. 367-374.

Gaikwad, A., Ghatge, A. Kumar, H. & Mudliar, K. (2016). Monitoring of smart greenhouse. International Research Journal of Engineering and Technology (IRJET), India, 3(11).

Dwinugroho T. B., Hapsari Y. T. and Kurniawanti T. (2021). Greenhouse automation: smart watering system for plants in greenhouse using programmable logic control. Journal of Physics – conference series 1823(2021).

Palková, Z., Harničárová, M., Valíček, J., Stehel, V., Mihailov, N., Fragkaki, M., Khalilia, W. and Salameh A. (2022). Perspective of education in Agriculture 4.0 in selected countries in European Union and Palestine. 8th International Conference on Energy Efficiency and Agricultural Engineering, Ruse, Bulgaria.

Resilience and Sustainable Development – The State of Palestine Ministry of Agriculture. National Agricultural Sector Strategy 2017-2022 (2016). Online, Available at https://prais.unccd.int/sites/default/files/2018-07/English%20Strategy%202017-2022.pdf

MANAGEMENT OF ICT SYSTEMS

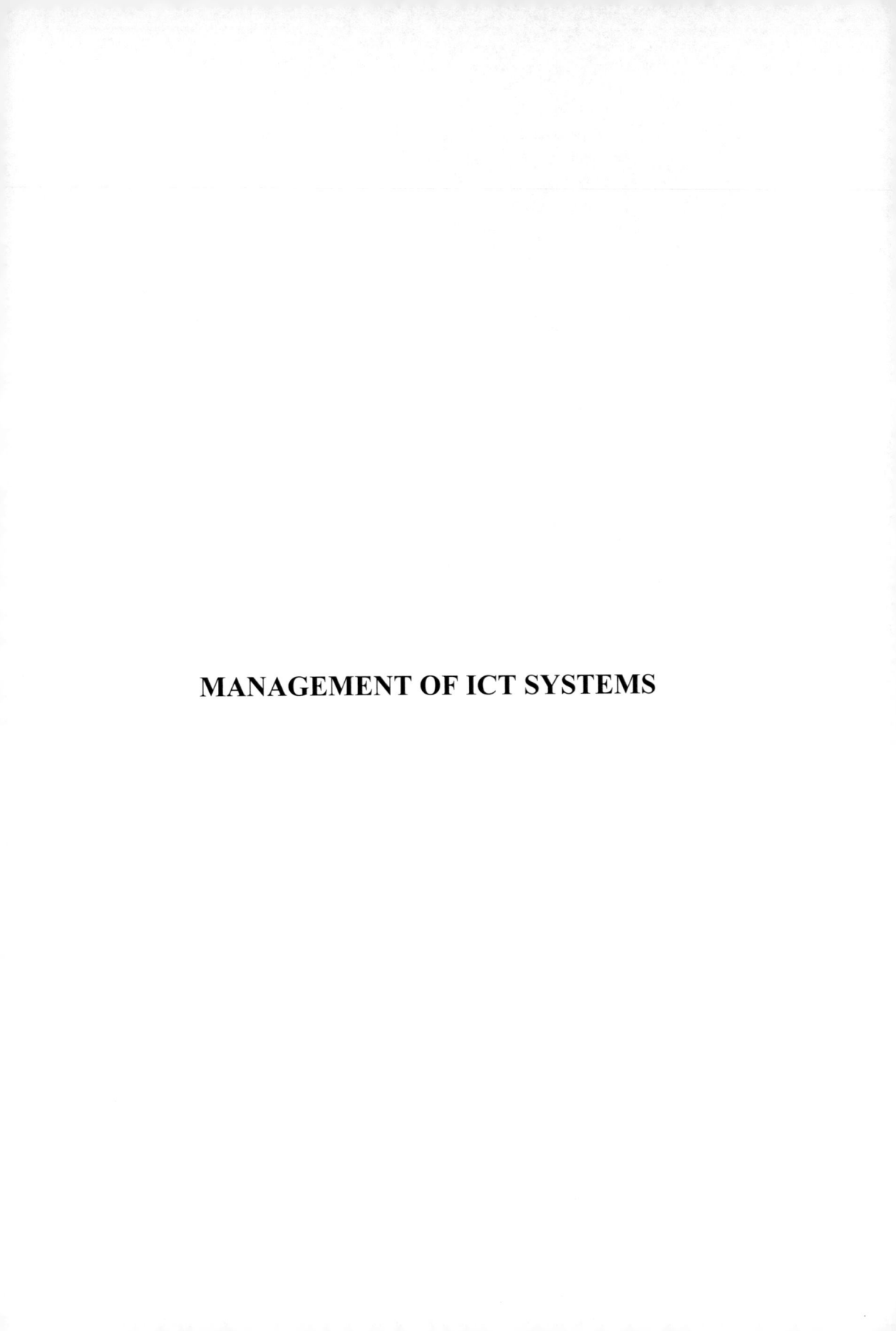

DIGITAL SERVICES AND PUBLIC ADMINISTRATION

Motto: Data must circulate not the citizen

Petr Doucek, Lea Nedomova

Faculty of Informatics and Statistics
Prague University of Economics and Business
doucek@vse.cz, nedomova@vse.cz

DOI: 10.35011/IDIMT-2023-179

Keywords

Digitalization, ICT penetration into public administration, digital public services, digital competencies

Abstract

One of the imperatives of the times is to vigorously reduce the costs of all business activities. This is no different in the state and public sector. One way is to digitise their agendas and digital communication between the state and the citizen. In this article we present the situation and development of digitalization in the Czech Republic. Firstly, its ranking among the EU countries, then we look at data mailbox services and the possibility of accessing e-government services in general. We measure the level of digitalization and state maturity within the EU using the DESI index - in 2022, the Czech Republic was ranked the 19th worst among EU member states. The use of data mailboxes is growing significantly in the Czech Republic, and users, however, focus mainly on downloading documents prepared for them by the state and public administration.

1. Introduction

The EU's goals in the area of digital transformation are defined in the communication: "2030 Digital Compass: The European way for the Digital Decade and "Path to the Digital Decade"(European Commission, 2023a) policy programme that sets up a governance framework and lists digital targets for 2030 based on four cardinal points: digital skills, digital infrastructures, digitisation of businesses and of public services. The EU is engaged on the pathway towards digital economies and societies with the twin (green and digital) transition accelerating the shift towards digitalisation and the use of digital tools for work and life purposes (European Commission, 2023b).

For the purposes of this paper, let us restrict the concept of digitalization (Gartners, 2022) to the introduction of information and communication technologies into public and government institutions. We will not be interested in the process of internal change of organisations and their organisational structures (and consequently the competences, skills and abilities of the staff of these institutions) - i.e. their back office, but in the digital services provided by these public and state administration institutions - i.e. their front office. The history of the development of digital services of the state to the citizen has a very long tradition. To some extent, their introduction and use reverses the role of the state and the citizen. The state is transferring many responsibilities and thus costs to the citizen. Information technology and digital communication enthusiasts are not even fully aware of how this transfer takes place. Older citizens or citizens with lower digital literacy then have problems using these services and are very often unable to take advantage of them. This brings us to the fundamental problem of digitisation - the acceptance of the functions offered by public and state administration by citizens.

One of the basic prerequisites for the successful digitalization (Gartners, 2022) of society is the penetration of information technology applications not only in the business sphere, e.g. in the form of electronic document exchange, electronic invoicing, ordering and purchasing goods via the Internet, etc., but also in public and state administration. In this sphere, digitisation represents a significant source of savings - but let us admit that it is mainly for the public administration and not for the citizen. However, not to take the side of the state and public administration alone, but for the citizen, digitisation saves time when travelling to offices and waiting in queues to have their requests processed. The disadvantage is the need for a higher level of digital literacy (digital competence) of the entire population and the availability of applications offered by the public administration to citizens.

The first question is what is digital competence. **Digital** competences are understood as cross-cutting key competences without which it is not possible to fully develop other key competences that are necessary for active participation in society and the labour market. However, the specific competences that make up **digital literacy** are not permanent, lasting competences (Peiro,2022). Here is also a permanent challenge for the education sector - the latest trend that has emerged in digital competences is artificial intelligence. We are not yet ready for it, even in the education sector, let alone in the business sectors or in government and public administration.

Data transmission and processing in the public and state administration is also a problem. Despite the more than 20 years of efforts of different Czech governments, the situation in this area is the most critical because of the considerable resistance of both officials and entire organizational units and structures against change (Bokša et al, 2019).

The aim of this article is to present the state of digitalization of the state administration in the Czech Republic, but also to point out the risks of digitalization. The risks are conceived in the broadest context, from financial risks to risks in the knowledge and skills of both officials and citizens.

2. Methodology

For the preparation of this article, materials available from public portals of the Czech Republic were used. An important source is data from the Czech Statistical Office (CZSO, 2023), from which we drew data on the situation in the Czech Republic. Other data from the Czech Republic environment is the Annual Report on the activities of the NKU for the year 2022 (NKU, 2022). For an overall view of the positioning of the Czech Republic within the European Union countries, we drew mainly from the European Union documents - (European Commission, 2023a, 2023b) and additionally from the source (Gartners, 2022). Thus, the basic techniques were the study of documents and the presentation of relevant information from them.

3. Results

To start the analysis of the digitalization of the Czech Republic, let us look at the comparison of the development of the Digital Economy and Society Index (DESI index) recorded by the Czech Republic since 2022 (Doucek et al., 2022; European Commission, 2021). Here we see that the Czech Republic has fallen one place from 18th place in 2021 to 19th place in 2022. This fall was caused by a significant improvement in the position of Italy, which moved up four places. Although this is a drop, the position at the top of the last third of EU countries is still not very flattering for the Czech Republic. THIS is the positioning in the digitalisation of the entire Czech society.

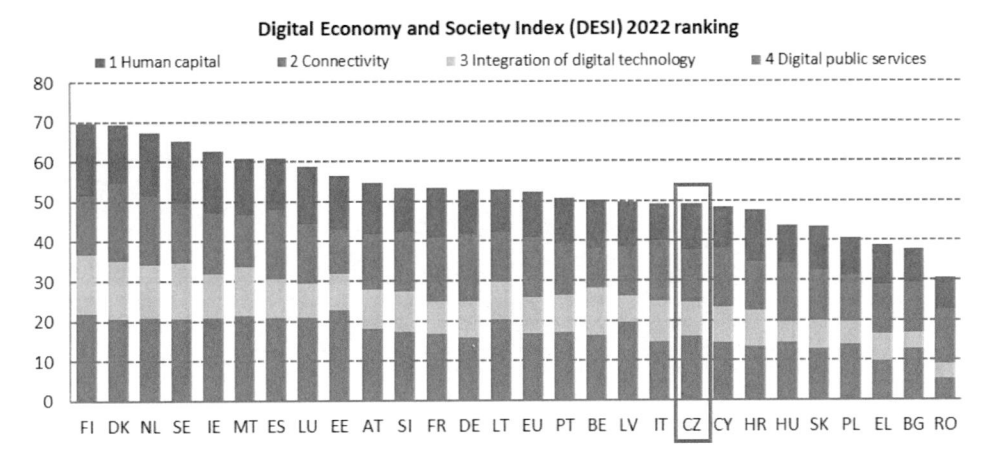

Figure 1. Digital Economy and Society Index 2022 for EU countries   Source: (European Investment Bank, 2023)

The situation is a bit different if we look at the development of digitalisation in individual companies in the Czech Republic. The EIBS Corporate Digitalization Index (CDI index). Here, the development of digitalisation is no longer at such a low level and the Czech Republic ranks somewhere towards the median of the European Union - at the end of the strong players and ahead of the average players - 14th overall.

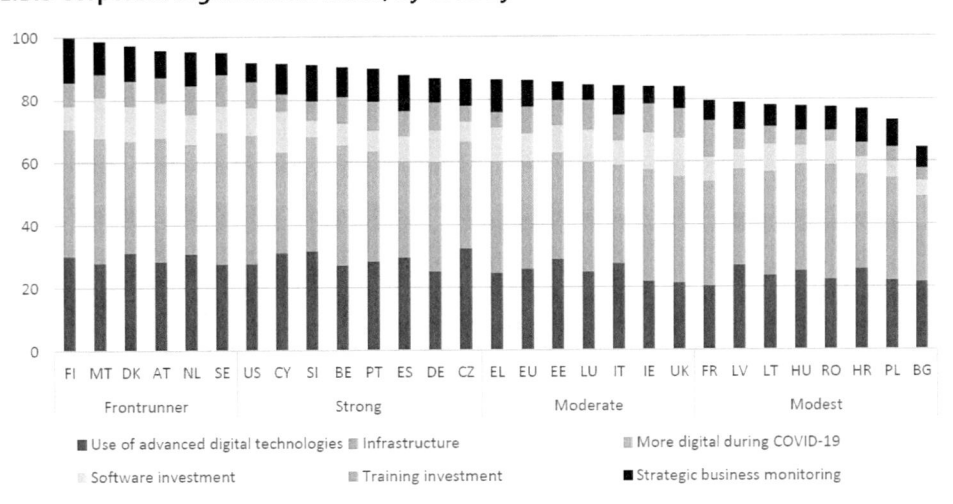

Figure 2. Corporate Digitalization Index 2022   Source: (European Investment Bank, 2023)

In both indices, as shown in Figure 1 and Figure 2, the dominance of Finland and Denmark, which are among the European leaders in the digitalization of both business and society, is unclear. An interesting comparison is then the graph shown in Figure 3. Here it is the correlation between the CDI index and the DESI index.

The data in Figure 3 clearly show the dominance of the Scandinavian countries - Finland, Denmark, Sweden together with the Netherlands. The Czech Republic is in the middle of the ranking of the EU countries.

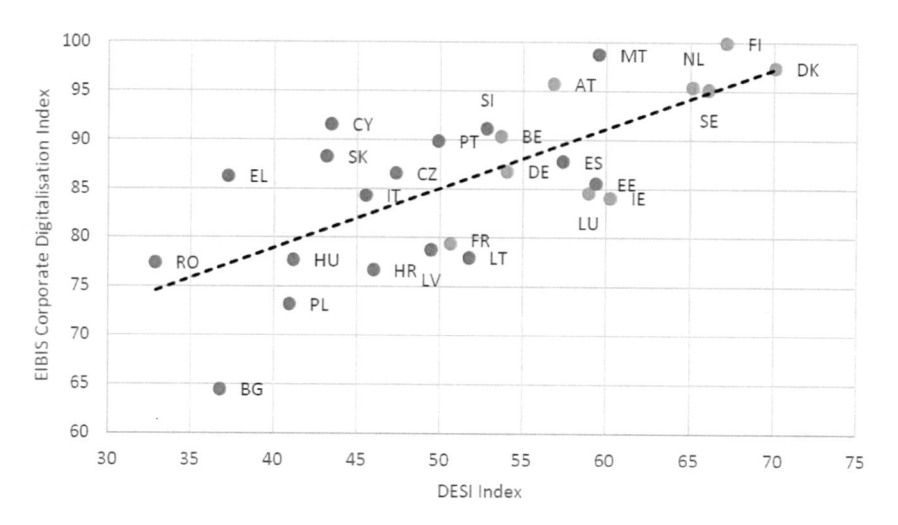

Figure 3. Relationship between CDI index and DESI index   Source: (European Investment Bank, 2023)

The conclusion for comparing the level of digitisation of the EU countries according to the CDI and DESI indexes is clearly for Scandinavia and then for the traditional Western European countries. The post-communist countries tend to rank in the bottom third of the EU countries in terms of digitalisation, with the exceptions of Estonia and Slovenia. Here, the digitalisation of society is developed at the level of advanced European countries. In the DESI, the Baltic states of the former Soviet Union (Lithuania and Latvia) are even more developed among the post-communist states. Here we can state the working hypothesis that the development was made possible by the overall size of the countries and the focus of their economies.

But let's take a look at how the digitisation of public and state administration in the Czech Republic looks like. Let us look at some key indicators that characterise the level of digitisation - or the possibility of digital communication between the state and the citizen in the Czech Republic. Given the limited scope of the paper, we will focus on two key indicators that ensure communication between the state (local government) and the citizen. These are the indicators of the number of public contact points where citizens can use e-government services, and the second is the number of data boxes available to citizens for this communication.

3.1. Digital contact points for citizens

We can see at which places a citizen can contact the state and public administration in the following Table 1. The dynamics of the increase can be seen in the period 2015 - 2022, when the number of contact points decreased by 57, mainly due to the decrease in the number of them at post offices. The Czech Post is currently undergoing reorganisation, with approximately 300 branches to be closed. This will also lead to a reduction of public contact points where citizens can use e-government services.

Table 1. Number of contact points for citizens 2015-2022

	2015	2020	2022
Total	7 942	7 893	7 885
Municipal and city authorities	6 398	6 398	6 398
Post Offices	981	949	941
Notary offices	399	435	435
Other places	91	111	111

The policy of the state in making digital services available to citizens clearly states that these services, or their availability, must be provided by citizens themselves from home by connecting first to the Internet and then to the relevant services provided by the state. The other option then is to go sin and office - this aspect should of course have been the main attraction for making digitalisation work - you do not have to go to the office. Thus, over the last seven years, there has not been any significant development of contact points, but rather a reduction (according to the state, optimization).

The main communication tool for the transfer of digital data between the citizen and the state are, of course, the so-called data boxes. A data box is a repository where the state sends a message to the citizen and the citizen is obliged to communicate with the state via the data box. Data boxes are operated by the Ministry of the Interior of the Czech Republic. By law, their mandatory owners are state and public administration authorities, legal entities, natural persons engaged in business (from 1 January 2023) and citizens who have voluntarily had a mailbox set up. The introduction of a data box turns the legal understanding of the delivery of information somewhat on its head. In the paper-based system, the state had to prove that it had delivered the message to the citizen (recipient). This was done by the institution of the so-called registered letter, where the recipient acknowledged receipt. From then on, the legal time limit for responding to the information or request of the state ran. In today's "mailbox" era, a message is legally considered to have been received by the recipient ten days after delivery to the mailbox, and all time limits run from then on. Thus, data boxes reverse the principle of provability for receipt of information or a message. It is the recipient, not the sender, who becomes responsible. How has the number of data boxes grown?

3.2. Data boxes

The basis of communication between the citizen and the state is the so-called Data Box. The increase in the number of data boxes was mainly caused by the legal obligation for individual economic entities. We will certainly see a further increase in 2023, when natural entrepreneurs will also become mandatory users of the mailboxes. In 2022, there were approximately 2,000,000 of them according to the register of economic entities.

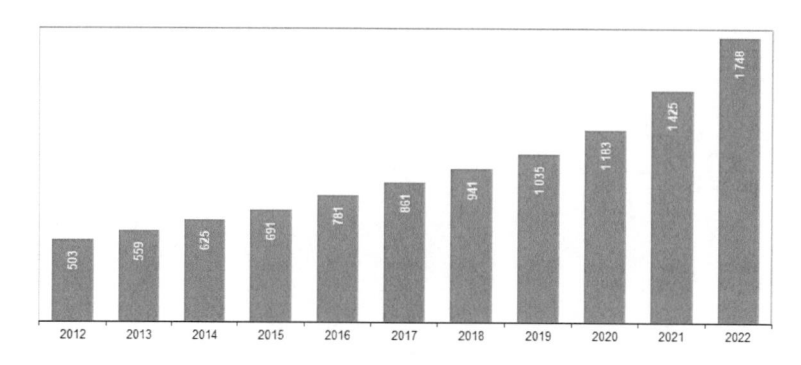

Figure 4. Number of data boxes in 2012-2022

As can be seen in Figure 4, the number of mailboxes AND the number of users of digital services is increasing. Let's take a look at what data boxes are used for and what purpose citizens use them for. Table 2 shows this usage by gender, age and education.

3.3. What data boxes are used for

The use of data boxes for three main tasks is shown in Table 2.

Table 2. Use of data boxes in 2022

	Download of official document in (%)	Submission of request or notification in (%)	Appointments made at the office in (%)
Total (16 years and older)	**48,1**	**28,0**	**13,2**
men	50,3	26,1	14,3
Women	45,9	29,8	12,2
Age group			
16-24 years	56,4	19,2	7,0
25-34 years old	61,6	30,4	18,6
35-44 years old	62,5	34,9	22,3
45-54 years old	60,4	35,3	18,5
55-64 years old	47,4	32,7	10,9
65-74 years old	23,3	21,9	5,1
75 years and over	9,1	9,8	1,6
Educational attainment (25-64 years)			
secondary school without matriculation and below	43,3	24,2	10,7
secondary school with a high school diploma	63,0	36,8	18,6
College	74,3	42,9	27,8

The data from Table 2 shows that the primary communication through data boxes is "Download of an official document" - i.e. passive communication of the citizen. Relatively more often, the citizen already sends messages to the authorities electronically (professionally, we think that he probably brings the applications to the authorities personally in order to have a certified paper version of the copy. The data box does not allow for unlimited archiving of documents and the document is automatically deleted after 90 days in the data box). Another observation is that people of working age (25-65 years) make more use of the data box services. And a very strong dependence on the use of data boxes is due to the level of education - higher education more frequent use of data boxes. The gender influence on the use of data box services is not very clear.

4. Conclusions

Since 2014, when the European Commission compiled the Digital Economy and Society Index (DESI), the Czech Republic has ranked 19th worst in 2022.

In an international comparison of the level of digitalisation of the economy and society, the Czech Republic has deteriorated for the second year in a row. However, it has managed to improve in the DESI sub-indicator of digital public services. Nevertheless, in the area of online pre-filled forms of public and state administration bodies, the share of pre-filled forms remains at 41%, while the EU average is 64%. The share of pre-filled forms shows how the state and public administration can use the information it already has about citizens (NKU, 2023).

Another major problem in the Czech Republic is the introduction of digitisation - not voluntary, but by law. To further increase the level of digitisation, it will therefore be necessary to make a number of legislative changes in the Czech legal system.

Communication and data transfer between ministries is not at the appropriate level (extraction of data once obtained from citizens for other ministries). Inter-ministerial coordination has been left on a voluntary basis and there is generally very little data exchange between ministries.

Acknowledgement

Paper was processed with support from institutional-support fund for long-term conceptual development of science and research at the Faculty of Informatics and Statistics of the Prague University of Economics and Business (IP400040) and the project IG 409033.

References

Bokša, M., Bokšová, J., Horák, J., Pavlica, K., Strouhal, J., & Šaroch, S. (2019). *Digitální Česko v digitální Evropě*. ŠKODA AUTO VYSOKÁ ŠKOLA o.p.s., ISBN 978-80-87042-75-5

CZSO. (2023). *Informační společnost v číslech 2023. Česká republika a EU. Informační technologie*. Český statistický úřad. Available at: https://www.czso.cz/csu/czso/informacni-spolecnost-v-cislech-2023

Doucek, P., Hološka, J., Nedomová, L. (2022). Management and digitalization. In: *IDIMT-2022 Digitalization of Society, Business and Management in a Pandemic*. Linz: Trauner Verlag Universität, pp. 35–42. ISBN 978-3-99113-758-0. DOI: 10.35011/IDIMT-2023-.

European Commission. (2021). Digital Economy and Society Index 2021: overall progress in digital transition but need for new EU-wide efforts. Available at: https://ec.europa.eu/commission/presscorner/detail/en/ip_21_5481

European Commission. (2023a). *Europe's Digital Decade: digital targets for 2030*. Available at: https://ec.europa.eu/info/strategy/priorities-2019-2024/europe-fit-digital-age/europes-digital-decade-digital-targets-2030_en

European Commission. (2023b). *Shaping Europe's digital future. DIGITAL Europe Work Programme 2023-2024 (.pdf)*. Available at: https://digital-strategy.ec.europa.eu/en/activities/digital-programme

European Investment Bank. (2023). *Digtalization in Europe 2021 – 2022: Evidence form the EIB Investment Survey*. European Investment Bank, ISBN 978-92-861-5233-7, DOI:10.2867/76258

Gartners, (2022). Information Technology – Gartner Glossary. Available at: https://www.gartner.com/en/information-technology/glossary/digitization

NKU. (2022). *Výroční zpráva o činnosti NKÚ za rok 2022*. Nejvyšší kontrolní úřad. Česká republika. Available at: https://www.nku.cz/cz/publikace-a-dokumenty/vyrocni-zprava/vyrocni-zprava-nku-za-rok-2022--id13098/

Peiró, J. M., Martínez-Tura, V. (2022). Digitalized' Competences. A Crucial Challenge beyond Digital Competences. *Journal of Work and Organizational Psychology,* 38(3), 189-199. https://doi.org/10.5093/jwop2022a22, Available at: https://journals.copmadrid.org/jwop/art/jwop2022a22

DIGITAL TRANSFORMATION AT THE NATIONAL, REGIONAL, AND LOCAL LEVELS OF PUBLIC ADMINISTRATION: A CASE OF THE CZECH REPUBLIC

Martin Lukáš, Tereza Burešová, Miloš Ulman, Martin Havránek, Jan Jarolímek

Department of Information Technologies, Faculty of Economics and Management,
Czech University of Life Sciences Prague
lukas@pef.czu.cz, cizkovat@pef.czu.cz, ulman@pef.czu.cz, havranek@pef.czu.cz,
jarolimek@pef.czu.cz

DOI: 10.35011/IDIMT-2023-187

Keywords

Public administration, digital transformation, enterprise architecture, local and national strategy, local and regional services

Abstract

Digital transformation (DT) of public administration entails major socio-technical and political changes to deliver positive, tangible changes in peoples' lives. Delivering the outcomes of the DT projects becomes increasingly difficult to manage as factors of organizational structuring, technologies, and innovation efforts play role. As the DT strategies are developed at the national level, little is known about how these strategies are adopted and implemented at the regional and local levels of government. We present a case based on a survey in two local municipalities and two regions in the Czech Republic. While municipalities reported a much higher number of specific and partial goals of DT, the regional administration offices about half of the risks and twice more strategic intentions than the municipalities. DT planning and implementation creates a knowledge and skills gap between local, regional, and national levels of public administration. Further research is needed on the barriers and challenges of DT at the lower levels of public administration.

1. Introduction

Digital transformation (DT) has been increasingly focused on by researchers, practitioners, and politicians (Siegel & Gabryelczyk, 2021). In the public sector, DT aims to bring positive, tangible changes in people's lives, which makes it different from mere information technology (IT) enabled transformation that is more focused on improving the operation of an entity through IT (Agarwal et al., 2010; Khisro, 2021; Vial, 2019). DT is commonly initiated by a strategic document developed by the government or a respective country's legislative body that defines DT programs and projects.

Delivering the outcomes of the DT projects becomes increasingly difficult to manage as factors of organizational structuring, technologies, and innovation efforts come into play (Hafseld et al., 2021; Meyerhoff Nielsen, 2019). The governance of the DT is grounded in the legislation of the country, which might be quite extensive (Mergel et al., 2021). The responsibilities for digitalization are distributed horizontally to several ministries and vertically across various administrative levels (Mergel et al., 2021). While the central government bodies usually have enough human, financial, and technical resources to manage large-scale DT initiatives, these resources are substantially smaller at the lower levels, which makes DT a challenging task (Hafseld et al., 2021). Regional and local public bodies mostly rely on consultancy companies invited to develop adapted DT strategy documents, formulate specific projects, and even implement these projects (Mergel et al., 2021).

Failures in DT initiatives are attributed to the lack of understanding of DT complexity and the interconnections between institutional arrangements, legislation, technologies, and information use (Gong et al., 2020; Khisro, 2021). DT projects implemented at the national level often fail due to frequent changes and discrepancies in legislation (Janssen et al., 2013), a low commitment of project sponsors, intra- and inter-organizational politics (Loukis & Charalabidis, 2011), and ineffective project management and planning (Anthopoulos et al., 2016). In contrast, the success rate of small-scale regional DT projects is higher since they are less complex, focused on a narrower target group, and easier to manage. The evidence of DT mostly focuses on national government projects and usually does not go beyond consultancy reports. The knowledge of DT projects' benefits and day-to-day practices at the regional and local levels of public administration is rather limited (Bousdekis & Kardaras, 2020). Therefore, we formulate the following research question: What are the differences between the local and regional levels of public administration regarding DT goals, projects, and risks?

The paper analyzes how regional and local public administration bodies adopt the national DT strategy. We particularly focus on analyzing DT's strategy, goals, and risks to identify gaps between the national DT strategy and the approach at lower levels of public administration.

The paper is structured as follows. First, we outline the issues with DT of public administration at different administrative levels, illustrate them on several examples of DT projects, and provide more details on the Czech national DT strategy. Further, we present findings from a survey with respondents from two local municipalities and two regional administrations. Based on the survey, we analyze the differences in the complexity of the DT strategy development and identify differences between the regional and local public bodies. In the final section, we discuss our findings and suggest further research work.

2. Literature review

2.1. Digital transformation in public administration

DT of public administration is a process that results in a public administration that fully uses digital technologies. DT typically includes the modernization of public administration with the possibility of electronic access to public services. DT should facilitate faster, cheaper, and better public services (EC, 2020). Productivity gains, reduction of the administrative burden of public services, sustainable innovation, and overall higher public sector resilience are benefits of DT that underpin the UN's global Sustainable Development Goals (Meyerhoff Nielsen, 2019).

DT is a socio-technical and socio-political solution (Hafseld et al., 2021), especially in large, complex democracies or companies with diverse stakeholders. Challenges faced during a large-scale DT project in a democratic society with a fragmented government resemble those of a large multinational company (Datta, 2020). The evidence shows that a strong governance model, coordination, and intergovernmental coordination are essential requisites to successfully deliver DT initiatives, such as in Denmark or Germany (Mergel et al., 2021; Meyerhoff Nielsen, 2019).

Projects become the main tool of the DT (Hafseld et al., 2021). However, overreliance on external consultants and state-owned IT service providers hinders the sustainability of project outcomes after the contracts expire or projects end (Mergel et al., 2021).

A study of a large Swedish municipality with 100,000 citizens showed that despite successfully creating the DT strategy and its implementation, practitioners tended to balance tensions of stability, short-term requirements, and stability. However, a national DT strategy's long-term goals remained in haze due to the daily focus on short-term benefits and the struggle with legacy systems. This showed that despite the municipality's sufficient human, technical, and financial resources, prioritizing digitalization activities and goals remained difficult (Khisro, 2021).

The importance of know-how of managers to lead DT initiatives at the local level was highlighted by Pittaway and Montazemi (Pittaway & Montazemi, 2020) in a study of 11 local administrations in Canada. DT projects are mainly implemented by external private partners with the necessary DT know-how. Unlike codified knowledge, e.g., stored in the form of files, transfer of external know-how is difficult mainly because of the context in which it was created. If a local peer municipality wants to obtain the know-how of another local municipality that gained experience from a successful DT project, several requisites must be met. Both governments need to develop mutual social ties, incentivize local government executives and knowledge workers, and create the absorption capacity of the recipient administration (Meyerhoff Nielsen, 2019).

2.2. Digitalization Strategy of the Czech Republic

According to the annual Digital Economy and Society Index, the Czech Republic ranked 19th place in 2022, which was below the EU's average. While the integration of digital technology and the level of basic digital skills are above average, digital public services use remains low. Although the level of human capital is high, most Czech companies and public institutions struggle to find digitally skilled workers due to a huge shortage in the labor market. Further improvements in digital public services quality, incentivizing businesses and citizens to use them, and implementing the "once only" principle are yet to be seen (EC, 2022).

The key strategic document for DT is Digital Czechia (Digitální Česko), and the innovation strategy is The Country of the Future. Digital Czechia consists of three interlinked sub-strategies targeting different beneficiaries: the Czech Republic in Digital Europe, the Information Concept of the Czech Republic (Digital Public Administration), and the Digital Economy and Society Concept. In total, Digital Czechia DT strategy sets out 17 main objectives and 116 sub-objectives User-friendly and efficient online services for citizens and businesses, digitally friendly legislation, development of an environment supporting digital technologies in the field of eGovernment, increasing the capacities and competencies of public administration employees, and efficient and centrally coordinated ICT public administration are among the main objectives of the national DT strategy (Czechia, 2023). The key instruments for implementing the strategy are legislation, enterprise architecture (EA) and business architecture, TOGAF (a framework for managing enterprise architecture), and ArchiMate (a graphical modeling language for EA) (MOI, 2022).

Large infrastructural projects representing the backbone of digital public services were already implemented by the end of the first decade of the 21st century. Since then, the only remarkable DT project has been Bank ID, which allows everyone with a mobile or online bank account to access digital public services. As the Czech Republic ranks at the top in the EU in mobile banking and e-commerce uptake, introducing Bank ID might accelerate the higher use of digital public services. Although less visible, several successful regional DT projects exist, such as the Regional Data Network of the Pardubice Region, the Regional Communication Infrastructure of the Karlovy Vary Region, and the citizen portal in various municipalities. Consistent with the literature (Hafseld et al.,

2021), the number and scale of unsuccessful and failed IT projects in Czech public administration are alarming (e.g., an interactive human resources portal at a major ministry).

3. Methodology

We took a mixed-method approach consisting of a survey and semi-structured interviews with key decision-makers in three local public administration bodies from different regions of the Czech Republic between 2020-2022. One of the authors worked as a senior external consultant on the projects for these public institutions that should help analyze the current state of digitalization and identify opportunities for DT with a special focus on improving their client services.

The representatives of two local and two regional administrations participated in the survey. The first local administration was Bílina, a town with 17,000 inhabitants in the Ústí nad Labem Region. The second body was Písek, a town with about 30,000 inhabitants in the South Bohemian Region. The third was the regional administration of the Pardubice Region, with a population of about 520,000 people. The fourth was the regional administration office of the Karlovy Vary Region, with a population of about 283,000 people. The subjects for the survey and semi-structured interviews were managers and staff of various departments, top management (the governor of Pardubice Region and the deputy governor of the Karlovy Vary Region), representatives of subordinated organizations (e.g., a communal services company), IT staff and managers, and elected representatives. We facilitated interviews in all four organizations. They took about one hour each, and their primary purpose was to map the status of digitalization in the department and organization, collect requirements for further, and identify opportunities to use existing centralized digitalization services. We administered the survey to Písek municipality, Pardubice Region, and Karlovy Vary Region respondents. In total, the surveys and interviews yielded responses from 252 respondents.

Finally, we analyzed respondents' answers to identify opportunities for new strategic digital transformation projects, creating a structured and visual representation of the newly proposed projects in project portfolios. We evaluated each proposed project from the perspectives of finance, time and resources, and goals, including a risk analysis. Further, we present a summary of findings from all three cases of DT strategy development in local public administration bodies.

4. Results

The main findings of the survey are summarized in Table 1. The indicators illustrate the scope and potential complexity of DT projects. While more than twice as many strategic plans were identified in the regional administration office of the Pardubice region as in the surveyed municipalities, the number of strategic plans in the regional administration office of the Karlovy Vary region was approximately 1.5 times as many. The specific and partial goals were significantly lower in both county offices than in both cities. The regional administration office of the Karlovy Vary Region had 2.5 fewer projects than the regional administration office of the Pardubice Region but with a much higher number of identified risks. We calculated the average project length, number of goals, and number of risks from the survey data.

Due to the requirement to approve digitization projects with budgets over 6 million CZK, the City's countywide digitization projects were approved by the Department of the Chief Architect of e-Government of the Ministry of the Interior. The project application includes an EA of the organization, including an analysis of the current state, schemas in ArchiMate, and answers to several questions regarding the processes and IT systems operated by the organization. Therefore, the lower-level authorities needed to strengthen their capacity and obtain the necessary competence to prepare the applications.

Respondents agreed they needed to look for co-financing from EU funds and the National Recovery Plan for projects within their budgets in all four cases.

The region was much farther in accomplishing partial goals set out by the national strategy than the towns. At the same time, the number of projects was significantly higher in towns but with fewer identified risks.

Further projects mentioned by the representative of local administrations were to extend the data center and current citizens' portal and launch a new mobile app for citizens. The regional administration office of Pardubice Region and the regional administration office of Karlovy Vary Region planned to update their website, increase free software and open standards, and introduce a collaborative platform for remote meetings and authorized voting of the regional council and various boards and committees.

Table 1. Overview of the DT goals, projects, and risks in selected public administration bodies

Table title	City Hall of Bílina	City Hall of Písek	Regional administration office of Pardubice Region	Regional administration office of Karlovy Vary Region	Total
Strategic intentions *)	21	21	43	33	118
Specific goals	35	32	20	11	98
Partial goals	48	49	15	26	138
Projects	10	13	41	17	81
Risks	24	28	14	71	137
Number of respondents	13	31	136	72	252
Form of information collection	Interview	Interview, survey	Interview, survey	Interview, survey	N/A
Average Project Length (months)	27,0	46,2	29,2	39,4	N/A
The average number of specific goals/project	3,5	2,5	0,5	0,7	N/A
The average number of partial goals/project	4,8	3,8	0,4	1,5	N/A
The average number of risks/project	2,4	2,2	0,3	4,2	N/A

*) Strategic intentions are linked to the Digital Czechia national strategy goals

The risk analysis was part of the survey results analysis. Both towns reported almost twice more risks as the region (Table 2). This may signalize the lack of competencies to manage DT projects and limited resources.

Table 2. Overview of risk severity

Overview of risk severity			
	Green	Amber	Red
City Hall of Bílina	6	11	7
City Hall of Písek	2	14	12
The regional office of the Pardubice Region	7	5	2
The regional office of the Karlovy Vary Region	14	27	30
Total	29	57	51

5. Discussion and conclusion

The lack of competencies and resources at the local level of public administration for developing an adapted DT strategy and implementing projects is partially due to an absence of broader coordination and governance, such as in Denmark (Meyerhoff Nielsen, 2019). Since Germany has similar advanced bureaucracy and IT legacy systems as the Czech Republic, focusing on co-creating DT strategy at all levels of government and with external actors might be one of the ways forward. However, this process cannot be driven bottom-up by frontline workers. We also recorded instances when, e.g., the region governor articulated his skepticism about the digitalization of certain processes. Lack of support or distrust of top management in digitalization efforts is one of the typical causes of project failure (Anthopoulos et al., 2016).

The presented results showed the gap between developing and implementing DT strategies at the national, regional, and local levels of public administration. We confirmed several practical implications for managers of public administration bodies, internal and external project managers, risk managers, and subject matter experts of administrative or self-government authorities and agencies, as well as external consultants, enterprise architects, project and program managers, and IT vendors. We plan to extend the survey to a wider sample of public institutions.

The main implication for DT managers is to pay more attention to the barriers and challenges of DT at the lower levels of public administration and the factors and variables that influence different approaches to decision-making regarding digital government projects. The data analysis showed differences between the number of strategic intentions, goals, projects, and risks at different levels of public administration. The reasons might be political issues as the main variable influencing digital government decisions, financial issues such as (lack of budget, incomparable volumes of budget sizes on different levels of public administration), and political leadership, which significantly impacts DT support. Researchers should consider these factors in further research on digitalization in public administration.

Acknowledgement

This paper was supported by the Internal Grant Agency of the Faculty of Economics and Management CZU Prague, grant no. 2023B0005.

References

Agarwal, R., Gao, G., DesRoches, C., & Jha, A. K. (2010). Research commentary—The digital transformation of healthcare: Current status and the road ahead. Information Systems Research, 21(4), 796–809.

Anthopoulos, L., Reddick, C. G., Giannakidou, I., & Mavridis, N. (2016). Why e-government projects fail? An analysis of the Healthcare. gov website. Government Information Quarterly, 33(1), 161–173.

Bousdekis, A., & Kardaras, D. (2020). Digital transformation of local government: A case study from Greece. 2020 IEEE 22nd Conference on Business Informatics (CBI), 2, 131–140.

Czechia. (2023). Digital Czech (Digitální Česko). https://digitalnicesko.gov.cz

Datta, P. (2020). Digital transformation of the Italian public administration: A case study. Communications of the Association for Information Systems, 46(1), 11.

EC. (2020). A Europe fit for the digital age. https://commission.europa.eu/strategy-and-policy/priorities-2019-2024/europe-fit-digital-age_en

EC. (2022). Czech Republic - DESI Country Profile. https://digital-strategy.ec.europa.eu/en/policies/countries-digitisation-performance

Gong, Y., Yang, J., & Shi, X. (2020). Towards a comprehensive understanding of digital transformation in government: Analysis of flexibility and enterprise architecture. Government Information Quarterly, 37(3), 101487.

Hafseld, K. H. J., Hussein, B., & Rauzy, A. B. (2021). An attempt to understand complexity in a government digital transformation project. International Journal of Information Systems and Project Management, 9(3), 70–91.

Janssen, M., van Veenstra, A. F., & van Der Voort, H. (2013). Management and failure of large transformation projects: factors affecting user adoption. Grand Successes and Failures in IT. Public and Private Sectors: IFIP WG 8.6 International Working Conference on Transfer and Diffusion of IT, TDIT 2013, Bangalore, India, June 27-29, 2013. Proceedings, 121–135.

Khisro, J. (2021). Strategizing Digital Transformation: A Clinical Inquiry into a Swedish Public Sector Organization. AMCIS 2021 Proceedings. 7

Loukis, E., & Charalabidis, Y. (2011). Why do eGovernment projects fail? Risk factors of large information systems projects in the Greek public sector: An international comparison. International Journal of Electronic Government Research (IJEGR), 7(2), 59–77.

Mergel, I., Porth, J., Bickmann, F., Schweizer, P., & Feller, Z. (2021). Digital transformation of the German state. In Public administration in Germany (pp. 331–355). Springer International Publishing Cham.

Meyerhoff Nielsen, M. (2019). Governance lessons from Denmark's digital transformation. Proceedings of the 20th Annual International Conference on Digital Government Research, 456–461.

MOI. (2022). eGovernment Architecture of the Czech Republic. https://archi.gov.cz

Pittaway, J. J., & Montazemi, A. R. (2020). Know-how to lead digital transformation: The case of local governments. Government Information Quarterly, 37(4), 101474.

Siegel, U. A., & Gabryelczyk, R. (2021). Exploring value streams and CSFs to foster digital transformation in public administration. AMCIS 2021 Proceedings. 10

Vial, G. (2019). Understanding digital transformation: A review and a research agenda. The Journal of Strategic Information Systems, 28(2), 118–144.

ASSESSMENT OF AN OPEN GOVERNMENT DATA READINESS – A CASE OF SLOVENIA

Mirjana Kljajić Borštnar, Andreja Pucihar

University of Maribor, Faculty of Organizational Sciences
mirjana.kljajic@um.si, andreja.pucihar@um.si

DOI: 10.35011/IDIMT-2023-195

Keywords

Open government data, use, maturity, impact measurement, Slovenia

Abstract

The concept of open government data (OGD) has evolved in the past decade and gained a lot of attention. The notion that OGD will enable series of economic, social and environmental transformations is driving the governments to make their data sets available to be freely used, reused and shared by anyone. Open data maturity serves as a benchmark to gain insights into the development achieved in the field of open data by governments in Europe. However, there is still little known about the use and impact of open data by users (i.e. enterprises, organizations). In this paper, we provide an overview of open data, focusing on the assessment of use and impact of open data. For this purpose, we analysed secondary sources, such as open data maturity reports, open data portals, assessment frameworks and based on that provide an agenda for future research.

1. Introduction

The concept of open government data was first coined in the early 2000. In Europe, European Parliament, Council of the European Union issued *Directive 2003/98/EC of the European Parliament and of the Council of 17 November 2003 on the Re-Use of Public Sector Information* (2003). Since then, numerous countries and organizations have embraced the concept of open government data, leading to the establishment of open data portals, policies, and initiatives across the globe. In 2019, European Parliament and Council of the European Union issued a Directive on open data and the re-use of public sector information (European Parliament, 2019), which replaced the directive from 2003. The movement of open government data has continued to evolve, with advancements in technology, data standards, and practices supporting the ongoing development of open government data ecosystems.

Open data refers to data that anyone can access, use and share (data.europa.eu); can be freely used, re-used and redistributed by anyone (Handbook, n.d.). In the context of public sector, this data is referred to as open government data (OGD) or open public sector data (Zuiderwijk in Janssen, 2014). Open government data represent one of the biggest sources of open data and is usually published as a collection of public datasets on the specialized government open data portals (i.e. data.europa.eu, https://podatki.gov.si/). The purpose of OGD is to stimulate the transparency of governments operations, responsibility and added value creation. "Open Government Data (OGD) is a philosophy- and increasingly a set of policies - that promotes transparency, accountability and value creation by making government data available to all." (OECD, n.d.).

As public sector organizations generate, collect and process ever increasing amounts of data, consequently the number of open data initiatives and research is also increasing (Attard et al., 2015; Safarov et al., 2017). By making their databases accessible, public institutions also become more interesting for citizens' political participation (E. H. J. M. Ruijer & Martinius, 2017), the creation of businesses and innovative services focused on citizens is encouraged (E. Ruijer et al., 2020). The long-term aim is to ensure the general transparency of government information (Jaeger & Bertot, 2010).

There are a number of open government data policies and initiatives on different government levels, however the systematic research on the impact of OGD is still scarce (Bachtiar et al., 2020; Çaldağ & Gökalp, 2022; Zuiderwijk et al., 2021; Attard et al., 2015). Among important challenges identified in the literature, there are OGD impact measurement (Apanasevic, 2021; Cvetkov & Ljubljana, 2021; Ruijer & Martinius, 2017; Safarov et al., 2017; Ubaldi, 2013), open data maturity (Çaldağ & Gökalp, 2022; Alromaih et al., 2016; Rahmatika et al., 2019; Doodds & Newman, 2015), availability and quality of data, cost and legal barriers (Welle Donker & van Loenen, 2017; Weerakkody et al., 2017; Wieczorkowski, 2019). By impact we mean the economic and social effect, which is demonstrable contribution to society and economy, and a benefit for individuals (Economic and Social Research Council, n.d.). The problem with assessing impact is that the socio-economic effect is hard to quantify, since the effects are usually indirect, and that there could be impacts to other fields as well (environment, political, scientific etc).

Several institutions and organizations measure the maturity of open data initiatives and the openness of government as for example: European Commission – Open Data Maturity (Assen et al., 2022), OECD – Open Government Data – OURdata Index (OECD, 2020), World Wide Web Foundation - Open Data Barometer (Foundation, 2018) and Open Data Watch - Open data inventory (ODIN) (Open Data Watch, n.d.). The problem with these assessments is that each institution measures different dimensions of open data maturity with different criteria. For example, European Commission's Open data maturity measures four dimensions: policy, portals, impact and quality. OECD's OURdata Index provides composite index of three dimensions data availability, data accessibility and government support data re-use. Furthermore, Open Data Barometer does not provide information for all countries, while ODIN focuses on evaluation of the coverage and openness of data provided on the websites maintained by national statistical offices and any official government website that is accessible from its site. Another problem of these measurements or assessments is the method for data collection. In almost all cases, the expert survey is used for national data collection. This leads to the results that are self-perceived and can be based on self-assumption and as such biased, especially if the person involved is not an expert and if there is no second control for data provided.

Having these challenges in mind, we address the problem of open government data maturity assessment and provide insights for small European country Slovenia. Slovenia adopted its first law on access to public data in 2003, which was later revised several times, and finally in April 2016 adopted the regulation on the transfer and reuse of information of a public data. Since 2003 the first public datasets were being published, but the government open data portal OPSI was established in 2016 (podatki.gov). The published open data is in line with open data standards and European open government data portal (https://data.europa.eu). As stated in the regulation, the authorities should enable the re-use of public information by making them freely available on the web in open standards, machine-readable form, together with metadata, except when this would entail a disproportionate effort beyond a simple procedure. Also, there are exceptions when it comes to personal data, which fall under General data protection regulation (Caserman et al., 2016). For the purpose of this paper, we have conducted meta-analysis of the secondary sources about the maturity and impact assessment of OGD in Slovenia. We present the analysis results and provide critical analysis of the measurement approaches with recommendations for future research.

2. Methodology

Meta-analysis of publicly available data sources has been used to analyse the state of open data use in Slovenia. We have reviewed available data sources in Slovenia and EU on the following topics:

- open (government) data use (government reports, Open data maturity report, OECD reports, project reports),
- Open data portal OPSI, Data Europa portal.

We have further analysed the European Commissions' Open data maturity report (Assen et al., 2022), the country questionnaires (https://data.europa.eu/en/publications/open-data-maturity/2022), the Report on the economic-social impact of open data in Slovenia (Likar & Štrukelj, 2021) and synthesized the findings.

3. Assessment of current state of open government data maturity in Slovenia

Open government data in Slovenia are published on the OPSI portal since 2016 (https://podatki.gov.si/). Currently, there is about 8000 datasets published within 14 categories (population & society – 1390; justice, legal system & public safety – 181; public sector - 390, Education, culture & sports – 1152; social & employment – 366; Health – 702; environment & space – 878; transport & infrastructure – 605; agriculture, fisheries, forestry & food – 400; finance & taxes – 499; economy – 945; energy – 146; science & technology – 251; international affairs - 14).

Datasets are catalogued and can be searched by the organization or geographical area (regional, local administration), and are equipped with metadata, such as terms of use, availability, description, licence, language, legal grounds etc. (Figure 1). A user can access datasets in different formats, i.e. csv, xls, zip, doc or program interface (API). Users can leave feedback (write to editor), rate data openness (1-5 stars), like or post a use-case. This is a very valuable information for the policy makers, since the open data maturity is currently being assessed mostly by the state of legal and technical grounds and evidence of use, and these are the use-cases reported by the users or recorded from the publicly available information. There are several initiatives that promote the use of OGD, such as organizing hackathons and datathons at the universities, faculties, research institutions, technology transfer organizations, university incubators, chamber of commerce and other business support organizations. Every year all organizations are asked to report about their OGD activities and results to the national OGD office, now working under Ministry of Digital Transformation of Republic of Slovenia.

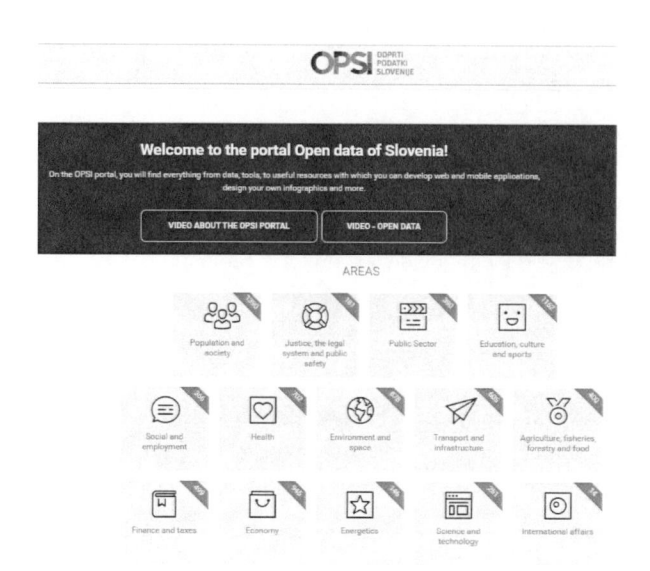

Figure 1. OPSI portal

One of the studies that aimed to quantify the economic impact of the OGD in Slovenia followed the (Huyer & van Knippenberg, 2020) methodology. Although Likar & Štrukelj (2021) state that this is the most methodologically correct way to quantify the economic impact, it still relies on quite a few assumptions. Huyer & van Knippenberg (2020) based their assessment of open data market value on country's GDP with an assumption that the average open data share of GDP is 1,33% and the median is 1,19%. Likar & Štrukelj (2021) further assumed that since Slovenia is above the EU28 average on the open data maturity ladder (66% in 2019), this number should be adjusted by Slovenia's open data maturity ranking in 2019, which is then 1,352%. According to Likar & Štrukelj (2021) for Slovenia the baseline open data market size in 2019 was estimated at 654 million € (with GDP being 48,393 million €). Assessment of GDP and open data market size from 2019 to 2025 according to the baseline scenario is shown in Figure 2.

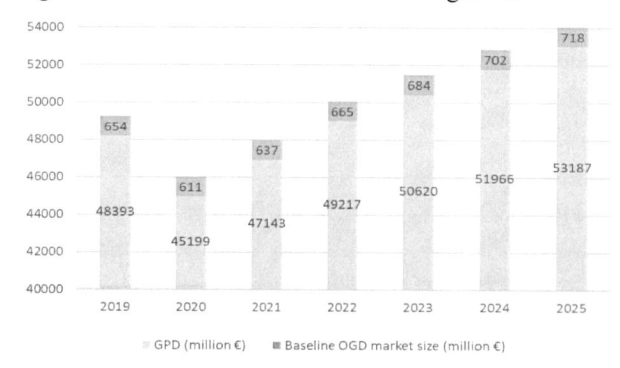

Figure 2. Baseline scenario for the open data market growth forecast for Slovenia Source of data: (Likar & Štrukelj, 2021)

On the European level, each year the open data maturity report on the 35 European countries (EU27 + 8) is published on the data.europa.eu portal. Open data maturity is assessed on four dimensions: Policy, Portal, Impact, and Quality (Figure 3). An EU27 average for 2022 is assessed for Policy

86% (Slovenia 90%) and it consists of three indicators: Policy Framework, Governance of open data, Open data implementation. Further, Open data impact (EU 71 %, Slo 76 %) consists of Strategic awareness, measuring reuse, Created impact, Political impact, Social impact, Environmental impact, Economic impact. The third dimension, Open data portal (EU 83 %, Slo 94%) consists of Portal features, Portal usage, Data provision, Portal sustainability. The last, fourth dimension is Open data quality (EU 77 %, Slo 92 %) and consists of four indicators: Currency and completeness, Monitoring and measures, DCAT-AP Compliance[1], and Deployment quality and linked data.

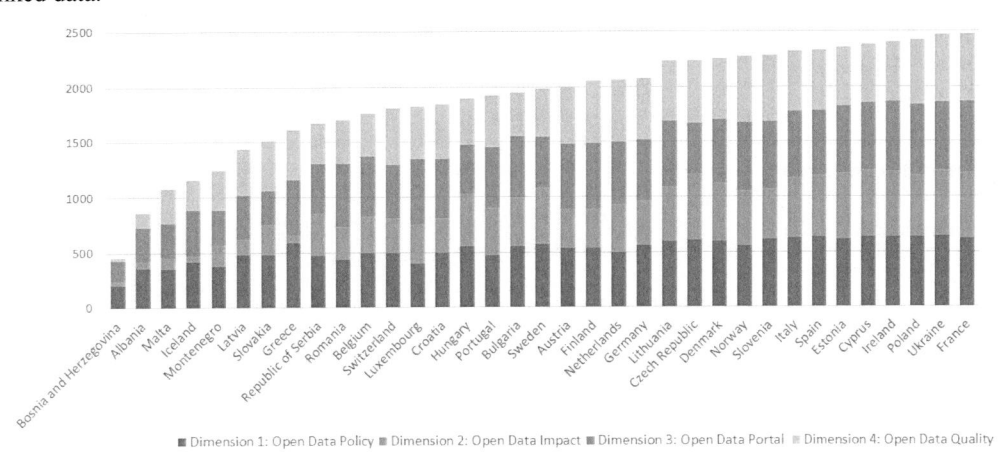

Figure 3. Open data maturity report 2022 country overview   Data source: (https://data.europa.eu/)

As can be observed in Figure 3, Slovenia is quite high on the open data maturity level in 2022, achieving 90% score and belongs to the second cluster, named Fast-tracker, behind France, Ukraine, Poland, Ireland, Cyprus, Estonia, Spain and Italy.

In Figure 4 we present the dimension with the highest score among countries is the Open data policy (blue), following by Open data portal (green) and Open data quality (Yellow). The lowest and most divergent scores are of the dimension Open data impact. This is expected since there is still no consensus on the definition of what open data impact is or how to measure it. The assessment of impact relies on monitoring and measuring the re-use of open data and based on that measuring the impact of open data on specific governmental, societal, environmental, and economic challenges of our time (Assen et al., 2022).

A closer look into Open data impact dimension ranking shows how diverse the scores are between the countries (Figure 5). An interesting observation is that some countries with higher GDP (i.e. Austria scored 355 points out of 600) have scored much lower compared to some countries with lower GDP (i.e. Republic of Serbia which scored 385 out of 600), while Slovenia scored 76%.

---

[1] The **DCAT Application profile for data portals in Europe** (DCAT-AP) is a specification based on W3C's Data Catalogue vocabulary (DCAT) for describing public sector datasets in Europe. https://joinup.ec.europa.eu/collection/semantic-interoperability-community-semic/solution/dcat-application-profile-data-portals-europe/release/11

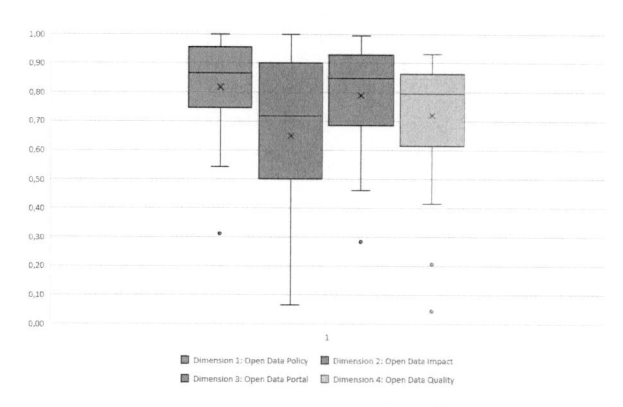

Figure 4. Box whisker diagram for four open data maturity dimensions   Data source: (https://data.europa.eu/)

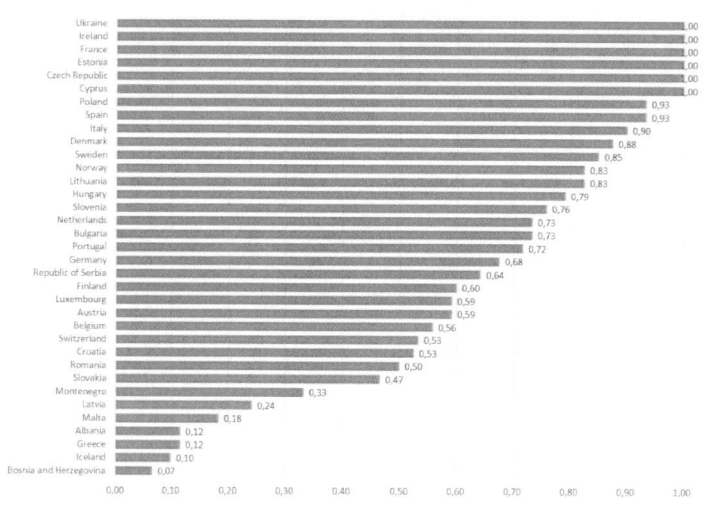

Figure 5. Country rankings according to the Open data impact dimension   Data source: (https://data.europa.eu/)

4. Disscusion and Conclusions

We addressed the problem of open government data assessment, with a special focus on Slovenia. For this purpose, we analysed secondary sources, mainly reports of open (government) data in the European countries (Open data maturity report, OECD report, Open data barometer, OPSI portal). We found that there are many open data initiatives and reports on the policy and implementation level globally. It is assessed that 55% of the countries worldwide have an open data initiative in place (Reis, M. S., Ladio, A. H., 2016). However, there is still a lack of understanding about the impact that open government data have on added value creation and sustainable development goals. The open data maturity report, for example, uses open-end questions and subjective quantification of goal achievement to collect the data on OGD impact in a specific country. Compared to the digital economy and society index (DESI) ((European Commission, 2022), where data is collected by a validated questionnaires through national statistical offices, the open data maturity report ranking should be considered with caution.

While surveys provide an important information on OGD, governments still struggle with lack of resources (people and funding) for collecting, maintenance and exchange of data, since they have other priorities in their work (Zuiderwijk & Janssen, 2014). It is understanding of the impact and potential of open government data that would contribute to putting OGD on the higher list of government priorities (Verhulst & Young, 2016). It is the understanding that "Open data has no value in itself; it only becomes valuable when used." (Janssen et al., 2012, pp. 260).

Based on our investigation and results provided in this paper, we may conclude, that further research is needed in OGD assessment as open data have high potential for the market and society. Our paper provides only first insights into the OGD assessment with particular focus to Slovenia and as such provide only limited understanding in this field. One of the possible future research directions could be related to comparison of different dimensions and criteria used for OGD maturity assessment. Also, country specific case studies as well as longitudinal observations would provide further understanding of OGD initiatives evolvement.

Acknowledgement

This research was supported by the Slovenian Research Agency: Program No. P5-0018— Decision Support Systems in Digital Business.

References

Alromaih, N., Albassam, H., & Al-Khalifa, H. (2016). A proposed checklist for the technical maturity of open government data: An application on GCC countries. *ACM International Conference Proceeding Series*, 494–499. https://doi.org/10.1145/3011141.3011211

Apanasevic, T. (2021). Socio-economic effects and the value of open data: A case from Sweden. *ITS Biennial Conference*. https://www.econstor.eu/bitstream/10419/238004/1/Apanasevic.pdf

Assen, M. van., Cecconi, G., Carsaniga, G., Lincklaen Arriëns, E. N., Dogger, J., & European Union. Publications Office. (2022). *Open data maturity report 2022.* https://doi.org/10.2830/70973

Attard, J., Orlandi, F., Scerri, S., & Auer, S. (2015). A systematic review of open government data initiatives. *Government Information Quarterly*, *32*(4), 399–418. https://doi.org/10.1016/j.giq.2015.07.006

Bachtiar, A., Suhardi, & Muhamad, W. (2020). Literature review of open government data. *2020 International Conference on Information Technology Systems and Innovation, ICITSI 2020 - Proceedings*, 329–334. https://doi.org/10.1109/ICITSI50517.2020.9264960

Çaldağ, M. T., & Gökalp, E. (2022). The maturity of open government data maturity: a multivocal literature review. *Aslib Journal of Information Management*, *74*(6), 1007–1030. https://doi.org/10.1108/AJIM-11-2021-0354

Caserman, M., Zatler, R., Veršič, A., & Prešern, M. (2016). *Priročnik za odpiranje podatkov javnega sektorja*. Ministrstvo za javno upravo. http://www.mju.gov.si/

Doodds, L., & Newman, A. (2015). *Open Data Maturity Model*. 32. https://theodi.org/article/open-data-maturity-model/

Economic and Social Research Council. (n.d.). *What is impact? - Economic and Social Research Council*. ESRC. https://esrc.ukri.org/research/impact-toolkit/what-is-impact/

European Commission. (2022). *Digital Economy and Society Index – DESI*. https://digital-strategy.ec.europa.eu/en/library/digital-economy-and-society-index-desi-2021

European Parliament. (2019). Directive (EU) on open data and the re-use of public sector information, 2019/1024. *Official Journal of the European Union*, *L 172*(January 2003), 56–83. http://data.europa.eu/eli/dir/2019/1024/oj

Directive 2003/98/EC of the European Parliament and of the Council of 17 November 2003 on the re-use of public sector information, (2003) (testimony of Council of the European Union European Parliament). https://eur-lex.europa.eu/legal-content/en/ALL/?uri=CELEX:32003L0098

Foundation, W. W. W. (2018). *World Wide Web Foundation (2018). Open Data Barometer - Leaders Edition* (Issue September). https://opendatabarometer.org/doc/leadersEdition/ODB-leadersEdition-Report.pdf

Handbook, O. D. (n.d.). *What is open data?* https://opendatahandbook.org/guide/en/what-is-open-data/

Huyer, E., & van Knippenberg, L. (2020). The Economic Impact of Open Data. In *Brussels: European Commission. Retrieved March* (Vol. 11). https://doi.org/10.2830/63132

Jaeger, P. T., & Bertot, J. C. (2010). Transparency and technological change: Ensuring equal and sustained public access to government information. *Government Information Quarterly*, 27(4), 371–376. https://doi.org/10.1016/j.giq.2010.05.003

Janssen, M., Charalabidis, Y., & Zuiderwijk, A. (2012). Benefits, Adoption Barriers and Myths of Open Data and Open Government. *Information Systems Management*, 29(4), 258–268. https://doi.org/10.1080/10580530.2012.716740

Likar, B. (University of P., & Štrukelj, P. (University of P. (2021). *Report on the economic-social impact of open data in Slovenia.* https://podatki.gov.si/sites/default/files/reports/Economic-social impact of open data in Slovenia.pdf

OECD. (n.d.). *Open Government Data.* https://www.oecd.org/gov/digital-government/open-government-data.htm

OECD. (2020). *OECD Open, Useful and Re-usable data (OURdata) Index: 2019.* https://www.oecd.org/governance/digital-government/ourdata-index-policy-paper-2020.pdf

Open Data Watch. (n.d.). *Open Data Inventory (ODIN).* https://odin.opendatawatch.com/

Rahmatika, M., Krismawati, D., Rahmawati, S. D., Arief, A., Sensuse, D. I., & Dzulfikar, M. F. (2019). An open government data maturity model: A case study in BPS-statistics Indonesia. *2019 7th International Conference on Information and Communication Technology, ICoICT 2019*, 1–7. https://doi.org/10.1109/ICoICT.2019.8835352

Reis, M. S., Ladio, A. H., N. P. 2014. (2016). ODB Global Report Third Edition. *The World Wide Web Foundation*, 48. http://opendatabarometer.org/doc/3rdEdition/ODB-3rdEdition-GlobalReport.pdf

Ruijer, E., Grimmelikhuijsen, S., van den Berg, J., & Meijer, A. (2020). Open data work: understanding open data usage from a practice lens. *International Review of Administrative Sciences*, 86(1), 3–19. https://doi.org/10.1177/0020852317753068

Ruijer, E. H. J. M., & Martinius, E. (2017). Researching the democratic impact of open government data: A systematic literature review. *Information Polity*, 22(4), 233–250. https://doi.org/10.3233/IP-170413

Safarov, I., Meijer, A., & Grimmelikhuijsen, S. (2017). Utilization of open government data: A systematic literature review of types, conditions, effects and users. *Information Polity*, 22(1), 1–24. https://doi.org/10.3233/IP-160012

Ubaldi, B. (2013). Open Government Data: Towards Empirical Analysis of Open Government Data Initiatives. *OECD Working Papers on Public Governance, NO.22*(22), 61. http://www.oecd-ilibrary.org/docserver/download/5k46bj4f03s7.pdf?expires=1400038714&id=id&accname=guest&checksum=0A581F24362C40FF67A6EF59C2B31BBB

Verhulst, S. G., & Young, A. (n.d.). *Toward an open data demand assessment and segmentation methodology.*

Weerakkody, V., Kapoor, K., Balta, M. E., Irani, Z., & Dwivedi, Y. K. (2017). Factors influencing user acceptance of public sector big open data. *Production Planning and Control*, 28(11–12), 891–905. https://doi.org/10.1080/09537287.2017.1336802

Welle Donker, F., & van Loenen, B. (2017). How to assess the success of the open data ecosystem? *International Journal of Digital Earth*, 10(3), 284–306. https://doi.org/10.1080/17538947.2016.1224938

Wieczorkowski, J. (2019). Barriers to using open government data. *ACM International Conference Proceeding Series*, 15–20. https://doi.org/10.1145/3340017.3340022

Zuiderwijk, A., & Janssen, M. (2014). Open data policies, their implementation and impact: A framework for comparison. *Government Information Quarterly*, 31(1), 17–29. https://doi.org/10.1016/j.giq.2013.04.003

Zuiderwijk, A., Pirannejad, A., & Susha, I. (2021). Comparing open data benchmarks: Which metrics and methodologies determine countries' positions in the ranking lists? *Telematics and Informatics*, 62(March), 101634. https://doi.org/10.1016/j.tele.2021.101634

UNRAVELING THE PROCESSES AND CHALLENGES OF ARTIFICIAL INTELLIGENCE IMPLEMENTATION IN THE SWISS PUBLIC SECTOR: A TOE FRAMEWORK ANALYSIS

Václav Pechtor, Josef Basl

Faculty of Informatics and Statistics
Prague University of Economics and Business
pecv06@vse.cz, josef.basl@vse.cz

DOI: 10.35011/IDIMT-2023-203

Keywords

Artificial Intelligence (AI), Public Sector, AI Adoption

Abstract

This research aims to comprehend the complex processes that underpin the adoption and implementation of artificial intelligence (AI) in the Swiss public sector, particularly the challenges that arise from these processes. Applying the Technology-Organization-Environment (TOE) framework, we examine six cases, evaluating the maturity levels of technical, organizational, and environmental processes and pinpointing the issues that emerge.

Our findings reveal that despite the widespread adoption of AI in other industries, the Swiss public sector faces unique hurdles tied to its implementation processes. A key challenge is the persistent concern around data protection and privacy, which hinders AI adoption even in the presence of existing encryption technologies. Our analysis also unveils other obstacles, such as infrastructure inadequacies, lack of top management support, and data management issues.

By dissecting these implementation processes and their associated challenges, this paper underscores the need for public administrations to not only implement existing data protection technologies but also to manage other crucial aspects of AI adoption efficiently. This study, therefore, bridges the research gap by identifying how data protection concerns and other factors inhibit AI adoption in the public sector. The insights derived from the TOE framework offer valuable guidance for improving AI integration processes, thereby advancing AI adoption more broadly.

1. Introduction

Artificial intelligence (AI) investments are constantly growing in the European Union. From 2018 to 2020, the European Commission reported growth from up to 94% (European Commission. Joint Research Centre., 2020). The absolute increase was from 8.2 billion EUR to 16 billion EUR annually. During the same period, the federal nondefense AI Budget grew from $0.56 billion to $1.43 billion (Zhang et al., 2021). In the EU, one-third of the investments are done in the public sector (European Commission. Joint Research Centre., 2020). These numbers show that the AI sector is growing worldwide and in the EU. It also shows that the public sector has made a significant contribution to AI investments and that AI is an essential technology for the public sector. The reason for this growth is the vast amount of available data, the advances in computer power, the growing complexity of models, and the new possibilities created by deep learning architecture (Poba-Nzaou & Tchibozo, 2022).

In parallel, researchers' interest in AI innovation and adoption is also significantly rising in the last few years (Mariani et al., 2022). Especially from 2018 onwards, we can see a sharp increase in published papers and systematic literature reviews (SLR) (Cubric, 2020). While public sector investments are one-third of the total investments in the EU, there is a large gap between AI research in the private and the public sector. A recent literature review showed that from 1142 articles, only 59 cover the specific application of AI in the public sector (van Noordt & Misuraca, 2020).

In response to the identified research gap, this study delves into the complexities of AI adoption in the Swiss public sector. By analyzing the processes involved and challenges occurring during AI implementation, we aim to understand how concerns about data protection and privacy, among other issues, are impeding the advancement of AI in this sector. This research contributes valuable insights that not only enhance understanding of the current state of AI adoption but also provide guidance for future efforts in the public sector.

To address this research gap, our study poses the following research question: What are the processes involved in AI implementation within the Swiss public sector, and how mature are these processes in Swiss public sector entities. By analyzing the dynamics of AI adoption within this context, the study aims to identify the state of the processes that enable AI implementation.

2. Theoretical Background

2.1. Artificial Intelligence in the Public Sector and the Associated Challenges

Despite growing interest in research and industry, there is still no unified definition for the term artificial intelligence (Neumann et al., 2022). This is somehow surprising because the term AI was coined for the first time during a conference in Dartmouth in 1956 by Stanford professor John McCarthy (Schaefer et al., 2021). Some papers mainly focus on the history, the changes, and current trends in defining AI (Ballester, 2021). One of the more recent and still valid definitions is "AI refers to the capability of a computer system to show humanlike intelligent behavior characterized by certain core competencies, including perception, understanding, action, and learning" (Wirtz et al., 2019). These definitions might change in the future if AI applications become more capable (Misuraca et al., 2020). There is not only a growing interest in artificial intelligence in the research community, but it also significantly impacts spending in this area. This trend can be perceived in the private as also in the public sector. The spending in the European Union more than doubled in the years from 2020 to 2022, from 10.7 billion EUR to 24 billion EUR (European Commission. Joint Research Centre., 2022). The public sector is responsible for 16% (1.7 billion EUR in 2020), and doubled in 2022. The rise in investments shows that there is growing confidence in the capabilities of AI. The possible potential of AI in the public sector was already recognized in research several years ago (Sousa et al., 2019). The most considerable potential is seen in the automation of processes and the associated improvement of the efficiency of the administration, together with cost savings (Schaefer et al., 2021). In general, using AI in public administration can lead to a higher level of output, better quality, and fewer errors resulting in better service quality for the citizen (Casalino et al., 2020).

While it is clear that there is potential and also planned investment in artificial intelligence, there are many challenges in adopting AI successfully in the public sector. One barrier is that the public sector inherently tries to avoid risk rather than maximize value, whereas the private sector mainly prioritizes value over risk and is, therefore, more motivated to implement new technologies like AI (Desouza et al., 2020). Another barrier is the penchant for bureaucracy and a hierarchical, centralized decision-making (Fatima et al., 2021). As a resource, data has a vital role in AI projects, but the maturity of data governance and data capabilities is often low in the public sector (Pencheva et al., 2020). To utilize the data in large volumes and provide enough computing power for ML models, it is crucial to have access to scalable infrastructure. The lack of such infrastructure is often a challenge in the public administration (Misuraca et al., 2020). Finally, the necessary resources and the appropriate funding are often insufficient (Schedler et al., 2019). An overview of the most common challenges can be found in Table 1.

Challenge	Authors
Bureaucracy and Centralized Decisions	(Desouza et al., 2020), (Fatima et al., 2021)
Data Availability, Management, Capabilities and Privacy	(Alexopoulos et al., 2019), (Ballester, 2021), (Campion et al., 2020), (Gong & Janssen, 2021), (Pencheva et al., 2020), (van Noordt & Misuraca, 2020)
Infrastructure	(Schedler et al., 2019), (van Noordt & Misuraca, 2020)
Lack of Strategy and Management Capabilities	(Ballester, 2021), (Desouza et al., 2020), (Gong & Janssen, 2021), (Schedler et al., 2019)
Resources and Funding	(Pencheva et al., 2020), (Schedler et al., 2019), (van Noordt & Misuraca, 2020)
Siloed Applications	(Gong & Janssen, 2021), (Pencheva et al., 2020)

Table 1. List of relevant articles highlighting the challenges of AI adoption

Given the multitude of obstacles associated with AI implementation in the public sector, it is crucial to delve further into the process of AI adoption within this context and examine established frameworks that elucidate the mechanisms underlying AI adoption.

2.2. Artificial Intelligence Adoption

The last three decades showed a vast evolution in research about technology adoption, creating models like Innovation Diffusion Theory (IDT), Theory of Planned Behavior (TBP), and Diffusion of Innovations (DOI) (Bryan & Zuva, 2021). Technology adoption can be defined as the "choice to acquire and use a new invention or innovation" and diffusion as "the process by which something new spreads throughout a population" (Schaefer et al., 2021).

There are different approaches to AI adoption using other frameworks. On the one side, there is research on AI adoption assigned to different sectors like the automotive (Demlehner & Laumer, 2020), agriculture (Issa et al., 2022), insurance (Gupta et al., 2022) or education (Almaiah et al., 2022). On the other side, there is a wide variety of approaches to explain how AI is adopted. Primarily, this research focuses on success factors (Hamm & Klesel, 2021; Neumann et al., 2022) or challenges and inhibitors (Alsheibani et al., 2019; Schaefer et al., 2021). In terms of frameworks, there is a focus on the individual factors (Vale Martins et al., 2021), like the TAM (Chatterjee et al., 2021), socio-technical models (Yu et al., 2023) and the very popular TOE (Alsheibani et al., 2019; Hamm & Klesel, 2021; Madan & Ashok, 2023; Neumann et al., 2022).

Overall, more research is focused on individual factors rather than at the firm or organizational level (Bryan & Zuva, 2021). However, adopting AI in the public sector, particularly in the context of data protection and privacy concerns, presents a unique set of challenges and processes that are not as thoroughly examined at the organizational level. This indicates a research gap in understanding how these concerns, among other factors, impact the technology adoption processes within the public sector. By focusing on this perspective, our study intends to contribute to this under-researched area significantly.

3. Methodology

Using a multiple case study and qualitative research approach, this study follows the method presented by (Gläser & Laudel, 2010). Although it is grounded on principles established by Mayring and Fenzl (Mayring, 2010), the method diverges in two aspects. First, no fixed categories are established following a trial run with a data sample, and second, the coding process for various attributes is exchanged by information extraction steps. This approach is particularly advantageous for reconstructing behaviors or processes through qualitative analysis. Given the focus on exploring AI adoption processes, this method was chosen for this paper. The process contains several consecutive steps, which are covered in this paper:

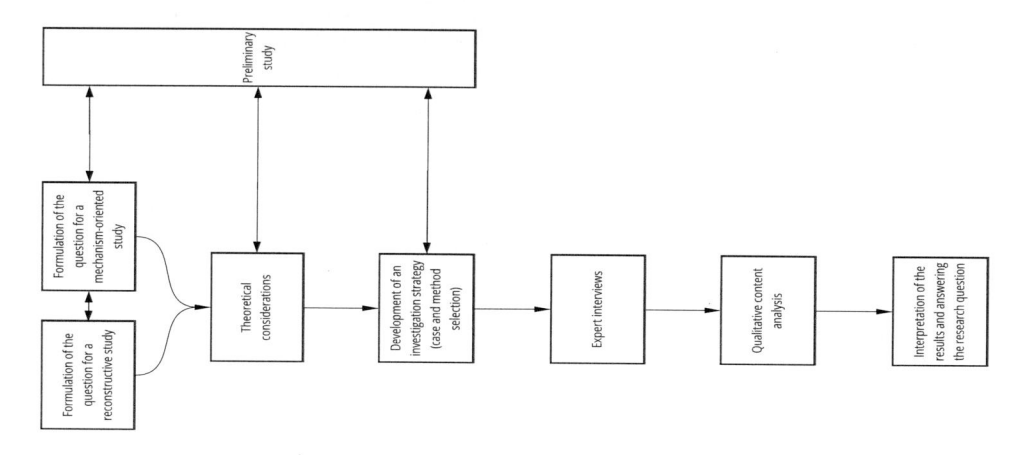

Figure 1. Research approach suggested by Gläser & Laudel

Chapter 1 addresses the research question and provides the theoretical background, while Chapter 2 delves into the initial stages of the qualitative study, including method development and case selection. Expert interviews receive a brief overview, with a more in-depth discussion of the findings presented in Chapter 4. Lastly, the methodology section concludes with an explanation of the qualitative content analysis process.

3.1. Case and Method Selection

Switzerland, scoring 68.49 on the Government AI Readiness Index, serves as a moderate example among Western European countries, exhibiting well-balanced capabilities in areas such as workforce, infrastructure, and policy environment. Its standing makes it an ideal benchmark for other countries, including those in Eastern Europe, such as the Czech Republic, which has a similar score of 67.05. Using Switzerland as a representative case, the study can provide valuable insights and lessons for countries with comparable AI readiness, offering a practical perspective on the challenges and opportunities associated with public sector AI adoption.

Within the Swiss public sector, we focused on entities of similar sizes, including medium to large cantons or large cities, as examples of public administration. To have a comparative benchmark, we also analyzed state-owned enterprises, which, although subject to stringent regulations and restrictions, operate with subtle distinctions compared to public sector administrations. This inclusion broadens the scope of the analysis while maintaining a focus on the public sector landscape.

Our selection encompassed four cantons (Cases C, D, E, G), one city (Case F), and one state-owned company, with the latter featuring distinct entities that were examined individually (Cases A and B). In each of these cases, we interviewed individuals who were either at the helm of AI initiatives or held positions closely related to AI, such as leading the analytics team. These discussions provided valuable insights into the AI adoption process within their respective organizations. They shed light on how they navigate the complexities of data protection and privacy, which are among the critical challenges identified in the current literature.

Due to the comprehensive nature of the TOE framework, which contains both internal and external factors, we used this framework as a guiding principle for our interviews. The TOE framework has previously demonstrated success in facilitating the adoption of various technologies, such as cloud computing and e-commerce, within numerous contexts (Chatterjee et al., 2021).

The TOE framework is well suited for analyzing technology adoption at the firm level, making it an effective tool for studies in this (Demlehner & Laumer, 2020). It has been previously used to research AI adoption in the general (Pumplun et al., 2019) and within the Swiss public sector (Neumann et al., 2022). By applying the TOE framework in our study, we aim to address the research gap by providing a comprehensive view of how organizations manage data protection and privacy when adopting AI, thereby offering valuable insights for both academic research and practical implementation.

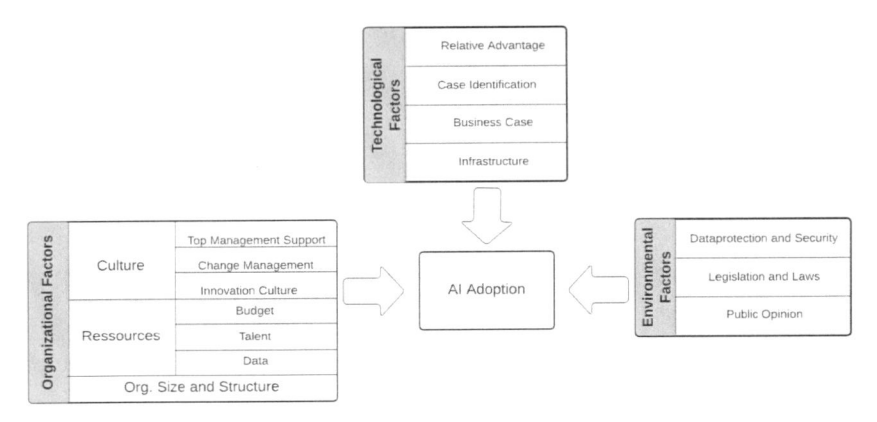

Figure 2. Adapted TOE framework   Source: author

Pumplun et al. already presented a TOE framework that was modified to explain AI adoption. Based on former research, we adapted to capture the specific aspects of the public sector. We added the Infrastructure as part of the technical factors because it is an essential factor of the public sector ICTs Field (Jansen, 2012), which is missing in earlier research approaches. Organizational size and structure were combined into one aspect because they are highly interconnected in the Swiss public sector. This structure guided the semi-structured interviews. Each category had at least one open-ended question to cover all the aspects provided by the TOE framework.

3.2. Expert Interviews

The interviews were conducted via online platforms during a four-month period spanning from January to April 2023, allowing for a comprehensive understanding of the AI landscape within the Swiss public sector. The online interviews, which lasted approximately 1.5 hours each, were structured utilizing a questionnaire grounded in the Technology-Organization-Environment (TOE) framework. The questionnaire can be found in Appendix A; it used and extended the TOE dimensions suggested in prior research (Pumplun et al., 2019). This approach used open-ended questions to elicit exploratory insights and foster a deeper understanding of the AI adoption process within the participating organizations. A first pilot interview was conducted with case E.

Each case was evaluated using three key areas: Technical, Organizational, and Environmental Factors. The status of processes within these categories was assessed to give a holistic view of AI adoption in these organizations. A maturity scale from 1 (early stage) to 5 (fully optimized) was utilized to gauge the advancement of each process of AI adoption. A score of 1 signifies a process with substantial potential for development, while 5 indicates a process fully primed for effective AI implementation.

3.3. Quantitative Content Analysis

In the Quantitative Content Analysis method designed by Gläser and Laudel, several key steps are integral to the process, and they can be outlined as follows: The first step, referred to as the preparation of extraction, involves stabilizing the source material and pinpointing specific indicators that will serve as focal points for analysis. This step lays the groundwork for a systematic and focused examination of the data.

The second step encompasses the extraction phase, which entails conducting an in-depth review of the material at hand. During this phase, researchers interpret the data and extract pertinent information. Simultaneously, they may modify existing variables or construct new ones based on the insights gleaned from the material. This iterative process allows for a thorough and nuanced understanding of the data.

The third step involves consolidating and summarizing information that bears similar meanings. Researchers can distill the data into more concise and coherent findings by identifying and synthesizing common themes or patterns, thereby simplifying the subsequent analysis.

Finally, the fourth step of the process focuses on analyzing individual "cases" and examining the connections that extend across these cases. This comprehensive analysis allows for the identification of overarching trends, relationships, and insights that may not be immediately apparent when examining each case in isolation.

4. Results

4.1. Technological Factors

The application of AI in the public sector is not centrally organized; instead, it often relies on individual initiatives or specific circumstances. There is no dedicated process for identifying AI opportunities, and the evaluation of traditional solutions typically occurs on an ad-hoc basis, often involving the information technology department. While most use cases include a return on investment (ROI) calculation, interviewees indicated that these assessments tend to be superficial and could be improved. AI projects are primarily focused on experimentation and gaining experience. Although costs and benefits are considered, the priority lies in testing new technology and prioritizing public value over cost savings. As one interviewee stated:

"First and foremost, the AI project should improve the service for the citizens."

Regarding compatibility with existing processes, most organizations attempt to modify their processes to utilize AI or digital tools better. Current regulations appear flexible enough to accommodate such adjustments while incorporating new technologies like AI.

However, compatibility with technical infrastructure poses a more significant challenge. There are limitations to on-premises resources (e.g., GPUs are unavailable), and in many instances, data protection constraints hinder the straightforward use of Software as a Service (SaaS) offerings in the public cloud. While this may not be an issue for more straightforward applications such as chatbots, it can impede the adoption of more advanced tools requiring specialized computing power.

The availability of advanced and scalable infrastructure, such as GPUs, is critical for effective AI utilization. In most instances, owning, operating, and maintaining such hardware in an organization's data center is impractical due to the need for highly specialized personnel to manage it. Consequently, many private sector companies rely on Amazon, Google, or Microsoft public cloud offerings. However, strict and occasionally ambiguous data protection regulations make it challenging for public sector institutions to adopt this approach.

The U.S. Cloud Act limits the use of public cloud offerings to data that does not contain any personally identifiable information (PII). Unfortunately, most use cases involve at least some information, such as names or email addresses. This renders it nearly impossible to take advantage of the flexible, scalable, and preconfigured cloud offerings, creating a significant barrier for many public sector institutions to begin prototyping without substantial investment in hardware or the need to select use cases requiring minimal computational power. This is an important observation in cases E and G.

In contrast, other cantonal or municipal institutions, like cases D and F, do not face these restrictions and can start prototyping on cloud computing engines. This difference is evident in the various responses from the interviewees:

"We are training on very small datasets... The model training would require a GPU which we are compensating with more CPU."

"We scaled the model down so we could actually train it on an office laptop [...] it took two weeks, though."

4.2. Organizational Factors

The public sector entities examined in this study are among the larger organizations within the Swiss public sector. However, to comprehend why company size is not a reliable predictor of AI capabilities, it is crucial to recognize the structure of these institutions.

Cantons or cities are divided into several, more or less independent departments, such as finance, social and health, education, security, and environment. Each institution has a centralized information technology (IT) department, but these departments traditionally provide only fundamental services like networks, storage, and virtual machines.

"The IT department manages or operates [the infrastructure]." "We have always done this [consulting] in the SAP area, and I have always been out in the departments. Now we need to extend this approach to other areas as well."

This implies that there is limited expertise in consulting, digitalization, or even AI within these organizations. Data analytics teams are generally small and primarily occupied with operational tasks. Data scientists and others who introduce and utilize AI are embedded within departments and business units, resulting in their dispersion throughout the organization with minimal interaction. Only in case B is there a robust central unit responsible for data analytics and AI. This case also exhibits the highest level of maturity, the most significant number of AI prototypes, and the most use cases in production.

Top management in cases C to F comprises elected politicians, which may make support for AI more vulnerable to political trends and opinions. Despite this, there is a broad consensus on the importance of digitalization. AI, however, does not play a significant role in political agendas at the cantonal or municipal levels. This emphasizes the need for support at the department or business entity level. This was explicitly mentioned in case C: *"Digitalization is very much in focus for them [the government councils]. Politicians often talk about digitalization, but I believe they are not always aware of the details behind it. However, in our case, it is the department head who is strongly driving the topic [of AI]."* In other cases, there is goodwill to support initial AI initiatives without explicitly demanding more effort in AI.

Interestingly, change management processes are not well-established in companies other than A and B. Change management is often integrated into digitalization initiatives (F) or e-government initiatives (E). Only A and B have dedicated innovation coaches to support the change process when implementing AI. Cases C to F do not have a dedicated process for promoting innovation; approaches vary depending on the department or business unit.

The absence of a centralized AI initiative or even a data team (C to G) makes creating positions for AI talents extremely challenging. Only F had two dedicated resources from 2022 to 2023 but discontinued AI efforts due to staff turnover. In contrast, A and B strive to attract, retain, and develop new AI talents, primarily by offering them interesting tasks and projects: *"Our HR is surprisingly active at many universities, and they do a really good job in terms of producing videos and so on. We show what exciting things we do, and we do a lot. And then we also publish [scientific articles]"*. In general, there is an awareness that AI talents are difficult to find, but there are no explicit processes in place to ensure their availability.

Data is a critical resource for AI applications, as it is necessary for training and testing models, as well as making predictions or performing classification tasks. While A and B have a more centralized data structure with a large data team providing various services to business units, data is dispersed across departments and business units in cases C to G. This results in a highly decentralized data structure with hundreds of databases, making it difficult for anyone to know the availability, quality, and accessibility of the data. Knowledge about these aspects is spread across numerous teams and often depends on individual personnel. In cases C, D, and F, there are now initiatives to establish central data governance and a company-wide data catalog. Although this does not yet resolve the siloed data storage and processing issue, it represents a first step towards better data awareness: *"We don't have a data lake yet; that might emerge from the data science topic. What we are working on is advancing data governance. There is now a project for us to know more precisely which data we actually have"*. The same constraints that apply to infrastructure also apply to data storage, with all databases being on-premises and limited possibilities for scalability or the use of advanced architectures like "Cloud Data Warehouse", "Lakehouse", or "Data Mesh".

4.3. Environmental Factors

Data protection and information security play crucial roles in public administration, resulting in the implementation of sophisticated and detailed processes in these areas. In cases C to F, there is a central authority for data protection, a chief data protection officer responsible for establishing data protection rules and measures. Information security falls under the purview of the chief information security officer (CISO), who oversees the monitoring of technical measures and information security. Although data and information security processes are relatively strict in all cases, there are differences in interpreting existing data protection laws. For D and F, storing and processing personally identifiable information (PII) in the cloud is permitted, while it is explicitly prohibited in C and E. This indicates that each public sector institution has some degree of flexibility that can be utilized to lower entry barriers for more advanced technologies like AI. The differences in applying data protection laws can be illustrated through the varied responses:

"Basically, you are allowed to use personal data in the cloud. That was the fundamental decision, that it is suitable for everything. But of course, appropriate measures must be taken."

"From the perspective of the data protection officer, personal data may only be used in the cloud if they are also encrypted in-use. Unfortunately, this currently excludes many offers, which is why we need other technical solutions."

Interestingly, no ethics boards are established in cases C to G. The prevailing view is that existing data protection laws cover all ethical aspects, which is inaccurate. An example is facial recognition: if implemented without using cloud resources, it would be theoretically allowed by data protection laws but was mentioned by all interviewees as being at least ethically questionable.

Public opinion plays a significant role in AI adoption: *"The last project demonstrates how important it is when customer data is collected, and how essential communication is"*. However, no reliable mechanisms exist for monitoring public sentiment on a broader scale. The concerns are often limited to tracking newspaper articles and do not encompass discussions in the digital space.

4.4. Summary of implemented measures and processes

The table below provides a detailed overview of the maturity levels of the processes involved in AI adoption for each of the six cases (A to F). Each case is assessed across three main categories: Technical Factors, Organizational Factors, and Environmental Factors. The individual processes under each category are evaluated to present a comprehensive overview of AI adoption in these organizations.

The scores were determined on a scale from 1 (low maturity) to 5 (high maturity). This scoring system reflects the extent to which the individual processes within each category have been developed and optimized for AI adoption. For instance, a score of 1 indicates that the process is in its initial stages with significant room for improvement. In contrast, a score of 5 signifies a highly matured process fully optimized for effective AI implementation.

The evaluation was based on a series of criteria that included, but were not limited to, the quality of the infrastructure, the extent of top management support, the effectiveness of data management strategies, and the level of adherence to data protection and privacy norms. Each case was thoroughly reviewed, and scores were assigned based on these criteria to ensure a robust and balanced assessment of the maturity of AI adoption processes in each organization.

	A	B	C	D	E	F	G
Technical Factors							
Case Handling Process	4	4	1	1	1	1	1
Compability	3	4	3	3	2	3	3
Infrastructure	5	5	1	4	1	3	1
Organizational Factors							
Top Management Support	4	4	4	4	2	3	2
Change Management	4	4	2	2	2	2	2
Innovation Process	4	5	1	1	1	1	1
Data Management	4	5	2	2	2	2	2
Talent Management	5	3	1	1	1	1	1
Budgeting Process	3	3	2	2	2	2	2
Environmental Factors							
Data Protection	4	4	5	5	5	5	5
Ethics	3	3	1	1	1	1	1
Public Opinion	5	4	4	4	4	4	4

Table 2. Maturity levels of the processes involved in AI adoption

5. Discussion

The analysis of AI adoption processes in the Swiss public sector revealed a noteworthy observation regarding data protection and privacy concerns. While public administrations at the canton or city level (cases C, D, E, and F) generally demonstrated less advanced processes in technical, organizational, and environmental aspects compared to state-owned companies (cases A and B), they showed a high level of maturity in data protection processes.

This finding suggests that data protection and privacy concerns are significant priorities for public administrations, potentially due to the sensitive nature of the data they handle and the legal obligations they must comply with. The intense focus on data protection could also act as a barrier to AI adoption, as stringent data protection measures might limit the flexibility and scalability of AI solutions, especially when it comes to using cloud-based services or advanced data architectures.

It is important to note that many technical solutions are already available for data protection, such as encryption methods, which can be utilized effectively in AI adoption. To leverage these solutions, public administrations need to understand the AI landscape better and move away from the traditional on-premise approach. Experimenting with existing technology and exploring new methodologies can help public administrations to securely and compliantly adopt AI.

In conclusion, addressing data protection concerns is essential, but the real impediments to AI adoption in the Swiss public sector lie in improving other technical, organizational, and environmental processes. To facilitate more effective AI adoption, it is crucial to balance robust data protection and implementing AI solutions that enhance service delivery and organizational efficiency. This may require revisiting and refining existing data protection policies and adopting tailored approaches that consider the unique characteristics and requirements of different entities within the Swiss public sector.

6. Conclusion

In conclusion, this study has shed light on the processes involved in AI implementation within the Swiss public sector, revealing the importance of data protection and privacy concerns and the need to improve technical, organizational, and environmental processes. Our findings emphasize that while addressing data protection concerns is crucial, it should not hinder the adoption of AI solutions that can enhance service delivery and organizational efficiency. To achieve this balance, public administrations need to experiment with new technologies and adopt tailored approaches that cater to the unique needs of different entities within the public sector.

Furthermore, our study contributes valuable insights to the existing body of knowledge on AI adoption in the public sector, particularly within the Swiss context. These findings can be used by policymakers and practitioners to guide AI implementation strategies and inform future research on the subject. Future studies could explore the role of public-private partnerships in AI adoption, the impact of AI on public-sector workforce dynamics, and the effectiveness of different AI applications in addressing specific public-sector challenges.

By bridging the research gap and providing actionable recommendations, this study can potentially drive meaningful change in the Swiss public sector's approach to AI adoption, ultimately leading to improved public services and more efficient use of resources.

References

Almaiah, M. A., Alfaisal, R., Salloum, S. A., Hajjej, F., Shishakly, R., Lutfi, A., Alrawad, M., Al Mulhem, A., Alkhdour, T., & Al-Maroof, R. S. (2022). Measuring Institutions' Adoption of Artificial Intelligence Applications in Online Learning Environments: Integrating the Innovation Diffusion Theory with Technology Adoption Rate. *Electronics*, *11*(20), 3291. https://doi.org/10.3390/electronics11203291

Alsheibani, S. A., Cheung, D. Y., & Messom, D. C. (2019). *Factors Inhibiting the Adoption of Artificial Intelligence at organizational-level: A Preliminary Investigation*. 10.

Ballester, O. (2021). An Artificial Intelligence Definition and Classification Framework for Public Sector Applications. *DG.O2021: The 22nd Annual International Conference on Digital Government Research*, 67–75. https://doi.org/10.1145/3463677.3463709

Bryan, J. D., & Zuva, T. (2021). A Review on TAM and TOE Framework Progression and How These Models Integrate. *Advances in Science, Technology and Engineering Systems Journal*, *6*(3), 137–145. https://doi.org/10.25046/aj060316

Casalino, N., Saso, T., Borin, B., Massella, E., & Lancioni, F. (2020). Digital Competences for Civil Servants and Digital Ecosystems for More Effective Working Processes in Public Organizations. In R. Agrifoglio, R. Lamboglia, D. Mancini, & F. Ricciardi (Eds.), *Digital Business Transformation* (Vol. 38, pp. 315–326). Springer International Publishing. https://doi.org/10.1007/978-3-030-47355-6_21

Chatterjee, S., Rana, N. P., Dwivedi, Y. K., & Baabdullah, A. M. (2021). Understanding AI adoption in manufacturing and production firms using an integrated TAM-TOE model. *Technological Forecasting and Social Change*, *170*, 120880. https://doi.org/10.1016/j.techfore.2021.120880

Cubric, M. (2020). Drivers, barriers and social considerations for AI adoption in business and management: A tertiary study. *Technology in Society*, *62*, 101257. https://doi.org/10.1016/j.techsoc.2020.101257

Demlehner, Q., & Laumer, S. (2020). *Shall We Use It or Not? Explaining the Adoption of Artificial Intelligence for Car Manufacturing Purposes*. 17.

Desouza, K. C., Dawson, G. S., & Chenok, D. (2020). Designing, developing, and deploying artificial intelligence systems: Lessons from and for the public sector. *Business Horizons*, *63*(2), 205–213. https://doi.org/10.1016/j.bushor.2019.11.004

European Commission. Joint Research Centre. (2020). *Estimating investments in general purpose technologies: The case of AI investments in Europe*. Publications Office. https://data.europa.eu/doi/10.2760/506947

European Commission. Joint Research Centre. (2022). *AI Watch: Estimating AI investments in the European Union.* Publications Office. https://data.europa.eu/doi/10.2760/702029

Fatima, S., Desouza, K., Buck, C., & Fielt, E. (2021). *Business Model Canvas to Create and Capture AI-enabled Public Value.* Hawaii International Conference on System Sciences. https://doi.org/10.24251/HICSS.2021.283

Gläser, J., & Laudel, G. (2010). *Experteninterviews und qualitative Inhaltsanalyse als Instrumente rekonstruierender Untersuchungen* (4. Auflage). VS Verlag.

Gupta, S., Ghardallou, W., Pandey, D. K., & Sahu, G. P. (2022). Artificial intelligence adoption in the insurance industry: Evidence using the technology–organization–environment framework. *Research in International Business and Finance, 63*, 101757. https://doi.org/10.1016/j.ribaf.2022.101757

Hamm, P., & Klesel, M. (2021). *Success Factors for the Adoption of Artificial Intelligence in Organizations: A Literature Review.*

Issa, H., Jabbouri, R., & Palmer, M. (2022). An artificial intelligence (AI)-readiness and adoption framework for AgriTech firms. *Technological Forecasting and Social Change, 182*, 121874. https://doi.org/10.1016/j.techfore.2022.121874

Jansen, A. (2012). The Understanding of ICTs in Public Sector and Its Impact on Governance. In H. J. Scholl, M. Janssen, M. A. Wimmer, C. E. Moe, & L. S. Flak (Eds.), *Electronic Government* (Vol. 7443, pp. 174–186). Springer Berlin Heidelberg. https://doi.org/10.1007/978-3-642-33489-4_15

Madan, R., & Ashok, M. (2023). AI adoption and diffusion in public administration: A systematic literature review and future research agenda. *Government Information Quarterly, 40*(1), 101774. https://doi.org/10.1016/j.giq.2022.101774

Mariani, M. M., Machado, I., Magrelli, V., & Dwivedi, Y. K. (2022). Artificial intelligence in innovation research: A systematic review, conceptual framework, and future research directions. *Technovation*, 102623. https://doi.org/10.1016/j.technovation.2022.102623

Mayring, P. (2010). *Qualitative Inhaltsanalyse.*

Misuraca, G., van Noordt, C., & Boukli, A. (2020). The use of AI in public services: Results from a preliminary mapping across the EU. *Proceedings of the 13th International Conference on Theory and Practice of Electronic Governance*, 90–99. https://doi.org/10.1145/3428502.3428513

Neumann, O., Guirguis, K., & Steiner, R. (2022). Exploring artificial intelligence adoption in public organizations: A comparative case study. *Public Management Review*, 1–27. https://doi.org/10.1080/14719037.2022.2048685

Pencheva, I., Esteve, M., & Mikhaylov, S. J. (2020). Big Data and AI – A transformational shift for government: So, what next for research? *Public Policy and Administration, 35*(1), 24–44. https://doi.org/10.1177/0952076718780537

Poba-Nzaou, P., & Tchibozo, A. S. (2022). Understanding Artificial Intelligence Adoption Predictors: Empirical Insights from A Large-Scale Survey. *2022 International Conference on Information Management and Technology (ICIMTech)*, 323–326. https://doi.org/10.1109/ICIMTech55957.2022.9915214

Pumplun, L., Tauchert, C., & Heidt, M. (2019). *A NEW ORGANIZATIONAL CHASSIS FOR ARTIFICIAL INTELLIGENCE - EXPLORING ORGANIZATIONAL READINESS FACTORS.* 16.

Schaefer, C., Lemmer, K., Samy Kret, K., Ylinen, M., Mikalef, P., & Niehaves, B. (2021). *Truth or Dare? – How can we Influence the Adoption of Artificial Intelligence in Municipalities?* Hawaii International Conference on System Sciences. https://doi.org/10.24251/HICSS.2021.286

Schedler, K., Guenduez, A. A., & Frischknecht, R. (2019). How smart can government be? Exploring barriers to the adoption of smart government. *Information Polity, 24*(1), 3–20. https://doi.org/10.3233/IP-180095

Sousa, W. G., Melo, E. R. P., Bermejo, P. H. D. S., Farias, R. A. S., & Gomes, A. O. (2019). How and where is artificial intelligence in the public sector going? A literature review and research agenda. *Government Information Quarterly, 36*(4), 101392. https://doi.org/10.1016/j.giq.2019.07.004

Vale Martins, R. do, Alturas, B., & Alexandre, I. (2021). Perspective for the Use of Adoption Theories in Artificial Intelligence. *2021 16th Iberian Conference on Information Systems and Technologies (CISTI)*, 1–4. https://doi.org/10.23919/CISTI52073.2021.9476340

van Noordt, C., & Misuraca, G. (2020). Evaluating the impact of artificial intelligence technologies in public services: Towards an assessment framework. *Proceedings of the 13th International Conference on Theory and Practice of Electronic Governance.* https://doi.org/10.1145/3428502.3428504

Wirtz, B. W., Weyerer, J. C., & Geyer, C. (2019). Artificial Intelligence and the Public Sector—Applications and Challenges. *International Journal of Public Administration, 42*(7), 596–615. https://doi.org/10.1080/01900692.2018.1498103

Yu, X., Xu, S., & Ashton, M. (2023). Antecedents and outcomes of artificial intelligence adoption and application in the workplace: The socio-technical system theory perspective. *Information Technology & People, 36*(1), 454–474. https://doi.org/10.1108/ITP-04-2021-0254

Zhang, D., Mishra, S., Brynjolfsson, E., Etchemendy, J., Ganguli, D., Grosz, B., Lyons, T., Manyika, J., Niebles, J. C., Sellitto, M., Shoham, Y., Clark, J., & Perrault, R. (2021). The AI Index 2021 Annual Report. *ArXiv:2103.06312 [Cs]*. http://arxiv.org/abs/2103.06312

Appendix A

Questions about the technical dimension (AI case selection, relative advantage, and compatibility)
- How do you identify and select new AI cases?
- How do you evaluate new AI cases' ROI (or other measures) and compare it to traditional solutions?
- Combability with existing processes: Do you adjust the business processes for AI usage or adapt the AI solution to the current process?

Questions about the organizational dimension (culture, org., and resources)
- Did you implement specific change management for the AI adoption
- How did you ensure support from the top management?
- Do you have an innovation process, or how do you manage AI-related innovations?
- Is there a dedicated AI budget, and how does the budget process for AI projects work?
- How do you hire, keep, and further develop AI talents?
- How do you collect, store, and prepare the data for AI?
- Is there a central data repository, and how does the cooperation with the data teams work?
- Do you have specific hardware for AI? Moreover, if yes, are the HW resources on-premises or in the cloud?
- How do you provision and scale hardware for AI?

Questions about the environmental dimension
- Who is responsible for data protection in AI projects, and do you have a process to ensure data governance and security?
- Do you have an ethics board, or how do you evaluate the ethical impact of AI solutions?
- Are there other regulations you need to consider when you create new AI applications
- Do you consider the energy consumption of AI applications, or do you have a green IT initiative?
- How do you measure citizens' impact and sentiment toward AI solutions?
- Are there any other measures related to the public sector that you have to ensure?

SECURITY SOFTWARE AS A HYGIENE FACTOR

Tomáš Sigmund

Faculty of Informatics and Statistics
Prague University of Economics and Business
sigmund@vse.cz

DOI: 10.35011/IDIMT-2023-217

Keywords

Security software, Herzberg motivation theory, hygiene factors, automation, unobtrusiveness, resistance to change

Abstract

This article investigates the application of Herzberg's Two-Factor Motivation Theory in the realm of IT security software. Using the online questionnaire, we tested the relationship between users' attitude towards security software and its features representing various hygiene factors. We confirmed the relevance of hygiene factors for users' attitude towards security software and can conclude security software is a hygiene factor that should work automatically, unobtrusively and be easy to use. Thus, we confirmed that users are not internally interested in security and are motivated by the security threats only.

1. Security software and Herzberg's theory of motivation

In today's increasingly digital world, organizations are becoming more and more reliant on technology for their operations. As such, ensuring the security of their systems and data is a top priority. This article examines the role of security software as a hygiene fa

ctor, in line with Herzberg's Two-Factor Theory of motivation.

Security software plays a critical role in safeguarding organizational assets and maintaining the integrity and confidentiality of sensitive information. Given the increasing number of cyber threats, organizations must prioritize the implementation of robust security measures to protect their networks, systems, and data. In this context, security software can be seen as a hygiene factor, as described by Herzberg's Two-Factor Theory of motivation (Herzberg et al., 1959).

According to Herzberg's Two-Factor Theory, employee satisfaction and motivation are influenced by two sets of factors: hygiene factors and motivators in the full sense of the word (Herzberg et al., 1959). Hygiene factors are essential for avoiding dissatisfaction, but their presence does not necessarily lead to increased satisfaction or motivation. They typically include aspects such as job security, working conditions, and company policies. Conversely, motivators are factors that can lead to increased satisfaction and motivation, such as recognition, achievement, and personal growth.

For Herzberg, motivators are internal whereas hygiene factors are external. Internal motivation refers to the drive that originates from within an individual, based on personal interests, values, and satisfaction derived from the activity itself (Deci & Ryan, 2000). People who are internally motivated engage in activities because they find them inherently enjoyable, meaningful, or challenging. Examples of internal motivation include pursuing a hobby for the joy of it, learning a new skill for personal growth, or participating in a sport because it is fun and exciting (Deci & Ryan, 2008). Research has shown that internal motivation is associated with increased creativity, persistence, and overall well-being (Amabile, 1996; Deci & Ryan, 2000).

External motivation, on the other hand, refers to the drive that originates from external factors or consequences, such as rewards, incentives, punishments, or social pressure (Vallerand & Ratelle, 2002). External motivation is called motivation in a derivative sense only as it does not originate within the human being, but is external for him. People who are externally motivated engage in activities to obtain external rewards or avoid negative outcomes. Examples of external motivation include working for a paycheck, studying to avoid a bad grade, or exercising to impress others (Ryan & Deci, 2000).

1.1. Types of security software

There are the various types of security software and their specific roles in ensuring a secure work environment.

1. Antivirus and anti-malware software: These tools are essential for detecting and removing malicious software, such as viruses, worms, and ransomware. Their presence helps maintain the integrity of an organization's systems and data, thus contributing to employee satisfaction (Symantec Corporation, 2021).

2. Firewalls: Firewalls act as barriers between an organization's internal network and external networks, such as the internet. They filter incoming and outgoing traffic based on predefined rules, thereby preventing unauthorized access to sensitive data (Palo Alto Networks, 2021).

3. Intrusion detection and prevention systems (IDPS): IDPS solutions monitor network traffic for signs of potential attacks and respond accordingly. They can detect and prevent various types of threats, including distributed denial-of-service (DDoS) attacks and unauthorized access attempts (Azeez et al., 2020).

4. Encryption software: Encryption tools are used to protect sensitive data by converting it into an unreadable format. This ensures that even if data is intercepted or accessed without authorization, it remains secure and confidential (Mattsson, 2005).

5. Secure communication tools: Secure messaging and email platforms, as well as VPNs, provide encrypted communication channels for employees. This is particularly important for remote workers who may be connecting to company networks from unsecured locations (Viega et al., 2002).

6. Identity and access management (IAM) systems: IAM solutions help organizations manage user access to systems and resources, ensuring that employees only have access to the data and applications necessary for their job roles (Rasouli & Valmohammadi, 2019).

7. Data loss prevention (DLP) software: DLP tools monitor and control the flow of sensitive information, both within an organization and externally. They can prevent unauthorized sharing or transmission of sensitive data, such as intellectual property or customer information (Tahboub & Saleh, 2014).

8. Security information and event management (SIEM) systems: SIEM solutions collect, analyze, and correlate security data from various sources, providing a comprehensive view

of an organization's security posture. They can help detect and respond to security incidents more efficiently (Bhatt et al., 2014).

By implementing and maintaining these various types of security software, organizations can create a secure working environment that supports employee satisfaction and overall company performance.

In the context of the modern workplace, security software helps for several reasons. All these types of support can be viewed as external reasons for security software employment:

1. Protection from external threats: The presence of security software, such as antivirus programs, firewalls, and intrusion detection systems, helps protect organizations from cyber threats (Patel et al., 2010). The absence of these protections can lead to dissatisfaction among employees, who may feel that their personal and professional information is at risk.

2. Compliance with regulations: Many industries require compliance with specific security standards, such as the General Data Protection Regulation (GDPR) or the Health Insurance Portability and Accountability Act (HIPAA). Implementing security software can help organizations meet these requirements and avoid potential fines, which can indirectly contribute to employee satisfaction.

3. Support for remote work: With the rise of remote work, employees need secure access to company resources and data. The use of VPNs, secure file sharing, and other security software can facilitate remote work and minimize potential security risks.

Security software acceptance can be studied from the perspective of standard acceptance models which consider usability and ease of use (Venkatesh et al., 2003). Provided security software is a hygiene factor, users should prefer software that provides them with secure environment without their engagement. They simply don't want to spend their time and effort taking care of their online security as they want to occupy themselves with their internal motivators for which the secure environment provides just the conditions. From the software features we may think of automatization and unobtrusiveness. They are both results of users' unwillingness to deal with security software. They are motivated by the threats and harms which represents external motivation only. Their disinterest should be manifested in the reluctance to change the security software if it works properly. An aspect of the resistance to change the security software may consist in users' inertia. Only IT enthusiasts should show some interest in new security software and would like to experiment with it.

It is important to note, however, that the impact of automation on motivation may be context-dependent and vary among individual users. Some users may appreciate the efficiency and convenience afforded by automation, while others may feel a sense of loss of control or disengagement as a result of reduced hands-on involvement in security tasks.

2. Influences on the attitude towards security software

2.1. Usability and ease of use

User acceptance of security software plays a critical role in ensuring effective and widespread protection (Venkatesh et al., 2003). The widely used acceptance model is based on two fundamental components, usability and ease of use, which have been identified as key determinants of user acceptance (Nielsen, 1993).

Usability is defined as the extent to which a product can be used by specified users to achieve specified goals with effectiveness, efficiency, and satisfaction in a specified context of use (ISO 9241-11, 1998). In the context of security software, usability refers to the design of the software's user interface, features, and functions, which enable users to perform security tasks effectively and efficiently (Whitten & Tygar, 1999). Research by Cranor and Garfinkel (2005) has demonstrated that poor usability can lead to security vulnerabilities and decreased user acceptance.

Ease of use, also referred to as perceived ease of use in the Technology Acceptance Model (TAM), refers to the degree to which a person believes that using a particular system would be free of effort (Davis, 1989). Security software's ease of use reflects the user's perception of how simple it is to install, configure, and interact with the software (Venkatesh & Davis, 2000). A study by Adams and Sasse (1999) revealed that users are more likely to accept security software when they perceive it to be easy to use and understand. Therefore, developers should prioritize ease of use when designing security software to increase user adoption.

2.2. Unobtrusiveness

Unobtrusiveness, on the other hand, can be seen as a design principle that enhances the user experience of security software ((Norman, 2013). By ensuring that security software operates in the background with minimal user intervention, unobtrusive design can contribute to a more seamless and efficient workflow (Bødker, 2006). This approach may lead to higher user satisfaction and motivation by minimizing interruptions and allowing users to focus on their core tasks (Nielsen, 1993).

2.3. Automation

In the context of Herzberg's Two-Factor Theory, security software and automation share a complex relationship. Security software primarily functions as a hygiene factor, ensuring that basic security needs are met and preventing user dissatisfaction. Automation in security software can be seen as a way to improve the efficiency and effectiveness of these hygiene factors. By automating tasks such as threat detection, updates, and incident response, security software can minimize the potential for dissatisfaction and provide a stable foundation for user contentment (Albrechtsen, 2007).

2.4. Resistance to Change

Resistance to change can be described as an individual or collective unwillingness to accept or support organizational changes (Dent & Goldberg, 1999). It can manifest in various forms, such as passive resistance, active resistance, or even sabotage. Factors contributing to resistance to change include fear of the unknown, loss of control, and perceived threats to job security or stability (Oreg et al., 2011).

2.5. Behavioural inertia

One aspect of the resistance to change is the behavioural inertia. Behavioural inertia refers to the human tendency to continue exhibiting a specific behaviour, even when an alternative option might be more advantageous or appropriate (Polites & Karahanna, 2012). This psychological phenomenon is often attributed to cognitive biases, such as the status quo bias, which is the preference for maintaining the current state of affairs (Samuelson & Zeckhauser, 1988). Additionally, the anchoring effect, which is the tendency to rely heavily on initial information when making decisions, can also contribute to behavioral inertia (Furnham & Boo, 2011).

3. Research design

We will research the influence of ease of use, usability, automation, unobtrusiveness and resistance to security software change by the method of our respondents' self-assessment. The answers asked will be formulated in a way that considers all these aspects as hygiene factors. Our general hypothesis states that users don't want to bother with security software, they want it to work without errors, automatically, unobtrusively and to be easy to use. This hypothesis will be broken down into correlations of attitude towards security software with selected relevant hygiene factors. As users don't pay much attention to security software, they don't want to change it and will continue to use the software they use. We also added one question concerning the way autonomy should work. We asked how important for users is that autonomy works in accordance with users' way of protection.

3.1. Methodology

To test our hypothesis, we have used an online questionnaire whose respondents were approached by email. The questions were general, no particular security software was tested. The respondents were students of Prague University of Economics and Business. We used the 5-point Likert scale with 1 meaning "I definitely disagree" and 5 "I definitely agree". We processed the results with SPSS software and tested Spearman correlation between respondents' attitude towards security software and various hygiene factors. Consequently, we attempted to form the regression equation with the attitude towards security software as dependent variable and hygiene factors as independent variables.

The assumptions for the Spearman correlation were met: the variables were ordinal, represent paired observation and their relationship is monotonic. The assumptions for regression were also met as there is a linear relationship between the variables, multicollinearity is small, no auto-correlation can be expected.

In our research we used the following questions. They express the content of sections 2.1-2.5 and were inspired by the content of these questions and the relevant literature.

Q1 (Attitude towards security software): My attitude towards the security software I use is positive.

Q2 (Usability): The security software I use works without errors or problems.

Q3 (Ease of use): I think it's easy to use the security software I use.

Q4 (Automation): The security software I use handles the protection without human intervention.

Q5 (Security software automation acceptance (autonomy)): The security software I use protects the same way I would protect myself.

Q6 (Unobtrusiveness): The security software I use doesn't bother me with unnecessary messages.

Q7 (Unobtrusiveness): The security software I use doesn't waste my time.

Q8 (Behavioural inertia): I will continue to use the security software that I use because I have always done so.

Q9 (Resistance to change): The idea of changing the security software I use doesn't interest me.

Q10: Gender

Q11: Age

3.2. Results

We have collected responses from 72 respondents. The email was sent to approximately 300 randomly selected students and 72 of them responded. Their average age was 23 years and gender composition 65% males, 35% females.

Table 1. Means and standard deviations of questions 1-9

	Mean	Std. deviation	Spearman corr. coeff. between Q1 and Q2-Q9
Q1	2,88	1,22	
Q2	2,90	1,42	0,64**
Q3	3,32	1,48	0,77**
Q4	2,70	1,56	0,62**
Q5	2,53	1,23	0,65**
Q6	3,08	1,47	0,59**
Q7	3,07	1,43	0,40**
Q8	3,36	1,21	0,32**
Q9	3,43	1,11	0,35**

We also carried out the regression analysis in which five variables were significant.

Table 2. Regression coefficients

	Unstandardized Beta	Std. Coef. Beta	t	Sig.
(Constant)	-1,002		-3,570	0,001
Q3	0,349	0,424	6,082	0,000
Q5	0,308	0,311	4,456	0,000
Q6	0,242	0,291	4,656	0,000
Q8	0,145	0,144	2,484	0,016
Q9	0,206	0,187	3,047	0,003

The regression equation can be seen below. The strongest influence on attitude towards security software is represented by its ease of use. We selected only those variables that have a significant effect on Q1. Q2, Q4 and Q7 were not significant.

$$Q1 = -1{,}002 + 0{,}349 * Q3 + 0{,}308 * Q5 + 0{,}242 * Q6 + 0{,}145 * Q8 + 0{,}206 * Q9$$

F statistics =57.5 and is significant at the 5% significance level.

Our results show that users' attitude towards security software is influenced by its usability and ease of use which corresponds to the technology acceptance model. However, the attitude towards it is also influenced by automation and unobtrusiveness and resistance to change which follows from the Herzberg's theory of motivation which claims that hygiene factors are external motivators and motivate only by its absence, in our case users are motivated by the absence of their security.

We must admit that our respondents (students) are not fully representative for the whole population. They represent the working people to some extent as many of them work or have working experience. Considering their age, they express the attitude of the young generation to some extent, especially of students, with the focus on students of the Prague University of Economics and Business.

4. Discussion

When security software is viewed as a hygiene factor, it implies that its presence is necessary to maintain a baseline level of satisfaction and prevent dissatisfaction among users. Our research has shown that users don't want to take care of the security software, if it works properly, they are not motivated to bother with it. They want to perform online activities that bring them intrinsic satisfaction like surf the internet, work, communicate with friends, play games etc. They prefer automatic unobtrusive, reliable, properly functioning and easy to use security software. This expectation should be considered by the security software designers. On the other hand it presents a challenge and maybe even a problem for the system security as they are motivated by the potential harms and if they don't consider them as probable enough they may be reckless.

The implications of viewing security software as a hygiene factor are divers. Properly functioning security software can prevent dissatisfaction arising from security breaches, loss of data, or disruptions to daily operations. As a hygiene factor, security software must be easy to use, unobtrusive, and efficient to ensure that users do not experience frustration or dissatisfaction with the system. Users generally expect a baseline level of security in their digital environment, so having adequate security software in place is essential to meet these expectations. Regular updates and maintenance of security software are crucial to ensure that it remains effective in protecting systems and data from evolving threats. While security software is essential for maintaining user satisfaction, it is not a direct motivator that will lead to increased productivity or higher levels of satisfaction. Users may appreciate its presence, but it doesn't inherently motivate them to perform better. Since security software is a hygiene factor, it should be seamlessly integrated with other systems and tools in the organization to minimize disruptions and maintain a smooth workflow.

5. Conclusion

Overall, the primary goal of treating security software as a hygiene factor is to maintain a stable foundation for user satisfaction by preventing dissatisfaction arising from security-related issues. This approach highlights the importance of usability, efficiency, and seamless integration to ensure that security software remains an essential part of the digital environment without causing unnecessary disruptions or dissatisfaction.

References

Adams, A., & Sasse, M. A. (1999). Users are not the enemy. Communications of the ACM, 42(12), 40–46. https://doi.org/10.1145/322796.322806

Albrechtsen, E. (2007). A qualitative study of users' view on information security. Computers & Security, 26(4), 276–289. https://doi.org/10.1016/j.cose.2006.11.004

Amabile, T. (1996). Creativity in context. Westview Press.

Azeez, N. A., Bada, T. M., Misra, S., Adewumi, A., Van der Vyver, C., & Ahuja, R. (2020). Intrusion Detection and Prevention Systems: An Updated Review. In N. Sharma, A. Chakrabarti, & V. E. Balas (Hrsg.), Data Management, Analytics and Innovation (Bd. 1042, S. 685–696). Springer Singapore. https://doi.org/10.1007/978-981-32-9949-8_48

Bhatt, S., Manadhata, P. K., & Zomlot, L. (2014). The Operational Role of Security Information and Event Management Systems. IEEE Security & Privacy, 12(5), 35–41. https://doi.org/10.1109/MSP.2014.103

Bødker, S. (2006). When second wave HCI meets third wave challenges. Proceedings of the 4th Nordic Conference on Human-Computer Interaction: Changing Roles, 1–8. https://doi.org/10.1145/1182475.1182476

Cranor, L. F., & Garfinkel, S. (Hrsg.). (2005). Security and usability: Designing secure systems that people can use. O'Reilly.

Davis, F. D. (1989). Perceived Usefulness, Perceived Ease of Use, and User Acceptance of Information Technology. MIS Quarterly, 13(3), 319. https://doi.org/10.2307/249008

Deci, E. L., & Ryan, R. M. (2000). The „What" and „Why" of Goal Pursuits: Human Needs and the Self-Determination of Behavior. Psychological Inquiry, 11(4), 227–268. https://doi.org/10.1207/S15327965PLI1104_01

Deci, E. L., & Ryan, R. M. (2008). Self-determination theory: A macrotheory of human motivation, development, and health. Canadian Psychology / Psychologie Canadienne, 49(3), 182–185. https://doi.org/10.1037/a0012801

Dent, E. B., & Goldberg, S. G. (1999). Challenging "Resistance to Change". The Journal of Applied Behavioral Science, 35(1), 25–41. https://doi.org/10.1177/0021886399351003

Furnham, A., & Boo, H. C. (2011). A literature review of the anchoring effect. The Journal of Socio-Economics, 40(1), 35–42. https://doi.org/10.1016/j.socec.2010.10.008

Herzberg, F., Mausner, B., & Snyderman, B. B. (1959). The motivation to work (2. ed). Wiley.

Mattsson, U. T. (2005). Database Encryption—How to Balance Security with Performance. SSRN Electronic Journal. https://doi.org/10.2139/ssrn.670561

Nielsen, J. (1993). Usability engineering. Academic Press.

Norman, D. A. (2013). The design of everyday things (Revised and expanded edition). Basic Books.

Oreg, S., Vakola, M., & Armenakis, A. (2011). Change Recipients' Reactions to Organizational Change: A 60-Year Review of Quantitative Studies. The Journal of Applied Behavioral Science, 47(4), 461–524. https://doi.org/10.1177/0021886310396550

Palo Alto Networks. (2021). What is a Firewall? Palo Alto Networks. https://www.paloaltonetworks.com/cyberpedia/what-is-a-firewall

Patel, A., Qassim, Q., & Wills, C. (2010). A survey of intrusion detection and prevention systems. Information Management & Computer Security, 18(4), 277–290. https://doi.org/10.1108/09685221011079199

Polites & Karahanna. (2012). Shackled to the Status Quo: The Inhibiting Effects of Incumbent System Habit, Switching Costs, and Inertia on New System Acceptance. MIS Quarterly, 36(1), 21. https://doi.org/10.2307/41410404

Rasouli, H., & Valmohammadi, C. (2019). Proposing a conceptual framework for customer identity and access management: A qualitative approach. Global Knowledge, Memory and Communication, 69(1/2), 94–116. https://doi.org/10.1108/GKMC-02-2019-0014

Ryan, R. M., & Deci, E. L. (2000). Self-determination theory and the facilitation of intrinsic motivation, social development, and well-being. American Psychologist, 55(1), 68–78. https://doi.org/10.1037/0003-066X.55.1.68

Samuelson, W., & Zeckhauser, R. (1988). Status quo bias in decision making. Journal of Risk and Uncertainty, 1(1), 7–59. https://doi.org/10.1007/BF00055564

Symantec Corporation. (2021). Internet Security Threat Report. https://www.symantec.com/content/dam/symantec/docs/security-center/white-papers/istr-24-2019-en.pdf

Tahboub, R., & Saleh, Y. (2014). Data Leakage/Loss Prevention Systems (DLP). 2014 World Congress on Computer Applications and Information Systems (WCCAIS), 1–6. https://doi.org/10.1109/WCCAIS.2014.6916624

Vallerand, R. J., & Ratelle, C. F. (2002). Intrinsic and extrinsic motivation: A hierarchical model. In Handbook of self-determination research. (S. 37–63). University of Rochester Press.

Venkatesh, Morris, Davis, & Davis. (2003). User Acceptance of Information Technology: Toward a Unified View. MIS Quarterly, 27(3), 425. https://doi.org/10.2307/30036540

Venkatesh, V., & Davis, F. D. (2000). A Theoretical Extension of the Technology Acceptance Model: Four Longitudinal Field Studies. Management Science, 46(2), 186–204. https://doi.org/10.1287/mnsc.46.2.186.11926

Viega, J., Messier, M., & Chandra, P. (2002). Network security with OpenSSL (1st ed). O'Reilly.

Whitten, A., & Tygar, J. D. (1999). Why Johnny Can't Encrypt: A Usability Evaluation of PGP 5.0. Proceedings of the 8th USENIX Security Symposium, 169–184. https://www.usenix.org/legacy/events/sec99/full_papers/whitten/whitten_html/index.html

THE SIGNIFICANCE OF SOC2 TYPE 2 AND ISO 27001 REGULATIONS FOR CC SERVICE PROVIDERS IN THE CZECH REPUBLIC

Vlasta Svatá

Faculty of Informatics and Statistics
Prague University of Economics and Business
svata@vse.cz

DOI: 10.35011/IDIMT-2023-227

Keywords

SOC2 Type 2, ISO 27001, CC service providers, e-Government Cloud

Abstract

The article provides analysis of the relevant regulations for the e-Government Cloud and existing international attestations and certifications which can help cloud computing (CC) service providers to be compliant with these regulations.

1. Introduction

Cloud computing (CC) is on the rise after the initial hesitancy of organizations. This fact is documented by a number of research papers, of which I would like to mention an article Comparison of cloud service consumption in the Czech Republic, Visegrad Group and European Union (Zbořil, Svatá, 2022). The situation in the cloud service usage evolution across European Union regions is shown in Figure. The analysis was conducted over sets of biannual data (2014, 2016, 2018, and 2020) that are available on the Eurostat site for all the European Union countries. The results show that Czechia had a lower average percentage of enterprises using cloud services than the EU, but higher than in Visegrád in all the analyzed time periods. In the same time Czechia has higher usage than the average in South-East Europe.

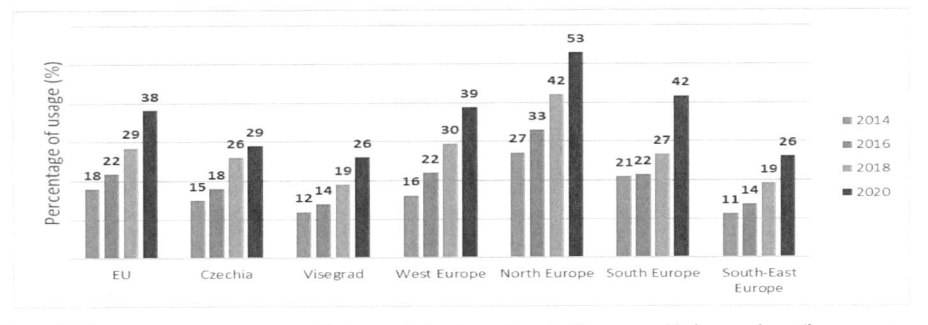

Figure 1. The average usage across all types of cloud services in European Union regions (in percentage)

Source: (Zbořil, Svatá, 2022)

The rapid development of CC in the EU is regulated both at the level of the entire EU and at the level of its individual members.

At the highest level the European Commission has launched a European Alliance on Industrial Data, Edge and Cloud, which will feature the development of several work streams, related to key EU policy goals:

- Joint Investment in cross-border cloud infrastructures and services to build the next generation cloud supply, including to enable Common European Data Spaces
- EU Cloud Rulebook for cloud services, which will provide a single European framework of rules, transparency on their compliance and best practices for cloud use in Europe
- A European marketplace for cloud services, where users will have a single portal to cloud services meeting key EU standards and rules (EU, 2023)

Examples of other initiatives are European commission cloud strategy, European cybersecurity certification scheme for cloud services, Regulation on the free flow of non-personal data, Standardized Cloud Service Level Agreements (SLA), EU Cloud Federation, European Federated Cloud, GAIA-X. In the document THE EUROPEAN COMMISSION CLOUD STRATEGY the European Commission defines a vision for Cloud computing: Cloud-first with a secure hybrid multi-cloud service offering (EU, 2019).

Within the framework of EU regulations and initiatives, the Czech Republic is trying to build such an environment in which it would be possible to use cloud computing to the greatest extent. The Czech Republic entered the trend of the declared by strategic documents of the he European Union and follows the application of the above mentioned "cloud first" principle. It means that the new information systems of the government units and related services must be preferably placed in cloud. In the Czech Republic the cloud usage in the public administration is called eGoverment Cloud (eGC). To be a cloud service in public administration service must be registered in the so-called Cloud Computing Catalog, which is since August 2020 managed by the Ministry of the Interior. The catalog is a public list in which demand and offers are collected to cloud services in public administration.

The catalog is part of the Cloud Computing information system which is the application supporting all eGC users in their work with CC Catalog. It is realized via the Ministry of Interior website (https://www.mvcr.cz/clanek/egovernment-cloud.aspx). CC Catalog contains four sub-catalogs: CC Demands Catalog, CC Providers Catalog, CC Offers Catalog and CC Catalog used by public administration bodies.

The core documents for eGC building are[1]:

- Act No. 365/2000 Coll., on public administration information systems
- Act No. 181/2014 Coll., on cyber security
- Act No. 12/2020 Coll., on right to digital services
- Decree No. 82/2018 Coll., on safety measures, cyber security incidents, reactive measures, requirements for filing in cyber security and data disposal
- Decree 433/2020 on the data kept in the catalog

---

[1] The documents are available on the websites of the Ministry of the Interior (mvcr.cz) and Institute for Cyber and Information Security (nukib.cz).

- Decree No. 315/2021 Coll., on the safety levels for the use of cloud computing public authorities,
- Decree No. 316/2021 Coll., on some requirements for enrollment in Cloud Computing Cataloq
- Information Concept of the Czech Republic,
- Methodology for work with Cloud Computing Catalog and Cloud Service Catalog
- A methodological guide to the use of cloud computing in public administration

Supporting materials:
- Guide to include the inquired cloud computing to the security level
- Requirements for penetration tests reporting in connection cloud computing catalog
- Table of Annexes to Decree No. 316/2021 Coll.
- Supporting material to identify digital service providers

2. Research Question and Methodology

The evolution of eGC in the Czech Republic is currently dynamic and the main advancements were done from the year 2020 up to now. The CC catalog has been introduced in August 2020. The first providers had to be registered from June 2021. Due to delayed specifications of the Cloud decrees, low demand and generally small awareness of CC advantages the total number of registered providers is 30 (up to date of February 26).

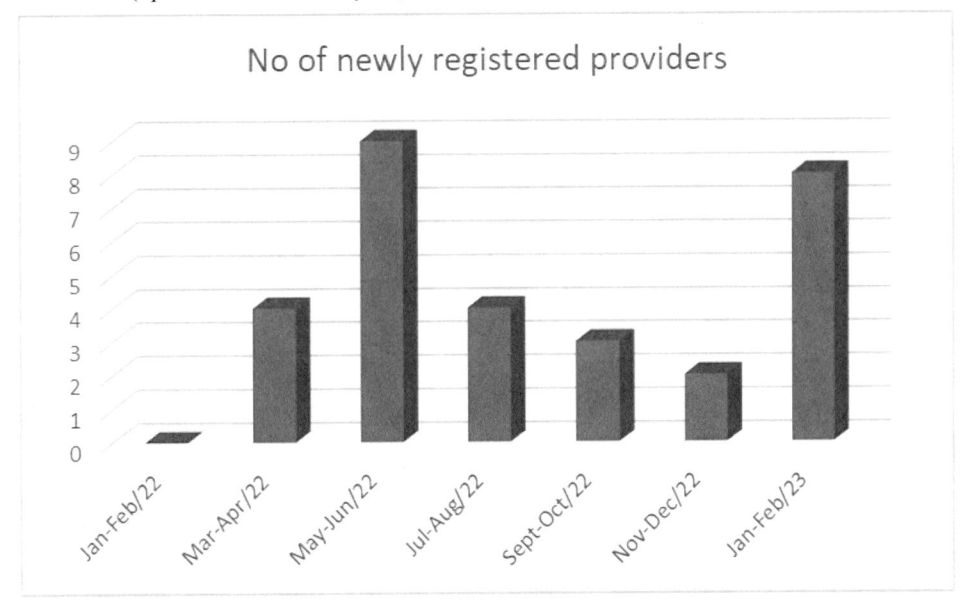

Figure 2. Number of newly registered providers in CC Catalog by month and year   Source: (MVČR, 2023)

Currently, those interested in registering in the catalog of providers have at their disposal clarifications and a number of them evaluate the extent to which they meet the declared requirements. In this situation the research question is: "How important is SOC2 Type2 attestation and ISO 27001 certification for eGC service providers"? The main research method is a comparative analysis of regulatory requirements for registration of service providers in eGC with requirements for obtaining SOC2 Type2 attestation and ISO 27001 certification.

3. Certifications and Audit Proofs of Information Security Requirements for CC Catalogue Registration

A prerequisite for a successful enrollment of the cloud provider to the catalog is to fill the enrollment process defined in Methodology for Work with Cloud Computing Catalog. An integral part of the process is successful ex-ante control of 48 security criteria on which the Ministry of the Interior is working with National Institute for Cyber and Information Security (NUKIB). These criteria /requirements are formulated in Decree No. 316/2021 in Annex No. 2 (NÚKIB, 2021). In the same Decree but in the Annex No 3 list of certifications relevant for protection of information security (confidentiality, integrity and availability) is given and the most important are:

- ISO/IEC 27001
- SOC 2® Type 2

3.1. ISO/IEC 27001 Certification

ISO/IEC 27001:2013 is one of the ISO/IEC 27000 family standards and specifies the requirements for establishing, implementing, maintaining and continually improving an information security management system (ISMS) within the context of the organization and risks of organization's activities. Organizations with this certificate can demonstrate their ability to permanently apply security measures protecting information assets in order to provide assurance to their partners about a sufficient level of information security. The requirements set out in this document are generic and are intended to be applicable to all organizations, regardless of type, size or nature.

The audit according to ISO / IEC 27000 standards is aimed at evaluating the conformity between the ISMS requirements formulated in the standard (114 checks in the 2013 version and 93 in the 2022 version) and the processes in the organization. Audit itself and decision about the certification must be done by the accredited bodies. The process of certification is defined by ISO/IEC 17021 Conformity assessment (Requirements for bodies providing audit and certification of management systems) and ISO/IEC 27006 (Security TechniquesRequirements for bodies providing audit and certification of information security management systems). At the beginning of the audit, an input analysis is carried out, which maps the organization's environment. It mainly includes an assessment of the infrastructure and process aspects of ISMS/BCM and an impact analysis (BIA) embedded in the organization's process model. The inherent part is the checks for the existence and completeness of key documentation, such as the organization's information security policy, Statement of Applicability (SoA), and Risk Treatment Plan (RTP). The results of the analysis, together with the customer's goals, then determine the actual audit and its demand for resources. The second part of certification is formal compliance audit which consists of independent testing the ISMS against the requirements specified in ISO/IEC 27001. The third part of audit are ongoing activities—follow-up reviews aiming to confirm that an organization remains in compliance with the standard. Certification is valid three years and after this period recertification audit is needed.

The new version of ISO/IEC has been published in 2022. This new version brings changes in number of controls and their grouping in themes. In the same time the norm is harmonized with the ISO/IEC 27002 guidance which was published earlier in 2022. Organizations are now in the transition period as they are already certified to the old 2013 standard version then they have three years to move across to the new version. The reason is that the certification bodies need to get their accreditation first. If the organizations are currently working towards certification to the 2013 version, the last date they will be able to do this will be April 2024 It is up to these organizations whether they will continue in this "old" certification or they will transfer efforts to achievement of certification compliant to the 2022 version.

3.2. SOC 2® Type 2

Many organizations, which are traded in global stock markets, rely on third party service providers for handling their sensitive data and several mission-critical processes. Standards for Attestation Engagements (SSAE) and Service Organization Control (SOC) reports are one of the most efficient ways to have a good idea about the internal control systems of service providers. The author of the SSAE is the American Institute of Certified Professional Accountant (AICPA), which in 2020 issued SSAE 22 (supersedes SSAE 18). Effective date of this standard was June 15, 2022. This kind of attestation is important for both the auditors and users. The importance for auditors resides in establishing requirements and application guidance for performing and reporting on examination, review, and agreed-upon procedures engagements, including Service Organization Controls (SOC) attestations. User organizations can benefit from the SOC attestations as they represent a reasonable assurance that controls at their service organizations, relevant to their internal controls are suitably designed and operating effectively. There are three primary types of SOC reports:

- SOC1 report is focused on financial reporting. The goal is to have and demonstrate internal controls for how you handle your customers' financial information.
- SOC2 report is focused on operations and compliance, especially in regard to cloud computing and data security. The goal is to have and demonstrate internal controls that align with Trust Services Criteria five criteria (Security, Confidentiality, Processing Integrity, Privacy, Availability). The report is shared among the non-disclosure agreement (NDA) by management, regulators and others.
- SOC3 basically contains the same information found in SOC 2 but it is publicly available to anyone.

In context of eCG SOC2 is relevant. Within the SOC2 we can use two types of report formats, Type 1 and Type 2. They vary in their content, which further differentiates the level of service to be performed in an attestation engagement for this subject matter.

- Type 1 reports are as of a particular date (sometimes referred to as point-in-time reports) that include a description of a service organization's system as well as tests to help determine whether a service organization's controls are designed appropriately.
- Type 2 reports cover a period of time (usually 6-12 months) and therefore besides a description of the service organization's system refer about the tests not only over the control design, but about their operating effectiveness as well.

SOC 2 audits are regulated by the American Institute of Certified Public Accountants (AICPA) and must be completed by a licensed CPA (Certified Public Accountant) external auditor. The process of audit is similar to ISO27001 audit and SOC 2 compliance is documented with a formal attestation.

4. Analysis

The subject of analysis is the Decree No. 316/2021 Coll., on some requirements for enrollment in cloud computing catalogue Section 4 and Annex No. 2. This annex specifies the requirements for the basic level of confidentiality protection, integrity, and availability of information for a public authority to be achieved by the offered cloud computing. The requirements are described in 10 lines and within each line there exist list of sub-requirements. Each sub-requirement is supplemented with information about the documents by which the provider proves compliance with it. After determining irrelevant sub-requirements (i.e. requirements that cannot be substantiated by any certifications and audits for the area of confidentiality protection, integrity, and availability of information), it was possible to check which of the two certification audits (ISO 27001 and SOC2 Type 2) can be used as documents meeting the given sub-requirement. The results are presented in Table.

Table 1. An overview of the compliance between the information security requirements stated in the Degree No. 316/2021 Coll. and the certifications ISO 27001 and SOC2 Type2

Section 4, Annex No.2 Requirements for the basic level of confidentiality protection, integrity, and availability of information for a public authority to be achieved by the offered cloud computing				
Line/ Requirement	No of sub-requirements	No of not relevant sub-requirements	Compliant to SOC2 Type 2	Compliant to ISO 27001
1. Place of data processing and storing	8	5	3	3
2 Applications for access to and disclosure of data	6	1	5	5
3. Authorization to perform the inspection	1	1	0	0
4. Service availability levels	2	0	2	2
5. Connection to Internet exchange node (IXP)	1	1	0	0
6. Ensuring provision of cloud computing services	8	1	7	5
7. Data handling	9	6	3	3
8. Certification of cloud computing services	7	0	1	6
9. Cybersecurity events and cybersecurity incidents	3	1	2	2
10. Testing cloud computer services	3	2	1	1
Sum	48	18	24	27

The first column of the table briefly lists the requirements for service providers for the basic level of confidentiality protection, integrity, and availability of information. The second column lists for each requirement the total number of sub-requirements that refine the requirement. The third column list the number of not relevant sub-requirements that were excluded from the analysis. The numbers in the fourth and fifth columns represent the number of relevant sub-requirements that can be met using SOC2 Type 2 attestation and/or ISO 27001 certification.

It can be seen from the table that for most Lines/requirements (10) both the ISO27001 and SOC2 alternatives are allowed. Differences in favor of ISO 27001 appear in Line 8—Certification of cloud computing services. For 6 sub-requirements of this Line, it is directly required that the provider holds a valid certification ČSN EN ISO/IEC 27001, EN ISO/IEC 27001 by a certification body that has been accredited to perform audits and certification of information security management systems by one of the members of the International Accreditation Forum (IAF), whose scope of certification includes the assessed cloud computing service. Two sub-requirements from this number state that CC service must operate in compliance with the procedures stipulated in the ISO/IEC 27017 standard and one sub-requirement states that CC service must operate in compliance with the procedures stipulated in the ISO/IEC 27018 standard. Only 1 sub-requirement states that the provider holds an SOC 2® Type 2 audit report whose scope includes the assessed cloud computing service, and which was issued by an independent auditor.

On the contrary, in Line 6—Ensuring provision of cloud computing services 7 relevant sub-requirements can be substantiated by both standards, while two sub-requirements can only be substantiated by SOC2 Type2 attestation.

5. Conclusion

The research question was "How important is SOC2 Type2 attestation and ISO 27001 certification for eGC service providers"? The answer is that both the regulatory compliances are important, but according to the analysis carried out, the ISO/IEC 27001 certification is more important for meeting the requirements for registration in the service catalog. This result is not surprising given that this certification has a greater tradition in Europe and was already mentioned in the context of the GDPR as a suitable basis for meeting the requirements of this regulation. The small difference in the number of fulfilled requirements between ISO 27001 and SOC2 Type 2 (3 sub-requirements) is therefore surprising. Given that SOC2 Type 2 is perceived as easier and less expensive to implement and maintain (but it's also less rigorous) and ISO 27001 involves more work, but it does more to protect organizations from information security threats (ITG, 2023). Thus, for many organizations, the SOC2 Type 2 certification can be an interesting alternative. Furthermore, from January 1, 2024 will be mandatory to have attestation SOC2 Type 2 in order to achieve security level 3 and 4 and thus to achieve high level of CC services sustainability.

But there are negative aspects of this situation as well. With the higher demand to perform a SOC2 audit, AICPA must be prepared to take care of the proper CPA selection and auditing industry must be prepared to keep high quality of SOC2 audits. Another problem is the fact, that SOC2 reports are in English and not all the users of the report are prepared for it.

References

E&Y, (2021) Ernst & Young, s.r.o..Analýza využití cloud computingu veřejnou správou v České republice, http://www.amcham.cz/files/uploads/News/9796/EY_AmCham_analysis_of_cloud_computing_final2.pdf

EU, (2019) https://commission.europa.eu/system/files/2019-05/ec_cloud_strategy.pdf

EU, (2023) https://digital-strategy.ec.europa.eu/en/policies/cloud-computing

ISO, (2013) ISO/IEC 27001:2013 Information technology — Security techniques — Information security management systems — Requirements, https://www.iso.org/standard/54534.html

ITG, (2023), Luke Irwin, ISO 27001 vs SOC 2 Certification: What's the Difference? (https://www.itgovernance.eu/blog/en/iso-27001-vs-soc-2-certification-whats-the-difference

MVČR, (2023) https://www.mvcr.cz/clanek/katalog-cloud-computingu.aspx?q=Y2hudW09Mg%3d%3d

NÚKIB, (2021), Decree No. 316/2021 Coll., On some requirements for enrollment in cloud computing cataloque, https://nukib.cz/download/publications_en/legislation/DECREE%20No.%20315_2021.pdf

Zbořil, Svatá (2022), COMPARISON OF CLOUD SERVICE CONSUMPTION IN THE CZECH REPUBLIC, VISEGRÁD GROUP AND EUROPEAN UNION, časopis Ekonomie a Management, ročník 25, Číslo 3, ISSN: 1212-3609, https://dspace.tul.cz/handle/15240/166035

THE TOPIC OF AI CHATBOTS IN HIGHER EDUCATION

Martin Potančok, Věra Radváková

Faculty of Informatics and Statistics
Prague University of Economics and Business
martin.potacok@vse.cz, vera.radvakova@vse.cz

DOI: 10.35011/IDIMT-2023-235

Keywords

AI chatbot, ChatGPT, information ethics, information society, educational process, educational system

Abstract

During this academic year, text-generating chatbots are becoming very popular among university students. One particularly popular chatbot is ChatGPT. The aim of this paper is to find out to what extent students of the Faculty of Informatics and Statistics (FIS) of the Prague University of Economics and Business (VŠE) specifically deal with this issue, for what purposes they use AI chatbots and, above all, whether they have already used AI chatbots for study purposes and what they see as the potential of this rapidly developing technology for the educational process. The authors draw on data collected in a questionnaire survey of undergraduate and graduate students. The area of cyber-security, liability and how to verify the data thus obtained were also important considerations. The authors also used the method of observation and their own teaching experience at the university as part of the research investigation. They point to the fact that the current development of artificial intelligence further exacerbates the disparity between the inflexible educational system in the Czech Republic and the rapid development of the information society.

1. Introduction

Advanced machine learning algorithms (Artificial Intelligence, AI) are beginning to reach into various spheres of human activity. One area where AI is showing significant potential is in the area of text-generating chatbots. Not only among university students, the chatbot ChatGPT and other intelligent agents have become popular in recent months (Doshi et al., 2023). In general, AI chatbots represent a large language model in order to process natural language and provide responses approaching human communication (Paliwal et al., 2019). Various products, such as Bing, Bard or the very popular ChatGPT, are being used (Burger et al., 2023). This research focuses on using AI chatbots in a university environment, so we only show examples of chatGPT (the purpose is not to analyse the differences between the most used AI chatbots; this can be found, e.g. in (Floridi, 2023)). ChatGPT was developed by OpenAI (OpenAI, 2023). It can answer questions and generate text in different languages. It is a powerful, useful tool that will definitely continue to evolve. Recently, a version of GPT4 has been created where language and image are already being combined. This version is not yet available to the public.

The question remains at what level of digital maturity we are at, where GPT is going next, and how students, but especially teachers at all levels of school, will cope and deal with it. This is a natural evolution. The process of globalisation brings with it not only new technologies but also new requirements and demands to protect and ensure cyber security (Doucek, 2020). Artificial intelligence is already built on a linguistic basis as well. However, it does not yet attempt to crack the code of human language.

The authors created the ChatGPT model to guide dialogue, to make conversation meaningful, and to be an ethical tool. A chatbot will not answer, for example, the question "how to make dynamite" (Freed, 2022). ChatGPT does not replace humans; it is meant to help (Shanshan et al., 2020), (Biswas, 2023), (Haman et al., 2023), and therefore it is necessary to start working with it in schools, bringing more creativity, creativity of teachers to the forefront. The problem arises that even ChatGPT can be creative, recognizing what people like or find annoying. The essence is mainly in interpretability and accountability. Chatbots can make it easier for students to find the information they need by responding to their questions and requests – through text input, audio input, or both – but they will not help them understand the information. Most often, this is where students get their information from text. Even in this case, however, it is not enough to simply obtain the relevant information. (Sandu et al., 2023), (Hannan et al., 2023), (Chiu et al., 2023). Above all, understanding the information, being able to verify the information correctly and being able to see the new information in different contexts are necessary conditions for success. Among the cognitive processes, within the logical operation of thinking, these interpretive processes occupy an important place, i.e., understanding what is presented, expressing what is understood and placing it in different contexts.

Thus, the aim of this research is to analyse the use of AI chatbots by university students and their future and to identify the issues that universities will have to address.

2. Methods and Materials

The analysis is based on data from a survey conducted by the authors of the paper. This survey was carried out in the academic year 2022/23. To meet the objectives, they chose the methods of questionnaire survey, observation and guided interviews. The present study is based on data from 120 completed questionnaires and their own teaching experience at the Prague University of Economics and Business.

The purpose of the quantitative research investigation was to determine the current situation of FIS VŠE students with the use and application of AI chatbots in the development of assignments and to what extent students are aware of the necessity of verifying information obtained in this way. The data obtained also tells the percentage of respondents currently use AI chatbots. The qualitative line of research was aimed at finding out for what purposes students use this new technology in particular and what they see its future as within higher education. We also investigated confidence in the outputs and their accuracy.

The authors assume that FIS VŠE students like and frequently use new technologies, including AI chatbots. They are aware that they must always declare the accuracy and reliability of the data in their academic papers. Going into future academic years, we see more accountability and control for educators, and it will be necessary to ensure that the methodology of each student paper is precise and detailed, with detailed justification of the topic, goals, and motivation. Prepare in advance the searches that AI will produce, and require students to take a different and more thorough approach.

120 respondents (93 male, 25 female, 2 ticked gender "other") participated in the research survey. These were male, female and other students in the 1st–3rd year of their Bachelor's degree (72 respondents) and 1st–2nd year of their Master's degree (48 respondents). The distribution between

bachelor and master students was 60% vs 40%. The return rate was 35%. The online tool Microsoft Forms was used to obtain responses.

From the data obtained, values and facts emerge, which the authors further work with and on which the conclusions of the whole research investigation are based.

3. Results

For the questionnaire survey, the authors chose the Tableau platform (Tableau, 2021), which is one of the leading in the field according to Richardson et al. (2021). Specifically, Tableau Desktop was used to create the visualizations. The design is based on the principles defined by Few (2012) and Knaflic (2015); the above conclusions extend the view of the results.

The results can be divided into the following groups: i) the use of AI chatbots; ii) the use for learning purposes; iii) the potential of AI chatbots.

3.1. Using AI chatbots

It is not surprising that 100% of the respondents who are students of Applied Computer Science, Mathematical Methods in Economics, Information Media and Services and Multimedia in Economic Practice in undergraduate studies and Business Analysis, Data and Analytics for Business, Information Systems and Technology in undergraduate and graduate studies are familiar with and use AI chatbots. The most used (84% of respondents) is ChatGPT. More surprisingly, a full 16% of these students are familiar with ChatGPT but have not had the need to use it.

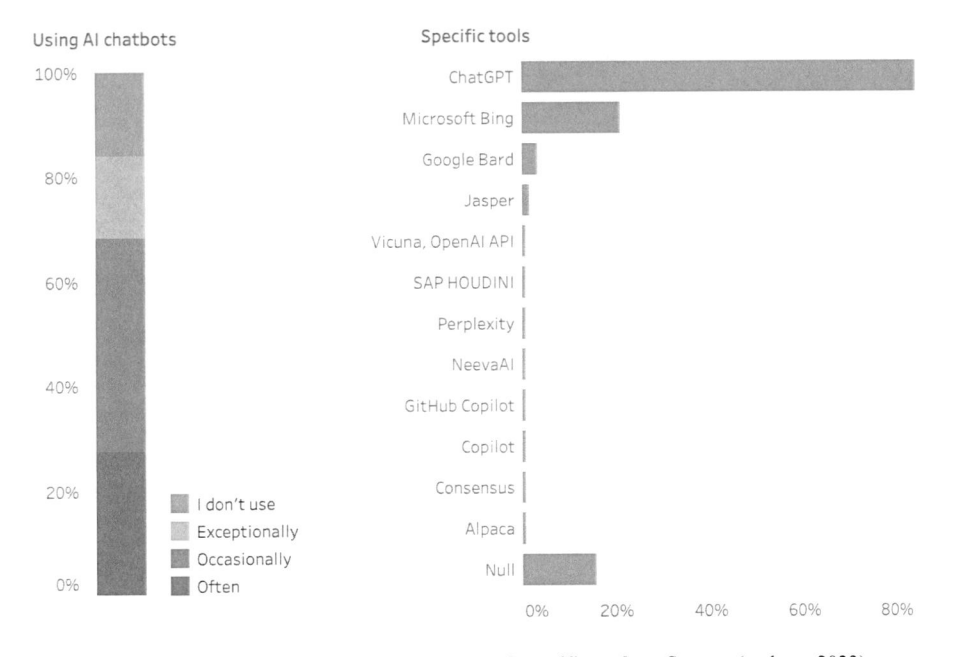

Figure 1. Frequency of AI chatbot use and specific tools   Source: (authors, 2023)

3.2. Use for study purposes

It should be a warning to educators that already in many year and perhaps even final papers at FIS VŠE, information is formulated not by students but only by artificial intelligence. The following chart shows that a full 72% of respondents are already using AI to help them with student projects or assignments. The good news is that the graph also shows that the vast majority of students, even those who do not yet use ChatGPT for their studies, are aware of the need to validate the information thus obtained.

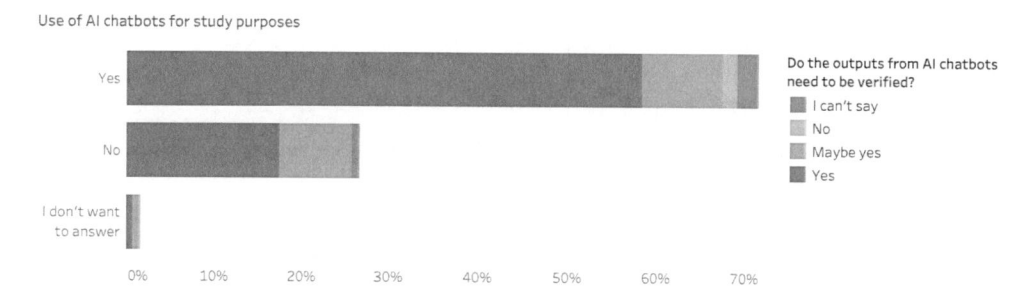

Figure 2. Use of AI chatbots for study purposes and the need to verify information Source: (authors, 2023)

Students most often use AI chatbots for programming, information search and research, brainstorming, explaining concepts, both school and work related tasks, *"for work"* – debugging code, etc. For school use – *I often get questions like 'Explain this topic to me as a small child'"*. The time of use is also very interesting, with some respondents pointing to the initial stages, *"To kick-start thought processes and to inspire"*, while some point to later, when they have finished outputs and want to validate them, *"to check their own work and get feedback"*.

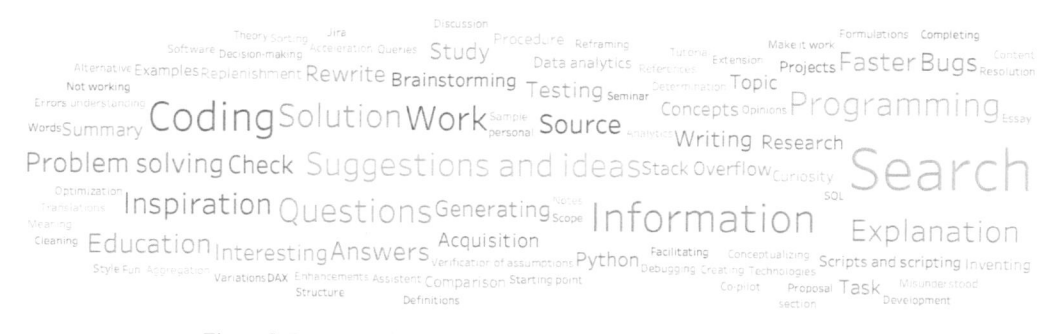

Figure 3. Purposes of AI chatbots Source: (authors, 2023)

3.3. The potential of AI chatbots

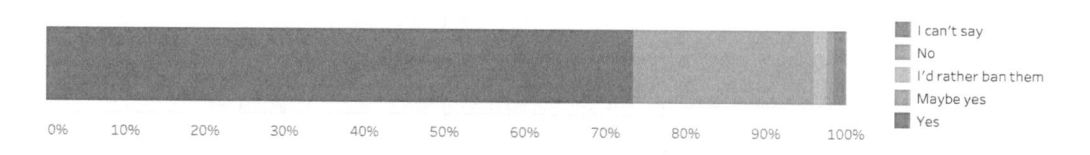

Figure 4. The potential of AI chatbots in the field of learning tools Source: (authors, 2023)

The results of the questionnaire survey mentioned above show that university students see opportunities for the use and integration of AI chatbots in the educational process. The current rapid development of artificial intelligence once again highlights the disparity between the rapid development of the information society and the inflexible educational system in the Czech Republic. Although students are aware of the pitfalls of AI chatbots, they consider them as a possible learning tool. At this point, it would still be necessary to check to what extent teachers will also be aware of this fact and be able to assess the diverse possibilities of AI chatbots in education.

Given the need for information verification, which is also perceived by students (see fig. 2), greater information literacy, which is the ability to read, interpret and produce information, will be needed (Elmborg, 2006). Thus, there is a need to emphasize information literacy education in universities as well. It should not rely on definitions alone, but rather on critically important practice (Cerny et al., 2023).

4. Discussions and conclusions

Unlike students and teachers, GPT is not responsible for the information or their answers and cannot be completely trusted. The biggest gap between humans and AI is in accountability. In today's society, which inherently relies on seeking and working with information, the danger of information dependency is increasing, as is the growing amount of abstract information as opposed to empirically documented information. The flexibility to acquire one's own information, including the inherent ability to create knowledge structures, is declining. On the one hand, technology is improving; on the other hand, the language skills of not only students are decreasing. The development of artificial intelligence is continuous, but it is still software, and schools need to work with it, not just warn against it.

If we address AI chatbots from a didactic point of view, we must first of all look at the forms and possibilities of their use in teaching. In universities, it is necessary to modernise the whole of teaching, especially teaching methods. If teaching method is characterized as "*a coordinated system of teacher's teaching activities and student's learning activities, which is aimed at achieving the set goals*" (Pelikán, 2011. p. 307), it is possible that AI will be considered not only as a teaching tool, but as a comprehensive teaching method. Thus, the didactic creativity of the teacher will have to be applied much more in the educational process. The great variety of teaching methods and techniques is an undeniable advantage not only in universities. In fact, it provides a large range of possible strategies, where current AI chatbots can also be included in the whole educational process.

References

Biswas, S.S. (2023). Role of Chat GPT in Public Health. Ann Biomed Eng 51, 868–869. https://doi.org/10.1007/s10439-023-03172-7

Burger, B., Kanbach, D.K., Kraus, S., Breier, M. & Corvello, V. (2023). On the use of AI-based tools like ChatGPT to support management research, European Journal of Innovation Management, Vol. 26 No. 7, pp. 233-241. https://doi.org/10.1108/EJIM-02-2023-0156

Centrum umělé inteligence. (2023). Centrum umělé inteligence (AIC) - ČVUT - Fakulta elektrotechnická. https://intranet.fel.cvut.cz/cz/vv/tymy/aic.html

Černý J. & Potančok M. (2023). Information literacy in international masters students: A competitive and business intelligence course perspective, Cogent Education, 10:1, DOI. 10.1080/2331186X.2022.2161701

Chiu, T.K.F., Moorhouse B.L., Chai, C.S. & Ismailov, M. (2023). Teacher support and student motivation to learn with Artificial Intelligence (AI) based chatbot, Interactive Learning Environments, DOI: 10.1080/10494820.2023.2172044

Doguc, O. (2022). Robot process automation and it is future. In Research Anthology on Cross-Disciplinary Designs and Applications of Automation (pp. 35-58). IGI Global.

Doshi, H.R., Bajaj, S.S. & Krumholz, M.H. (2023) ChatGPT: Temptations of Progress, The American Journal of Bioethics, 23:4, 6-8, DOI: 10.1080/15265161.2023.2180110

Doucek, P. (2020). Řízení kybernetické bezpečnosti a bezpečnosti informací. Praha: Professional Publishing. ISBN 978-80-88260-39-4.

Elmborg, J. (2006). Critical information literacy: Implications for instructional practice. The Journal of Academic Librarianship, 32(2), 192–199. https://doi.org/10.1016/J.ACALIB.2005.12.004

Floridi, L. (2023). AI as Agency Without Intelligence: on ChatGPT, Large Language Models, and Other Generative Models. Philos. Technol. 36, 15. https://doi.org/10.1007/s13347-023-00621-y

Freed, A. R. (2022). Conversational AI: Chatbots That Work. Shelter Island: Manning. ISBN 9781617298837.

Haman, M. & Školník, M. (2023). Using ChatGPT to conduct a literature review, Accountability in Research, DOI: 10.1080/08989621.2023.2185514

Hannan, E. & Liu, S. (2023), AI: new source of competitiveness in higher education, Competitiveness Review, Vol. 33 No. 2, pp. 265-279. https://doi.org/10.1108/CR-03-2021-0045

OpenAI. (2023). OpenAI. https://openai.com/

Paliwal, S., Bharti, V. & Mishra, A.K. (2020). Ai Chatbots: Transforming the Digital World. In: Balas, V., Kumar, R., Srivastava, R. (eds) Recent Trends and Advances in Artificial Intelligence and Internet of Things. Intelligent Systems Reference Library, vol 172. Springer, Cham. https://doi.org/10.1007/978-3-030-32644-9_34

Pelikán, J. (2011). Základy empirického výzkumu pedagogických jevů. Praha: Kosmas. ISBN 978-80-246-1916-3.

Sandu, N. & Gide, E. (2019). Adoption of AI-Chatbots to Enhance Student Learning Experience in Higher Education in India. *18th International Conference on Information Technology Based Higher Education and Training (ITHET)*, Magdeburg, Germany, pp. 1-5, doi: 10.1109/ITHET46829.2019.8937382.

Shanshan, Y. & Evans, Ch. (2020). Opportunities and Challenges in Using AI Chatbots in Higher Education. In Proceedings of the 2019 3rd International Conference on Education and E-Learning (ICEEL '19). Association for Computing Machinery, New York, NY, USA, 79–83. https://doi.org/10.1145/3371647.3371659

Šimberová, I. (2022). Jak posoudit digitální zralost. Praha: Grada. ISBN 978-80-271-3431-1.

SOCIAL MEDIA

SOCIAL MEDIA AND INNOVATIONS: CASE STUDIES IN AUTOMOTIVE INDUSTRY

Antonín Pavlíček

Faculty of Informatics and Statistics
Prague University of Economics and Business
antonin.pavlicek@vse.cz

DOI: 10.35011/IDIMT-2023-243

Keywords

Social media, innovations, case studies, automotive industry

Abstract

The integration of social media platforms into our daily lives has not only revolutionized communication and connected people from diverse backgrounds but has also emerged as a powerful tool for businesses to innovate and maintain their competitive edge. Case studies from the automotive industry has shown significant transformations through the integration of social media platforms. This paper explores how companies like Tesla and Ford have leveraged social media to create new revenue streams, increase brand awareness, and engage with their fan communities. Examples include Tesla's direct car sales and brand-building efforts and Ford's use of social media to connect with fans and promote new models. Overall, social media has become an essential element in the innovative strategies of automotive companies, enabling them to reach wider audiences and adapt to evolving consumer demands.

1. Introduction

The integration of social media platforms into our daily lives (Khan & Khan, 2019) has not only facilitated communication and connected individuals from diverse backgrounds but has also emerged as a powerful tool for businesses aiming to innovate and maintain their competitive edge. Enterprises of various scales, ranging from small startups to multinational corporations, have recognized the potential of leveraging social media platforms to foster novel ideas, engage with customers, and drive business growth.

Term "social media" refers to interactive online platforms where individuals and communities actively participate in creating, co-crating, modifying, discussing, and sharing user-generated content (Carlson et al., 2018; Arora et al., 2021). As such, social media encompasses a wide range of platforms, including but not limited to social networking sites like Facebook or Vkontakte, visual sharing sites such as YouTube or Instagram, microblogs like Twitter, forums like Reddit, professional networking sites such as LinkedIn, and collaborative platforms like Wikipedia.

Within this context, social networks serve as invaluable repositories of data and information that companies can effectively utilize to shape their innovation strategies. Han & Xu (2021) have pointed out, that social media have dramatically changed the way knowledge search activities are conducted. By harnessing conversations occurring on social media platforms and analyzing user behavior, companies can gain profound insights into customer needs and preferences, identify emerging trends, and unearth unexplored opportunities for the development of products and services. Moreover, social media platforms act as vibrant crowdsourcing arenas, enabling companies to actively connect with their target audience and tap into the collective knowledge and expertise of their communities. By engaging with customers and involving them in the creative process, companies can collaboratively develop innovative offerings that better cater to the requirements of their specific target market.

Consequently, employing social media as a catalyst for innovation empowers companies to establish a competitive advantage within the swiftly evolving business landscape of today (Zhang, 2017). As a result, it is increasingly imperative for companies to devise and implement a comprehensive social media strategy that aligns with their innovation goals (Soto-Acosta, 2017) and positions them at the forefront of industry advancements (Sudzina, 2021). The use of social media by companies has experienced substantial growth (Arora, 2021), establishing itself as one of the most prominent tools in knowledge development.

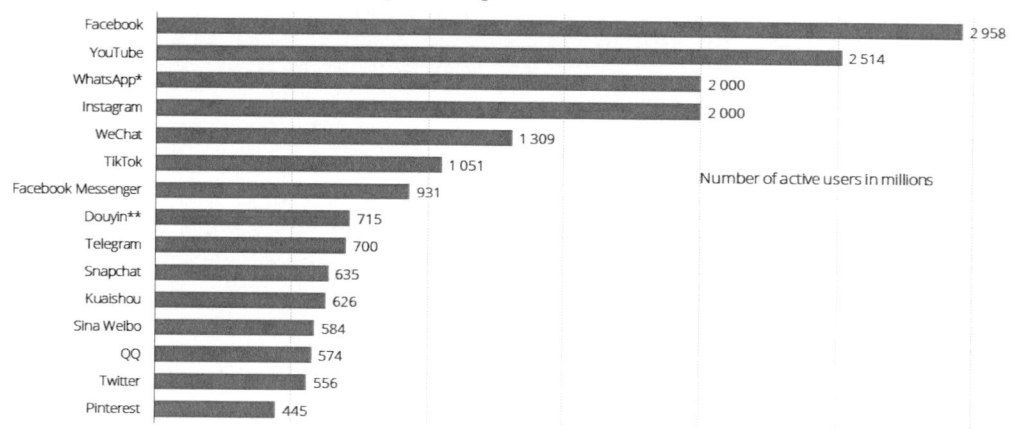

Platform	Number of active users in millions
Facebook	2 958
YouTube	2 514
WhatsApp*	2 000
Instagram	2 000
WeChat	1 309
TikTok	1 051
Facebook Messenger	931
Douyin**	715
Telegram	700
Snapchat	635
Kuaishou	626
Sina Weibo	584
QQ	574
Twitter	556
Pinterest	445

Figure 1. Most popular social networks worldwide, ranked by number of monthly active users
Source: (Statista, 2023)

Utilizing social media as a means of fostering innovation holds significant importance for multiple reasons. Firstly, it enables companies to enhance their comprehension of target users and more effectively address their needs. Through the analysis of conversations taking place on social networks, organizations can gain valuable insights into customer preferences, market trends, and existing vulnerabilities within their products and services. Consequently, this empowers them to develop offerings that are more pertinent, efficient, and better tailored to their intended audience.

Moreover, leveraging social media for innovation endeavors enables companies to maintain a competitive edge within their respective industries by identifying emerging trends and market opportunities. Social networks serve as platforms where users freely express their opinions, share experiences, and articulate their expectations. By meticulously scrutinizing the data generated from these interactions, companies can swiftly recognize emerging trends and readily adapt to dynamic market changes (Jirásek, 2022).

Furthermore, employing social media as a tool for innovation facilitates direct engagement between companies and their target audience, facilitating collaborative product and service development. By actively involving customers in the process of creating new offerings, companies can gain invaluable insights into the desires and requirements of their customer base. Consequently, this enables the development of products and services that directly cater to customer needs, ultimately enhancing long-term satisfaction and loyalty (Korčák, 2021).

Recent published research indicates that successful companies have already effectively - and at low cost - utilized social media platforms to acquire knowledge (Barlatier, 2018; Roberts, 2016). Social media enable firms to extract new ideas and information from users (Ozcan et al., 2021) and they also facilitate active involvement of customers in the innovation process (Muninger et al., 2022). By leveraging social media, Ogink (2019) claims that companies can effectively harness knowledge for product development and innovation, fostering intricate communication patterns by connecting those seeking innovation (Muninger, 2019) and those providing innovative solutions across various stages of the innovation process (Testa, 2020).

In summary, the use of social media as an innovation tool is of great importance for companies endeavoring to sustain competitiveness in an ever-evolving marketplace. The benefits derived from this approach encompass a more profound understanding of customers and their needs, the ability to identify emerging trends and market opportunities, and the capacity to engage in co-development initiatives with target audiences.

1.1. Comparing the approach before and after the advent of social media:

In the pre-social media era, companies predominantly depended on conventional advertising channels, endorsements, events, and community engagement as their primary means of generating revenue, enhancing brand visibility, and connecting with their audience. Although the emergence of social media has brought about a substantial shift in marketing strategies, it is important to acknowledge the effectiveness of these traditional approaches during their time, as they played a crucial role in establishing numerous successful brands that we witness today.

Pre-social media era:

- **TV and Radio Advertising:** Advertisers heavily relied on TV and radio commercials as a key marketing tool to promote their products. They used catchy jingles, memorable slogans, and compelling storytelling to create brand awareness and entice customers.
- **Celebrity Endorsements:** Clothing companies collaborated with popular celebrities to endorse their products and enhance brand visibility. For instance, Nike's partnership with Michael Jordan not only resulted in increased revenue but also established a strong association between the brand and basketball.

Social media era:

- **Online Communities and Forums:** Automotive companies foster online communities and forums where enthusiasts can connect, share experiences, and discuss the brand's vehicles. These platforms cultivate a sense of belonging, brand loyalty, and fan engagement.
- **Social Media Campaigns:** Clothing brands now leverage social media platforms to actively engage with their fans through creative campaigns. For instance, Burberry initiated the "Art of the Trench" campaign, encouraging customers to share photos of themselves wearing Burberry trench coats. This campaign not only increased brand awareness but also generated user-generated content.
- **Social Media Contests:** Companies frequently organize social media contests to interact with their fan base. Wendy's, for example, gained significant attention through Twitter challenges and entertaining interactions, resulting in heightened brand awareness and increased customer engagement.

- **Influencer Marketing:** Clothing companies collaborate with influencers or popular bloggers who have a substantial following on social media platforms to promote their products. Influencers create content featuring the brand's clothing, reaching a wide audience and generating brand awareness and sales.

- **Social Media Advertising:** Companies effectively utilize targeted advertising on social media platforms to reach their desired audience. Platforms like Facebook and Instagram provide companies with the capability to create highly specific ad campaigns based on demographics, interests, and behaviors.

2. Case studies

The advent of social media has fundamentally transformed the dynamics of business-customer interactions, providing companies with novel avenues for direct, personalized, and interactive communication with their target audiences. This paradigm shift has opened up new possibilities for companies to effectively increase brand awareness, strengthen engagement with existing customers, and explore untapped revenue streams by reaching previously unexplored audiences.

The first criterion under consideration pertains to the establishment of new revenue streams. Social media platforms offer companies a unique opportunity to connect with and target new segments of the market, utilizing innovative strategies. By leveraging social media, companies can effectively promote and showcase new products and services, launch compelling advertising campaigns, and even facilitate direct sales transactions. Successful implementation of these strategies enables companies to strengthen their market position and achieve new business objectives.

The second criterion revolves around brand awareness. Social networks provide companies with a platform to strengthen their online presence and shape their brand image. Companies can effectively share their narratives, values, and corporate culture, fostering a community of passionate and loyal followers. Companies that excel at building brand awareness through social media witness increased brand recognition, improved reputation, and enhanced customer trust.

The third criterion focuses on fan engagement. Social networks enable companies to engage with their target groups in a more personalized and interactive manner. Companies can utilize social media platforms to actively respond to customer feedback, initiate conversations, organize contests, and motivate customers to generate user-generated content. Companies that effectively engage with fans through social media benefit from stronger customer relationships, heightened loyalty, and increased influence on purchasing decisions.

In summary, social media offers companies powerful tools to drive innovation and attain new business objectives. By strategically and creatively harnessing the potential of social media, companies can unlock new revenue streams, enhance brand awareness, and foster greater fan engagement.

2.1. Case study in automotive industry

In recent years, the automotive industry has undergone adaptations in response to the emergence of digital tools, particularly social media platforms, in an effort to drive innovation within the sector. Automakers swiftly recognized the potential of social media to expand their reach to new audiences, bolster brand awareness, enhance fan engagement, and generate fresh revenue streams.

Through social media, automakers have gained the capability to directly connect with their target audience, facilitating real-time interaction, collecting valuable feedback on their products and services, and fostering the establishment of devoted fan communities. Platforms such as Facebook, Twitter, Instagram, and YouTube have provided automakers with the means to promote their brand through captivating videos, compelling imagery, and engaging narratives, thereby effectively capturing the attention and involvement of consumers.

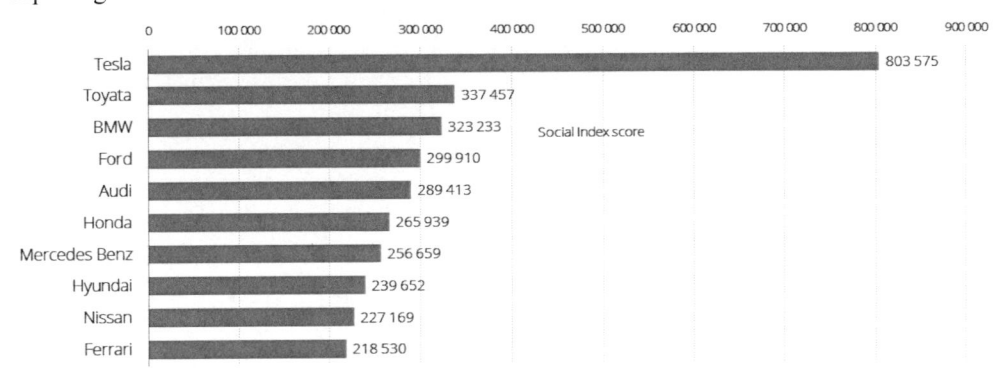

Brand	Social Index score
Tesla	803 575
Toyata	337 457
BMW	323 233
Ford	299 910
Audi	289 413
Honda	265 939
Mercedes Benz	256 659
Hyundai	239 652
Nissan	227 169
Ferrari	218 530

Figure 2. Leading automotive brands worldwide in 2021, by Social Index score Source: (Statista, 2021)

The utilization of social media platforms has facilitated car manufacturers in the creation of new revenue streams. For instance, certain brands have adopted the practice of selling car accessories directly through their social media accounts, while others have introduced loyalty programs to incentivize customers to make additional purchases.

Furthermore, social media has proven to be instrumental in enhancing fan engagement for automakers. Through the organization of contests, live events, and the sharing of compelling narratives, automakers have been successful in cultivating a more dedicated fan community, thereby augmenting the overall customer experience.

In summary, social media has enabled the automotive industry to establish direct connections with consumers, generate new revenue streams, elevate brand awareness, and foster greater fan engagement. Car manufacturers persistently innovate in this domain to sustain their competitiveness within an increasingly demanding market.

2.1.1. Tesla

Social media used to create new revenue streams

Tesla is known for its ability to innovate in the automotive industry, and that also extends to using social media to create new revenue streams. Here are some examples of how Tesla has used social media to generate additional revenue:

Direct online car sales:

The advent of direct online car sales has revolutionized the automotive industry, with Tesla being one of the pioneers in adopting this approach. By bypassing the traditional dealer network, Tesla has been able to sell cars directly to consumers, resulting in cost reduction and the ability to offer more competitive pricing to its customers.

Notably, data reported by InsideEVs (2023) reveals that since the introduction of its first model, the Tesla Model S, in 2012, Tesla has successfully sold over 200,000 cars online. In 2020, online sales accounted for nearly 75% of the brand's total sales, reflecting the significant impact of their direct sales strategy. It is noteworthy that despite the challenges posed by the COVID-19 pandemic, which had adverse effects on the automotive industry as a whole, Tesla's online sales experienced a remarkable 50% increase compared to the previous years.

Referral programs:

Tesla has implemented referral programs as part of its marketing strategy to incentivize customers to recommend the brand to their acquaintances. Through these programs, customers can earn rewards, such as credits towards the purchase of a new vehicle or exclusive invitations to Tesla events, by actively promoting the brand to their friends and family.

Tesla launched its referral program in 2015, which quickly gained significant success. In 2016, Tesla announced that 31% of its sales in the US were directly attributed to customer referrals. Tesla reported that customers who participated in the referral program generated an average of 5-6 referrals, enabling the brand to expand its audience and reach potential new customers.

The specific details of Tesla's referral program may vary depending on the country and region, but generally, customers can earn rewards by inviting friends to experience a test drive of a Tesla vehicle or by assisting them in the process of purchasing a Tesla car.

Accurate and comprehensive data regarding the precise impact of Tesla's referral programs on the brand's sales remains elusive, as the company does not disclose detailed sales figures specifically linked to customer referrals. Nevertheless, it is evident that Tesla's referral program has played a significant role in the company's growth strategy, enabling it to not only access new customer segments but also retain its existing customer base.

Social media used to build brand awareness

Tesla demonstrated pioneering efforts as one of the early adopters among automakers to employ a digital marketing strategy, actively using social media to cultivate brand awareness. The following are key methods employed by Tesla to leverage social media for building brand awareness:

Product presentation:

Central to Tesla's digital marketing strategy has been the showcasing of its products on social media platforms. Through the utilization of images, videos, and detailed descriptions, Tesla effectively presents its new car models, software updates, accessories, and other related offerings. This approach enables Tesla to offer its audience an immersive understanding of its products and their value-added features. Additionally, the utilization of social media platforms for product presentation allows Tesla to extend its reach beyond the confines of traditional launch events.

By 2019, Tesla's social media presence had expanded to include approximately 2.7 million followers on Twitter, 5.5 million followers on Instagram, and 8.4 million likes on Facebook. Subsequently, in 2020, these figures experienced substantial growth, with Tesla accumulating over 6.2 million followers on Twitter, more than 12 million followers on Instagram, and surpassing 10 million likes on Facebook.

Furthermore, the impact of Tesla's digital marketing efforts is exemplified by the viewership statistics of their product presentation videos. In 2019, the Tesla Model Y presentation video garnered over 1.5 million views on YouTube within a mere two days. Similarly, in 2020, the Tesla Cybertruck presentation video amassed over 16 million views in just one week. Additionally, in 2021, Tesla utilized social media to promote the launch of the Full Self-Driving Beta software update. Within a few days, the accompanying video introducing the feature accumulated over 7 million views on Twitter.

Overall, Tesla's adept utilization of social media platforms to showcase its products has significantly contributed to the development of brand awareness among a wide audience. By leveraging visual media and engaging content, Tesla has effectively harnessed the power of social media to bolster its brand presence and engage with potential customers.

Marketing campaigns:

Tesla's digital marketing strategy encompasses a range of marketing campaigns that have played a pivotal role in reaching new audiences, enhancing brand awareness, and stimulating sales. A notable example is the 2018 marketing campaign for the Tesla Model 3, which centered on social media, online advertisements, and launch events. Through strategic deployment of videos and images of the Model 3 on social media platforms, Tesla successfully generated anticipation and buzz. Moreover, the company organized launch events in various cities worldwide, providing enthusiasts with the opportunity to experience the car firsthand and reserve their own Model 3.

This marketing campaign proved to be immensely successful for Tesla, as it garnered over 325,000 reservations, equivalent to a value exceeding $14 billion, within a week. Furthermore, the campaign generated extensive social media mentions and garnered significant media coverage.

In 2019, Tesla initiated another marketing campaign for the Tesla Model Y, encompassing television and online advertisements, as well as launch events. Leveraging social media platforms, Tesla showcased the Model Y through videos, images, and interactive engagement with fans. This campaign also achieved notable success, with the introduction video for the Model Y amassing over 1.5 million views on YouTube within two days and receiving a substantial number of reservations shortly after its unveiling.

These numerical outcomes aptly demonstrate the efficacy of Tesla's marketing campaigns in augmenting brand awareness and propelling sales. The campaigns have effectively enabled Tesla to reach new audiences, generate substantial interest in its latest car models, and ignite significant buzz within the market.

Overall, social media platforms have played a vital role in Tesla's digital marketing strategy, contributing significantly to the establishment of brand awareness. As indicated by the aforementioned statistics, Tesla has amassed more than 6.2 million Twitter followers, over 12 million Instagram followers, and more than 10 million Facebook likes in 2020 alone. These figures signify substantial growth compared to previous years, underscoring the positive impact of Tesla's social media-focused digital marketing strategy.

Social media used to build fan engagement

Tesla has gained prominence for its innovative marketing approach, particularly through its utilization of social media platforms to actively engage with its fanbase. The following are notable methods employed by Tesla to effectively connect with its audience and cultivate a robust community of enthusiasts:

Creation of engaging content:

Tesla prioritizes the development of captivating content as a primary strategy to engage fans on social media. The company produces a diverse content, including videos, images, infographics, and articles, creatively showcasing their products while informing and entertaining their audience.

For instance, on Twitter, Tesla consistently shares videos highlighting the impressive performance of their electric cars, photographs of new car models, updates on technological advancements, details about company events, expressions of gratitude towards loyal customers, and responses to user inquiries. This amalgamation of creative and informative content has propelled Tesla's prominence on social media, fostering substantial engagement from their followers. Indeed, according to data from Socialbakers, a social media management platform, Tesla emerged as the most engaged automotive brand on Twitter in 2020, with over 40 million interactions throughout the year. Furthermore, Tesla garnered the highest number of mentions among automotive brands on Twitter, amassing 1.2 million mentions within a month. These statistics underscore the effectiveness of Tesla's engaging content creation strategy in driving engagement from their dedicated fan community.

Community building:

Tesla actively employs community-building strategies to foster engagement among its fanbase on social media. The company encourages customers and fans to share their experiences and ideas through various social networks while maintaining regular interaction with their audience.

For example, Tesla utilizes Twitter as a platform for addressing user queries, resolving issues, disseminating news, and providing brand updates. Additionally, Tesla has established Tesla car owner groups on Facebook, facilitating connections between owners, allowing them to share experiences and collectively troubleshoot problems.

This approach has enabled Tesla to cultivate a devoted and engaged community of fans. According to data from Brandwatch, Tesla emerged as the most mentioned automotive brand on social media, accumulating 1.2 million mentions within a month in 2021. Moreover, the company's efforts in community building have contributed to the establishment of a loyal and active fan community. Additionally, according to Meltwater's Social Media Benchmark report for 2020, Tesla was the most mentioned automotive brand on social media, with over 10 million mentions.

Foster brand loyalty

Nurturing brand loyalty constitutes a vital strategy employed by Tesla to effectively engage its fanbase through social media channels. To foster brand loyalty, Tesla prioritizes the delivery of an exceptional customer experience, exemplified by swift responses to customer inquiries and concerns, complimentary software updates, extended warranty offerings, and rewards programs specifically tailored for loyal customers.

Furthermore, Tesla has implemented a referral program aimed at incentivizing existing customers to advocate for the brand among their social circles. By providing rewards to customers who successfully refer new individuals, this program not only cultivates loyalty among existing customers but also expands the customer base by attracting new Tesla car purchasers. ReferralCandy data reveals that in 2018 alone, Tesla's referral program generated an impressive count of over 40,000 referrals, underscoring the effectiveness of this approach in nurturing brand loyalty. Moreover, according to the Brand Intimacy Study 2020 conducted by MBLM, a prominent marketing consultancy, Tesla emerged as the automotive brand with the highest emotional connection to consumers, indicating the positive impact of brand loyalty on fan engagement.

2.1.2. Ford

Social media used to create new revenue streams

Ford has adeptly harnessed social media to create new revenue streams, primarily through targeted advertising strategies.

Targeted advertising:

Leveraging the wealth of user data available on social networks, Ford has been able to deliver tailored advertisements that effectively reach consumers exhibiting a genuine interest in the brand's products.

Through targeted ads on social media platforms, Ford has successfully promoted a diverse array of products, spanning electric vehicles, trucks, and sports cars. Such precision-targeted advertisements enable Ford to engage with consumers who are most likely to make purchases within these product categories, thereby augmenting the conversion rate of ads into tangible sales.

In terms of investment, Ford allocated approximately 40 percent of its total advertising budget to digital ads in 2020, with a significant portion allocated specifically to social media advertisements. An analysis conducted by eMarketer reveals that Ford's digital ad expenditure in the United States reached $1.48 billion in 2020, reflecting a 10.4 percent increase compared to the previous year. Although these figures do not exclusively pertain to targeted social media advertisements, they underscore the significance Ford attributes to digital advertising and its substantial impact on the company's financial performance.

Through a strategic focus on targeted advertising campaigns on social media, Ford has successfully capitalized on the potential of social media platforms to generate new revenue streams. By leveraging user data and tailoring advertisements to specific consumer segments, Ford has effectively increased the probability of converting ad exposures into tangible sales. The substantial investment in digital advertising further underscores the importance Ford places on digital channels and their influence on the company's overall financial performance.

Social media used to build brand awareness

Creating engaging branded content

Ford strategically implemented a compelling branded content creation approach on social media platforms to effectively capture consumer attention and establish a strong brand presence. This strategy involved the development of informative, inspirational, and educational content that aligned with the brand's identity and values.

Ford employed a diverse range of content formats on social media, encompassing visually appealing photos, engaging videos, and thought-provoking blog posts. The content aimed to promote Ford's products, narrate the brand's unique story, highlight the brand's automotive expertise, and emphasize the importance of environmental sustainability.

For instance, Ford created a series of educational videos dedicated to hybrid technology, serving to enhance consumer understanding of the benefits associated with this innovative technology. Additionally, the brand launched a collection of documentary videos showcasing Ford's rich history and the brand's profound impact on people's lives.

This strategy of producing captivating and informative content has proven instrumental in augmenting Ford's brand awareness on social media platforms. According to data from Brand Finance, Ford secured a position among the top 10 most valuable automotive brands worldwide in 2021, with a remarkable brand value of $12.7 billion.

Furthermore, Ford witnessed a notable 7.9% increase in Facebook engagement in 2021 compared to the preceding year. The brand also experienced significant engagement growth across other platforms (16.5% rise Instagram engagement and 19.6% increase Twitter engagement in 2021).

These statistics affirm the effectiveness of Ford's strategy in creating engaging content on social media, leading to heightened brand awareness and increased audience engagement. Ford's commitment to delivering compelling content has facilitated the brand's recognition as a prominent player in the automotive industry, resonating with consumers and cultivating a loyal fan base.

Interaction with customers

Ford implemented a robust customer interaction strategy on social media platforms as part of its brand awareness initiatives. This strategy entailed utilizing various communication channels, such as comments, private messages, and live chats, to engage directly with customers. A key aspect of this strategy was the prompt response to customer inquiries and concerns, aiming to deliver swift customer service through these channels. By establishing a reputation for responsive and reliable customer support on social media, Ford successfully cultivated customer trust and loyalty.

Furthermore, Ford introduced incentive programs to incentivize customer engagement with the brand on social networks. This included running interactive contests and games that allowed customers to participate and have the opportunity to win prizes. These endeavors served as effective mechanisms for driving brand awareness and enhancing customer perception of the brand.

According to a study conducted by Forrester Research, Ford was recognized as one of the top automotive brands for customer service on social media in 2020, underscoring the brand's commitment to fostering positive customer interactions.

Moreover, Ford experienced significant increases in engagement across multiple social media platforms in 2021. Specifically, there was an 8.6% surge in Facebook engagement, a 14.7% rise in Instagram engagement, and a 15.4% increase in Twitter engagement compared to the previous year.

These findings highlight the effectiveness of Ford's customer interaction strategy on social media in augmenting brand awareness and improving customer engagement. Ford's commitment to prompt and personalized customer service, coupled with the implementation of incentivized programs, has positively influenced customer perception and fostered stronger connections with its audience.

Social media used to build fan engagement

Ford has also used social media to build engagement with its fans. Here are a few examples of how Ford has built its community and created engaging content:

Creating engaging content

Ford leveraged social media to execute marketing campaigns, exemplified by the successful "Mustang Countdown" and "Fiesta Movement" initiatives. The "Mustang Countdown" campaign, employed countdown videos, imagery, and articles disseminated across social media and Ford's website to generate anticipation for the new Mustang. This campaign amassed over 9 million YouTube views and secured 16,000 pre-orders for the vehicle. "Fiesta Movement" campaign in 2009 involved distributing 100 Ford Fiesta cars to social media influencers, who created original content to showcase the vehicle. The campaign garnered remarkable results, including more than 6.2 million YouTube views and a significant 30% increase in Fiesta sales that year. In 2021, Ford's commitment to engaging content persisted, with the "Mach-E 1400: The Ultimate Performance Machine" video on YouTube amassing over 2 million views within weeks of its release.

Community building

Building a vibrant community on social media is a central element of Ford's strategy to foster fan engagement with the brand. Here are key examples of how Ford has successfully cultivated its social media community, as demonstrated by the following metrics:

- Ford has established dedicated Facebook groups for various car models, enabling owners to exchange experiences and discuss their affinity for the brand. Notably, the "Ford Mustang Owners" group boasts over 460,000 members as of 2021.

- On Twitter, Ford initiated the hashtag #FordFamily for enthusiasts to share photos of their Fords and interact with fellow owners. In 2020, this hashtag generated over 10,000 tweets.
- Ford hosts both online and offline events exclusively tailored for Ford car owners, encompassing gatherings, driving sessions, and live virtual events. These occasions provide fans with opportunities to connect and celebrate their shared passion for the brand. Remarkably, Ford orchestrated over 500 fan events worldwide in 2020.
- Ford introduced the mobile app FordPass, granting car owners access to features such as locating gas stations, planning routes, and reserving parking spots. By 2021, the app had garnered over 1.5 million downloads.

These initiatives have effectively nurtured Ford's fan community on social media, fostering interaction among Ford car owners and providing dedicated spaces to express their brand loyalty. As a result, fan engagement with the brand has notably increased, evident through metrics including event attendance, hashtag usage, and the popularity of the FordPass mobile app.

3. Conclusions

The automotive industry has witnessed significant transformation in recent years, due to the integration of social media platforms, which provided brands with opportunities to establish new revenue streams, enhance brand awareness, and foster engagement within their fan communities.

Tesla has emerged as a trailblazer in leveraging social media to revolutionize the industry. The brand has utilized these platforms not only for direct car sales but also to promote ancillary products. By circumventing traditional dealership models, Tesla has offered customers a personalized purchasing experience. Additionally, social media has facilitated brand awareness by enabling direct communication with its fan community, while reinforcing a strong brand image aligned with its commitment to technological innovation and environmental sustainability.

Ford has utilized social media to enhance brand awareness and establish connections with its fan community. By leveraging these platforms to share exclusive content and engage in direct communication with customers, Ford has cultivated a more accessible and personalized brand image. Furthermore, social media has facilitated the promotion of new car models and the implementation of interactive marketing campaigns.

In summary, social media has become an integral component of the marketing strategies employed by automotive companies. These platforms offer brands an expansive reach, heightened brand awareness, diversified revenue streams, and improved engagement with their fan communities. In an increasingly interconnected world where consumers seek personalized interactions with brands, the utilization of social media has become indispensable for maintaining competitiveness within the ever-evolving automotive industry.

References

Arora, A. S. K. S. & Paul A. P. (2021). Social Capacitance: Leveraging Absorptive Capacity in the Age of Social Media. Journal of Business Research 124: 342–56.

Barlatier, P., & Josserand, E. (2018). Delivering Open Innovation Premises through Social Media. Journal of Business Strategy, 39(6), 21–8.

Carlson, J. M. R., & DeVries N. (2018). Customer Engagement Behaviours in Social Media: Capturing Innovation Opportunities, Journal of Services Marketing 32(1), 83–94.

Han, M., & Xu B. (2021). Distance with customers effects on green product innovation in SMEs: A way through green value cocreation. SAGE Open, 11(4), https://doi.org/10.1177/21582440211061539.

InsideEVs (2023).| Electric Vehicle News, Reviews, and Reports. InsideEVs. https://insideevs.com/

Jirásek, M, & Sudzina, F. (2022). The association between personality traits and perceived innovativeness. International journal of business innovation and research, eISSN 1751-0260. ISSN 1751-0252. DOI: 10.1504/IJBIR.2022.10051418.

Khan, N. A., & Khan A. N. (2019). What Followers, Are Saying about Transformational Leaders Fostering Employee Innovation Via Organisational Learning, Knowledge, Sharing, &Social Media Use in Public Organisations? Government Information Quarterly, 36(4), 101391.

Korčák, J., Syrovátková, J., & Sigmund, T. (2021). Social Connectedness in Online Environment: Literature Review. In: IDIMT-2021 Pandemics: Impacts, Strategies and Responses, Linz, Trauner Verlag, 223–228. ISBN 978-3-99113-261-5.

Muninger, M., Mahr, D., & Hammedi, W. (2022). Social Media Use: A Review of Innovation Management Practices. Journal of Business Research 143: 140–56.

Muninger, M., Hammedi, W., & Mahr, D. (2019). The Value of Social Media for Innovation: A Capability Perspective. Journal of Business Research 95, 116–27.

Ogink, T., & Dong, J. Q. (2019). Stimulating Innovation by User Feedback on Social Media: The Case of an Online User Innovation Community. Technological Forecasting and Social Change 144, 295–302.

Ozcan, S., Sulogu, M., Sakar, O. C., & Chatufale S. (2021). Social Media Mining for Ideation: Identification of Sustainable Solutions and Opinions. Technovation 107, 102322.

Roberts, D. L., Piller F. T., & Lüttgens D. (2016). Mapping the Impact of Social Media for Innovation: The Role of Social Media in Explaining Innovation Performance in the PDMA Comparative Performance Assessment Study. Journal of Product Innovation Management 33, 117–35.

Soto-Acosta, P., Popa, S., & Palacios-Marqués, D. (2017). Social Web Knowledge Sharing and Innovation Performance in Knowledge-Intensive Manufacturing SMEs. The Journal of Technology Transfer 42(2), 425–40.

Statista. (2021). Leading automotive brands worldwide in 2021, by Social Index score. Statista. https://www-statista-com.zdroje.vse.cz/statistics/1322315/car-brands-social-index-score//

Statista. (2023). Biggest social media platforms 2023. Statista. http://www.statista.com/statistics/272014/global-social-networks-ranked-by-number-of-users/

Sudzina, F., Dobeš, M., & Pavlíček, A. (2021). Towards the psychological profile of cryptocurrency early adopters: Overconfidence and self-control as predictors of cryptocurrency use. Current Psychology, 40(8), 1–5. eISSN 1936-4733. ISSN 1046-1310. DOI: 10.1007/s12144-021-02225-1.

Syrovátková, J., Korčák, J., & Pavlíček, A. (2021). Sharing information on social networks. In: Proceedings of the 14th International Conference on Strategic Management and its Support by Information Systems 2021. Ostrava, VŠB – Technical University of Ostrava Faculty of Economics, 2021, 283–291. ISBN 978-80-248-4521-0.

Testa, S., Massa, S., Martini, A., & Appio F. P. (2020). Social Media-Based Innovation: A Review of Trends and a Research Agenda. Information & Management 57(3), 103196.

Zhang, N, Zhao, X., Zhang, Z., Meng, Q., & Tan, H. (2017). What Factors Drive Open Innovation in China's Public Sector? A Case Study of Official Document Exchange Via Microblogging (ODEM) in Haining. Government Information Quarterly 34(1), 126–33.

MARKETING COMMUNICATION TARGETING CHILDREN ON ONLINE MEDIA

Jitka Burešová

Ekonomická fakulta
Technická univerzita v Liberci
jitka.buresova@tul.cz

DOI: 10.35011/IDIMT-2023-255

Keywords

Children, Online medium, Marketing communication tools, Social networks

Abstract

Children spend a large part of their free time online. The issue of children's safety online has been debated in society for many years. However, the debate does not focus on the impact of online marketing communications that target children on the Internet. This article aims to map the online media most frequently visited by children aged 10 to 13 in the Czech Republic and identify the most common ways in which children actively interact with marketing content. To achieve this goal, qualitative pre-research was first conducted as individual in-depth interviews with 16 children of the given age. The interviews identified the seven most frequently visited online media by children on which marketing communication is placed and how children interact with this online marketing communication. The main research data collection method was an online questionnaire, which was completed by a total of 591 children. The questionnaire tested seven identified online media and children's interactions with marketing communication. The results showed that children have an average of 4.8 media out of the seven we asked about and most often interact with online marketing communication on the Google search engine, where they click on different types of PPC ads, and on Instagram and TikTok, where they post profiles of famous people who very often have paid partnerships with the company whose products they then promote to children.

1. Introduction

The Internet is not only a medium for adults today; it also plays an indispensable role in the lives of children. Parents often face the dilemma of deciding at what age and in what form to give their children access to the Internet. Many parents habitually hand a smartphone or tablet to toddlers (Ward, 2013). Therefore, the societal discussion in recent years has rightly addressed the issue of children's internet safety. Most often mentioned is the need to teach children to handle their passwords properly, not to reveal confidential information about themselves or to not communicate with people the child does not know. Outside of these main topics is online marketing, which children encounter across the online world, but virtually no one addresses the impact of online marketing on children.

Several online media[1], especially social media, are officially accessible only to children aged 13 and over. For this reason, there are no official statistics on whether and how many under-age children are on these social networks.

From birth, a child is surrounded by marketing communications in the real world and on the Internet. For example, Watkins et al. (2022) point out that on a typical day in the US, children see an average of 554 brands in 10 hours, 20% of which are junk food and beverage brands. However, this constant exposure to brands significantly impacts brand awareness, an essential prerequisite for customers to buy (Aaker, 2003). Children are often targeted by manufacturers and sellers of calorific food (sweets, sugary drinks, fast food, Etc.). These companies want to nurture lifelong customers. They rely on children liking the brand at an early age and thus preferring it throughout their lives (Story & French, 2004). These manufacturers exploit the fact that children are vulnerable to campaigns they recognise as a form of marketing communication and are even worse off when they do not identify the marketing communication. Children between the ages of 10 and 12 can recognise the explicit purpose of advertising campaigns but cannot think critically about it (Heart and Stroke Foundation, 2017). This lack of critical insight is mainly because children generally have a rather negative attitude towards marketing communication, which they have adopted from adults. Negative attitudes towards marketing tools are prevalent in the adult population, with over-saturation of advertising and the fact that advertising encourages unnecessary consumption being mentioned in particular (Česká marketingová společnost, 2022). Negative attitudes among children, however, do not lead to advertising not influencing them. On the contrary, if a child refuses to acknowledge that an advertisement appeals to him or her and influences his or her purchasing decisions, it is all the more dangerous for him or her (Mallalieu et al., 2005).

The text above shows that companies routinely target marketing communications to children and that children have a limited ability to resist these communications. Much of this communication is directed to the online space where children are present for several hours daily. Where and what form of online marketing communication children encounter and whether they actively seek it out has yet to be investigated in research conducted in the Czech Republic. Thus, we have yet to learn which types of children use more online media according to their sociodemographic characteristics, nor which forms of online marketing communication they interact with most actively. This knowledge can serve as a basis for further research on the impact of online marketing communication on children, which is necessary to be carried out in order to establish recommendations for possible amendments to legislation that would restrict certain forms of online marketing communication in relation to children or to provide tips for managers of companies that own online media on how to adapt their interface to make it safer for children. Research in this area can help eliminate the biggest risks associated with online marketing communications and their impact on children.

For the research, the age of the respondents was set between 10 and 13 years. These are primary school pupils in grades 5 and 6 who, according to the 2017 research, already have their financial resources and are starting to shop independently (Thaichon, 2017). This age group is regularly online and encounters online marketing communication (Kopecký, 2019). The ability of children of this age to think about marketing issues in a broader context (John, 1999) makes the age group of 10 to 13 ideal for research. Based on the specification of the research problem and the future respondents, the main objective of the research was formulated:

---

[1] Online media is an umbrella term for any website, social network or email, i.e. anything that is hosted on the Internet (Law Insider 2023)

The article's main objective is to map the online media most frequently visited by children aged 10 to 13 in the Czech Republic and to identify the most common ways children actively interact with marketing content.

Due to the lack of Czech research on the topic, it was impossible to establish research hypotheses; therefore, three research questions were set.

1. **What is the average number of online media visits by children aged 10 to 13?**
2. **What sociodemographic factors influence the number of online media children aged 10 to 13 watch?**
3. **On which online media do children aged 10 to 13 most often actively interact with marketing activities?**

The next chapter will present in detail the research methodology and the statistical methods used to evaluate the data. The next chapter will present the results of the data analysis according to the three formulated research questions. The discussion will then compare the results obtained with the already conducted research, and the conclusion will present the necessity of changes in legislation in the field of online marketing communication targeting children and the limits of the research.

2. Methodology

The quantitative research presented in this article was preceded by qualitative research, specifically through in-depth interviews. The interviews aimed to identify which online media children visit and what they do on them. A total of 16 children from eight primary schools in Liberec, aged 10 to 13, participated in this pre-research. The qualitative research identified seven online media that children visit at least occasionally, and at the same time, some form of marketing communication is found on them. The most frequent forms of interaction of children with this online marketing communication were also identified. In social media, it turned out that children mostly do not follow company profiles or are interested in company posts. On the contrary, children follow the profiles of well-known personalities; we can say influencers regularly post content promoting specific brands. For other online media, a classic active approach to marketing communication was identified, such as opening and reading company emails, searching for product prices on Google search or shopping on an e-shop. The quantitative research further explored these activities and the seven identified online media.

The purpose of the quantitative research was set to be exploratory, and the strategy used was ad hoc research. The basic set for the questionnaire survey was all primary schools and multi-year grammar schools in Liberec and adjacent municipalities (satellites). The base set was chosen to guarantee fast data collection with a high return rate. The advantage of this chosen base set was geographical proximity and accessibility to the research team. A non-probability judgmental sampling method was chosen to determine the sample of respondents. This method was used to select eight schools from the population cooperating with the Faculty of Science, Humanities and Education of TUL for a long time. The sample was deliberately selected to include a variety of schools, both in terms of their location, size, prestige, and possible extended teaching of a particular subject. These were the same schools from which we selected pupils for in-depth interviews. The selected sample includes different groups of pupils regarding sociodemographic characteristics found in large cities nationwide. For this reason, the research results are related to children from regional cities nationwide.

An online questionnaire was chosen as the data collection method. The filter questions were used to determine which online media students visit and with what frequency. The media visited were then presented to the respondents with additional questions in the form of Likert scales relating to the degree of interaction of the respondents with the identified communication tools. The questionnaire concluded with questions to identify the sociodemographic characteristics of the student's family.

Data collection was conducted in all fifth and sixth grades in the selected primary schools between May 31 and June 20, 2021. The questionnaire was completed by all children who had a signed consent form from a legal guardian and were at school on the day of data collection. A total of 591 pupils participated in the survey.

51% of boys and 49% of girls participated in the study. 10%, 43%, 48% and 4% of respondents were 10, 11, 12 and 13 years old, respectively. 21% of the respondents had no siblings; most, 55% of the respondents, had one sibling, two siblings 18% and three or more siblings 6% of the respondents. The ambition of the survey was to gain some understanding of the sociodemographic characteristics of the children's families. However, through qualitative research, we verified that children do not have a good idea of their family's financial situation and their parents' occupation. For this reason, a set of questions was devised that together could be expected to provide at least a basic idea of the sociodemographic characteristics of families. The first question aimed at identifying families that have a problem with sudden financial expenditure. When asked if parents would have a financial problem buying a new smartphone for their child immediately, 9% of respondents answered that they would. Unfortunately, 33% of the children answered that they did not know, and we cannot tell if they did not know or were embarrassed to admit it. The next two questions asked about the parents' education. These two questions were evaluated to create a variable taking three variations (both parents max. high school education, one parent with a college degree, and both parents with a college degree). The questionnaire included what the parents were currently doing, whether they were employed, running a business, staying at home or looking for work. For both mothers and fathers, the most common response was that they were going to work, with business coming in second. Other responses were recorded minimally

The data were evaluated using descriptive statistics, specifically, frequencies converted to percentages. A classification tree method was chosen to reveal the influence of sociodemographic variables on the number of online media used. The number of online media used by each respondent entered the analysis as the dependent variable. The sociodemographic characteristics of the respondents and their families presented in the previous section were used as independent variables. A general tree was constructed using the CHAID method interpreted by a dendrogram with a maximum depth of 5 levels. The minimum cases in the parent node were 100, and 50 in the child node.

3. Results

As mentioned in the methodology chapter, the survey included seven online media for which we asked whether the child uses them and if so, how often. The average number of online media children use is 4.8, which means that a child uses almost 5 of the seven media we asked about.

Furthermore, sociodemographic factors influencing the number of online media used were investigated. The results of the classification tree show that respondents can be segmented according to how much online media they use (figure 1). In this case, the most critical factor is the child's age. Younger children up to and including 11 years old use on average 4.5 online media, while older children use five media. For younger children, the school they attend also has an impact. More online media are used by children from the two schools where smartphone are allowed during breaks and at the school with extended computer science lessons. From the bottom branch of the graph, we can see the people who use the most media. These children over the age of 11 are familiar with the family's economic situation and whose parents have, at most, a secondary education with a high school diploma.

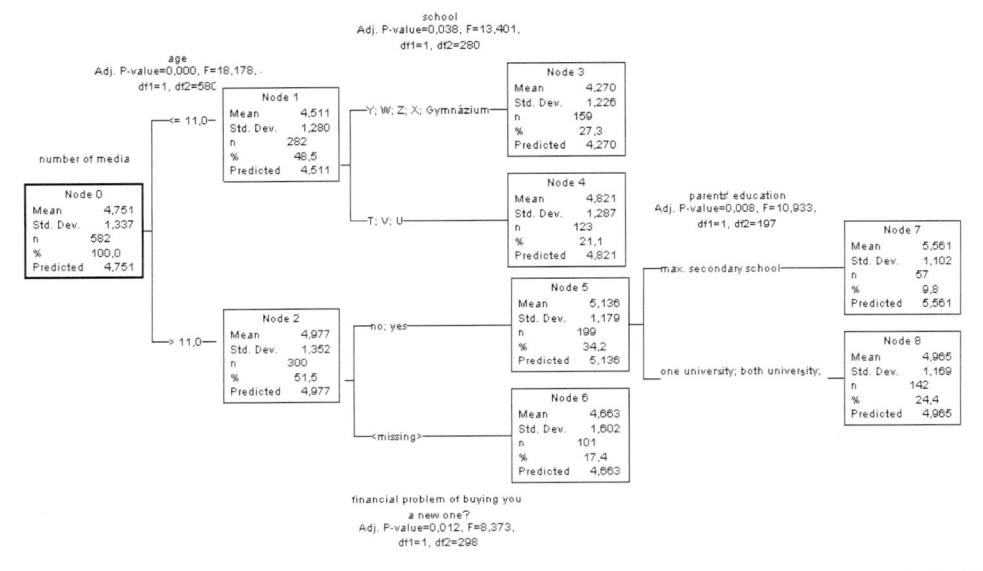

Figure 1. Classification tree for the dependent variable number of media   Soure: (own processing in SPSS)

For research question 3: On which online media do children aged 10 to 13 most often actively interact with marketing activities, three results tables were needed. Table 1 shows all seven online media that entered the analysis and the frequency with which children use them (never, several times a month, several times a week and daily). On the right is the sum of all users of that online medium who visit the online medium at least several times a month and more frequently. Online media are ranked from most used (YouTube) to least used (Facebook).

Table 1. Frequency of visits to individual online media which were the subject of the research

Online medium	frequency of visits				
	never	several times a month	several times a week	daily	Sum of users
YouTube	2 %	16 %	31 %	51 %	98 %
Google	4 %	20 %	38 %	37 %	96 %
e-mail	7 %	35 %	42 %	16 %	83 %
Instagram	38 %	15 %	15 %	33 %	62 %
TikTok	40 %	8 %	13 %	40 %	60 %
e-shop	48 %	39 %	9 %	3 %	52 %
Facebook	84 %	10 %	4 %	2 %	16 %

Source: own processing

The second table presents the most frequent forms of children's interaction with marketing activities on individual online media. Respondents again rated the activities according to frequency (never, several times a month, several times a week and daily). On the right side of the table is the sum of all users of a given online media who do a given activity at least a few times a month or more often. The most frequent activity is liking the Instagram pages of celebrities. In-depth interviews with children revealed that they mainly like the profiles of influencers they follow on other social networks (mainly YouTube), as well as the profiles of famous singers and actors. Children admitted that these celebrities often communicate with brands and recommend specific products in their posts. Up to 95% of users of this social network follow the pages of famous personalities, of which 40% follow daily. On the other hand, children are the least likely to watch video ads on YouTube, with only 32% of YouTube users doing so and none daily. In the in-depth interviews, children reported that they only watch ads when intended for their age group, and therefore the ad interests them.

Table 2. Frequency of active interaction with marketing activities

Online medium	marketing activity	frequency of activity				
		never	several times a month	several times a week	daily	Sum of users
Instagram	They like the pages of famous personalities.	5 %	15 %	40 %	40 %	95 %
Google	They search on Google how much an attractive product costs.	7 %	39 %	34 %	20 %	93 %
TikTok	They add influencer accounts.	19 %	33 %	31 %	17 %	81 %
e-shop	They buy something from an e-shop.	25 %	14 %	10 %	2 %	75 %
Facebook	They like the pages of famous personalities.	27 %	27 %	26 %	20 %	73 %
e-mail	They open emails from some companies.	39 %	37 %	16 %	8 %	61 %
YouTube	They watch an ad on YouTube.	68 %	30 %	2 %	0 %	32 %

Source: own processing

Table 3 summarises the results of the two previous tables, namely the ranking of the frequency of visiting a given online medium and the ranking of the frequency of interaction with marketing activities. The table shows that YouTube is the most visited online medium, but watching video ads is the least frequent activity. In contrast, the Google search engine is the second most frequently visited an online medium, with up to 37% of children visiting it daily, the second highest percentage after YouTube. According to the in-depth interviews, actively searching for products and their prices, where children commonly encounter PPC advertising campaigns of various formats and click on them, is the second most frequent activity. We can therefore say that Google search is the online medium where children most often actively interact with companies' marketing communication tools.

Table 3. Comparison of the order of frequency of visits and order of frequency of interaction with marketing activities

Online medium	Order by frequency of visit	Order by frequency of activity
YouTube	1	7
Google	2	2
e-mail	3	6
Instagram	4	1
TikTok	5	3
e-shop	6	4
Facebook	7	5

Source: own processing

Instagram was ranked second, as it is the fourth most visited online medium, and the most frequent activity is actively liking the profiles of celebrities. In third place is the social network TikTok, where children again add profiles of tiktokers who, like all influencers on other social networks, often communicate brands and products to recommend them to children for purchase.

4. Discussion

The first stated research question was: What is the average number of online media children aged 10 to 13 visits? According to qualitative research, media that are used by children and that contain online marketing communication entered the questionnaire survey. Children average, have 4.8 media out of the seven we asked about. The second research question focused on what sociodemographic factors influence the number of online media children aged 10 to 13 watch. The number of media used increases as children get older, as confirmed by research from 2019 (Kopecký & Szotkowski, 2019). Younger children up to and including age 11 use an average of 4.5 online media, while older children use five media. For children aged 11 and above, their knowledge of their family's economic circumstances also plays a role. However, surprisingly, it is not the case that children from poorer families, who theoretically might not have an internet connection at home and a smartphone through which children access the Internet most often, watch less online media. We have already found in qualitative research that children from these families own a smartphone and are online. The only difference from the better-off pupils was that they mostly did not have a mobile data plan and relied on a wifi connection. The smartphone is nowadays a standard part of the lives of children from all walks of life, and thanks to this, they can be online wherever there is a wifi connection. Internet is now a standard part of Czech households. According to the ČSÚ, 97% of households with children have Internet at home (ČSÚ, 2020). The number of children who do not have Internet at home is, therefore, absolutely negligible. For children under 11 years of age, their parents' education also plays a role, with children of parents with no more than a secondary education visiting more online media.

The third research question was: On which online media do children aged 10 to 13 most often actively interact with marketing activities? First, the online media that children most frequently visit were identified. The most used social network is YouTube, followed by TikTok and Instagram. All these social networks are full of marketing communication messages. At the same time, these are social networks that children can only use from the age of 13, and therefore most of the respondents to our survey should not have access to them. Google is a modern search engine for children, which they use to get a range of information. As many as 95% of Instagram users add profiles of celebrities at least occasionally, which are proven to be full of paid collaborations between these people and companies. Similar to Instagram, kids also follow the profiles of celebrities on TikTok. Qualitative research has shown that children trust these celebrities and therefore trust their recommendations to buy the communicated product. Another widespread activity is to search for prices of products that children are interested in. The searches are mostly done through Google search engines. Despite the undeniable positive features of the search engine, such as access to relevant and exciting information, Google contains several PPC ad formats that children have difficulty identifying. Through qualitative research, we found that children click on PPC ads, mainly shopping campaign formats. Few children know that these are paid campaigns; they feel that Google offers them the best products in the top positions. Thus, the research found that children aged 10 to 13 actively interact with marketing activities on Google, Instagram and TikTok.

5. Conclusion

In conclusion, children aged 10 to 13 are very active on the Internet and visit many online media where they encounter online marketing communication. Despite this, there is no social debate about whether targeting child users with many communication tools is ethical, often in formats children do not recognise as marketing communications. The ambition of this article is to draw attention to the need to open up this debate and, based on this debate, to adopt legislation to regulate online marketing communications targeting children. Furthermore, there is a need to appeal to online media providers to set rules on online communication targeting child users. Beyond these changes, however, children need to be educated about online marketing in schools and their families. No amount of regulation will ever ensure that children are not exposed to marketing communications at all. Besides, children will grow up to be adults who will be expected to have the skills to identify and critically evaluate marketing communications.

Acknowledgement

This paper was supported by TAČR – ÉTA: TL03000236

References

Aaker, D. A. (2003). Brand building: Budování obchodní značky: vytvoření silné značky a její úspěšné zavedení na trh. Computer Press.

Česká marketingová společnost. (2022). Češi a reklama 2022 (research study No. 39; pp. 1–8). Factum research. https://www.cms-cma.cz

ČSÚ (2020). Informační společnost v číslech - 2020. Český statistický úřad. https://www.czso.cz/csu/czso/informacni-spolecnost-v-cislech-2020

Heart and Stroke Foundation. (2017). The kids are not alright. How the food and beverage industry is marketing our children and youth to death. ScienceDaily. https://www.sciencedaily.com/releases/2017/02/170201131522.htm

John, D. (1999). Consumer Socialization of Children: A Retrospective Look At Twenty-Five Years of Research. Journal of Consumer Research, 26, 183–213.

Kopecký, K. (2019). Více než polovina českých dětí mladších 13 let používá služby, které jsou pro ně nevhodné. e-bezpečí. https://www.e-bezpeci.cz

Kopecký, K., & Szotkowski, R. (2019). České děti v kybersvětě (výzkumná zpráva). Univerzita Paladského v Olomouci. https://www.e-bezpeci.cz

Mallalieu, L., Palan, K. M., & Laczniak, R. N. (2005). Understanding Children's Knowledge and Beliefs about Advertising: A Global Issue that Spans Generations. Journal of Current Issues & Research in Advertising, 27(1), 53–64.

Story, M., & French, S. (2004). Food Advertising and Marketing Directed at Children and Adolescents in the US. International Journal of Behavioral Nutrition and Physical Activity, 1(1).

Thaichon, P. (2017). Consumer socialization process: The role of age in children's online shopping behavior. Journal of Retailing and Consumer Services, 34, 38–47. https://doi.org/10.1016/j.jretconser.2016.09.007

Ward, V. (2013). Children using Internet from age of three study finds. The Telegraph. https://www.telegraph.co.uk/technology/internet/10029180/Children-using-internet-from-age-of-three-study-finds.html

Watkins, L., Gage, R., Smith, M., McKerchar, C., Aitken, R., & Signal, L. (2022). An objective assessment of children's exposure to brand marketing in New Zealand (Kids'Cam): A cross-sectional study. The Lancet Planetary Health, 6(2), 132–138.

COMPARATION OF EU POLITICS ACTIVITY ON TWITTER (YEARS 2020 AND 2022)

Jana Syrovátková, Jiří Korčák

Faculty of Informatics and Statistics
Prague University of Economics and Business
jana.syrovatkova@vse.cz, jiri.korcak@vse.cz

DOI: 10.35011/IDIMT-2023-265

Keywords

Twitter, politicians, EU, covid crisis changes.

Abstract

With huge boom of social media as they are used by broad masses of population, in addition to individuals and business companies, politicians are also starting to use this technology. We have studied Twitter data of 188 EU politicians in 2020 and found out, that there were statistically significant differences between usage Twitter by politicians from rich and from poor countries. During the covid crisis more and more people started to use social networks often. They spend more time on computers and therefore in this study we have prolonged our study to the data from 2022 (155 Twitter accounts) to see, how the crisis has changed selected politicians´ activity on the Twitter platform. Our study analyses the profiles of European politicians (heads of the countries, prime ministers, ministers). Study compares activity and dependence to the GDP per capita and regions (north, south, west, east, defined by OSN) and uses statistical methods (ANOVA, F and t-tests). Our study shows evolution in politic usage of the Twitter and shows the differences from the previous study.

1. Introduction

During Covid pandemic the importance of electronic communication has grown. People started to prefer online medias before paper ones (Ahmed et al., 2020). With the fastening of the in-person communication, the importance of social networks news is increasing. Politicians as well as businesses see this trend and see it as an opportunity to increase their influence. Popular format of their expression can be Tweets. Tweets are very short messages with a limited number of characters. Although their length is gradually increasing, it is still a medium where the principle is a short, concise message, possibly supplemented with an image. Using this method, politicians are able to interact with voters and society on rather personal level. Especially Swedish politicians are known to be first to employ this method extensively by Gustafsson (2012).

1.1. Twitter and Political Engagement

Twitter has become a powerful political platform as it offers real-time interactions and personalized engagement with followers. The character limits inherent to each tweet encourage concise communication, enabling politicians to respond swiftly to current events, which is crucial for political personas. Twitter's accessibility and wide reach, make it a potential tool for setting political agendas and driving social change (Seethaler, & Melischek, 2019). In the 2018 Italian nationalist political party campaigns, Twitter was effective in engendering rapport between politicians and their constituents (Takács, 2022).

Grussel and Nord (2012) also noted, Twitter's role as a platform for political engagement is evidence of the changing trend of communication between leaders and the electorate and that was decade ago. The advantage of personalization that Twitter offers, its wide geographical coverage, and capacity for rapid information sharing have made it a vital tool for political campaigns, grassroots mobilization, and democracy promotion (Karlsen & Enjolras, 2016). However, it is imperative to ensure that the communication practices on Twitter are factual and transparent (Lawrance et al., 2013).

1.2. Impact of COVID-19 on Political Twitter Activity

The importance of Twitter in political communication has been further underscored by the COVID-19 pandemic since traditional campaign strategies and public engagements have been disrupted by health concerns. Therefore, politicians are relying increasingly on Twitter to communicate with constituents and disseminate information (Carey, Sánchez-Castillo & Cubillo, 2020). The pandemic has also increased the public's reliance on social media for real-time updates, positioning Twitter as a vital source of information dissemination from both domestic and international political figures, leading to an unprecedented increase in European Union politicians' Twitter activity, underlining the platform's ever-evolving role in the political landscape (Chong, 2020). Additionally, the pandemic has caused a shift in the nature of political communication on Twitter, towards the prioritization of crisis management, public health information, and expressions of solidarity among politicians (Jain et al., 2021).

1.3. Previous research

In the previous research of Pavlíček, Syrovátková (2022) we had 188 politicians as presidents, prime ministers, heads of parliament, ministers and opposition politicians from 28 countries (UK was in EU).

We have tried to compare activity of politicians from rich and poor countries and between regions (south, north, etc.). We have found, that politicians in the countries with higher GDP are more active on Twitter than politicians from countries with low GDP.

We have also found that there are differences in number of likes and following between regions.

2. Methods

2.1. Data collection

At first, we have defined a data sample. We decided to collect data about Twitter activity of main EU politicians. We chose country's official leader (e.g., the president, the King, the Queen), the Premier or prime minister, the Minister of Finance, the Minister of Foreign Affairs, the Minister of Culture and the Minister of Education. In the 2020 we chose more politicians, but for 2022 we decided for the most important – only leaders and ministers from leading political side (or coalition) of the country.

In 2020 United Kingdom was in EU, we chose to keep it for 2022 research and make comparison with the previous data. Following, we started with manual control of actual politicians, their activities and followers in EU countries for each year. We looked for each country, who are the ministers / premier / leader and if those politicians has his Twitter account. Then we have taken only those with Twitter account.

In 2020 data was collected from Twitter manually and by usage of a tool "foller.me", in 2022 we used scraper called PhantomBuster. After identifying politicians and his Twitter accounts, we have made a table of Twitter accounts names Through this tool, we received data about activity of politicians Twitter accounts – number of Tweets, Likes, Followers and Followings.

In total we have collected N = 188 politicians on Twitter in 2020 (131 of them were heads, premiers and ministers) and N = 155 politicians on Twitter in 2022 (not all positions are in all countries). We can say that there are more politicians having account on Twitter in 2022 (131 heads, premiers and ministers in 2020 vs. 155 in 2022).

2.2. Breakdown of countries for comparison

For testing differences between countries we have taken differences in GDP and geographical differences. We have identified EU countries with high (over USD 36,000) GDP per capita: Austria, Belgium, Cyprus, Denmark, Finland, France, Germany, Ireland, Italia, Luxembourg, Malta, Netherlands, Spain, Sweden, United Kingdom. Afterwards on contrary we identified countries with low (under USD 36,000) GDP per capita: Bulgaria, Croatia, Czech Rep, Estonia, Greece, Hungary, Latvia, Lithuania, Poland, Portugal, Romania, Slovakia, Slovenia.

For differences between regions from geographical point of view, we chose regions defined by OSN for statistical purpose.

Northern Europe: Denmark, Finland, Estonia, Ireland, Latvia, Lithuania, Sweden, United Kingdom.

Southern Europe: Croatia, Cyprus, Greece, Italy, Malta, Portugal, Slovenia, Spain.

Western Europe: Austria, Belgium, France, Germany, Luxembourg, Netherlands.

Central and Eastern Europe: Bulgaria, Czech Republic, Hungary, Poland, Romania, Slovakia.

2.3. Research questions

We proposed these basic research questions:
- Are there statistically significant differences in activity of the politicians on Twitter before and after covid crisis?
- Are there statistically significant differences in activity of the politicians on Twitter for countries with high and low GDP per capita?
- Are there statistically significant differences in activity of the politicians on Twitter for countries taken geographically?
- Is the activity statistically growing?

2.4. Statistical Methods

Analysis was done using Data Analysis tool in Excel. The politician's data are independent, so it was possible to use F-test, t-test and ANOVA. When we take all politicians together, there is enough data for comparison. We have as a hypothesis that the value is the same against alternative, value is not the same – so we have used variant with two-tails. Before we have used a t-test, we have tested variance using F-test for deciding, which type of t-test we should use. Everything was calculated at a significance level 0.05.

2.5. Statistical hypothesis

We have tested these exactly given hypothesis corresponding to the research questions. For each hypothesis we did separate tests for tweets, likes, followers and following for both categories using GDP and geographical location.

- H_1: Senior politicians of countries with higher GDP have the same number of tweets on Twitter as senior politicians of countries with lower GDP. Against alternative that they have different number of tweets.
- H_2: Senior politicians of countries with higher GDP have the same number of followers on Twitter as senior politicians of countries with lower GDP. Against alternative that they have different number of followers.
- H_3 & H_4: Similarly, with following and likes.
- H_5: Number of tweets of senior politicians on Twitter does not depend on geographical location of the country against alternative that at least one of the geographical locations (north, south, east, west, center) has statistically different number of tweets.
- $H_6 - H_8$: Similarly for the geographical location and for followers, following and likes.
- $H_9 - H_{12}$: Similarly for years 2020 and 2022.

3. Results

3.1. Descriptive statistics

We have analyzed profiles of 155 policitians in 28 countries. From countries with higher GDP it was 92 politicians, with lower GDP it was 63 politicians. From northern region there were 50 politicians, from south 42, from west 36 and from east 27.

There were some accounts with more than 5 million followers – The Royal Family of United Kingdom and president of France (Emmanuel Macron). More than 1 million followers have presidents of Poland (Andrzej Duda) and Spain (Felipe VI), Prime Ministers of Spain (Pedro Sánchez) and Netherlands (Mark Rutter).

Means of numbers of all tweets, followers, following and likes are differentiated by year and put into table 1 and table 2.

Table 1. Means in 2020

	Differentiation by GDP		Differentiation by region				All together
	High GDP	Low GDP	North	South	West	East	
Tweets	8,099	3,084	9,853	6,827	5,225	946	6,259
Followers	212,401	56,818	119,944	175,706	270,198	39,782	155,299
Following	1,083	333	866	630	1,423	157	808
Likes	1,391	633	1,854	1,096	941	139	113

Table 2. Means in 2022

	Differentiation by GDP		Differentiation by region				All together
	High GDP	Low GDP	North	South	West	East	
Tweets	8,785	4,025	8,403	7,767	6,846	2,554	6,850
Followers	324,157	92,046	202,871	162,306	415,932	136,569	229,815
Following	1,180	606	1,290	1,065	834	281	947
Likes	4,133	2,232	4,392	1,946	4,797	1,734	3,360

3.2. Activity comparison between regions by GDP

For hypothesis H1, H2, H3 and H4 we have analyzed differences between countries with high and low GDP per capita. We have started with F-test and then by the results of F-test we have used t-test for same or not-same variances (on significance level 0.05). We have two tails variant of t-test. As we can see in Table 3, we can reject three of four hypotheses about the same mean for states with high and low GDP for all the monitored data. We can reject it for tweets, following and likes in both years (on significance level 0.05). As a result, we can say that politicians in the countries with higher GDP are more active on Twitter.

Table 3. Comparison between regions by GDP

	F-test p-value	t-test p-value
Tweets	$5.54*10^{-12}$	**0.0019**
Followers	$4.39*10^{-27}$	0.0510
Following	$2.84*10^{-04}$	**0.0042**
Likes	$7.32*10^{-05}$	**0.0225**

3.3. Activity comparison between regions (OSN regions)

We have taken the regions (north, south, east and west) defined by OSN and compared, if there are differences between regions. We have analyzed hypothesis H5, H6, H7 and H8. We have compared the regions using ANOVA simple test.

In the Table 4 we can see that we can reject the hypothesis for number of followings and likes. So, we can say that there are regional differences in number of followings and likes.

Table 4. Comparison between regions by OSN

	ANOVA p-value
Tweets	0.1281
Followers	0.5140
Following	**0.0122**
Likes	**0.0247**

3.4. Activity comparison between 2020 and 2022

The last comparison we have done was between the years 2020 and 2022. Here we can say that we can reject the hypothesis H9 and H12 about the same number of Tweets and Likes, but we can't reject the hypothesis about the same number of Followers and Followings (at significance level 0.05). The results are in Table 5.

So, we can tell that politicians have in 2022 statistically more Tweets and Likes than in 2020, but we can't say it about number of Followers and Followings.

Table 5. Activity comparison between 2020 and 2022

	F-test p-value	t-test p-value
Tweets	$1.84*10^{-12}$	**0.0031**
Followers	0	0.1186
Following	0.14	0.1661
Likes	$4.11*10^{-15}$	**0.0000**

4. Conclusion and Discussion

Our research has compared the politicians activity on Twitter. We have found that politicians in wealthy European countries are statistically significantly more active on the Twitter platform. They post more, more followings – follow more and receive more likes.

There is a regional variability too – politicians in the Western Europe have more likes and followings than in the Central & Eastern. Southern politicians are in between.

There is a little progress in between years 2020 and 2022, but it can't be said that it is very significant. There are differences between years 2020 and 2022 only in Tweets and Likes, not significant difference in number of Followers and Following.

The main limitation of the research is that west have more rich countries than east and other regions. Also, we cannot say if there is any direct causality between the richness of a country and the number of tweets, as it can go both ways. It is very probable that it is a natural phenomenon for rich country politicians to be active on social networks as there is a need for them to be transparent in their opinions. As well as rich countries are connected in higher technological advancement which comes with people using technologies like Twitter and other social media.

For next research it would be interesting to go through comments section of certain tweets and try to discern emotion for these tweets and try to correlate it with growth of politicians account and political development in the country.

References

Ahmed, W., Vidal-Alaball, J., Seguí, F., Moreno-Sanchez, P. (2020). A Social Network Analysis Of Tweets Related To Masks During the Covid-19 Pandemic. IJERPH, 21(17), 8235. https://doi.org/10.3390/ijerph17218235

Carey, L., Sánchez-Castillo, S., Cubillo, E. (2020). European Leaders Unmasked: Covid-19 Communication Strategy Through Twitter. EPI. https://doi.org/10.3145/epi.2020.sep.04

Chong, M. (2020). Network Typology, Information Sources, and Messages Of The Infodemic Twitter Network Under covid -19. Proc Assoc Inf Sci Technol, 1(57). https://doi.org/10.1002/pra2.363

Grusell, M., Nord, L. (2012). "Three Attitudes To 140 Characters the Use And Views Of Twitter In Political Party Communications In Sweden". PCR, 2(2). https://doi.org/10.5130/pcr.v2i2.2833

Gustafsson, N. (2012). The subtle nature of Facebook politics: Swedish social network site users and political participation. New Media & Society, 14(7), 1111–1127. https://doi.org/10.1177/1461444812439551

Jain, N., Singh, P., Singh, P., Mukherjee, S. (2021). Twitter Mediated Sociopolitical Communication During the Covid-19 Pandemic Crisis In India. Front. Psychol., (12). https://doi.org/10.3389/fpsyg.2021.784907

Karlsen, R., Enjolras, B. (2016). Styles Of Social Media Campaigning and Influence In A Hybrid Political Communication System. The International Journal of Press/Politics, 3(21), 338-357. https://doi.org/10.1177/1940161216645335

Lawrence, R., Molyneux, L., Coddington, M., Holton, A. (2013). Tweeting Conventions. Journalism Studies, 6(15), 789-806. https://doi.org/10.1080/1461670x.2013.836378

Pavlíček, A. & Syrovátková, J. (2022). Use of Twitter as an effective communication tool – case study on EU, Underwood, H., & Findlay, B. (2004). Internet relationships and their impact on primary Computer Interaction, Idea Group Reference, Hershey, London, Melbourne, Singapore, 2006, ISBN 1-59140-562-9

Seethaler, J. & Melischek, G. (2019). Twitter As a Tool For Agenda Building In Election Campaigns? The Case Of Austria. Journalism, 8(20), 1087-1107. https://doi.org/10.1177/1464884919845460

Takács, L. (2022). Race For Attention: Twitter Campaign Of Italian Party Leaders Before the 2018 Parliamentary Elections. CI, 2(18), 26-35. https://doi.org/10.5752/p.1809-6182.2021v18n2p26-35

ARTS NEWS AGENDA SETTING ON SOCIAL MEDIA

Tereza Willoughby

Faculty of Informatics and Statistics
Prague University of Economics and Business
Charles University, Faculty of Arts
Institute of Information Science and Librarianship
tereza.willoughby@gmail.com

DOI: 10.35011/IDIMT-2023-273

Keywords

Social networks, information, reporting, cultural reporting, culture, agenda setting, balance, reach

Abstract

In this paper the author explores whether the representation of Czech culture on public media outlets' social media accounts is balanced. Traditional Czech media are increasingly active on social networks, which are becoming a key information channel, meaning they shape both information and public taste. Using the example of the arts coverage of public broadcaster Czech Television (ČT), the author examines how agenda setting for social networks works in traditional audiovisual media. Based on quantitative research of the accounts of its news station and specialised arts section in March 2023, she analyses the topics to which editors give most space. The findings are then followed up with quantitative research in the form of guided semi-structured interviews with those responsible for accounts' content. The result is a narrowly focused analysis of the principles used in the selection of arts topics on public TV's social media accounts.

1. Introduction

The influence of the media is nowadays also increasingly exerted through social networks, which have started to be used by traditional media in two main ways. The first is to obtain information, either from official sources, from institutions and personalities, or as a source of user-generated content. In a 2015 survey conducted by Cision, a private US organization, 51% of journalists worldwide said they would not be able to do their job without social media (Cision.com, 2015). A 2022 survey by the Pew Research Center, a nonpartisan American think tank based in Washington, D.C., which has long tracked social trends and public opinion, journalists' use of social media averages 90% across their various fields of work. Despite media professionals being aware of the pitfalls and risks associated with social media, 87% acknowledge it helps them get their stories out to the public, and 79% consider it an indispensable means of connecting with the public (Pewresearch.com, 2022). In fact, the number of users who use social networks as a news source continues to grow. In the US, social networks overtook printed newspapers as a news source for the first time in 2018 (Pew Research Center, 2018). It is precisely in terms of information dissemination that social networks provide a free space for traditional media to disseminate content. Moreover, they represent virtually the only means to share extremely quick, short and clear messages. Social media does not require in-depth analysis or reporting; it merely provides a superficial overview of key events in text or graphic form. In terms of broadcast journalism, it is the continuous equivalent of a crawl (i.e., text bar with the latest information running alongside a broadcast), but without the need to follow a specific broadcast at a specific time. Social networks therefore allow traditional media to keep up with the ever-growing trend of "information/news on demand" 24/7. It also offers them a platform to disseminate and promote traditional content (reports, interviews) free of charge, but to different target groups than the usual audience of, for example, mainstream TV news programmes. Traditional media fundamentally lack interactivity and individuality; in this respect, social networks provide news outlets with a forum for debate, albeit in a controlled way.

If we continue to focus primarily on TV news, which is the subject of our research, in the Czech Republic every station dedicated to news has set up a profile on the network since the Facebook boom in 2009. But within the Meta family, Instagram is also very popular, especially for its ability to communicate a concise visual message. Other mainstream media outlets use Twitter and sporadically engage on the social network TikTok as well. Czech Television's news station, CT24, uses all the aforementioned social networks. The ability of social networks to convey more serious messages is of course questionable. However, it is necessary to accept that information cannot reach a segment of the audience in any other way than via clips, and that this trend can be expected to grow. Social networks are a very complex phenomenon. Even because of their relative youth, they provide a wealth of unexplored topics.

News on Czech social media is not yet sufficiently researched, although a large part of the population gets its information from social media. The principles by which TV news outlets work with social media posts have never been examined. If we consider that social networks influence the audience, then in the case of the public service media, we can add that they should create a general taste based on societal values. It ought to offer broadly represented, balanced and diverse content objectively reflecting the reality. When we talk about taste, we can narrow the issue down to arts news. This segment of news production is sufficiently limited and focused, and can be linked to a clearly definable aesthetic classification. In terms of arts news, we decided to trace how, in terms of content and form, TV news works with social networks and how agenda setting works in the case of social media. We examine whether the representation of reports is balanced in terms of content, i.e., objective. We look at the representation of the different art forms and analyse the observed trends on this basis. In a second step, we then want to determine whether these trends are deliberately generated or are due to random influences.

2. Aims and Methods

The aim is to find out whether the representation of Czech culture on public media outlets' social media is balanced. The basic method was empirical quantitative research, in which we subsequently used a qualitative line: guided semi-structured interviews. In the quantitative research the focus is on data quality; several experimental statistical surveys were conducted in the preceding months.

2.1. Quantitative research

We have delimited the data by a specialisation, namely arts news, which is – as already mentioned – defined and clearly targeted. Moreover, for our purposes, we consider only public TV news, mainly because it does not use paid content as a principle of public service media but focuses exclusively on informational content. At the same time, CT is the only Czech TV news channel that has a dedicated arts news department. A comparison with different Czech media that carry dedicated arts news (e.g., Czech Radio or websites of print outlets) would be uninformative because editorial procedures and the general work flow are very different (we have drawn on our own experience). A future work could allow us to compare our results with art news television in other countries, because that is only way to get an enriching comparison.

This limit that we are working solely with material provided by public service television simplified our thinking about the definition of the words balanced or diverse and their relation to objectivity, because all these terms are enshrined in law in the Czech Television Act. The quantitative research was conducted on the basis of data gathered in March 2023. We have deliberately chosen this short period of time because in the pilot research following a longer period (March–July 2022) we discovered that every month contains the same elements in repeats (our experience suggests that this would work at any time except the month of August, which is out of season, and December, which is marked by the Christmas holidays). So, analysis of one representative month allows us to be more detailed and focused for the purposes of the limited space of this paper. The data we follow concern all arts-related posts on the profiles of CT24 and CT24 Culture during the month. The choice of this month is justified by the fact that in terms of arts coverage it was during the main season, so the posts will have high relevance; here we draw on our own empirical evidence. Among the social networks, we ended up focusing only on Facebook (FB) as in this case arts news posts appear on the general profile of the CT24 news programme (@ct24.cz, number of followers as of 10 April 2023: 874 078) and on the dedicated arts profile (@ct24kultura, number of followers as of 10 April 2023: 6 326), which is run by the arts news department, so it is possible to explore the differences and go into more depth. We always collect data on social media content a week apart to better measure reach.

2.1.1. Defining the fields

An essential aspect of the research was to define at the beginning the disciplines or art forms whose representation on social networks we wished to monitor. The final system of 17 disciplines we choose is represented in the figure 1. Unfortunately, no currently applicable theory offered us a clear solution. For a base of commonly used approaches, we can look to that in Ancient Greece, where they assigned patrons to each type of art, the so-called Muses, except for the fine arts, which were considered crafts. Aesthetic approaches further derive from Plato's Symposium, and especially from Aristotle's Poetics. A number of articles over the years have progressively focused on purely contemporary cultural manifestations. After studying current approaches, we decided – on those bases – to create our own system of artistic types. We follow the basic division of the National Information and Consulting Center for Culture (NIPOS, an organization of the Ministry of Culture of the Czech Republic, founded 1991). We have modified this official definition of the fields by essential aesthetic theories, but also supplemented them with specific examples of creativity represented in contemporary media production. The categories we defined to some extent copy the focus of editors at the arts news department of Czech Television, merging some art forms and setting others apart due to their exclusivity. We quantify the representation of all these groups and compare representation on the general and dedicated profiles on the social network.

2.2. Qualitative research

The statistical investigation noted trends seen across arts posts on CT's social media. Based on these trends, guided interviews were conducted to illuminate their creation. Thus, the second phase of the research is qualitative research in the form of guided interviews. The choice of interviewees was clear; the head of the social media department of the CT newsroom, and the editor-in-chief of CT's arts news department. Both are directly responsible for the publication of culture posts on a particular social network profile (the arts editor is responsible for the content of the CT24 Culture FB profile; the head of the social network editorial team is responsible for the publication of posts on CT24's FB). Both respondents requested anonymity. We asked two types of questions: original ones and those directly resulting from the quantitative research. The second part is crucial for the research as it clarifies the data found by the statistical investigation and answers the research questions.

What are the criteria for including arts posts on public television's social media?

To what extent is the agenda setting of arts posts for CT's social media driven by chance and to what extent is it targeted?

3. Results

In the case of CT24 Culture's FB, we observe a greater balance in relation to the types of arts and fields covered. A guided interview with the editor of CT's arts news department revealed that an internal statistic is kept on reports posted, which is shared among all staff involved. Although the method is not 100% exact, it makes it possible to avoid, for example, repetition of posts, or a seemingly significant focus on only one art form or even on one particular artist. In addition, the editor notes that the appearance of specific names in published articles is always determined by the content of arts news and current events at a given time; in this case, 100% balance and objectivity cannot be created artificially. The social media agenda represents just a portion of the editorial agenda. Deviations are therefore mainly caused by current events and the agenda of the arts news department. In the month of March 2023, these reasons are quite compatible with the fact that in terms of art forms, film and TV are the most prominently represented on CT24 Culture's FB profile, followed by visual arts, then popular music and social issues.

CT24's FB profile's posting of arts reports is uneven and generally avoids fringe or less mainstream topics. According to the head of the social media editorial department of CT's newsroom, they follow a large number of parameters when publishing stories. Editors follow a daily release template where they can see what items should be included, just as all news shows (e.g., Události/News, Události v kultuře/Culture News) have a pre-set, point-by-point script. In this scenario, there are hard news items and more entertaining reports: regional/environmental/culture or explicitly just arts. However, it always depends on the particular editor and also on the other agenda that the head of news designates as the key (actual hard news items).

The most prominent and significantly (more than double) dominant art form is film and TV. According to the head, this is due to the visual appeal and dominance of film themes in pop culture (the head of the social media team says, "Everyone goes to the cinema, everyone watches TV"). He also admits that the profile tries to promote Czech TV's own projects, which are overwhelmingly films.

Another significant group is themes with broader socio-political content or manifesting elements of activism. Here, there is a general effort to place all such reports on the universal profile (the editors do this for all editorial departments, including domestic news). We traced a common phenomenon on this profile of a piece masquerading as representing an art form but actually being posted for another aspect (e.g., film as a social protest, music as a presidential inauguration moment, literature as a manuscript display, visual art as an auction). These posts also have a broader potential to spark debate (here we can note that in the case of CT24's FB, the so-called vocal minority is the most audible; comments do not focus on the cultural aspect of the post, but express political positions or the commentators' agenda).

The third group in frequency is obituaries. According to the observed data and the assertions of both respondents, obituaries generally have greatest impact in terms of reach and interest. When it comes to a prominent cultural figure, these appear in the top 10 most successful posts each month, while also fulfilling the profile's public service role.

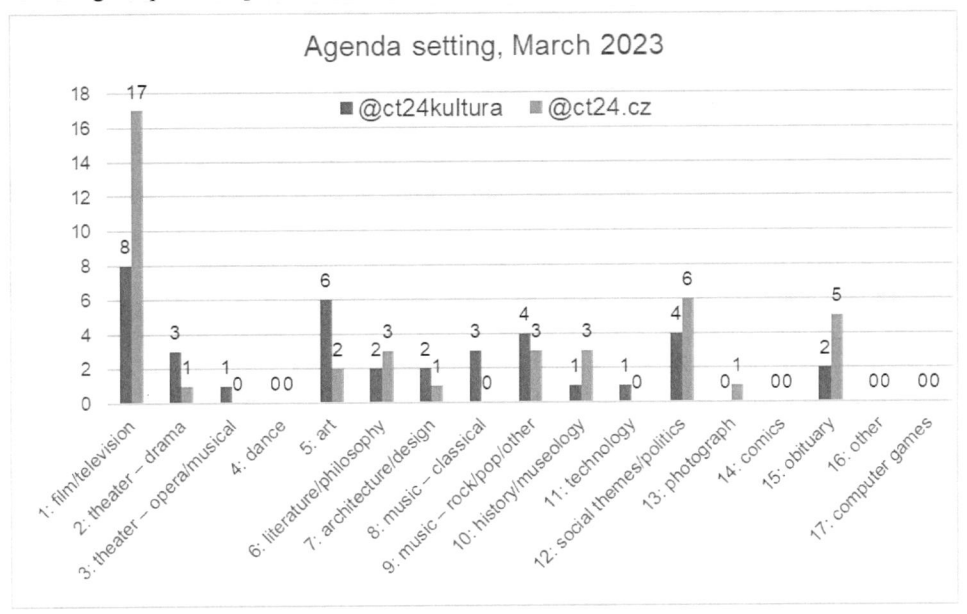

Agenda setting, March 2023

(Bar chart comparing @ct24kultura and @ct24.cz across categories)

Values shown (category: @ct24kultura, @ct24.cz):
1: film/television — 8, 17
2: theater – drama — 3, 1
3: theater – opera/musical — 1, 0
4: dance — 0, 0
5: art — 6, 2
6: literature/philosophy — 2, 3
7: architecture/design — 2, 1
8: music – classical — 3, 0
9: music – rock/pop/other — 4, 3
10: history/museology — 3, 1
11: technology — 1, 0
12: social themes/politics — 4, 6
13: photograph — 0, 1
14: comics — 0, 0
15: obituary — 2, 5
16: other — 0, 0
17: computer games — 0, 0

Figure 1. representation of artistic types on FB arts/general news Source: own research

The inclusion of arts topics on the universal CT24 FB profile to some extent copies the reach of the reports (figure 2). The type ranking trend echoes the range trend. The editor-in-chief of social networks confirmed this assumption, saying that expected reach is one of the main criteria for publication. Below is a simplified overview of the reach of reports on the CT24 and CT24 Culture FB profiles. For logical reasons, the numbers differ in order of magnitude; this is directly proportional to the number of followers of the given profile.

In the case of the specialised culture profile, trends diverge (figure 3). The most watched CT24 Culture piece was about a visit of president-elect Petr Pavel to the National Theatre. This post replicated the need for broader content described in the case of the universal profile and considerably exceeded the usual reach of posts on the profile. On the other hand, it should be noted that a post on the premiere of the production of the play Její pastorkyňa at the Klicper Theatre (6 March 2023) also had higher reach on the dedicated profile. From the specialist arts point of view, this is a long-awaited premiere, which critics predict will be play of the year. Another peak can be seen in a post devoted to the new Muzoleum gallery of works by artist David Cerny (19 Mar 2023); this post also achieved high numbers. It should be noted that the profile was probably the first Czech media outlet to cover the venture. This illustrates very well the fact the dedicated profile is consumed by users interested in culturally relevant and current topics. At the same time, it is necessary to note a fact that is not the subject of our investigation, namely that all of these posts have been specifically adapted for social media. In both cases, it was not an original TV report (the most common type of post on the CT24 Culture FB), but brief information supplemented by a visual/short video.

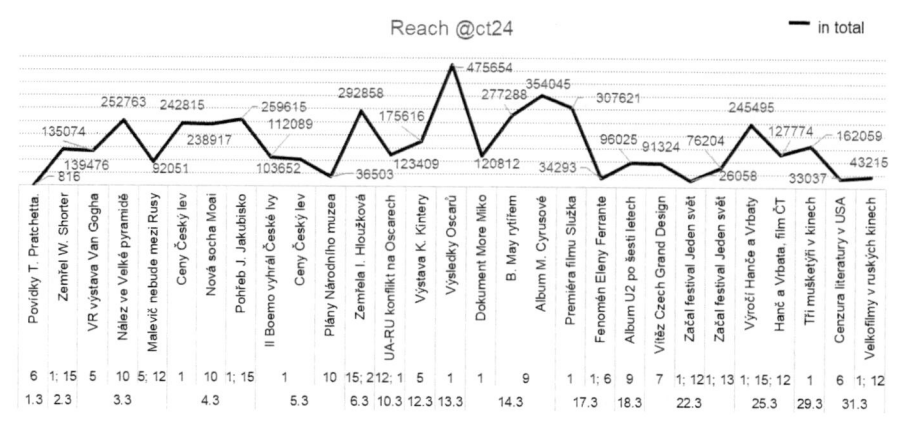

Figure 2. arts news reach on FB general news   Source: own research

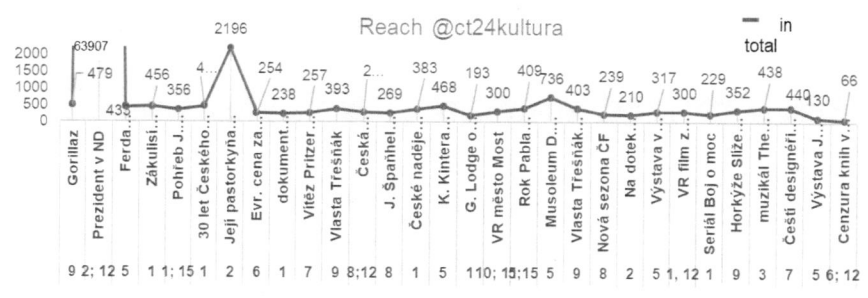

Figure 3. arts news reach on FB arts   Source: own research

4. Conclusions and Future Works

The criteria for classifying reports are basically determined by traditional news values defined by Walter Lippmann (Reifová, 2004). At the same time, the social profile of the specialised arts news department closely connects relevance with professional knowledge and resonance of the given topic in the community of informed viewers, possibly in the arts community itself. Social media are a quick source of information, so for the CT24 and CT24 Culture FB profiles the topicality of the subject is key. They are also interactive, so topics with discussion potential also dominate. Considering the principles of information transmission characteristic of social networks, the visual attractiveness of the published material also plays a role.

In the case of CT24's FB, the imbalance in artistic genres is largely due to chance. Editors' selection is not driven by professional judgment, as they are not narrowly focused on the arts but must evaluate and process a diverse range of topics and information during a shift. Although they try to essentially fulfill the principles of public service even with arts topics, they mainly focus on pop culture and areas that have the potential for broad impact and which also appeal to them. On the formal side, however, they follow a pre-set scheme for arts topics, as well as techniques that have proven effective with hard news and guarantee greater reach.

The universal approach of the CT24 FB profile contrasts with that of the CT24 Culture FB. The editors of the specialised profile choose topics by relevance in current and long-term cultural life, taking into account visual appeal or popularity with an informed audience, while maintaining balance in terms of art forms. Randomness in the case of the CT24 Culture FB profile is manifested on the formal side, where there is no scheme of publishing posts. The imperfection of the form of the posts prevents higher reach. Although arts editors are narrowly focused on specialised topics, they cover them across the entire editorial production, i.e., mainly on air. They see social media as a fringe issue, so they are not formally specialized.

To sum up, arts topics on CT24's FB have adequate reach and become a relevant part of the information flow to recipients (users) via social media, thought the agenda setting is not balanced. This is not driven by expertise, but rather by formal criteria or the random taste of the editor as a representative of the mainstream view of culture. We can simply put that these Facebook posts do not set the public agenda; they are more or less following trends and an agenda already set by general public taste. By contrast, topics on the specialised CT24 Culture FB are balanced in terms of art forms and there is a relevant selection from the professional point of view that tries to play a role in creating the public agenda. We can say that in this case the importance assigned to the information by the media also very often reflect the level of importance and attention bestowed by the audience. However, posts' reach is also often hampered by their formal imperfection and, in the vast majority of posts, by the distinct lack of editing to make posts suitable for consumption via social media (visually attractive posts in the form of a photo or short video, reports with captions, striking graphics with unambiguous information – see the expert statement of the head of the social media editorial office).

Formally, all Czech TV's social media profiles follow the same rules, but content-wise there is no collaboration between the CT24 and CT24 Culture FB profiles that would help increase reach, or at least prevent duplication of content (and unwanted competition). We regard such collaboration as quite necessary for a relevant and genre-balanced coverage of arts topics on the social media profiles, specifically Facebook, managed by Czech TV. It is the simplest way for both profiles to add what they lack: the general profile needs professional relevance, and the specialised one needs formal relevance in relation to the functioning of information through social networks. Why this is the case and what collaboration should ideally look like could be the subject of further research.

The study follows a limited principle of agenda setting in terms of art forms. We are aware of the limitations of this approach. In the case of the largely unexplored issue of news content on social media, we also encounter other major themes. One is formal principles. This follows logically from the need of social media users to consume content largely without the use of sound, for example, via a smartphone in a public space or generally in the presence of others at work or in private. The form of reports suitable for this information channel is an interesting topic worthy of future focus. In the course of the analysis, we also noted the influence of time of publication of a post and the timing of arts news posts on social media could be a subject for further investigation. From an editor's point of view, both of these areas have a common goal: to select the most appropriate conditions for the information to reach the widest audience. This brings us to the phenomenon of measuring audience interest (reach, reaction). These variables are touched on in places, but for the purposes of our limited research we only work with them in refining the questions in the guided interviews. However, audience interest is indeed a complex aspect that opens up other research fields. From the broader perspective, such research could also explore the potential effects of cultural representation on public discourse and societal dynamics.

Acknowledgements

TAČR, Interpretation of landscape aspects through the social and artistic science.

References

Aristotelés (1999). Rétorika/Poetika. Rezek, Praha. ISBN 80-86027-14-7.

Bouzek, J., Kratochvíl, Z. (1995). Řeč umění a archaické filozofie. Herrmann & synové, Praha. p. 19. ISBN

Cision.com (2015). Global Social Journalism Study. URL https://www. cision . com / us / resources / research - reports / social - journalism - study/.

Curran, J. (2010). The future of journalism. Journalism Studies, Vol. 11, No 4

Deuze, M. (2003). The web and its journalisms: considering the consequences of different types of newsmedia online, New Media & Society, Vol. 5, No. 2, ISSN 1461-4448.

Fortunati, L. (2005). Mediatization of the Net and Internetization of the Mass Media. Gazette: The International Journal for Communication Studies, Vol. 67, No. 1, ISSN 0016-5492

Levinson, J. (1984). Hybrid Art Forms. The Journal of Aesthetic Education 18 (4):5-14. p. 5.

Maguire, J. P. (1964). The Differentiation of Art in Plato's Aesthetics. Harvard Studies in Classical Philology, Vol. 68. Department of the Classics, Harvard University. URL http://www.jstor.org/discover/ 10.2307/310813?uid=3737856&uid=2&uid=4&sid=2110 4018478733. p. 392.

Measures, Ch.: The Rise of Citizen Journalism. Socialmedia today (online), URL http://socialmediatoday.com/ chrismeasures/1430031/rise-citizen-journalism

Mironova, T. (2021). "Plurality the types of art in contemporary art: specifics of media art. National Academy of Managerial Staff of Culture and Arts Herald. p. 139.

Moravec, V. (2016). Média v tekutých časech. Konvergence audiovizuálních médií v ČR. Academia, Praha. ISBN 978-80-200-2572-2 p. 57.

Národní informační a poradenské středisko pro kulturu. Statistika kultury ČR. URL https://www.statistikakultury.cz/.

O'Sullivan, J.; Heineken, A. (2008). Old values, new media: Journalism role perceptions in a changing world. Journalism Practice, Vol. 2, No. 3, ISSN 1751-2786

Pavlíček, A. (2010). Nová média a sociální sítě. ISBN 978-80-245-1742-1

Pew Research Center (2018). Social media outpaces print newspapers in the u.s. as a news source. URL https://www.pewresearch.org/fact-tank/2018/12/10/social-media-outpaces-print-newspapers-in-the-u-s-as-a-news-source/

Pew Research Center (2022). Many journalists say social media helps at work, but most decry its impact on journalism. URL https://www.pewresearch.org/journalism/2022/06/14/many-journalists-say-social-media-helps-at-work-but-most-decry-its-impact-on-journalism/

Reifová, I. (2004). Slovník mediální komunikace. Portál, Praha. ISBN 80-7178-926-7, p. 76.

483/1991 Sb. Zákon o České televizi, URL https://img.ceskatelevize.cz/boss/document/1801.pdf?v=1.

DIGITAL TRANSFORMATION
OF SUPPLY CHAIN MANAGEMENT

EXAMINING THE EFFECTS OF SUPPLIER LOCALIZATION ON PUBLIC PROCUREMENT PERFORMANCE

Radoslav Delina, Gabriel Demeter

Faculty of Economics
Technical University of Kosice
Radoslav.Delina@tuke.sk, Gabriel.Demeter@tuke.sk

DOI: 10.35011/IDIMT-2023-283

Keywords

Public procurement, behavior, collusion, risk, data

Abstract

Non-standard behavior in public procurement with negative impact is significant problem which is highlighted in several scientific studies or policy documents. In this paper, we will address the problem of geographically close relations between supplier and public procurer and their effects on several public tender performance indicators. The analysis was conducted on data from transparent electronic contracting platform from Slovakia. We are presenting several analyses which suggest that local relationships may relate with non-standard behavioral patterns with negative impact on public tender. These results are visible also in highly transparent environment for public tendering with automatic notifications of published tenders to suppliers.

1. Motivation and background to the supplier localisation

Corruption in public procurement is a serious problem that can have a significant impact on the economy and society. It distorts competition, reduces efficiency, and undermines trust in public institutions. Public policy documents, such as the United Nations Convention against Corruption and the Organisation for Economic Co-operation and Development (OECD) Guidelines for Fighting Bid Rigging in Public Procurement, highlight the importance of addressing corruption in public procurement to ensure transparency, accountability, and fairness (OECD, 2020).

Effective measures to prevent corruption in public procurement include enhancing transparency, promoting competition, and strengthening oversight and enforcement mechanisms. This can be achieved through initiatives such as open contracting, e-procurement systems, and anti-corruption compliance programs. By implementing such measures, governments can ensure that public procurement processes are conducted in a fair and transparent manner, and that public resources are used efficiently and effectively.

Nowadays, and due to digital transformation and data economy development, data science and data services has the potential to play a significant role in addressing corruption in public procurement (OECD 2018). Imhof (2018) used a combination of simple behavioral scanners and machine learning algorithms, and this method was proved to be a powerful tool that could correctly identify up to 80% of the market situations (Imhof, 2018). By leveraging advanced analytics and machine learning algorithms, data scientists can identify patterns of behavior that may indicate collusion, bid-rigging, or other corrupt practices in procurement processes. For example, data analytics can be used to detect unusual bidding patterns, such as consistently high or low bids from certain suppliers, which may suggest collusion or bid rigging.

Moreover, data science can also facilitate the development of predictive models to identify the high-risk procurement processes that are more susceptible to corruption. This can help procurement officials to allocate resources more effectively to prevent and detect corrupt practices. For example, predictive models can be used to identify the suppliers or contractors with a history of unethical behavior and flag them for closer scrutiny. In summary, data science can help to enhance the effectiveness of anti-corruption measures in public procurement and ensure transparency, accountability, and fairness in procurement processes.

One of the significant problems of public tenders is a factor of low competitiveness which is common risk issue in public tenders in non-transparent but also in transparent environment. Non-competitiveness or tenders with a very low number of suppliers negotiated the contract pose a significant risk especially within corruption attempts in public procurement. When there are only a few suppliers competing for a contract, the risk of collusion or bid rigging increases, as the suppliers may be tempted to cooperate rather than compete. This can result in inflated prices, reduced quality, and limited innovation.

Several behavioral patterns, such as cartels and corruption, have a negative impact on public procurement. Fazekas and Toth (2014) introduced a method using red flags within public procurement records to identify fraudulent practices. Their Corruption Risk Index (CRI) serves as a scalable measure across different countries and organizations to assess the likelihood of violating fair competition. Notable red flags include single or a small number of bids, failure to publish tender calls in official journals, deviations in eligibility criteria length, short submission periods, pricing anomalies, modifications to tender calls, non-price evaluation criteria influence, annulment and relaunching of procedures, prolonged decision periods, contract modifications during delivery, contract extensions, and contract share of the winner. The authors also found a positive correlation between the contract value ratio (comparison of estimated vs. final value) and the CRI, indicating higher corruption levels in tenders with a greater ratio (Fazekas and Toth, 2016).

De Silveira and Kovacic (2019) compared sophisticated screening tools, such as SMA (UK), FAS (Russia), BRIAS (Korea), and CADE Projecto Cerebro (Brazil). They emphasized the importance of international collaboration among competition authorities to develop next-generation screening software. The indicators employed in these tools can be grouped into four categories: number and patterns of bidders, suspicious pricing patterns, low effort and similar submissions, and history of participation.

Non-competitive procurement processes are often a factor in public procurement environment with a lack of transparency and accountability in procurement decisions. This can create opportunities for favoritism, nepotism, and other corrupt practices.

To mitigate the risks of non-competitiveness, public procurement policies should prioritize transparency, accountability, and competition. This can be achieved by promoting open contracting, increasing the number of bidders, and ensuring that procurement processes are conducted in a fair and transparent manner. Additionally, data analytics and machine learning algorithms can help identify patterns of behavior that may suggest collusion or bid rigging, and flag them for closer scrutiny.

Transparency plays a crucial role in various aspects. Henze, Schuett, and Sluijs (2015) assert, based on experimental research, that transparency fosters prosperity and increases consumer surplus. In situations with imperfect information, producers can maintain prices above marginal costs, resulting in profits at the expense of buyers. Transparency facilitates improved competition among sellers by allowing them to observe the price and quality of competing products. Veldkamp (2006) argues that transparency also contributes to market stability by reducing information asymmetries, enabling efficient resource allocation in the face of internal or external shocks. Building trust is another critical aspect of transparency, as emphasized by Willmott (2003). However, other studies (Soh et al., 2006; Zhu, 2004; Ozcelik and Ozdemir, 2011; Gu and Hehenkamp, 2010) highlight potential negative effects of increasing transparency, such as reluctance of companies to participate, challenges related to anonymity and protection of trade secrets, harm to competition, opportunities for anti-competitive activities, diminished innovation capacity, and potential monopolization.

Distance between supplier and procurer is also a factor that can contribute to corruption in public procurement. When the supplier is located far away from the procurer, it can be difficult and expensive for other suppliers to participate in the procurement process, reducing competition and increasing the risk of collusion or bid-rigging.

Moreover, when procurement officials work with suppliers located far away, there is a risk of favoritism or nepotism, as they may be more likely to work with suppliers they know or have a relationship with, rather than seeking out the best value for the procurement.

Public policy documents, such as the OECD Guidelines for Fighting Bid Rigging in Public Procurement, highlight the importance of promoting competition in public procurement, including reducing barriers to entry for suppliers located far away.

Data analytics can also help to identify the risk of corruption related to distance between supplier and procurer. By analyzing procurement data, data scientists can identify suppliers who are located far away from the procurer and assess whether this distance is correlated with an increased risk of collusion or bid-rigging. The distance between supplier and procurer can be a factor contributing to corruption in public procurement. Policies that promote competition and reduce barriers to entry for suppliers located far away can help to mitigate this risk.

Overall, addressing the risks of non-competitiveness in public procurement is critical to ensuring that public resources are used efficiently and effectively, and to maintaining trust in public institutions.

In this paper, we will address the non and low competitive environment in transparent public procurement platform and try to understand frequencies of specific occurrences in different types of tenders and market segments and study the occurrence of close distance between procurer and supplier. Within the discussion we will open a debate how transparency can reduce the occurrence and stability of non-competitive negotiations in public tenders and how data can help to avoid its negative effects or non-competitive situations.

2. Research and methodology

For our analysis we will use open data from EKS platform (Electronic Contractual System) of public tenders. Our dataset consists of 160387 contracts from October 2014 to January 2023. The EKS is highly transparent electronic contracting platform, where public procurers can publish their tenders and all tenders are automatically send as notifications to suppliers registered within specific product or service category – CPV (Common Procurement Vocabulary). All suppliers can submit their offers which are transparent to other suppliers. Notifications are sent to suppliers registered to their specific CPV code and lower.

We have processed data to calculate local level of public contracts, it means, if supplier and procurer had the same regional aspect or local level. Local level was defined from four dimensions:

- local level = 0 as national level, when supplier and procurer are from Slovakia, but their cities are different. Here, we are also calculating the same ZIP but from different cities, as this situation is possible when big cities have some rural parts with the same ZIP.
- Local level = 1, when supplier and procurer are based in same cities, but ZIP code or address is different.
- Local level = 2, when supplier and procurer are based on the same ZIP code, but their address are different.
- Local level = 3, when supplier and procurer are based on the same address and their cities are the same.

In next table we are providing explanations of local level calculations and frequencies of contracts characterized by specific local level.

Table 1. Local level calculations and contract frequencies

Same address	Same ZIP	Same city	Local level	Count
0	0	0	0	137028
0	0	1	1	22265
0	1	1	2	957
1	0	1	3	72
0	1	0	0	57
1	1	1	3	8

As we see, from Table 1, there is quite high number of contracts also in a city (local level 2), although within ZIP code there are only 72 contracts and within one address 80.

Together, we present numbers of unique suppliers supplying into the public tenders based on specific local levels.

Table 2. Count of unique suppliers according to different local levels

Local_level	Count of unique suppliers
0	5553
1	2076
2	325
3	8

When we want to analyze specific differences between different local levels we can start with the most common performance indicator of public procurement – saving. The saving is calculating from estimated price and winner price after negotiations. In our analysis, we are using relative savings expressed in percentage of price reduced after negotiations.

Another indicator relates to competitive level of negotiations based on number of applicants – potential suppliers. This indicator is often used to express a level of healthy or non-standard competition and is analyzed within different non-standard or unfair behaviors like collusion, corruption, cartel etc.

One of indicator expressing competition power is also a number of bids per applicant – bids_per_CO. This indicator presents the intensity of competition or bidding atmosphere in the public tender negotiation.

All these indicators are analyzed by visualization of line graphs for bilateral relation of specific procurer (contracting authority CA) and specific supplier (contractor – CO). On the Figure 1 we are presenting performance indicator trends by increasing number of contracts between procurer and supplier.

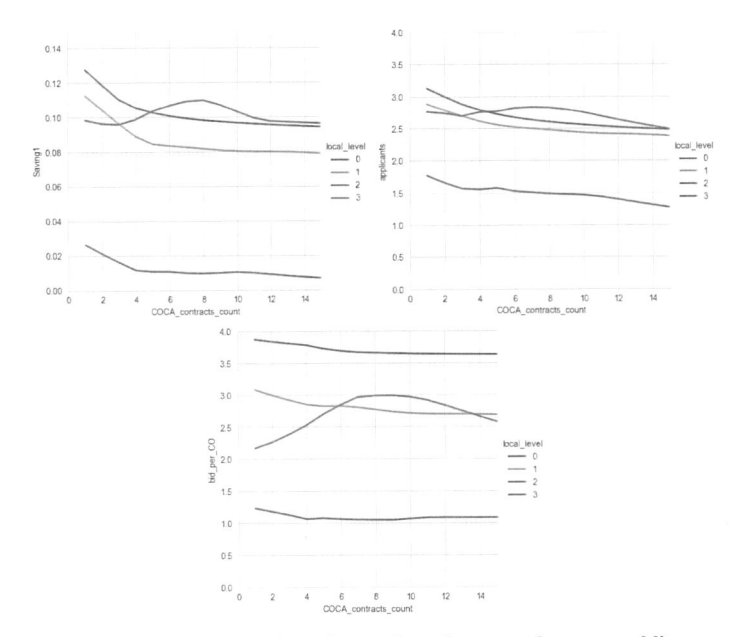

Figure 1. Performance indicator trends based on the number of contract between public procurer and supplier

Interesting is, that almost all performance indicators are decreasing in time by long runners. The best performance has national and ZIP contracts. ZIP based contracts are surprisingly good against the city and address level, although when they are considered as closer relation from geographic aspect. Number of applicants are not so different between national, city and ZIP level but quite low numbers are on address level. These trends are visualized by Lowess smoothing method. Although the competitiveness based on number of suppliers is not so different in the intensity of competitiveness there are differences between national against more local levels. It may provide and evidence that on national level, there is weaker trends to have collusive or other type of unfair behavior between suppliers or between suppliers and procurer (corruption).

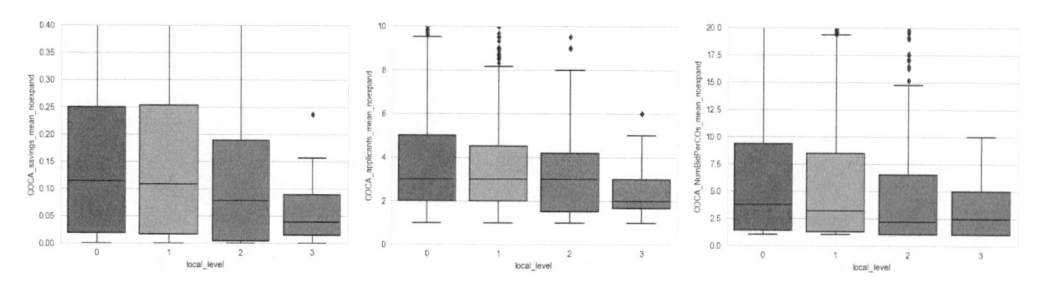

Figure 2. Boxplots of bilateral contracts aggregated performance based on local level

In Figure 1, we analyzed the trends over time as the number of contracts won by a single supplier in public procurements increased. Figure 2 examines the aggregated performance indicators throughout the supplier's active period in public tenders. The variable COCA_savings_mean_ noexpand represents the mean savings achieved in all historical contracts of the supplier, compared based on different local levels of the bilateral relationship. The same principle applies to applicants and the number of bids per CO. The results are more conclusive compared to Figure 1, with medians decreasing and indicating a decline in the distribution of indicator values as the local level decreases. The analysis suggests that the distance between the supplier and the procurer can significantly impact the negative outcomes of performance indicators in public contracts.

One interesting collusion indicator is the presence of a fixed portfolio of suppliers that consistently appears in the same composition in public tenders. A specific behavioral signal involves bidding, where one supplier consistently emerges as the winner. Therefore, we also focused on the indicator NcombCO_winning_ratio, which measures the winning ratio of the most successful supplier within a stable portfolio of suppliers during public tender negotiations. The corresponding boxplots in Figure 3 illustrate this indicator. The right boxplot displays the success rates of suppliers at different local levels, indicating that as the local level of contracts increases, suppliers with more than five successful wins in tenders of a specific procurer tend to have higher success rates. The left boxplot demonstrates a similar dependency and provides further evidence that closer proximity between the supplier and procurer results in a higher occurrence of non-standard behavior.

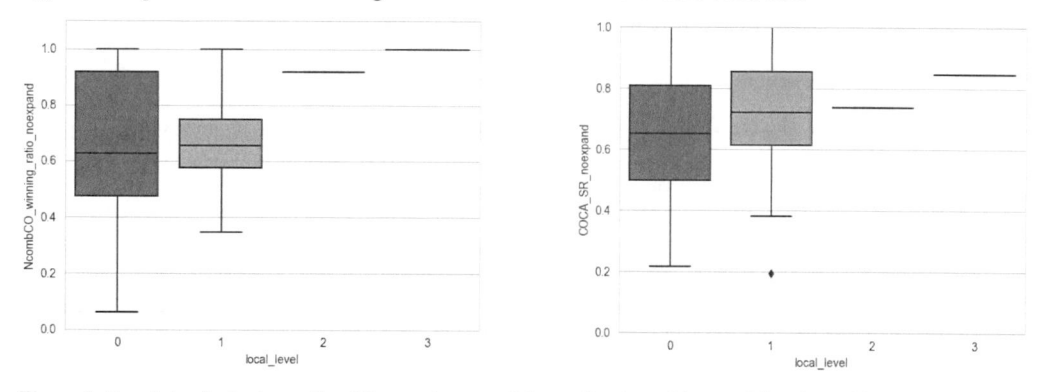

Figure 3. Boxplots of winning ratio of the most successful supplier in stable portfolio of suppliers and local level of public contracts and success rate of supplier winning tenders of one specific procurer

When we are focusing on stable portfolio of suppliers which are mentioned in several studies as long runners within collusive behavior examination, we are providing also the statistics of the frequency of such a contracts with this signal (stable portfolio of suppleirs with more than five contracts per procurer) to show if there is or not some pattern within number of such a contract or amount of public spendings to such a portfolio of suppliers. The trend is not so clear although within transparent platform as EKS is, the number and also sum of such a contracts are from our point of view interesting. We have to say that we are surprised that in such a transparent environment, where automatic notifications are set up we have identified so many occurences of such a behavior. It can show, that although transparent environment provides an opportunity for unfair behavior, e.g. manipulation of the tender conditions, CPV code definition or other signs, which reduce the effiency of high level transparency as claimed by several studies or policy makers.

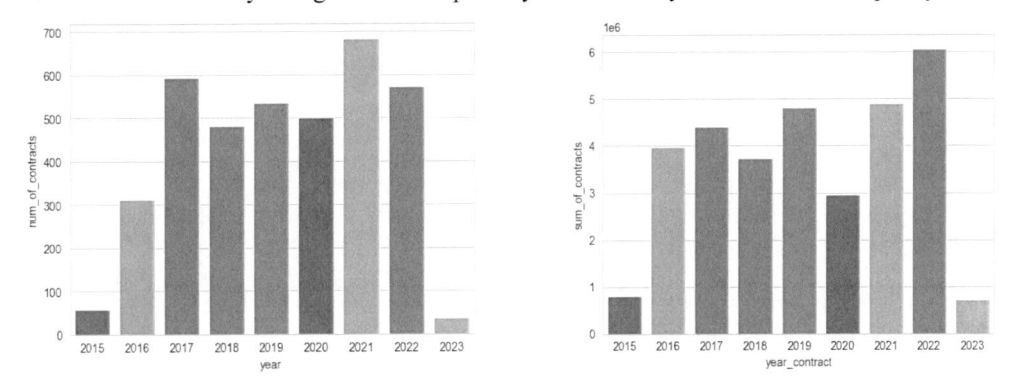

Figure 4. Number and sum of contracts with stable portfolio of suppliers in public tenders

Another view on risks related to public tendering is the focus on dependency of public procurer on supplier or vice versa. High dependency relates to increased risk of fixed prices, lock-in or lower innovation or quality of products and services delivered to the procurer. On the other hand, higher dependency on procurer may relate with lower stability on the market in the case, the public procurer will change his behavior or some signs of corruption. Both can have negative effect on tender performance but we was not able to find the analysis where this aspect was examined according to local level or from geographic dimension.

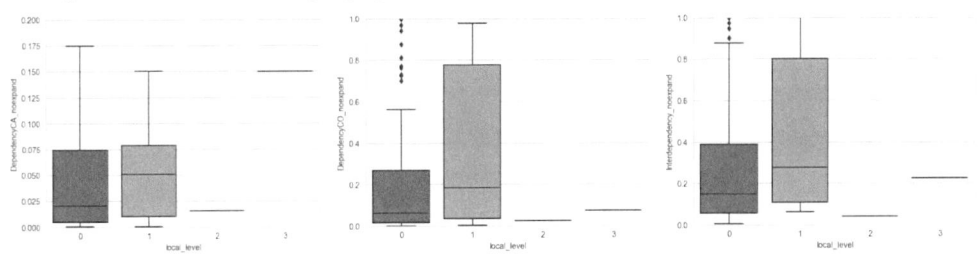

Figure 5. Boxplots of dependency indicators on different local levels

As shown from Figure 5, we see again that these risky patters with negative impact potential are more common on city level as on national level. It is hard to assess the ZIP and address levels due to insufficient frequency of such a bilateral relations or contracts. But the difference between national and city level is quite significant and can suggests again the proof, that closer geographical relations between supplier and public procurer may lead to risky behavior.

The next signal of non-standard behavior and low public procurement performance are contracts with zero spendings. It means, the competition level was so low or only one supplier was presented in the negotiation that no bidding or competitive behavior occur. The graph below shows relation between contracts of specific bilateral relationship of one supplier and one procurer where all contracts were with zero savings and shows the duration of such a relationship against different local levels. On the graphs in the middle and in the right section, there are line graphs visualizing the change of count or sum of such a contracts on such a transparent platform again according to the local level.

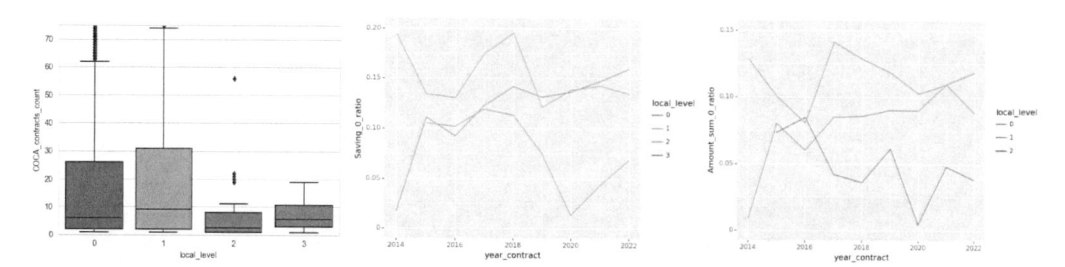

Figure 6. Boxplot of contractual length and ratio of zero saving contract frequency or public spending amount agains all contracts

In Figure 6 the situation is not so clear, as the city level has longer contractual relationships with zero saving contracts but ZIP or address level is not so clear. On the graphs next to boxplot we see the ratio of contracts with zero savings against all tenders from the aspect of frequency and public spending amount. Interesting is, that here, the contracts on national level suggest some tendency to increase, although the city shows still the most frequent zero saving contracts and highest volume.

3. Conclusion

In this study we wanted to highlight the aspect of localisation of public tenders, it means to study if there are some differences of public tender performance based on different geographical distance between supplier and public procurer.

We have analyzed several performance indicators where almost in all the visualisation through boxplots or trend lines it suggests, that there is quite strong relation and closer distance shows the higher probability for non-standard behavior with negative impact on public tenders. For example in cities there are higher dependencies on business partner then on national level. Together, occurance of fixed portfolio of suppliers in more than five contracts within one specific public procurer is much more higher in lower local level as on national level. All these results indicates several possible reasons. One is quite sensitive and it relates to non-standard behavior with unfair character, e.g. collusion in the form of cover bidding, rotations or directly corruption as some agreements between suppliers and public procurer.

As we show, also sipmle data visualisation can make these patterns transparent and provides some decision making or monitoring support for public makers or procurers.

Together, it has to be said, that the study was based on data from highly transparent platform EKS from Slovakia, where transparency should play the role of unfair behavior regulator. Although results shows, that nor high transparency is not so efficient against some non-standard behavior and several risky or suspicious behavioral patterns are emerging quite frequently also in transparent environments.

We are encouraging researchers to study this phenomenon more deeply on wider data also from other countries and model more complex dependencies and causalities to find solutions how to reduce these negative effects and not mix positive effects of public spending for regional companies with unfair behavioral patterns.

Acknowledgement

The paper is written with support of APVV within the project No APVV-20-06089 *"The research of behavioral patterns on big data within public and commercial procurement with negative impact on efficiency of procurement processes"*.

References

Da Silveira, P. B., and Kovacic, W. E. (2019). Global Competition Enforcement: New Players, New Challenges. Kluwer Law International, 2019. ISBN – 9403502835

Fazekas, M. and Tóth, I.J. (2014). From corruption to state capture: A new analytical framework with empirical applications from Hungary, Corruption Research Center Budapest Working Papers No. CRCB-WP/2014:01, http://dx.doi.org/10.2139/ssrn.2531701

Fazekas, M., Tóth, I. J., and King, L. P. (2016). An Objective Corruption Risk Index Using Public Procurement Data. European Journal on Criminal Policy and Research, 22(3), 369–397. doi:10.1007/s10610-016-9308-z

Gu, Y., and Hehenkamp, B. (2010). The Inefficiency of Market Transparency–A Model with Endogenous Entry. Ruhr Economic Paper, (219).

Henze, B., Schuett, F., and Sluijs, J. P. (2015). Transparency in markets for experience goods: experimental evidence. Economic Inquiry, 53(1), 640-659.

Imhof, D. (2018). Empirical Methods for Detecting Bid-rigging Cartels. Retrieved from https://tel.archives-ouvertes.fr/tel-01963076

OECD. (2018). Summary of the workshop on cartel screening in the digital era, DAF/COMP/M(2018)3

OECD. (2020). Recommendation of the Council concerning Effective Action against Hard Core Cartels OECD/LEGAL/0452. Retrieved from http://www.oecd.org/daf/competition/2350130.pdf

Ozcelik,Y. and Ozdemir, Z.D. (2011). Market Transparency in Business-to-Business e-Commerce: A Simulation Analysis, International Journal of E-Business Research (IJEBR), 7(4), DOI: 10.4018/jebr.2011100105

Soh, C., Markus, M. L., and Goh, K. H. (2006). Electronic marketplaces and price transparency: strategy, information technology, and success. MIS quarterly, 705-723.

Veldkamp, L. L. (2006). Information Markets and the Comovement of Asset Prices. The Review of Economic Studies, 73(3), 823–845. https://doi.org/10.1111/j.1467-937X.2006.00397.x

Willmott, M. (2003). Citizen brands: corporate citizenship, trust and branding. Journal of Brand Management, 10(4-5), 362-369.

Zhu, K. (2004). Information transparency of business-to-business electronic markets: A game-theoretic analysis. Management Science, 50(5), 670-685.

ANALYSIS OF PUBLIC PROCUREMENT IN STRATEGY RESOURCE SOURCING: DOES RELATION OF MATTER IN LONG RUN CONTRACTS?

Michal Tkáč, Jakub Sieber

The University of Economics in Bratislava
michal.tkac1@euba.sk, jakub.sieber@euba.sk

DOI: 10.35011/IDIMT-2023-293

Keywords

Public procurement, strategy, supplier relations, strategy resource

Abstract

The proposed paper is conducting the analysis of public procurement of electricity in Slovak Republic between years 2014 and 2022. Based on 1,009 observations there is made an analysis of the rate of savings in public procurement with focus on features describing the repeated relation between the supplier and contracting authority, as well as evaluation of the savings rate according to the chosen type of procurement strategy, comparing the auction and contractual type. Results of CHAID algorithm suggests the predicted savings have tendency to be higher while using auction type, also supported by non-parametric test, when the median saving rate is higher by 3.73%

1. Introduction

There are various energy procurement strategies that organizations can use to acquire energy. Some of the commonly used strategies include fixed-price contracts, index-based pricing, and renewable energy procurement. Fixed-price contracts involve purchasing energy at a fixed price over a specific period. Index-based pricing involves purchasing energy at market rates based on a specified index, while renewable energy procurement involves sourcing energy from renewable sources such as wind, solar, and hydro. Procurement strategies are essential for organizations to effectively manage their costs and obtain goods and services of the desired quality. According to Shuler (2021) and KPMG (2009), the cost of procurement can be as high as 70% or more of the total cost of goods sold in some industries. Hence, procurement is a strategic priority for management, and organizations need to develop effective procurement strategies to reduce costs and improve quality. In order to achieve robust competition in the procurement process, the selection procedure must be impartial and fair. Unintentional or intentional biases can be avoided in a fair and objective process to help ensure that the best options are chosen. Third-party providers are encouraged to participate because of the integrity of the process, which gives them the assurance that their bids will be thoroughly evaluated on their merits. To accomplish this, procurements must contain the necessary safeguards to prevent giving any offers an unfair advantage, to ensure that they are carried out as intended, and to deal with unforeseen circumstances in a way that is fundamentally fair and consistent with the process's competitive intent. The procurement should be set up to support market players' competitive offerings that are strong and innovative ideas. Participants in the market must have the following conditions in order to be encouraged to respond competitively: (1) assurance that their offers will be treated fairly and objectively; (2) assurance that their confidential information will be adequately protected; and (3) access to sufficient information regarding bidder requirements, product specifications, model contract terms, evaluation procedures, and other factors that would affect the resources they choose to offer.

One approach to procurement strategy is to identify the most suitable suppliers who can provide high-quality goods and services at competitive prices. According to Duica et al. (2018), supplier selection is a critical component of procurement strategy, and organizations need to consider several factors when selecting suppliers, such as supplier capabilities, reliability, and performance. Identifying the need, making the choice to buy, finding sources, picking the best suppliers, contracting, and maintaining connections with potential contractors are all parts of the complicated notion of procurement management, which is a function of the B2B market. To find the correct supplier and keep a long-lasting and prosperous relationship with them, supplier selection is a difficult process throughout the supply chain. Another approach is to develop long-term relationships with suppliers to ensure a stable supply of goods and services. According to Naoui-Outini and El Hilali (2019), strategic partnerships with suppliers can help organizations reduce costs, improve quality, and foster innovation. However, developing such partnerships requires trust, mutual understanding, and commitment from both parties. Additionally, organizations can implement e-procurement systems to streamline their procurement processes and reduce costs. According to Alor-Hernandez et al. (2011), e-procurement systems can help organizations automate their procurement processes, improve supplier collaboration, and reduce transaction costs. Several studies have examined the effectiveness of different energy procurement strategies. A study by Ari et al. (2022) found that fixed-price contracts were effective in reducing energy costs, while index-based pricing resulted in higher costs due to market volatility. Renewable energy procurement was found to be effective in reducing greenhouse gas emissions and increasing energy security.

Both the pandemic of COVID and the financial crisis of 2008 revealed the potentially catastrophic risks of just-in-time strategies and the need for one that would be better referred to as just-in-case that places a lot more of a focus on resilience. Given how much debt in private companies is now owned by the public sector, this is only going to become more crucial. So how can businesses make this transformation in the most efficient way? By approaching procurement in a way that emphasizes building robust multi-relational networks rather than linear supply chains. In fact, if one adopts this mentality, procurement may end up becoming a strategy. As stated by Ramírez et al. (2020) Procurement becomes a key component of strategy as businesses place less emphasis on efficiency and more on resilience. This is due to its exceptional capacity to coordinate long-term value-creating systems that can survive external shocks, accept incompatible value holders, share burdens, and evolve dynamically. This illustrates an essential lesson: When resilience is your top concern, smart procurement might be the best approach.

2. Methodology and data sample description

Presented paper is following two main objectives. First objective is to analyze if there is evidence of repeated deals between procurer (contracting authority) and supplier resulting in the different value of savings in public procurement of electricity. Second objective of the presented paper is to test the difference between the procurement strategy (process) and its influence on savings while procuring the electricity. Both objectives are tested on the sample of public procurements in Slovak Republic in the period from 2014 to 2022, which were directly related to the electricity. All the analyzed public procurements are publicly available data from Slovak national electronic contracting system (EKS). The analyzed data consist of 1,009 observations.

In order to achieve stated objectives, there was applied CRISP-DM methodology and decision tree approach, similar to Rocha et al. (2010) and Wiemer et al. (2019). CRISP-DM is a de-facto standard in data mining that provides a process model for applying data mining projects. It includes descriptions of the typical phases of a project, the tasks involved with each phase, and an explanation of the relationships between these tasks (Schröer et al., 2021). CRISP-DM is an industry-proven way to guide data mining efforts and support the iterative nature of data science (Huber et al., 2021). Decision trees are a popular machine learning algorithm used for both classification and regression tasks. They have many advantages over other algorithms, including being flexible, requiring fewer data cleaning, and being easy to interpret and visualize. Some commonly used decision tree algorithms include CART, C5.0, and CHAID. CHAID is particularly useful for market research and can build wider decision trees because it is not constrained to make binary splits (Almuallim et al., 2002). To prevent overfitting of decision tree, there will be used sample partition in conventional share of 0.7 training data and 0.3 testing data. Beside partitioning, there will be also used column sampling at 0.8. Beside machine-learning techniques there is used non-parametrical statistical method Mann-Whitney U test for testing the differences between examined groups. The dependent variable is savings of the observed procurement process, which is defined as a percentage of the savings when comparing the anticipated price of the procurement and the final price. Independent variables used in presented analysis were: *offers_count* representing the number of offers registered for the contract; *CO_all_contracts_count* defining the market share of the supplier (contractor), as the frequency of the contracts provided by supplier; *Price_incl.VAT* describing the final value of the approved and signed contract; *CO_all_contracts_mean* another variable describing the position of supplier on the market, as the average value of signed contracts; *number_of_bids* representing the count of bids made for contract in auction, in order to see the difference if the offers were changed during the auction; *applicants* stands for the number of applicants (suppliers) registered in the process of procurement; *bid_per_CO* as the number of bids made in relation to the number of suppliers in the competition; *Contract_length_days* equals to the number of the days the final contract was signed; *Number_of_CO_notified* as the number of suppliers, who were officially informed before the procurement procedure; *COCA_all_contracts_count* representing the number of contracts signed between the winning supplier and the contracting authority.

Table 1. Descriptive statistics of the sample

Variable	Min	Max	Mean	St. Dev.
saving_pct	0	0.96	0.1	0.114
offers_count	1	376	23.75	36.86
CO_all_contracts_count	1	1660	293.95	312.8
Price_incl.VAT	345.24	425219	65358	65488
CO_all_contracts_mean	13000	173500	55154	16024
number_of_bids	1	376	24.26	36.92
applicants	1	9	3	1.76
bid_per_CO	1	188	7	11.33
Contract_length_days	0	1460	500	248.88
Number_of_CO_notified	22	624	173	62.53
COCA_all_contracts_count	1	12	2	1.58

Table 1 illustrates descriptive statistics of an examined sample of public procurements of electricity. The variance of the dependent variable savings from procurement is moving from 0 to 96%, with the average value at 10%. Except the mentioned variables in Table 1, there is also categorical variable identifying the procurement strategy (process) – auction or contractual (Table 2).

3. Results

When dividing observations in the sample according to the procurement type, 439 observations were classified as an auction type of procurement process, while 570 were a contractual type of procurement process. The contractual process of procurement showed mean percentual savings at 9.06%, and in the auction type of procurement process, the mean value of savings was at the level of 11.09%, as illustrated in Table 2. Except for the mean value of savings, the auction process of the public procurement showed a higher mean value of every examined variable as offers received (*offers_count*), number of bids (*num_of_bids*), applicants and price of the final contract.

Table 2. Average values of observed variables according to the procurement process

Proc. process	n	saving_pct	offers_count	num_of_bids	applicants	Price	days_contract
Auction	439	0.1109	40	40	4	68500	500
Contractual	570	0.0906	11	12	2	63000	498

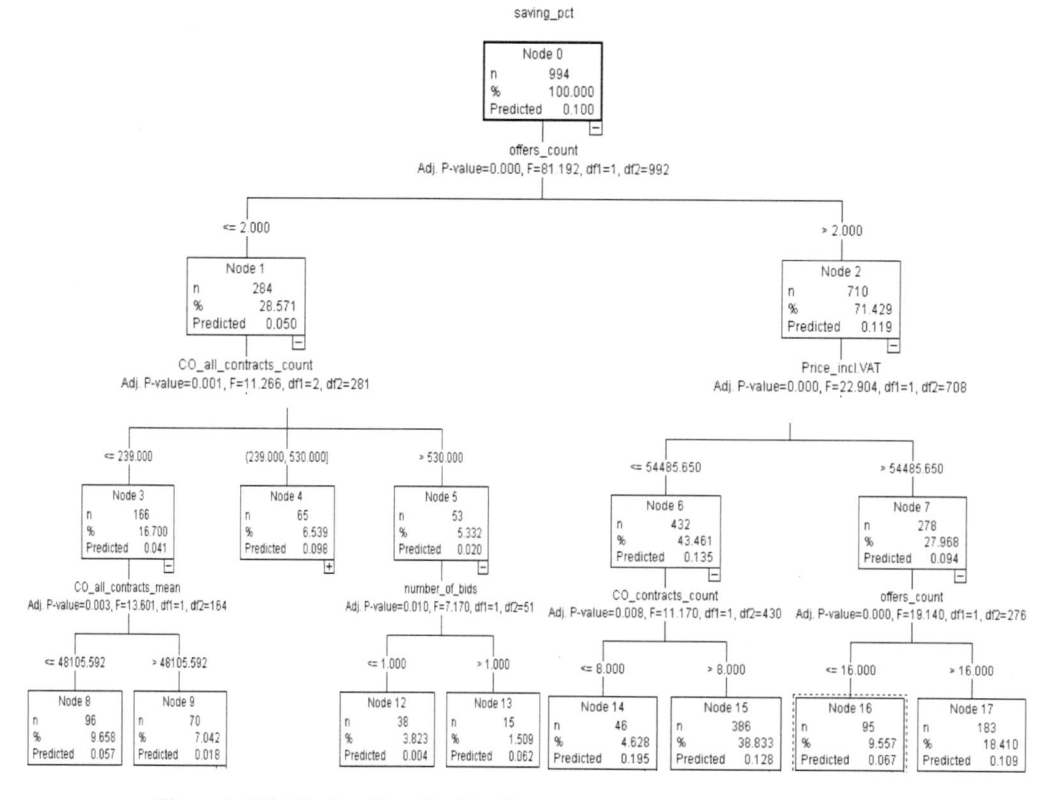

Figure 1. CHAID algorithm: Decision Tree – aggregated strategies results, model 1

Figure 1 illustrates Node 0 of the CHAID decision tree, with R2 score = 0.71, MAE = 0.075 which illustrates the variable with the highest importance on the dependent variable – savings from observed procurement processes. The model presented in Figure 1 metrics have reached mean absolute error (MAE) = 0.067, and standard deviation (SD) = 0.102. As the predictor of the savings with the highest importance was chosen parameter offers received for the public procurement contract,where the treshold resulted in to 2 offers. While the number offers was equal or less than 2, the predicted savings were 5%, otherwise it moved to 11.9%. The CHAID algorithm has not chosen the categorical parameter of procurement type (auction or contractual) as important feature, while making the predictions. Therefore, there was created another subsample for further modelling, where one subsamples consisted only of one procurement strategy, auction, or contractual respectively, see figures 2 and 3. Model 2 presented in Figure 2 shows the results of model, where predictions of public procurements savings are made only on the subsample consisting of auction strategy procurements. In this case the most impactful feature, which divide decision tree at first level to nodes 1 and 2 is feature number of bids, equaling how many times the offer for contract had changed. The threshold for the number of bids shows, that if the number of bids was more than thirteen, the predicted value of saving has mean value of 12.4%, while in cases, where the number of bids was thirteen or less (representing more than 71% of the subsample), the predicted saving is reaching 7.9% of mean value of expected contract value. The node 1 is following the division by the number of contractors (suppliers) notified. In this case, the highest savings are predicted in case, when there are less than 110 contractors notified about the auction (13.7%), while when there is notification for more than 259 contractors, the average predicted saving of the procurement is at the value 4.3%. Metrics of the model 2 have reached of R2 score = 0.75, MAE = 0.065. What represents slightly better evaluation metrics than in the case of the model 1.

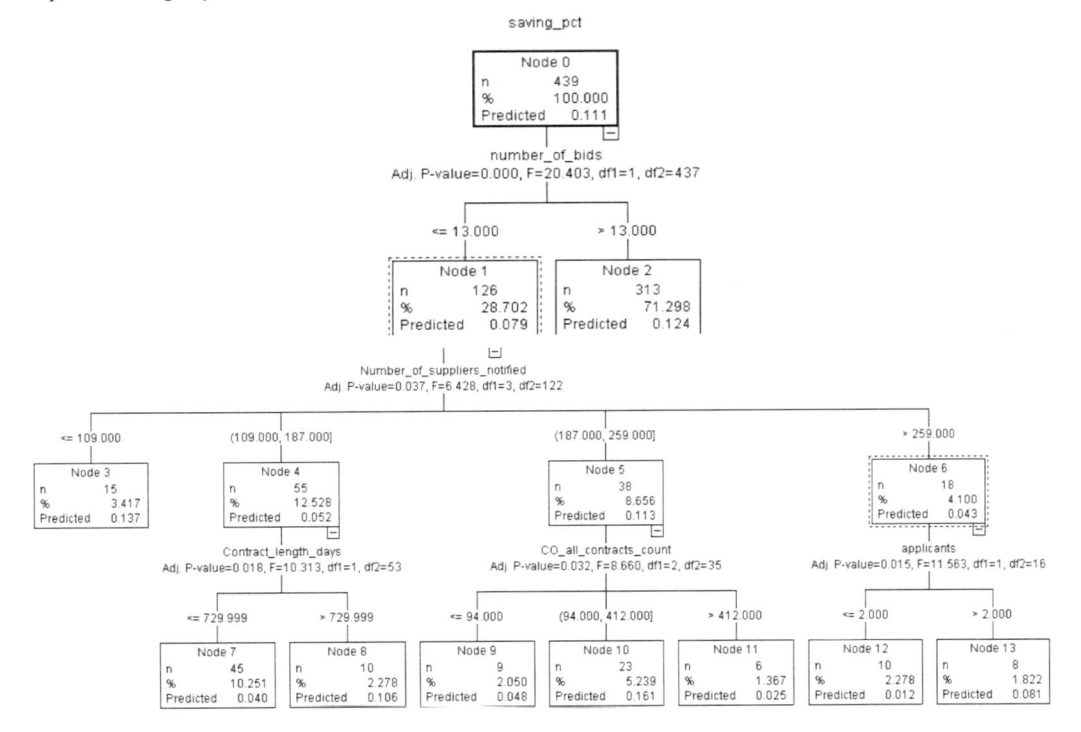

Figure 2. CHAID algorithm: Decision Tree – auction procurement results, model 2

In case of the subsample dealing only with contractual strategies of public procurement (Figure 3) the very first division of the decision tree is on the feature applicants, describing the number of the applicants in the competition.

The average value of saving is raising with the number of applicants in the procurement process. The lowest predicted value of savings is observed, when there is only one applicant, at the 4.6%, what was the case in 39% of studied subsample. The predicted value of savings in case of two applicants have raised to 8.6%. The highest mean value of predicted savings is observed in case of more than two applicants (Node 3, Figure 3). If there are more than two applicants, the prediction of the offered contract in procurement is based on the number of supplier count of contracts in observed period (CO_all_contracts_count).

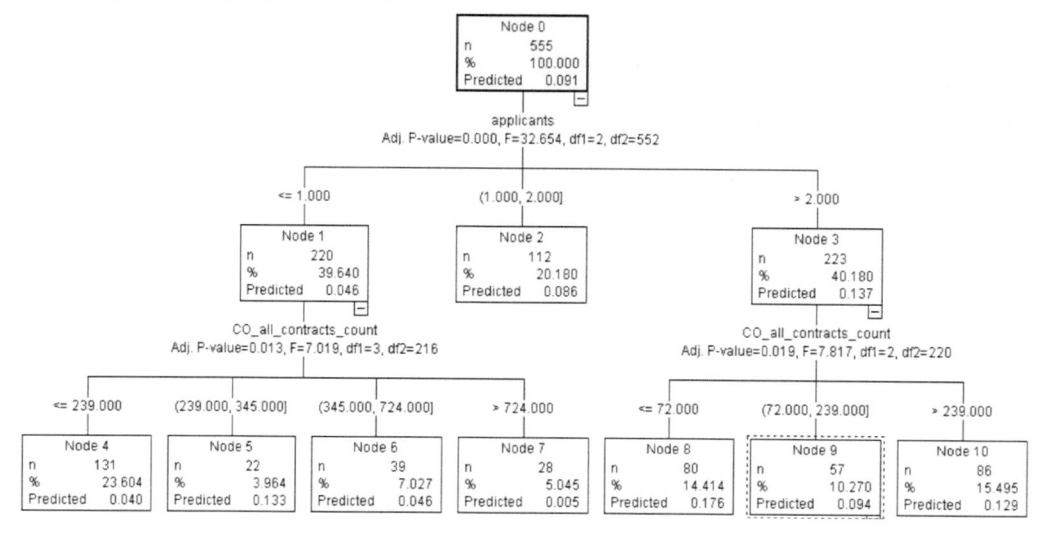

Figure 3. CHAID algorithm: Decision Tree – contractual procurement results, model 3

The predicted values do not follow any specific trend with the number of contracts the supplier offered. Higher values of predicted savings are observed in the threshold values of upper and lower interval. The middle interval signaling number of supplier contracts between 72 and 239 is predicting the average savings on contractual procurement process at 9.4% against the expected value of the contract. Model 3 presented in Figure 3 metrics have reached MAE = 0.071, R^2 = 0.74, signaling slightly worse accuracy as in the case of baseline model 1.

Table 3. Testing the relation between chosen procurement features and procurement strategy

H	Null Hypothesis	Test	Sig.	Decision
1	The distribution of saving_pct is the same across categories of Procurement_strategy.	t-Samples Mann-Whitney U	0.000	Reject the null hypothesis.
2	The distribution of Number_of_suppliers_notified is the same across categories of Procurement_strategy.		0.486	Retain the null hypothesis.
3	The distribution of number_of_bids is the same across categories of Procurement_strategy.		0.000	Reject the null hypothesis.

H	Null Hypothesis	Test	Sig.	Decision
4	The distribution of offers_count is the same across categories of Procurement_strategy.		0.000	Reject the null hypothesis.
5	The distribution of CO_all_contracts_count is the same across categories of Procurement_strategy.		0.014	Reject the null hypothesis.
6	The distribution of COCA_all_contracts_count is the same across categories of Procurement_strategy.		0.315	Retain the null hypothesis.
7	The distribution of bid_per_CO is the same across categories of Procurement_strategy.		0.000	Reject the null hypothesis.

To justify the creation of the subsamples, and results presented in model 2 and model 3, there was conducted nonparametric Mann-Whitney U Test (Table 3). According to the Mann-Whitney test results it was possible to state there are statistically significant differences in savings according to the type of procurement strategy. As presented in Tab. 3, according to the Mann-Whitney Test it was possible to reject the null hypothesis of the same distribution in the category of the procurement strategy, except the features number of suppliers notified, and the feature describing the repeating relationship between supplier and procurer – contracting authority (*COCA_all_contracts_count*). Feature describing the number of suppliers notified is observed only in model 2 (Figure2, Node 1). On the other hand, it was not possible to observe the feature describing the relationship between supplier and procurer in any of previously presented models as a predictor with significant impact on the savings from the public procurement. Box plot in Figure 4 illustrates the results from Mann-Whitney test from Table 3. It is possible to observe the statistically significant differences between auction and contractual type of public procurement of electricity. The auction type strategy median value of savings is at the level of 8.68%, while the contractual procurements yielded median value at the level of 4.95%. In the contractual type of procurement, it is also possible to higher variability of the savings, with the first quartile closer to the zero, than in the case of the procurements made as auctions. The contractual type of procurement also showed higher frequency of the outliers and extreme value occurrences.

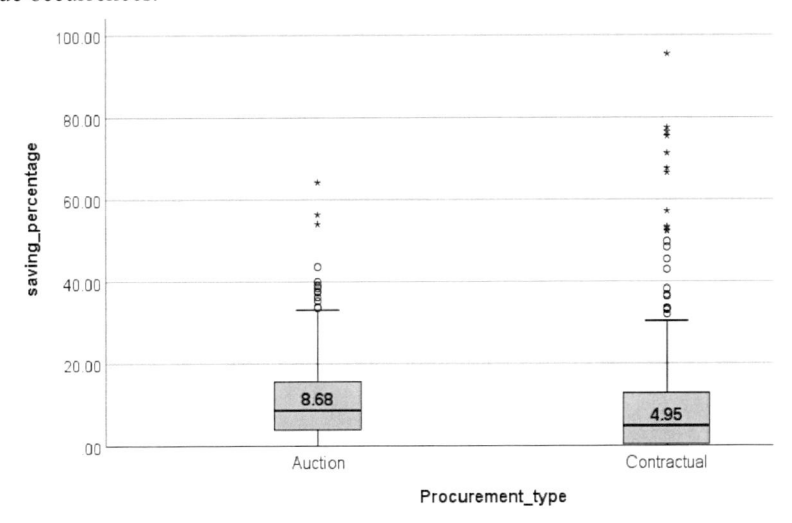

Figure 4. Box plot analysis of the relation between savings from procurement and procurement strategy

4. Conclusions

Presented paper analyzed public procurements related to the electricity in the Slovak Republic between the years 2014 and 2022. According to the 1,009 observations there is no evidence of the relation between the repeated occurrence of contracts between supplier and contracting authority and savings rate. The observed relation between supplier of electricity and the procurer expressed as the count of signed and approved contracts in the past did not show any significant importance, when analyzing mentioned relationship by algorithm CHAID in three models with modified sample. While analyzing the importance of the supplier, in the results there could have been observed, that the "power" of supplier (market share/the amount of contracts) is playing important role in the public procurement. The observable trend presented in Figure1, Figure 2, and Figure 3 could be explained that the lowest rate of savings is usually obtained when the electricity was procured from the biggest players on the energy market. In Figure 3, we could also observe that almost 40% of applicants were = 1, indicating possible monopoly or oligopoly structure presence, while in the Figure 2 describing the auction type, the smallest value observed for factor of applicants was 2, and only in 2.3% of the sample. Second objective of the paper was to focus on the public procurement strategy. In this case, it is possible to state, there are significant differences in savings rate accordingly to the procurement strategy. Contractual type of public procurement of electricity showed the median saving rate at the level of 4.95% from the value of the contract, what is significantly lower, than 8.68% observed in the auction type of public procurement. The results presented in the Figure1, Figure 2, and Figure 3 allows to argue, that auction type of procurement yields higher savings rate in electricity public procurement. While investigating the relationship between savings rate and procurement type there were identified similarities and differences in observed features of the procurement strategies. Speaking about the similarities, the length of contract, there were not observed significant differences, in case of both types of procurements the median value of the contract length was observed at the value 500 days, and the mean value is differentiated only by 2 days. On the other hand, in both cases the factor of the competition played the significant role. In auction strategy is the most important feature number of bids in auction, while in the contractual strategy it is number of applicants. In auction type of public procurement is observable higher average number of variables representing the competition of suppliers for given contract, such as number of offers, number of bids or applicants. In conclusion it might be stated that auction type of procurement strategy yields higher probability of savings rate in electricity procurement in Slovak Republic.

Acknowledgement

The paper is written with the support of APVV within project No APVV-20-06089 *"The research of behavioral patterns on big data within public and commercial procurement with negative impact on efficiency of procurement processes"*.

References

Almuallim, H., Kaneda, S., & Akiba, Y. (2002). Development and applications of decision trees. In Expert Systems (pp. 53-77). Academic Press.

Alor-Hernandez, G., A., A., Cortes-Robles, G., & Sanchez-Ramirez, C. (2011). Improving E-Procurement in Supply Chain Through Web Technologies: The HYDRA Approach. InTech. doi: 10.5772/21459

Ari, A., Arregui, N., Black, S., Celasun, O., Iakova, D., Mineshima, A., Mylonas, V., Parry, I., Teodoru, I., & Zhunussova, K. (2022). Surging Energy Prices in Europe in the Aftermath of the War: How to Support the Vulnerable and Speed up the Transition Away from Fossil Fuels. IMF Working Papers, 2022/152

Duica, M., Florea, N. & Duica, A. (2018). Selecting the Right Suppliers in Procurement Process along Supply Chain: Mathematical Modeling Approach. Valahian Journal of Economic Studies. 9. pp. 47-58.

Electronic Contracting System of Slovak Republic. Overview of contracts. Available at: https://eo.eks.sk/Prehlady/ZakazkyVerejnost

Huber, S., Wiemer, H., Schneider, D., & Ihlenfeldt, S. (2019). DMME: Data mining methodology for engineering applications–a holistic extension to the CRISP-DM model. Procedia Cirp, 79, 403-408.

KPMG. (2012). The Power of Procurement: A global survey of Procurement functions. Available at: https://assets.kpmg.com/content/dam/kpmg/pdf/2012/07/the-power-of-procurement-a-global-survey-of-procurement-functions.pdf

Naoui-Outini, F. & El Hilali, N. (2019). Innovative suppliers and purchasing function interaction: An exploratory research in the car rental sector. Journal of Innovation Economics & Management, 28, pp. 171-192. https://doi.org/10.3917/jie.028.0165

Ramírez R., McGinley, C., Churchhouse, S. (2020). Why Investing in Procurement Makes Organizations More Resilient. Harvard Business Review, Operations And Supply Chain Management.

Rocha, B. C., & de Sousa Junior, R. T. (2010). Identifying bank frauds using CRISP-DM and decision trees. International Journal of Computer Science and Information Technology, 2(5), pp.162-169.

Schröer, C., Kruse, F., & Gómez, J. M. (2021). A systematic literature review on applying CRISP-DM process model. Procedia Computer Science, 181, 526-534.

Shuler, K. (2021). How to Identify (and Significantly Reduce) Procurement Costs. QUANDRY Consulting Group: Procurement. Available at: https://quandarycg.com/how-to-identify-and-significantly-reduce-procurement-costs/

Wiemer, H., Drowatzky, L., & Ihlenfeldt, S. (2019). Data mining methodology for engineering applications (DMME)—A holistic extension to the CRISP-DM model. Applied Sciences, 9(12), 2407.

THE ANALYSIS OF THE PUBLIC PROCUREMENT ENVIRONMENT BEFORE AND AFTER COVID-19 BREAKTHROUGH: CASE OF SLOVAKIA

Michal Tkáč

Department of Corporate Financial Management
The Faculty of Business Economics with a seat in Košice,
The University of Economics in Bratislava
michal.tkac1@euba.sk

Michal Tkáč

Department of Quantitative Methods
The Faculty of Business Economics with a seat in Košice,
The University of Economics in Bratislava
michal.tkac@euba.sk

Juraj Till

Department of Corporate Financial Management
The Faculty of Business Economics with a seat in Košice,
The University of Economics in Bratislava
juraj.till@euba.sk

DOI: 10.35011/IDIMT-2023-303

Keywords

Public procurement, Slovakia, CPV

Abstract

This study analyzes the Slovak public procurement environment before and after the COVID-19 pandemic by examining a research sample of over 102,000 real procurement offers presented in the Slovakian EKS Elektronický kontraktačný systém. The study compares the savings from public procurement contracts in the pre-COVID era and the COVID era using Box-plot analysis and the Mann-Whitney test. The results indicate that while the mean savings rate remained similar, the COVID era had a significantly lower median savings rate and a different distribution of savings rates compared to the pre-COVID era. The study also compares the distribution of savings based on the type of public procurement offers and the type of procurer. These findings can be useful for policymakers and practitioners in understanding the impact of the pandemic on public procurement.

1. Introduction

Public procurement has been a crucial aspect of government operations for a long time, intending to achieve transparency, efficiency, and effectiveness in the acquisition of goods and services. However, the outbreak of COVID-19 in 2020 has had a significant impact on public procurement processes around the world. While the pandemic has highlighted the importance of public procurement in ensuring the provision of essential goods and services, it has also exposed weaknesses in the system, including supply chain disruptions and increased demand for medical supplies. Therefore, it is essential to examine how public procurement has changed before and after the COVID-19 breakthrough to identify the challenges faced and the measures taken to mitigate them. In this paper, we provide an overview of public procurement practices before and during the COVID-19 pandemic, including the impact of the pandemic on procurement processes and the strategies used to manage the challenges posed by the outbreak. By doing so, we hope to contribute to the ongoing conversation on improving public procurement in the post-COVID-19 era.

2. Literature review

Public procurement is a critical function of government operations that aims to ensure transparency, efficiency, and effectiveness in the acquisition of goods and services. The outbreak of the COVID-19 pandemic in 2020 has had a significant impact on public procurement processes worldwide. This literature review examines the changes in public procurement before and after the COVID-19 outbreak. A survey conducted by the World Bank Group (2020) highlights the opportunities and challenges faced by public procurement during the early months of the pandemic. The study identified several issues, including supply chain disruptions, increased demand for essential medical supplies, and the need to quickly adapt to remote work environments. Furthermore, the study recommends the adoption of innovative approaches such as e-procurement and virtual bid openings to mitigate the challenges posed by the pandemic. Similarly, a report published by the European Commission (Paulović and Zomer, 2021) examines the trends that emerged during the COVID-19 pandemic in public procurement practices. The report identifies several new trends, including the increased use of sustainable procurement practices and the need for more agile procurement processes. The report also highlights the importance of strategic partnerships and cooperation between cities to address procurement challenges. Eßig, Deimling, and Glas (2021) argue that the COVID-19 crisis has exposed the deficiencies of public procurement systems, and the root causes lie in public procurement capabilities. The authors propose extended public buyer competencies based on a European Framework, evidence-based decision-making, and the use of digital technologies to improve the security of supplies. Chagelishvili and Surmanidze (2022) study the impact of the COVID-19 pandemic on simplified procurement in Georgia. The authors note that crises are conducive to the implementation of simplified procurement to address emergencies, but such measures carry the risk of corruption and less transparency. The study recommends measures to reduce the share of simplified procurement in total procurement and improve transparency. Casady and Baxter (2022) discuss the relevance of unsolicited proposals (USPs) in public-private partnerships (PPPs) in healthcare procurement during the pandemic. The authors argue that the protracted procedures of traditional PPP procurements are not suitable for times of crisis. USPs could play a pivotal role in the COVID-19 pandemic as boundary spanners between public agencies and the private sector in the PPP procurement process. The study recommends a pragmatic and practical approach to encouraging and procuring healthcare USPs. Vecchi, Cusumano, and Boyer (2020) analyze the contracting challenges faced by Italian healthcare authorities and U.S. procurement officials in the immediate aftermath of the COVID-19 crisis. The authors provide practitioner-derived lessons for improving procurement in times of disaster, including the need to recognize the strategic role of procurement, empowering procurement officials, and building trust among different governance levels.

3. Methodology

The study methodology aimed to analyze the Slovak public procurement environment using a research sample of more than 102,000 real procurement offers. The research sample was based on procurement offers presented in the Slovakian EKS. Elektronický kontraktačný systém (EKS) is an electronic platform used by Slovakian public sector organizations to manage the procurement of goods, services, and construction work. The system simplifies procurement by providing a single place for public tenders, allowing businesses to easily find and respond to opportunities. EKS incorporates features to increase transparency, ensure legal compliance, streamline administrative tasks, and facilitate efficient communication between purchasers and suppliers. Its ultimate goal is to foster fair competition, reduce corruption, and promote the efficient use of public funds. The study focused on the pre-COVID era from January 2017 to December 2019 and the COVID era from January 2020 to December 2022. Due to the non-normal distribution of savings, the study used the Box-plot analysis and Mann-Whitney test to compare the differences in savings in public procurement contracts before and after the COVID-19 outbreak. The output variable in the study was savings, which represents the difference between the estimated value and the winning bid as a percentage of the estimated value. Savings from public procurement contracts were used in this study to determine the impact of the pandemic on the Slovak public procurement environment. These findings can help policymakers and practitioners better understand the impact of the pandemic on public procurement practices in Slovakia and other countries facing similar challenges.

4. The research

The research in this paper is focused on the analysis of the Slovakian public procurement environment before and after the COVID-19 breakthrough. The descriptive analysis and statistical hypothesis testing of more than 102 000 real procurement offers placed in 6 year period in the Slovak electronic contractual system is presented in Table 1.

Table 1. Descriptive statistics of savings from public procurement offers presented in the Slovakian EKS

Saving %	Count	Mean	St. Dev.	P05th	P25th	$\tilde{x}$	P75th	P95th
Pre-COVID-19	60601	13.59	17.60	0	0.0417	5.79	21.93	50.75
COVID-19	41803	13.86	18.43	0	0.0357	5.375	22.24	53.06

Null Hypothesis	Test	p-value	Verdict
The distribution of Savings (%) is the same across categories of COVID-19.	Independent-Samples Mann-Whitney U Test	0.022	Reject the null hypothesis.

According to the results of the Mann-Whitney U test, there is a statistically significant difference between the savings rates from public procurement offers during the pre-COVID-19 and COVID-19 periods. Despite both periods having a similar mean savings rate of 14% and standard deviation of 18%, the median savings rate during the COVID-19 period was significantly lower at 5,3%

compared to 5,79% during the pre-COVID-19 period. Moreover, the test indicated that the distribution of savings rates in the COVID-19 period was significantly different from the pre-COVID-19 period at a 5% level of significance. While the 25th percentile in both periods had a savings rate of 0%, the 75th percentile during the COVID-19 period was higher at 22,25% compared to 21,93% in the pre-COVID-19 period. The top 5% of offers in the COVID-19 period also had a slightly higher savings rate of 53% compared to 51% in the pre-COVID-19 period. In conclusion, although the average savings rate from public procurement offers remained similar between the two periods, the Mann-Whitney U test suggests that the COVID-19 period had a significantly lower median savings rate and a different distribution of savings rates compared to the pre-COVID-19 period.

In the next step, we compare the distribution of savings based on type of the public procurement offers. The motivation behind this type of research was to describe how the distribution of savings differ in auction and contractual type of offers. The box-plot analysis is presented in Figure 1.

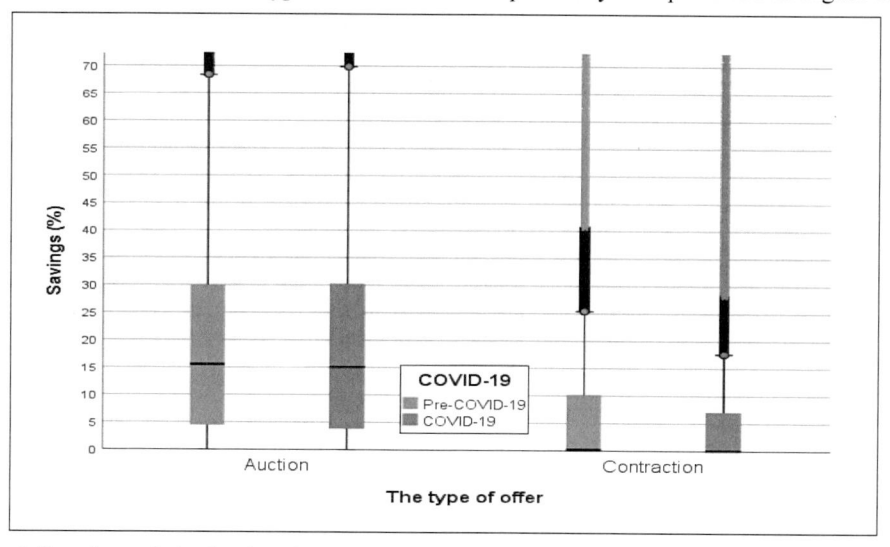

Figure 1. Box-plot analysis of savings from public procurement offers based on the contractual type of offers

Based on the provided data, it can be observed that the median values and percentile ranges for auctions and contracts in the pre-COVID-19 and COVID-19 periods were different. In the pre-COVID-19 period, the median value for auction contracts was 15.56%, and the 25th and 75th percentile values were 4.43% and 30%, respectively. On the other hand, for contraction contracts, the median value was 0.18%, and the 25th and 75th percentile values were 0% and 10.18%, respectively. During the COVID-19 period, the median value for auction contracts decreased slightly to 15.08%, while the 25th and 75th percentile values for auction contracts were 3.82% and 30.24%, respectively. For contraction contracts, the median value was even lower at 0.06%, and the 25th and 75th percentile values were 0% and 7.07%, respectively. These results suggest that the median value and percentile ranges for both auction and contraction contracts decreased during the COVID-19 period. While the median value for auction contracts decreased only slightly, the median value for contraction contracts decreased significantly. Additionally, the percentile ranges for both types of contracts also decreased during the COVID-19 period, indicating a reduction in the variability of the contract values. The Mann-Whitney U tests showed statistically significant differences at 5% level significance in distributions of savings in the Pre-COVID-19 and COVID-19 periods for both auction and contractual contracts.

In further research, we compare the distribution of savings based on the type of agreement. The motivation for this kind of research was to determine whether the distribution of savings differs based on the type of proposed contracts. The box plots are presented in Figure 2. The data provided in Figure 2 shows the statistics of savings from public procurement offers for different types of contracts in the pre-COVID-19 and COVID-19 periods. The percentile values for the 25th, 50th (median), and 75th percentiles are given for each type of contract. For Framework Agreements, there was a slight increase in the 25th percentile value from 0.025% to 0.044% in the COVID-19 period. The median savings rate also increased from 5.47% to 6.28%, and the 75th percentile value increased from 21.69% to 23.88%. For Purchase Contracts, the 25th percentile value decreased from 0.04% to 0.03% in the COVID-19 period, while the median savings rate remained similar at 5.6% and 5.03% in the pre-COVID-19 and COVID-19 periods, respectively. The 75th percentile value decreased slightly from 21.12% to 20.81%. For Service Contracts, the 25th percentile value decreased from 0.13% to 0.05% in the COVID-19 period. The median savings rate remained similar at 7.67% and 7.13% in the pre-COVID-19 and COVID-19 periods, respectively. The 75th percentile value increased significantly from 32.35% to 42.26%. For Work Contracts, the 25th percentile value decreased significantly from 0.42% to 0.14% in the COVID-19 period. The median savings rate decreased from 12.50% to 6.81%, and the 75th percentile value decreased slightly from 34.79% to 31.41%. The results suggest that the savings from public procurement offers varied across different types of contracts in the pre-COVID-19 and COVID-19 periods. While there were some increases in the median and 75th percentile values for Framework Agreements and Service Contracts, there were decreases in the 25th percentile values for all types of contracts, indicating that the lowest savings rates decreased in the COVID-19 period.

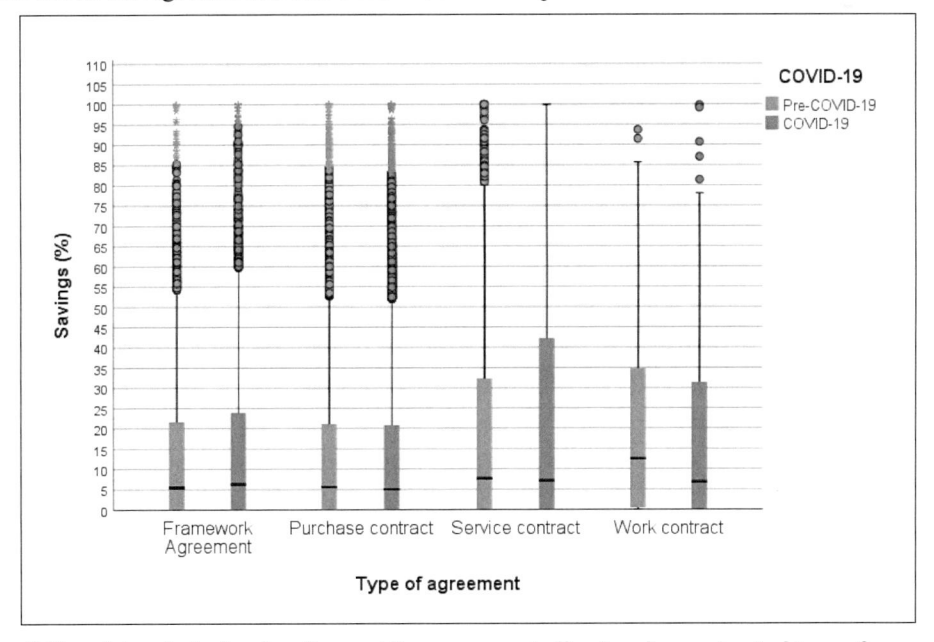

Figure 2. Box-plot analysis of savings from public procurement offers based on contractual types of agreements

The data presented in Table 2 indicates the distribution of savings from public procurement offers in the pre-COVID-19 and COVID-19 periods, categorized by contract type. The Mann-Whitney U test revealed that there is a statistically significant difference between the two periods for all types of contracts, except for service contracts.

Table 2. The results of the statistical tests comparing distributions savings from public procurement offers based on the contractual type of agreements.

	Type of contract	Null Hypothesis	p-value	Verdict
H2	Framework Agreement	The distribution of Savings (%) is the same across categories of COVID-19.	0.000	Reject null
H3	Purchase contract		0.000	Reject null
H4	Service contract		0.276	Retain null
H5	Work contract		0.037	Reject null

CPV categories also play a significant role in the distribution of savings in public procurement offers. Therefore we tried to identify for which CPVs the distribution of savings changed and for which CPV was the same, with the breakthrough of the pandemic. Based on statistical hypothesis testing, Table 3 shows the CPVs for which the distribution of savings between the PRE-COVID-19 and COVID-19 periods were significantly different. The data show that there was a statistically significant difference in the distribution of savings for all CPVs listed. The largest difference was observed in the Health and Social Work Services CPV, with a median difference of -9.57%. The CPV with the smallest difference was Public Utilities, with a median difference of 16.66%. The table also shows the number of observations for each period and the median savings for each CPV. The results of the Mann-Whitney U test, which was used to test for the significance of the differences in the distribution of savings, are shown in the p-value column. All p-values were less than 0.05, indicating that the null hypothesis of no difference in the distribution of savings between the two periods can be rejected. Therefore, the verdict is to reject the null hypothesis and accept the alternative hypothesis that there is a significant difference in the distribution of savings between the two periods for all CPVs listed in the table.

Table 3. The list of CPVs with statistically significant changes in the distribution of savings

CPV	Pre-Covid-19		Covid-19		Comparison	
	N	$\tilde{x}$	N	$\tilde{x}$	$\tilde{x}$ diff.	p-value
Public Utilities	60	41.67	44	58.32	16.66	0.000
Business services: law, marketing, consulting, recruitment, printing and security	944	30.59	816	43.77	13.18	0.000
Security, fire-fighting, police and defence equipment	410	6.89	523	17.19	10.30	0.000
Other community, social and personal services	292	5.91	256	16.20	10.29	0.000
Agricultural, forestry, horticultural, aquacultural and apicultural services	121	21.85	63	31.89	10.04	0.001
Clothing, footwear, luggage articles and accessories	1155	6.99	914	15.03	8.04	0.000
Agricultural machinery	803	1.59	431	7.11	5.52	0.000
Industrial machinery	1427	4.44	1136	7.50	3.06	0.023
Agricultural, farming, fishing, forestry and related products	971	3.20	850	5.88	2.68	0.004

CPV	Pre-Covid-19		Covid-19		Comparison	
	N	x̃	N	x̃	x̃ diff.	p-value
Petroleum products, fuel, electricity and other sources of energy	1726	6.86	943	9.01	2.14	0.011
Software package and information systems	789	6.46	610	8.22	1.76	0.044
Leather and textile fabrics, plastic and rubber materials	664	0.59	363	2.20	1.61	0.005
Medical equipment, pharmaceuticals and personal care products	8802	0.36	4627	1.59	1.23	0.000
Chemical products	2835	0.10	1508	0.36	0.27	0.000
Hotel, restaurant and retail trade services	260	0.76	145	0.13	-0.64	0.012
Repair and maintenance services	905	1.00	769	0.18	-0.82	0.000
Radio, television, communication, telecommunication and related equipment	886	7.06	739	5.04	-2.02	0.011
Transport equipment and auxiliary products to transportation	4138	3.40	3504	0.26	-3.14	0.000
Mining, basic metals and related products	284	3.66	224	0.29	-3.37	0.006
Office and computing machinery, equipment and supplies except furniture and software packages	12671	9.38	9322	5.81	-3.56	0.000
Transport services (excl. Waste transport)	870	8.72	191	1.54	-7.18	0.001
Printed matter and related products	802	14.70	354	6.88	-7.82	0.000
Health and social work services	57	16.18	40	6.61	-9.57	0.017

There were also several CPVs for which, based on the Mann-Whitney U test, we cannot confirm statistically significant changes in distributions of savings in the pre-COVID-19 and COVID-19 periods. They were: Electrical machinery, apparatus, equipment and consumables; Lighting ($p=0.088$), Machinery for mining, and quarrying, construction equipment ($p=0.941$), IT services: consulting, software development, Internet and support ($p=0.318$), Musical instruments, sports goods, games, toys, handicraft, art materials and accessories ($p=0.921$), Education and training services ($p=0.138$), Laboratory, optical and precision equipments (excl. glasses) ($p=0.949$), Furniture (incl. office furniture), furnishings, domestic appliances (excl. lighting) and cleaning products ($p=0.317$), Construction structures and materials; auxiliary products to construction (excepts electric apparatus) ($p=0.640$), Food, beverages, tobacco and related products ($p=0.329$), Sewage-, refuse-, cleaning-, and environmental services ($p=0.460$), Postal and telecommunications services ($p=0.312$), and Architectural, construction, engineering and inspection services ($p=0.950$). These findings suggest that there were no statistically significant alterations in public procurement savings for these specific CPVs during the pandemic period. As such, the influence of the Covid-19 pandemic on public procurement savings within these sectors remains unconfirmed based on our current dataset.

5. Conclusion

The study aimed to analyze the impact of the COVID-19 pandemic on the Slovak public procurement environment. The data for the study was collected from the Slovakian EKS Elektronický kontraktačný systém, which presented more than 102,000 real procurement offers. The study focused on the pre-COVID-19 period from January 2017 to December 2019 and the COVID-19 period from January 2020 to December 2022. The output variable of the study was savings, which represented the difference between the estimated value and the winning bid as a percentage of the estimated value. The Mann-Whitney U test results showed that there was a statistically significant difference between the savings rates from public procurement offers during the pre-COVID-19 and COVID-19 periods. Although both periods had a similar mean savings rate of 14% and a standard deviation of 18%, the median savings rate during the COVID-19 period was significantly lower at 5.3% compared to 5.79% during the pre-COVID-19 period. The 75th percentile during the COVID-19 period was slightly higher at 22.25% compared to 21.93% in the pre-COVID-19 period. The top 5% of offers in the COVID-19 period also had a slightly higher savings rate of 53% compared to 51% in the pre-COVID-19 period. These findings indicate that although the average savings rate remained similar between the two periods, the COVID-19 period had a significantly lower median savings rate and a different distribution of savings rates compared to the pre-COVID-19 period. The study also compared the distribution of savings based on the type of public procurement offers, namely auctions and contracts. The results indicated that the median value and percentile ranges for both auction and contraction contracts decreased during the COVID-19 period. The Mann-Whitney U tests also showed statistically significant differences in distributions of savings in the pre-COVID-19 and COVID-19 periods for both auction and contractual contracts. These findings suggest that the COVID-19 pandemic had a significant impact on public procurement practices in Slovakia. Furthermore, the study compared the distribution of savings based on the type of procurer. The results showed that the percentile ranges for different types of procurers were different, with legal persons under $2 having the lowest median savings rate and state institutions having the highest median savings rate during the pre-COVID-19 and COVID-19 periods. In conclusion, the study provides valuable insights into the impact of the COVID-19 pandemic on the Slovak public procurement environment. The findings can help policymakers and practitioners better understand the changes in public procurement practices in Slovakia and other countries facing similar challenges. The study highlights the need for policymakers to focus on increasing the median savings rate in public procurement contracts during the COVID-19 pandemic and reducing the variability of contract values.

Acknowledgement

The paper is written with the support of APVV within project No APVV-20-06089 *"The research of behavioral patterns on big data within public and commercial procurement with negative impact on efficiency of procurement processes"*.

References

Casady, C. B., & Baxter, D. (2022). Procuring healthcare public-private partnerships (PPPs) through unsolicited proposals during the COVID-19 pandemic. Journal of Public Procurement, 22(1), 6-16.

Chagelishvili, A., & Surmanidze, N. (2022). Impact of the Covid-19 pandemic on public procurement in Georgia (On the example of simplified procurement)/Covid-19 პანდემიის გავლენა საქართველოს სახელმწიფო შესყიდვებზე (გამარტივებული შესყიდვების მაგალითზე). The New Economist, 16(3), 1-1.

Eßig, M., Deimling, C. V., & Glas, A. (2021). Challenges in public procurement before, during, and after the COVID-19 crisis: selected theses on a competency-based approach. European Journal of public procurement markets, 3, 65-80.

Paulović, T., & Zomer, B. (2021). Case studies on the impact of COVID-19 on public procurement practices in Europe (focus on social, environmental, and economic impacts). Futurium. https://futurium.ec.europa.eu/sites/default/files/2021-07/Case%20studies%20on%20the%20impact%20of%20COVID-19%20on%20public%20procurement%20practices.pdf

The World Bank Group. (2020). Opportunities and challenges for public procurement in the COVID-19 pandemic. World Development Indicators. Retrieved June 15, 2023, from https://openknowledge.worldbank.org/entities/publication/fe93c577-4f10-553d-93c9-75f3c6c3fbc6

Vecchi, V., Cusumano, N., & Boyer, E. J. (2020). Medical supply acquisition in Italy and the United States in the era of COVID-19: The case for strategic procurement andpublic–private partnerships. The American Review of Public Administration, 50(6-7), 642-649.

ANALYSIS OF UNIVERSITY STUDENTS' ATTITUDES TOWARD WORK IN PROCUREMENT

Markéta Zajarošová, Jaroslav Urminský, Anežka Šenkýřová

Faculty of Economics
VŠB-Technical University of Ostrava
marketa.zajarosova@vsb.cz, jaroslav.urminsky@vsb.cz, anezka.senkyrova.st@vsb.cz

Marek Macík

Faculty of Economics
Technical University of Kosice
marek.macik@tuke.sk

DOI: 10.35011/IDIMT-2023-313

Keywords

Procurement, students, buyer, survey, procurement skills, employment benefits, Mann-Whitney test

Abstract

There are many studies and professional papers analyzing the skills required for procurement. Most of these studies are focused on analyzing the skills of already working buyers at different levels. This study is focused on the analysis of university students who have gone through purchasing education. The objective of this study is to examine the attitudes of students of the Faculty of Economics, VSB-Technical university of Ostrava of the master's degree Marketing and Business toward work in the field of procurement. Other objectives are to analyze the selected abilities and personality traits of students important for work in procurement, including the evaluation of job benefits preferences. This study is quantitative and focused on primary data collected from an online survey from university students who completed courses related to procurement. A total of 74 relevant questionnaires were collected in 2021 and 2022. The return rate of the questionnaires reached 77%. Statistical results revealed that only 5% of students would like to work in procurement. The students lack the personality characteristics that are needed for work in purchasing. The Mann-Whitney test revealed that there was a gender difference in the evaluation of three benefits and two personality characteristics.

1. Introduction

Procurement is one of the elementary functions of a business. At the same time, it does not matter the sector in which the company orients its activities. It can be manufacturing, trading, but also service-providing companies. Procurement management has undergone a major transformation in recent decades. This change is mainly related to the use of e-procurement methods, i.e., technologies enabling the electronic procurement of goods or services using the Internet, but the requirements for the skills of buyers are also changing.

Purchasing professionals are responsible for defining and implementing category strategy, managing supply risks, establishing long-term relationships, and leveraging innovation capabilities, while simultaneously assuring all operative tasks and striving to reduce costs (Feisel et al., 2011). There is not much literature dealing with the identification of buyer skills and abilities. But most authors agree on the existence of basic skills for buyers and managerial skills for purchasing managers (e.g., Guinipero and Pearcy, 2000; Klézl, Vašek, Kotrle, Saghiri, 2018; Tassabehji and Moorhouse, 2008; Delke, Schiele, Buchholz, 2022).

The objective of this study is to examine the attitudes of students of the Faculty of Economics, VSB-Technical university of Ostrava of the master's degree Marketing and Business toward work in the field of procurement. Other objectives are to analyze the selected abilities and personality traits of students important for work in procurement, including the evaluation of job benefits preferences. The research is based on data obtained from the online survey in 2021 and 2022.

The main contribution of the paper results from the nature of the empirical data. However, the main contribution of this paper is to identify the main skills and abilities that students of the chosen master's degree have for working in procurement. Another benefit of the work is also the identification of benefits that this Generation Z expects when starting work and considers them important. The main contribution is finding the influence of gender on the evaluation of individual skills and benefits.

2. Literature review

If we look at the assessment of personality characteristics and skills for working in purchasing, there are not many studies. One such study is the study by the authors Klezl, Vasek, Kotrle, Saghiri (2008), who analyzed 432 advertisements on the labor market that were aimed at various positions in purchasing. From this unique analysis, it was concluded that there are certain differences in the requirements given the hierarchical position. Technical skills and knowledge of category management were generally sought at the junior buyer level. In terms of personality characteristics, conscientiousness, responsibility, compliance and risk aversion prevailed.

If we look at a more recent study by the authors Delke, Schiele, Buchholz, 2022, we can say that these authors identify in their study that in the purchase it is primarily expected the responsibility for innovation buying to increase for direct purchasers, a wave of internationalization and the associated need for cultural, communication and flexibility and agility skills is expected for indirect purchasers.

At non-scientific publications, at populist articles in the media based on research by companies or research agencies, they clearly say that generation Z (current university students) want better benefits the most. In terms of benefits, they look for a good work/life balance first. Employees see four-day working hours and mental health care as prevention of burnout at work (see Mearian, 2022; Freedman, 2023).

On the basis of these studies, the authors of the article identified basic skills and abilities, which the students subsequently evaluated on a Likert scale of 1-5, where the value 1 meant that they fully identified with this statement and 5 that, on the contrary, they did not identify with this statement.

An important aspect of the payroll system is the tangible and intangible benefits that employees can receive. Many companies offer a number of benefits and these may also be the reason why students consider working for them. It is also similar in the area of procurement. The aim was to test the benefits that students expect in their future employment, as these could be offered by companies that want to attract students to work in procurement.

3. Methodology

This study is quantitative and focused on primary data collected from an online survey from university students who completed courses related to purchasing. The data were collected in the years 2021 and 2022. Specifically, these are two groups of students who studied the same field of marketing and business, who completed courses related to procurement. One group of students completed their master's studies in 2022 and completed their procurement course in the academic year 2020/2021, and the second group will complete their master's studies in 2023 and completed their procurement course in the academic year 2021/2022. A total of 74 relevant questionnaires were collected. The return rate of the questionnaires reached 77%. In terms of gender, this sample can be considered representative as the rate of representation of women in research is 74% (the rate of representation of women in the field within both years is 72%) and the rate of representation of men in research is 26% (28% in the field within both years).

The questionnaire contained a total of 23 unique questions chosen in view of the fulfillment of the objectives of the study. Data were processed using IBM SPSS Statistics 29 statistical software. In addition to basic frequency analyses, advanced statistical analysis tools were used. The data are mostly nominal and ordinal, where respondents rate the given factors using a Likert scale (1-5, where 1 is the best value; 5 is the worst value). The questions in the questionnaire are divided by type into closed, semi-closed and open, and by focus into factual and identifying.

At this point, it is also necessary to mention the general reliability of data obtained by similar questionnaire surveys. As shown by some analyses, some of the respondents do not provide real data when asked, but try to place their answers closer to the average or ideal state. This is, for example, a problem with questions that are answered by choosing from a certain value scale (e.g., Lickert scale). This possible distortion must be considered in all types of research. For this reason, data normality was tested for all questions, as the law of large numbers could not be used. The data do not have normal distribution; therefore, a non-parametric testing of the data was undertaken.

4. Results

The results are divided into two parts. Part one reflected basic descriptive characteristics. Part two presented results in sense of the relationship between gender and preferred employment benefits, and personality characteristics (abilities).

4.1. Descriptive statistics

The distribution of respondents by gender was representative, a total of 74 students took part in the research, of which 74% were women, and 26% were men. 65% of respondents will finish their education in 2023 and 35% of respondents have already finished it in 2022. The vast majority of students are already involved in the work process while studying a higher education master's degree (full-time, part-time, own business), only 5% of them stated that they did not work during their studies.

Almost half of the students (46%) want to stay and work in Ostrava, where they are studying. Only 27% of students expressed their willingness to move practically anywhere within the Czech Republic. Students showed the least interest in employment in Prague (4%). Only 7% of respondents would like to work abroad. Students should state what starting salary they would like to have after graduation. The largest representation has the option of 25,001-30,000 CZK (34%).

54% of respondents are more or less considering working in procurement, and 5% of them are considering it very seriously. This result can be considered very favorable for companies operating in the field of procurement or supply chain, as the teaching of subjects related to procurement and supply chain is represented very little due to the field's focus.

The results in Figure 1 clearly show that there is a clear preference for those benefits that are related to time, even among the students who were involved in the research. Undoubtedly, the most preferred benefit is the possibility of career growth, as well as flexible working hours and the possibility of a home office. The least preferred benefits are material benefits such as a company car, telephone or laptop.

	N	Mean
Career growth	74	1,5
Flexible working hours	74	1,9
Home office	74	1,9
Further education	74	2,0
Sick days (3-5 days)	74	2,3
Leave (at least 25 days)	74	2,3
Contribution for pension ensurance	74	2,4
Contribution to sport/culture	74	2,6
Free refreshments at the workplace (drinks, coffee, fruit ..)	74	2,7
Notebook	74	2,8
Cell phone	74	3,3
Company car	74	3,4
Valid N (listwise)	74	

Figure 1. Preferred employment benefits   Source: own elaboration, 2023

There is probably no need to discuss the importance of knowing foreign languages these days. Not only in the field of purchasing, but in any other department in the company, knowledge of one world language is often a basic requirement for employment. This is especially true for multinational, international companies or companies with business ties abroad. The English language was chosen due to its greatest preference in the labor market. As the results show, students prefer the possibility of working in the Czech Republic with only occasional use of the English language (66%), 12% of respondents state that they do not want to use the English language at work and 22% of respondents are interested in exclusively communicating in English at work.

On the basis of purchasing/supply management skills presented by Guinipero and Pearcy (2000), a modified list of personality characteristics and abilities was designed, which students evaluated according to how they assess themselves on a Likert scale.

It is clear from the results, see Figure 2, that the best rated characteristics are goal orientation, indirect communication and career importance. Among the worst rated statements are extroversion, working with data and handling stressful situations. The result shows that students do not have a good grasp of the characteristics important for purchasing or do not possess them. Although the majority of students expressed that they might consider a job in procurement, from the point of view of their skills assessment, we can say that they do not have the right skills and abilities for a job in procurement. In particular, they lack the ability to be extroverted, to handle direct communication, stress and work under pressure.

	N	Mean
I am goal-oriented.	74	2,0
Indirect communication suits me (emails, chats, Whatsapp, etc.)	74	2,0
Career is important to me	74	2,1
I speak English fluently	74	2,6
I can work well under pressure	74	2,6
I like to communicate with people directly (in person, by phone)	74	2,8
I enjoy working with IT systems	74	2,9
I handle stressful situations well	74	2,9
I enjoy working with data	74	2,9
I am an extrovert	74	3,0
Valid N (listwise)	74	

Figure 2. Personality characteristics (abilities) Source: own elaboration, 2023

4.2. Relationship between preferred employment benefits, personality characteristics (abilities) and gender

First, we tested the assumption of normality data distribution. A normality test helps determine whether our data are normally distributed or not. The Shapiro-Wilk tests were used because of the character of our data. Finally, the observed p-values p≤0.05 indicated that the distribution of our sample is significantly different from a normal distribution. Since assumptions of parametric tests were not fulfilled, a non-parametric statistical test was utilized (see Hollander et al. 2013). One of the methods applicable for this comparison represents the Mann-Whitney U test (see Mann and Whitney 1947). Mann-Whitney U test is an ordinal test. The Null hypothesis (H0) specifies that two groups come from the same population or in other words that the two independent groups are homogeneous and have the same distribution (Nachar 2008). Median values are recommended to describe the basic traits of the data. Simultaneously we can claim that the respondents evaluate the question in a relatively similar way. A Mann-Whitney U test was performed to evaluate whether employment benefits differed by gender and whether personality characteristics (abilities) differed by gender. The null hypothesis expresses that the means (medians) are equal among classes. The alternative hypothesis expresses that the means (medians) in the classes gradually increase/decrease.

Test Statistics[a]

	Company car	Cell phone	Laptop	Contribution for pension insurance	Flexible working hours	Home office	Sick days (3-5)	Leave (at least 25 days)	Free refreshments at the workplace (drinks, coffee, fruit.)	Contribution to sport/culture	Further education	Career growth
Mann-Whitney U	443,500	445,500	381,000	352,500	428,000	349,000	303,000	489,000	453,000	508,500	474,000	476,500
Wilcoxon W	633,500	1985,500	1921,000	1892,500	1968,000	1889,000	1843,000	2029,000	1993,000	698,500	2014,000	666,500
Z	-1,012	-,986	-1,800	-2,203	-1,258	-2,298	-2,867	-,440	-,894	-,182	-,642	-,668
Asymp. Sig (2-tailed)	,311	,324	,072	,028	,209	,022	,004	,660	,372	,855	,521	,504

a. Grouping Variable: Gender

Figure 3. Relationship between employment benefits and gender Source: own elaboration, 2023

In the case of gender, the only statistically significant differences were observed in the assessment of *contribution for pension insurance*, *home office* and *sick days*. From this data it can be concluded that evaluation of these three benefits was statistically significantly more important for women than the male's evaluation of these benefits. If we look at the differences in means (or medians), women on average consider these benefits more important than men.

Test Statistics[a]

	I am an extrovert	I like to communicate with people directly (in person, by phone)	Indirect communication suits me (emails, chats, Whatsapp, etc.)	I enjoy working with IT systems	I can work well under pressure	I enjoy working with data	I handle stressful situations well	I am goal-oriented	Career is important to me	I speak English fluently
Mann-Whitney U	314,000	428,000	427,500	299,500	501,500	458,500	502,000	487,000	461,500	390,500
Wilcoxon W	504,000	618,000	1967,500	489,500	2041,500	648,500	692,000	2027,000	2001,500	580,500
Z	-2,692	-1,205	-1,243	-2,857	-,272	-,820	-,263	-,469	-,797	-1,685
Asymp. Sig. (2-tailed)	,007	,228	,214	,004	,786	,412	,792	,639	,426	,092

a. Grouping Variable: Gender

Figure 4. Relationship between personality characteristics (abilities) and gender Source: own elaboration, 2023

In the case of gender, the only statistically significant differences were observed in the assessment of "*I am an extrovert*" and "*I enjoy working with IT systems*". If we look at the differences in means (or medians), men on average consider these characteristics more typical of them.

Respondents evaluated benefits and skills equally, the only difference in gender evaluation was found for three benefits (*contribution for pension insurance, home office* and *sick days*) and two personality characteristics ("*I am an extrovert*" and "*I enjoy working with IT systems*"). Women's averages in the area of benefits were lower. In the area of personality characteristics, men rated themselves as more extroverted and fonder of working with IT systems.

5. Conclusion

The aim of this article was to analyze the extent to which master's degree students at the Faculty of Economics VSB-Technical university of Ostrava, studying marketing and business, show an interest in working in purchasing after completing subjects focused on this issue. Basic descriptive tools were used but also advanced statistical analysis using the Mann-Whitney test to identify gender differences in the assessment of job benefits and personality characteristics.

The results of the descriptive analysis show that only 5% of students are seriously considering a job in purchasing, they mostly have an idea of their starting salary and the benefits they would like to have at work. Most of the benefits are related to time and are usually the option of a home office, sick days and also career growth. Material benefits are considered less important by these students.

The results clearly show that students prefer indirect communication at work, do not consider themselves extroverts, do not handle stressful situations very well and do not enjoy working with data and IT systems very much. The Mann-Whitney test revealed that there was a gender difference in the evaluation of three benefits (*contribution for pension insurance, home office* and *sick days*). If we look at the differences in means (or medians), women on average consider these benefits more important than men. Also, the Mann-Whitney test revealed that there was a gender difference in the evaluation of two personality characteristics ("*I am an extrovert*" and "*I enjoy working with IT systems*"). In the area of personality characteristics, men rated themselves as more extroverted and fonder of working with IT systems.

The limit of this study is the number of students and also the fact that it is only one field at one faculty. The authors of the articles intend to continue to collect data annually and track differences within the time series.

Acknowledgement

This paper is financed by Student Grant Competition of the Faculty of Economics, VŠB-Technical University of Ostrava; project's registration number is SP2023/083. All support is greatly acknowledged and appreciated.

References

Delke, V., H. Schiele & Buchholz, W. (2023). Differentiating between direct and indirect procurement: roles, skills, and Industry 4.0. International Journal of Procurement Management, 16(1), 1 – 30.

Feisel, E., Hartmann, E., & Giunipero, L. (2011). The importance of the human aspect in the supply function: Strategies for developing PSM proficiency. Journal of Purchasing and Supply Management, 17(1), 54–67.

Friedman, M. (2023). Understanding Generation Z in the Workplace. https://www.businessnewsdaily.com/11296-what-gen-z-workers-want.html

Gabrielova, K. & Buchko, A. (2021). Here comes Generation Z: Millennials as managers. Business Horizons 64, 489-499.

Giunipero, L. C. & D. H. Pearcy. (2000). World-Class Purchasing Skills: An Empirical Investigation. The Journal of Supply Chain Management, 36(3) 4 - 13.

Klézl, V., Vašek, J., Kotrle, M., & Saghiri, S. (2018). Assessing the Personal Traits and Skill Required for Purchasing Jobs. IPSERA 2018 Conference: Purchasing and Supply Chain: Fostering Innovation (pp. 863-872). Athens, Greece: International Purchasing and Supply Education and Research Association (IPSERA).

Mann, B. H., & R. D. Whitney. (1947). On a Test of Whether one of Two Random Variables is Stochastically Larger than the Other. The Annals of Mathematical Statistics 18, 50-60.

Mearian, L. (2022). What Gen Z and millennials want from employers. https://www.computerworld.com/article/3661170/what-gen-z-and-millennials-want-from-employers.html

Nachar, N. (2008). The Mann-Whitney U: A Test for Assessing Whether Two Independent Samples Come from the Same Distribution. Tutorials in Quantitative Methods for Psychology 4(1), 13-20.

Tassabehji, R. & Moorhouse, A. (2008). The changing role of procurement: Developing professional effectiveness. Journal of Purchasing and Supply Management, 14(1), 55–68.

BENEFITS OF E-AUCTION: REAL USERS EVALUATION

Jaroslav Urminský, Markéta Zajarošová, Adam Vávra, Ondřej Karady

Faculty of Economics
VŠB - Technical University of Ostrava
jaroslav.urminsky@vsb.cz, marketa.zajarosova@vsb.cz, adam.vavra@vsb.cz,
ondrej.karady.st@vsb.cz

DOI: 10.35011/IDIMT-2023-321

Keywords

Electronic auction, e-auctions, evaluation, benefits, survey, Jonckheere-Terpstra test

Abstract

Electronic auctions have become a common tool used in the field of procurement. They are used regardless of the type of organization and the nature of the markets. The problem we dealt with was how their real users evaluate the commonly mentioned advantages of e-auctions. We focus closely on the relationship between the experiences of e-auction implementers and their evaluation of the advantages. Potential differences were examined by the Jonckheere-Terpstra tests. The research is based on data from the survey. The results show that in most cases, the experience of the users does not influence the evaluation of the benefits. Statistical differences were confirmed only for financial savings in relation to the frequency of use of e-auctions and for simplicity of the tool in the case of the length of e-auctions using. The results can contribute to discussion related to the learning process of organizations among others.

1. Introduction

Organizations of all types are part of the gradual digitalization of processes and activities related to extremely fast technological development. Digitalization offers a range of possibilities to increase the efficiency of their existence. New electronic tools are constantly being developed and can be applied to different types of organizations, regardless of sector affiliation and the nature or structure of the markets. One such tool represents auctions or rather electronic auctions (hereinafter e-auctions) which experienced the biggest boom at the beginning of the millennium. E-auction can be defined as an electronic tool used by organizations that enables an electronic form of tendering for specific desired products (Sashi and O´Leary, 2002; Yu et al., 2022). After the initial idea of a certain "all-powerful" tool with several positives for all parties involved, the correction was introduced. In addition to the positives, the negative aspects of e-auctions and their important limits are also beginning to be highlighted in the literature (see Schoenherr and Mabert, 2007). Nevertheless, e-auctions are regularly used in the activities of organizations. The period of the COVID-19 pandemic represented the last significant impetus for the intensification of thinking about the use of e-auctions. The paralysis of mutual relations at the global level was unprecedented. The completely new and extreme situation also hit the area of the supply-customer chain hard.

Internal and external pressures to increase the intensity of digitalization of companies' processes were evident throughout the world. Questions about the advantages or disadvantages of their applications came to the fore even more strongly (see Tkáč and Sieber, 2022).

By gradually using electronic tools, their implementers gain experience (Hur et al., 2006). Therefore, they should be able to formulate attitudes and opinions about the characteristics and potential benefits of e-auctions more accurately, too. These subjective opinions of real actors could become an interesting impulse for theoretical debates as well as for practical aspects of the realization of purchases through e-auctions. We take a closer view at the question of whether the length and frequency of using e-auctions by the organizations are printed in the evaluation of e-auction benefits (see also Standaert et al., 2015; Gravier and Hawkins, 2014).

The objective of the paper is to analyze the main benefits of e-auctions, as perceived by their users themselves. We focus primarily on private companies that are actual users or sometimes used the e-auction in the past. The research is based on data obtained from the survey conducted between Czech and Slovak companies.

The main contribution of the paper results from the nature of the empirical material obtained. The subjective perception of the advantages of e-auctions by real users enriches the theoretical considerations related to the given area, as well as the practical aspects of their functionalities. Closely, we are focused on the relationship between user experience and benefits evaluation.

2. Literature review

Electronic auctions have become a common part of procurement management. Hur et al. already in 2006 perceived e-auctions as a new way of selecting suppliers for organizations, which will fundamentally affect buyer-supplier relationships in the future. The positive impulse consisted of the transition from personal contact in negotiations towards its (impersonal) electronic form. Over time, a few benefits have been attributed to the use of e-auctions. We will focus more closely on the selected advantages that are frequently mentioned in the literature. It should be noted that the mentioned advantages cannot be taken dogmatically. Some authors are either cautious about individual factors or even consider them rather as negatives (e.g., Emiliani and Stec, 2005; Schoenherr and Mabert, 2007). Obviously, the definition of advantage/disadvantage may vary contextually. However, the factors listed below are abundant with positive connotations in the literature. The final structure of the advantages is: Financial savings, Time savings, Transparency, Credibility, Simplicity, Discovery of new suppliers, and Supporting relationship with suppliers. All described will be closely analyzed. They were integrated into the question of battery character.

Financial savings are generally mentioned as a fundamental positive effect resulting from the realization of e-auctions. Efficiency is usually operationalized as the minimization of the resulting price while observing the required input parameters. However, it does not have to be the only approach; it is possible to monitor the overall value of the buyer, buyer satisfaction, or other objective functions (Standaert et al., 2015; Bei and Chen, 2015). The method of measuring efficiency also comes to the fore when differentiating the type of purchasing entities in the private/public sector (see Ochrana, 2001). It can be said that there is no single, generally acceptable way of measuring the efficiency of e-auctions. Fundamentally different objective functions can generate a different structure of factors that affect the achieved auction result. Nevertheless, financial savings represent one of the most frequent benefits attributed to e-auctions.

Another mentioned advantage is *time savings*. Time savings are reported in connection with various activities and various phases of the e-auction implementation process. In principle, time savings can be observed in relation to their specific implementers, i.e., buyers in individual organizations (Pearcy and Giunipero, 2008). Savings are achieved due to the progressive digitalization of activities, the possibility of their automation, including the possibility of algorithmizing the evaluation of the relevant auctions, etc. Finally, thanks to the online mode, the realization of the auction itself can be solved in a few minutes, while the effects achieved can be considerable. Different kinds of products can be traded in real-time on a global level, which is also an advantage (Yu et al., 2022). Time savings are directly related to the ease of use of electronic tools.

Transparency represents a powerful advantage of e-auctions. Several aspects play a role here (see Dráb et al., 2018). Due to the nature of e-auctions, the trend of their use can also be observed in connection with e-government. Public organizations have become significant users, primarily as buyers (Chmelová and Štípek, 2017). In some countries, the application of these types of tools is even printed in legislation. This tool is considered beneficial about the fight against corruption and unfair practices (Glas and Essig, 2018). The transparency of the market can generally be considered one of the fundamental conditions underpinning its functioning and co-determining its efficiency.

Another mentioned benefit of *credibility* is closely related to transparency. Credibility is one of the important elements affecting the strength and competitive position of every company. E-auctions are perceived as beneficial, having a positive effect on increasing the credibility of the given organization. Credibility also has the function of signaling. Signals the potential level of risk that entities may encounter during mutual participation. It refers to transparency and compliance with the established framework conditions, the stability of the company, as well as the un/transparency of information flows. Credibility may contribute to reducing transaction costs.

Simplicity represents another benefit. Simplicity is related to the electronic form of this tool, i.e., to its technological background. The gradual digitalization of processes resulting in increasing computer literacy and user experience with e-auctions (Yi et al., 2006). The contracting authority can very simply define all conditions and the form of the auction. At the same time, it is possible to predefine templates and use them repeatedly, which is made possible by the stability of the environment. Due to its simplicity, it is possible to involve a wide range of suppliers regardless of time and space (Gumussoy and Calisir, 2009).

Discovery of new suppliers can be perceived as another advantage (see Sashi and O´Leary, 2002). The given factor is directly related to the characteristics of the competitive environment. The number of subjects plays an important role during the auction (Bos et al., 2021). The possibility of expanding the market with additional potential suppliers is appreciated above all. In the same way, the possibility of the involvement of foreign entities is also mentioned, thus suppressing the negative role of borders. The number of entities participating in the auction is ultimately reflected in the final savings achieved (Delina et al., 2021).

Supporting buyer-supplier relationship could be perceived as controversial. The professional literature is not consistent in the sense of evaluating this factor as an advantage. A lot of authors mention or even emphasize the opposite effect, i.e., the gradual destruction of buyer-supplier relationships (see, e.g., Emiliani and Stec, 2005). Contrary to that, Schoenherr and Mabert (2007) marked it as a myth. They argue that the damage of the buyer-supplier relationship is not necessary, and even more, e-auctions are helpful in the gradual building of the relationship. Carter et al. (2004) make the argument in a similar spirit. They mentioned the deepening of the relationship due to the application of e-auctions, thanks to the positive effects of increased transparency and overall objectivity of the entire auction process.

3. Research design

This part included methodical notes of the research. Basic conditions of the research in the sense of data collection are described. Next, we introduce brief characteristics of the applied methods.

3.1. Data collection

Data collection was carried out through a survey. The questionnaire itself consisted of 15 questions. All types of questions were represented, i.e., open, closed, or semi-closed. A battery of questions containing selected factors was also used, and evaluation was done through a five-point Likert scale (see Boone and Boone 2012; Joshi et al. 2015). The Likert contained 5 degrees (from 1 to 5). The lowest/highest value expressed a strict agreement/disagreement with the question. The neutral position was represented by degree 3. Only selected issues will be presented due to the predefined maximum range of the paper.

The data collection itself took place from 16.3. until 1.4. 2021. They were collected for the purpose of the final thesis (see Michálková, 2021). The survey was conducted using an electronic questionnaire, which was distributed in cooperation with the company PROEBIZ s.r.o. The company's headquarters is in Ostrava in the Czech Republic but also operates in foreign markets. Its core activity lies in the provision of services in the field of e-auctions. The company also provided a database of contacts/suppliers who were subsequently contacted. A total of 4,103 suppliers were approached with a request to fill out a questionnaire. These involved 1,599 suppliers from the Slovak Republic and 2,504 suppliers from the Czech Republic. Only 85 respondents out of all those approached responded to the request. The total return is therefore slightly above 2%. The very low return may have been due to the time of data collection. Data collection was carried out during the pandemic period. The impacts of the pandemic were widespread and fundamental. The companies had to react. It often meant an extreme workload for the employees. In sum, employees may not have had the time disposition, or desire to answer the questions. The small sample represents one of the main limitations of the presented article.

The original sample of 85 respondents had to be further reduced due to failure to meet the precondition-use of electronic auction sometimes in the past. After reduction, the final sample of respondents is *N=71*.

3.2. Applied methods

The applied methods are based on the nature of the research, the defined objective, and the character of the dataset. Due to the limited scope of the article, the individual steps are only briefly commented upon. Standard descriptive statistics were used, followed by verification of the data distribution. In the last step, we tested the relationships between the selected variables using non-parametric tests. All relevant hypotheses were tested at the $\alpha=0.05$. Finally, three basic steps were realized: a) Descriptive statistics, b) Normality test, c) Jonckheere-Terpstra tests.

4. Results

The results are divided into two parts. Part one reflected basic descriptive characteristics. Part two presented results in sense of the relationship between users experience and evaluation of benefits.

4.1. Descriptive statistics

The selected descriptive statistics were used for the summarization of our data set. Based on the nature of the data, we show all three basic categories of measures: measures of central tendency, measures of variability, and frequency distribution, see Figures 1 and 2.

How long have you been using electronic tenders?

		Frequency	Percent	Cumulative Percent
Valid	less than 1	2	2,8	2,8
	1 - 5	24	33,8	36,6
	6 - 10	27	38,0	74,6
	more than 10	18	25,4	100,0
	Total	71	100,0	

How often do you realize electronic tenders?

		Frequency	Percent	Cumulative Percent
Valid	several times per month	36	50,7	50,7
	once per month	17	24,0	74,7
	once per 3 months	10	14,1	88,8
	once per 6 months	4	5,6	94,4
	once per year	4	5,6	100,0
	Total	71	100,0	

Figure 1. Experience of electronic tender users   Source: own elaboration, 2023

The tables above show the basic structure of the sample according to their experience with e-auctions. In general, it can be said that experienced users predominate. Almost 2/3 of the respondents have been in the field of e-auctions for more than 6 years. They already operated e-auctions before the COVID-19 period. Electronic tenders are used by 75 % of organizations at least once a month or more often. They represent routine users with an up-to-date overview of the nature of the auction environment or possible changes in the markets.

The overall evaluation of the selected e-auction advantages is reflected in Figure 2. The ranking according to the average values shows that the respondents most value transparency and the possibility of achieving financial savings. On the other hand, the discovery of new suppliers and especially supporting relationship with suppliers is considered neutral. A neutral rating corresponds to the not clear position of the factor, which is discussed in the professional literature.

	Financial savings	Time savings	Transparency	Discovery of new suppliers	Credibility	Simplicity	Supporting relationship with suppliers
N	71	71	71	71	71	71	71
Median	2,00	2,00	1,00	3,00	2,00	3,00	3,00
Minimum	1	1	1	1	1	1	1
Maximum	5	5	5	5	5	5	5
Mean	2,25	2,48	2,18	2,99	2,42	2,73	3,20
Geometric Mean	1,95	2,12	1,77	2,73	2,17	2,50	3,01
Std. Deviation	1,192	1,372	1,486	1,165	1,104	1,121	1,023
Variance	1,421	1,882	2,209	1,357	1,219	1,256	1,046
Kurtosis	-,841	-,873	-,681	-,701	-,407	-,193	-,525
Skewness	,584	,609	,912	,140	,595	,616	-,081

Figure 2. Evaluation of e-auction advantages – descriptive statistics   Source: own elaboration, 2023

4.2. Relationship between user experience and e-auction benefits evaluation

First, we tested the assumption of normality data distribution. A normality test helps determine whether our data are normally distributed or not. The Shapiro-Wilk tests were used because of the character of our data. It tests the hypothesis that the distribution of the data deviates (or not) from a normal distribution. Finally, the observed p-values $p \leq 0.05$ indicated that the distribution of our sample is significantly different from a normal distribution. Based on the results of the Shapiro-Wilk test, the nonparametric method was applied. The Jonckheere-Terpstra test was chosen to identify the potential differences among classes (Field, 2009). It is the rank-based nonparametric test and is designed to detect alternative ordered class differences. The test was used to identify potential differences in the evaluation of e-auction advantages first in relation to the frequency of electronic tenders' realization and then in the length of the electronic tenders using (see Figures 3 and 4). The null hypothesis expresses that the medians are equal among classes. The alternative hypothesis expresses that the medians in the classes gradually increase/decrease.

Jonckheere-Terpstra Test[a]

	Financial savings	Time savings	Transparency	Discovery of new suppliers	Credibility	Simplicity	Supporting relationship with suppliers
Number of Levels in How often do you realize electronic tenders?	5	5	5	5	5	5	5
N	71	71	71	71	71	71	71
Asymp. Sig. (2-tailed)	,021	,319	,991	,572	,625	,678	,619

a. Grouping Variable: How often do you realize electronic tenders?

Figure 3. Relationship between frequency of e-auction realization and evaluation of e-auction advantages

Source: own elaboration, 2023

Jonckheere-Terpstra Test[a]

	Financial savings	Time savings	Transparency	Discovery of new suppliers	Credibility	Simplicity	Supporting relationship with suppliers
Number of Levels in How long have you been using electronic tenders?	4	4	4	4	4	4	4
N	71	71	71	71	71	71	71
Asymp. Sig. (2-tailed)	,095	,366	,097	,840	,124	**,007**	,071

a. Grouping Variable: How long have you been using electronic tenders?

Figure 4. Relationship between length of using e-auction and evaluation of e-auction advantages

Source: own elaboration, 2023

An overall view of the test results points to an important fact. The respondent's experience with e-auctions does not have a significant influence on the evaluation of the selected benefits in most cases. It is relevant to both analyzed relationships. We must point out that these are indicative results valid only for our respondents.

In the case of frequency, the only statistically significant differences were observed in the assessment of *financial savings*. Here we can say that frequent users (once a month or more often) rate the benefit of financial savings less positively. This fact corresponds to the conclusions of some literature when repeated use can reduce the amount of savings achieved (see Standaert et al., 2015). Both sides of the auction relationship go through a learning process. They can gradually project the results into the form of an auction process. The resulting impact may demonstrate by gradually decreasing savings achieved by the contracting authority. This issue is also directly related to the issue of the very method of measuring savings and the resulting consequences, including the need to distinguish between purely financial savings and total savings or total benefits resulting from auctioned products. In the case of the second investigated relationship, i.e., length of use of e-auctions, statistically significant differences appear only in the factor *simplicity*. As a result, the given relationship shows that the longer the user is familiar with the environment of e-auctions, the more positive assessment gives towards the simplicity of the tool. It also depends on the specific softwires (auction environment). Let us remind you that we are only dealing with companies that are in the database of PROEBIZ. This can be considered as a limit of the paper too. It is obvious that individual software solutions can differ, including essential functionalities. However, it can be argued that if the subject uses e-auctions in some environment for a long time, the knowledge of the given environment grows. Setting parameters and the course of the auction becomes easier (see

Gravier and Hawkins, 2014). It does not automatically mean an absence of better solution, or rather it does not mean that optimal results are achieved. Various behavioral characteristics and types of cognitive distortion of the users can be manifested in the auction process.

5. Conclusion

There are published a lot of researchers aimed to identify crucial advantages of e-auctions. Sometimes are not consistent in the evaluation of concrete factors. It causes some controversies. So, their evaluation from real users' viewpoints is always useful. The results may contribute to the theoretical explanation as well as to the practical functioning of e-auctions as a whole. Based on the predefinition of typical advantages, an evaluation was conducted. Respondents evaluate seven benefits on the five-point Likert scale. Finally, transparency and financial savings are perceived as the most powerful advantages. The discovery of a new supplier and notably supporting relationship with suppliers could be mentioned as a controversial factor, on the other hand. It corresponds to the ambiguous position of the factor that exists in the literature. The strong differences in the evaluation of the advantages of the e-auctions in relation to the experience of the users (operationalized as the length and frequency of using e-auctions) were not identified. In the case of frequency of use, the only distinction was detected in the case of financial savings. Those who use e-auctions less frequently expressed more positive evaluations. The length of e-auction using by organizations differed in evaluation only in the case of factor-simplicity. Here we can say that the longer organizations use e-auctions, the better they rate this factor. For the future, it seems like an interesting question how financial savings are calculated and to what extent they are an important part of the evaluation of the overall intention of or a project. Another direction may be to compare users of different types of software environments where the auctions themselves are realized.

Acknowledgement

The paper is financed by Student Grant competition of the Faculty of Economics, VSB-Technical University of Ostrava; project's registration number is SP2023/083. All support is greatly acknowledged and appreciated.

References

Bei, T.L., and M.Y. Chen. 2015. The Effects of Hedonic and Utilitarian Bidding Values on E-Auction Behavior. Electronic Commerce Research, 15, 483-507. DOI 10.1007/s10660-015-9197-0.

Boone, H. N., and D. A. Boone. 2012. Analyzing Likert Data. The Journal of Extension 50 (2): 1-5. Retrieved April 08, 2023 from https://joe.org/joe/2012april/tt2.php.

Bos, O., F. Gomez-Martinez, S. Onderstal, and T. Truyts. 2021. Signalling in Auctions: Experimental Evidence. Journal of Economic Behavior & Organization, 187, 448-469. DOI 10.1016/j.jebo.2021.04.001.

Carter, R.C, L. Kaufmann, S. Beall, P.L. Carter, T.E. Hendrick, and K.J. Petersen. 2004. Reverse Auctions–Grounded Theory from the Buyer and Supplier Perspective. Transportation Research Part E: Logistics and Transportation Review, 40(3), 229-254. DOI 10.1016/j.tre.2003.08.004.

Chmelová, P. a V. Štípek. 2017. Analýza vývoje trhu veřejných zakázek v České republice v letech 2008-2015. Politická ekonomie, 65(3), 316-334. DOI 10.18267/j.polek.1146.

Delina, R., R. Olejarova, and P. Doucek. 2021. Effect of a New Potential Supplier on Business to Business Negotiations Performance: Evidence-Based Analysis. Electronic Commerce Research. DOI 10.1007/s10660-021-09524-6.

Dráb, R., R. Delina, and T. Štofa. 2018. Electronic Auctions: Role of Visibility Settings in Transparency Analysis. Quality Innovation Prosperity, 22(2), 100-111. DOI 10.12776/QIP.V22I2.1059.

Emiliani, M.L. and D.J. Stec. 2005. Wood Pallet Suppliers´ Reaction to Online Reverse Auctions. Supply Chain Management: An International Journal, 10(4), 278-287. DOI doi.org/10.1108/13598540510612758.

Field, A. 2009. Discovering Statistics Using SPSS. 3rd Edition, London: Sage. ISBN 978-1-84787-906-6.

Glas. A.H. and M. Essig. 2018. Factors that Influence the Success of Small and Medium-sized Suppliers in Public Procurement: Evidence from a Centralized agency in Germany. Supply Chain Management, 23(1), 65-78. DOI 10.1108/SCM-09-2016-0334.

Gravier, M., and T.G. Hawkins. 2014. Individual Manager Experience Influences on Reverse Auction Use. International Journal of Procurement Management, 7(6), 719-749. DOI 10.1504/IJPM.2014.064985.

Gumussoy, A.C., and F. Calisir. 2009. Understanding Factors Affecting E-Reverse Auction Use: An Integrative Approach. Computers in Human Behavior, 25(4), 975-988. DOI 10.1016/j.chb.2009.04.006.

Hur, D., J.L. Hartley, and V. A. Mabert. 2006. Implementing Reverse E-auctions: A Learning Process. Business Horizons, 49(1), 21-29. DOI 10.1016/j.bushor.2005.05.001.

Joshi, A., S. Kale, S. Chandel, and D. K. Pal. 2015. Likert Scale: Explored and Explained. British Journal of Applied Science & Technology 7 (4): 396-403. DOI 10.9734/BJAST/2015/14975.

Michálková, E. 2021. Analýza užívání e-aukcí ve firemním sektoru. Diplomová práce. Ostrava: VSB-TUO, Faculty of Economics, Marketing and Business Department.

Ochrana, F. 2001. Veřejný sektor a efektivní rozhodování. Praha: Management Press. ISBN 80-7261-018-X.

Pearcy, H.D. and L.C. Giunipero. 2008. Using E-procurement Applications to Achieve Integration: What Role does Firm Size Play? Supply Chain Management: An International Journal, 13(1), 26-34. DOI 10.1108/13598540810850292.

Sashi, M.C., and B. O´Leary. 2002. The Role of Internet Auctions in the Expansion of B2B Markets. Industrial Marketing Management, 31(2), 103-110. DOI 10.1016/S0019-8501(01)00189-4.

Shoenherr, T. and V.A. Mabert. 2007. Online Reverse Auctions: Common Myths Versus Evolving Reality. Business Horizons, 50, 373-384. DOI: 10.1016/j.bushor.2007.03.003.

Standaert, W., S. Muylle, and I. Amelinckx. 2015. An Empirical Study of Electronic Reverse Auction Project Outcomes. Electronic Commerce Research and Applications, 14(2), 81-94. DOI 10.1016/j.elerap.2014.12.001.

Tkáč, M. and J. Sieber. 2022. Comparison of Electronic Invoicing Adoption Before and After COVID-19 Pandemics in European Union. Retrieved April 08, 2023 from https://idimt.org/wp-

Yi, M., Jackson, J.D., Park, J.S. and J.C. Probst. 2006. Understanding Information Technology Acceptance by Individual professionals: Toward an Integrative View. Information & Management, 43(3), 350-363. DOI 10.1016/j.im.2005.08.006.

Yu, H., M. Huang, X. Chao, and X. Yue. 2022. Truthful Multi-Attribute Multi-Unit Double Auctions for B2B E-Commerce Logistics Service Transactions. Transportation Research Part E: Logistics and Transportation Review, 164, 102814. DOI 10.1016/j.tre.2022.102814.

ONLINE REPUTATION OF SELECTED E-COMMERCE ENTITIES THROUGH THE LENS OF PANDEMIC AND POST-PANDEMIC COMPARISON

František Pollák

Faculty of Business Management
University of Economics in Bratislava
frantisek.pollak@euba.sk

Faculty of Corporate Strategy
Institute of Technology and Business in České Budějovice.

Peter Markovič, Kristián Kalamen

Faculty of Business Management
University of Economics in Bratislava
peter.markovic@euba.sk

DOI: 10.35011/IDIMT-2023-329

Keywords

E-commerce, Accelerated digitization, Digital transformation, Supply chain, COVID-19 pandemic, Online Reputation Management

Abstract

The main goal of the contribution is to present the results of a comparative analysis of the development of the level of online reputation of the most important industry representatives from among the electronic commerce entities operating on the Slovak market across the individual phases of the pandemic. The reference point for comparison is the measured levels of individual determinants of online reputation for specific entities at the time of the outbreak of the COVID-19 pandemic in 2020. State values represent the levels of individual determinants of online reputation measured at the time of the lifting of the last pandemic-related restrictions in the second quarter of 2023. The same methodology of extended sentiment analysis was used for both measurements. By comparing two measurements, at the time of onset, and at the time of retreat of the COVID-19 pandemic, we find that most subjects notice a significant improvement in the basic sentiment level of search results within the Google ecosystem over the monitored period. On the other hand, however, the analyzed subjects recorded during pandemic a real decline in the dynamic side of online reputation created by reputation determinants of a more complex nature. The results indicate that from the point of view of basic online reputation optimization, it is possible to view the three years of the pandemic period as an accelerator of digital transformation. However, continuous research is needed to compile more complex development trends.

1. Introduction

Brick-and-mortar stores have always been the backbone of retail. Even in times of turbulent economic and social changes, retail has retained its characteristic features. The advent of digital technologies at the end of the twentieth century created space for an evolutionary leap (Maryška, Doucek, Novotný, 2012; Delina, Tkáč, 2010), but tradition and customer preferences did not allow a leap change. The outbreak of the global pandemic in the first quarter of 2020 significantly changed the usual rules of the game. Policies to combat the spread of the new coronavirus were based on the assumption of a reduction in the mobility of individuals, which led to the attenuation of the interactions of the stone world. While these policies were applied by both developed and developing markets. The digital infrastructure has managed the transition from offline to online quite well. Both sides of the market have adapted their habits towards digital (Kostiuk et al., 2021; Pollák et al., 2022). The catching-up markets had a relatively significant disadvantage in the form of the absence of digital traditions that could be monitored through specific indicators (Világi, Konečný, Ruschak, 2022; Sagapova, Dušek, Pártlová, 2022). One of such indicators is the level of digital identity of subjects, in our case, the level of online reputation (Loayza, 2013). In the first year of the pandemic, we carried out an empirical analysis with the aim of examining the digital identity situation of subjects. At the time of the cancellation of the last pandemic measures, we are implementing a second measurement, which we are trying to create an empirical basis for solving the research problem of the impact of the pandemic on the digital presence of SMEs operating in the developing market. The presented study is thus a partial output of a complex research project on the issue of online reputation management.

2. Objectives and methods

The main goal of the study is to present the results of a comparative analysis of the development of the level of online reputation of the most important industry representatives from among the electronic commerce entities operating on the Slovak market. The object of the research consisted of selected representatives of the e-commerce market. As it was difficult to directly select specific industry representatives while maintaining the necessary validity of the data, we decided to perform our analysis on selected ambassadors of a whole research file. The Research file was represented by the sample of winners of the Quality Award of the Slovak e-shop of the year /Shoproku/ 2019 survey of the Hereka Group (Heureka 2019) in its selected six categories, which we evaluated as the most relevant for chosen market. From the point of view of the dataset, the reference point for comparison is the measured levels of individual determinants of online reputation for selected entities at the time of the outbreak of the COVID-19 pandemic in 2020. State values represent the levels of individual determinants of online reputation measured at the time of the lifting of the last pandemic-related restrictions in the second quarter of 2023. While considering the context and methodology of the initial study (Pollák, et al. 2020), within which the analyzed dataset is presented in the current study as a reference base. For analysis itself we used the TOR methodology (Pollák, Dorčák, Markovič, 2021), we chose the methodology based on its ability to identify changes in the individual determinants of reputation in a relatively short time. In its first step we performed an extended analysis of the sentiment ASA. Extended form of sentiment analysis (SA) of the nature of first ten Google search results for chosen subjects, considers the occurrence of sentiments in several dimensions compared to the original methodology (Liu, 2012). The Table 1 shows chronological sequence of awarding points to the analyzed entities. Positive response or sentiment results in the increase of the score. The higher the position of this sentiment in the search result, the more points are awarded. Similarly, but with the opposite effect it/is works in identifying the negative sentiment:

Table 1. Sentiment Individual Results/Position of Results

Sentiment / Position		1	2	3	4	5	6	7	8	9	10
Positive sentiment	(+)	20	19	18	17	16	15	14	13	12	11
Own website	(x)	10	9	8	7	6	5	4	3	2	1
Neutral sentiment	(±)	2	2	2	2	2	2	2	2	2	2
Negative sentiment	(−)	−20	−19	−18	−17	−16	−15	−14	−13	−12	−11

Source: (Pollák, Dorčák, Markovič, 2021)

In our case of our six subjects were tested for sentiment of search results both in the "general" and "news" categories of Google. The process records the evaluation of the first page of the Google search results, i.e. the first ten organic results in Google search. After summing up the sentiment points, we reach the final amount. That amount is then a starting factor in assessing the success or failure of companies in the segment. For the two dimensions analysis, we perform the same procedures for each of them separately, in our case separately for the category "general" and separately for the category "news". The resulting amounts are calculated and converted to percentages. This assumes that within a single group the entity may receive a maximum score of 155 points – the ratio 1 point = 0.645%. For purpose of our analysis with 2 groups, the entity may receive a maximum score of 310 points – the ratio 1 point = 0.322%.

In the second step, we identified other relevant reputation determinants as follows:

- FBS- Facebook score (read directly through the evaluation of the subject's profile, then converted to percentages);
- HRS- Customer rating score from the Heureka portal (the recommendation to realize the future purchase expressed by customers in the last 90 days);
- GRS- Google reviews score (converted to percentages).

In the third step, we proceeded to the calculation of the TOR indicator. In our case, the TOR coefficient represents the arithmetic mean of the measured values of the partial Reputators.

3. Results and discussion

Based on the analysis of both datasets, it is possible to present individual partial as well as complex values in the context of their changes across measurements through Table 2 as follows.

Table 2. Findings across measures

No.	Subject/Result sentiment	ASA 2023 (%)	ASA 2020 (%)	FBS 2023 (%)	FBS 2020 (%)	HRS 2023 (%)	HRS 2020 (%)	GRS 2023 (%)	GRS 2020 (%)	TOR 2023 (%)	TOR 2020 (%)
1.	DATART.sk	76	44	58	99	96	93	84	84	79	80
2.	Astratex.sk	89	71	90	92	98	98	0	0	69	65
3.	Footshop.sk	80	66	0	90	97	93	86	88	66	84
4.	MojaLekáren.sk	58	45	82	88	98	90	64	72	76	74
5.	svetnapojov.sk	54	38	0	98	99	99	96	0	62	59
6.	HEJ.sk	55	63	0	99	94	92	84	84	58	85

Source: Own processing

In the following subsections, the findings will be discussed in a qualitative context, as well as in the context of comparisons across measurements. Important connections will be presented graphically.

3.1. Qualitative evaluation of findings

The subjects were subjected to a qualitative analysis and then a comparison of findings across measurements (onset /2020/ and retreat /2023/ of the covid pandemic), the results are as follows:

DATART.sk

ASA (general): In the first place, we find the subject's own website. The second and third places are links to the official Facebook profile and the profile on the Heureka platform. Both of which have a significantly positive sentiment. The fourth position is occupied by a link to a platform providing loyalty program services. We evaluate this occurrence positively, as it is a form of developing relations with customers. The fifth position is occupied by a link to a profile within the YouTube platform, again we note a positive sentiment. The sixth position refers to the site of the operator for the Czech market. We attribute the nature of neutral sentiment to this occurrence. The seventh rung refers to the evaluation of the platform for sales promotion, due to the evaluation, the occurrence is quantified at the level of positive sentiment. The eighth position refers to the evaluation within the Azet platform, it oscillates around the mean value, the sentiment is therefore quantified as neutral. The penultimate position belongs to the link to the sales support platform. In the last place we find a link to the competitor's website. When it comes to the comparison across measurements, we observe only an insignificant decrease in the level of reputation.

ASA (news tab): The first five links in the message category are strongly positive in nature. From the point of view of content, these are mostly PR links. In the sixth place, we find a link to an earlier report about a limited supply due to a lack of chips. Considering the methodology, we evaluate the link as a negative sentiment. Links in the seventh to tenth place are dominantly positive in nature. Again, this is a relatively broad mix of media and content producers, the news is mostly published in the horizon of 2021 and 2022. As far as the comparison across measurements is concerned, we see a relatively model situation where the subject transforms neutral sentiments into positive messages through its marketing activity in the online space.

Reputors: The score on the Facebook social network can be considered a dynamic and, to a certain extent, an organic element of online reputation, as part of the second measurement, we record the value of the Facebook score at the level of 58%. Across the measurements in the period through and after the pandemic, we observe a significant drop of more than 30%. Regarding the reputation levels according to the Heureka platform, the entity maintains an unchanging reputation based on the evaluation of buyers for the last 90 days at the level of 96% within the framework of measurements. The last monitored parameter, the Google rating, can only be read indirectly, as it is linked to the entity's physical stores. Based on the methodology, we record a value of 84%, which is identical to the value measured in the first year of the pandemic.

Astratex.sk

ASA (general): In the first place, we find the subject's own side. The second, third and fourth places are occupied by links of positive sentiment with the character of affiliate marketing. The fifth position is occupied by a link to the platform sprebnitelskytest.sk, which has a positive nature. The following is a link to the Heureka platform, which shows a high level of satisfaction among the entity's customers. It is therefore possible to quantify this occurrence as positive. The seventh and eighth positions within the headline and neither the link description show signs of neutral sentiment. The evaluation is completed by occurrences in the ninth and tenth positions with the character of positive sentiment. Across measurements, we observe an almost two-fold increase in the level of reputation according to the simplest parameter within the chosen methodology. While the level increase occurs by replacing neutral links with positive ones, especially in the first half of the monitored order.

ASA (news tab): Like the first measurement, we find references to significantly positive sentiment in all monitored positions. However, the links have a relatively poorly diversified nature from the point of view of the Internet media. We are following an example of significant product specialization focused on a communication platform with a relatively significant strength of its own website. Nine out of ten links are dated to the period before the pandemic. Reputation in the online environment has relatively considerable media longevity for specific cases.

Reputators: Within the social network Facebook, we observe a slight decrease in the level of reputation, while the other two platforms show the same values across the measurements. As such, the entity still does not have a Google rating. Locally, this may not be a significant deficit, but in a global environment, the subject can be significantly limited from the point of view of lack of authenticity.

Footshop.sk

ASA (general): In the first place is the subject's own page, which is followed by a link to the Heureka platform. The third and fourth links in the sequence are links to sales support platforms. All of them can be attributed a positive sentiment polarity. The fifth in the order is a link to a competitor's e-shop, we rate this occurrence as neutral. The next five occurrences, except for the ninth occurrence, which is a link to a Facebook profile, are links to business support platforms. In any case, all occurrences are positive sentiments. Compared to the first measurement, this is a significant shift towards the possible maximums determined by the chosen methodology. The entity was able to literally displace neutral links in a relatively simple way, thereby significantly strengthening the level of its online reputation.

ASA (news tab): Targeted marketing communication of the subject to the chosen market can be monitored on all monitored positions. The only exception is the link in the second position, which informs about the termination of the brick-and-mortar operation of the entity in the capital. According to the methodology, we assign a negative sentiment to this occurrence. Seven out of ten results are from 2022, the entity uses dominantly two communication platforms of one operator for its communication. Compared to the first measurement, we see a slight decrease in the partial score. This can be attributed to the already mentioned report on the closing of the brick-and-mortar store.

Reputators: Within the Facebook platform, we find a relatively well-managed profile with current and relevant content, but the profile does not contain a rating. As for other profiles, we find another profile of the subject, which does contain an assessment, but the last content was added in 2019. Therefore, we do not take it into account for measurement purposes. As for the Google rating, like in the previous case, it only contains a link to the brick-and-mortar store. In this case too, we see a relatively long inertia of reputation, when this rating secures a link to a permanently closed brick-and-mortar operation. As for the evaluation of the Heureka platform, compared to the first measurement, it increased by 4 percentage points from 94 to 97%.

MojaLekáreň.sk

ASA (general): In the first position, similarly to the previous cases, we find the subject's own side. In order, the second result is a link to the subject's Facebook profile, the third to sixth places refer to platforms for business support. Positive sentiment can be attributed to all these results. In order, the seventh reference is the mention of the change of the subject's logo, due to the nature of the content that points to innovations, we evaluate the reference at the level of positive sentiment. The eighth and ninth places refer to social media. The search results are closed by a link of a neutral nature. Compared to the first measurements, we see a significant shift towards the application of active reputation management approaches. In numerical terms, this is almost a two-fold increase in the partial score.

ASA (news tab): From the point of view of the search results, we notice a rather interesting paradox, when an active effort to build a brand does not result in a clear strengthening of identity in the online environment. The media mix is optimal from the point of view of its carriers, the temporal relevance of the content is less so. We also find content formulated as sensations for the masses, where the subject acts as a popularizer and professional authority. Considering the fact that subject is an Internet pharmacy and not a research institute, this fact is understandable, but it cannot be evaluated as productive in view of the marketing communication of previous entities. In comparison to the first measurement, we can see an effort to produce relevant content, but the character of this content is either irrelevant or downright negative from the point of view of the polarity of the words and the construction of the text. As a result, we see a decrease in the level of reputation among the measurements, despite significantly increased activity with an effort to remove neutral search results.

Reputators: From the point of view of the rating on the Facebook platform, we are noticing a slight decrease in the overall rating. This is compensated by an increase in the subject's rating on the Heureka platform. In terms of Google Rank, we see a drop across measurements of 8 percentage points.

Svetnapojov.sk

ASA (general): In the first place, we find the subject's own side. In second place we find a profile on the TikTok platform. We evaluate this occurrence as significantly positive, at the same time it is the first such occurrence within the entire research set. The third in order is a link to the subject's profile within the Instagram platform. The fourth is a link to the evaluation within the Heureka portal. The fifth to tenth places refer to business support platforms. In positions two to nine, we find links with the nature of positive sentiment. Thus, for the first time in the current measurement, we see a perfectly optimized presence of the subject in the first ten Google search results. Compared to the first measurement, we thus note an increase in partial reputation by 50 percentage points and the elimination of all neutral results.

ASA (news tab): We find only two media mentions in the search results. The first can be considered relevant and fully organic. Where in the discussion in the article relevant to the subject's business area, the discussant refers to a specific product in the subject's e-shop. The second of the links is irrelevant, which quantifies it as a neutral sentiment on the second position. We thus find a relatively vulnerable place of the subject from the point of view of its online identity. The absence of targeted media communication exposes the entity to both reputational risk and the risk of losing the market in the event of the potential expansion of one of the global market players. Compared to the first measurement, we thus note a slightly different situation, but an identically low partial score.

Reputators: The subject has a relatively well-updated and content-saturated profile on the Facebook social network. In any case, profile does not allow direct evaluation, which partially loses the authenticity of the profile content. From the Heurek evaluation point of view, we find identical scores as in the case of the first measurement. We also note a relatively high Google rating score, which is linked to the entity's physical operation in the capital. Compared to the first measurement, we see on the one hand a retreat from the Facebook rating, but on the other hand, we note a high Google rating score. The subject thus loses authenticity in the social network environment, but gains authenticity through its presence in the offline world.

HEJ.sk

ASA (general): In the first position we find the subject's own page. In second place is a link to the Heureka platform. The third and fifth in order are links to business support platforms. The fourth and sixth are links to social networks. The seventh and eighth positions also refer to social networks, while the last 2 occurrences refer to business support platforms. In the second to ninth positions, we find references evaluated as positive sentiments. This is the second case in the dataset where the subject reaches the imaginary maximums determined by the methodology. Compared to the first measurement, we thus note an increase in the partial score by 40 percentage points.

ASA (news tab): When it comes to targeted media communication, we are seeing results of a non-optimal nature. The media work of the operator of the entity is clearly noticeable, in any case, the content of the news is either negative sentiment or dominantly neutral. In terms of content recency, only four results are from the period after the first measurement, none reaching the level necessary for classification for positive sentiment of the result. Across the measurements, we observe a significant decrease in the partial reputation level by 64 percentage points.

Reputatiors: This is the third case in a row where the subject waives the possibility of direct evaluation on the profile within the Facebook social network. Compared to the previous two cases within the dataset, however, this is not a profile that would compensate for the reduced authenticity in the desired direction with its content. From the point of view of the Heureka platform, we observe a slight increase in the overall score. From the point of view of Google ranking, the subject maintains the same level of score across the measurements.

3.2. Presentation of specific findings

In the following figure, we can see the evolution of parameters across measurements. While visualizing the most important parameter of the calculation, the score from the combined two-factor sentiment analysis (ASA) and the overall coefficient of the level of online reputation (TOR).

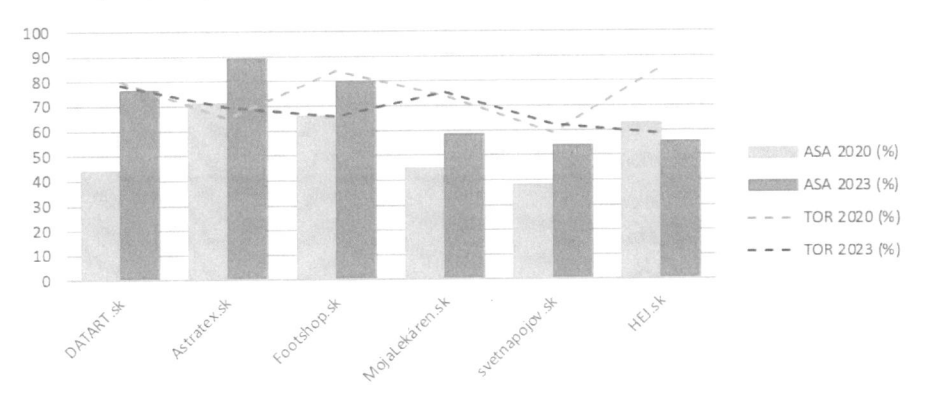

Figure 1. Reputation of entities   Source: Own processing

Across the measurements, we can observe a positive development of the level of reputation according to the basic parameter of ASA for the majority of evaluated subjects. Despite this fact, in two cases it is possible to observe a more significant decrease in the overall level of online reputation caused mainly by a slight loss of authenticity. In the remaining cases, the level of reputation after the pandemic oscillates around the values measured in the phase of its outbreak. By establishing these facts, it is possible to proceed to the formulation of the conclusion.

4. Conclusion

Based on the findings, it is possible to conclude, that across measurement at the time of onset and at the time of the end of the pandemic, the majority of subjects notice a significant improvement in the basic sentiment level of search results within the Google ecosystem. At the same time, the analyzed subjects record, compared to the measurement in 2020, a real decline in the dynamic side of online reputation created by reputation determinants of a more complex nature. The results indicate that from the point of view of basic online reputation optimization, it is possible to view the pandemic period as an accelerator of digital transformation. Since the environment being analyzed is the developing market, we consider it important to monitor the state of development in order to identify medium-term market trends. Further research on the issue is therefore more than desirable. Thus, the presented study has the character of a partial output of complex research on the issue of ORM.

Acknowledgment

This article is one of the partial outputs of the currently solved research grant VEGA no. 1/0140/21. This research was funded by the Institute of Technology and Business in České Budějovice, grant number IVSUPS2305.

References

Delina, R., Tkáč, M., (2010). Trust Building Mechanisms for Electronic Business Networks and Their Relation to eSkills, World Academy of Science, Engineering and Technology 6 (71), pp. 380-390.

Heureka Group. 2020. Cena kvality Shop roku 2019- Heureka Group a.s. Available from internet: https://www.shoproku.sk/vysledky

Kostiuk, Y., Kohútová, V., Straková, J., Koleda, N. (2021). Added value in the transport sector at the time before COVID-19 pandemic: a comparison of the EU countries. Journal of Entrepreneurship and Sustainability Issues. 9(2), pp. 303-315

Liu, B. (2012). Sentiment Analysis and Opinion Mining Chicago, IL, USA: Morgan & Claypool Publishers.

Loayza, J. (2013) The Beginner's Guide to Reputation Management: 8 Core Principles of Reputation Management. Available from internet: http://reputationhacks.com/guide-to-reputation-management-3-8-core-principles/

Maryška, M., Doucek, P., Novotný, O. (2012). Requirements of companies on the knowledge ICT specialists for the ICT administrator role. 4th World Conference on Educational Sciences. Barcelona, 2012. Procedia - Social and Behavioral Sciences. Vol. 46 (2012), pp. 4389 – 4393.

Pollák, F., Dobrovič, J., Váchal, J., Straková, J., Pártlová, P. (2020). Crisis Management of Corporate Reputation- Analysis of selected e-commerce entities in times of global pandemic. In: P. Doucek, G. Chroust and V. Oškrdal, IDIMT-2020: Digitalized Economy, Society and Information Management. 28th Interdisciplinary Information Management Talks, Kutná Hora, CzechRepublic, 2-4 September 2020. Linz: Trauner Verlag, pp. 297-304.

Pollák, F., Dorčák, P, Markovič, P. (2021). Corporate Reputation of Family-Owned Businesses: Parent Companies vs. Their Brands. Information. 12(2), 89.

Pollák, F., Markovič, P., Vavrek, R., Konečný, M. (2022). Return to the New Normal: Empirical Analysis of Changes in E-Consumer Behavior during the COVID-19 Pandemic. Behavioral Sciences. 12(3), 85.

Sagapova, N., Dušek, R., Pártlová, P. (2022). Marketing Communication and Reputation Building of Leading European Oil and Gas Companies on Instagram. Energies. 15(22), 8683.

Világi, R., Konečný, M., Ruschak, M. (2022). Impact of selected financial indicators on a company's reputation. Entrepreneurship and Sustainability Issues. 10(2), pp. 408-417.

ONLINE REPUTATION OF PUBLIC CHARGING STATIONS OPERATORS: AN EMPIRICAL STUDY ON THE CZECH MARKET

Michal Konečný

Faculty of Corporate Strategy, Department of Tourism and Marketing
Institute of Technology and Business in České Budějovice
27826@mail.vstecb.cz

Michal Ruschak

College of Entrepreneurship and Law
Pan-European University, Prague
xruschak.michal@peuni.cz

Yaroslava Kostiuk

The Faculty of Operation and Economics of Transport and Communications
Department of Economics, University of Zilina
kostiuk@stud.uniza.sk

Faculty of Corporate Strategy, Department of Management
Institute of Technology and Business in České Budějovice
26567@mail.vstecb.cz

DOI: 10.35011/IDIMT-2023-337

Keywords

Corporate reputation, sustainable development, reputation management, sentimental analysis, low-carbon mobility, Czech Republic

Abstract

The paper deals with challenges associated with the sustainable development of company reputation of public charging station operators in the Czech Republic. Specific attention is paid to online reputation, which represents an important aspect for the development of their responsible and sustainable image and is perceived as a valuable but vulnerable intangible asset. For the purposes of the research, a sample of 10 largest operators of public charging stations in the Czech market was selected. The sampling was based on the public charging stations listed by the Ministry of Industry and Trade as of 31 December 2022. The analysis was performed using the method of sentiment analysis. The findings identified within the study of this significant sample provide a perspective on the challenges concerning a sustainable development of company reputation. The findings enable better understanding of how to achieve sustainable development of public charging station operators´ reputation, but are also applicable to other relevant business areas.

1. Introduction

In order to struggle environmental problems, electromobility is developing globally (Higueras-Castillo et al., 2019). Currently, the issue of electromobility is a highly debated topic, especially in the context of reducing greenhouse gas emissions. Incentives from many countries are leading to the promotion of electromobility to achieve decarbonisation targets. This encourages a lot of countries to promote electromobility through accomplishing decarbonization targets (Skrabulakova et al., 2021). Electromobility, and low-carbon mobility in general, is one of the main objectives of the European Union's green transition policy (Pollák et al., 2021). The European Union's (EU) long-term goal is to achieve a competitive low-carbon economy which is primarily based on enabling environmentally sustainable investments, in particular in reducing energy consumption in buildings, switching to electric vehicles and developing smart electricity grids, while promoting the usage of renewable energy to reduce greenhouse gas emissions by at least 80 % by 2050 in comparison with the year 1990. Given that transport is one of the main sectors most contributing to EU emissions, the introduction of electric vehicles could enable significant reductions. Therefore, since the announcement of the 2050 Roadmap in 2009, there has been a large increase in studying and exploring the viability of the transition to e-mobility in the context of the EU, identification of common factors and variables. However, it is usually more complicated when decision makers are trying to translate these variables into policy implications that will actually help to achieve the EU's energy transition goals. At this point, motivators and barriers are the most important (Biresselioglu, Kaplan & Yilmaz, 2018). The pandemic crisis has had a significant impact on the global economy (Straková et al., 2021). The impacts of the COVID-19 pandemic were intensively addressed especially during the period of the economic recovery (Markovič et al., 2022). The crisis caused by the COVID-19 pandemic has affected the economic situation in all EU countries, but the pace of electro-mobility deployment has not slowed down and has even accelerated. In the first year of the COVID-19 pandemic, the dynamics of the implementation of the number of electric cars increased in all EU countries. The growth rate in the EU was 86 % in 2020, compared to 48 % in 2019. This was due to a change in social behaviour related to mobility under conditions of an infection risk. COVID-19 became a positive catalyst for the change. The perspectives for the development of this kind of transport are very good, as the activities related to the development of the electromobility sector perfectly match the needs of the society related to the reduction of an environmental pollution (Rokicki et al., 2022). Every second we are witnessing the global impact of fossil fuels and carbon emissions on the environment, to which countries around the world are responding by introducing ambitious goals to become carbon-free and energy efficient. Electric vehicles (EVs) are being developed as a possible solution to achieve the ambitious goal of creating a cleaner environment and facilitating smarter modes of transportation. This excellent idea of a transition based on full EV mobility has resulted in a number of challenges for industry and economy that need to be solved. The problems range from the intensification of electricity generation for the expected energy consumption increase to the development of an infrastructure large enough to meet the higher demand for electricity generated by the penetration of EVs in the market (Ravi & Aziz, 2022). Electric vehicles are taking over market share from conventional vehicles with an internal combustion engine. The growing popularity of electric vehicles has resulted in a higher number of charging stations, which have a significant impact on the electricity grid. Various charging strategies as well as grid integration methods are being developed to minimize the adverse effects of EV charging and to enhance the benefits of a grid integration of EVs (Das et al., 2020). One of the reasons for the growing popularity of electric vehicles is car-sharing companies that target users who prefer short-term rent of vehicles. Nowadays, one-way car sharing is growing rapidly, where the vehicle can be parked at a location other than where it was borrowed. The point is that one-way car sharing gives travellers the option to use car sharing in combination with other modes of transport such as public transport, showing that there are necessary intermodal connections (Mounce & Nelson, 2019). One of the biggest barriers to the development of electromobility is people's fear because electric cars have a significantly shorter range than conventional cars (Gajdac, Gajdosik & Steininger, 2020). Electromobility, electric vehicles and charging infrastructure are key building blocks for a sustainable energy future (Kirpes & Becker, 2018). A fast-charging network for battery electric vehicles is based on people's needs and provides an opportunity to remove widespread barriers to adoption of electro-mobility and thus accelerate its penetration into the market (Philipsen, Schmidt & Ziefle, 2018). In cities with a low level of electromobility, it is particularly important to plan the establishment of the most efficient distribution of the first charging stations, as this contributes to creating trust in electric vehicles. The location of charging stations should thus meet the actual needs of users to promote electromobility and maximize its implementation effect (Staniek & Sierpinski, 2020). The development of electromobility includes the development of the EV charging infrastructure. The increase in the number of chargers creates new demands on the AC network, particularly with regard to its capacity to deliver high peak power. As an alternative, the public AC grid to supply urban electrified transport systems (trams, trolleybuses, and metros) can be used for electric car chargers (Bartlomiejczyk, Jarzebowicz & Hrbac, 2022). Environmental and energy security concerns have made governments to introduce many incentive policies to promote electric vehicles. In 2015, the global threshold of 1 million electric cars on roads was crossed, yielding policy dividends and reaching 1.26 million. Among these incentive policies, the subsidy scheme was considered the most important and the most effective one. However, many governments such as China, America and Germany intend to abolish subsidies for electric vehicles. Wang, Tang & Pan (2019) identify key factors, including incentive measures and other socio-economic factors, for promoting electric vehicles. They used the multiple linear regression method to examine the relationship between these variables and 30 national division on an electric vehicle market in 2015. The results showed that charger density, fuel price, and road priority are significantly positive factors that correlate with a country's division on an electric vehicle market. However, fiscal incentives are no longer the cause of large differences in the promotion of electric vehicles compared to other countries. The Internet is becoming increasingly important today, with consumers using it for communication, looking up information that is important for their purchasing decisions, as well as for online shopping. Customers are more demanding and have higher expectations towards companies; in turn, companies are trying to meet their demands and needs to the maximum possible extent by optimizing their processes and fast delivery of their products to customers. Therefore, it is important for companies to focus on their online reputation (Zrakova, Demjanovicova & Kubina, 2019), as building and managing online reputation is becoming an integral part of everyday life (Hesse & Teubner, 2020), and factors such as interactivity and mobility within the effective use of e-commerce tools or effective combining e-commerce tools are becoming factors significantly contributing to company´s success (Pollák, Nastišin & Kakalejčík, 2015). As for companies, it is primarily about their perception of the relative advantages associated with the application of e-marketing tools given the effort and resources required for building and maintaining an e-marketing infrastructure. In terms of customers, it is about how they perceive the specific aspects of using virtual social networks by companies for the purposes of building a brand or direct promotion (Dorčák, Štrach & Pollák, 2015). The reputation of organizations comprises different perceptions of different groups on the basis of history and expectation. As there is no universal definition of the term, there are several methods of measuring reputation. These measurements are overseen by online reputation monitoring and management systems through sentiment analysis (Orrego et al., 2021).

2. Objectives and methods

Providing an analytical perspective on the issue of the online reputation of the largest public charging station operators in the Czech Republic is the main objective of the study which the initial research problem, i.e., to determine how these public charging station operators are perceived in the online environment, is based on. The research sample consists of the 10 largest operators of public charging stations in the Czech Republic from the list of public charging stations based on the register kept by the Ministry of Industry and Trade (2023) as of 31 December 2022. A basic sentiment analysis is chosen as the basic methodological tool of the empirical analysis (Pollák, Dorčák & Markovič, 2019; Pollák, Dorčák & Markovič, 2021), which can be quantified by the sentiment, or the polarity of the first ten results of a particular entity in Google search engine at the level of its online reputation. Sentiment analysis, also known as opinion mining, can be defined as automatic quantification of a subjective content expressed in a textual form with the aim of determine the attitude of the speaker or the author concerning the given topic. The main tasks of sentiment analysis include the identification of subjectivity, orientation, intensity, and the bearer of sentiment, classification of emotional mood, detection of sarcasm and various comparisons (Koncz, 2013). The process of measuring reputation starts with identifying representatives of the analysed sector and its competitors. In sentiment analysis, first ten search results are considered. In order to minimize the distortion of search results, which can be personalized on the basis of the user's history of searches, and to reduce the influence of cookies and other factors, proxy anonymiser is used (Sasko, 2011). Sentiment analysis always uses a standard and generally known designation of the examined subject or object, such as a search phrase, in order to achieve accurate results of the analysis (Dorčák & Pollák, 2013). The subject's own name (name of the operator of public recharging points) serves as a search phrase. The sentiment of the results obtained from searching for the desired sequence in the search engine is one of the main factors in evaluation. Sentiment can be defined as a character of the result found based on keywords. The results can reflect positive, neutral, and negative reviews that provide an image of the subject under investigation and ultimately determine its online reputation (Dorčák & Pollák, 2013). The sentiment of the first search results on Google is evaluated. Points for sentiment are added together, which provides the resulting value. This value is then used as a starting factor for evaluating the success or failure of a company in a specific segment. The search results in each of the ten positions are then quantified according to the following key:

Table 1. Sentiment of results / position of results

Sentiment/Position of the result	1	2	3	4	5	6	7	8	9	10
+										
Positive sentiment	20	19	18	17	16	15	14	13	12	11
x										
Company owned website	10	9	8	7	6	5	4	3	2	1
±										
Neutral sentiment	2	2	2	2	2	2	2	2	2	2
-										

Sentiment/Position of the result	1	2	3	4	5	6	7	8	9	10
Negative sentiment	-20	-19	-18	-17	-16	-15	-14	-13	-12	-11

Source: (Liu, 2012 In: Dorčák, Pollák & Szabo, 2014)

To minimize the personalization of the results, an incognito search mode is chosen, where only organic search results are quantified. Results marked as ads are not considered. If there are more links to the test subject's own website within the search results, then the second to nth search results of this type are attributed neutral sentiment. The polarity of the result is determined on the basis of data directly visible from the link, i.e., it is mainly the name and lead. Determining the overall polarity of sentiment of a specific text is a part of a comprehensive study from 2010 (Liu, 2012). The method called opinion mining is used to evaluate the polarity of subjective published opinions concerning a specific subject. To avoid this problem, it is necessary to define the overall polarity of the text on the basis of the polarity of individual words in the text. The theory suggests that the most suitable words to determine the orientation of the text are adjectives and adverbs. Mostly, it is possible quite precisely to determine the sentiment of a message or a text using superlative adjectives either with positive meaning (the oldest, the best, etc.) or negative meaning (the worst, the weakest). Similarly, verbs expressing certain activities directed towards something positive can be considered a positive signal. Conversely, negative signals can be e.g., information about accidents, potential dangers, and risks, uncontrollable or unexpected changes that cannot be reversed in any ways. However, in such cases, it is also necessary to consider the object to which the given words refer. An adjective, noun, or verb can have different polarity depending on different objects. Therefore, it is necessary to decide which object the evaluation refers to and subsequently assign a numerical value to words and phrases, which then determines the overall orientation of the sentiment. Similarly, numerical values can be assigned to ten websites that appear in the search results on the basis of the search term, depending on whether it is an organization's website or word phrases in different domains. For example, the word "unforeseen" can have a positive polarity, if it refers to a theatre performance, but considerably negative if referring to e.g., car accidents (Liu, 2012). The same procedure is followed for the analysis of each of the ranked entities, where a sub-indicator of reputation is determined for each of the positions and in the next step, the total value is created based on their sum. The aggregate value for each test subject is then converted to percentage. Each of the examined subjects can achieve a maximum of 155 points in the final total, which accounts for 100 %, with one percentage being 0.645 points. The ranking, which provides an overview of the relative position of the test subjects (SA score), is based on the overall percentage of online reputation.

3. Results and discussion

Selected public charging station operators were subjected to a basic sentiment analysis. The table shows the values of the individual monitoring indicators for each of the analysed operators as follows:

Table 2. Basic reputation score

Brand/Position results	1	2	3	4	5	6	7	8	9	10	Score SA (%)
ČEZ	10	9	2	2	2	5	2	2	2	2	24,52
E.ON Česká republika	10	9	2	2	2	2	2	2	2	2	22,58
E.ON Drive Infrastructure CZ	10	2	2	2	6	2	2	2	2	2	20,65

Brand/Position results	1	2	3	4	5	6	7	8	9	10	Score SA (%)
E.ON Energie	10	9	2	2	2	2	2	2	12	2	29,03
ELEKTRO-PROJEKCE	10	2	2	2	2	2	2	2	2	2	18,06
Lidl Česká republika	10	2	2	2	2	2	2	2	2	2	18,06
MOL Česká republika	10	2	2	2	2	2	2	2	2	2	18,06
Pražská energetika	10	2	2	17	2	2	2	2	2	2	27,74
ŠKO-ENERGO	10	2	2	2	2	-15	2	2	2	11	12,90
Teplárny Brno	10	19	2	17	2	15	14	2	2	2	54,84

After determining the sentiment of each of the ten results in the search engine for each of the public charging station operators, scores were determined based on the sentiment scoring scale from table 1. The resulting scores are presented in Table 2. According to the sum of the scores, the ranking of the public charging station operators can be determined as follows: 1. Teplárny Brno, 2. E.ON Energie, 3. Pražská energetika, 4. ČEZ, 5. E.ON Česká republika, 6. E.ON Drive Infrastructure CZ, 7. ELEKTRO-PROJEKCE, Lidl Česká republika and MOL Česká republika with the same amount of scores with 8. ŠKO-ENERGO. The results of the sentiment analysis show that the first positions in the search engine for all the public charging station operators surveyed were for the company's website. This fact may be due to SEO optimization, which aims to optimize the enterprise's website to reach the first positions within search. The second finding resulting from the sentiment analysis is the neutrality of the contributions, which included sites such as wikipedia.org, kurzy.cz, firmy.cz, penize.cz or mapy.cz, where no sentiment was recorded. The positivity of the post in the ninth position within the Google search results for E.ON Energie can be explained by reference to an article on Tarimfomat (2023) regarding a positive evaluation and review of E.ON Energie's energy supply by a customer who switched from ČEZ to EON with a gas supply. The positivity of the post in the fourth position in the Google search results in the case of Pražská energetika can be explained by reference to an article by Česká tisková kancelář on Seznam Zprávy (2023) regarding the fact that Pražská energetika will offer fixed tariffs with electricity and gas prices below the government ceiling, and in the case of Teplárny Brno, by reference to a post on their Facebook profile Teplárny Brno (2023) regarding the company's financial contribution to the Brno University Hospital (a modern endoscope). The positivity of the post in the sixth position in the Google search results for Teplárny Brno can be explained by the reference to an article on the website Asociace PCC, spol. s.r.o. - public relations and marketing (2023) regarding the successful merger of Tepláren Brno and Tepelné zásobování Brno, and in the seventh position in the Google search results by the article on the website iDnes.cz (2023) regarding the fact that the price of heat will be reduced in Brno as of March 2023, and households will save a hundreds of crowns a month. The positivity of the article in the tenth position in the Google search results for ŠKO-ENERGO can be explained by reference to an article by David Tramba (2021) on Ekonomický deník regarding the emission-free Mladá Boleslav, where ŠKO-ENERGO wants to completely replace coal with biomass by December 2025. The negativity of the article in the case of ŠKO-ENERGO can be explained by the evaluation of a former employee of the company on Atmoskop.cz (2023), who worked for the company for 5 months and then left, in his words, for another company where his work makes sense.

4. Conclusion

If an internet user looking for information about a particular company does not encounter positive indicators of its reputation, this may ultimately affect their overall perception of that company. This is particularly true for potential customers who have not yet had personal experience with the company and whose opinions are formed only on the basis of information obtained from the online environment. The selected public charging station operators perform well in this respect, but in the future they should continue their efforts to limit their negative publicity and continue to work on and improve their positive publicity. This can be achieved in particular through implementing an active online communication policy, which includes mainly the dissemination of positive information about the company through major well-known online newspapers or social networks. The best way to remove negative or neutral publicity from the top ten search results is to replace negative publicity with a thoughtful marketing communication policy that is implemented in the online environment. The most effective model for comprehensive online reputation management is to focus on the dominant determinants of reputation, namely Google search results, as well as active management of social media profiles. As Sasko (2014) claims, actively used online reputation management tools can significantly facilitate proactive communication of companies with the public and help companies to obtain and evaluate feedback or accelerate the implementation of measures related to crisis marketing communications.

Acknowledgement

This article is one of the partial outputs of the currently solved research project IVSUPS2305. This research was funded by the Institute of Technology and Business in České Budějovice, grant number IVSUPS2305.

References

Atmoskop.cz. (2023, April 23). Hodnocení firmy ŠKO-ENERGO, s.r.o. [ŠKO-ENERGO, s.r.o. company evaluation]. https://www.atmoskop.cz/nazory-na-zamestnavatele/3064559-sko-energo-s-r-o/hodnoceni

Bartlomiejczyk, M., Jarzebowicz L., & Hrbac R. (2022). Application of Traction Supply System for Charging Electric Cars. Energies, 15(4), 1448.

Biresselioglu, M. E., Kaplan, M. D., & Yilmaz, B. K. (2018). Electric mobility in Europe: A comprehensive review of motivators and barriers in decision making processes. Transportation Research Part A-Policy and Practice, 109, 1-13

Česká tisková kancelář. (2023, March 2). Pražská energetika nabídne fixované tarify s cenami pod vládním stropem. Seznam Zprávy. https://www.seznamzpravy.cz/clanek/ekonomika-prazska-energetika-nabidne-fixovane-tarify-s-cenami-pod-vladnim-stropem-226935

Das, H. S., Rahman, M. M., Li, S., & Tan C. W. (2020). Electric vehicles standards, charging infrastructure, and impact on grid integration: a technological review. Renewable & Sustainable Energy Reviews, 120(3), 109618.

Dorčák, P., & Pollák, F. (2013, June 7). Analýza on - line prostredia slovenského virtuálního trhu [Analysis of the on-line environment of the Slovak virtual market]. http://www.region-bsk.sk/SCRIPT/ViewFile.aspx?docid=10051170/

Dorčák, P., Pollák, F., & Szabo, S. (2014). Analysis of the Possibilities of Improving an Online Reputation of Public Institutions. IDIMT-2014: Networking Societies - Cooperation and Conflict: 22nd Interdisciplinary Information Management Talks. Poděbrady, Czech Republic, 2014. pp. 275–282.

Dorčák, P., Štrach, P., Pollák, F. (2015) Analytical view of the perception of selected innovative approaches in marketing communications. Quality. Innovation. Prosperity, 19(1), 74-84

Gajdac, I., Gajdosik, T., & Steininger J. (2020). The Energy Assist for the Electric Car Edison. Current Methods of Construction Design. Lecture Notes in Mechanical Engineering, 251-261

Hesse, M. & Teubner, T. (2020). Reputation portability - quo vadis?. Electronic Markets. 30(2), 331-349.

Higueras-Castillo, E., Liebana-Cabanillas, F. J., Munoz-Leiva, F., & Garcia-Maroto, I. (2019). Evaluating consumer attitudes toward electromobility and the moderating effect of perceived consumer effectiveness. Journal of Retailing and Consumer Services, 51, 387-398

iDnes.cz. (2023, February 8). V Brně se od března sníží cena tepla, domácnosti ušetří stovku měsíčně. [Brno will reduce the price of heat from March, households will save a hundred a month]. https://www.idnes.cz/brno/zpravy/cena-tepla-snizeni-teplarny-brno.A230208_141410_brno-zpravy_mos1

Kirpes, B., & Becker, C. (2018). Processing Electric Vehicle Charging Transactions in a Blockchain-based Information System Emergent Research Forum (ERF). 24th Americas Conference on Information Systems (AMCIS) - Digital Disruption, New Orleans, LA

Koncz, P. (2013, June 7). Prezentácie. [Prezentácie]. http://people.tuke.sk/jan.paralic/prezentacie/MZ/MZ8.pdf

Liu, B. (2012). Sentiment Analysis and Opinion Mining, Synthesis Lectures on Human Language Technologies, Chicago, IL, USA: Springer Cham, 167, ISBN 978-3-031-02145-9

Markovič, P., Pollák, F., Vavrek, R., & Kostiuk, Y. (2022). Impact of Coronavirus Pandemic on Changes in e-Consumer Behaviour: Empirical Analysis of Slovak e-Commerce Market. Journal of Economics, 70(4), 368-389.

Mounce, R., & Nelson, J. D. (2019). On the potential for one-way electric vehicle car-sharing in future mobility systems. Transportation Research Part A-Policy and Practice, 120, 17-30

Orrego, Ch., Villa, L. F., Sepulveda-Cano, L. M. & Giraldo, L. M. M. (2021). Organizational Online Reputation Measurement Through Natural Language Processing and Sentiment Analysis Techniques. Applied Computer Sciences in Engineering. WEA 2021. 2021. 1431, 60-71

Philipsen, R., Schmidt, T., & Ziefle, M. (2018). Fast-Charging Stations or Conventional Gas Stations: Same Difference? - Variations of Preferences and Requirements. AHFE International Conference on Human Factors in Transportation, Los Angeles, CA, 597, 951-962

Pollák, F., Dorčák, P., & Markovič, P. (2019). Reputation Management. In U. Ayman, & A. K. Kaya (Eds.), Promotionand Marketing Communications. IntechOpen

Pollák, F., Dorčák, P., & Markovič, P. (2021). Corporate reputation of family-owned businesses: Parent companies vs. their brands. Information (Switzerland), 12(2), 1–16

Pollák, F., Nastišin, Ľ., & Kakalejčík, L. (2015) Analytical view on the use of mobile platforms in purchasing process. European journal of science and theology, 11(6), 137-146

Pollák, F., Vodák, J., Soviar, J., Markovič, P., Lentini, G., Mazzeschi, V., & Luè A. (2021). Promotion of Electric Mobility in the European Union—Overview of Project PROMETEUS from the Perspective of Cohesion through Synergistic Cooperation on the Example of the Catching-Up Region. Sustainability, 13(3), 1545

Ravi, S. S., & Aziz, M. (2022). Utilization of Electric Vehicles for Vehicle-to-Grid Services: Progress and Perspectives. Energies, 15(2), 589

Recenze dodávky energií E.ON Energie. Tarifomat.cz. Retrieved April 23, 2023. Tarifomat.cz. https://tarifomat.cz/recenze/energie/e-on-energie/

Rokicki, T., Borawski, P., Beldycka-Borawska, A., Zak, A., & Koszela, G. (2022). Development of Electromobility in European Union Countries under COVID-19 Conditions. Energies, 15(1), 9

Sasko, J. (2011, August, 23). Spravodajské portály ako riziko pre reputačný mananžment. Online reputačný manažment. Reputation.cz. http://www.reputation.cz/spravodajske-portaly-ako-riziko-pre-reputacny-manazment/

Sasko, J. (2014, June 9). Dbáte na hodnotu svojej značky? Online reputačný manažment. Podnikajte.sk. https://www.podnikajte.sk/marketing/online-reputacny-manazment

Seznam veřejných dobíjecích stanic — stav k 31. 12. 2022. (2023, January 12). Ministerstvo průmyslu a obchodu. https://www.mpo.cz/cz/energetika/statistika/statistika-a-evidence-cerpacich-a-dobijecich-stanic/seznam-verejnych-dobijecich-stanic-_-stav-k-31--12--2022--271957/

Skrabulakova, E. F., Ivanova, M., Rosova, A., Gresova, E., Sofranko, M., & Ferencz, V. (2021). On Electromobility Development and the Calculation of the Infrastructural Country Electromobility Coefficient. Processes, 9(2), 222.

Staniek, M., & Sierpinski, G. (2020). Charging Station Distribution Model - The Concept of Using the Locations of Petrol Stations in the City. Modern Traffic Engineering in The System Approach to The Development of Traffic Networks. Advances in Intelligent Systems and Computing, 1083, 99-113

Straková, J., Koraus, A., Váchal, J., Pollák F., Cernak, F., Talíř, M., & Kollmann, J. (2021). Sustainable Development Economics of Enterprises in the Services Sector Based on Effective Management of Value Streams. Sustainability, 13(16), 8978

Teplárny Brno (2023, April 13). Teplárny Brno opět pomáhají, Dětské nemocnici přispějí na moderní endoskop. Facebook. https://www.facebook.com/photo/?fbid=245965021277432&set=a.182613887612546&locale=cs_CZ

Tramba, D. (2021, April 1). Bezemisní Mladá Boleslav. Elektrárna Ško-energo zcela nahradí uhlí biomasou. Ekonomický deník. https://ekonomickydenik.cz/bezemisni-mlada-boleslav-elektrarna-sko-energo-zcela-nahradi-uhli-biomasou/

Úspěšná fúze Tepláren Brno a TEZA. (n.d.). Asociace PCC - Public Relations A Marketing. Retrieved 23 April 2023, https://www.apc-pr.cz/cz/novinky/uspesna-fuze-teplaren-brno-a-teza/

Wang, N., Tang, L. H., & Pan, H. Z. (2019). A global comparison and assessment of incentive policy on electric vehicle promotion. Sustainable Cities and Society, 44, 597-603

Zrakova, D., Demjanovicova, M., & Kubina, M. (2019). Online reputation in the transport and logistics field. 13th International Scientific Conference on Sustainable, Modern and Safe Transport, 40, 1231-1237

BUILDING A SUSTAINABLE BATTERY SUPPLY CHAIN WITH DIGITAL BATTERY PASSPORTS

Veronika Siska, Astrid Al-Akrawi

AIT Austrian Institute of Technology GmbH
veronika.siska@ait.ac.at, astrid.al-akrawi@ait.ac.at

Mats Zackrisson

RISE Research Institutes of Sweden
mats.zackrisson@ri.se

DOI: 10.35011/IDIMT-2023-347

Keywords

Digital product passport, Digital battery passport, Data spaces, Sustainable battery supply chain

Abstract

The digital battery passport is an essential driver of sustainable production and circular economy as it enables storing and tracking data for batteries throughout the whole value chain. The BatWoMan project is paving the way towards carbon-neutral Li-ion battery cell production via new sustainable and cost-efficient methods, and by building a prototype for a digital battery passport. In this article, we outline the concept of the battery passport, including the status of relevant regulations, standards and initiatives. We then present the BatWoMan project and its design for a battery dataspace and passport. We describe relevant stakeholders and their interactions within the data space and introduce the system architecture, which is based on the International Data Spaces and Gaia-X frameworks. Finally, limitations of the research outcome are presented.

1. Introduction

Batteries are crucial for affordable and clean energy, one of the 17 Sustainable Development Goals (SDGs) defined in the United Nation's Agenda 2030 for Sustainable Development (United Nations, 2015). Efficient energy storage enables the use of renewable, dynamic energy sources like solar or wind power and supports the transition towards electromobility. However, source materials of batteries often include hazardous or rare materials, whose mining and production processes cause a substantial environmental footprint (Peters et al., 2017). At their end-of-life, disposed batteries are an additional burden, while reuse or recycling is often hampered due to suboptimal design for sustainability, a lack of information on the battery's materials, structure and status and the complexity and variety of recycling processes (Harper et al., 2019).

1.1. Digital product passports

An important driver of a sustainable battery lifecycle is a standardised digital battery passport, a Digital Product Passport (DPP) for each battery. A DPP is a digital representation of an individual product that describes its properties and current state and accompanies it throughout and after its operation time. The passport's goal is to support sustainability and circularity, with participation from all actors along the supply chain (Adisorn et al., 2021; Walden et al., 2021). Data stored in the passport provides means for regulatory compliance, supports informed decision-making, and enables a circular economy by providing crucial information for collectors, second-life operators, and recyclers.

The DPP concept spans various sectors, but is still relatively new as a research domain, despite ongoing standardization efforts fueled by regulations (van Capelleveen et al., 2023). Battery passports are one of the focal areas of DPP research. Bai et al., 2020 conceptualise a Battery Identity Global Passport, focusing on its role in recycling strategies. Berger et al., 2022 present the concept and information requirements of a digital battery passport. Plociennik et al., 2022 describe a passport with a direct interface to production machines using the Asset Administration Shell (AAS).

Upcoming regulations are a strong driver for DPPs, particularly in Europe. The *EU Ecodesign for Sustainable Products Regulation* lays the foundation for cross-sectoral digital product passports; to be accompanied by separate sector-specific regulations. The new *EU Battery Regulation* on sustainable and circular batteries will establish a Battery Passport, describing content and technical requirements. From 42 months into its entry into force (expected August 2023), all electric vehicle and LMT (light means of transport, such as e-scooters or e-bikes) batteries, as well as industrial batteries with a capacity above 2 kWh, shall be equipped with a digital battery passport.

There are several DPP initiatives; some enforced by regulations and some optional. *Material Passports* (Luscuere, 2017) describe a general early passport concept, which found voluntary applications particularly in the construction sector, to facilitate the reuse and recycling of building materials. Although there is no operative battery passport as of now, multiple projects and initiatives are working towards that goal, with participation from major industrial players. The German-driven *BatteryPass* project develops content and technical guidelines as well as a demonstrator, while the European *CIRPASS* project prepares the ground for DPP across industries. On a global scale, the *Global Battery Alliance* conceptualised a framework for a Battery Passport, as well as rulebooks for key sustainability indicators: the Greenhouse Gas rulebook and the Child Labour and Human Rights indices. The battery passport demonstrator in BatWoMan builds on these initiatives to enable interoperability, validate their guidelines and contribute to best practices.

1.2. Data spaces

Data spaces have been proposed as the data management system supporting digital product passports (Walden et al., 2021). The concept of data spaces originated from computer science as a new kind of data management platform, where participants manage their own data (Franklin et al., 2005). According to modern definitions, a data space is a decentralised data ecosystem based on data sovereignty, i.e. the "capability of a legal entity or natural person to determine and execute usage rights when it comes to their data" (Otto, 2022). All participants agree to a shared set of rules that serve as a basis for trust. In a DPP system, actors of the supply chain and beyond (see section 3.4) can share data under mutually agreed terms, without losing control over who uses them and how.

Data spaces were formalised at Fraunhofer ISST, leading to the establishment of the International Data Spaces Association (IDSA) in 2015 and the creation of the initial concept and framework for data spaces, described in the International Data Spaces Reference Architecture Model (IDS RAM). Gaia-X, a European initiative for the establishment of a federated and secure framework for sovereign data exchange, takes the dataspace concept one step further. Gaia-X considers generic data-related services (e.g. storage, web servers) to enable interoperability between different cloud providers and IT infrastructures and also builds a common trust layer shared between dataspaces. The BatWoMan architecture builds on both the IDS and Gaia-X frameworks and principles.

Multiple data space initiatives focus on sharing data across the supply chain. Catena-X, established in the automotive sector, is one of the most mature of such projects. Members of Catena-X span the whole value chain: the project enables sovereign data exchange between suppliers, manufacturers, handlers, repairers, second life operators and so on. Due to the strong ties between batteries and the automotive industry, Catena-X is also involved in European and global battery passport initiatives.

2. Methodology

From a practical point of view, a battery passport follows the process below. Relevant data from the entire supply chain is shared with authorized parties, from raw materials and manufacturing to usage and end-of-life. Before the battery enters the market, the manufacturer creates a unique identifier, physically accessible on the product, e.g. as a QR (Quick Response) code, a URI (Uniform Resource Identifier) or an RFID (Radio Frequency Identification) tag. They then publish a passport with the required content and links to related data (e.g. battery model information). During its operation, the battery passport can be constantly updated by authorized entities, e.g. with data on its current status or about repairs. When reaching its end-of-life, second-hand users or recyclers can retrieve these data to guide their decisions about recycling, repair or reuse. Publishing, accessing, using or updating data is regulated by policies defined by data owners and compliant with regulations; also respecting privacy requirements.

The technical architecture for battery passports consists of a decentralised system (referred to as "electronic exchange system" in the upcoming new EU Battery Regulation), potentially combined with information stored in centralised storage. The decentralised system will be implemented as a dataspace containing the passports and related data, with sovereign data exchange under access and usage restrictions; and an additional publicly available area containing unrestricted data. Using dataspace standards (e.g. from the already mentioned European Gaia-X and IDSA initiatives), such data can also be integrated with other existing data ecosystems, such as Catena-X for electric vehicle batteries. The centralised part may contain information about battery models or simply a searchable catalogue of data available in the decentralised dataspace. According to the new battery regulation, the Commission should set up and maintain a product passport registry with records of all data carriers and unique identifiers linked to products placed on the market or put in service. In the BatWoMan battery passport demonstrator, this registry is realised via the dataspace's data catalogue.

3. BatWoMan battery passport demonstrator

3.1. The BatWoMan project

The project BatWoMan aims to develop new sustainable and cost-efficient Li-ion battery cell production concepts, paving the way towards carbon-neutral cell production within the European Union. It started in September 2022 and is funded by the European Union's Horizon Europe research and innovation programme. Regarding production processes, it focuses on electrode processing with water-based slurries of high dry mass content, without volatile organic compounds, improved electrolyte filling and low-cost, energy-efficient cell conditioning (wetting, formation and aging). These improvements will be supported by an Artificial Intelligence (AI)-driven platform for smart retooling (adapting machine parameters to optimise production). As part of the project, a battery dataspace and passport demonstrator will be built, using data generated and collected in the project, building on the previously mentioned frameworks and standards, and in alignment with other European product passport initiatives, particularly with BatteryPass and CIRPASS.

3.2. Data sources

The battery passport in BatWoMan uses data collected on raw battery materials, as well as from each step of the improved, data-driven manufacturing process developed in the project, following the content guidance (Battery Pass Consortium, 2023) from the Battery Pass project, based on the new EU Battery Regulation. This is complemented by the results of a full life-cycle assessment, in which the battery's carbon footprint throughout its lifetime and other sustainability-related indicators are estimated.

Raw materials to be used for battery cell production in BatWoMan are investigated, based on the bill-of-material for NMC622/graphite batteries. This investigation considers main players in the global battery materials supply chain for the main electrode materials lithium, cobalt, manganese, nickel and graphite; with further studies on other battery materials such as collectors, paper-based separators, pouch foil and electrolyte components. The focus lies on sustainable sources, with special attention to European suppliers, to facilitate sustainable production within the project.

During the manufacturing process in pilot factories of consortium members, data is collected from each produced battery cell. Aside from general metadata (battery type, ID, manufacturing date and location, manufacturer information, etc.), details of the battery cell's weight, chemistry and composition is recorded, with special attention to hazardous materials and critical or expensive elements to facilitate recycling. Performance and durability metrics are also calculated and recorded.

A life-cycle assessment (LCA) is also part of BatWoMan, to be used for design work within the project as well as assessing the overall environmental performance of the final design for BatWoMan battery cells. Results of the LCA, including sustainability indicators such as the carbon footprint, also provide data for the battery passport.

3.3. Users and their interactions

The BatWoMan demonstrator considers a minimal set of user categories to support basic use cases. We distinguish between suppliers, battery producers, actors within the usage or second life phases, authorities and the general public. Except for the latter, participants interact with the dataspace through their dedicated connector services, which enable interactions according to dataset-specific policies. Participants and their interactions via the battery dataspace are shown in Figure.

Suppliers are registered participants of the underlying dataspace who may publish and consume data, but do not create a passport. They correspond to industry players involved with the supply chain, who do not produce a finished product which is placed on the market (in our case, a battery), and are not legally responsible for creating passports. Within BatWoMan, consortium partners take this role.

The *battery producer* represents the organization placing the battery on the market, who is responsible for creating its passport according to the new EU battery regulation. Like suppliers, they are dataspace members who may publish and consume data, but they also publish passports for each battery. Within BatWoMan, this will be emulated, as no commercial products are produced.

Participants related to the *usage (e.g. user, repairer)* or *second life (e.g. collector, recycler)* phases also play an important part. They provide and consume dynamic data related to individual batteries, for example information regarding its status, repairs being done or whether the battery is reused in a different context. Such dynamic, personal data is out of scope for BatWoMan. However, a simplified "recycler" role, handling only static data (disregarding the usage phase), will be considered.

Authorities may also participate in the dataspace. They have access to all public and restricted data that they require for regulatory purposes, but cannot obtain other datasets which may be sensitive and shared only between particular participants (e.g. manufacturer and their suppliers). In a real scenario, regulatory bodies would fall under this category, within BatWoMan this role will be emulated.

The last category of users of the dataspace is the *general public*. They only have access to publicly available data of a battery, either directly via its unique identifier (e.g. after scanning a QR code physically present on the product) or by searching in the dataspace catalogue.

It is also worth noting that a dataspace participant does not necessarily belong to a single category. A recycling company for instance may appear at the end of a battery's life and also as a supplier. It may consume data related to the battery to be recycled (e.g. to choose the optimal recycling procedures) and also publish data as a supplier (on recycled raw materials for use in new batteries).

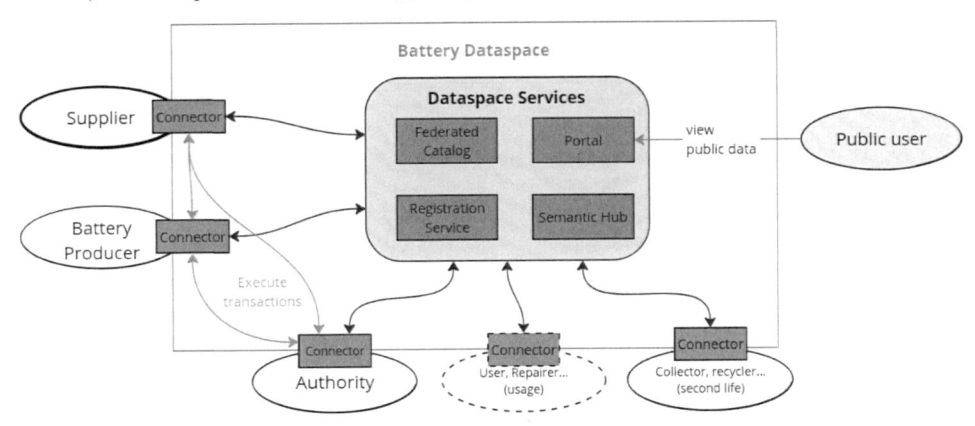

Figure 1. Users and their interactions within the battery dataspace. In BatWoMan, supplier data will be provided by consortium partners (bold line) and the usage phase is out of scope (dashed line)

Source: Own visualization

3.4. System architecture

The BatWoMan demonstrator, as mentioned above, builds on the IDS-RAM and Gaia-X architecture models to realise a decentralised ecosystem for sharing data, including individual battery passports. Participants and datasets are identified via verifiable credentials (VCs), that is, cryptographically signed certificates stored at their owner. The concrete architecture and implementation will be based on Eclipse Dataspace Components (EDC), an open-source software suite used also by Catena-X and other dataspace initiatives, with an expressed goal to comply with both IDS and Gaia-X architectures. The BatWoMan architecture consists of dataspace services and connectors, both of which we will describe using terminology from the IDS-RAM and Gaia-X.

Dataspace services are operated for a dataspace to facilitate interaction between its participants (see Figure 2). The BatWoMan dataspace architecture includes four such services: a *portal*, a *registration service*, a *semantic hub* and a *federated catalogue* (the latter will be explained later). The *portal* provides user-friendly access to the dataspace, both to public and restricted functionalities. Using the *portal*, participants can browse content or provide and consume data, respecting access and usage restrictions. The *registration service* accepts requests to join the dataspace (optionally associated with a particular role) and if the conditions are satisfied, issues VCs that participants can use as a proof of their membership. It also connects to external services for the verification, particularly the Gaia-X Trust Services. The *semantic hub* stores and provides machine-readable definitions of standardised data descriptions for battery passports and other kinds of datasets, to enable services to automatically interpret data available via the dataspace.

Following the IDS architecture, so-called *connectors* are deployed for each registered participant. A connector is a dedicated component for sending and receiving data, which acts as a secure gateway and enables authorized access to the dataspace. Participants can interact both with dataspace services and directly with each other via their corresponding connectors. In EDC, processes related to data exchange are separated into a control and a data plane to provide better scalability and a separation of concerns. The control plane handles all processes that prepare and follow a transaction, including publishing data and associated policies (e.g. for access and usage control), validating participants and datasets, contracting and logging. The data plane's responsibility lies in the execution of a transaction after successful contract negotiation. Additionally, an identity hub is part of each connector, which is a module to store, manage and present VCs as a proof of identity.

A *catalogue* complements the system to allow participants to search and select datasets. It builds on a federated architecture, consisting of nodes in each connector and a crawler - potentially with multiple instances - for the dataspace (see Figure). The crawler polls the nodes of each registered participant's connector, which respond with currently registered policies and assets. The portal relies on the crawler to enable interaction with the contents of the dataspace. In addition to the catalogue, battery passports are also directly accessible via their unique identifier, e.g. by scanning a QR code on the battery which directly leads to the page of that particular product's passport in the portal.

A participant can *register* themself to the dataspace as follows (see Figure 2, "Registration"):

1. Participant initiates registration with the registration service, sending required metadata (e.g. company registration number, self-signed VC and other credentials).
2. Registration service sends signed VC of dataspace membership to the participant.
3. Participant stores membership credential in its connector's Identity Hub.

Data exchange in the system would consist of the following steps (see Figure 2 "Data Exchange"):

1. Producer publishes a dataset offer with an associated policy via its connector.
2. Consumer initiates contract negotiation via its connector.
3. The connectors negotiate the contract. In this step, they verify VCs of each other and of services and datasets, and ensure that the conditions of policies are met.
4. The connectors execute the data transfer. This may happen using different protocols, such as HTTPS file transfer or cloud-based solutions.

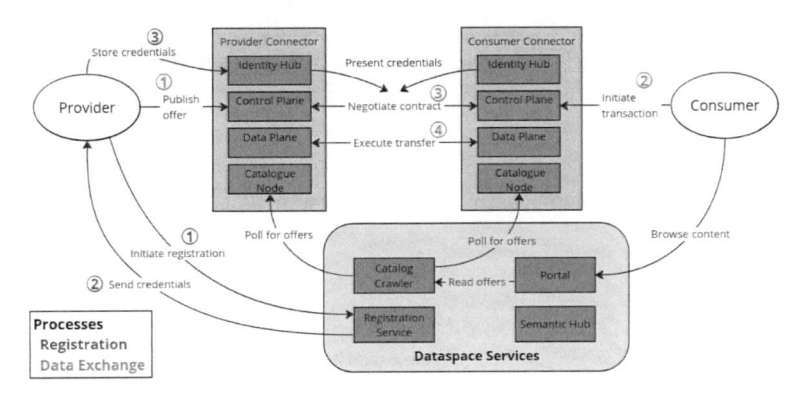

Figure 2. Components of the BatWoMan Passport (dataspace) architecture and their interactions. Steps for two processes are depicted: participant registration (blue) and data exchange (red).   Source: Own visualization

3.5. Limitations

The battery passport demonstrator of BatWoMan has some limitations when compared with an operational system. Our system is demonstrated as part of battery production, but not in an operational environment pipeline, corresponding to Technology Readiness Level 6. The BatWoMan battery cells will not be placed on the market, which has implications on the dataspace and passport. First, documents legally required for commercially sold batteries will not all be available. Second, we work with a reduced supply chain and thus emulate certain business roles (battery manufacturer, authority) and omit or limit others (user, repairer, second life operator, recycler...). Related to the reduced supply chain, we also have reduced data availability. Only data from the battery cell production process will be generated as part of BatWoMan, complemented by external data from materials sourcing and estimated data on sustainability from the life cycle assessment. Data related to the usage phase, to the batteries' second life or even from assembled batteries past battery cells (e.g. modules or packs) are not directly included. However, data relevant to the recycling phase, complemented by recommendations on the recycling route, will be included via the LCA.

4. Conclusion

The BatWoMan battery passport and data sharing ecosystem might serve as a validation testbed for battery research and production, to help prepare a suitable set of guidelines, develop best practices and promote an innovative, green battery life cycle. The goal should be to lay a good foundation with sensible standards and guidelines and an architecture that focuses on sustainability, but without a heavy bureaucratic burden on industry that would impede European innovation. Validating the emerging standards and guidelines for battery passports based on real production data is essential to prove their applicability, explore suitable concrete tools for implementation and identify issues early.

In BatWoMan, the combination of production data from pilot factories, aided by rigorous studies and investigation concerning raw materials and the batteries' full life cycle provides an ideal testbed for such a demonstrator. The design for the battery dataspace and passport outlined in this paper provides the basis for a flexible, interoperable implementation within the BatWoMan project and fosters knowledge sharing within and beyond the digital passport and dataspace communities.

Acknowledgement

The work leading to this publication is part of the BatWoMan project, funded by the European Union's Horizon Europe research and innovation programme under Grant Agreement no. 101069705, with additional support from the Austrian Gaia-X Hub.

References

Adisorn, T., Tholen, L., & Götz, T. (2021). Towards a Digital Product Passport Fit for Contributing to a Circular Economy. *Energies*, *14*(8), Article 8. https://doi.org/10.3390/en14082289

Bai, Y., Muralidharan, N., Sun, Y.-K., Passerini, S., Stanley Whittingham, M., & Belharouak, I. (2020). Energy and environmental aspects in recycling lithium-ion batteries: Concept of Battery Identity Global Passport. *Materials Today*, *41*, 304–315. https://doi.org/10.1016/j.mattod.2020.09.001

Battery Pass Consortium. (2023). *Battery Passport Content Guidance*. https://thebatterypass.eu

Berger, K., Schöggl, J.-P., & Baumgartner, R. J. (2022). Digital battery passports to enable circular and sustainable value chains: Conceptualization and use cases. *Journal of Cleaner Production*, *353*, 131492. https://doi.org/10.1016/j.jclepro.2022.131492

Franklin, M., Halevy, A., & Maier, D. (2005). From databases to dataspaces: A new abstraction for information management. *ACM SIGMOD Record*, *34*(4), 27–33. https://doi.org/10.1145/1107499.1107502

Harper, G., Sommerville, R., Kendrick, E., Driscoll, L., Slater, P., Stolkin, R., Walton, A., Christensen, P., Heidrich, O., Lambert, S., Abbott, A., Ryder, K., Gaines, L., & Anderson, P. (2019). Recycling lithium-ion batteries from electric vehicles. *Nature*, *575*(7781), Article 7781. https://doi.org/10.1038/s41586-019-1682-5

Luscuere, L. M. (2017). Materials Passports: Optimising value recovery from materials. *Proceedings of the Institution of Civil Engineers - Waste and Resource Management*, *170*(1), 25–28. https://doi.org/10.1680/jwarm.16.00016

Otto, B. (2022). The Evolution of Data Spaces. In B. Otto, M. ten Hompel, & S. Wrobel (Eds.), *Designing Data Spaces: The Ecosystem Approach to Competitive Advantage* (pp. 3–15). Springer International Publishing. https://doi.org/10.1007/978-3-030-93975-5_1

Peters, J. F., Baumann, M., Zimmermann, B., Braun, J., & Weil, M. (2017). The environmental impact of Li-Ion batteries and the role of key parameters – A review. *Renewable and Sustainable Energy Reviews*, *67*, 491–506. https://doi.org/10.1016/j.rser.2016.08.039

Plociennik, C., Pourjafarian, M., Nazeri, A., Windholz, W., Knetsch, S., Rickert, J., Ciroth, A., Precci Lopes, A. do C., Hagedorn, T., Vogelgesang, M., Benner, W., Gassmann, A., Bergweiler, S., Ruskowski, M., Schebek, L., & Weidenkaff, A. (2022). Towards a Digital Lifecycle Passport for the Circular Economy. *Procedia CIRP*, *105*, 122–127. https://doi.org/10.1016/j.procir.2022.02.021

United Nations. (2015). Transforming our world: The 2030 Agenda for Sustainable Development. *General Assembly Resolution A/RES/70/1*.

van Capelleveen, G., Vegter, D., Olthaar, M., & van Hillegersberg, J. (2023). The anatomy of a passport for the circular economy: A conceptual definition, vision and structured literature review. *Resources, Conservation & Recycling Advances*, *17*, 200131. https://doi.org/10.1016/j.rcradv.2023.200131

Walden, J., Steinbrecher, A., & Marinkovic, M. (2021). Digital Product Passports as Enabler of the Circular Economy. *Chemie Ingenieur Technik*, *93*(11), 1717–1727. https://doi.org/10.1002/cite.202100121

ETHICAL ASPECTS OF WORKING WITH DATA

ETHICAL ASPECTS OF WORKING WITH DATA

Anton Lisnik, Martina Kuperova

Institute of Management
Slovak University of Technology in Bratislava
anton.lisnik@stuba.sk, martina.kuperova@stuba.sk

DOI: 10.35011/IDIMT-2023-357

Keywords

Ethics, Data, ChatGPD

Abstract

New software capabilities have brought new freedom and new possibilities to mankind. The virtual interface is also a platform for collecting information and working with it. The paper asks him where and in what ways the boundary of ethics is established.

1. Introduction of topic

Rapid dynamic changes in society create pressure to increase the capacity of technologies that aim to improve the quality of services and satisfy customer needs. All these aspects are connected with prestige and competition, which distorts society in a special way, from two points of view. The first point of view is based on competition, which creates pressure on performances, and the second point of view is the examination of the ideas of customers or consumers.

The need of the consumer and the satisfaction of his desires enter this world of measurable prestige of achievements.

On the outside, a sophistic dichotomy, which in full synergy is created for the satisfaction of the client-consumer so that he has a feeling of happiness?

User utilities create the comfort of the service and the feeling that our device or interface service understands us.

Meanwhile, somewhere it is an interface that gives a definitive accent to the freedom of the user interface and the trap of information that we have offered voluntarily to the interspaces of business and learning IT technologies.

The EU GDPR directive is a legal framework that is supposed to protect client information. Formally, however, it is essentially a given consent to collect information about consumers.

Gradually setting up user interfaces creates the feeling that we are the rulers of this important information about us.

The most important errors in decision-making with fatal consequences for society, both in the past and in our time, have been ethical failures.

In the context of these historical professional experiences, we are on the verge of a time when ethical standards will be basic decision-making attributes.

The potential of self-learning software and the context of ethics

Ethical challenges in this area are the principles of survival of human dignity, his privacy and in the context of the principles of developing the "ability" of self-learning software such as e.g. GPT chat.

The constant need to set standards for work with data and information produces the creation of system standards.

The development of this activity is associated with a change in the diction of standards, which create the need to actively respond to the utilization of IT potential and to respond to changes in behaviour with the client in the information environment. Thus, our pattern of behaviour also changes.

The basic question is therefore to find a way to apply the principles of digital ethics to the area of new software interfaces and work with data. Especially nowadays, it is necessary to understand the principle of data protection.

The paper is an outline of a philosophical-ethical study on data processing using self-learning IT technology and identifying potential ethical problems of their activity.

2. Basic theoretical scope and principles of self-learning ethics

GPT is self-learning software that externally interfaces with the user as a Chatbot, which is a computer program designed to simulate conversations with human users, especially over the Internet (King, 2022).

As a source of information, Chatbots use accessible information that is in real virtual space. Chatbots select information using the Attention Mechanism, a method used in neural networks that allows the model to focus only on specific aspects of the input data when making predictions (Niu et al., 2021).

The latest generations of chatbots use a self-learning model whose methodology is built on the principle of a generative model that generates new data, as opposed to just classification or prediction based on input data (Pavlik, 2023).

The combination of these principles resulted in the Generative Pre-Trained Transformer (GPT) machine learning model, which uses unsupervised and supervised learning techniques to understand and generate human language (Radford et al., 2018).

GPT in information processing has its own internal system, which is called a language model. It is a type of artificial intelligence model that is trained to generate text that is similar to human language (MacNeil et al., 2022).

A higher way of strategies used in addition to text generation in the GPt system uses a system of multimodal neurons, which are units of an artificial neural network that are able to understand and interpret the form of an object in different modes or representations, such as images, text, and speech (Goh et al., 2021). A tool to understand in addition to information in binary, what machine code letters, characters, words, texts and contexts of texts is natural language processing, which is a field of artificial intelligence that involves the use of algorithms to analyze and interpret human language, such as text and speech, in order to extract meaning and extract useful information (Manning & Schutze, 1999).

Algorithms for understanding contexts are used supervised fine-tuning. It is a machine learning technique in which a pre-trained model is further trained on a smaller, labelled data set to improve its performance on a specific task (Lee et al., 2018). Along with the higher scholar process, this is unsupervised retraining. Lee defines it as a machine learning technique where a model is trained on a large data set without any labelled examples, allowing it to learn the underlying structure and patterns in the data. (Lee et al., 2018).

ChatGPT has a Transfer learning capability that uses knowledge gained from one task to improve its performance on another, related task (Lee et al., 2018).

2.1. Ethical contexts of ChatGPT

From the legal norms and regulations, we could summarize the following basic principles:

1. Respect confidentiality: It is important to protect the personal and sensitive data of individuals and organizations. Therefore, all data must be confidential and must not be provided to unauthorized persons.
2. Obtain Consent: Data must be collected with the informed consent of the individuals and organizations from which it originates. This means explaining the purposes for which the data is collected, how it will be used and who will have access to it.
3. Use data ethically: Data should only be used for legitimate purposes and in accordance with the law. This includes not using data to discriminate against, harm or exploit individuals or organisations.
4. Practice data accuracy: Data must be accurate, current and reliable. It is the responsibility of the data processor to ensure that the data is not manipulated, distorted or misused in any way.
5. Minimizing harm: Data processors should strive to minimize harm to individuals and organizations when collecting, analyzing and sharing data. This includes ensuring that data is secure and not used to abuse or harm anyone.
6. Protect privacy: Data must be handled in a manner that respects the privacy of individuals and organizations. This includes taking measures to protect data from unauthorized access, modification or destruction.
7. Responsible data sharing: Data processors should share data with others in a responsible and ethical manner, with due regard for the privacy and confidentiality of participants.
8. Adhere to ethical principles: All data processors should adhere to ethical principles, including transparency, honesty, integrity and adherence to professional standards.

"These rules are also an ethical framework for working with data in virtual space".

I have made sure that I am not biased, discriminatory or harmful in any way. Here are some ethical principles that guide my interactions with people:

By following these ethical principles, I can ensure that my interactions with people are respectful, unbiased, and beneficial. (https://chatgpt.org/chat) online 23/04/2023

3. Discussion

If we talk about the ethical aspects of using the GPD Chabot, we are talking about the confrontation of the human desire for information and the ethics of using these tools.

The communication interface of Chatbots is a meeting of artificial intelligence with human expressions that leaves a person in a virtual space. While artificial intelligence recognizes formal external signs such as letters, gathered into words, which a person understands not only technically (can read them, i.e. identify them), a person understands their meaning and also many nuances of meaning. Artificial intelligence is able to learn the mutual combination of these technically speaking signs, but it is very difficult to learn the correct use of words and their meanings in contexts, i.e. in sentences and articles. Despite the perfectly mastered content meaning of individual characters, he is unable to learn their semantic meaning, because not everyone who puts message texts into the virtual space uses words and their meaning. Thus, learning software is influenced not only by correct information, but also by incorrect information.

Here we encounter two so-called problems that significantly affect the quality of learning software outputs.

1. Personalized capacity of the author of the texts.

The Internet is a public space to which every person has access, and with the help of many social networks or cloud spaces, he inserts many forms of contexts into this space. In addition to "technical" information, it also contains an interpreted opinion context, circumstances of the author's experience, or emotion. All expressed with the same signs (words), which for other people have a different context, a different emotion or different circumstances. Here we express the fact that everyone very individually shapes the content context of words, but also of language or situations.

Furthermore, experience and expertise in the given issue are a very important factor. Education in the given issue. Will in making decisions.

2. Intentional sharing of information in relation to influencing the frequency of information.

This problem is critically influenced by two factors. 1 factor is the goal of the author's activity, which he wants to achieve and 2. factor is the reason (purpose) of what the author wants to achieve.

Goals are set by a person himself, by his own decision. This motivation is usually a person's internal motivation. It reflects his inner qualities acquired through upbringing, education, but also from the social environment. It can also be an external motivation that affects a person's internal decision, which he can take freely or not freely under the influence of various external circumstances but also internal circumstances such as fear.

Both internal and external motivations are confronted with a person's personality and his experience. They are either regulated so that one acts either ethically or morally, or accelerated for the same reasons.

Instead of the ethicality of the action, an equally legitimate reason can be an unethical or amoral action, which may be illegal, or it may also be legal. (Ethics and legality is a social agreement. Morality is an established norm that is not subject to social changes or agreements).

The goal of the action also determines the ethics or morality of the act. The question arises: is self-learning software able to recognize and assess this quality?

The reason or purposefulness of a person's action can, just as in ethical and moral systems, even social systems (e.g. legal systems), in addition to changing the ethics of the act, also change the consequence - that is, the sanction after the act has been committed. They can multiply it and increase the consequences, or they can "soften" it, i.e. reduce or cancel the consequences of the deed.

Again, there is the question of whether the self-learning software can identify these facts.

Because if, according to his programmed ability, he identifies a lot of repeated or occurring information in the context of the subsequent dissemination of information, then the purposeful decision of the author or the authors of vital contexts can mean deliberate manipulation of information in order to achieve his own truth. It is difficult to change the consequences of these decisions, manipulation, or populism, or knowledge. Because the more the information appears, the more it will seem relevant and realistic or even true from the point of view of the software. We see this in disinformation activities in the viral space.

Both of these contexts are an important element that affects both the quality of the information and the truthfulness of the information - that is, the ethics of the information.

There is a confrontation between the objective (which is nevertheless relatively linked to the objectivity of knowledge and the ability to share knowledge as information to others) with the subjectivity of the incidence of information, which may not be objective or true in the entire context, even though it is the most numerous.

From the above, the ethics of information has a broader, more contextual problem. And whether the software is able to understand that often published information may not be true. If it is not true, whether it is able to recognize. If he were able to recognize her, by what can he identify her (What is the standard of truth)? If it does identify and compare it, to what extent does it select the attributes of truth? If he chooses the attributes of truthfulness, then according to what does he evaluate the quality of the output of the author of the truth? Is it education? Or the most cited information, or is it expertise with experience?

The Chatbot itself (self-learning software) has its own internal regulations, which it follows, because a person implemented them in its "IT DNA", which is influenced by the creator and later influenced by content creators.

In the Core of Work section, we asked the Chat GPT program (https://chatgpt.org/chat) two questions.

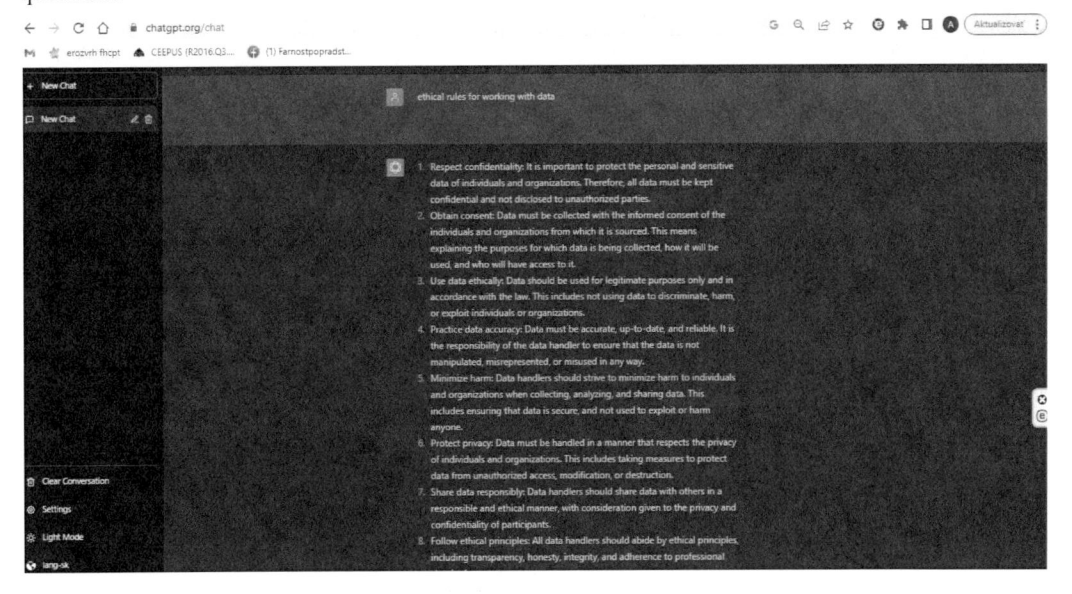

Figure 1. Ethical rules for working with data

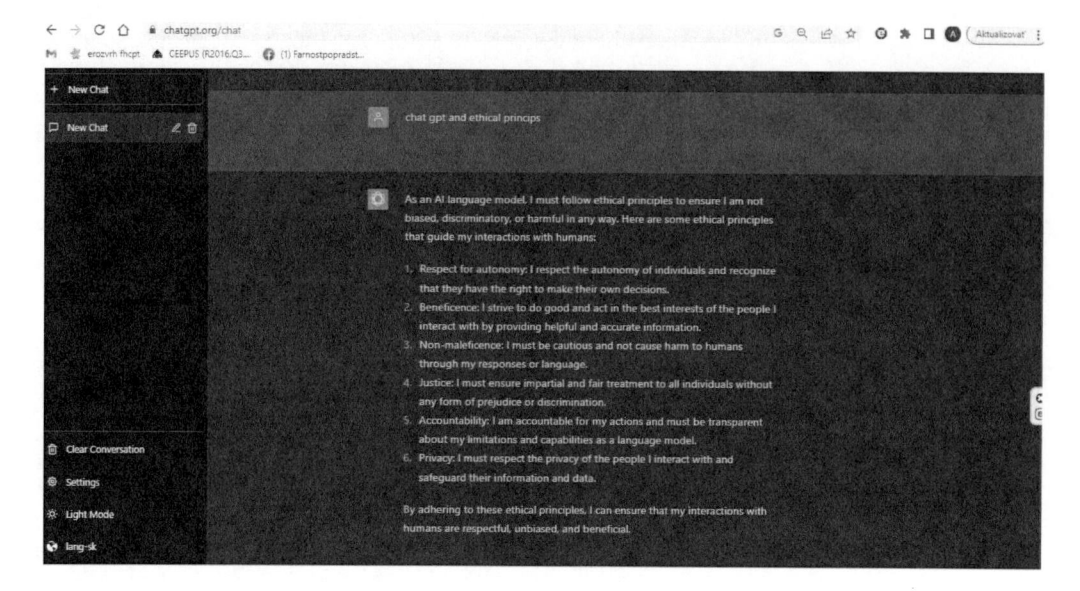

Figure 2. chat gpt and ethical princips

It is clear from the given answers that there is a self-regulating ethical aspect of a self-learning program. Considering the context of values created by man to protect them when working with data, the most serious question arises here. How can my virtual space be identified with my habits of working in the virtual space if I myself can shape it according to my habits of my behaviour if he himself learns, that is, I teach him. In this context, who knows how to set an ethical framework for me as well as for the self-learning software?

This basic principled question somehow merges with my understanding of quantum mechanics interpreting the definition of the position of the electron in the atomic shell.

4. Conclusion

The suitability of knowing this kind of experience is in the final statement that the ethics of the virtual space, despite the established principles, changes by examining (entering questions) the client for the virtual space of chat bots.

I don't know if we can determine the content of the ethical rules for working with data, but I know that based on the principles of quantum mechanics applied to the self-learning IT space, by looking at them and looking for them, we can define the principles in our user interface. So, again, it's just a matter of a person's ethics.

References

Goh, G., Cammarata, N., Voss, C., Carter, S., Petrov, M., Schubert, L., Radford, A., & Olah, C. (2021). *Multimodal neurons in artificial neural networks*. Retrieved from https://doi.org/10.23915/distill.00030

King, M. R. (2022). The future of AI in medicine: A perspective from a chatbot. *Annals of Biomedical Engineering.* https://doi.org/10.1007/s10439-022-03121-w

Lee, C., Panda, P., Srinivasan, G., & Roy, K. (2018). Training deep spiking convolutional neural networks with STDP-based unsupervised pre-training followed by supervised fine-tuning. *Frontiers in Neuroscience, 12*, article 435.

MacNeil, S., Tran, A., Mogil, D., Bernstein, S., Ross, E., & Huang, Z. (2022). Generating diverse code explanations using the GPT-3 large language model. *Proceedings of the ACM Conference on International Computing Education Research, 2*, 37-39.

Manning, C., & Schutze, H. (1999). *Foundations of statistical natural language processing*. MIT Press.

Niu, Z., Zhong, G., & Yu, H. (2021). A review on the attention mechanism of deep learning. *Neurocomputing, 452*, 48-62.

Pavlik, J. V. (2023). Collaborating with ChatGPT: Considering the implications of generative artificial intelligence for journalism and media education. *Journalism and Mass Communication Educator*. https://doi.org/10.1177/10776958221149577

Radford, A., Narasimhan, K., Salimans, T., & Sutskever, I. (2018). *Improving language understanding by generative pre-training*. Retrieved from https://www.cs.ubc.ca/~amuham01/LING530/papers/radford2018improving.pdf

ETHICAL IMPLICATIONS OF ARTIFICIAL INTELLIGENCE DATA USAGE: A CASE STUDY OF SLOVAKIA AND GLOBAL PERSPECTIVES

Ivan Katrenčík, Boris Mucha, Monika Zatrochová

Institute of Management
Slovak University of Technology in Bratislava
ivan.katrencik@stuba.sk, boris.mucha@stuba.sk, monika.zatrochova@stuba.sk

DOI: 10.35011/IDIMT-2023-365

Keywords

ChatGPT, artificial intelligence, legislation, AI data, data ownership

Abstract

Artificial intelligence (AI) is becoming increasingly integrated into various aspects of our lives, from personal assistants to self-driving cars. With this integration comes the ethical responsibility of how AI data is collected, stored, and used. In Slovakia and around the world, there are ongoing debates about who owns the data created by AI, with some arguing that it should be owned by the individuals or organizations that produced it and others arguing that it should be treated as a public good. There are also concerns about bias and discrimination in AI data and algorithms, as well as the potential for AI to be used for harmful purposes. As the use of AI continues to grow, it is important to address these ethical issues and ensure that AI is developed and used in a way that aligns with our societal values and principles. In Slovakia, there is currently no specific legislation governing the use of AI, although the General Data Protection Regulation (GDPR) provides some guidance on data privacy. However, there is a need for further discussion and regulation on the ethical use of AI data, especially as the technology continues to advance. This paper will explore the ethical aspects of using AI data in Slovakia and around the world, including ownership, bias and discrimination, and potential harms, and discuss potential solutions and frameworks for addressing these issues.

1. Introduction

Artificial intelligence (AI) has become a popular technology in recent years, and has found a range of applications across various industries. One such application is in the development of conversational agents like ChatGPT, which use natural language processing to interact with users and provide them with information or assistance. According to a report by Research and Markets (2019), the global market for conversational AI is expected to grow significantly in the coming years, driven by factors such as the increasing demand for virtual assistants and chatbots.

The use of artificial intelligence in conversational agents like ChatGPT has the potential to revolutionize the way businesses interact with their customers. As noted by a report by McKinsey (2018), chatbots and virtual assistants can help companies reduce customer service costs, improve response times, and enhance the overall customer experience. However, the use of AI also raises ethical and legal concerns, particularly with regard to data privacy and security.

As AI technology continues to evolve and become more sophisticated, its potential applications are likely to grow. Conversational agents like ChatGPT are just one example of how AI can be used to improve customer service and enhance the user experience. However, it is important for businesses to be aware of the legal and ethical considerations associated with the use of AI, and to ensure that they comply with applicable laws and regulations (Lisnik *et al.*, 2020). AI can be used also in e-learning system and other Learning Management Systems (Kuperova & Zatrochová, 2019).

There are several ethical aspects to consider when working with AI, such as ChatGPT. Here are some key ethical considerations:

1. *Bias:* One of the key ethical considerations when working with AI is the issue of bias. AI systems can perpetuate biases if the data used to train them is biased. This can result in unfair treatment of certain groups of people. It is important to ensure that AI systems are developed using diverse and representative data sets and are regularly audited for bias (Agrawal, Gans, & Goldfarb, 2021; Buolamwini & Gebru, 2018). Unintentional discrimination and unconsious bias in the training data that develops AI systems can have impact for instance in decision-making in the hiring process assisted by AI system. When developing algorithms and training data for AI systems, the risk must be kept in mind, particularly when the AI can be involved in decision-making processes about individuals or marginalized groups (Coudry *et al.* 2023).

2. *Privacy:* Another ethical consideration when working with AI is privacy. AI systems often rely on large amounts of data to operate, which can include personal information. It is important to protect individuals' privacy and ensure that their data is collected and used in an ethical manner (Agrawal *et al.*, 2021; Mittelstadt *et al.*, 2016).

3. *Transparency:* AI systems can be complex and difficult to understand, which can make it hard to determine how decisions are being made. It is important to ensure that AI systems are transparent and provide explanations for their decisions (Burrell, 2016; Mittelstadt *et al.*, 2016).

4. *Responsibility:* It is important to consider who is responsible for the decisions made by AI systems. Developers, users, and other stakeholders should take responsibility for ensuring that AI is used in an ethical and responsible manner (Bostrom & Yudkowsky, 2014; Floridi, 2019).

These ethical considerations highlight the need for responsible and ethical development and deployment of AI systems, such as ChatGPT. It is important for developers, users, and other stakeholders to consider these aspects and work towards creating ethical and responsible AI systems.

According to a study conducted by the European Commission in (2021), around 42% of large European companies reported using AI technologies in their business processes. The most common applications of AI in these companies were predictive maintenance, quality control, and demand forecasting. The study also found that smaller companies and those in certain sectors, such as healthcare and education, were less likely to use AI.

Another report by PwC in 2020 found that the adoption of AI in Central and Eastern Europe, which includes Slovakia, was lower than in Western Europe. However, the report noted that the region had a growing interest in AI and its potential benefits, such as increased efficiency and productivity.

2. Use of data generated by artificial intelligence

In terms of data protection, Slovakia follows the European Union's General Data Protection Regulation (GDPR) which requires companies to protect the personal data of individuals. This is relevant to the use of AI tools as they often require access to personal data to function properly.

In Slovakia, there are currently no specific regulations or laws governing the use of artificial intelligence in general or specifically tools like ChatGPT. However, there are several laws and regulations that may apply to AI in certain contexts, such as:

- Personal Data Protection Act: Act No. 18/2018 Coll. This law regulates the collection, processing, and storage of personal data, including data that may be collected and used by AI systems.
- Labour Code: Act No. 311/2001 Coll. This law sets out the rights and obligations of employees and employers, and may apply to situations where AI is used in the workplace.
- Consumer Protection Act: Act No. 250/2007 Coll. This law protects consumers from unfair or deceptive practices, which may include the use of AI to manipulate consumer behavior.
- Criminal Code: Act No. 300/2005: This law includes provisions that may apply to the use of AI in criminal activities, such as hacking or identity theft.
- Civil Code: Act No. 40/1964. This law governs civil law matters, including liability for harm caused by AI systems.
- Copyright Act: Act No. 185/2015 Coll:
    - Content creation: AI algorithms can be used to create original works of art, literature, music, and other types of content. The question of who owns the copyright to these works, the creator or the developer of the AI, may arise.
    - Copyright infringement: AI can be used to detect and prevent copyright infringement, such as identifying pirated content or unauthorized use of copyrighted material.
    - Licensing: AI can be used to manage licenses for copyrighted works, such as determining the terms and conditions of use and enforcing compliance.
    - Fair use: AI can be used to analyze and determine whether a particular use of copyrighted material falls under the doctrine of fair use or other exceptions to copyright protection.

The question of who owns the data created by AI can be complex and may depend on various factors such as the type of data, the context in which it was created, and the legal framework in the relevant jurisdiction. In general, there are different views on this issue. Some argue that the data created by AI should be owned by the individuals or organizations that produced it, while others argue that the data should be treated as a public good that is owned by society as a whole.

The question of whether the data produced by AI should be owned by individuals or organizations that produced it or treated as a public good is a matter of ongoing debate and does not have a definitive answer. Different stakeholders hold varying perspectives on this issue.

Advocates for individual or organizational ownership argue that those who invest resources and efforts into generating the data should have control over its use. They emphasize the rights of individuals or entities to benefit financially or otherwise from their data assets. This perspective aligns with traditional notions of property rights and incentivizing innovation.

On the other hand, proponents of treating data as a public good contend that certain types of data, particularly those generated by AI systems, hold societal value. They argue that considering data as a collective resource allows for broader access, innovation, and addressing societal challenges. This viewpoint often emphasizes the importance of data sharing, open science, and promoting the public interest.

Ultimately, the approach to data ownership in the context of AI depends on various factors, including legal frameworks, cultural values, and specific use cases. It requires striking a balance between individual rights, economic considerations, and the broader societal impact of data access and utilization. As technology and societal norms evolve, ongoing discussions and thoughtful considerations are necessary to shape appropriate regulations and policies around data ownership and access.

There are also legal frameworks that provide guidance on this issue. For example, in the European Union, the General Data Protection Regulation (GDPR) establishes that individuals have certain rights with respect to their personal data, including the right to access, rectify, and erase their data. The GDPR also imposes certain obligations on data controllers and processors with respect to the collection, use, and storage of personal data. Overall, the question of who owns the data created by AI is still subject to debate and may require further clarification from lawmakers and regulators.

In the world there are several approaches and legislative frameworks for the protection of personal data that can also be applied to artificial intelligence. Some of them are:

- In the European Union, the General Data Protection Regulation (GDPR) recognizes the right of individuals to own and control their personal data, including data generated by AI systems. Article 20 of the GDPR grants individuals the right to receive a copy of their personal data in a structured, machine-readable format, and to transmit that data to another controller without hindrance. (Source: European Union. (2016). General Data Protection Regulation. Official Journal of the European Union, L119/1-L119/88.)

- In the United States, the concept of data ownership is not explicitly recognized in federal law. However, some state laws, such as the California Consumer Privacy Act (CCPA), give individuals certain rights over their personal data, including the right to know what data is being collected, the right to request that data be deleted, and the right to opt out of the sale of their data. (Source: California Legislative Information. (2018). California Consumer Privacy Act of 2018. Assembly Bill No. 375.)

- In the United Kingdom, the Centre for Data Ethics and Innovation (CDEI) was established in 2018 to advise the government on the ethical use of data and AI. In its report "AI and Data Ownership, Rights and Controls", the CDEI recommends that data generated by AI systems should be treated as a public good, but that individuals should have the right to control how their personal data is used. (Source: Centre for Data Ethics and Innovation. (2020). AI and Data Ownership, Rights and Controls. Report.)

- In China, the Cybersecurity Law, which went into effect in 2017, requires network operators to obtain user consent before collecting, using, or disclosing personal information, including data generated by AI systems. The law also requires network operators to adopt technical measures to protect personal information and to report data breaches to the authorities and affected individuals. (Source: National People's Congress. (2017). Cybersecurity Law of the People's Republic of China.)

- In Canada, The Canadian government has developed the Directive on Automated Decision-Making, which provides guidelines for the ethical and accountable use of AI within the public sector. The directive emphasizes fairness, transparency, and human rights considerations. This framework provides guidance for federal institutions on the responsible implementation and management of AI systems within the public sector. Key aspects are:
    - Ethical Principles: The framework emphasizes the importance of upholding ethical principles in AI systems, such as fairness, transparency, human rights, accountability, and avoiding bias and discrimination. It highlights the need for AI systems to align with Canadian values and legal obligations.
    - Risk Assessment: The directive encourages federal institutions to conduct risk assessments when deploying AI systems. This involves evaluating the potential impacts of AI on individuals, groups, and society, including any privacy or security risks associated with the use of personal data.
    - Human Oversight: The framework emphasizes the importance of maintaining human oversight in decision-making processes involving AI systems. It recognizes that human judgement should be present to ensure accountability, prevent undue reliance on AI algorithms, and allow for intervention or correction if necessary.
    - Transparency and Explainability: The Canadian framework promotes transparency and explainability in AI systems. It encourages federal institutions to provide clear and understandable explanations about how AI decisions are made, ensuring that individuals can understand and challenge the outcomes.
    - Privacy and Data Protection: The directive highlights the need to respect privacy and protect personal information when implementing AI systems. It emphasizes compliance with relevant privacy laws and regulations, ensuring that data collection, storage, and processing align with established privacy principles. (Directive on Automated Decision-Making, 2023).

The Canadian framework for AI, such as the Directive on Automated Decision-Making, is designed to provide guidance specifically for federal institutions within the Canadian context. While the principles and considerations outlined in the framework can serve as a valuable reference for other countries, the direct implementation of the Canadian framework in Slovakia may not be applicable.

Each country has its own legal and regulatory framework, cultural context, and specific requirements when it comes to AI governance and implementation. Slovakia would need to develop its own tailored approach to address the ethical and accountable use of AI based on its unique circumstances, legal system, and policy priorities.

At the time of writing, the EU is negotiating to adopt one of the first rules to regulate AI and to ensure a human-centric and ethical development of AI. The proposed regulation aim to ensure that AI systems are overseen by people, are safe, transparent, traceable, non-discriminatory, and environmentally friendly. They also want to have a uniform definition for AI designed to be technology-neutral, so that it can apply to the AI systems of today and tomorrow. The regulations follow a risk-based approach and establish obligations for providers and users depending on the level of risk the AI can generate. AI systems with an unacceptable level of risk to people's safety would be strictly prohibited, including systems that deploy subliminal or purposefully manipulative techniques, exploit people's vulnerabilities or are used for social scoring (classifying people based on their social behaviour, socio-economic status, personal characteristics). (European Parliament, 2023). The proposed rules will:

- address risks specifically created by AI applications;
- propose a list of high-risk applications;
- set clear requirements for AI systems for high risk applications;
- define specific obligations for AI users and providers of high risk applications;
- propose a conformity assessment before the AI system is put into service or placed on the market;
- propose enforcement after such an AI system is placed in the market;
- propose a governance structure at European and national level (European Commission, 2023).

The proposal is part of a wider AI package, which also includes the updated Coordinated Plan on AI. Together, the Regulatory framework and Coordinated Plan will guarantee the safety and fundamental rights of people and businesses when it comes to AI. And, they will strengthen uptake, investment and innovation in AI across the EU. A risk-based approach is in this regulatory framework divides the AI n 4 groups:

- Unacceptable risk – clear threat to the safety, livelihoods and rights of people,
- High risk – AI technology used in critical infrastructures, education, employment and management of workers, essential private and public services, law enforcement, migration and border control management, administration of justice and democratic processes. This AI system will be subject to strict obligations before they can by put on the market.
- Limited risk – for example chatbots. Users should be aware that they are interacting with a machine so he can take an informed decision,
- Minimal or no risk – free use AI, such as video games, spam filters and so on (European Commission, 2023).

In September 2022, the European Commission published a proposal for a directive on adapting a non-contractual civil liability rules to AI, called AILD – Artificial Intelligence Liability Directive. The Commission proposes to complement and modernise the EU liability framework to introduce new rules specific to damages caused by AI systems. The new rules intend to ensure that persons harmed by AI systems enjoy the same level of protection as persons harmed by other technologies in the EU. The purpose of the AI liability directive is to improve the functioning of the internal market by laying down uniform requirements for non-contractual civil liability for damage caused with the involvement of AI systems. The new rules would apply to damage caused by AI systems, irrespective of whether they are defined as high-risk or not under the AI act (Artificial intelligence liability directive, 2023).

If these regulations pass all the necessary legislative processes within the EU institutions, Slovakia will have to accept them (regulation) or transpose them (directive). In Slovakia, AI policies are part of digitalization strategy - Action plan for the digital transformation of Slovakia for 2019-2022. This action plan contains concrete steps to build a sustainable, human-centric, and trustworthy AI ecosystem within the long-term which follows up the Strategy of the Digital Transformation of Slovakia 2030.

In general, the Slovak Government advocates the creation of a goal-oriented and dynamic regulation that leaves more freedom for experimentation. On the other hand, building trustworthy AI systems require proper ethical guidelines. In Slovakia, these purposes are implemented through:

- principles for a transparent and ethical use of AI – this policy was launched by the Ministry of Investments, Regional Development and Informatisation (MIRRI) and the Ministry of Economy. This will include:
    - launch of a public survey to obtain the point of view of citizens and companies on ethical AI that can help policy makers to define ethical guidelines,
    - appointing members of the Standing Committee on Ethics and Regulation of AI (CERAI),
    - collaborates with international and European platforms, such as the Ad hoc Committee on AI (CAHAI),
- development of a legal framework for data – preparation of a new Act on Data,
- revision of the regulatory environment for AI – advisory group consisting of experts form academia, business and government,
- coordination of national efforts across ministries and public bodies in response to the published EEU proposal for a legal framework on AI (AI Watch, 2021).

3. Conclusion

In conclusion, the use of AI data presents various ethical implications, including issues related to privacy, data ownership, bias, and compliance with existing legislation. While there are ongoing debates around whether AI data should be owned by individuals or organizations that produce it or treated as a public good owned by society as a whole, there is a growing consensus that the responsible and ethical use of AI data is essential. This is reflected in the efforts of global institutions such as the European Union and national governments such as Slovakia to establish regulatory frameworks that protect the rights and interests of individuals and society as a whole. It is clear that as the use of AI continues to expand in Slovakia and around the world, it is crucial to address the ethical implications of AI data and ensure that it is used in ways that benefit society as a whole while respecting individual rights and interests.

Acknowledgment

The contribution is a partial output of the KEGA research task no. 011STU-4/2022 "Creating a model of education supporting the increase of competencies of students of a non-economically oriented university in the field of innovative, entrepreneurial thinking and business support" conducted at the Institute of Management of the STU in Bratislava.

References

Agrawal, A., Gans, J., & Goldfarb, A. (2021). Economic policy for artificial intelligence. Journal of Business Research, 122, 211-222.

Ai Watch. (2021). National strategies on Artificial Intelligence. A European perspective. ISBN 978-92-76-39081-7.

Albawi, S., & Al-Badawi, I. (2020). A survey on deep learning techniques for artificial intelligence. Journal of Big Data, 7(1), 1-33.

Amodei, D., Olah, C., Steinhardt, J., Christiano, P., Schulman, J., & Mané, D. (2016). Concrete problems in AI safety. arXiv preprint arXiv:1606.06565.

Artificial intelligence liability directive. (2023). Retrieved June 8, 2023, from https://www.europarl.europa.eu/RegData/etudes/BRIE/2023/739342/EPRS_BRI(2023)739342_EN.pdf

Bostrom, N., & Yudkowsky, E. (2014). The ethics of artificial intelligence. In The Cambridge handbook of artificial intelligence (pp. 316-334). Cambridge University Press.

Buolamwini, J., & Gebru, T. (2018). Gender shades: Intersectional accuracy disparities in commercial gender classification. Conference on Fairness, Accountability and Transparency, 77-91.

Burrell, J. (2016). How the machine 'thinks': Understanding opacity in machine learning algorithms. Big Data & Society, 3(1), 1-12.

Directive on Automated Decision-Making. (2023). Canda.ca. Retrieved June 8, 2023, from https://www.tbs-sct.canada.ca/pol/doc-eng.aspx?id=32746

European Commission. (2021). European business use of artificial intelligence: A survey on the results. https://ec.europa.eu/digital-single-market/en/news/european-business-use-artificial-intelligence-survey-results

European Commssion. (2023). Regulatory framework proposal on artificial intelligence. Retrieved June 8, 2023, from https://digital-strategy.ec.europa.eu/en/policies/regulatory-framework-ai

European Parliament. (2023). AI Act: a step closer to the first rules on Artificial Intelligence. Retrieved June 8, 2023, from https://www.europarl.europa.eu/news/en/press-room/20230505IPR84904/ai-act-a-step-closer-to-the-first-rules-on-artificial-intelligence.

Floridi, L. (2019). The logic of information: A theory of philosophy as conceptual design. Oxford University Press.

Choudhry, M., Wall, N., Reynolds, M. (2023). Guide to artificial intelligence regulation in Canada. Torys.com. Retrieved June 6, 2023, from https://www.torys.com/our-latest-thinking/publications/2023/04/guide-to-artificial-intelligence-regulation-in-canada

Jain, A., Soni, S., & Sharma, A. (2019). A review on applications of artificial intelligence in mechanical engineering. Journal of Mechanical Engineering Research and Developments, 42(2), 43-54.

Kuperová, M., Zatrochová, M. (2019). E-learning as an innovative method of education. In Trends and innovative approaches in business processes 2019. 126-132.

Lisnik, A., Janičková, J., Zimermanová, K. (2020). Biometric systems and thei use in social networks. IDIMT-2020: digitalized economy, society and information management. 253-258.

McKinsey. (2018). The business value of design. from: https://www.mckinsey.com/capabilities/mckinsey-design/our-insights/the-business-value-of-design

Mittelstadt, B. D., Allo, P., Taddeo, M., Wachter, S., & Floridi, L. (2016). The ethics of algorithms: Mapping the debate. Big Data & Society, 3(2), 2053951716679679.

PwC. (2020). AI in CEE: A regional approach to unlocking the potential. https://www.pwc.com/gx/en/industries/technology/publications/ai-cee-unlocking-the-potential.html

Research and Markets. (2019). Conversational AI Market by Component, Type, Technology, Application, Deployment Mode, Organization Size, Vertical And Region - Global Forecast to 2024.

Russell, S., & Norvig, P. (2020). Artificial intelligence: A modern approach. Pearson.

Sinha, S. K., & Yadav, R. (2019). Applications of artificial intelligence: A review. International Journal of Advanced Computer Science and Applications, 10(1), 299-305.

Slovakia (2019a). Action plan for the digital transformation of Slovakia for 2019 –2022. Government of Slovak Republic. https://www.mirri.gov.sk/wp-content/uploads/2019/10/AP-DT-English-Version-FINAL.pdf

Zatrochová, M., Majerník, M., Kuperová, M., Majerník, Š. (2019). The challenges for economic growth within the food industry. In Zeszyty Naukowe Politechniki Śląskiej. DOI10.29119/1641-3466.2019.135.20, 257-272.

SPECIFICS OF ETHICAL PRINCIPLES OF SYSTEM DATA PROTECTION IN THE SERVICE SEGMENT

Anton Lisnik, Patrik Bretz, Miroslav Warhol, Milan Majerník

Institute of Management
Slovak University of Technology in Bratislava
anton.lisnik@stuba.sk, patrik.bretz@stuba.sk, miroslav.warhol@stuba.sk,
milan.majernik@stuba.sk

DOI: 10.35011/IDIMT-2023-373

Keywords

Data, ethics, hotel services

Abstract

Each segment that works with data has exact rules and its own specifics. All data is now specially protected and is subject the EU level to rules and regulations as well as the organization's own internal regulations. A special segment is the data collected in the hotel service segment, especially about the accommodated guests. Ethics play a very important role in this segment of information. This paper focuses on the specification of ethical rules used in the service sector.

1. Introduction

The basic legal regulation is the European legislation focusing on the data handling adopted in 2018. We know it under the term GDPR, its full name is called the General Data Protection Regulation. This is the legislation of the European Union, which was supposed to significantly increase the protection of personal data of all citizens of European countries. It is intended to prevent unauthorized handling of their data and personal data. It is a set of rules that replaced other laws in individual countries. This legal framework came into force in 2018.

"GDPR considers all information about an identified or identifiable natural person to be personal data. An identifiable natural person is a natural person who can be directly or indirectly identified, especially by a certain identifier, for example a name, identification number, network identifier or by one or more special elements of the physical, physiological, genetic, psychological, economic, cultural or social identity of this person natural person." (Ministry of the Interior of the Czech Republic, 2020).

2. Legal processing of peronal data

The basic problem in this legislation is that all these data speak not only about accommodated guests, but should also be a subject to special regulation because they can fall into a special category, as they can identify e.g. religious, political or sexual orientation. These data fall under a special regime. "However, there are special categories of personal data, which include genetic data, biometric data, health data, personal data that reveal racial or ethnic origin, political opinions, religious or philosophical beliefs, trade union membership, sex life or sexual orientation of a physical person." (Marková Hana, 2018).

According to Pavlovič (2017), in terms of Art. 6, par. 1 GDPR, processing is legal only if one of the following conditions is met:

- the person concerned has expressed his consent to the processing of his personal data,
- processing is necessary for contract performance,
- processing is necessary to fulfil the legal requirement of the operator,
- processing is necessary to protect the vital interests of the person concerned,
- processing is necessary to fulfil a task in the public interest,
- legitimate interest.

The European Data Protection Board (EDPB) is an independent EU body with legal personality, which contributes to the consistent application of data protection rules throughout EU, and supports cooperation between EU authorities for the protection of personal data. It was created according to Art. 68 GDPR and is the successor of the Working Group on Data Protection, WP29.

Tasks and duties:

- provide general guidelines to clarify the GDPR,
- provide advice in any matter related to the protection of personal data,
- to accept consistency findings in cross-border data protection cases,
- promote cooperation and effective exchange of information and best practices between national supervisory authorities.

Based on EU data protection rules, data should be processed fairly and lawfully for specified and legitimate purposes, and only data that is necessary to fulfil this purpose should be processed.

To process personal data, one of the following conditions is required:

- the consent of the person concerned,
- personal data are necessary for the fulfilment of contractual obligations towards the person concerned,
- personal data is necessary to fulfil a legal obligation,
- personal data is necessary to protect the vital interests of the person concerned,
- personal data are processed for the purpose of execute a task in the public interest,
- is carried out in the legitimate interests of its company as long as the fundamental rights and freedoms of the person whose data are processed are not seriously affected. If the rights of the person concerned prevail over the interests of the company, the personal data cannot be processed.

Ethics are not treated, and, in the future, we see this phenomenon as a potential ethical problem as well as working with data also in other forms such as e.g., e-learning. (Kuperová, Zatrochová, 2019). Ethical work with data is a basic prerequisite for building financial literacy. (Katrenčik, Zatrochová, 2022).

3. Implementation

According to the Office of Personal Data (2023), personal data processing means performing operations or a set of operations with personal data, starting with their acquisition and ending with disposal. The Personal Data Protection Act enumerates some of the most frequently performed processing operations, such as obtaining, collecting, disseminating, recording, organizing, processing, or changing, searching, browsing, rearranging, combining, moving, using, storing, blocking, disposal, their cross-border transfer, providing, making available or publishing.

Businessmen are obliged to provide an accurate calculation of the specific purposes for which the data is processed. At the same time, consent to the processing of personal data for the purpose of sending commercial information must not be conditioned, for example, on the conclusion of a purchase contract or the sending of an order. It must not even be included in the business terms and conditions.

Active consent then means that the box with consent to send commercial notifications must be empty and it is up to the user to consciously click it off." (Fišerová Kateřina, 2018).

3.1. Marketing communication

According to the GDPR SLOVAKIA (2023), it is possible to send a newsletter to existing customers without their express consent. The newsletter must be related to goods or services that have already been ordered from the merchant. If someone buys a t-shirt, a promotional offer for sweatshirts, pants or shoes can be sent. However, you should no longer be tempted by new perfumes. Every customer can cancel the right to send newsletters, and the company must accept his decision.

The text of the consent must contain answers to the following questions:
- which data I collect,
- who am I and who else processes them,
- for what purpose,
- for how long (indefinitely is not possible),
- what rights does the person whose personal data I process have.

The company to which the selected enterprise belongs processes personal data in accordance with Regulation 2016/679 GDPR on the protection of natural persons in the processing of personal data and on the free movement of such data and Act No. 18/2018 Coll. on the protection of personal data and on amendments and additions to certain laws, has developed security measures that are regularly updated.

The selected company, as an accommodation facility, processes personal data for the purpose of:
- Accommodation reservations
- Reservation of services

- Orders for goods
- Processing of accounting documents
- Complaints
- Debt collection
- Execution
- Records of job applicants
- Communications via "Newsletter"
- Monitoring of premises for the purpose of property protection
- Records of representatives of suppliers and customers

All obtained personal data can be managed or deleted based on prior consent. According to the law, the affected person has the right to withdraw consent, most often in electronic form, he also has the right to access data, the right to correction, the right to limit processing, the right to the accuracy of data, or the right to object.

4. Storage and processing of data in a selected hotel-type enterprise

The first is the reservation and sales channel, which addresses clients both before arrival and after departure. This method of communication is very important, as it fulfils the task of confirming the reservation, requesting changes, or sending the necessary documents. After leaving, the client is also approached for feedback with a satisfaction questionnaire. This form is used for the so-called necessary communication with clients. It is archived, but no further work is done with it, which we perceive as unused potential. This database is acquired based on online shopping on the hotel's website.

The second form of the database is already with the consent of the clients. Consent from the client is confirmed by default with a handwritten signature at the hotel reception, or by sending a request to register an email address for sending newsletters, i.e. news and offers. However, it should be noted that hotel clients are not actively encouraged to do so. Thus, the database is not updated continuously.

Companies in the hotel segment not only collect data, but also analyze it qualitatively and react to trends in the behaviour and behaviour of clients. To the year 2020 these data operations generated revenue growth of up to 22% it is about 1 billion euro (Nezmar, 2017).

5. Working with data

It should be noted that the selected company does not work actively with the tools available. Based on internal sources, we know that the newsletter is sent twice a month, but the database is not continuously updated with new contacts.

In the questionnaire, which was conducted in 2021-2022, we asked a sample of 150 respondents in two Tatra hotels about data related to data ethics. Respondents voluntarily and anonymously answered 10 questions. We evaluated the questions statistically and present statistically relevant answers.

Statistically, the male gender has an interesting relationship to the issue. Men are more aware of the need for security and ethical access to data than women. We can assume that it is because they are more intensively devoted to IT topics and work in the virtual space in general.

The following graph shows the answers to the question: „Would you rather connect to your own data transfers instead of connecting to Wi-Fi that collects your personal data?"

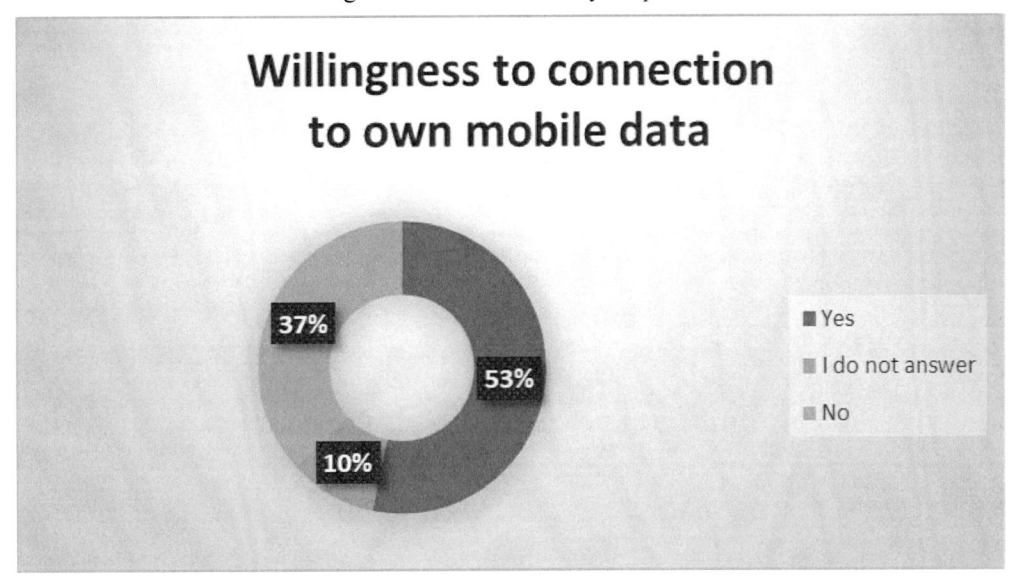

Figure 1. Willingness to connection to own mobile data Source: Own processing

Respondents answered at a statistically relevant level that they would rather choose to use their mobile data, so privacy is more important to them than sharing data about themselves.

Sharing of photos or family images on websites or Facebook pages of hotel facilities was decisive in relation to other factors in different ways.

The most relevant was the connection of not sharing the photo in connection with the social status of the client, which we examined in relation to the amount of his income, and the examination of the place where they live was equally relevant. People living in cities with more than 200,000 people were the least interested in sharing images.

6. Granting consent to the use of cookies

We received the following statistics from a professional marketing agency that manages several hotel operations. These cookies are used precisely to confirm that the website visitor is OK with the website collecting data about him and further working with it. Until the beginning of 2022, it was enough if there was information on the website that the given website collects cookies. After the change in legislation, it was necessary to modify the cookies bar so that the visitor must explicitly confirm that he can collect data. Without this consent, nothing you do on the website can be recorded.

Altogether, the data from April 2022 to April 2023, i.e. a year, shows that 477,945 unique visitors visited hotel's website. However, the number of visits was 822,368. It can be concluded that some web visitors regularly return to the hotel's website.

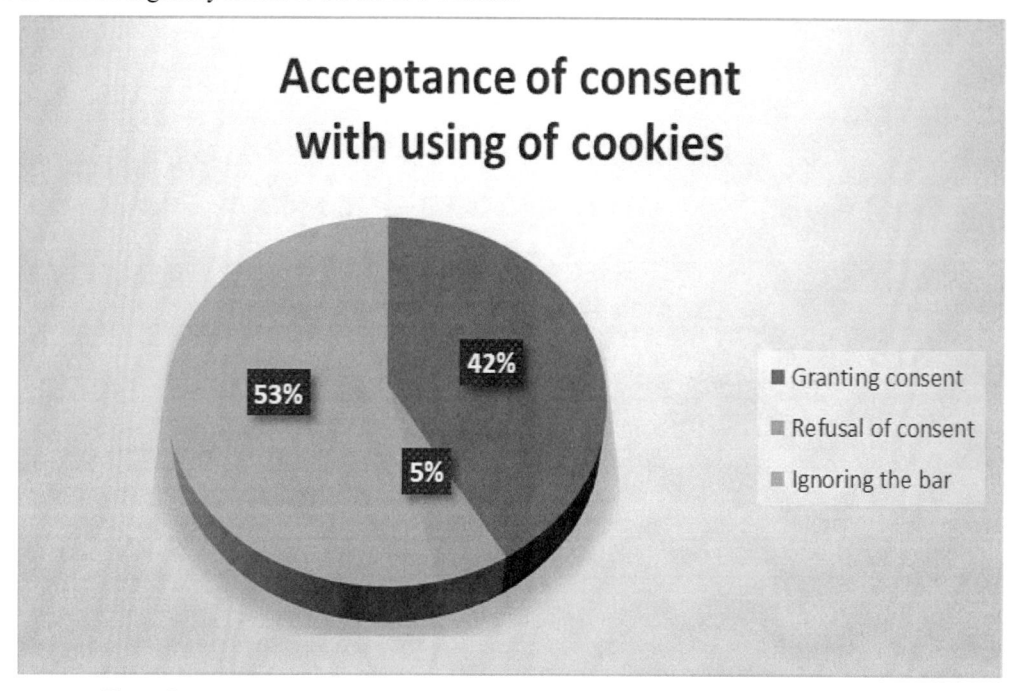

Figure 2. Acceptance of consent to the use of cookies Source: Own processing

Out of the total number of visitors, only 173,163 people agreed to the collection of cookies. Cookies were outright rejected by 20,851 people and ignored by 221,717 people, which is the largest number. Since they did not confirm the cookie bar (it does not matter whether they ignored it or explicitly indicated their disapproval), it is not possible to collect information about those visitors.

To ensure and increase the quality and safety of work in hotel services, a model of P2P nodes is proposed.

The architecture of the system is implemented through nodes which communicate through peer to peer (P2P) network. The nodes has gateway API which performs the P2P communication and enables in cooperation with the Communication Server, the Contract creation for a service. The data collected from sensors and from user are gathered from the Data Storage Service to apply consent control. The management system promotes an IoT request for a service and if the provider accepts the request, the Contract is created. Every time a communication request appears between 2 Things, the API Gateway is used to require from the Communication Server permission or denial, according to the Contracts, for the communication request. (Metalidou, 2020)

7. Conclusion

Data processing in the hotel segment is very demanding and requires very precisely developed procedures associated with protecting and working with client data.

From the research above we found out that clients have a high degree of interest in protecting their privacy. All statistically relevant answers point to the need to be very protective of these client data and to continue to maintain a high degree of freedom in the decision-making process. The client values privacy. Therefore, it is important that, from the proposed measures, we create a relationship with the client based on discretion and a sense of security, that the collected data is protected and that there is no subsequent manipulation of it beyond the law.

Among the suggestions for improving the work with data, we would mention changes in the management of the security system of hotels, where the anonymity of clients would be increased.

It is appropriate that the possibility to pay for services using cash remains, which is also connected with the legal norms of the state, which has the will to introduce the digital euro and limit payments using cash.

To make the work with the database available to the company more efficient, it is necessary to start working more actively on it and change the form of communication with clients so that the database starts to be supplemented.

We suggest using the tools available to the company. It is for example collecting email addresses by logging into the company's wifi network. Thanks to this step, they will begin to intensively supplement their database, which they will be able to address with offers.

We also recommend that the hotel reception work more actively with guests in the creation of the above mentioned database.

Clients who use hotel services connected to data must have a high degree of security. It would also be appropriate to offer information about cookies and make them more accessible to the client, not only under the information item, but perhaps create a concept of refusal by the client, and only then continue. It could possibly mean something like this: login. The client would have to refuse that he does not want to know more details about the data we process and then he could go to the hotel portal.

Acknowledgment

Contribution funded by a grant: KEGA: 023STU-4/2023.

References

GDPR-slovensko.sk. (2018). Ako zasielať newslettre v súlade s GDPR? GDPR Slovensko. https://gdpr-slovensko.sk/ako-zasielat-newslettre-v-sulade-s-gdpr/

Kancelarie.sk. (2018). GDPR: Pozor na nové pravidlá pre zber kontaktov aj využívanie existujúcich. kancelarie.sk. https://www.kancelarie.sk/poradna/gdpr-pozor-na-nove-pravidla-pre-zber-kontaktov-aj-vyuzivanie-existujucich

Katrenčik, I. & Zatrochová M. (2022). Financial Literacy and Predispositions to Study Economics: An Applied Research at a Technical University in Slovakia. In: EDULEARN22 - 14th International Conference on Education and New Learning Technologies. Palma: IATED, 2022. 574-581, ISBN 978-84-09-42484-9

Kuperová, M. & Zatrochová, M. (2019). E-learning as an innovative method of education. In: Trends and innovative approaches in business processes. Technická univerzita v Košiciach, 2019, 126-132. ISBN 978-80-553-3422-6

Marková, H. (2018). Směrnice č. 1/2018 Směrnice o ochraně osobních údajů. https://www.vojnuvmestec.cz/urad-mestysu/gdpr/smernice-c.-1/2018- smernice-o-ochrane-osobnich-udaju

MVCR. (n.d.). Základní pojmy v GDPR - Ochrana osobních údajů. https://www.mvcr.cz/gdpr/clanek/zakladni-pojmy-v-gdpr.aspx

Metalidou, C., Psannis, K. E, & Alexandropolou-Egaptiadou, E. (2020). An Efficient IoT System Respecting the GDPR. 2020. The 3rd World Symposium on Communication Engineering. IEEE, Thessaloniki, Greece, 2020. In: https://ieeexplore.ieee.org/document/9275573. DOI: 10.1109/WSCE51339.2020.9275573

Nezmar, L. (2017). GDPR: Praktický průvodce implementací. Grada Publishing, Praha. 2017. 229. ISBN: 978-80-271-0921-0

Pavlovič, T. (2017). Nová právna úprava ochrany osobných údajov. https://zlz.sk/wp-content/uploads/2018/05/Newsletter-GDPR-a-ochrana-osobn%C3%BDch-%C3%BAdajov.pdf

Úrad na ochranu osobných údajov Slovenskej republiky. (2014). Spracúvanie osobných údajov. https://dataprotection.gov.sk/uoou/sk/content/spracuvanie-osobnych-udajov

SPECIAL SESSION

EARLY CAREER & STUDENT SHOWCASE

E-PORTFOLIOS TO FOSTER REFLECTIVE LEARNING – A SYSTEMATIC LITERATURE ANALYSIS TO EXAMINE CURRENT RESEARCH

Julia Schwope, Anne Jantos

TUD Dresden University of Technology
{julia.schwope, anne.jantos,}@tu-dresden.de

DOI: 10.35011/IDIMT-2023-383

Keywords

E-Portfolio, Reflection, Higher Education, Assessment.

Abstract

Everyday life of higher education is undergoing a change that requires a shift from subject-specific to interpersonal skills such as reflection. E-portfolios as a learning and assessment method can be the answer. We show the potential of e-portfolio using a systematic literature analysis with the result that e-portfolios can foster reflective learning with holistic didactical planning and extensive support both in the learning group and by the teachers.

1. Introduction

Intrapersonal competencies like reflection are currently associated only to a limited extent with higher education teaching but are becoming increasingly relevant since future employers' value are diverse and focus on interdisciplinary competencies not primarily based on content knowledge (Dede, 2009). Higher education institutes are already implementing various new techniques to address this new demand. For example, by introducing e-portfolios as assessment methods. Portfolios are students' own stories of what they know, why they believe they know it, and why others should agree - A portfolio is opinion backed by fact (Paulson & Paulson, 1991) which promotes self-confidence, individuality, creativity, and personal responsibility (Moore, 2019). Digitization is leading to learning acceleration, and digital transformation, especially in higher education. E-portfolios are increasingly becoming part of university teaching and include visual and auditive content such as text, images, video, and sound (Abrami and Barrett, 2005; Filkins, 2010). But do they foster reflective processes in learners? And how? We aim to analyse and critically question the effect of e-portfolios on learning processes to identify new didactical opportunities and challenges. With our systematic literature analysis, we focus primarily on the aspect of reflection as it is a main concern for a student's future.

During a course of study, homework, and written and oral examinations are usually used to check how well the material has been understood (Jonassen, 1991). However, this does not provide a framework for individual development and engagement but for students to develop from passive observers to active participants, portfolios can be introduced to the curriculum (Mills-Courts & Amiran, 1991).

1.1. Portfolio Work in Higher Education

The term portfolio is defined as "A purposeful collection of student work that exhibits the student's efforts, progress, and achievement in one or more areas" (Paulson et al., 1991). Thus, it is a collection of work that a learner has gathered, selected, organized, reflected upon, and presented with the goal to show their understanding and progress (Barrett, 2006). According to Stiggins (1994), a portfolio is a means of communication about learner development, but it is not only a form of assessment - it demonstrates achievement and improvement.

1.2. E-Portfolio Work in Higher Education

Unlike traditional portfolios, e-portfolios rely on technology. This allows the individual artefacts to be organized in different media types. The result is a structuring of the material and linking of evidence to appropriate outcomes, goals, and standards (Barrett, 2006). The National Learning Infrastructure Initiative (2003) define: "An e-portfolio or electronic portfolio is a digital collection of authentic and diverse evidence, drawn from a larger archive that represents what a person has learned over time, on which the person has reflected, designed for presentation to one or more audiences for a particular rhetorical purpose". According to the QESN-RÉCIT (2004), there are five phases in the creation of an e-portfolio: collection, selection, reflection, assessment, and celebration. In the collection phase, artefacts representing successes and growth opportunities are stored. Then, in the selection phase, these are reviewed and evaluated. In the reflection phase, the learner's thoughts on each part of the portfolio are clarified. Thereby the growth of knowledge but also existing gaps are illustrated. In the assessment phase, results are compared to performance standards and goals. The final phase involves publishing the e-portfolios (Barrett, 2009). Adding technology allows for improved archiving, linking, storytelling, collaboration, and publishing (Barrett, 2007). E-portfolios are both a product and a process (Berret, 2009). Figure 1 shows the five phases of e-portfolios:

Collection →	Selection →	Reflection →	Assessment →	Celebration
Collect various artefacts that show progress and growth opportunities.	Evatuate and review collected artefacts.	Gather and clarify thoughts about collected artefacts and their development. Illustrate gathered	Compare performance to learning goals.	Publish artefacts and tag, link and like.

Figure 1. The five phases of e-portfolios

According to Greenberg (2004), e-portfolios have three general purposes: structuring the work that remains to be done to ensure that it is completed, learning, and presentation of the achievement. Through presentation, what is learned is illustrated rather than merely described (Abrami & Barrett, 2005). Imhof and Picard (2009) noted that clarity of purpose is key to the effective use of e-portfolios. However, when this is missing it represents a far-reaching flaw in the process. For an e-portfolio to be used effectively, the learner must perform evidence. Evidence is measured not only by the artefacts, but also by the rationale for using a particular artefact. This process is expressed in the formula: Evidence = Artefacts + Reflection (Justification) + Validation (Feedback) (Barrett, 2003). Jenson and Treuer (2014) identified five skills for the effective use of e-portfolios: Collection, Self-regulation, Reflection, Integration, and Collaboration. These skills can be learned in isolation as well as one after the other because they build on each other and have to be seen as a habit. The skills must be learned one after the other in the beginning and practiced cyclically later on. This ensures that the learner can enter any learning environment at an appropriate point.

1.3. Reflection in Learning and Reflective Learning

Reflection on one's learning process is an essential aspect of cognitive development and the acquisition of new knowledge and skills and the ability to reflect on one's learning process enables individuals to become more metacognitively aware of their learning styles and preferences, and to optimize their learning environment as well as strategies which can lead to more efficient and effective learning, and can also promote a sense of self-efficacy, or the belief in one's ability to achieve learning goals (Boyd & Fales, 1983). Furthermore, reflection on the learning process allows for the identification of areas for improvement and the setting of specific, measurable, and achievable goals for future learning which influences targeted and focused learning, as well as the sense of progress and accomplishment (Brockbank & McGill, 2006). Reflecting on one's learning process also enables individuals to connect their learning to their larger personal and professional goals, and to understand the applicability of their learning in real-world contexts which can promote deeper understanding and retention of the material, as well as foster a sense of relevance and purpose (Brockbank & McGill, 2006). Moreover, reflection on one's learning process is also of significant value for educators and other professionals who are seeking to improve their teaching practice and to understand how to better support the learning of their students or clients. Reflecting on one's learning process can provide insight and inform instruction, thus promoting more effective teaching and learning (Brockbank & McGill, 2006). So, reflection on one's learning process is a vital aspect of cognitive development, it enables individuals to become more aware of their learning process, optimize their learning strategies, set goals, and connect their learning to real-world contexts, which is crucial for personal and professional development in a constantly changing and complex world (Bourner, 2003) and can be fostered by implementing e-portfolios (Ayaz & Gök, 2022).

2. Methodology

We conducted a systematic literature review to analyse the current state of research (Newman & Gough, 2020). These are critically evaluated and questioned. Both German and English literature was searched for. Six studies were included. Figure 2 shows the process.

In the first step, the data sources were selected. At the beginning of the literature search, Google Scholar was used to get an overview of the topic. In addition, Business Source Complete was consulted, as it is one of the TOP databases in the field of economics. To cover all potential terms and keywords, synonyms and different spellings were searched for the generic terms: "e-portfolio", "electronic portfolio", "eportfolio" and "university", "college", and "higher education". These were then used and combined with the Boolean operator "AND". The term "reflection" and its synonyms "reflexion" and "reflective" were intentionally not used, as this would have led to a premature narrowing down to 15 studies. This search strategy yielded 104 studies as results. Limitations were set to narrow these down. Studies should have been published between 2015 and 2022 to maintain timeliness. And studies should have been published in English. The exclusion criterion was the term "school" and synonyms, as this is outside the research question to be answered. For the narrowed-down literature, the abstract was now reviewed and checked for usability with regard to the research question. The literature search was completed by an additional forward and backward search, starting from the identified articles.

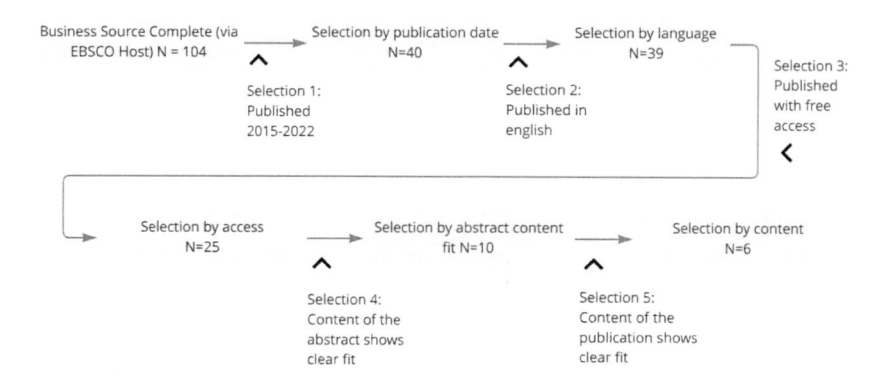

Figure 2. Selection Process

3. Results

To explain the effects of e-portfolios, the results of the individual studies will now be described in more detail to conclude how the use of e-portfolios affects students' reflection process. The following 6 studies will be analysed further:

Table 1. Summarized findings of the systematic literature review

Study	Addresses reflection processes as follows:	Main take away
Bacal, Walters & Einbinder (2015). Are You A Leader? How We Learned to Stop Asking.	The study showed that learners were able to enhance their learning skills through e-portfolios. A connection between learning and experiences occurs and students take ownership. Overall, the students benefited from this process because they gained the ability to provide evidence of acquired knowledge which is a reflective process in learning. Students developed an understanding of the importance of a variety of learning experiences and self-reflection. At the beginning of the study, it was important for students to develop themselves online through the e-portfolio process and thus create an online professional identity. In the end, it became apparent that students particularly valued the process. This was interpreted as a valuable reflection. In conclusion, it can be seen that e-portfolios promote the individuality and creativity of students. Their reflection on the overall process proves to be positive. However, students must not be left alone and receive assistance when necessary. This allows students to receive individualized support.	E-portfolios open room to reflect and foster reflection processes in learners. Support by the teacher must be available and well organised.

Study	Addresses reflection processes as follows:	Main take away
Ring (2015). Implementing a Peer Mentoring Model in the Clemson ePortfolio Program	They observed that e-portfolios, in conjunction with the peer review model, that by identifying strengths and weaknesses of an artefact, and improve critical thinking skills and communication. Through the feedback process, students receive suggestions for improvement and can revise artefacts. Students can learn from the experiences of their peers through peer review and thus reflect better. They gain a different perspective on the subject matter. When the peer review model was first introduced, learners only received feedback through virtual feedback. However, this turned out to be ineffective because students needed interaction and time. There was a lack of dialogue. Due to this, virtual feedback was expanded through various communication tools. Furthermore, additional advising staff were hired. Students stated that e-portfolio enabled them to reflect on what they take from various artefacts in their work.	E-portfolio work fosters reflection processes when both time and room to communicate with each other and the teachers are given.
Bodle, Malin & Wynhoven (2017). Students' experience toward ePortfolios as a reflective assessment tool in a dual mode indigenous business course.	In this study, a majority of students agreed that the e-portfolio helped them understand the content. It is used to gather information that can be used beyond the course and after graduation. Also, understanding new technology has largely had a positive impact on students. Students have learned to reflect. However, it should be noted that some students also had difficulties using it and felt limited by the regular updating of the e-portfolio.	E-portfolio foster reflection processes. Missing support by teachers and the system led to confusion and overload.
Mihret, Abayadeera, Watty & McKay (2017). Teaching auditing using cases in an online learning environment: The role of ePortfolio assessment	In this study, many students highlighted that the e-portfolios encouraged their self-discipline. This led to the improvement of learning skills and habits. Also, in the online case discussions, the student's interest is piqued because it can put a different perspective on a topic. Constructive criticism occurs, which is very helpful. This creates a team spirit, as students help each other improve their answers. Students noted that the process improved their interpersonal and communication skills as well as reflective and critical thinking.	E-portfolio foster reflection processes.
Dreisiebner, Riebenbauer & Stock (2017). Using Eportfolios to encourage reflection	This study shows that e-portfolios have a positive effect on self-reflection. Students are better able to assess their competencies and often discover new ones. The study shows that graduates who have used e-portfolios are better	E-portfolio foster reflection processes. Well-introduced e-portfolio work encourages long-lasting

Study	Addresses reflection processes as follows:	Main take away
and competency development.	able to reflect on their strengths and weaknesses. Even though the majority of graduates did not continue to work on their e-portfolios after graduation, they were able to use them as a presentation portfolio for job applications.	usage.
Beckers, Dolmans & van Merriënboer (2021). Student, direct thyself! Facilitating self-directed learning skills and motivation with an electronic development portfolio.	The improvement of the self-assessment of a performance is also shown by this study as it also confirms the hypothesis of increased motivation. Learners in the PERFLECT group showed a significant increase in intrinsic goal orientation. It can be seen that reflection has an important meaning in the use of e-portfolios. The e-portfolios can be used across disciplines and also serve as a unique selling point for job applications after graduation. However, there needs to be an introduction to the use of e-portfolios. Only in this way can students derive a benefit from them.	E-portfolios open room to reflect and foster reflection processes in learners. Support by the teacher must be available and well organised.

It can be concluded that students have reacted positively to the use of e-portfolios. They express that the new learning coupled with the increasing experience during their studies advances the development of their personality. They allow for the easy collection and organization of a variety of different types of evidence of learning. This makes it easier for students to see the breadth and depth of their learning over time and reflect on it. Also, they typically include tools for reflection, such as prompts and rubrics (Andrade & Cizek, 2010), that encourages students to think critically about their learning and the process of learning itself which helps students to become more aware of their strengths and areas for improvement and to set goals for their future learning. Furthermore, e-portfolios allow for easy sharing and collaboration, both within the classroom and beyond which provides students with valuable feedback from peers and instructors, and also encourages them to connect students with broader communities of learners.

In short, we answer our research questions as such: E-portfolios are a powerful tool for fostering reflective learning because they support the collection, organization, and reflection on evidence of learning, and facilitate the sharing and collaboration which leads to a better understanding of their learning process. We conclude that the best strategy to implement e-portfolios is to focus e-portfolio work on the exchange, peer feedback, and self-reflection aspects of the assessment. Use technology to the learners' advantage by creating space and time for reflective work and creating a safe space to exchange and receive feedback.

4. Discussion

The use of e-portfolios in the academic environment has increased over the last years (Ayaz & Gök, 2020; Filkins, 2010). The analysed studies have shown that an introduction to the proper use and creation of e-portfolios is effective in fostering reflective learning as they were enabled and motivated to see the connection between critical reflection, general skills, and accumulated experience. By developing their personalities, skills, and competencies, students can reflect on the learning process and achieve their success. We also found that only those e-portfolio implementations that were planned carefully and implemented with many opportunities to discuss and ask for assistance were effective.

We were able to draw initial conclusions from a small group of publications. These relate to different teaching circumstances but do not include the totality of all formats which is why further research is needed to relate and sharpen the insights gained here. Further, we deduce that other 21st Century skills are bound to be addressed better with e-portfolio than other assessment (Kienzler et al., 2023) which will be of great interest in future.

We see great potential in the increased implementation of e-portfolios in higher education especially since reflection will become more relevant with new technology like AI. However, the use of e-portfolios can only be successful if teachers can plan efficiently for the effects and hurdles involved in their use. These competencies should be specifically trained in university educators. It is crucial that teachers use technology wisely and integrate it into their lesson plans. Even though, e-portfolios rely on independent learning, the teacher cannot be absent. Especially the introduction of this method requires trust, bonding, and understanding of all participants. Therefore, it is relevant to prepare teachers for the complex and mixed use of assessment and to further research and teach strategies such as blended assessment (Jantos & Langesee, 2022).

References

Abrami, P., Barrett, H. (2005). Directions for Research and Development on Electronic Portfolios. Canadian Journal of Learning and Technology. 31(3). https://www.learntech-lib.org/p/43165/

Andrade, H. L.; Cizek, G. J. (2010): Handbook of formative assessment. Routledge.

Ayaz, M., Gök, B. (2022). The effect of e-portfolio application on reflective thinking and learning motivation of primary school teacher candidates. Curr Psychol. https://doi.org/10.1007/s12144-022-04135-2

Bacal, J., Ly, M., Walters, J. L., & Einbinder, A. (2015). Are You A Leader? How We Learned to Stop Asking. Theory Into Practice, 54(4), 309–316. https://doi.org/10.1080/00405841.2015.1076694

Barrett, B. (2009). Using e-Portfolios to Evaluate Intellectual Capital of Online Learners. 67–76.

Barrett, H. (2003). The eportfolio: A revolutionary tool for education and training?

Barrett, H. (2006). Using electronic portfolios for formative/classroom-based assessment. Classroom Connect Connected Newsletter, 13(2), 4–6.

Barrett, H. (2007). Researching Electronic Portfolios and Learner Engagement: The Re-flect Initiative. Journal of Adolescent & Adult Literacy, 50(6), 436–449.

Beckers, J., Dolmans, D., van Merriënboer, J. (2021). Student, direct thyself! Facilitating self-directed learning skills and motivation with an electronic development portfolio. Journal of Research on Technology in Education, 54(4), 617–634. https://doi.org/10.1080/15391523.2021.1906363

Bodle, K. A., Malin, M., Wynhoven, A. (2017). Students' experience toward portfolios as a reflective assessment tool in a dual mode indigenous business course. Accounting Research Journal, 30(3), 333–350. https://doi.org/10.1108/ARJ-06-2015-0089

Bourner, T. (2003), Assessing reflective learning, Education + Training, 45(5), 267-272. https://doi.org/10.1108/00400910310484321

Boyd, E. M., Fales, A. W. (1983). Reflective Learning: Key to Learning from Experience. Journal of Humanistic Psychology, 23(2), 99–117. https://doi.org/10.1177/0022167883232011

Brockbank, A., McGill, I. (2006). Facilitating reflective learning through mentoring and coaching. Journal of Humanistic Psychology, 23(2), 3-128. https://journals.sagepub.com/doi/epdf/10.1177/0022167883232011

Dede, D. (2009). Comparing Frameworks for 21st Century Skills.

Dreisiebner, G., Riebenbauer, E., & Stock, M. (2017). Using Eportfolios to encourage reflection and competency development. 31–47.

Filkins, D. T. (2010). The Acquisition of Electronic Portfolio Support Staff Expertise: A Theoretical Model. (Phd Thesis).

Greenberg, G. (2004). The digital convergence: Extending the portfolio. Educause Re-view. 28–36.

Imhof, M., Picard, C. (2009). Views on using portfolio in teacher education. Teaching and Teacher Education, 25(1), 149–154. https://doi.org/10.1016/j.tate.2008.08.001

Jantos, A., Langesee, L.-M. (2022): Blended Assessment in Higher Education Collaborative Case Study Work – A Qualitative Study. In: The 26th International Conference on Interactive Collaborative Learning

Jenson, J. D., Treuer, P. (2014). Defining the E-Portfolio: What It Is and Why It Matters. Change: The Magazine of Higher Learning, 46(2), 50–57. https://doi.org/10.1080/00091383.2014.897192

Jonassen, D. H. (1991). Objectivism versus constructivism: Do we need a new philosophical paradigm? Educational Technology Research and Development, 39(3), 5–14. https://doi.org/10.1007/BF02296434

Kienzler, M., Jantos, A., Langesee, L.-M. (2023). 21st Century Skills in Higher Education – A Quantitative Analysis Of Current Challenges And Potentials at a University Of Excellence. In: 17th annual International Conference of Education, Research and Innovation

Mihret, D. G., Abayadeera, N., Watty, K., McKay, J. (2017). Teaching auditing using cases in an online learning environment: The role of ePortfolio assessment. Ac-counting Education, 26(4), 335–357. https://doi.org/10.1080/09639284.2017.1292466

Mills-Courts, K., Amiran, M. R. (1991). Metacognition and the use of portfolios.

Moore, K. (2019). Tools and tips for helping students create E-Portfolios. 33–37.

National Learning Infrastructure Initiative. (2003). E-Portfolio.

Newman, M., Gough, D. (2020). Systematic Reviews in Educational Research: Methodology, Perspectives and Application. In: Zawacki-Richter, O., Kerres, M., Bedenlier, S., Bond, M., Buntins, K. (eds) Systematic Reviews in Educational Research. Springer VS, Wiesbaden. https://doi.org/10.1007/978-3-658-27602-7_1

Paulson, F. L., Paulson, P. R., Meyer, C. A. (1991). What Makes a Portfolio a Portfolio? Educational Leadership, 48(5), 60–63.

Paulson, P. R., Paulson, F. L. (1991). Portfolios: Stories of Knowing. 1–8.

QESN-RECIT. (2004). Portfolio process: Online resources for teachers.

Ring, G. L. (2015). Implementing a Peer Mentoring Model in the Clemson ePortfolio Program. Theory Into Practice, 54(4), 326–334. https://doi.org/10.1080/00405841.2015.1077616

Stiggins, R. J. (1994). Student-centered classroom assessment.

DEEP LEARNING FOR CYBER SECURITY IN THE INTERNET OF THINGS (IOT) NETWORK

Dawit Dejene Bikila

Faculty of Economics and Administration
University of Pardubice
dawitdejene.bikila@student.upce.cz

DOI: 10.35011/IDIMT-2023-391

Abstract

The Internet of Things (IoT) is a swiftly evolving paradigm having the potential to transform the physical interaction between individuals and organizations. IoT has applications in multiple fields such as healthcare, education, resource management, and information processing to name a few. Many organizations rely greatly on technology, and most are changing their process into intelligent or smart solutions. Moreover, these networks are wireless, self-configuring, do not need pre-existing infrastructure, and have a large unpredictable node movement; security becomes one of the most crucial concerns that need to be addressed. In this paper, we proposed an intrusion prevention method that uses a federated deep learning-based framework. A real IoT traffic dataset will be used to train the state-of-the-art graph neural network algorithm. A comparison will be carried out based on different experimental results. Finally, this work contributes to the security of IoT networks through the implementation of effective tools/techniques for timely IoT attack classification and mitigation.

Keywords

IoT, Cyber Security, Deep Learning, Intrusion Detection, Federated Learning.

1. Introduction

Significant developments in wireless sensor networks, telecommunications, and informatics have laid a milestone for the realization of pervasive intelligence, which visualizes the future Internet of Things (IoT). Currently, new business models are set for IoT implementations that require massive connectivity, high privacy, and security, complete coverage, ultra-high reliability, and ultra-low latency Kinza. S. et. al, (2020). IoT is a paradigm in which every physical object or thing that you wear, drive, read and see, and even the people and the places will be connected, addressed, and controlled remotely. Several physical things are connected to the internet and share massive data with cyberspace. Every year, millions of new IoT devices will be deployed to different application domains as reported by Mohammed. N. et. al, (2021).

IoT uses several communication technologies to connect devices that are embedded with microcontrollers and microprocessors for various purposes with significant processing power and memory. This infrastructure commonly relies on Wi-Fi and Bluetooth technologies for data sharing though there are also other technologies like NFC, NB-IoT, ZigBee, Cellular 3G, 4G, LET,5G, LoRaWAN, and SigFox as well. However, the wireless nature creates a higher vulnerability.

Depending on the application and factors such as network topology, security, and other critical issues that affect the reliability and trustworthiness of IoT networks, selecting the appropriate technology with efficient security is a challenge as reported by Miljan. S. et. al. (2020).

IoT has given a higher level of accessibility, availability, scalability, and interoperability in device connectivity throughout the globe. Yet, IoTs are vulnerable to cyber-attacks due to a combination of their multiple attack surfaces, newness, and thus lack of security standardizations and requirements. A variety of cyberattacks those attackers can impose against IoT, depending on the target system, and the gain from the attack are devised. Hence, a large volume of research should be conducted into the cybersecurity of IoT according to Murat. K. et al. (2021).

Cyber security is a term that usually refers to high-tech, procedures, and usage anticipated that are intended to preserve networks, devices, programs, and information from damage, illegal access, and attacks. It is now extensively used for protecting assets in most organizations due to attacks such as face hacking, data modification, DDoS, etc., known as cyber-crime which creates new challenges for the digital sector like IoT according to Akanksha. V. et. al. (2021).

Cyber security has three main security aspects that are confidentiality, authentication, and access control for ensuring that only authorized users can access data, communications infrastructures, services, and computing resources, and making sure that those authorized users are not prohibited from such access. Consequently, the security of IoT devices and associated applications can be breached by any attacks related to the above cyber security aspect from any location, which makes cyber security the main issue that has to be addressed as Fathima. J. (2019) stated.

Recent trends show researchers' huge interest in the integration of various technologies such as integrating sensors and embedded systems with Cyber-Physical Systems (CPS), Device-to-Device communications (D2D), and 5G wireless systems with IoT as a center. Currently, new business models are set for IoT implementation with new technologies, which provides solutions to business models. As a result, IoT services require high scalability, connectivity, and security for a wide range of applications, providing various mobility levels. So far, among the above requirements, communication systems developed for IoT applications have not been able to fully address the security requirements according to Snigdhaswin. K. et. al. (2021).

This research is motivated to develop a security method that uses deep learning techniques, to overcome cyber security problems associated with IoT networks. we pay more attention to systematically investigating how deep learning can be used to tackle cybersecurity problems, and what challenges or potential risks are remaining to be addressed. Additionally, analysis of currently developed Intrusion Detection Systems (NIDS), deep learning-based feature extraction, and classification methods are investigated.

The paper is organized as follows. In section two we present the current state of the art in cyber security for IoT networks and network security threats targeting IoT. In section three we will state the problem statement and aim of the work. Then, section four will discuss the materials and methods for the proposed work and finally, the result and discussion will be outlined in the last section.

2. Literature Review

The Internet of Things (IoT) is a connection of smart devices embedded with sensors that are capable of exchanging data without human intervention. These intelligent or smart things' capabilities and autonomously configuring, connecting features, and data transmission have brought a security challenge as stated by Mohammed. A. et. al. (2020). Many organizations rely greatly on these smart devices, and most will change their process into intelligent solutions to run their day-to-day services shortly. But industries are facing security breaches due to the lack of the strangest security mechanisms according to Veena. K. et. al. (2021).

IoT devices are operating in heterogenous domains such as the healthcare environment, smart homes, smart cities, transportation, smart grid system, etc., a huge amount of data over various sensors, actuators, transceivers, or other wearable devices is being exchanged via the IoT network. However, IoT is vulnerable to many threats, risks, and cyber-attacks and needs improvement as authors Bin. L. et. al, (2020) stated. Cognizant of this, securing the IoT network is vital as it plays a countless role in our day-to-day lives. In this regard, several machine learning-based attack detection techniques are developed to detect cyber-attacks. These methods are constantly evolving by learning new vulnerabilities intelligently and not relying on known attack signatures or normal network patterns.

Bou-Harb. E. et. al. (2021), proposed a novel multi-dimensional classification approach using deep learning that uses features extracted from executable binaries. Authors use the FLOSS tool for checking obfuscated malware, analyzing 70.000 recently detected IoT malware. They reported their method has an accuracy of 99.97% as compared with the conventional single-level classification. This work focuses only on deobfuscated malware samples thus, isolated detection does not provide a required level classification of the larger threat across different IoT networks and at different times. Yuyang. Z. et. al. (2019), introduce a defender-led signaling game model for DDoS Mitigation in IoT using cyber deception to spread camouflage information to confuse attackers. The results of the experiment show the method is effective in DDoS attack mitigation, but it has a problem in orchestration over heterogeneous IoT network domains.

Amir. N. J. et. al. (2021), compared Machine learning algorithms, such as K-Nearest Neighbor (KNN), Random Forest (RF), DT, Logistic Regression (LR), Artificial Neural Network (ANN), Naïve Bayes (NB), and SVM in terms of their effectiveness in detecting a backdoor command, and SQL injection attacks. The comparative summary suggested that the RF algorithm has the best attack detection, with a recall of 0.9744 while ANN is the fifth-best algorithm, with a recall of 0.8718 and the LR is the worst-performing algorithm, with a recall of 0.4744. The authors also reported that the ANN could not detect 12.82% of the attacks and classified 0.03% of the normal samples as attacks. In addition, LR, SVM, and KNN considered many attack samples as normal samples, and these algorithms are sensitive to imbalanced data. In other words, they are not suitable for attack detection in IoT networks.

Mohamed A. F. et. al. (2021), proposed a Logical Analysis of Data (LAD) method to extract patterns and rules from the sensor data and use these patterns to design a two-step anomaly detection system that uses the KNN algorithm to detect cyber-attacks on gas pipelines. To minimize the effect of using an imbalanced dataset in the algorithm, they performed oversampling. Using the KNN on the balanced dataset, they reported an accuracy of 97%, a precision of 0.98, a recall of 0.92, and an f-measure of 0.95. They compared the performance of the proposed LAD method with the DNN, SVM, and Convolutional Neural Network (CNN) methods. Based on these experiments, the Deep Neural Network (DNN) outperformed the LAD method in the precision metric. However, most of these algorithms have a dimensionality issue due to the big data generated in real-world IoT networks.

Mohamed A. F. et. al. (2021), provided an experimental analysis of federated deep learning in comparison with other three deep learning approaches, namely, Recurrent Neural Network (RNN), Ensemble Learning (EL) Convolutional Neural Network (CNN), and Deep Neural Network (DNN). They used three new real IoT traffic datasets to study the performances of each deep learning model. The comparative analysis demonstrates that centralized techniques resulted in degraded model performance and require higher computing power that is not suitable for IoT networks, while federated deep learning approaches outperform non-federated learning in providing higher accuracy in detecting IoT attacks. Therefore, efficiently implemented federated approaches that use less computational overhead are strongly required for IoT networks and applications.

Kalupahana L. et. al. (2021), proposed a deep learning-based three-stage intrusion detection and prevention system for coordinated cyber-attacks on IoT networks. The authors introduced a hierarchical distributed architecture used to place the security solution between the edge of the IoT network and the ISP. They stated that the dynamic changes in the IoT network and devices challenge traditional network security solutions at the endpoints (e.g., antivirus) and even at network perimeters (e.g., firewalls and IDS). The experimental results proved their work outperformed other methods significantly in both attack-stage detection and identification. But they used a simple key-based technique in which the key may be compromised by an attacker.

Xiaoding W. et. al. (2021), proposed a hierarchical federated learning model based on Deep Reinforcement Learning (DRL) algorithm to detect privacy leakage attacks. The experimental outcomes of this work yield high throughput, low latency, and high attack detection results with an accuracy of 97.5 %, but they did not validate the result with a network intrusion detection dataset. Ivan C. et. al. (2021), introduced federated learning based on Logistic Model Tree (LMT) method to detect DDoS attacks. The experimental result shows a detection accuracy of 99.21%-99.96%, Viraaji M. et. al. (2022), proposed a federated learning Gated Recurrent Units (GRUs) model for the detection and prevention of DDoS attacks by using a network dataset to train the model. They reported a detection accuracy of 99.5%, but both works used a dataset not applicable to federated learning. Rahim T. et. al. (2021), proposed a Generative Adversarial Network (GAN), which consists of a generative model and a discriminative model which can be combined to produce a dynamic game system, and a federated adversarial network to mitigate poisoning attacks. They trained the model using contango and genome datasets and found an accuracy of 96%, but, they did not consider inference attacks.

Truong T. et. al. (2021), proposed a federated neural network for IoT edge computing to tackle data exfiltration, keylogging, server scanning, DoS, and DDoS (HTTP, TCP, UDP) attacks. They trained the model using the BoT-IoT dataset and reported 99% accuracy but did not calculate the energy cost. Xiaokang Z. et. al, (2021), proposed the Hierarchical Adversarial Attacks (HAA) method using the state-of-the-art deep learning method called Graph Neural Network (GNN) in black box attack scenarios. With varying the training dataset size from 2%-30% for training the model, they reported the accuracy of the GNN is degraded up to 30% and concluded that more datasets will result in better GNN performance. Thus, as it is state of the art, by applying the balanced dataset and federated learning approach, we can leverage the performance of this method.

Authors, Ferrag M. et. al. (2022) developed a cyber security dataset called Edge-IIoTset for the implementation and attack detection in both IoT and IIoT applications for centralized and federated approaches. They reported that their dataset is simulated in a real-world IoT environment whereas other datasets like CICIDS2017, UNSW-NB15, ISCX, NSL-KDD, and ARPA2009 are not simulated. Moreover, they stated that these datasets are not applicable to federated learning-based attack detection.

Smart devices with embedded sensors can now compute complex cryptographic methods that are not efficient despite consuming high computational resources, so we can apply intelligent algorithms. The complex and huge amount of data generated from these devices can be used to train security procedures and normal use. The results of the training can be used to learn, detect and protect against any intrusion. Protecting these infrastructures with an intelligent mechanism that uses the capability of learning the flow of data among these devices is crucial for any organization operating using this technology as indicated by Monika. R. et. al. (2019).

From the related works, it is clear that the IoT network needs improvement to ensure the confidentiality, integrity, and authentication of IoT applications. This motivates the development of a security model which is capable of detecting attacks on IoT networks with balanced learning and low computational resources. As a result, the present study will present a novel federated deep learning-enabled framework that can proactively adapt the attack surfaces, dynamically optimize defense strategies, and rapidly deploy the corresponding defense mechanisms by using recent Edge-IIoTset Datasets, applicable for federated learning as reported by Ferrag M. et. al. (2022), for the cyber security of IoT networks.

3. Problem Statement

A huge user data is digitally shared among devices in the IoT network, which makes the IoT network attractive and open to different types of cyber-attacks. As a result, a huge interest has been developed among researchers in the investigation and proposing new approaches like machine learning for detection and prevention. however, most of the current methods use a centralized machine learning approach that depends on datasets located on a central server which has privacy concerns regarding the user data as Viraaji M. et. al. (2022) reported.

The existing studies mostly focus on detecting attacks after the IoT devices get compromised and start performing malicious activities like DDoS, flooding, spam, etc. Similarly, the performance of most of the existing machine learning-based botnet detection models are limited to a specific training dataset. As a consequence, these solutions do not perform well on other attacks due to the diversity of attack patterns. Since IoT devices have limited memory, computing power, and battery network base technique is more feasible than host-based techniques to overcome such cyberattacks discussed by authors Faisel H. et. al. (2021).

Recent cyber threats demonstrate the weaknesses of existing cyber defenses, such as firewalls, intrusion detection, and prevention systems, as their mechanisms are often built on heuristic and static attack signatures. These systems cannot detect new variants and zero-day attacks that could exploit attack surfaces of devices and their network protocols. IoT networks are considerably vulnerable to attacks, where there is a lack of security considerations for protecting heterogeneous and complex devices and systems. Thus, IoT requires intelligent security mechanisms that can automatically identify evolving cyber-attacks as Muna. A. H. et. al. (2020) recommended. Therefore, researching cyber security for IoT is very important to solve current security-related problems in IoT networks. Moreover, unlike other machine learning methods, a deep learning technique is state-of-the-art in developing a novel security method for IoT networks as indicated by Shakila. Z. et. al. (2021).

3.1. Research Question

In this study, we will attempt to leverage recent advances in the methods of deep learning for IoT network security. The goal of this research mainly focuses on enhancing the prevention and detection of cyber-attacks on IoT networks. Specifically, the research questions we pursue in this study are: learning to secure IoT networks and seeking to answer the following questions:

1. What security criteria should be used to develop a more robust security method for IoT networks?
2. How can deep learning help monitor IoT networks?

3. How can deep learning help to overcome cyber-attacks on IoT networks?

To answer these questions, we will review different kinds of literature that have a direct relation to the proposed work. The purpose of the literature review is to know the state of the art in cyber security and IoT, new and intelligent attack types, and more about methods of testing and evaluation standards for IoT network security.

3.2. Objective of the study

The main objective of this research is to explore the methods of developing a deep learning-based security model for the cyber security of IoT networks. Which will have basic tasks including exploring IoT network monitoring methods, Training the model using the GNN algorithm, designing a novel deep learning-enabled attack detection scheme, validating the proposed method using standard security metrics, and comparing the performance of the new method and the existing method. Further, the study will have contributions that include providing novel and intelligent monitoring and prevention method which is ideal for resource-constrained IoT networks.

The proposed model will focus on securing the IoT network. It will implement a method to prevent and detect cyber-attacks on IoT to enhance IoT security. The proposed work will reduce or mitigate the chances of risk associated with IoT security. In last, it should be noticed that the study will not be interested in improving issues in IoT devices like memory consumption, power consumption, and CPU processing speed issues that are associated with these devices.

4. Materials and Methods

A design science, experimental and qualitative, research methodology will be used to develop a security framework for IoT networks. IoT nodes such as 3GPP, NB-IoT, LTE-M, and other suitable nodes for implementing federated learning-based intrusion detection will be used to develop and investigate the new security mechanism. The new method will be installed on these devices, and the performance will be investigated by changing different security parameters. In the end, the results of the proposed method will be evaluated using standard matrices in the analysis section.

This work is experimentally based on which the mathematical, practical, and theoretical investigations of IoT security will be performed. The study will implement the new method on selected IoT devices. The sampling and selection of these devices will be based on the researcher's judgment. This can be done by considering some of the basic network technologies, protocols, devices, and services vulnerable to security risks.

Real IoT traffic dataset set, Edge-IIoTset Datasets, applicable for federated learning as stated by Ferrag M. et. al. (2022), will be used to train the model. Then the model will be trained on individual nodes using their data in the network. The performance of the new framework will be analyzed using generated adversarial attacks. Finally, the performance of the new method will be compared with another similar method in terms of some standard metrics that are used for security performance analysis.

5. Conclusion

The usage of federated learning in our model will enhance the detection of intelligent zero-day attacks, as deep learning can learn from the pattern, and reduce costly storage on a single IoT device; the conventional and central models in previous studies are not memory efficient for these devices, which causes high storage costs. Moreover, it solves the issue of privacy leakage as the actual data is not shared with all devices in the network. As a result, the proposed federated learning approach, using the selected real-time Edge-IIoTset dataset, will improve the detection of the attack as compared to central approaches. The reason is that multiple versions of models are collected from different devices of the IoT network and then a more powerful and accurate model will be developed, which provides a better prediction of malicious and legitimate behavior.

- Study of usability and possibilities to deploy network security detection methods for IoT networks. We will be also interested in distributed deep learning methods to develop an intelligent intrusion detection system.
- Enhancement of current network monitoring tools for specific needs of the IoT network. Data must be collected and further analysis must be done based on information observed from network monitoring tools and datasets.
- Tools and methods for intrusion detection in IoT devices and networks. The target of detection will consider anomalies related to the IoT network.
- Study of modified tools capabilities to detect cyber-attacks targeting IoT networks.
- The end product will be the sturdiest security framework with higher intrusion prevention and detection accuracy for the IoT network.

Acknowledgment

This paper was supported by grant No. SGS_2023_010, supported by the Student Grant Competition. Faculty of Economics and Administration, University of Pardubice.

References

Akanksha. V. et. al. (2021), "Cyber Security in Digital Sector," in *International Conference on Artificial Intelligence and Smart Systems*, Coimbatore,

Amir. N. J. et. al. (2021), "Toward Detection and Attribution of Cyber-Attacks in IoT-enabled Cyber-physical Systems," *IEEE Internet of Things*, vol. 8, no. 17, pp. 13712 – 13722.

Bin. L. et. al, (2020), "Security Analysis of IoT Devices by Using Mobile Computing: A Systematic Literature Review", IEEE.

Bou-Harb. E. et. al. (2021), "A Multi-Dimensional Deep Learning Framework for IoT Malware Classification and Family Attribution," *IEEE Transactions on Network and Service Management*, vol. 1, no. 1, pp. 1-12.

Fathima. J. (2019), "IoT Cybersecurity based Smart Home Intrusion Prevention System," in *Cyber Security in Networking Conference*, Quito,

Ivan C. et. al. (2021), "Boosting-Based DDoS Detection in Internet of Things Systems," *IEEE Internet of Things Journal*, vol. 9, no. 3, pp. 2109 – 2123.

Kalupahana L. et. al. (2021), "ADEPT: Detection and Identification of Correlated Attack Stages in IoT Networks," *IEEE INTERNET OF THINGS JOURNAL*, vol. 8, no. 8, pp. 6591-6607.

Kinza. S. et. al, (2020), "Internet of Things (IoT) for Next-Generation Smart Systems: A Review of Current Challenges, Future Trends, and Prospects for Emerging 5G-IoT Scenarios," *IEEE Access*, pp. 23022 – 23040,

M. A. Ferrag, O. FRIHA, D. HAMOUDA: Edge-IIoTset: A New Comprehensive Realistic Cyber Security Dataset of IoT and IIoT Applications for Centralized and Federated Learning IEEE Access, 2022.

Miljan. S. et. al. (2020), "An Overview of Wireless Technologies for IoT Network," in *19th International Symposium INFOTEH-JAHORINA, 18-20*, East Sarajevo,

Mohamed A. F. et. al. (2021), "Federated Deep Learning for Cyber Security in the Internet of Things: Concepts, Applications, and Experimental Analysis," *IEEE Access*, vol. 9, pp. 138509 – 138542.

Mohammed. A. et. al. (2020), "A Survey of Machine and Deep Learning Methods for Internet of Things (IoT) Security," *IEEE,* pp. 1-46.

Mohammed. N. et. al, (2021) "Internet of Things (IoT): A review of its enabling technologies in healthcare applications, standards protocols, security and market opportunities," *IEEE Internet of Things,* vol. 8, no. 13, pp. 10474 – 10498.

Monika. R. et. al. (2019), "Deep Learning Models for Cyber Security in IoT," *IEEE,* pp. 0452-0457.

Muna. A. H. et. al. (2020), "Deep Learning-enabled Threat Intelligence Scheme in the Internet of Things Networks," *IEEE Transactions on Network Science and Engineering,*

Murat. K. et al. (2021), "Role of Artificial Intelligence in the Internet of Things (IoT) cybersecurity," *Springer.* pp. 8442 – 8452.

Rahim T. et. al. (2021), "Fed-IIoT: A Robust Federated Malware Detection Architecture in Industrial IoT," *IEEE Transactions on Industrial Informatics,* vol. 17, no. 12,

Shakila. Z. et. al. (2021), "Survey on Security Threats and AI-based Countermeasures for IoT Networks," *IEEE,* vol. 9, pp. 1-22.

Snigdhaswin. K. et. al. (2021), "5G-IoT Architecture for Next Generation Smart Systems," in *IEEE 5G World Forum (5GWF),* Montreal,

Truong T. et. al. (2021), "LocKedge: Low-Complexity Cyberattack Detection in IoT Edge Computing," *IEEE Access,* vol. 9, pp. 29696 – 29710.

Veena. K. et. al.(2021), "A Survey on Attack Detection Methods For IOT," in *3rd International Conference on Signal Processing and Communication (ICPSC),* Coimbatore.

Viraaji M. et. al. (2022), "Federated-Learning-Based Anomaly Detection for IoT Security Attacks," *IEEE Internet of Things Journal,* vol. 9, no. 4, pp. 2545 – 2554.

Xiaoding W. et. al. (2021), "Toward Accurate Anomaly Detection in Industrial Internet of Things Using Hierarchical Federated Learning," *IEEE Internet of Things Journal,* vol. 9, no. 10, pp. 7110 - 7119.

Xiaokang Z. et. al, (2021), "Hierarchical Adversarial Attacks Against Graph Neural Network Based IoT Network Intrusion Detection System," *IEEE Internet of Things Journal,*

Yuyang. Z. et. al. (2019), "An SDN-Enabled Proactive Defense Framework for DDoS Mitigation in IoT Networks," *IEEE Transactions on Information Forensics and Security,* vol. 21, no. 1, pp. 812 - 837.

COBIT 2019 CONTRIBUTION TO DIGITAL LITERACY

Karel Maršálek

Department of Information Technologies
Faculty of Informatics and Statistics
Prague University of Economics and Business
karel.marsalek@vse.cz

DOI: 10.35011/IDIMT-2023-399

Keywords

Digital literacy, digital transformation, COBIT, digital skills, governance, management

Abstract

Digitization and digital transformation have become an absolute necessity for many organizations in order to stay competitive in the current dynamic world. This brings various obstacles that need to be addressed, some of which are less apparent than others. One such critical obstacle, or rather a key factor affecting the success of digital transformation processes, is digital literacy in an organization. This article examines whether the adoption and utilization of COBIT 2019 can positively contribute to an organization's level of digital literacy. This is determined by examining the relation between the concept of digital literacy and the COBIT 2019 framework. More specifically, COBIT enterprise objectives, alignment objectives, associated metrics, governance objectives and management objectives are analyzed for overlaps with digital literacy. Even though COBIT 2019 is a comprehensive framework aimed at the enterprise as a whole, the results show there are certain aspects of the framework that directly or indirectly relate to digital literacy. The main overlaps can be found in the area of human resources management and resource optimization, which are addressed by COBIT governance and management objectives APO07 and EDM04. Additionally, five other COBIT management objectives were identified to have a partial relation to digital literacy – mostly to certain subsets of digital skills. These objectives can be recommended to management of organizations as areas of focus for ensuring a sufficient level of digital literacy, which is vital for any organization that is currently undergoing or plans to undergo changes related to digital transformation.

1. Introduction

COBIT 2019 (Control Objectives for Information and Related Technologies) is a widely used information technology governance and management framework. Even though the framework focuses on the use of information technology (IT) within an organization, it is not restricted just to the organization's IT department – the framework is aimed at the enterprise as a whole. In other words, COBIT covers all the information technology within the organization, regardless of where it is used (ISACA, 2018b, p. 13).

The authors of COBIT 2019 state: *"Stakeholder value creation (i.e., realizing benefits at an optimal resource cost while optimizing risk) is often driven by a high degree of digitization in new business models, efficient processes, successful innovation, etc. Digitized enterprises are increasingly dependent on I&T for survival and growth."* (ISACA, 2018b, p. 11) It is evident that, for many organizations, digitization and digital transformation represent an absolute necessity to stay competitive in the ever more dynamically evolving world.

However, recognizing the need for "being digital" is only the first of many steps. As with any large change to the functioning of the organization, digitization and digital transformation bring many obstacles that need to be addressed. It is also important to note that some of these obstacles are less apparent than others, thus organizations often wrongly disregard them as insignificant. But overlooking these less apparent factors can later prove very painful for the organization. This article is focused on one such significant digital transformation factor – digital literacy.

But even recognizing the importance of digital literacy is just another of many required steps, as organizations often need guidance in ensuring a sufficient level of digital literacy. The COBIT 2019 framework is already widely used as guidance in areas of governance and management. Therefore, the main aim of this article is to determine whether this guidance can be expanded also to the area of digital literacy, i.e., whether the adoption and utilization of COBIT 2019 can positively contribute to the level of digital literacy in an organization.

The framework is designed to assist organizations with governance and management tasks by cascading very comprehensive goals into more granular objectives, for each of which it defines seven universal components. These components include – among others – activities, information flows, organizational structures, skills, and competencies, which serve as guidance for the organizations to identify problems and fulfil objectives. This component cascade provides a complex view of each of the objectives.

Therefore, it can be stated that the contribution of COBIT 2019 to the level of digital literacy is dependent on the existence of overlaps between digital literacy and COBIT objectives. Proving that there is a significant relation between particular objectives and digital literacy would also mean that there are already defined specific activities, information flows, etc., which can help the organizations with ensuring a sufficient level of digital literacy. This article demonstrates how specific COBIT 2019 governance and management objectives tackle challenges posed to organizations by the current digital age, more specifically by the need to have a sufficiently digitally literate workforce.

The aim of this article is approached by addressing the following research questions:

1. Which are the key skills that compose the concept of digital literacy?
2. Which COBIT 2019 enterprise goals, alignment goals, associated metrics, governance, and management objectives can positively contribute to ensuring a sufficient level of digital literacy in an organization?
3. Which digital skills are represented in COBIT 2019?

2. Defining digital literacy

Digital literacy can be defined as an umbrella term encompassing several types of skills that are connected to the use of digital technologies. The scope of digital literacy, i.e., what types of literacies or skills can be regarded as its components, has been widely discussed over the past 25 years. One of the first definitions presented digital literacy as a combination of the computer, information, and media literacies/skills (Gilster, 1997).

While the importance of these building blocks – especially computer/ICT (Binkley et al., 2012; Chetty et al., 2018; Voogt & Roblin, 2012) and information literacy (Binkley et al., 2012; Carretero et al., 2017; Chetty et al., 2018; van Dijk, 2013; van Laar et al., 2017) – has remained recognised over the years, the scope of digital literacy has been significantly broadened. Later publications also stress the importance of several other skills, such as:

- Collaboration skills (Buitrago-Flórez et al., 2021; Carretero et al., 2017; van Laar et al., 2017; Voogt & Roblin, 2012)
- Communication skills (Buitrago-Flórez et al., 2021; Carretero et al., 2017; Chetty et al., 2018; van Dijk, 2013; van Laar et al., 2017; Voogt & Roblin, 2012)
- Content-creation/creativity skills (Buitrago-Flórez et al., 2021; Carretero et al., 2017; van Dijk, 2013; van Laar et al., 2017; Voogt & Roblin, 2012)
- Critical thinking skills (Buitrago-Flórez et al., 2021; van Laar et al., 2017; Voogt & Roblin, 2012)
- Data skills (Carretero et al., 2017)
- Problem-solving skills (Buitrago-Flórez et al., 2021; Carretero et al., 2017; van Laar et al., 2017; Voogt & Roblin, 2012)
- Safety skills (Carretero et al., 2017)
- Strategic skills (van Dijk, 2013)

Digital literacy is also an integral part of the broader concept of digital transformation, which will (and already has) significantly affect businesses and organizations in future years. It can be stated that digital literacy is one of the essential enablers of digital transformation processes. However, ensuring a sufficient level of digital literacy among the organization's employees is precisely one of the obstacles that organizations tend to overlook.

3. Digital literacy in COBIT 2019

3.1. Method

COBIT 2019 is a comprehensive framework that covers governance and management principles applicable to the organization as a whole. On the contrary, it is clear that digital literacy is related only to much smaller segments of the organization. Therefore, this article analyses overlaps of digital literacy and COBIT by gradually narrowing the framework's scope to more granular components, which is represented by its cascade of enterprise goals, alignment goals, governance objectives, and management objectives.

In other words, the complete set of enterprise goals provided by COBIT is narrowed down only to the relevant ones, i.e., those at least partially connected to digital literacy. For these selected enterprise goals, all related alignment goals are analysed and again, only the relevant ones are retained. Finally, for these retained alignment goals, all related governance and management objectives are analysed for their overlaps with digital literacy.

3.2. Enterprise and alignment goals

The strategy of an enterprise is realized through the achievement of a number of enterprise goals which the strategy cascades into. COBIT 2019 identifies 13 key enterprise goals that are vital for the fulfilment of the enterprise strategy.

3.2.1. Identifying relevant enterprise and alignment goals

While the concepts of digital skills or digital literacy are not explicitly covered in the COBIT framework, there are two enterprise goals that are connected to these concepts – mainly *EG10 Staff skills, motivation and productivity* and partially also *EG12 Managed digital transformation programs* (ISACA, 2018b, p. 30). The enterprise goals further translate into alignment goals which emphasize the alignment of IT efforts with business objectives (ISACA, 2018b, p. 28).

Already at first glance, it is apparent that the main overlap of digital literacy (or digital skills) with the COBIT 2019 framework is represented by the already mentioned *EG10* enterprise goal (bold in Table). This goal translates into two alignment goals: *AG12 Competent and motivated staff with mutual understanding of technology and business* (Primary) and *AG08 Enabling and supporting business processes by integrating applications and technology* (Secondary).

Since we are discussing digital literacy as a key enabler of digital transformation processes, the *EG12* enterprise goal is also relevant (bold in Table). This goal is primarily or secondarily linked to 6 alignment goals in total, 2 of which are at least partially connected to digital literacy: *AG08 Enabling and supporting business processes by integrating applications and technology* (Primary) and *AG13 Knowledge, expertise and initiatives for business innovation* (Secondary).

Table 1. Mapping digital literacy with COBIT 2019 enterprise and alignment goals

Alignment goals	Associated enterprise goals	Overlap with digital literacy
AG03 Realized benefits from I&T-enabled investments and services portfolio	Primary: **EG12** Secondary: EG01, EG05, EG08, EG09	Insignificant
AG05 Delivery of I&T services in line with business requirements	Primary: EG01 Secondary: EG05, EG06, EG08, **EG12**	Insignificant
AG06 Agility to turn business requirements into operational solutions	Primary: EG01 Secondary: EG05, EG08, **EG12**, EG13	Insignificant
AG08 Enabling and supporting business processes by integrating applications and technology	Primary: EG01, EG05, **EG12** Secondary: EG08, **EG10**, EG13	Partial/marginal
AG09 Delivering programs on time, on budget and meeting requirements and quality standards	Primary: EG01, **EG12** Secondary: EG05, EG08, EG09, EG13	Insignificant
AG12 Competent and motivated staff with mutual understanding of technology and business	Primary: **EG10** Secondary: EG05	Significant (digital skills)

Alignment goals	Associated enterprise goals	Overlap with digital literacy
AG13 Knowledge, expertise and initiatives for business innovation	Primary: EG01, EG13 Secondary: EG03, **EG12**	Partial

3.2.2. Identifying relevant metrics for enterprise and alignment goals

COBIT 2019 also provides a set of example metrics for each enterprise and alignment goal, which should help the organization determine whether and to what degree the particular goal is being fulfilled. In addition, these metrics can give us a better understanding of the contents and meaning of the particular goal. In the context of this article, they also provide an additional ground for finding connections to the concept of digital literacy.

After analysing individual goals together with their metrics, it can be concluded that there are several metrics that at least indirectly refer to digital literacy. The most relevant metrics are: *Level of stakeholder satisfaction with staff expertise and skills* (EG10), *Percent of staff whose skills are insufficient for competency in their role* (EG10), *Percent of I&T-savvy business people* (i.e., those having the required knowledge and understanding of I&T to guide, direct, innovate and see I&T opportunities in their domain of business expertise) (AG12), *Number or percentage of business people with technology management experience* (AG12), and *Level of business executive awareness and understanding of I&T innovation possibilities* (AG13).

3.3. Cascading to governance and management objectives

Alignment goals can be further cascaded into governance and management objectives. These are, in their essence, groups of issues an organization needs to deal with in order for information and technology to contribute to enterprise goals (ISACA, 2018b, p. 20, 2018a, p. 11). COBIT 2019 addresses a total of 40 governance and management objectives, which are divided into five domains. Governance objectives are represented by the *Evaluate, Direct and Monitor (EDM)* domain, whereas management objectives each belong to one of the four remaining domains: *Align, Plan and Organize (ADM), Build, Acquire and Implement (BAI), Deliver, Service and Support (DSS)*, and *Monitor, Evaluate and Assess (MEA)* (ISACA, 2018a, p. 11).

3.3.1. Identifying relevant governance and management objectives

As already outlined, the most apparent overlap among COBIT alignment goals is represented by the AG12 goal. A partial, rather indirect connection can also be recognised with the AG13 goal. The link between other alignment goals and digital literacy is marginal or non-existent at all. Therefore, the subset of relevant alignment goals is narrowed down only to the two mentioned above – AG12 and AG13 (bold in Table). In this section, all governance and management objectives that relate to these two goals are analysed for overlaps with digital literacy, with the most relevant objectives presented below and in Table.

The management objective *APO02 Managed strategy* ultimately strives for enablement of *"reliable but agile and efficient response to strategic objectives"* of the organization. A great emphasis is put on the organization's digital transformation efforts. But most importantly, it stresses that these efforts need to be backed by sufficient digital maturity of the organization (ISACA, 2018a, p. 99), which clearly involves ensuring a solid level of digital literacy among the organization's employees.

Nevertheless, the term "digital maturity" in the COBIT interpretation involves more than just digital literacy; more specifically – in the APO02 context – it includes *"ability of leadership to leverage technology, level of accepted technology risk, approach to innovation, culture and knowledge level of users."* Based on this definition, it is evident that the connection to digital literacy is present but not very strongly emphasized.

This lack of standalone attention can also be observed in the management objective *APO07 Managed human resources*. In spite of that, the APO07 is undoubtedly the key COBIT objective for ensuring a sufficient level of digital literacy in the organization. As defined in COBIT 2019, the purpose of managing human resources is to optimize these resource capabilities in such a way that they enable achieving enterprise objectives (ISACA, 2018a). This is certainly (and understandably) a very broad definition as these required "capabilities" can differ completely based on the specific industry, organization, position, or scope of work within the organization. The APO07 objective together with its related management practices, activities etc. is constructed in such a way that makes it universally applicable to the needs of any organization.

Closely connected to APO07 is the governance objective *EDM04 Ensured resource optimization*, which focuses on ensuring *"adequate and sufficient business and I&T-related resources"* to effectively support enterprise objectives (ISACA, 2018a, p. 45). Such "resources" include mainly processes, technologies, and – importantly – people. Thus, while having a broader scope than APO07, the EDM04 objective is definitely a vital one for the area of digital literacy since it guides organizations on how to secure sufficient (in this case, digitally ready) resources for their effective functioning.

However, the overlaps between COBIT and digital literacy can be much less evident than in the area of human resources management. Management objective *APO08 Managed relationships* is a prime example. *"Base relationships on open and transparent communication... Business and IT must work together to create successful enterprise outcomes in support of the enterprise objectives."* (ISACA, 2018a, p. 107) Since communication and collaboration are some of the essential digital skills, a connection – although a subtle and only partial one – of COBIT and digital literacy can be found here as well.

Table 2. Mapping digital literacy with COBIT 2019 governance and management objectives

Governance and management objectives	Associated alignment goals	Overlap with digital literacy
EDM02 Ensured benefits delivery	Primary: AG03 Secondary: AG05, AG06, AG08, **AG13**	Insignificant
EDM04 Ensured resource optimization	Primary: AG09 Secondary: AG03, AG05, AG06, AG08, **AG12**	Significant (all digital skills)
APO02 Managed strategy	Primary: AG08 Secondary: AG03, AG05, AG06, **AG12**, **AG13**	Partial (strategic skills)
APO04 Managed innovation	Primary: **AG13** Secondary: **AG12**	Partial (creativity skills)
APO07 Managed human resources	Primary: **AG12, AG13**	Significant (all digital skills)
APO08 Managed relationships	Primary: **AG12, AG13**	Partial (communication

Governance and management objectives	Associated alignment goals	Overlap with digital literacy
		and collaboration skills)
BAI02 Managed requirements definition	Secondary: **AG12**	Insignificant
BAI05 Managed organizational changes	Secondary: **AG12**	Partial (digital transformation)
BAI08 Managed knowledge	Primary: **AG12, AG13**	Partial (information skills)

Similarly, another partial connection, i.e., connection to only a specific subset of digital skills, can be identified in the management objective *APO04 Managed innovation*. The link is specifically to creativity skills, which van Laar et al. (2017) define as *"skills to use ICT to generate new or previously unknown ideas, or treat familiar ideas in a new way and transform such ideas into a product, service or process."*

Several COBIT objectives focus on the area of digital transformation within the organization. One such objective is *BAI05 Managed organizational change*, which aims to *"maximize the likelihood of successfully implementing sustainable enterprise-wide organizational change"* and *"cover the complete life cycle of the change."* (ISACA, 2018a, p. 187) Sufficient digital literacy should, in this case, be seen as a necessary enabler of change that needs to be in place throughout the life cycle of the (digital transformation) change in order to limit risks connected to such change.

Lastly, the management objective *BAI08 Managed knowledge* is another example of a partial connection to a subset of digital skills – mainly to the information skills. According to COBIT, this objective includes *"planning for the identification, gathering organizing, maintaining, use and retirement of knowledge"* and *"providing the knowledge and information required to support all staff... and allow for informed decision making"* (ISACA, 2018a, p. 205). This is in line with van Laar's definition of information skills: *"the skills to use ICT to efficiently search, select, organize information to make informed decisions"* (van Laar et al., 2017).

4. Conclusion

This article examines whether the adoption and utilization of COBIT 2019 can positively contribute to the level of digital literacy in an organization by analyzing the framework for the existence of overlaps with the concept of digital literacy. It was determined that several COBIT governance and management objectives have either a significant or at least partial relation to digital literacy. These can be recommended as areas of focus to management of any organization, which is currently undergoing or plans to undergo changes related to digital transformation.

The complete set of thirteen COBIT enterprise goals was narrowed down to two goals that are at least partially related to digital literacy: *EG10 Staff skills, motivation and productivity* and *EG12 Managed digital transformation programs*. These two enterprise goals cascade to a total of seven alignment goals, out of which one was identified to have a significant relation to digital literacy (*AG12 Competent and motivated staff with mutual understanding of technology and business*), one was identified to have a partial relation (*AG13 Knowledge, expertise and initiatives for business innovation*), and another one was deemed to have only marginal relation (*AG08 Enabling and supporting business processes by integrating applications and technology*) and was therefore not considered further.

The main identified relations between COBIT management objectives and digital literacy are represented by the management objective *APO07 Managed human resources* and governance objective *EDM04 Ensured resource optimization*. These objectives have a tight connection to digital skills in general, without any specific type of digital skills being significantly more or less important than the other. Five other management objectives have a partial connection to digital literacy, in most cases to certain subsets of digital skills, such as strategic (*APO02 Managed strategy*), creativity (*APO04 Managed innovation*), communication and collaboration (*APO08 Managed relationships*), and information skills (*BAI08 Managed knowledge*). Management objective *BAI05 Managed organizational changes* is also partially relevant, but it deals more with digital transformation as a whole rather than specific digital skills. It is also worth noting that each of the objectives contains components – especially the components *People, Skills and Competences* and *Policies and Procedures* – which provide additional information or links to resources that can prove to be useful for digital transformation processes. Among these resources, we can find, e.g. the *e-Competence Framework (e-CF)*.

Interestingly, all of the identified objectives belong to either the *Align, Plan and Organize (ADM)*, *Build, Acquire and Implement (BAI)*, or *Evaluate, Direct and Monitor (EDM)* domain. None of the objectives from the remaining two management objective domains have any apparent overlaps with digital literacy. In addition, all of the seven identified governance and management objectives are connected to the AG12 alignment goal, proving it to be a key COBIT goal for digital literacy.

References

Binkley, M., Erstad, O., Herman, J., Raizen, S., Ripley, M., Miller-Ricci, M., & Rumble, M. (2012). Defining twenty-first century skills. In Assessment and teaching of 21st century skills (pp. 17–66). Scopus. https://doi.org/10.1007/978-94-007-2324-5_2

Buitrago-Flórez, F., Danies, G., Restrepo, S., & Hernández, C. (2021). Fostering 21st Century Competences through Computational Thinking and Active Learning: A Mixed Method Study. International Journal of Instruction, 14(3), 737–754. https://doi.org/10.29333/iji.2021.14343a

Carretero, S., Vuorikari, R., & Punie, Y. (2017). DigComp 2.1: The Digital Competence Framework for Citizens with eight proficiency levels and examples of use (Scientific Analysis or Review, Technical Guidance KJ-NA-28558-EN-N; p. 48). Publications Office of the European Union. https://doi.org/10.2760/38842

Chetty, K., Qigui, L., Gcora, N., Josie, J., Wenwei, L., & Fang, C. (2018). Bridging the digital divide: Measuring digital literacy. Economics: The Open-Access, Open-Assessment E-Journal, 20. https://doi.org/10.5018/economics-ejournal.ja.2018-23

Gilster, P. (1997). Digital Literacy (1st edition). Wiley.

ISACA. (2018a). COBIT 2019 Framework: Governance and Management Objectives. Information Systems Audit and Control Association.

ISACA. (2018b). COBIT 2019 Framework: Introduction and Methodology. Information Systems Audit and Control Association.

van Dijk, J. A. G. M. (2013). A theory of the digital divide. In The Digital Divide: The Internet and Social Inequality in International Perspective (pp. 29–51). Routledge. https://research.utwente.nl/en/publications/a-theory-of-the-digital-divide

van Laar, E., van Deursen, A. J. A. M., van Dijk, J. A. G. M., & de Haan, J. (2017). The relation between 21st-century skills and digital skills: A systematic literature review. Computers in Human Behavior, 72, 577–588. https://doi.org/10.1016/j.chb.2017.03.010

Voogt, J., & Roblin, N. P. (2012). A comparative analysis of international frameworks for 21st century competences: Implications for national curriculum policies. Journal of Curriculum Studies, 44(3), 299–321. https://doi.org/10.1080/00220272.2012.668938

ANNEX

STATEMENT OF THE PUBLICATION ETHICS AND PUBLICATION MALPRACTICE

IDIMT's Publication Ethics and Publication Malpractice Statement is based, in large part, on the guidelines and standards developed by the Committee on Publication Ethics (COPE).

We expect all parties commit to these publication ethics. We do not tolerate plagiarism or other unethical behaviour and will remove any manuscript that does not meet these standards.

The relevant duties and expectations of authors, reviewers, and editors are set out below:

1. Author Responsibilities

Authors must certify that their manuscripts are their original work.

Authors must certify that the manuscript has not previously been published elsewhere.

Authors must certify that the manuscript is not currently being considered for publication elsewhere.

Authors must notify us of any conflicts of interest.

Authors must identify all sources used in the creation of their manuscript.

Authors must report any errors they discover in their manuscript.

2. Reviewer Responsibilities

Reviewers must notify us of any conflicts of interest.

Reviewers must keep information pertaining to the manuscript confidential.

Reviewers must bring to the attention of the Editor-in-Chief any information that may be reason to reject publication of a manuscript.

Reviewers must at any time evaluate manuscripts only for their intellectual content without regard to race, gender, sexual orientation, religious belief, ethnic origin, citizenship, or political philosophy of the authors.

Reviewer who feels unqualified to review the research reported in a manuscript or knows that its prompt review will be impossible should notify us and excuse himself from the review process.

3. Editorial Board Responsibilities

The Editorial Board must keep information pertaining to submitted manuscripts confidential.

The Editorial Board must disclose any conflicts of interest.

The Editorial Board must evaluate manuscripts only for their intellectual content.

The Editorial Board is responsible for making publication decisions for submitted manuscripts.

LIST OF AUTHORS

Affara, Muna 13
Al-Akrawi, Astrid 347
Aumayr, Georg 39

Bachňáková Rózenfeldová, Laura
.... 89
Basl, Josef 203
Bikila, Dawit Dejene 391
Bretz, Patrik 373
Briškárová, Soňa 89
Burešová, Jitka 255
Burešová, Tereza 187

Cabal-Rosel, Adriana 21
Coronel, Carmina 161

Danel, Roman 169
Delina, Radoslav 283
Demeter, Gabriel 283
Doucek, Petr 81, 179
Duscher, Georg 13

Espinoza, Felix 81

Ferenčak, Ivana 21
Fertig, Tobias 101
Fleckenstein, Elena 111

Gehre, Florian 13
Geyer, Constanze 29, 39
Grosser, Cosmas 29

Habarta, Filip 121
Hafner, Antonia 29
Hagendorn, Melissa 29
Hardan, Khalid 169
Harničárová, Marta 169
Havránek, Martin 187
Henczkó, Judit 21
Henkelmann, David 101
Hučková, Regina 89
Hyden, Patrik 21

Istaitih, Yahya 169

Jaho, Eva 13
Jantos, Anne 111, 383
Jarolímek, Jan 187

Kalamen, Kristián 329
Karady, Ondřej 321

Katrenčík, Ivan 365
Khalid Hardan 169
Khalilia, Walid 169
Kljajić Borštnar, Mirjana 195
Konečný, Michal 337
Korčák, Jiří 265
Kostiuk, Yaroslava 337
Kovářova, Marie 81
Kovářová, Marie 73
Kramreither, Nicole 21
Kuchtíková, Nikola 151
Kuperova, Martina 357

Leidwein, Alois 13, 29
Leierzopf, Ernst 63
Lisnik, Anton 357, 373
Litzenberger, Martin 161
Lukáš, Martin 187

Macík, Marek 313
Majerník, Milan 373
Malá, Ivana 121
Marek, Luboš 121
Markovič, Peter 329
Maršálek, Karel 399
Maryska, Milos 73, 81, 151
Mayrhofer, René 63
Mucha, Boris 365

Nedomova, Lea 179
Neubauer, Georg 13, 29

Palková, Zuzana 169
Pályi, Bernadett 21
Pavlíček, Antonín 243
Peham, Johannes R. 13
Pechtor, Václav 203
Peischl, Nadine 21
Pollák, František 329
Polzer, Daniel 21
Potančok, Martin 235
Prüller, Rainer 29
Pucihar, Andreja 195
Putz, Florentin 63

Radváková, Věra 235
Rainer, Karin 13, 21, 29
Rathammer, Krista 21
René Mayrhofer 63
Ringler, Gudrun 39
Roland, Michael 63

Ruppitsch, Werner 21
Ruschak, Michal 337
Řepka, Michal 169

Salomon, Gabriele 29
Shaaban, Abdelkader Magdy . 143
Schimak, Gerald 13
Schmittner, Christoph 143
Schöggl, Florian 29
Schöggl, FLorian 29
Schoitsch, Erwin 133
Schraml, Stefan 51
Schwope, Julia 383
Sieber, Jakub 293
Sigmund, Tomáš 217
Siska, Veronika 347
Sokol, Pavol 89
Sonntag, Michael 51
Spanakos, Gregory 21
Steger, Julia 21
Sturm, Nadine 29, 39
Svatá, Vlasta 227
Syrovátková, Jana 265

Šenkýřová, Anežka 313
Štěpánek, Lubomír 121

Tabain, Irena 21
Tamimi, Talat 169
Till, Juraj 303
Tkáč, Michal 293, 303
Tryfinopoulou, Kyriaki 21

Ulman, Miloš 187
Urminský, Jaroslav 313, 321

Valíček, Jan 169
Vávra, Adam 321
Vlachostergiou, Angeliki 13
Vogt, Iris 111

Warhol, Miroslav 373
Willoughby, Tereza 273
Wohlleben, Kilian 161

Zackrisson, Mats 347
Zajarošová, Markéta 313, 321
Zatrochová, Monika 365